ROUTLEDGE HANDBOOK OF DISCOURSES IN AFRICAN LITERATURE

This handbook provides a critical overview of literature dealing with groups of people or regions that suffer marginalization within Africa.

The contributors examine a multiplicity of minority discourses expressed in African literature, including those who are culturally, socially, politically, religiously, economically, and sexually marginalized in literary and artistic creations. Chapters and sections of the book are structured to identify major areas of minority articulation of their condition and strategies deployed against the repression, persecution, oppression, suppression, domination, and tyranny of the majority or dominant group.

Bringing together diverse perspectives to give a holistic representation of the African reality, this handbook is an important read for scholars and students of comparative and postcolonial literature and African studies.

Tanure Ojaide is the Frank Porter Graham Professor of Africana Studies at the University of North Carolina at Charlotte, USA.

Joyce Ashuntantang is an Associate Professor of English at the University of Hartford, USA.

ROUTLEDGE HANDBOOK OF MINORITY DISCOURSES IN AFRICAN LITERATURE

Edited by Tanure Ojaide and Joyce Ashuntantang

Routledge
Taylor & Francis Group

LONDON AND NEW YORK

First published 2020 by Routledge

2 Park Square, Milton Park, Abingdon, Oxon OX14 4RN

605 Third Avenue, New York, NY 10017

Routledge is an imprint of the Taylor & Francis Group, an informa business

First issued in paperback 2022

British Library Cataloguing-in-Publication Data
A catalogue record for this book is available from the British Library

Library of Congress Cataloging-in-Publication Data
A catalog record for this book has been requested

ISBN: 978-0-367-36834-0 (hbk)
ISBN: 978-1-03-233629-9 (pbk)
DOI: 10.4324/9780429354229

Typeset in Bembo
by Apex CoVantage, LLC

We dedicate this book to the memory of Pius Adesanmi who had agreed to submit a contribution to this Handbook before the tragic crash. Pius always affirmed the African humanity in all he did. And that is an everlasting truth.

CONTENTS

Contents

Contents

NOTES ON EDITORS
AND CONTRIBUTORS

Editors

Tanure Ojaide

A Fellow in Writing of the University of Iowa, Tanure Ojaide was educated at the University of Ibadan, where he received a bachelor's degree in English, and at Syracuse University, where he received both M.A. in Creative Writing and Ph.D. in English. He has published over twenty collections of poetry, four collections of short stories, three memoirs, four novels, and nine scholarly books. His literary awards include the Commonwealth Poetry Prize for the Africa Region (1987), the All-Africa Okigbo Prize for Poetry (1988, 1997), the BBC Arts and Africa Poetry Award (1988), the Association of Nigerian Authors Poetry Award (1988, 1994, 2003, and 2011), and the 2016 African Literature Association Folon-Nichols Award for Excellence in Writing. Ojaide taught for many years at The University of Maiduguri (Nigeria), and is currently The Frank Porter Graham Professor of Africana Studies at the University of North Carolina at Charlotte. He received a National Endowment for the Humanities fellowship in 1999, the Fulbright Senior Scholar Award in 2002/2003 and 2013/2014, and the University of North Carolina's First Citizens Bank Scholar Medal Award for 2005. In 2016 he was awarded both the Folon-Nichols Award and the Nigerian National Order of Merit for the Humanities. He was co-winner of the 2018 Wole Soyinka Prize for Literature in Africa.

Joyce Ashuntantang (Joyce Ash)

Born in Cameroon, Central Africa, Joyce Ashuntantang is a poet, actress, librarian, interdisciplinary scholar and Associate Professor of English at the University of Hartford, Connecticut. A graduate of universities on three continents, Dr. Ashuntantang received a B.A in English with a minor in Theater Arts from the University of Yaoundé Cameroon, a Master's in Library and Information Science from the University of Aberystwyth, UK, and Ph.D. in English/African Literature from the City University of New York. She is the author of many scholarly and creative publications, which include *Landscaping Postcoloniality: The Dissemination of Anglophone Cameroon Literature* (2009) and three poetry collections, *Their Champagne Party will End: Poems in Honor of Bate Besong* (co-edited, 2008), *A Basket of Flaming Ashes* (2010) and *Beautiful Fire* (2018). She has appeared as an invited poet in many countries around the world including England, Germany, Nicaragua, Greece, Costa Rica, Colombia, Bangladesh, Cameroon, and United States. She has also contributed to several international anthologies of poetry highlighting the plight of minority groups including: *Peace for Afrin, Peace for Kurdistan* (2019), *Hiraeth-Erzolirzoli: A Wales - Cameroon Anthology* (2018), *Poems for the Hazara* (2014), *Reflections: An Anthology of New Work by African Women Poets* (2013) and *We Have Crossed Many Rivers: New Poetry from Africa* (2012). Her poems have been translated into Spanish, Greek, Hebrew, Turkish, Bangla, Arabic and Romanian. Her awards include Spirit of Detroit Award for Leadership (1987), Ministry of Culture, Cameroon, Award for Outstanding Performance in Theater (1989, 1994), Belle K. Ribicoff Prize for Excellence in Teaching and Scholarship (2012), and Kathrak-Bangladesh Literary Award (2018).

Contributors

Saeedat Bolajoko Aliyu is Lecturer in the Department of English of the Kwara State University, Malete, Kwara State, Nigeria where she teaches African literature and literary criticism. She obtained a Ph.D. in Literature in English in 2015 from the University of Ilorin, Ilorin, Nigeria. Her research interests include African cultural studies, environmental literary studies, gender, and film studies. She has published in these areas in books and journals both locally and internationally.

Charles Cantalupo is the author of three books of poetry, three books of translations of Eritrean poetry, four books of literary criticism ranging from Thomas Hobbes to Ngũgĩ wa Thiong'o, and a memoir, *Joining Africa – From Anthills to Asmara* (2012). His work has received support from the Ford and Rockefeller Foundations and the World Bank. Two of his most recent books are *Where War Was – Poems and Translations from Eritrea* (Mkuki na Nyota) and *Non-Native Speaker: Selected and Sundry Essays* (Africa World Press). Co-author of the historic Asmara Declaration on African Languages and Literatures, he is a Distinguished Professor of English, Comparative Literature, and African Studies at Penn State University.

Rajendra Chetty is Professor of Language Education at the University of the Western Cape. His primary research interest is the intersectionality of race, class, and inequality. In 2015/6 he was Fulbright visiting professor at the Graduate Centre, City University of New York. His most recent books are *Narrating the New Nation: South African Indian Writings* (2018),and the literary biography *At the Edge: The Writings of Ronnie Govender* (2018).

Ernest Cole is Professor and Chair of English at Hope College, Holland, Michigan, where he teaches Postcolonial Literatures of Sub-Saharan Anglophone Africa, India, and the Caribbean. Previously he taught African literature at Fourah Bay College, University of Sierra Leone, The Gambia College, Brikama; and the University of The Gambia. He has published two monographs – *Theorizing the Disfigured Body* (2014) and *Space and Trauma in the Writing of Aminatta Forna* (2017) and two collected volumes: *Emerging Perspectives on Syl Cheney Coker* (with Eustace Palmer), and *Ousmane Sembene, Writer, Filmmaker, & Revolutionary Artist* (with Oumar Cherif Diop, 2015).

Oumar Chérif Diop is Professor of French and English at Kennesaw State University in Georgia, USA. His field of research is the study of representations of violence and trauma in African literature. His publications include two books, *Violence and Trauma in Selected African Literature* (2018) and *Ousmane Sembene: Writer, Filmmaker, and Revolutionary Artist* (co-edited with Ernest Cole, 2015); "Traumatics: The Representation of Trauma in Yvonne Vera's *Without a Name*" in *Managing Conflicts in Africa's Democratic Transitions* (Akanmu Adebayo, ed.); "Violence and the Ethics of Reading: The Body as Site of Violence and Resistance in Alex Laguma's *In Fog of the Season's End* and Sony Labou Tansi's *La Vie et Demi*." in the *Journal of Third World Studies*.

Sule Emmanuel Egya is Professor of African Literature and Cultural Studies at Ibrahim Badamasi Babangida University, Lapai, Nigeria. His research interests include literature and the environment, literature and politics, and literary theory. He is also an award-winning poet and novelist who writes under the pen name E. E. Sule. His latest books are *Power and Resistance: Literature, Regime and the National Imaginary* and *Makwala* (a novel).

Frieda Ekotto is Professor in the Department of Afroamerican and African Studies and of Comparative Literature and Francophone Studies at the University of Michigan, Frieda Ekotto is the author of ten books, the most recent scholarly monograph being *What Color is Black? Race and Sex across the French Atlantic* (Lexington Press, 2011). Her early research traced interactions between philosophy, law, literature, and African cinema, and she currently works on LGBT issues, with an emphasis on West African cultures within Africa as well as in Europe and the Americas. In 2017, she co-produced the feature-length documentary *Vibrancy of Silence: A Discussion with My Sisters,* which premiered at the University of Michigan. She has won many outstanding awards including the Nicolàs Guillèn Prize for Philosophical Literature in 2014, an Honorary Degree from Colorado College in 2018, and the 2018 Zagora International Film Festival of Sub-Sahara Award for her work in African cinema.

Maximilian Feldner is a postdoctoral researcher and lecturer at the University of Graz. He recently published a study on Nigerian diaspora literature, *Narrating the New African Diaspora: 21st Century Nigerian Literature in Context* (Palgrave Macmillan, 2019). Having studied in Graz, New York City, and Limerick, he holds a doctorate in English and American Studies from the University of Graz.

Obari Gomba is Honorary Fellow in Writing of the University of Iowa (USA), as well as a recipient of Rivers ANA Distinguished Writer Award and a two-time winner of both the Best Literary Artiste Award and the First Prize for Drama of the English Association of the University of Nigeria. He has been shortlisted three times for the Nigeria Prize for Literature. His works include *Thunder Protocol* (Winner of ANA Poetry Prize), *For Every Homeland* (Winner of ANA Poetry Prize), and *Guerrilla Post* (Winner of ANA Drama Prize). He teaches Literature and Creative Writing at the University of Port Harcourt in Nigeria.

Stephen Ese Kekeghe teaches creative writing, African and European literature at the Department of English, College of Education, Warri, Nigeria. He obtained a B.A in English from Delta State University, Abraka; M.A and Ph.D. degrees in English from University of Ibadan, Nigeria. Dr. Kekeghe's scholarly articles and poems have appeared in a variety of print and online publications. His play, *Pond of Leeches* (Kraft Books, Ibadan, 2015), has been interpreted on stage in the University of Ilorin, Kwara State, and Niger Delta University, Bayelsa State, respectively. Dr. Kekeghe is a member of Literary Society of Nigeria (LSN), Madness and Literature Network, International Society for Oral Literatures of Africa (ISOLA), and Association of Nigerian Authors (ANA).

Mwenda Mbatiah is a creative writer and literary scholar specializing in Swahili literature. He has published widely in the area, and his papers have appeared in various journals in both English and Swahili. Currently, he is an associate professor of Swahili literature in the Department of Kiswahili, University of Nairobi. So far he has published eight novels in Swahili, a play, and numerous short stories. His books have won several national awards. For instance, he is the latest winner of the Text Book Centre Jomo Kenyatta Prize for Literature, awarded in 2019 for his novel: *Watoto wa Mwelusi* (2018). His book, a historical study of the Swahili novel entitled: *Riwaya ya Kiswahili: Chimbuko na Maendeleo Yake* was published in 2016.

Daniela Merolla is Professor in Berber Literature and Art at the Institut National des Langues et Civilisations Orientales (Sorbonne Paris-Cité). She taught and did research in African Literatures and Media at Leiden University (NL) until 2015. She published among others: "Space, time, and culture on African/diaspora websites" in the *Journal of African Cultural Studies* (2020) ; *Les cinémas berbères. De la méconnaissance aux festivals nationaux* (edited with Kamal Naït Zerad and Amar Ameziane, Karthala, 2019); *Searching for Sharing: Heritage and Multimedia in Africa* (edited with Mark Turin, Open Book Publishers, 2017); *De l'art de la narration tamazight (berbère)* (Éditions Peeters, 2006).

Honoré Missihoun is Research Scholar and Senior Lecturer in Africana Studies Department at UNC Charlotte. He received a combined Romance Languages and Comparative Literatures doctorate from UNC Chapel Hill, USA, and Universidade de Coimbra, Portugal. He was awarded MAT in Teaching Portuguese as a Second Language from Coimbra, MAT in language acquisition and curriculum design from Kent State, and MA/MED in English and African Literature, Spanish Linguistics and Education from Universités Nationales de Côte d'Ivoire and Bénin and Pontificia Católica de Salamanca, Spain.

Razinat Talatu Mohammed is Associate Professor of Feminist Literary Criticism and Theoretical Approaches at the University of Maiduguri. She is the award winning author of *A Love Like a Woman's and Other Stories* (Kraftbooks, 2006). Her first novel, *Habiba* (Kraftbooks, 2013), was a finalist for the ANA prize for prose 2014. She is also the author of *The Travails of a First Wife* (Origami, 2015), *Intra-gender Relations Between Women: A Study of Nawal El-Saadawi and Buchi Emecheta's Novel* (Lambert Academic Publication, 2012) and *Female Representation in Nigerian Literature* (www.africanwriter.com), among others.

F. Fiona Moolla is Lecturer in the English Department at the University of the Western Cape, South Africa. She is the author of *Reading Nuruddin Farah: The Individual, the Novel & the Idea of Home* (James Currey, 2014), and the editor of *Natures of Africa: Ecocriticism and Animal Studies in Contemporary Cultural Forms* (WITS UP, 2016), among other academic and non-academic publications. She currently heads a project on romantic love in African and South African literature and culture.

Gĩchingiri Ndĩgĩrĩgĩ is Professor in the Department of English at the University of Tennessee, Knoxville. He has published journals articles in *Mũtiiri, Ufahamu, The Drama Review, Journal of the African Literature Association* (JALA), *Indian Journal of Ecocrticism, Canadian Review of Comparative Literature, African Theatre Journal, Journal of African Cultural Studies*, and *Research in African Literatures*. His book chapters appear in the MLA's *Approaches to the Work of Ngũgĩ, Unmasking the African Dictator, Chimamanda Adichie: An Anthology of Works and Criticism*, and *Cultural Archives of Atrocity*, in addition to encyclopedia entries in the *Cambridge Encyclopedia of Stage Actors and Acting*.

Maik Nwosu is Professor of English at the University of Denver, Colorado. His research areas include African, African Diaspora, postcolonial, and world literatures; semiotics and critical theory. Nwosu has published three novels (*Invisible Chapters, Alpha Song,* and *A Gecko's Farewell*); a poetry collection (*Suns of Kush*); two critical studies (*Markets of Memories: Between the Postcolonial and the Transnational* and *The Comic Imagination in Modern African Literature and Cinema: A Poetics of Laughter*); and a coedited anthology (*The Critical Imagination in African Literature: Essays in Honor of Michael J. C. Echeruo*).

Enajite Eseoghene Ojaruega is Associate Professor of African Literature and Chair, Department of English and Literary Studies at Delta State University, Nigeria. Her areas of academic interest and specialty include: Modern African Literature, African Prose Fiction, Gender Studies, and Post-Colonial Literatures. She has published scholarly articles on contemporary African literature in reputable peer-reviewed journals like *Tydskrif Ver Letterkunde, Matatu, Journal of African Literature Association* and *The IUP Journal of Commonwealth Literature.* She is a Fellow of The Italian Academy for Advanced Studies in America, Columbia University, New York.

Dike Okoro is Associate Professor of English and Chair of the Department of Humanities at Harris-Stowe State University. His book chapters, scholarly essays, and works of nonfiction have appeared in reputable books, anthologies, and encyclopedias, including *Emerging African Voices, World Literature Today, Dictionary of Literary Biography: African Writers Series, Far Villages: Welcome Essays for New & Beginner Poets, Black Issues Book Review, Imbizo: International Journal of African Literary and Comparative Studies, Chimurenga,* and elsewhere. A Newberry Scholar-in-Residence and Sam Walton Fellow, his research interests include the intersection of literature and politics in Africa, Afrofuturism, ecocriticism, disability studies, and film studies.

Chike Okoye is Associate Professor of the Department of English, Nnamdi Azikiwe University, Awka, Nigeria. He has published book chapters, essays, and articles. His books include *Essentials of Poetry, Introduction to Commonwealth and Postcolonial Literatures* and *The Mmonwu Theatre: Igbo Poetry of the Spirits.* He is co-editor for *Liminal Margins: Performance Masks, Masquerades and Facekuerades* with Sunday Ododo. A university orator, he belongs to the Association of Nigerian Authors (ANA), Literary Society of Nigeria (LSN), Igbo Studies Association (ISA), and African Literature Association (ALA). His major research interests include Poetry, Cultural Studies, and Postcolonial Literatures.

Tijan M. Sallah is a Ph.D.-trained economist, former professor and retired sector manager at the World Bank. He is the Gambia's most famous living poet and one of Africa's most significant writers. His poems and short stories appear in several major African poetry and short story anthologies. Prof. Wumi Raji edited a book of critical perspectives on his works in 2014 published by Cambria Press. Among his recent books are *Dream Kingdom: Selected Poems* and *Chinua Achebe: Teacher of Light* (a biography). His forthcoming book of literary essays is titled *Saani Baat: Aspects of African Literature and Culture, Senegambian Essays.*

Pamela J. Olubunmi Smith is Professor Emerita, The Goodrich Scholarship Program, University of Nebraska at Omaha, where she taught English and Humanities for over three decades. She earned a Ph.D. in Comparative Literature from the University of Washington. Her body of published critical works includes: three major literary Yoruba-English translations of leading contemporary Yoruba writers Adebayo Faleti and Akinwumi Isola's novels, numerous critical essays on literary translation issues, as well as review essays in Yoruba studies.

Maurice Taonezvi Vambe is Professor of African Literature in the Department of English Studies at the University of South Africa. He has published scholarly articles on critiques of African nationalism, identity politics, memory and the poetics of cultural representations in the African post colony. Professor Vambe has published *African Oral tradition and the Zimbabwean in English* (2004). Vambe's most recent work is *Genocide in African Fiction* (2019) and this book will be published in March 2020 by Africa World Press. Vambe is working to edit an *Encyclopedia of Genocide in Africa*. His other academic interests are in popular culture and film studies.

Hein Willemse is Professor of Literature and Literary Theory in the Department of Afrikaans at the University of Pretoria. He has published widely on Black Afrikaans literature and the Afrikaans Oral Tradition. His publications include *Aan die ander kant: Swart Afrikaanse Skrywers in die Afrikaanse Letterkunde* (2007), and edited volumes such as *More than Brothers: James Matthews and Peter Clarke at 70* (2000), and Achmat Davids's *The Afrikaans of The Cape Muslims* (2011). HE is a past President of the International Society for the Oral Literatures of Africa (ISOLA) and the former editor of *Tydskrif vir Letterkunde*.

PART I

Background

1

INTRODUCTION

Tanure Ojaide and Joyce Ashuntantang

The project that resulted in *The Routledge Handbook of Minority Discourses in African Literature* started several years back as two of us discussed peculiar situations in our respective countries. Joyce is from Anglophone Cameroon and Tanure from Nigeria's Niger Delta region. Anglophone Cameroon constitutes two regions, South Southwest and Northwest, out of the republic's ten. It suffers marginalization in political representation and economic development from the Cameroonian government, which is dominated by Francophones. The Anglophone area has been so subjected to neglect by the pro-Francophone government that many on that side have called for either an autonomous region within Cameroon as existed from 1961-1972, or a separate independent nation. This situation is compounded by the fact that Anglophone Cameroon is rich in natural resources including oil and is regarded as the breadbasket of Cameroon. The Niger Delta region, geopolitically the South-South in Nigeria, produces the oil and gas whose joint revenues fund the 744 local governments, 36 states, and the Federal Capital Territory, as well as the federal government. In addition to suffering environmental degradation which imperils their health, the Niger Delta people are also helpless as the powerful federal government and multinational oil companies take away their resources to develop other parts of the country and make staggering profits, respectively. This happens as the people of the region remain among the poorest in Nigeria, if not the entire world. The current minority status of Anglophone Cameroon and the Niger Delta dates back to French and British colonial policies which have condemned them to the domination of political units (Cameroon and Nigeria) created for the profit and interest of the colonialists.

We at first thought of a project to compare and contrast the literatures of the two relatively small but multiethnic regions. However, we decided to start from the comparative areas of exploitation, marginalization, and resistance in Anglophone Cameroon and the Niger Delta. We, the editors, are scholars and writers: Joyce writes poetry, plays, fiction and non-fiction; Tanure writes poetry, fiction, and non-fiction. As writers, we found that initial option very tempting. However, also as academics, with more discussions, we felt there were many other "minorities" whose plight needs to be part of the project that has to do with marginalization, political activism and resistance, expressing solidarity of the oppressed by a dominant power, and suffering as a result of the minority status. It was then that we started to have a growing conviction that many forms of "minorities" reflected in literature could gain entry into our project. We realized that we needed more scholars to do a more comprehensive and profound job. What could be more appropriate for a project that advocates diversity and inclusion than drawing scholars knowledgeable about African literature to look at the manifold levels of "minority" status expressed in it? We then researched for weeks on whom to invite into the team of scholars to tackle each "minority" situation. That is, the genesis of this project grew out of two regions of neighboring countries to embrace other situations and conditions that we will describe as "minority discourses."

As Africans but also products of the American/Western academy, we had to fashion our project in the light of earlier studies which we want our work to expand upon and also to show that African literature does not always follow Western theoretical constructs. Working from the premise that literature, like the other artistic creations of art and music, is a cultural production, we settled on interrogating African literature as reflecting the African experience through Africa's particular culture and society. We acknowledge African culture as dynamic and changing with forces from within and without. These changes have become more rapid with the forces of globalization that have made local happenings in other places influence Africa and perhaps caused Africa's local happenings to have global significance. Tanure knows that any disturbance in Warri or Port Harcourt in Nigeria affects the world oil prices and the Stock Exchange in New York and elsewhere. At the same time, a government crackdown in any part of Anglophone Cameroon catches the attention of social justice protesters abroad. The world has become intertwined, and while accepting what is needed from outside, the African should not surrender to foreign forces so as to lose his identity.

We thus had our notions of "minority" and diversity before we did more research, after which we assigned topics to contributors from across different regions of Africa, the United States and Canada, and Europe. We would discover works on "minorities" that in general terms tallied with or differed a little from what we had in our minds. While some scholars, including Homi Bhabha in "DissemiNation: Time, Narrative, and the Margins of the Modern Nation," have written on minority discourse, the focus here is on two texts inspired by different historical circumstances that have received great academic attention and which some of the contributors to this Handbook have read and referred to. Gilles Deleuze and Felix Guattari, in their *Kafka: Toward a Minority Literature*, use Franz Kafka's work to define what they term "minority literature." They see Kafka, then a member of the Jewish minority in Prague writing about the Jewish experience in the majority German language, as writing minority literature. That leads them to make the categorical statement that "a minor literature doesn't come from a minor language; it is rather that which a minority constructs in a major language" (16). Maybe because of the historical context of Kafka's works, we do not accept this statement as true of all minor literatures in the case of African literature. In this book, works of minority ethnic groups in their own languages that are marginalized by overarching colonial languages or dominant majority groups are taken as minor literatures.

Three quick examples of such minor literatures language-wise represented in this book are the Jola of the Casamance region of Senegal and The Gambia, the Berbers/Amazigh of North Africa, and Pidgin English from Nigeria. It is true there are "minorities" in the majority languages of English, French, and Portuguese, but literary works do not need to be written in them to qualify as minority literature or discourse in African literature. The emphatic words of Deleuze and Guattari – "a minor literature doesn't come from a minor language" – do not adequately describe the minority literatures in Africa, where the term "minority" is more amplified in the multifarious way of looking at things.

Deleuze and Guattari name two other features of "minority literature": being political and taking on a collective value (17). These are also some of the features of the "minority" groups that constitute the marginalized groups in Africa whose reflections in literature are our concern in this Handbook. What could be more political than the cases of the Anglophone Cameroon and Niger Delta already mentioned? And, of course, the rhetoric of the collective aspirations of marginalized or exploited people to express their position in the face of a dominant group or power stands out in its passion and emotive language.

It is interesting to note that Franz Kafka wrote in German in the early part of the 20th century. It is also noteworthy that Gilles Deleuze and Felix Guattari's *Kafka: Toward a Minority Literature* was originally published in French in 1975 in Paris before being re-published in English in 1986 by the University of Minnesota Press. It is in the period of the American academy's fascination with multiculturalism and diversity that Abdul R. JanMohamed and David Lloyd's *The Nature and Context of Minority Discourse* came out in 1990. The authors see in "minority" "the political and cultural structures that connect different minority cultures in their subjugation and opposition to the dominant culture" (ix). While English is the majority language in the United States of America, there are literatures in English that the American academic establishment calls "ethnic literatures" in advertisements for faculty positions. The mainstream/majority Anglo-American literature, with its canon closely guarded by its literary scholars, is not described as "ethnic literature." The "ethnic literatures" probably include African-American literature, Native American literature, Chicana literature, and literatures written in English by Americans outside the Anglo-American literary tradition. It is in this context that JanMohamed and Lloyd's book has chapters on race, culture, ethnic, white, Asian-American, African, and Hebrew topics. It is a deliberate effort to use these different/diverse groups' discourses to subvert the hegemonic monolith of Anglo-American literature.

Africa is not a superpower country but a continent of fifty-four countries. Thus, the issues that informed "minority discourse" in a work meant for the American/Western academy are different from what inform African literature and other cultural productions. Race may be a problem in South Africa and North Africa, but generally, other issues loom large in the African experience. For instance, in this Handbook, we are taking issues of disability, the environment, gender, sexuality, and others as equally important rather than a black-and-white notion in which "white" is the dominant power, institution, and attitude and "black" the subjugated minority. Africa is not homogenous culturally, but for the most part, sub-Saharan Africa tends to have a fairly comparable culture; hence, Africa is culturally a subregion among such other cultural areas as the Western/European and Oriental. In any case, on the theoretical side, JanMohamed and Lloyd strike a common chord on minorities:

> By "minority discourse", we mean a theoretical articulation of the political and cultural structures that connect different minority cultures in their subjugation and opposition to the dominant culture. This definition is based on the principle that minority groups, despite all the diversity and specificity of their cultures, share the common experience of domination and exclusion by the majority.
>
> *(ix)*

Minority discourse in African literature is not aimed at multicultural objectives in administrative and pedagogical remediation as in the West as such. It is not meant to show diversity where one has to fill in one's race as black, white, or otherwise. Like us, many Africans did not have to identify themselves as black until they landed in the United States, where race is a mark of identity. In the African experience of literature, diversity is a reaffirmation of the multifarious nature of the people and their ontology. As explained in the first chapter, most African cultures, such as those of the Yoruba, Ashanti, Dogon, and Igbo, place a premium on diversity or the multiplicity of representations.

We want to be mindful that interest in minority discourses is not only in Africa but universal. Our work in literature has an intellectual convergence with a work like Al Gedicks's *Resource Rebels: Native Challenges to Mining and Oil Corporations* on pollution and exploitation of the weaker peoples and regions by multinational companies in which the likes of Nigeria's Niger Delta exist all over the world, especially in Latin America and Asia. "Resource rebels" who seek to have control over their resources are many in the world. There are other forms of minoritization, including languages spoken and lifestyles. The contexts of diversity are, however, different, and what contemporary society expects from the exhibition of the minority beside the majority may also be different. In the West, it could be aimed at excoriating the conscience of the exploiting, dominant, hegemonic structure towards acceptance and ceding of space to the constricted minority status group. Each struggle for minority rights is a contribution to humankind for a world in which all are accepted and treated equally, ensuring social justice.

To better understand the content of this Handbook, it is thus important to see diversity in cultural perspectives and also the role of literature in sociocultural perspectives. From traditional to contemporary times, literature in Africa has been utilitarian and transformative. Folktales are told to imbibe young ones with morals and ethics, as epics are used to express through the hero or heroine the virtues that humans look up to in their respective communities or societies. In modern and contemporary times, literature has been a medium of expressing the vision of writers towards sociopolitical and economic development and equality of their respective countries. There is no doubt that African literature is on the whole geared towards activism, unlike contemporary literature in the West, where writers do not seem to be bothered by the happenings in their societies. In Africa, writers could be questioned, arrested, jailed, and even executed by the government or the ruling class for pointing out the truth, but something like that will likely never happen in the Western world. Thus, literature is used by many African writers as a sociopolitical weapon, quite unlike in North America and Europe, where it is merely for intellectual reflection. With that role of literature in society, the study of African minority literature could combine traditional and modern roles as a form of transformative and advocative agent in society.

* * *

We have sought balance in the chapters which make up the book. Some of the chapters deal with general or wide topics, and others are very specific. Tanure Ojaide's opening chapter on theory and aesthetics is general and encompasses some of the issues that other contributors write on more specifically later in the book. At the same time, both Gĩchingiri Ndĩgĩrĩgĩ and Honoré Missihoun write on Wangari Maathai's memoir, *Unbowed*, and Tanella Boni's *Matins de couvre-feu*, both of which respectively deal with the environment. Both Maximilian Feldner and Stephen Kekeghe write on several short stories of Chimamanda Ngozi Adichie and Tanure Ojaide, respectively, though on specific works, Feldner and Kekeghe start with general concepts relevant to their chapter. There are also specific examples in the general topics. Feldner, in his chapter, begins with the concept of "African culture," as interpreted in North America and Europe, which influences the African literary works they publish, promote, and market, before focusing on Adichie's short stories, which in her fictional work form a "minority discourse." Similarly, Kekeghe compares the relationship between the psychiatrist and patient with the creative writer and his fictional characters with mental disorders before discussing specific Ojaide short stories dealing with mental illnesses and concluding that the short stories form a "minority discourse" in Ojaide's writings.

Each chapter justifies the minority status of that literature. For a long time, African literary scholars have talked of "literatures," and, in fact, one of the leading literature research journals is called *Research in African Literatures*. Many "literatures" exist in Africa, and they make up African literature. There are discourses of minority regions such as the Niger Delta, Anglophone Cameroon, Jola/Casamance, and Amazigh/Berber. While these are parts of nations, there are other minority literatures passionately articulated in the book. Two examples stand out. Sule Egya writes on Northern Nigerian literature as a minority literature within Nigerian literature. Even though the population of Northern Nigeria is said to exceed that of the South, the modern literature in English has been produced almost entirely by Southern writers. Egya gives the historical indirect rule of the British colonial system which allowed the North to implement its own laws, the Islamic religion, and the low rate of Western education as major reasons for the scarce literary productions in English in the North. This is evidently a case in which the majority people have a minority status in Western education and literary production. This does not take into consideration the fact that there are other literary works in the North written in Fulfulde and Hausa but which are not given the same exposure as literary publications in English.

Also within a nation, there are minority discourses when the national government alongside a specific majority ethnic group could minoritize other groups in the sense of using the government's power and resources to create a dominant discourse at the expense of groups that are victims of government reprisals. Maurice Vambe's chapter deals with the separate responses to nationhood within Zimbabwe after Robert Mugabe's government violently suppressed the Ndebele people of Mashonaland. According to Vambe, the majority Shona writers see things differently from the minority Ndebele writers. He uses many fictional texts to debunk the government and Shona's attitude to the military action as creating a false sense of one nation, when in fact is not so. The majority Shona dominated the Zimbabwean government under Mugabe. The Ndebele responses in imaginative works in English become a minor literature within Zimbabwean literature.

There are minority literatures as far as language is concerned, such as the chapters by Daniela Merolla on Amazigh/Berber literature, Ernest Cole on Krio drama in Sierra Leone, Chike Okoye on Pidgin English poetry in Nigeria, Mwenda Mbatiah on Swahili literature, and Hein Willemse on Afrikaans literature. As explained in the opening chapter, each language creates a linguistic community which binds its speakers emotionally and politically. There are chapters on gender and sexuality as well as on disabilities and religion. The issues that constitute minority status interrelate, as on region and language in the case of Anglophone Cameroon, religion and gender as seen in Saeedat Aliyu's discussion of female Muslim writers in Nigeria, Enajite Eseoghene Ojaruega on gender and a traditional poetic genre, and Hein Willemse on race and language in Afrikaans literature. The minority status becomes the raison d'être of each chapter when directly or indirectly expressed. This brings cohesion to the work as the respective minority statuses of the literatures bring out the subjectivities that in totality form African literature.

We have also paid attention to disability as a minority discourse, as well as migration and others. Pamela Olubunmi Smith deals with the presentation of madness and psychiatric disorders in female characters in African literature. Dike Okoro deals with a disabled boy who, despite being shunned by the community, gains redemption by saving the people from a disastrous flood in Meshack Asare's *Sosu's Call*. Okoro introduces Afro-futurism as a discourse in African literature.

Clearly, the Handbook takes a panoramic view of African literature. There are instances of minority literatures in the precolonial or traditional period through postcolonial to contemporary/ global times. Razinat Talatu Mohammed writes on Afropolitan writers who are not bound by national boundaries but see their identity in transnational and global terms. Such writers include Chimamanda Ngozi Adichie, Taiye Selasi, and NoViolet Bulawayo. Enajite Eseoghene Ojaruega writes on *udje*, a Nigerian Urhobo oral poetic performance genre that sings about women but excludes women in composition and performance and leaves them to marginal activities such as handclapping and fanning the *ebo-ile*, the lead performers. Mwenda Mbatiah takes a sweep of Swahili literature from about the 13th century to the present. The postcolonial period seems to have exacerbated issues of feminism and sexuality and current global concerns about the environment and climate change.

Let us expatiate on some of these issues. African patriarchy seems to have been exacerbated by the colonialists. The Western culture which traces its values to Judeo-Christian tenets is a patriarchy. In the British colonial period in Africa (and we believe the same of the French and Portuguese), there was not a single female administrator in all the colonies. This attitude reinforced the patriarchy in Africa that was mitigated with some matriarchal and matrilineal societies as among the Akan in West Africa and many small groups in Central Africa. There were set roles for men and women in the agrarian society in Africa which modernity appears to have disrupted. There are African subtleties which the West, by its own expressive openness, tends to see in their light and label as denial or suppression. Frieda Ekotto's chapter touches on this. There might have been women loving women in Africa before the coming of Europeans but not necessarily in the manner of European women, so that throwing Western terms of sexuality at Africans may not be right. Cultures are different, and none are more so than African and European cultures.

Literature, through this study of minority discourses, has excavated or salvaged African practices lost through four to five generations of European colonization of Africa. In addition to differences that seem to appear on the nature of sexuality are African and Western/European attitudes to the environment. This Introduction does not have room to do a detailed comparison, but it suffices to know that Africans have always paid attention to their environment, with a lot of regard for the non-human beings with whom they shared their lands. It is only in the late 1980s and early 1990s that ecocriticism started as a focus of scholarly interrogation of literature. The current interest in the environment and climate change has been integrated into the traditional life of the African. Wangari Maathai's *Unbowed* and the work of the Green Belt Movement reflect traditional Africa's concerns for the environment which other cultural groups are just waking up to.

We have divided the book into sections as an organizational strategy and to give a sense of order to the structure. In some cases, the chapters within sections could be switched because of the fluidity of some issues that intertwine with others. It is an arrangement that gives meaning to the project of "minority" discourses. The broad areas covered thus are in these sections: 1: political and racial forms of marginalization; 2: culture and language; 3: patriarchal domination, gender, sexuality, and other sociocultural minorities; 4: intranational, national, and international marginalization; 5: literature and disability; and 6: recent trends of marginalities: timely and timeless. We have attempted to frame each chapter within these broad outlines of minority literatures. However, the case of Eritrea in Charles Cantalupo's writing is a unique case where the entire national literature becomes a part of the national experience "against all odds" in light of the Horn of Africa and especially Eritrea's secession from Ethiopia.

The editors want to emphasize that despite a minority discourse leaving the impression of a binary situation of majority-minority with the "minority" always vulnerable, it is not always so in African literature. Maurice Vambe argues that "Minority discourses are in perpetual flux," and there could be minority within minority discourses. As Vambe further explains and as also already mentioned in the case of majority Northern Nigeria producing a minor literature in English compared to the minority Southern Nigeria producing a majority discourse in literature, "minority discourse" is not in numbers. Vambe gives the example of there being a very few colonialists compared to natives and yet the colonialists being dominant. In that case, "a numerical minority might be a numerical majority in the control of the publishing industry." And "By the same logic," according to Vambe, "a numerical majority might be a numerical minority in the field of knowledge production, management, and its dissemination."

We have attempted to engage all literary genres of literature. Fiction in the form of novels seems to have engaged minority discourse the most among the contributors. Essays on gender, sexuality, disability, and many more areas of minority statuses are based on fictional works. It is interesting that Okoro focuses on Meshack Asare's children's storybook, *Sosu's Call*. Ernest Cole writes on Yulisa Maddy's use of Krio in his plays, and Mwenda Mbatiah has plays in Swahili among his literary texts for discussion. Feldner and Kekeghe work on short stories. Ojaruega writes on traditional poetry, Chike Okoye on Ezenwa-Ohaeto's Pidgin English poetry, and Cantalupo on Eritrean poetry. The chapter on Swahili literature has memoirs and autobiographies as some of the texts. Ndĩgĩrĩgĩ focuses on Wangari Maathai's memoir, *Unbowed*, as Missihoun quotes copiously from Boni's non-fictional works. The Handbook is a reflection of the critical/scholarly attention to different African literary works.

Some chapters give a detailed historiography before focusing on specific texts to give background to the minority situation being discussed. Tijan M. Sallah does this on the Jola, who are split into Senegal, The Gambia, and Guinea Bissau. Merolla does the same for the Amazigh, the Berbers, of North Africa, who appear erased from Moroccan, Algerian, and North African literatures mostly in Arabic and French. Willemse details the history of Afrikaans and its change from minority to majority and back to minority language in the new dispensation of South Africa. It is also worth mentioning Fiona Moolla's discussion of "Coloured" and Rajendra Chetty's history of Indians, both in South Africa. Reading African literature through the lenses of these contributors takes one through a multidisciplinary path to a sudden awareness of why things are what they are: the source of every minority status and its resort to literature as a form of resistance against domination.

The editors have not interfered with each contributor's opinion or ideology, to reflect the multifaceted nature of knowledge inherited from Ananse's pot of wisdom which broke and spread out to be gathered by as many people as possible! It is a process meant to encourage a vibrant and healthy scholarly expression to show the diversity of opinions in critical discourse. In fact, each contributor's view is itself a "minority discourse," and the totality of the views approximates the reality of diverse views, emotions, and aesthetic appreciation. The editors are only facilitators of the discussion, and each chapter is a contribution to the palaver of minorities in the congress of African literature.

Works cited and references

Deleuze, Gilles and Felix Guattari. *Kafka: Toward a Minority Literature*. Minneapolis: University of Minnesota Press, 1986.

Gedicks, Al. *Resource Rebels: Native Challenges to Mining and Oil Corporations*, Cambridge, MA: South End Press, 2001.

JanMohamed, Abdul R. and David Lloyd. *The Nature and Context of Minority Discourse*. Oxford, UK: Oxford University Press, 1990.

2

THE THEORY AND AESTHETICS OF MINORITY DISCOURSES IN AFRICAN LITERATURE

Tanure Ojaide

Introduction

In literature, theory and aesthetics have become protean terms whose definitions or meanings seem to shift from what were previously thought to be their limited spaces into new scholarly vistas. Theory and aesthetics often function in a partnership that brings out the unity of a text or a collection of works that form a discourse. Jeffrey R. Di Leo, in his review of Vincent B. Leitch's *Literary Theory in the 21st Century: Theory Renaissance*, taunts us with "Word on the street is that theory is dead – superseded by a multitude of studies" (412). He goes on to quote Leitch as writing that "theory in recent times has become a crossover interdiscipline fusing literary criticism, linguistics, philosophy, history, anthropology, sociology, psychoanalysis, and politics" (29). The profusion of "studies" in the 21st century has given rise to the "renaissance" of what can also be called theories.

Though the study of "minorities" or minority studies has been popular in the Western academy, especially since the 1990s, when there was general encouragement of multicultural-ism, "minority literature" predated that decade. Franz Kafka, writing about Jewish experience in German, a mainstream language, was producing "minor literature" at the beginning of the twentieth century. Gilles Deleuze and Felix Guattari, in *Kafka: Toward a Minor Literature* (1986), start by emphasizing that "A minor literature doesn't come from a minor language; it is rather that which a minority constructs within a major language" (16). They then go on to say: "The three characteristics of minor literature are the deterritorialization of language, the connection of the individual to a political immediacy, and the collective assemblage of enunciation" (18). Abdul R. JanMohamed and David Lloyd, in their edited *The Nature and Context of Minority Discourse* (1990) write that:

> By "minority discourse", we mean a theoretical articulation of the political and cul-
> tural structures that connect different minority cultures in their subjugation and oppo-
> sition to the dominant culture. This definition is based on the principle that minority
> groups, despite all the diversity and specificity of their cultures, share the common
> experience of domination and exclusion by the majority.
>
> *(ix)*

The definitions from these two books will constitute a major part of the understanding of "minority" discourse or literature in this chapter.

Minority studies, minor literature, and minority discourse are used to mean the same thing in this chapter to discuss theory and aesthetics in African literature. Minority discourse has to do with the conception of minority groups, as opposed to majority, with different identities or traits in specific spatiotemporal settings, and often relating to power in political and social issues. It is thus minor in not being dominant but different from the mainstream. Minority studies is therefore unique in its discourse, which is eclectic as it relates to political, social, economic, ethnic, racial, and other ideological and identity issues that may be set in contexts of place or time. It is panoramic in its "crossover" and interdisciplinary attributes and focuses on the specificity of its minority status.

African literature has undergone scrutiny through various theoretical approaches, including structuralism, deconstruction, Marxism, historicism, postcolonialism, and feminism. The substrata of African literature comprise minority literatures whose discourses exhibit comparative features in countering majority or dominant institutions or attitudes, especially in social, cultural, political, and economic spheres of the African experience. It is significant to note from the beginning that most minority discourses are themselves counter-discourses, but they are not always or necessarily so. For example, as argued by B. Weiss in "Utter(ing) Silences," though "women have crossed the borderline of restricted spheres and have thrown their voices for everyone to hear" (Smith and Ce 8), sometimes "women deliberately choose to refuse to throw their voice. They, in the true sense of the word, decide to be voiceless, yet as a means of subversion" (Smith and Ce 9). Thus, while feminism could be a minority discourse attempting to subvert patriarchal orthodoxies, there is another discourse within feminism in which it is not only "voice-throwing" but also silence that could be a more potent weapon against male or patriarchal domination. It appears therefore that even within a minority discourse, there can be a counter-discourse or discourses, while in a majority discourse, the counter-discourse could be a minority discourse. I work under the premise that "minority discourse" avails itself of a set of ideas that can lead to a meaningful discussion of African literature. Furthermore, these minor literatures have in their particular ways aesthetic features that make them of interest and value to their writers and readers.

The study of the minority discourses in African literature is bound to elicit some conclusions on the theory and aesthetics, however tentative they may be. It offers the critical inquirer ample opportunity to have this array of discourses from whose panoply one can proffer remarks that constitute not only a form of reiterating its theoretical attributes but also aesthetic conclusions on African literary minority discourses. Certain ideational patterns emerge in an exploration of literatures that are not in the mainstream but have their respective bodies of work which are intrinsic parts of African literature. Interestingly, these different discourses are parts of a larger unit in literary traditions that contextually distinguishes itself as African literature and is distinct as a literary tradition or canon from, for instance, European, Asian, or Latin American literatures. I am aware of Anthony Giddens's argument about the effects of the forces of globalization in the remapping and reconfiguration of the cultures that produce the "continental" literatures. However, African literature remains very much an African cultural production from traditional to modern times because it is itself a part and vehicle of African mores, history, sensibility, worldview, and realities, which it reflects and records in the literary genres of poetry, drama, and fiction. Thus, as a cultural production, literature, through its content and deployment of figurative language, has characteristic features and functions, which Stein Haugom Olsen says "must display those features which define and justify that interest which members of the culture take in its literature" (521). To him, the properties of literature "constitute their aesthetic nature and thus their aesthetic worth" (Olsen 521). The aim of this chapter, therefore, is to establish a pattern of the theory of minority discourses and simultaneously examine the aesthetics that drives these discourses as vibrant parts of African literature and without which the literature itself is not complete as the comprehensive reflection in writing of the experiences and living realities of the people.

Theory and African literature

Theory and aesthetics have long been bandied about in African literary scholarship without definitions, and sometimes they become buzzwords in literary essays and presentations that leave one wondering what these terms really mean. I use "literary theory" in this chapter as defined by Gregory Castle "in terms of principles and concepts, strategies and tactics needed to guide critical practice" (2). Castle defines theory as *"the capacity to generalize about phenomena and to develop concepts that form the basis for interpretation and analysis"* (2). To him, the:

> mode of thought suggested by this working definition involves first the ability to think generally about a given set of phenomena (language, social relations, women's experience, the novel as a form); second to develop theoretical concepts (or models) based on assumptions and principles governing the inclusion of elements within the set and the relations between those elements; and, finally, to use these concepts as the starting point from which to interpret and analyze specific instances within a set.
>
> *(3)*

By "set," he means "the function of metaphor, capitalism, female gender roles, the *Bildungsroman*" (3). These "sets" in African literature form minority literary traditions whose discourses present their respective "elements." Castle also points out that theory grows out of ideology (3). It is a mode of thought related to society, politics, language, history, psychology, and gender, among others. Theory is thus the idea through which the literary scholar can look at the binding contents and forms of texts and also interrelate and exclude them from other bodies of work that do not open themselves to particular modes of interpretation or types of scrutiny.

While complaining of "a near absence of clear theoretical moorings" (2) and "theoretical anaemia" (5) in African literature in the later part of the 20th century, Chidi Amuta makes a significant point that "the interpretations of the literary products of a given society can only command validity if they are rooted in theoretical paradigms that either organically derive from or are most directly relevant to the objective conditions of life in the society in question" (6). To the Nigerian Marxist critic, "it is the socio-economic, political and ideological contradictions which define the life and historical experiences of the African people that must form the basis of a new and more functionally relevant theoretical approach to African literature" (vii–viii). Amuta's alignment of the African reality to only class conflicts is ideologically suitable for his materialist discourse but does not allow theory to involve power, gender, social, and other paradigms of the African experience. Minorities in politics, culture, gender, language, economic and psychological states, and more seek to express their disaffection with the perceived majorities and affirm their own identity. In this sense, each minority discourse becomes a "theoretical articulation of the political and cultural structures that connect different minority cultures in their subjugation and opposition to the dominant culture" (JanMohamed and David Lloyd ix). With the long history of postcolonialism and now globalization, this chapter affirms the accommodation of the plurality and diversity of African experiences that form minority discourses.

Aesthetics and African literature

Aesthetics has been a contentious term to use to describe literature outside of poetry for a long time. Peter Lamarque says, "If aesthetics is to be at all relevant to literature it must deploy recognizable features of aesthetic appraisal as applied more widely but it must also capture something distinctive about literature as an art form" (5). The point is that aesthetics is not only about beauty but has come to include interest, value, meaning, and literary devices such as form and realism that help the reader to grasp the content of a literary work. It is in light of this definition of "aesthetics" that the term is not only relevant but also helps to mark out any literary discourse by both the pleasure and the meaning of the experience expressed.

In his *Ideology & Form in African Poetry* (1990), Emmanuel Ngara defines "aesthetic ideology" as "the literary convention and stylistic stances adopted by the writer" (12). To the Kenyan Marxist literary scholar, "The reader and the text enter into a relationship similar to that of a man and a woman making love" (16–17). Many African scholars have examined African literary texts or genres with particular attention to their respective aesthetics. For example, in my book, *Contemporary African Literature: New Approaches* (2012), there is this observation:

> One can say that the aesthetics of a people's literature inform the features that make that literature unique. The literary artist and readers/audience have a symbiotic relationship as producer and consumer, each with expectations that make the literary work contribute to the spiritual and intellectual delight and a manifestation in creative terms of the socio-cultural and political condition as it affects the individual. In the end, the literary work pleases the more it performs a function that brings and affirms the values and virtues that the people hold dear.
>
> *(Ojaide 188)*

Going by this statement, each minority discourse in African literature has its "expectations" for "the spiritual and intellectual delight" of the minority group ranging against the dominant group. In this discussion of minority discourses in African literature, the focus is more on experience expressed as a discourse in the multiplicity of discourses that are subsumed in African literature than in literary techniques per se in the texts. In any case, however much has been done earlier on the aesthetics of African literature as a literary tradition, one still needs a broader definition of aesthetics to separate minority discourses from majority literature.

Josette Attard posits several points in connecting literature and aesthetics. She sees aesthetic characteristics as "a special kind of values, which can lead to experiences of interest and desire" (81). After identifying form as relevant to aesthetics in literature with particular attention to poetry, she says that "an aesthetic experience can result from the detection of the expressive qualities of a literary work" (81). Attard sees a core aesthetic experience in literature which "consists of the contemplation of the conceptions the work presents to the imagination and this is done for the sake of pleasure arising from such an experience" (83). So each minority discourse presents an "experience" to which many writers respond. For instance, Niger Delta, Anglophone Cameroon, North African Amazigh/Berber, and the Senegambian/Casamance Jola (Diola) literatures all interrogate experiences of particular peoples or groups with specific conditions which cast them as minorities or marginalized peoples among the respective dominant groups they struggle against. Their unique experiences are borne by a literature whose form lends its discursive power to tropes or expressions that carry certain values and at the same time bring about some measure of emotional and intellectual pleasure.

In addition, there are experiences in African societies based on languages such as Nigerian Pidgin English, Sierra Leonean Krio (Creole), Congolese or Ivorian patois, Central Africa's Lingala, South African Afrikaans, and East and Central African Swahili. The speakers of each of these languages see themselves as minorities, since these languages are not the generally or majority-spoken languages in their respective nation-states. Each language speaker is connected imaginatively to the speakers of the same language, and all the speakers create a linguistic community in which they share common interests that bind them socioculturally, politically, psychologically, and sometimes economically. I believe there is a certain political affinity among Anglophone Cameroonians who speak English and see themselves as marginalized by the majority Francophone Cameroonians who control the central government in Yaounde. Though the official language of Tanzania and despite millions of speakers in East and Central Africa, Swahili is still a minority language compared to the inherited colonial languages of English, French, and Portuguese which are widely spoken and adopted as official languages. Afrikaans is a minority language largely spoken by "whites" of Dutch origin in South Africa and was identified with the constitutional change to apartheid in South Africa from 1948 until it ended on May 10, 1994, when Nelson Mandela became the first black president and officially ended the noxious separation of races in the country. It is instructive to note that Coloureds and many blacks speak and write in Afrikaans and the language has fluctuated from majority/official status to minority depending upon the political swing of the country.

Each of these languages has its aesthetic structures that make it peculiar for writers to deploy the diction, figures, and other phonological ploys in the language to express their thoughts and feelings. A body of literature has coalesced around each of these "minor" languages and, put together, they too all form many of the "minority discourses" in African literature. Nigeria's Pidgin English, for instance, is mainly used by the less educated in society, especially traders and the common folks in urban areas. To a large extent, Pidgin is the lingua franca of the Niger Delta in Nigeria, despite the language's spread to other parts of the country. It is a "language" that is very humorous and used by comedians and writers to say serious things in a lighthearted manner. Pidgin English has been dexterously deployed in Nigerian literature. In the poetry of Aig Imokhuede, Chinua Ezenwa-Ohaeto, Akachi Ezeigbo, and Eriata Oribhabor, among many poets, its aesthetic features powerfully manifest themselves in the frivolous banter for which the language is known. The same could be said of a long history of Nigerian fiction with Pidgin English dialogue, from Cyprian Ekwensi's *Jagua Nana* through Ken Saro-Wiwa's *Sozaboy: A Novel in Rotten English* (1985) to more recent works like Chimamanda Adichie's *Half of a Yellow Sun*. In fact, Saro-Wiwa's *Sozaboy* is written entirely in Pidgin English that the author calls "rotten English."

Similarly, there is a huge body of work in Swahili literature which bears Arab and African cultural traits. Abdilatif Abdalla's collection of prison poems, *Sauti Ya Dhiki*, has been praised for the manner in which form and language fuse to convey meaning. In any case, the elocution of Pidgin English, like the other African languages, in poetry, drama, and fiction gives them a distinctive mark in the plethora of languages in Africa outside the officially adopted foreign English, French, and Portuguese whose speakers, writers, and readers ironically form the majority discourse as far as languages are concerned in Africa.

African folkloric affirmation of multiple/minority discourses

African folklore, through many examples, seems to affirm fragmentation rather than homogeneity and so privileges diversity over conformity or oneness. The examples of Yoruba orishas – a thousand and one godheads – and Ashanti Ananse's pot of wisdom breaking and dispersing wisdom seem to demonstrate this affirmation. The Dogon also have myths woven out of multiple godheads emanating from Amma. Furthermore, among the Igbo people, as Achebe emphasized, one is not enough, and there is tolerance of "another" or "others" in the saying that "Where one thing stands, there can also stand another." There are likely many other examples of folkloric myths of fragmentation and multiplicity of one, but these mentioned examples are some of the most powerful mythical representations of the psychic acceptance of pluralities of the African essence, or rather the diversity of oneness. Deploying these myths to understand the familiarity with diversity, one can say that there is one African literature made up of many parts, subdivisions, or discourses.

African literature, especially in its traditional and oral form, has long been broadly described as being mainly for entertainment and education. However, today, one is aware of the multiplicity of characteristics, forms, or sets of the literature. As the literature grew and with more texts availing themselves of different sociocultural, political, economic, and psychological spectra, African literature was bound to display its many parts in the countless "discourses" which stand alongside each other in their differences and against their respective majorities in the African imaginary. One can infer that there is a proclivity to the diverse and multiple, as nothing solidly uniform can be as vibrant, strong, and lasting as something made of different parts that continue to reproduce and by doing so engage in self-rejuvenation.

African literature may have established itself as a literary tradition with its canons as different from literatures of other cultural regions of the world. However, what is evident is that even within a canon or tradition, there are disruptions and the "fragments" can be assembled into a whole. African literature is thus made up of multiple discourses that carry the totality of the African experience, identity, reality, and worldview and a sense of African-ness or Africanity. After all, a human being is made up of many limbs or parts and each part contributes to a healthy body. Culture is the heart and language the blood that give life to the body. It is in the same light that the minority discourses play out in African literature.

Interestingly, each "minority discourse" unit has a body of work to it so that the "minor literature" has its own identity in the wider field of African literature. For instance, there is a body of work that constitutes each of the minority languages I earlier discussed. Similarly, marginalized groups in African countries have their literatures, such as Anglophone Cameroonian literature, Niger Delta literature, Amazigh/Berber literature, and Senegambian Jola literature. Niger Delta literature includes numerous collections of poetry, dozens of plays, and many fictional works. It also has many scholarly works on this literature of a Nigerian marginalized people whose region has valuable resources of petroleum and gas whose sale forms the main earnings sustaining the Nigerian federal government. Many of these literatures are subnational literatures, too. Anglophone Cameroon has a very vibrant literature of its own that equally has an identity of its own through the works of such writers as Mbella Sonne Dipoko, Bate Besong, Bole Butake, Anne Tanyi-Tang, and Joyce Ashuntantang. Connected to this set or subset are literatures related to intranational conflicts such as the South Sudan and Zimbabwean Shona-Ndebele problems. Civil war conflicts such as the Nigeria-Biafra war have a large body of work in fictional representations of war activities, as shown in the works of Flora Nwapa, Isidore Okpewho, Festus Iyayi, and Elechi Amadi. The genocide in Rwanda, the Boko Haram insurgency in Nigeria and adjoining countries, and the Eritrean-Ethiopian war have also generated their own literatures that form minor literatures.

Historical forces and minority discourses

African minority discourses embrace historicist backgrounds. We are at this time at the confluence of postcolonialism and globalization, and African literature is evolving into manifold directions and forms. Postcolonialism and globalization have their impact in bearing testimony to the multifarious discourses that make up African literature. For a long time, the discourse of African literature concerned both the oral/traditional and the written/modern. The oral/traditional literature itself is made up of a variety of forms. The modern/written form of African literature assumed the nomenclature of "postcolonial," which by its implication is a never-ending discourse. The "postcolonial" seems unipolar in the sense that it sees all the literary productions resulting from the European imperial interventions of the 19th century in Africa and elsewhere in the world through that historical lens. However, things are changing, since all those who had been once colonized could not be tied forever to their far-past history. Inevitably, this change has affected the realities of Africans and their cultural productions. African literature has asserted its uniqueness and has a tradition and a canon of its own. Globalization has exacerbated the disruptions in Africa from the postcolonial unipolarity into minority subdivisions of liberalized African cultural productions. Kwame Anthony Appiah's "Is the Post- in Postmodernism the Post- in Postcolonial?" (McKeon, ed. 882–897) touches on the changing realities of Africa which have given rise to expression of multiple states of being.

Let me use two discourses that have changed drastically because of the intellectual climate of the liberalization and exposure brought about by democracy and increased movements of peoples across borders. It is not that some of the experiences did not exist even when not talked about. Issues of sexuality and migration show how globalization has highlighted and brought into the open African internal contradictions in expressions of experiences that at some time in the past would have been taboos. This is in addition to the internal forces driving people to migrate out of the continent. I hope to discuss these subjects later as aspects of contemporary African experiences. Being African as well as the African experience are no longer uniform or have a specific essence as such but are now quite multidimensional. One is not even sure Africans are one people! They are peoples whose unique experiences divulge the elasticity of current and future discourses that cannot be classified in one small space but many small spaces. To put it in a popular way, the genie has come out of the bottle!

Modern African literature might have started as reactive, which is what postcolonial literature is in its response to being under the rule of a foreign power whose motive is the economic wellbeing of the imperial government and not the interests of the subjected people. In most of the literary works, African writers depicted how Africans suffered in colonial times, whether in the forms of racial discrimination, economic exploitation, and political marginalization, among other woes. Then the literature evolved to what we really are and on to an affirmative literature. In other words, it developed from a conscious response to those who disrupted African life with their imperial ambitions to a period of subconscious expression of being African. Literature has become increasingly responsive to our environment, our biology, our inner being, and our living realities. I am a human being who has choices and is living the consequences of my being in a particular environment. People(s) are not the same and so do not behave the same way and do not have the same needs. Identities have become more fluid and complicated in Africa now than in past decades. The expression of disparate experiences is at the core of multiple discourses. Most in society will follow conventional ways, but others will have their own individual ways. So there are majorities and there are minorities. The dominant group wants order, peace, and harmony which favor it, but some may feel constrained by the needs of the majority and so seek to disrupt their constraints.

Even African folklore also affirms this. The tortoise, spider, and other trickster characters undermine the majority ethos of society, whether for self-centered individual needs or not, and so express alternative views. The communal needs and the individual or personal needs do not always converge in the same ethical directions; hence the majority and the minorities. There is alterity that contends with any form of accepted ways. Even when ways of life are forbidden, people will still practice them!

Countering domination

The societal apprehension of dissent or dissident ways may not be unique to only African society but appears to be a universal human trait. In a way, these multiple discourses can be related to Michel Foucault's concepts of "power," "madness," and "resistance." The unconventional, rebel, deviant, or abnormal folks of society are shamed so as to conform, but many will resist the strong tactics of power. The minorities are perceived as "mad" by the majority groups. For instance, most Nigerians far from "the drilling fields" with the apocryphal devastation of the Niger Delta because of the exploitation of its oil and gas will wonder why there is such a loud cry for resource control. Of course, the impoverished people of the oil-rich region "resist" the powerful multinational companies and the complicit federal Nigerian government with gun and pen; hence the struggle of the Egbesu Boys, Movement for the Emancipation of the Niger Delta, Niger Delta Defense Force, and other militant groups to seize control of their land's resources. The same case of dissent could be seen in minority Anglophone Cameroon, which the dominant Francophone side could say is "mad" in its attempt to shed minority status by becoming a self-governing region or a sovereign country of its own. One can posit that in the more liberal climate of today, there are bound to be many "madmen" fighting a war of "resistance" against the "power" of the establishment, which could be an authoritarian government, patriarchal system, or homophobic society.

Patriarchy is the dominant sociocultural structure in Africa. Men's control of power leads to gender biases. In a literary work like Tsitsi Dangerembga's *Nervous Conditions*, the men enjoy privileges that women are excluded from. For instance, young Nhamo is sent to live with Baba Mukuru, the educated and wealthy family patriarch. He does not sit near women in the bus because he says they smell of reproductive odors. He leaves his luggage at the bus stop and expects his sister to come and get it for him. One is not surprised that when he dies, his sister does not grieve. Baba Mukuru and his wife go abroad and have virtually the same level of educational qualification, but it is only the man who is celebrated upon their return. Similarly, Nyasha and her brother Chido are treated differently. The father allows the boy to go out as he likes and to even sleep at his friend's place, but he is very harsh on Nyasha, complaining about her style of dressing and lateness in coming from parties. The domination of the male gender thus leads to rebellion by the female gender as a result of being kept down. Since the males see themselves as superior to women, there are grumblings and protests by the female characters to counter male domination. *Nervous Conditions* is emblematic of feminist voices that include Mariama Ba's *So Long a Letter*, Chimamanda Ngozi Adichie's *Purple Hibiscus*, and Sindiwe Magona's *Beauty's Gift* that speak against male domination.

As a minority discourse, feminism empowers female characters to free themselves from men-ordained sociocultural traditions and exercise all their agencies to be full human beings who can live towards self-fulfillment. Feminist literary texts have value in inspiring female readers to summon their agency rather than living as victims in a patriarchal society. They provide female models to female readers. At the same time, feminist texts, by exposing the exploitation and oppression of women by men, sensitize male readers towards treating women as equals and helping to bring equity to representation on gender, economic, and political levels. The aesthetics of feminist discourse embraces the use of irony and other tropes to undermine the assumed superiority of men over women because of gender. In Dangarembga's *Nervous Conditions*, Nhamo is not as brilliant as Tambu, but when things are hard financially, the family only pays his school fees because he is male. The girls are seen as only needing to be trained to cook and be good wives. And that is why a boy like Nhamo is able to eat his chicken and still have it!

Closely related to the silence or paucity of women's voices is sexuality. African writers, male and female, heterosexual or not, now express themselves more openly. In this context of sexuality, heterosexuality becomes the dominant set that other kinds of sexual orientation contend with. Conventional society does not encourage deviation from the norm and sees LGBTQ folks as abnormal. There are now African works that problematize heteronormativity. Jude Dibia's *Walking with Shadows* presents Adrian Njoko, a gay protagonist, who, after living a hidden life by marrying and having children, has to choose between the false life and what he really is, a gay man, in a society that will shun him if he exposes his true being. The conflict he experiences appears treated with authorial empathy. Uzodinma Iweala's *Beasts of No Nation*, a civil war novel, has gay practice among the soldiers. Similarly, Chris Abani's *GraceLand* describes homosexual practice in the Afikpo section of the novel. Tess Onwueme, in *Tell It To Women: An Epic Drama* (1995), describes two female characters, Ruth and Daisie, in a lesbian relationship.

The increasing body of literary work on gay lifestyle tells the experience of a minority group that wants its voice to be heard and its experiences to be acknowledged. Times have passed when many gay men and women or writers hid their experiences, and they now openly show off their lifestyles in literary works as well as in parades in major African cities. Theirs is the literary representation of their living reality as gay, and they also express their criticism of homophobic behaviors in most African societies. Thus, there are many dimensions of whatever subject is talked about. The plurality of involvement, however far from the majority's, shows the diversity of the African experience which can only be fully comprehended through attention to many other discourses.

Trending periods in African literature

The indigenous oral and modern written traditions have managed over decades to fuse into the subconscious stream. African writers in poetry, fiction, and drama no longer want to prove themselves to be as good writers as their Western counterparts. This was, however, not the case in the initial stage of modern African literature, when many of the writers modeled their works on Western writers. For instance, that generation of African poets that includes Leopold Sedar Senghor, Tchicaya U Tam'si, Christopher Okigbo, Kofi Awoonor, Wole Soyinka, and J.P. Clark, among others, is in fact African "modernist" since the writers exhibit many of the features of Western modernist poetry such as allusiveness, fragmentation, and the focus on individualism. How could one read Okigbo without strong echoes of Paul Verlaine, Arthur Rimbaud, or Stephane Mallarme? The same could be said of Clark with Gerald Manley Hopkins, whose "sprung rhythm" he adopts in some of his poems. Senghor writes about the African experience of his time, but he deploys the poetic techniques of French Symbolists to express himself in many of his poems. So there was a time when African poets wrote as if they were part of the European/Western modernist poetry tradition.

There are parallels in fiction and drama of what was happening on the poetry scene. There have been studies of Chinua Achebe's indebtedness to Thomas Hardy's form of the tragic novel. The Nigerian writer might have also learned from the craft of Joseph Conrad, whose *Heart of Darkness* he denounced on many occasions as a racist novel. Greek tragedies like Orpheus and Eurydice informed Ofeyi and Iriyise in Soyinka's *Season of Anomy*. Soyinka may have learned from not only Bertolt Brecht but also other European practitioners of the theatre of the absurd, resulting in a play like *The Road*.

The reactive streak of modern African literature includes Negritude that aimed at affirming African-ness as opposed to the European. Of course, there were writers and scholars of Anglophone Africa who did not accept the philosophy that Negritude tried to preach. Soyinka's famous or rather infamous retort that a tiger does not proclaim its "tigritude" shows the lack of uniformity on African ways of regaining an African identity after colonization has attempted to destroy it or make Africans look down on their own culture and "assimilate" Western ways. Negritude is different from the expression of the African Personality which takes pride in the African as a being of his own. Like in the mode of models, many writers seemed to have fallen in line with the literary tradition of the country that colonized them. In this manner, the Negritude writers were from Francophone countries, and many of them studied in France. The African Personality novelists were from Anglophone Africa. One can say that there has never been a uniform tradition as far as African literature is concerned, as there are always writers pitching their writing tents on some turf that is not universally followed in the continent. So the issues of what are majority and what are minority literatures have always been there but have become exacerbated by more open expressions of "minority" experiences.

Following the generation of writers already mentioned are the "Alter/Native" poets who rose to prominence in the 1980s following Chinweizu's strong and persistent criticism of the African "euromodernists" as not writing from the African tradition. *Towards the Decolonization of African Literature* played a role in separating the African "modernist" writers from the writers that followed and looked to their oral traditions to model their techniques. The Alter/Native poets do not have to prove themselves as their predecessors did but express themselves as they see fit from the perspective of their African-ness. These writers do not look backwards for reaction to the past of European expansionist imperialism. They are more concerned with the living realities in Africa that involve class conflict. The writers attempt to transform the inadequacies of the present into a society that cares for its underprivileged. They conceive of poetry as comprehensible with use of such devices as irony, personification, metaphors, and other figures that expose the class differences so as to bridge the gap between the haves and the have-nots. The early resort to oral literature features might have been responsible for the label of "Alter/Natives."

There are thus major movements in African literature, but there are many still outside such movements and giving space to diversity. There seems to be in every period of African literature a form of majority trend which has reacting against it multiple counter-trends that may not be as strong. What is significant is that at one time or the other, there is a mainstream or popular discourse or assumption of the major trend which many other discourses attempt to counter or subvert. It must be stated that these counter-discourses to majority subjects, positions, situations, and traditions may not be deliberate but individual responses reflecting the views of others or efforts to go along with the zeitgeist or otherwise. For instance, if we were to take Frantz Fanon's concept of the development of the literature of a colonized people with its three stages in *The Wretched of the Earth*, there are many varieties and diverse or counter-movements within broad development periods. Fanon conceives three developmental periods in the history of colonized nations. In the first phase, the writers write like their counterparts in the metropolis to show that they are as creative and good as nationals of the colonizing country. The African "euromodernists" seem to fit into that category of writing almost within the Western tradition of the time. The second phase has to do with a resort to nationalism and the stubborn application of literature to nation-building. The "Alter/Natives" appear to represent that phase by borrowing much from the indigenous oral traditions. By Funso Aiyejina's nomenclature of this group of writers, they are not only "alternatives" to the "euromodernists" but also fostering a new form of "native" literary tradition.

The blind spots of Frantz Fanon's third stage of literature development

Fanon posits the third phase of literature of the colonized people as affirming themselves without recourse to lamenting, whining, or criticizing "others," the Western imperialists, forever. The people at this stage have to assume responsibility for their respective destinies and express their subconscious or emotive state of being. We live in history but also outside of it; not the broad history of Western imperialism and its consequences (colonialism) but within a history of subnationalism and transnationalism, even though it could be argued that these current developments were earlier created by imperialist forces. However, Africans now express themselves in thoughts and feelings in areas of migration, sexuality, disability, and the environment. These are issues consonant to their humanity. Thus, while Fanon projects what the third phase of the literature of a colonized people would be, he projected it in "postcolonial" and "post-postcolonial" perspectives which did not take into account the many "studies" that would occupy the attention of Africans in the later 20th and current 21st centuries. Yes, African literature is "postcolonial" but cannot remain forever in the continuum of that post-imperialist conundrum and so has to reflect the living realities of the people whose experiences are the subjects of literary works.

Fanon could not anticipate many of the concerns that would preoccupy writers in former colonies of European powers in so many decades to come. Many of the discourses that prevail in African literary scholarship today can be said to be the blind spots of Fanon's theoretical assumption of the final phase of the literature of the people who were once colonized. These are minor areas in the major postcolonial history and all are subsumed into modern African literature. Migration, sexuality, and the environment in particular have become important issues not only in the lives of the people but also in literary representations. Many of these issues have tangential connections to postcolonialism in the sense that the migration of people from the once-colonized nations seeking better lives in Europe, the liberal lifestyle that gives rise to free expression of sexuality, and sensitivity to environmental issues can still be traced to the former European powers and the West. In any case, these areas have become areas of concern among many others in Africa.

Migration literature

Migration has always been part of modern African literature because Africans have always been traveling or migrating to other countries. The traffic has always been to former European imperial powers and new Western economic powers; hence the popularity of Western Europe and North America as destinations of choice. In Cheikh Hamidou Kane's *Ambiguous Adventure*, set in Senegal, a colony of France then, the young and impressionable Samba Diallo, who has been trained in an Islamic school, is sent to Paris, the French capital, to study philosophy. He develops psychological problems which take him back home, and that conflict drives him to become a psychological wreck. The experiences of the 21st-century new-wave migrants have provided materials for the content of works of writers. Nigerian diaspora writers have established a subcategory of literature called Afropolitan literature about experiences of migrants to and from the North (Europe and North America). These texts reflect historical, sociocultural, economic, and philosophical contexts. The wave of African migrants dying in the Mediterranean in efforts to get to Lampedusa or other parts of Europe has become a regular television event. Chimamanda Ngozi Adichie's *Americanah*, Chika Unigwe's *On Black Sisters' Street*, and Taiye Selasi's *Ghana Must Go*, among many others, carry the experiences of migration in contemporary Africa. In recent times, there is a generation of Africans who are global citizens who see themselves as Africans and more. Their identities go beyond borders of specific countries, especially where they migrated or decided to settle. These experiences form a minority discourse in contemporary African literature.

It is significant that the migration from the continent tells of the lack of jobs and other socioeconomic opportunities in Africa. In some places, civil conflicts are responsible for the exodus of mainly youths to take risky journeys to other lands for a peaceful life. The texts draw attention to the need for African leaders to pursue policies that will create jobs, have non-dictatorial policies, and give hope to their citizens, especially youths, who only leave for the North because they have no hope in their futures in their respective African homelands.

African eco-critical literature

Literature about the environment, or eco-critical literature, has gained attention in recent decades. Nigeria's Ken Saro-Wiwa exposed the environmental degradation of the Niger Delta where oil and gas-exploring and exploiting multinational companies such as Shell BP and Chevron did not care about preventing oil spills or managing them with the same standards as in the companies' home countries in Europe and the United States of America. Gas flares continue in the Niger Delta over two decades after its banning by the United Nations. Within the Niger Delta, there have been literary responses to the pollution which affects human and non-human lives. Wangari Maathai's Green Belt Movement in Kenya; her works, especially *Unbowed*; and her winning the Nobel Prize for Peace have promoted the environmental struggle in Africa. Eco-critical literature has a body of work that also includes the works of Niyi Osundare such as *The Eye of the Earth*, Tanure Ojaide's *The Activist* and *The Tale of the Harmattan*, and Zakes Mda's *The Heart of Redness*. What is significant is that while the literature could be postcolonial or post-postcolonial, there are many issues that converge into it. After all, Africa's living realities comprise not only one situation but multifarious situations.

The rhetoric of minority discourses

Rhetoric is used here as the device in establishing the emotive and intellectual space of a minority discourse. It is the "expressive qualities" of a text that Attard talks about (81). In a way, it marries theory and aesthetics into a set that not only brings delight but also intellectual delimitation of the discourse. There are expectations of a discourse, majority or minority, and in those expectations are the delight, interest, and value of the literary texts that fall within that corpus of discourse. The literature of blacks, for instance, in North Africa where Arabs form the majority brings to the center black characters that are often represented as victimized or marginalized by the majority group and so resist oppression by self-assertion. The minority in almost every discourse casts itself as the wronged and virtuous side against a villainous majority. In a gay fictional work, one will expect the gay characters to be portrayed in a sympathetic manner by the gay writer as asserting independence of sexuality in the midst of homophobic assault. The mere fact that a gay writer or reader can identify with gay characters in the narrative is a matter of interest, delight, and value. How can there be a feminist discourse without issues of women's marginalization, oppression, or solidarity? How can there be a Marxist discourse without issues of socioeconomic stratification?

Aesthetics involves the delight or pleasure derived from the text or group of texts that constitute a discourse. In these minority discourses, there is a certain sincerity of the writer in pursuing a cause or advocacy that generates a rhetoric that becomes consonant with that minority's resistance, collective solidarity, and the politics of its wellbeing. The situation of a minority discourse is often a response against a dominant or majority position it counters for its individual affirmation. Each minority discourse goes against the grain of a dominant culture. It directly or indirectly condemns the tyranny of the dominant group that is often described as unethical, unfair, and even immoral. It is an effort to shake off the majority's perception of the minority as deviant, rebellious, and abnormal. The rhetoric that gets associated with minority discourse involves tropes that represent the situation being expressed so as to be acceptable to the reader. The different metaphors that define minority from majority are carefully selected to assert its raison d'être.

The form deployed for the expression becomes a paradigm that unites all the voices of the minority into a single discourse. The aptness of the tropes comes in the beauty of the metaphors and other types of figurative language used. Often repetition, irony, and hyperbole are other figures deployed. The minority discourse counters the majority or dominant tradition, whether it is in sociocultural, political, economic, racial, or other terms, as already mentioned in this discussion. It turns things upside down and often expresses a revolutionary ethos to affirm its identity and relevance.

Conclusion

From the foregoing discussion, theory appears inseparable from aesthetics in the sense that it is the organizing principle based on incorporating ideas to approach a text, group of texts, or "studies" towards making meaning of the human experiences that the writers present in their respective works. It is a way of thinking differently from the majority or dominant group; a counter-discourse that wants to be seen or heard outside the majority voice. Theory of any-thing or, in this case, minority situations, has semi-autonomy of its own existence. Theory and aesthetics say something that delight intellectually through the artistic rendition of human experiences in literature.

Minority studies of African literature does not show a contestation of different discourses but a growing polyvocality and emergence of differences in a postmodern and global world of which Africa is a part. The African experience has begun to manifest the subdivision that allows Derrida's wish for a thousand flowers to bloom. Small or minor discourses are now seen as important in an inclusive and multicultural world; hence this study to show how there is strength in differences and many voices.

In conclusion, theory and aesthetics in African minority discourses are intertwined. The form and language of each minority discourse mark it in a unique way that makes readers enjoy the craft and meaning of the particular body of texts that constitute that discourse. There is no doubt that these minority discourses are the subjectivities of super-constructs such as politics, nation, gender, race/ethnic group, and other assumed or accepted norms that minorities resist to create their own spaces where they want to be left alone to enjoy their humanity. Humanity becomes a complex entity whose body and emotions differ within groups. The suspicion of the monolith could not have been stronger than what it is today that has expanded every field to many reflections and interpretations. Meaning and value become the main aesthetic features that promote minority status into a self-propelling agency that stands out as different to affirm a new identity within a bigger identity that solemnizes oneness for strength but which oppresses. From this discussion, African literature's strength arises from a multiplicity of thoughts and feelings that coalesce into groups, one major and many minorities resisting the dominant force. As Gilles Deleuze and Felix Guattari have written, "There is nothing that is major or revolutionary except the minor. To hate all languages of masters" (26). The different African minority literatures are in every sense "revolutionary" and deploy the languages of their dominant groups to achieve their aesthetic fulfillment.

Works cited and references

Amuta, Chidi. *The Theory of African Literature: Implications for Practical Criticism*. London: Zed Books, 1989.

Appiah, Kwame Anthony. "Is the Post- in Postmodern the Post- in Postcolonial?" in McKeon, Michael, ed. *Theory of the Novel: A Historical Approach*. Baltimore: Johns Hopkins University Press, 2000, pp. 882–897.

Attard, Josette. "The Connection between Literature and Aesthetics: Is It Problematic?" in *Symposia Melitensia*, Number 14 (2018); https://www.um.edu.mt/library/oar/handle/123456789/30002

Castle, Gregory. *The Blackwell Guide to Literary Theory*. Malden, MA and Oxford, UK: Blackwell Publishing, 2007.

Chinnweizu, Onwuchekwa Jemie and Ihechukwu Madubuike. *Toward the Decolonization of African Literature*. Washington, DC: Howard University Press, 1983.

Deleuze, Gilles and Felix Guattari. *Kafka: Toward a Minor Literature*. Trans. Dana Polan. Minneapolis: University of Minnesota Press, 1986.

Dibia, Jude. *Walking with Shadows*. Birmingham, Alabama: Black Sands Books, 2005.

Di Leo, Jeffrey R. "Vincent B. Leitch, *Literary Theory in the 21st Century: Theory Renaissance*. New York: Bloomsbury, 2014, 174 pp." (review). *The Comparatist*, vol. 39, 2015, pp. 412–415.

Fanon, Frantz. *The Wretched of the Earth*. New York: Grove Press, 1963.

Foucault, Michel. *Discipline and Punish: The Birth of Prison*. Grans. Alan Sheridan. New York: Vintage, 1995. Print. *The Consequences of Modernity*. Stanford: Stanford University Press, 1991.

Foucault, Michel. *Madness and Civilization: A History of Insanity in the Age of Reason (Folie et Déraison: Histoire de la folie à l'âge classique)*. Paris: Librairie Plon, 1964; in French 1961).

Foucault, Michel. *History of Madness*. Trans. Jean Khalfa Jonathan Murphy. Ed. Jean Khalf. London and New York: Routledge, 2006. Print.

Foucault, Michel. *History of Sexuality*. Trans. Robert Hurley. New York: Pantheon Books, 1978. Print.

Fukuyama, Francis. "The End of History?" *The National Interest*, vol. 16, 1989, pp. 3–18.

Giddens, Anthony. *The Consequences of Modernity*. Stanford: Stanford University Press, 1991.

JanMohamed, Abdul R. and David Lloyd, eds. *The Nature and Context of Minority Discourse*. New York and Oxford: Oxford University Press, 1990.

Kane, Cheikh Hamidou. *Ambiguous Adventure*. London: Heinemann, 1972.

Lamarque, Peter. "Aesthetics and Literature: A Problematic Relation?" *Philosophical Studies*, vol. 135, no. 1, 2008.

Maathai, Wangari. *Unbowed*. New York: Alfred A. Knopf, 2006.

Ngara, Emmanuel. *Ideology & Form in African Poetry*. London: James Currey, 1990.

Novitz, David. "*Philosophy and Fiction: Essays in Literary Aesthetics*" (review). *Philosophy and Literature*, vol. 8, no. 1, April 1984, pp. 144–145.

Ojaide, Tanure. *Contemporary African Literature: New Approaches*. Durham, NC: Carolina Academic Press, 2012.

Ojaide, Tanure. "Literary Aesthetics: Continuity and Change." *Journal of the African Literature Association*, vol. 6, no. 2, 2012, pp. 114–132.

Ojaide, Tanure. *Literature and Culture in Global Africa*. New York and London: Routledge and Francis and Taylor, 2018.

Ojaide, Tanure. *Theorizing African Oral Poetic Performance and Aesthetics: Udje Dance Songs of the Urhobo People*. Trenton, NJ: Africa World Press, 2009.

Olsen, Stein Haugom. "Literary Aesthetics and Literary Practice." *Mind*, vol. 90, no. 360, 1981, pp. 521–541.

Saro-Wiwa, Ken. *Sozaboy: A Novel in Rotten English*. Port Harcourt, Nigeria: Saros International Publishers, 1985.

Smith, Charles and Chin Ce, eds. *Counter Discourse in African Literature*. Lagos, Nigeria: Progeny Press International, 2014.

Vierke, Clarissa. "'What Is There in My Speaking': Re-Explorations of Language in Abdilatif Abdalla's Anthology of Prison Poetry, *Sauti Ya Dhiki*." *Research in African Literatures*, vol. 48, no. 1, Spring 2017, pp. 135–157.

PART II

Political and racial forms of marginalization

3

AMAZIGH/BERBER LITERATURE AND "LITERARY SPACE"

A contested minority situation in (North) African literatures

Daniela Merolla

Are the Imazighen/Berbers in a "situation of minority" in the Maghreb and in (North) African literatures? Although raising such a question may seem paradoxical in the case of language groups that suffered censure and gross violence in colonial and postcolonial times, the notion of Amazigh/Berber minority can be tricky to discuss and is largely rejected by the Imazighen themselves. Such an interrogation leads to questioning the relationships among historical actors and to avoiding essentialist interpretations of minority and majority groups in North Africa. The assigned "situation of minority" or majority needs to be reconstructed in the light of reciprocal historical dynamics by looking at cultural interaction and change and retracing inequality in power relationships which are not simply dichotomic (dominant/dominated) but very much articulated (Bertheleu 2008: 29). Reflecting on "minor," "minority," and "minorization" in literature offers an entrance to such dynamic constructions. This article investigates Amazigh/Berber literature and "literary space" by looking at the articulation of identity construction and at discourses on minority and majority in North Africa.

Both the terms Amazigh and Berber are used because, since the end of the 20th century, the Amazigh (sg.) and Imazighen (pl.) tend to stand out in society and in current studies, while the term Berber remains inscribed historically in the discourse of the research domain.[1] The geographical space of the communities using Amazigh/Berber vernaculars extends from Morocco to the oasis of Siwa in Egypt and passes through Algeria, Tunisia, and Libya. It also includes the Tuareg Berber-speaking populations in Mali, Niger, and the north of Burkina Faso.

Contested population figures

The estimated population figures for Imazighen were and are *loci* of political and scientific debate in both colonial and postcolonial sociopolitical contexts. The range of estimates indicates that censuses and any existing sources are either old or unreliable: Amazigh people are presently estimated to number between 12 and 25 million. The latter figure depends upon recalculation based on colonial sources, while the former derives from recent censuses that are unreliable concerning language use.[2] Moreover, the large migrant communities in Europe are not always taken into account. While the colonial sources indicated about 40% Amazigh/Berber-speaking population in Morocco and 25% in Algeria, recent studies agree on lower figures today and with huge differences, as indicated previously. According to the *Atlas des minorités dans le monde* (Atlas of the World's Minorities), Amazigh speakers number 17 million, and in 2008, they constituted 35% of the population in Morocco (Rif, Middle and High Atlas, Sous), 17% in Algeria (Kabylia, Aurès, Mzab), 2% in Tunisia (Isle of Djerbaa and Chenini, Douz, Tozeur), 1% in Mauritania (Zenaga), and 6% in Libya (Djebel Nefusa). Such figures are much lower than those recalculated respectively by activists and by scholars, the latter usually working on the basis of colonial sources. The Tuaregs, who live in a wide Saharan and sub-Saharan area across Algeria, Libya, Mali, Niger, and Burkina Faso, are estimated to be 83% of the inhabitants of such an enormous area, which is, however, very little inhabited: Tuaregs are estimated to be around two million speakers in all.

Even when all the difficulties are taken into account, it seems safe to say that the number of Amazigh/Berber speakers steadily decreased in the 20th century, as it is also doing in the present one. Considering the figures, Salem Chaker (1989a: 834) wrote: *"la berbérité, la conscience d'être berbère, est liée à la berbérophonie et ne concerne plus qu'une minorité (importante) de la population"* (Berber-ness, the consciousness of being Berber, is linked to the Berber language and concerns only a [significant] minority of the population).[3] At the same time, the high percentages of Amazigh/Berber speakers in Morocco and Algeria make them "bulky minorities," as Chaker writes in a later article (2003) reflecting on the fact that, as large and geographically concentrated groups, they are difficult to manage in national terms. Moreover, the notion of being in a situation of minority is not just linked to demographics but is characterized by inequality in power relationships and by the reciprocal representation of the minority/majority discourse over time (Bertheleu 2008: 25). Subsequently, I attempt to delineate the historical relationships between and among linguistic communities in North Africa in the *long durée* and in the recent past.

Linguistic and cultural arena: the dynamics of the *long durée*

It is useful to remember what linguistic and cultural arena is being discussed here. The Amazigh/ Berber vernaculars, such as Taqbaylit and Tachawit in Algeria or Tarifit and Tasoussit in Morocco,[4] have existed in environments where writing and literacy were diffused since antiquity. The interaction of Mediterranean cultures and languages is pointed to by archeological findings (e.g. bilingual Libyan and Punic or Latin stelae), by the Punic origin of the Tifinagh alphabet among the Tuareg Berbers in the Sahara, and by literary elements, such as the motif of "the ants helping Psyche" in the famous *Metamorphoses* of Apuleius (Plantade and Plantade 2014), who wrote in Latin but was born in Madaura (M'daourouch in present-day Algeria) around 123–125 CE. Historical sources, such as Procopius' *Vandal War*, confirm the social and cultural interactions after the dissolution of the Roman empire, often in terms of violent clashes, and the presence of autochthonous populations called *Mauri* (Camps 1984). Although it is difficult to ascertain whether archeological findings and Latin sources point to the ancestors of present-day Berber speakers in North Africa (Millar 1968: 128, quoted in McDougall 2003: 70; Rouighi 2011), many studies find it plausible that – on the basis of linguistic elements present in the sources – at least some of the groups called *Mauri* used vernaculars that are called today Amazigh/Berber (Camps 1984; Modéran 2003; Lee, Finkelpearl, and Graverini 2014).

Since the mid-7th century CE, after the Arab conquest of North Africa, one finds the use of terms such as *al-Barbar* (the Berbers), *lisân al-barbarî* (Berber language), and *al-barbariyya* (the Berber) in Arab sources (Chaker 2013: 227). According to Ramzi Rouighi (2011), the *Mauri* of the Latin sources do not correspond to the *Barbar* of the Arab ones, the latter term being used in a usually vague way: Arab authors began to create their "Other" during the progressive conquest of North Africa and Andalusia by "tagging," under the label *Barbar*, heterogeneous groups and confederations of unclear origin, possibly tribal as well as political alliances, and by developing the idea of the autochthony of the *Barbar* in the 9th century CE.

Linguistic elements, on the other hand, point to the existence and use of vernaculars today called Amazigh/Berber by the Almoravid and Almohad dynasties in western North Africa. Building on previous studies, Ghouirgate (2015) shows, for example, that a "Berber" variant played a central role in the preaching as well as in the military action of the founder of the Almohad dynasty, Ibn Tumart – who, using it in writing, promoted it as a language for religious texts:

> The language used by the Almohads was called *al-lisān al-garbī* (the Western language). The Almohads made the choice not to designate as "Berber" the idiom they used because this was a too derogatorily connoted term linked to the long-standing heresies of this people.
>
> (*Ghouirgate 2015: 580*)

The use of the "Western language" by religious preachers and scholars in the 12th century led to the development of orthographic norms which continued to be used under the following dynasties, and an advanced bilingualism is expressed in linguistic elements that appear in historical and literary sources of this period.[5] Ghouirgate (2015: 596) concludes by indicating that the use of the Western language and Arabic in religious, military, and administrative tasks under the Almohads opposes the leitmotif of the Berbers as a minority since the Arab conquest of North Africa and of the Berber language as only an oral language.

In the field of the literary tradition, the acquisition of Arabic literacy led to a religious written production in Amazigh/Berber not only in regions under the Almohad dynasty, such as the Souss (south Morocco) but also in the Mzab in Algeria and at Djerba in Tunisia.[6] Several Berber manuscripts written in the Arabic script present religious commentaries, poems, and admonitions. Most of these manuscripts are preserved thanks to versions from the 19th and 20th centuries.

Over time, the diffusion of the Arabic language (Arabization) increased, and Arabic was acquired by larger strata of the population in North Africa. The social and political changes brought about by the diffusion of Islam and Arabic led to the formation of multilingual contexts, where oral languages were used for daily communication and literary production (Amazigh/Berber vernaculars and dialectal Arabic) as well as for commerce and communication between distant individuals and groups (dialectal Arabic), while a written, prestigious language (classical Arabic) increasingly became the vehicle for religion, scholarly literary production, and urban administrations. Judeo-Arabic languages were also spoken and written in North Africa. As noted before, writing in Amazigh/Berber disappeared or became limited, while Amazigh/Berber vernaculars, as oral languages, became subordinated to the prestige of written Arabic, the sacred language of the Koran.

When one looks at the cultural arena in the *long durée*, the notions of majority/minority are inadequate when applied to the relationships between Arab speakers and Amazigh/Berber speakers, since they convey the idea of homogeneous and separate groups and of the Berbers as a historically minorized group. Such notions do not take into account the long process of creolization of the Maghreb. The examples given previously illustrate the presence of Berber dynasties in present-day Morocco, the role of the Berber variant called "Western language" as court language and written tool of religious communication, and the interconnectedness of the "Western language" and Arabic. Also, in the area corresponding to present-day Algeria, speaking a local Berber vernacular did not always mean being a member of a minority: pre-colonial relationships were governed by political and lineage affiliation, although language could play a role in these relationships. For instance, one can take the case of two large and powerful Kabyle Berber confederations (also called "kingdoms" in colonial texts) established at the beginning of the 16th century (Kuku, roughly located in present central Kabylia, and Beni Abbas, roughly corresponding to present maritime Lesser Kabylia). These confederations were rival and strategically allied with or opposed to the Ottoman empire in Algiers and the latter's enemies (the Hafsid dynasty of Tunis and the Spanish army) in order to maintain their own power positions (Roberts 2014; Genevois 1974). At alternating moments, they even defeated the Ottomans and imposed themselves in Algiers.

The making of minorities and majorities in North Africa

As developed subsequently, the minorization of Amazigh/Berber languages and communities is a colonial and postcolonial phenomenon linked to the creation of national states. The use of language as ethnic marker was applied – among other categories such as rural and urban, nomad and sedentary – during colonization, and the construction of communities united (and divided) by language increased under the postcolonial Arabization policy.

From the first half of the 19th century, the situation described in the colonial studies was that of a mosaic of Muslim Arab- and Berber-speaking populations, whose alliances and loyalties intersected and went beyond language groupings. Where Berber vernaculars were spoken, usually a limited number of Muslim literates used Arabic as written support for religious activities. Colonization superimposed the French language (written and spoken) in the Maghreb and introduced a divisive policy of communities defined as Arab, Berber, Muslim, and Jew.

Public and religious schools disseminated French-language instruction in Algeria and Morocco. Arabic teaching was suppressed in Algeria after 1870 and partially maintained in Morocco during the protectorate but for a very low percentage of the population.[7] Berber teaching was designed to train military personnel, administrators, and interpreters for the conquest and management of Berber areas. There was no French colonial teaching of Berber to Berber-speaking populations, notwithstanding the creation of the so-called Franco-Berber schools that were "Berber" only for the recruitment areas of pupils and some teachers (Knibiehler 1994: 493). These schools were successful, however, in creating "a new francophone rural Berber elite" (Maddy-Weitzman 2011: 58).

The colonial discourse on the Berbers was Janus faced. On the one hand, Berbers were depicted as the *bons sauvages* of North Africa and as the Roman civilization's heirs, who aspired only to be reintegrated into Western civilization thanks to assimilation to French colonization. On the other hand, Berber society was stigmatized as being more retrograde than the Arab one was. Women's status was presented as particularly retrograde, since women were disinherited and they could be married off before puberty and even "sold" to their husbands (which Berber intellectuals denied). The Berber language and literature supposedly also expressed such a backward sociocultural position.[8] The representations of Berber society in and by colonial writings were called into question by a number of Berber writers, students, schoolteachers, and local intellectuals who had been educated in the French school system (such education was also diffused among their Arabic-speaking fellow countrymen). A number of these individuals – professionals, semi-professionals, and amateurs – began to learn and teach how to write in Berber, and to collect, transcribe, translate, and re-diffuse (in writing) Berber oral poetry and narratives. These activities, in synergy with the overall social changes, constituted a productive framework for the self-production of "Berber" local identities.

The divisive colonial policy aimed at opposing two imagined homogeneous groups ("Arabs and Berbers") did not succeed, and anticolonial forces from all sides and regions joined political parties and military actions. Berber-speaking areas were often bastions of the anticolonial movements in Algeria and Morocco, such as in the case of Kabylia, the Aurès, and the Rif. In the latter region, a powerful military rebellion led to the constitution of the short-lived Republic of the Rif (1921–1926) under the leadership of Abdelkrim El Khattabi. Although various interpretations of the rebellion are possible (Pennel 2017), the Republic of the Rif was proclaimed in the name of Islam and of freedom from Spanish and French domination. Maddy-Weitzman (2011: 85) writes: "Berber population acted neither as a large cohesive unit, nor in the name of a specific Berber-Moroccan identity." This applies by and large to North African anticolonial movements. The language question, however – although not explicitly mentioned – was probably involved in the conflicts within the Algerian FLN (National Liberation Front), which set the Kabyle Berber leaders on the margins of the revolutionary movement during the anticolonial war and during the unrest that took place just after independence, ending with the military occupation of Kabylia.[9] A similar pattern developed in the Rif region where, in 1958, the Moroccan army under the leadership of future king Hassan II repressed an uprising which had aimed at safeguarding the local economy and tribal autonomy. Although language was not a factor in the rebellion or in the repression, Hassan II strategically chose two spouses of Berber origin (from the Middle Atlas) to indicate the integration of such communities into his kingdom and, at the same time, enforced the *damnatio memoriae* of the Republic of the Rif from public spaces and supported the Moroccan Arabization policy aimed at replacing Berber with Arabic in the whole country.[10]

In the post-independence period, the linguistic policy in the Maghreb indeed centered on the adoption of Arabic. If Arabization was seen as a form of national affirmation against the colonizer, the previous subordination of Berber (as oral vernacular) to Arabic as the sacred written language acquired a political connotation. Berber was stigmatized as the bygone language of local ancestors and denied vitality and public space. At the same time, Berber-speaking activists and writers started to demand recognition for Berber as a component of the national culture and its integration into school programs. Such demands were interpreted by Algerian and Moroccan governments and national elites as a risk to national identity and unity, which were represented by Arabic. Activists were accused of "localism" and of French "acculturation." Their activism in favor of the Berber language and of improved political and economic conditions of life in Berber-speaking areas was presented as "Berberism," manipulatively interpreted as foreboding requests for regional independence. As indicated previously, the large Amazigh/Berber-speaking communities – geographically concentrated and, one can add, with a history of military action as confederations of lineages and villages – posed a question of management to national centralized states. Inclusion and federation could have been a strategy but, instead, the label of "Berberism" became a weapon for police and military repression by authoritarian governments aiming to control and to suppress all political opposition.

Considering the post-independence policy, it is no surprise that until the late 1990s there was no Berber school education in Algeria, Morocco, Libya, and Tunisia. University studies on Berber developed mainly outside the Maghreb, which contributed to configuring Berber speakers as a minority. Such a school policy was a consequence of the colonial politics of division as well as the expression of the authoritarian character of the nationalist governments in North Africa. The exception of the recognition of Tuareg Berber as a "national" language in Mali and Niger from 1961 led to limited activities of schooling and an alphabetization policy, though this did little to contribute to modifying the difficult power relationships, and repeated violent clashes between national armies and Tuaregs occurred.[11] The epitome of the confrontations was the attempt, linked to long-standing socioeconomic marginalization and the diffusion of global radical Islamic movements, to create the independent state of Azawad in 2012.[12]

The recognition of Amazigh as a national and official language in Algeria (respectively, from 1995 and 2016) and in Morocco (from 2001 and 2011) was brought about after long years of activism, mass demonstrations, and state repression.[13] Although it is impossible to speak of a homogeneous movement – because individuals with diverse political views and various fragmented groups participated in it – it is safe to say that, by and large, Amazigh/Berber activism has increased the production of identity discourses locally and nationally. At the same time, the transnational approach to "Amazigh-ness" has been strengthened by organizations aiming to cross national borders – such as the Berber Academy in the 1970s and later on the Amazigh World Congress – and was emblematically represented by the creation of the Amazigh flag in the late 1990s.[14] Decades of Algerian state repression and economic deprivation of Kabylia led to the development of an activist discourse in terms of autonomy (MAK, Mouvement pour l'autonomie de la Kabylie; RPK, Rassemblement pour la Kabylie) and, in 2013, of self-determination (MAK) – somehow taking up the Catalan model (Tilmatine 2017). It seems sadly ironic that the fear of national division led to repressive policies that turned out to be a self-fulfilling prophecy. It should be clear, however, that the MAK is just one of the political organizations in Kabylia and that the choice for self-determination is questioned by other parties – such as the FFS (Socialist Forces Front), the RCD (Rally for Culture and Democracy), and, recently, the RPK (Rally for Kabylia) – which inscribe regional autonomy in the national state framework.[15] In Morocco, the Amazigh/Berber language and identity were not among the demands of the Hirak movement in the Rif[16] – somehow a follow-up to the previous national 20 February Movement.[17] Hirak leaders asked for a solution to the economic problems and corruption in the region, but Amazigh flags were often visible during the demonstrations. This latter element was used by the authorities to accuse the Hirak movement of separatism – which is denied by activists (Wolf 2018: 5) – adding such an accusation to the reasons devised to crush the movement violently and arrest hundreds of participants.

If the minorization of Berbers/Imazighen coalesces in postcolonial times, the idea of separate minorities and majorities is at the same time countered by the Moroccan central authority's strategy to manage Amazigh/Berber areas through the integration of the Berber elites and rural middle classes into the national politics and in the "patronage/spoils of power" system (*système de cooptation* in French) (Maddy-Weitzman 2011: 88, 96). Also, the postcolonial Algerian policy has strategically included individuals and families of the rural middle class in the power system. The consequences of the spoils system (linked to the economic boom of the 1970s) are differently interpreted as contributing to shaping an elitist Berber consciousness or, conversely, creating a class interested in its own social benefits and its own integration into the national power system (Roberts 1982; Chaker 1989b: 71–81). Either way, the consciousness of being Amazigh/Berber developed among local elites and the wider strata of population in regions such as Kabylia, the Souss, and the Rif, which renewed and modified previous identities derived from local lineages and confederations. Such consciousness developed under the impact of a number of intertwined processes: the divisive colonization policy and the anticolonial fighting, the social changes and migration flows caused by colonization and by postcolonial crises, the expected "death" of oral languages due to factors such as literacy and "modernization," nationalism and Arabization, centralizing policies, economic marginalization, and postcolonial police and military repression.

A contested situation of minority

The inequality in power relationships and the economic and political marginalization of Amazigh/Berber-speaking regions in North African postcolonial states has led some activists to claim the status of "minority." For example, the association Tamaynut and one of its leading founders, Hassan Id Belkassem, linked their demands for the recognition of the Amazigh/Berber language in Morocco to the United Nation's legal status and definition of "indigenous minority people" (Maddy-Weitzman 2011: 132). The previously mentioned position of the MAK can also be seen as the implementation of the idea of a minority (or rather a regional "majority") aspiring to self-determination.

On the other hand, most activists refuse to be seen as, and to be confined by the definition of, a minority. Taking the history of Arabization of the Maghreb as a starting point, such a position affirms that Imazighen/Berbers cannot be presented as a minority, because most of the North African population is composed of Arabized Berbers who "lost" their original language. Hence, in such an approach, Imazighen/Berbers are *de facto* the majority. Presenting themselves as the "autochthonous" people of North Africa, pre-existing the process of Arabization, activists challenge their minorization within their national borders. As indicated previously, a transnational approach to a pan-Amazigh/Berber identity has also developed. A widespread idea among Amazigh activists is their affiliation to *Tamazgha*, a North African autochthonous cultural space, *politically* and territorially unified, which is hoped for in the future and which otherwise has no historical existence. There is a weakness in this approach: presenting the Imazighen/Berbers as the autochthonous people of North Africa aiming to (re)construct a utopian cultural and territorial unity disregards the creolization of the Maghreb. As indicated by Karima Dirèche (2017: 81), presenting "Berber culture as original and authentic . . . would suggest that all those who claim an Arab genealogy must now assume altered, if not inauthentic, ancestry." Moreover, activists tend to dismiss or ignore the contradiction between the national pluralistic model maintained by the Amazigh associations and the idea of the cultural continuity of a *Tamazgha* whose existence is justified by the autochthony of Imazighen (with respect to other groups) (Oiry-Varacca 2012–2013: 12; Jay 2016: 72). The intellectually more extreme consequences of such an approach are limited, however, by the positions claiming Amazigh as part of the nation state. Many Amazigh associations and trends "consider Amazighity as a basis of identity common to all Moroccans and not as a substrate that devalues that which would come afterwards or as a prerequisite of an ethnical or cultural group" (Oiry-Varacca 2012–2013: 12). Such a moderate position attempts to maintain the demands in favor of Amazigh/Berber languages and communities without posing them as internal "minorities."

In summary, the process of minorization of Amazigh/Berber speakers and communities in the sense of limited rights and unbalanced political power is historically a modern phenomenon, developed in the colonial and postcolonial periods. Such a minorization is resented and opposed by several currents of Amazigh/Berber activism. The formation of an internationally shared Amazigh/Berber identity is also a modern phenomenon, which is articulated to equally modern local identities emerging from past linkages and strong feelings of belonging to specific villages and confederations. It is undeniable that the notions of majority/minority fail to take into account the long process of creolization of the Maghreb as well as the activist discourse reclaiming that the Imazighen/Berbers are the majority when the North African territory is seen as overlapping with an "autochthonous" Amazigh/Berber cultural space. As indicated previously, the latter cultural space is utopian and contested in the studies because it also tends to disregard creolization.

What Amazigh/Berber literature can tell us about minority, multilingualism, and transnationalism is the topic of the following sections.

Minorization and literature

Taking Franz Kafka as an example, Gilles Deleuze and Felix Guattari (1975) developed their famous definition of "minor" literature, which refers not to what is produced in the language of a linguistic or other minority but to works written in the mainstream (dominant or national) language by authors who belong to a group that finds itself in a situation of minority or marginalization. Writers do not need to live in the place where the majority language is spoken (Kafka wrote in German and lived in Prague), but they express an "other" sensibility or consciousness *vis-à-vis* the canonical literature produced in the mainstream language. The definition of "minor" literature is not directly linked to demographics or to the idea of a "lesser" literature. On the contrary, Deleuze and Guattari celebrate the expressive and innovating force of "minor" voices creating counter-discourses to hegemonic, majoritarian, national narratives.

Literary and cultural studies agree on three main characteristics of minority literature, descending from Deleuze and Guattari's work: deterritorialization, politics, and collective discourse (for instance, JanMohamed and Lloyd 1987; Bensmaia 1994; Buchanan and Marks 2000; Ponzanesi 2004; Haines 2015; Laurie and Khan 2017). By deterritorialization is meant the distance of the "minor" voice from the mainstream literary language, which disrupts canonical ways of expression and creates a new literary language. This literary disruption can take place through an "accented" language, such as the use of Prague German in Kafka; through extreme forms of playfulness or gravity; and through questioning and weakening the sociological link between national territory, language, and identity (Lauri and Khan 2017: 3). The political character of minority literature is provided by the attention paid to the holistic relationship between the individual and his/her community. Because of such a holistic relation, all events become collective in the form of a social and political drama – which allows the interpretation of minority literature as revolutionary with regard to mainstream literature which is (seen as more) individualistically oriented. According to such an approach, an aspect of this political character is that minority works are characterized by collective discourse, as the writers tend to express communal values and ideas more than individual ones. The latter characteristic strengthens the political effect of writing by inventing a collectivity which takes form in the minority literature.

The articulation of minority literature and cultural difference within the nation is to be found in Homi Bhabha's chapter "Time, narrative and the margin of the modern nation" (1994: 199–244). Bhabha writes:

> Cultural difference, as a form of intervention, participates in a logic of supplementary subversion similar to the strategies of minority discourse. . . . The aim of cultural difference is to rearticulate the sum of knowledge from the perspective of the signifying position of the minority that resists totalization.
>
> *(1994: 232)*

As in the case of "minor" voices, cultural difference exposes the contradictions of the national, unifying, and homogenizing narration:

> The very possibility of cultural contestation, the ability to shift the ground of knowledges, or to engage in the "war of position," marks the establishment of new forms of meaning, and strategies of identification. Designations of cultural difference interpellate

forms of identity which, because of their continual implication in other symbolic systems, are always "incomplete" or open to translation.

(Bhabha 1994: 233)

Bhabha's reflection on cultural difference and minority discourse helps us to understand that the characteristics of "minor" literatures mentioned previously intersect and overlap with those of the so-called postcolonial literatures. Postcolonialism, as it is known, refers to art and literature produced after the encounter/clash following European invasions in Asia, Africa, America, Australia, and Oceania.[18] Nowadays, the label "postcolonial literature" is criticized as yet another form of ethnocentrism, because it seems to say that European colonialism was, and still is, the most important moment in global history and in world literature. In fact, the opposite is apparent: many contemporary works are not at all concerned with colonialism and postcoloniality. Despite the criticism, some characteristics of "postcolonial" texts can be identified: thinking and writing beyond national, cultural, and social borders, with transnationalism as a central characteristic; questioning notions of "home," identity, and cultural affiliation, including fragmentation, alienation, and hybridity; rediscovering local knowledge (as opposed to dominating "Western" theories); exploring diversity and equality within a community, between communities, and between minorities and majorities; blurring genre and language boundaries; and bringing language creativity to the extreme by, among other devices, interacting with mother tongues when writing is in a mainstream language.

Studies largely refer to "minor" voices and cultural difference in literatures produced in the European languages of the colonial domination – and by extension in the languages of other dominations – but some studies have begun to apply postcolonial research to African language literatures.[19] In the following section, a reflection is offered on Amazigh/Berber literature and "literary space" in the light of the characteristics attributed by theoretical approaches to postcolonial and minority literatures.

Amazigh/Berber literature: beyond minority voices

As indicated in the previous sections, when one looks at the *longue durée*, both the religious manuscripts written in Amazigh/Berber and Berber as a court language oppose the stereotypes of Amazigh as an exclusively oral language and as a language reduced to a minority situation since the Islamization and the Arabization of the Maghreb. Moreover, literary analysis shows that Amazigh oral poetry and narratives are solidly anchored in their own vernacular and territory. Lexical loans (from Arabic and to a lesser extent from French) in narratives told in Amazigh and collected since the 19th century are indications of social and political interactions of such vernaculars with the broader context. Specifically, the use of poetic verses in Arabic shows the prestige of the Arabic language. There is also a tension between Muslim universal culture and local heroes and values. For example, Camille Lacoste-Dujardin (1970), analyzing a corpus of the Kabyle folktales collected and published in 1893–1898, shows the presence of two kinds of heroes: the first a "traditional" defender of the local group and the second a "conquering" hero emblematically represented by the stories concerning Harun al-Rashid, the famous caliph of the Abbasid dynasty in Baghdad (8th century CE) and renowned personage of the *Arabian Nights*. Nevertheless, one does not find a questioning of belonging or a language "deterritorialization" in Amazigh folktales – rather the negotiation of multilingualism and Islamic references integrated into the narration of one's world and identity. At the same time, such intellectual negotiations challenge the assimilation to homogenizing literary models arising from Muslim universal culture. The language of Amazigh poems and tales confirms esthetic codes and traditions, while their literary strategies sustain the ideal of social cohesion, the moral values, and the reproduction of the conventional norms of the local societies which produced such oral genres and shared the Berber vernaculars. Studies show that Kabyle, Chaouia, and Riffian folktales, for example, create and affirm, respectively, Kabyle-, Chaouia-, and Rif-centered worlds, while itinerant bards contributed to create a common and highly appreciated literary language and tradition in the whole of the Souss region.[20]

Innovation and change do exist in Amazigh oral genres, as they do overall in other oral literatures. An example is given by the introduction of the poem composed by a strophe of nine verses in the Kabyle poetry of the second half of the 19th century. As Lahlou's research (2017) exemplary shows, the emergence of such a poetry can be explained in the context of the upheaval and disorientation induced by colonization. The colonizers' expropriation of the land belonging to Kabyle villages and confederations; the later military defeat after the uprising of 1871; and the consequent disruption of previous social, political, and economic structures led to a weakening of the role of the professional "tribal" poets and their styles.[21] The poet Si Mohand ou Mhand innovatively adopted the nine-verse strophe as an autonomous form of poem and intensified the literary language, in his case through sobriety and lapidary style, as in the definitions of minor literature. However, in contrast with the latter, Si Mohand ou Mhand also continued to use his mother tongue and developed themes leading to an "individualization" of his poems, not to a promotion of collective values. Moreover, although oral genres are usually marginalized on the national and global literary scenes, the poetry of Si Mohand ou Mhand is still well known, diffused, and appreciated among the Kabyles. His nine-verse strophe, or Mohandien *asefrou*, is today widespread in Kabyle poetic production, thus having become "mainstream" within such a cultural context (Mammeri 1969; Lahlou 2017):

Si Mohand ou Mhand's poems differ and oppose the long tradition of epic, didactic, hagiographic, and narrative poetry – for it is first of all an individual, personal, and spontaneous poetry, which essentially expresses the shocks of its existence and the echoes of its interior universe.

(Lahlou 2017: 376)

Another example of innovation and change is provided by the "modern" Amazigh songs and music groups. Although some oral genres tend to disappear along with their contexts of production, new forms have also arisen at the intersection of oral, written, audiovisual, and digital modes. Increasingly, the overwhelmingly varied and enormously popular genre of modern songs incorporates "classical" musical styles and poetry with inspiration and instruments from around the world. Singers such as Idir, Aït Menguellet, Matoub, and Khalid Izri and the bands Djurd-jura and Izenzren have innovated in terms of music, abandoning the orchestration diffused in the 1940s under the influence of Andalusian and Egyptian music and adopting the sound of acoustic and electric guitars, drums, and synthesizers. Another example is the music of the Tuareg band Tinariwen, whose members play *teherdent* (lute), *imzad* (violin), *tinde* (drum), and electric guitar. Morgan (2007) argues that Tinariwen merge the Tuareg style of *assouf* ("solitude" or "nostalgia") with influences from Kabyle Berber contemporary songs (for instance, from Idir and Aït Menguellet), Malian blues, Algerian urban *raï*, Moroccan *chaabi*, pop, rock, and Indian music.[22]

In term of language, all these singers and bands sing in the Amazigh vernaculars of their families and communities, contributing to maintaining and developing them and resisting the enforcement of homogenization by Arabization and international global languages. Others, however, may increasingly participate in the global multilingual scene, as in the case of Hindi Zahra, who sings in English and Chleuh Berber and incorporates Chleuh sounds with blues, jazz, American folk, Egyptian music, and the influence of African singers such as Ali Farka Touré and Youssou' Ndour.[23] In terms of themes, a large number of the Amazigh lyrics can be labeled "protest songs," but without pointing to didactic or pamphlet-like styles. Abdellah Bounfour (2006: 4438) aptly summarizes it as follows:

> The contemporaneity of such poetry resides essentially in its renewed themes and, among them, that of identity is haunting: Who are we? Why are we dominated? Who is responsible for this state of affairs? The answers to such questions are given by re-reading ancient and/or recent history, by sociology, and so on. It can be said, without hesitation, that sung poetry popularized the ideas that Berber intellectuals, their creators, could not carry beyond their own circles.

Skillfully analyzing the song "*A vava inouva*," Jane E .Goodman (2005: 49–68) shows that the singer Idir and the poet Ben Mohamed were able to vivify a traditional tale and refrain to engage the feeling of homeliness and at the same time to contest "the Algerian state's discourse which positioned Berber culture as backward and at odds with the state's modernizing projects" (49).[24] Goodman adds that Ben Mohammed sees such an innovation as deriving from their internal gaze "informed by neither the East nor the West but by indigenous modes of knowledge" (Goodman 2005: 49). Blending a traditional story with new attributed meanings and traditional sounds with European instruments, Idir and Ben Mohamed were able to counter the folklorization of Berber culture through an original synthesis of ethnographic continuity and change: "*A vava inouva*" became "an emblem of Berber identity, a sign of the rich heritage, legitimacy, and modernity of Kabyle culture" (Goodman 2005: 68). "*A vava inouva*" became a hit not only for the Kabyles but also in Algeria and in France, selling around 200,000 copies (Humblot 1978, quoted in Goodman 2005: 65). The Tuareg band Tinariwen also received international acclaim: in 2005, their album *Amassakoul* (The Traveler) had sales of more than 100,000 copies, and they were awarded the Best World Music Grammy in Los Angeles in 2012. Nadia Belalimat (2010: 155) explains that Tinariwen became internationally known for their particular style of music and for presenting a contemporary image of Tuareg society. Their songs are effective in creating internal bonding by expressing (past) military experience and a real political engagement (Belalimat 2010: 7) – for example, when songs and music gatherings were used to convey militant ideas and to spread them through cassettes and other media, such as radio and later on cell phones and the Internet:

> Friends hear and understand me
> You know, there is one country
> One goal, one religion
> And unity, hand in hand
> Friends, you know there is only one stake to which you fettered
> And only unity can break it.
>
> ("*Imidiwen segdet teslem*," 1978)[25]

At the same time, the blend of Tuareg classic music style and instruments with electronic and international sounds, the images of four-wheel drives, camels, beautifully clothed men with veils and turbans, electronic guitars, and the marketing of "rebel" music have fascinated the international public, refashioning previous imagery of the Tuaregs as the grand warriors of colonial fantasies. If a recurrent theme is the nostalgia linked to the desert and the fatherland (Belalimat 2010), a major theme of the Tinariwen's songs is indeed "rebellion" against Malian state oppression. Their songs castigate the harsh repression of the Tuareg uprisings particularly in the 1960s, recalling a courageous military image in terms of rightful rebellion against authoritarian governments. Besides themes of military bravery, Belalimat (2010: 5) shows that the Tinariwen also address the situation of exiles and refugees in Algerian and Libyan camps and contemporary complaints, such as in the song *Ahimana* (Oh My Soul):

> Oh mother! Since I left for Libya persevering,
> I finally arrived! But I cannot settle in no way
> I search for the necessary money through all means
> But it desperately refuses to accumulate.
> Tinariwen, "*Ahimana*" (track 4), 2008[26]

Women as singers participate in the construction of contemporary Amazigh identities (such as in the case of the band Djurdjura and the singer Fatima Tabaaramte), but they also complain about and reflect on life from their own "minor" position vis-à-vis men, presenting or discussing the roles attributed to women and the norms concerning femininity in their own communities (Nouara, Cherifa, Tabaaramte, Djurdjura). This is something that one can also recognize in some of the Amazigh songs of Hindi Zahra, whose texts primarily speak of intimate experiences and urban youth culture. For example, her song "Oursoul" – a wordplay which can be interpreted as both "Our soul" in English and "Ursul" in Amazigh Tasoussit (Never again) – tells the story of her parents' marriage but can be interpreted as a more generalized complaint against arranged marriages:

> They told me: "Rest, your husband will come."
> They said to me: "Rest, he will come."
> I will never have what I want!
> They told me: "It will work out."
> I will never have what I want!
> (Hindi Zahra, "Oursoul,"
> *Handmade*, 2010)

I choose English because it is a way to create a space from the things I say. It would be very hard for me to sing my love stories in my mother's tongue. In the Berber [language], I talk about different stories. Especially in "Oursoul," when I talk about the story of my parents. They had to get married, not really forced, but the system was like this in the village. You had to get married. Berber was the easiest way to express and talk about this.

> (*Hindi Zahra*. "Discovery: Hindi Zahra." *Interview*,
> August 29, 2011)

A more complicated relationship to language than that of "minor" vs "major," or hegemonic language, is expressed by Hindi Zahra in the previous interview: "another" language can also offer a space of liberty to express that which, in the eyes of the singer, is not legitimate or socially acceptable in her vernacular and in the community that such a language creates. This was a well-known point in literary criticism concerning Francophone literature (Bounfour 1990; Déjeux 1994: 130; Dehane 1992: Le Rouzic 1996; Gans–Guinoune 2010: 70; Yacine 1995). For example, the famous writer Assia Djebar says in an interview "the norm is not to talk about oneself . . ., one never says 'I'" (Dehane 1992: TC 00:02:30 – 00:03:31)

The previously mentioned examples of innovations in oral genres and changes in literary and musical registers point to a process of literary and musical acquisition, negotiation, and subversion, which can be interpreted in term of cultural difference and global postcolonial features. If it is clear that contemporary poets and singers create in response and reaction to the pressure of hegemonic languages and political systems, at the same time, the focus on using their own vernaculars (or combining them with other languages) and on shared literary/music styles derived from still-loved literary traditions shows the will, and the practice, to affirm their "internal" gaze and cultural difference, even when participating in increasingly global scenes.

Writing in Amazigh vernaculars and in other languages

With the significant exception of the *Cahiers de Belaïd*, posthumously published in 1963 and 1964 (Aït Ali/Dallet and Degezelle, eds.), a new production of novels written in Amazigh/ Berber started in the last decades of the last century as the engaged effort of writers who had been educated either in French or in Arabic. The first novels (*ungal/ungalen*) in Kabyle appeared in the 1980s. The interweaving between literary creation and historical context (the repression of the so-called Berber Spring) was underscored by the militant and identity tone of the novels *Asfel* (The Ritual Sacrifice, 1981) and *Faffa* (La France, 1986) by Rachid Aliche and *Askuti* (Boy Scout, 1983) by Said Sadi, as well as of the novels published later, such as *Iḍ d wass* (Day and Night, 1990) by Amar Mezdad and *Tafrara* (Dawn, 1995) by Salem Zénia. Among the features of these novels, as analyzed by Abrous (1989: 81–100, 1992), are that they avoid loan words from Arabic and preserve the language through the use of Berber neologisms and ancient expressions, while, on the other hand, they show a lexical and syntactic influence from French. As Salhi (2014: 151) aptly notes:

> the elements borrowed from Islam and the Arabic language and, more recently, from Western culture, particularly from the French language and culture, to mention only the most important elements, have been integrated and adapted by the Kabyle to such an extent that at present they constitute structuring parameters of their lived culture.

The Mammeri Prize (Tizi Ouzou), established for writing in Kabyle, and more recently new contests have helped to stimulate young writers. In the last decade, novels and short stories show a greater variety of themes, such as love, infidelity, children/parent conflicts, radicalism, and "recalcitrant" Islamists. If the language of the Kabyle novels is often difficult because of the high recurrent number of neologisms and the syntactic influence of French, some novels are more readable and close to spoken Kabyle (Salhi 2005) – such as *Salas d Nuja* (Salas and Nuja 2003, names of characters) by Brahim Tazaghart, *Lwerd n tayri* (The Rose of Love, 2004) by *Igli n tlelli* (Horizon of Freedom, pseud.), *Bururu* (Owl, 2006) by Tahar Ould-Amar, and the collection of short stories *Ger zik d tura* (From the Past and Today, 1993/2008) by Saïd Chemak. The theme of family relations in a poor and harsh Kabyle context is taken up in the text by Fatima Merabti, *Yir Tagmat* (Bad Brotherhood, first two chapters of a novel that were published in the journal *Tizir* in 1997 and 1998) and in *Aâecciw n tmes* (The Fire Hut, 2009), the first published novel of a Kabyle woman writer, Lynda Koudache. Koudache presents women's magic opposing "love" in a traditional world in which, as in the world of tales, marriage is more than a meeting of hearts because it involves the social and economic roles of, and within, the extended family.

Amazigh written production in Morocco has seen the appearance of plays, novels, and short stories by Riffian and Souss writers. However, publication is limited, as the works are often self-published or scattered in small periodicals. After Ali Mimoun Essafi's plays published in the

1980s, the first novel in Souss Berber is *Tawargit d imik* (A Dream and a Little More), authored by Mohammed Akunad. Published in 2002, this novel concerns the unforeseen consequences of an imam's decision to pray and to teach in Amazigh. Currently, there are at least 20 novels and 20 collections of short stories published in Souss Berber, such as *Amussu n umalu* (The Movement of the Shadow, 2008) by Lahacem Zaheur, *Ijjigen n tidi* (The Flowers of Sweat, 2007) by Mohamed Akunad, and *Igdad n Wihran* (The Birds of Oran, 2010) by Lahoucine Bouyaakoubi. The first novels in the Rif vernacular were published in the diaspora. As in the case of Kabyle literature, there is a continuity of cultural production between the country of origin and the Riffian emigration in Belgium, the Netherlands, and Spain. Emigration, travel, and memory are central themes – for example, in *Rez ṭṭabu ad d teffegh tfukt* (Breaking the Taboo and Letting the Sun Appear, 1997) by the late Mohamed Chacha (who also has collections of short stories and poems to his name). Several writers active in Morocco and the Netherlands have produced novels and short stories as well as theatrical productions and films, such as Mohamed Bouzaggou, Omar Boumazzough, and Ahmed Ziani. The first novel published by a woman writer appeared in Tarifit: *Tasrit n wezru* (The Bride of the Rock) by Samira Yedjis n Idura n Arrif (pseud.), published in Morocco (Oujda) in 2001.

As a consequence of the colonial and postcolonial school policy, it is not surprising that a large proportion of Amazigh/Berber-speaking authors wrote in other languages until about the 1990s. An example is the genre of the novel. The novels of the first Berber writers were often written in French, such as in the case of the Algerian Mouloud Feraoun (1913–1962), Mouloud Mammeri (1917–1989), Fadhma Amrouche (1882–1967), and Taos Amrouche (1947–1976), and by the Moroccan Mohamed Khaïr-Eddine (1941–1995), or in Arabic by the Moroccan Mohamed Choukri (1935–2003) and Mohamed Mrabet (1936), and by the Libyan Ibrahim Al-Kûnî (1948). Several studies have highlighted the use of Kabyle words and expressions and the transposition of oral genres in the works of Mouloud Feraoun, Mouloud Mammeri, Fadhma Amrouche, and Taos Amrouche, linked to Kabylia as geographical and cultural space. Jacqueline Arnaud (1986) wrote that it was necessary to speak of "Francophone" Berber-speaking and Arabic-speaking authors "if one is interested in the linguistic substratum of the French language . . . and the perspectives envisaged." Writer and researcher Nabile Farès (1987: 94, 96) raised this issue by referring to the Berber-ness of some works, even though they are written in French. Salem Chaker (1989b: 23) speaks of "French-speaking Kabyle writers" by considering the Kabyle roots of their works, the reception of the public, and the promotion of the Berber language by these writers through the collection and translation of poems, songs, and oral tales; in a number of cases, one can also add their production of grammars and dictionaries. Such a trend does not fade after independence but, on the contrary, continues in the production of writers who revendicate a Kabyle origin (see Merolla 1995). Similarly, there are several references to Berber languages and communities in *Légende et vie d'Agoun'chich* (The Legend and Life of Agoun'chich, 1984) by the Moroccan writer Mohamed Khaïr-Eddine and in literary texts written in Arabic by the Libyan writer Ibrahim Al-Koni. In more recent times, the productions of migrant authors in Europe have been largely written in the languages of these countries: in addition to the vast production in French, there are new writings in Dutch, in Catalan, and in Italian by authors of Amazigh origin. However, the language and cultural references to Amazigh languages, contexts, cultural imaginary, and characters are never isolated from a broader context and reveal intercultural elements and references. More than an "ethnic" Amazigh/Berber discourse, these works narrate a quest for identity which resists cultural homogeneity endorsed by national and international intellectual and political powers. As said previously, the novels narrating such a quest for identity were accused of "localism" and of French "acculturation". Notorious debates around the works of Mouloud Feraoun and Mouloud Mammeri included the nationalist critique of the supposed acculturation, regionalism, self-ethnography, and lack of patriotism of the authors.[27] The nationalist critique in turn has been debunked in its ideological elements.[28]

Writing in Amazigh Berber is a definitively "territorialized" endeavor. As in the case of Amazigh oral poetry and narratives, writing is solidly anchored in the vernacular, in the sense that authors use and promote their own linguistic variation and that their readers are usually speakers/readers of the same vernacular. As Salhi and Sadi (2016: 32) note:

> Written in one of the Berber variants, its [the Berber novel's] reception is realized only within the limits of this variant. Thus, we will speak of Kabyle novel (Kabylia and Kabyle diaspora especially in France), Chleuh novel (mainly the region of Souss where the Tachelhit [a Berber variant] is spoken and Chleuh diaspora mainly in France), and Riffian novel (the region of Rif and Riffian diaspora especially in the Netherlands). . . . We will say that the Kabyle novel, the Riffian novel, and the Chleuh novel compose the Maghreb novel written in Berber.

At the same time, one recognizes an Amazigh transnational effort, as neologisms are created from other Amazigh variations and from common linguistic roots. The questioning of national belonging and of cultural affiliation are central themes, as well as language creativity and the blurring of genre and language boundaries, as in the case of other postcolonial literatures. As mentioned previously, the influence of the languages of school education, such as French and Arabic, often appears in the syntactic structures, and the blending of genres, for instance, is revealed by the scientific debate on what can/should be defined as *ungal* or *tullist*, which are the usual translations, respectively, for "novel" and "short story" (Salhi 2011: 86–87; Ameziane and Salhi 2014). However, when one looks at the institutional side, notwithstanding local and individual efforts, the recognition of Amazigh in Algeria and Morocco in the last two decades has not yet translated into organized support of literary writing in Amazigh (Salhi 2011). While this latter aspect is linked to the still-continuing status of "minority" attached to the Amazigh/Berber language, the territorializing, transnational, and identity discourse of the novels in Amazigh point to a cultural difference and, in Bhaba's terms, to literature as a form of intervention aimed at resisting totalization. On the other hand, the choice of a written – and (inter) national – language in the arena of oral and written communication is symptomatic of the prestige and hegemony of literacy and an indication of the "situation of minority" experienced by oral languages and by the speakers of Amazigh/Berber vernaculars who were often educated in languages other than their mother tongue. Their novels in French and in Arabic, and later on in other languages of the diasporic locations, reveal the search for linguistic interaction with their vernaculars and for a renewed literary expression. This language interaction destabilizes the mainstream language and, at the same time, also establishes a form of "reterritorializing" the novels, which contributes to creating a community not only narratively but also in public reception.[29] Such a reception also impacted nationalist criticism (see previously) and state censure, because these novels were perceived, whatever the themes treated, as politically motivated. The novels written in other languages by speakers of Amazigh/Berber vernaculars can therefore be interpreted as those of "minor" voices, characterized, as we saw, by destabilization of the mainstream language, community building, and political tenor. However, the production in French, Arabic, and other languages should not be understood as isolated from writing in Amazigh and from the cultural project to promote Amazigh/Berber locally, nationally, and transnationally, which to various extents is shared by those who narrate and sing in Amazigh vernaculars.

Conclusion: Amazigh/Berber literary space

The definition of Amazigh/Berber literature is usually considered equivalent to "literature in Amazigh/Berber" by the immediate identification of the literary corpus on the basis of the language of creation. Although it may seem simple and immediately applicable, language-based identification can be problematic. Questions arise from the combination of political and theoretical approaches to literature definitions – for instance, in the case of British and American literature using the same language or in the case of the so-called Francophone/Anglophone literatures deriving from an imperial, nowadays rejected, distinction between the centers of colonial empires and their ex-colonies. Language-based definitions are justified through a form of relativism which sees language as the vehicle of a specific worldview and by nationalist ideas about the uniqueness of a language to express the feeling of national unity in literature.

Regarding the Amazigh/Berber literary productions, theoretical approaches and nationalism have led to an ignoring – for different and sometimes opposite reasons – of the fact that there have been multiple lines of literary creation. The usual definition of Amazigh/Berber literature tends to isolate texts that maintain intra- and extra-textual relations with several languages and literatures within one language field. Reflecting on multimediality (oral, written, audiovisual, and digital modes) and multilingualism, one sees that the oral and written texts discussed previously present the following traits: the "territorializing" of the texts by the use of Amazigh vernaculars in spoken, sung, or written form and by the marked reference to such vernaculars and their oral genres in another mainstream language (e.g. Arabic, Dutch, French, Italian, Spanish, and so forth); the linguistic interaction characterizing the texts, whatever the language, the media, and the location of the literary productions; and the reference to *tamurt* (the land and its inhabitants) and to its history as a form of intervention that creates an identity narrative and establishes the intertextuality of a variety of literary productions. Literary genres with such narrative characteristics belong to a continuum in which the Berber/Amazigh references and the discourse of its identity construction constitute one of the relevant readings (Merolla 1995, 2006: 13–16, 28–40). This continuum is a domain of multiple affiliations, which partially overlaps and interacts with different artistic traditions of the multilingual context of North Africa (Amazigh/Berber, classical Arabic, dialectal Arabic, French, Judeo-Arabic, and so forth). I define such a continuum by the notion of "Amazigh/Berber literary space," a term which aims to go beyond the limits of the usual definition of Amazigh/Berber literature and to acknowledge the creolization of the North African context (Merolla 2006: 73; Merolla 2014).

A theoretical point needs to be mentioned here. The term "literary space" seems more appropriate for our approach than the notion of "field" commonly used in literary studies (Bourdieu 1991). The notion of field implies a rigid autonomy of "literature," bestowed with a coherent economic and intellectual structure, a linguistically homogeneous readership, and common shared institutions (Magdelaine-Andrianjafitrimo 2006; Mouralis 2001). A shared language (one of the vernaculars) is therefore not sufficient to establish a field without the other structuring elements. The Amazigh case, moreover, presents cleavages among literary institutions related to different languages and different forms of "habitus" provided by oral, written, audiovisual, and digital media. I consider the Amazigh "literary space" a vague and floating continuum. On the one hand, the literary institutions of such a continuum are unequal and in competition; on the other hand, the range of individual positions is also differentiated and unequal. The situation is therefore at the same time more complex than, and less representable by, a structured "field" where each "atom," each text or author, can be directly related to the others. What the continuum presents is the play of intertextuality and the evocation of a discourse of identity – through references to the histories, scenes, and characters attached to a specific Amazigh/Berber vernacular referring to (and, eventually, redefining) a specific cultural region. As seen previously, a transnational Amazigh community also takes form in many contemporary sung and written productions. The relations among the media of expression (oral, written, audiovisual, and digital media) and the languages (Amazigh/Berber, Arabic, French, English, and so forth) determine multiple dialectics of power among texts and authors. In other words, one can adopt the notion of field for the "literature written in Kabyle," with shared literary forums and with works and writers who define each other, but it is more complicate to speak of the "field" of oral and written productions in Amazigh/Berber which do not share such forums and do not have a common "habitus." The notion of "literary space" develops from this point and indicates the continuum provided by all the productions which, whatever the language (Kabyle, Tasoussit, Arabic, French, English . . .) and the medium (orality, writing, audiovisual, digital . . .) used, do share the Amazigh-Berber problematic and construction of "identity," without being compelled to share literary institutions and the other structuring elements characterizing a "field" in Bourdieu's definition.

In conclusion, the situation of minority attributed to the Amazigh/Berber language is a product of colonial and postcolonial historical processes. As indicated previously, territorializing, transnationalism, and identity discourse in literary (oral and written) genres in Amazigh/Berber point to cultural difference and to literature as a form of intervention which challenge totalization and (so-called) universal cultures in the present and in the past. Literary productions in mainstream languages, on the other hand, show the traits attributed to "minor" voices, such as deterritorialization, community building, and political tenor. However, there is also the re-territorialization of these productions, which should be understood in a much larger "literary space" and not as isolated from the cultural project to promote Amazigh Berber, which is shared by those who sing, narrate, and write in Amazigh. The production of contemporary identities, local and transnational, in the Amazigh Berber literary space expresses a long process of re-appropriation and subversion of linguistic and cultural data produced during colonization and in the postcolonial period and is an example of the effort to discuss manipulative visions of cultural homogeneity promoted by various centers of intellectual and political power.

Notes

1 "Berber" was increasingly rejected by activists because of its etymological links with "barbarous" in European languages and in Arabic. Complex political issues are involved in the state appropriation of the term "Amazigh" in Morocco and in Algeria; see Chaker (2013).
2 Maddy-Weitzman (2017).
3 All translations of items listed only in French in the References are mine.
4 Tamazight is spoken in the Middle Atlas. In Algeria, the term "Tamazight" is used to refer to the Berber language as a whole, whereas in Morocco, to avoid confusion with the variant of the Middle Atlas, the term "Amazigh" was chosen when the IRCAM, the Royal Institute of the Amazigh Culture, was founded in 2001. Taqbaylit (Kabyle) is spoken in Kabylia and Tachawit (Chaouia) in the Aurès Mountains (north Algeria); Tarifit (or Tarifiyt, also called Chleuh by its speakers) is the vernacular in the Rif (north Morocco) and Tasoussit (also called Tachelhiyt/Tachelhit or Chleuh) in the Souss (southwestern Morocco).
5 Ghouirgate (2015: 598–599, 603).
6 See *Études et Documents Berbères* 2016.
7 Zouggari (2005) and Kateb (2004).
8 Hanoteau (1867), Basset (1920), and Coulon (1930).
9 Roberts (1982: 334), Chaker (1984: 174), and Carlier (1984: 347–371).
10 Maddy-Weitzman (2011: 86, 89–90) and Mouline (2016).
11 The uprisings in 1962–1964, 1985–1990, and 1990–1996 were repressed harshly by national armies. Long-term disquiet and international pressure brought a relatively stable peace agreement in 1995 (Niger) and in 1996 (Mali), until new insurgent acts in 2007–2009 and 2012.

12 See "Mali Tuareg rebels' call for independence rejected," *BBC News* (3 June 2012).
13 See the "Berber Spring" in 1980 and the "Black Spring" in 2001 and 2002.
14 The Amazigh flag presents three colors, yellow, green, and blue, with the red Tifinagh character ⵣ (Z).
15 Ilikoud (2006) and Tilmatine (2017).
16 The movement was triggered in 2016–2017 by the dramatic death of Mouhcine Fikri while he tried to salvage his fish confiscated by the police in Al Hoceima. (Masbah 2017; Akarkach 2018; Wolf 2018).
17 Following the wave of demonstrations which swept through Tunisia in December 2010.
18 The following reflections are drawn from Schipper, Merolla, and Brinkman (2019: 341–342).
19 Barber (1995), Bourlet (2013), Irele and Gikandi (2004), and Merolla (1995, 2006).
20 Lacoste-Dujardin (1970), Galand-Pernet (1998), Bounfour (1999, 2005, 2018), Kossmann (2000), and Merolla (2006).
21 Lahlou (2017: 376).
22 Culshaw (2007).
23 Hindi Zahra, interview, 2009 (stage name of Zahra Hindi) and Tanti (2011).
24 "Oh my father"—standard transcription is *a baba-inu ba*, where the last *ba* is an alliteration on *baba*, father.
25 "Companions . . .". Translation by Belalimat (2010: 7).
26 Translation by Belalimat (2010: 5).
27 Lacheraf (1953), Sahli (1953), and Achour (1986).
28 Adam (1987), Khadda (1991), Elbaz and Mathieu-Job (2001), and Merolla (2006).
29 Berrichi (2013), El-Zein (2015), and Kizzi (2019).

References

Abrous, D. 1989. *La production romanesque kabyle: une expérience de passage à l'écrit*, Mémoire en vue du Diplôme d'Etudes Approfondies, Université de Provence.

Abrous, D. 1992. La production romanesque kabyle: un aperçu sur la thématique, *LiAF*: 105.

Achour, Christiane. 1986. *Mouloud Feraoun, Une voix en contrepoint*. Paris: Silex.

Adam, Jeanne. 1987. "Influence d'un conte kabyle et de quelques romans coloniaux sur 'Le Fils du pauvre' de Mouloud Feraoun." In *Actes du colloque Jean Amrouche, l'éternel Jugurtha*, 539–546. Marseille: Du Quai, Laffitte.

Ait Ali, Belaïd. 1963, 1964. *Les Cahiers de Belaïd*, ed. by Jean-Marie Dallet and Jules-Louis Degezelle. Fort National: FDB [1963 (texts), 1964 (translation)].

Akarkach, Btisam (ed.). 2018. *Opstand in de Rif* [Rebellion in the Rif]. Berchem: EPO.

Akunad, Mohammed. 2002. *Tawargit d imik* [A Dream and a Little More]. Rabat: Tizrigin Bouregreg.

Akunad, Mohammed. 2007. *Ijjigen n tidi* [Flowers of Toil]. Agadir: Aqlam.

Aliche, Rachid. 1981. *Asfel* [The Ritual Sacrifice]. Lyon: Fédérop.

Aliche, Rachid. 1986. *Faffa* [La France]. Lyon: Fédérop.

Ameziane, Amar and Mohand Akli Salhi. 2014. "Tullist kabyle: réflexions préliminaires sur le corpus." In *Actes du 3ème colloque international sur la problématique des genres littéraires amazighes: définitions, dénominations et classifications*, 114–120. Bouira: Université de Bouira.

Arnaud, J. 1986. *La littérature maghrébine de langue française*. Paris: Publisud.

Barber, Karin. 1995. "African Language Literature and Postcolonial Criticism." *Research in African Literatures*, 26(4): 3–30.

Basset, Henri. 1920. *Essai sur la littérature des Berbères*. Algiers: Carbonnel. New edition: 2001. Paris: Awal-Ibis Press.

Belalimat, Nadia. 2010. "The Ishumar Guitar: Emergence, Circulation & Evolution from Diasporic Performances to the World Scene." In *Tuareg Society within a Globalized World*, ed. by Anja Fischer and Ines Kohl, 155–170. London and New York: Tauris Academic Studies.

Bensmaia, Réda. 1994. "On the Concept of Minor Literature." In *Gilles Deleuze and the Theater of Philosophy*, ed. by Constantin V. Boundas and Dorothea Olkowski, 213–228. London and New York: Routledge.

Berrichi, Boussad. 2013. "Émergence d'une nouvelle littérature en Afrique du nord." In *Trajectoires et dérives de la littérature-monde. Poétiques de la relation et du divers dans les espaces francophones*, ed. by Cécilia Francis and Robert Viau, 255–272. Amsterdam and New York: Rodopi.

Bertheleu, Hélène. 2008. "Pour une approche sociologique de l'insertion des nouveaux venus." *Glottopol, Revue de sociolinguistique en ligne*, 11. www.univ-rouen.fr/dyalang/glottopol

Bhabha, Homi. 1994. *The Location of Culture*. London and New York: Routledge.

Bounfour, Abdellah. 1990. "Autobiographie, genre et croisement des cultures. Le cas de la littérature fran-cophone du Maghreb." *Itinéraires et contacts de cultures*, 10: 85–90.

Bounfour, Abdellah. 1999. *Introduction à la littérature berbère. 1. La poésie*. Paris and Louvain: Peeters.

Bounfour, Abdellah. 2005. *Introduction à la littérature berbère. 2. Le récit hagiologique*. Paris and Louvain: Peeters.

Bounfour, Abdellah. 2006. "Littérature berbère contemporaine." *Encyclopédie berbère*, 28–29: 4435–4439. Aix-en-Provence: Edisud.

Bounfour, Abdellah. 2018. *Introduction à la littérature berbère. 3. Le conte merveilleux*. Paris and Louvain: Peeters.

Bourdieu, Pierre. 1991. " Le champ littéraire." *Actes de la recherche en sciences sociales*, 89: 3–46.

Bourlet, Mélanie. 2013. "L'acte d'écrire: sur la performativité de l'écriture littéraire en pulaar." *Journal des Africanistes*, 83(1): 106–132.

Bouyaakoubi, Lahoucine (Anir). 2010. *Igdad n Wihran* [Birds of Oran]. France: Privately Printed.

Buchanan, Ian and John Marks (eds.). 2000. *Deleuze and Literature*. Edinburgh: Edinburgh University Press.

Camps, Gabriel. 1984. "Être berbère." *Encyclopédie berbère*, 1: 7–26.

Carlier, Omar. 1984. "La production sociale de l'image de soi. Note sur la 'crise berbériste' de 1949." *Annuaire de l'Afrique du Nord*: 347–371.

Chaker, Salem. 1984. "Langage et identité berbère (Algérie/migration): un enjeu de société." *Annuaire de l'Afrique du Nord*: 173–180 (a).

Chaker, Salem. 1989a. "Arabisation." *Encyclopédie berbère*, 6: 834–843. Aix-en-Provence: Edisud.

Chaker, Salem. 1989b. *Berbères aujourd'hui*. Paris: L'Harmattan.

Chaker, Salem. 2003. "Le berbère." In *Les langues de France*, ed. by Bernard Cerquiglini, 215–227. Paris: PUF.

Chaker, Salem. 2013. "Amazigh/Berbère/Tamazight: dans les méandres d'une dénomination." *Revue des Etudes berbères*, 9: 221–239.

Chemak, Saïd. 2008 [1993]. *Ger zik d tura* [From the Past and Today]. Alger: Asqamu Unnig n Timmuzgha (High Commission for Amazighity).

Coulon, Alfred. 1930. "La femme kabyle." *Bulletin de la société géographique d'Alger et de l'Afrique du Nord*, 124: 553–575.

Culshaw, Peter. 2007. "Desert Storm [Tinariwen]." *Songlines*, 42, March–April: 20–25. www.eyefortalent. com/eft-press/T-N%20SonglinesMarApr07.pdf

Dehane, Kamal. 1992. *Assia Djebar, entre ombre et soleil* (Documentary). France: Zeaux Productions, 52 min.

Déjeux, Jean. 1994. *La littérature féminine de langue française au Maghreb*. Paris: Karthala.

Deleuze, Gilles and Felix Guattari. 1975. *Kafka: Pour une littérature mineure*. Paris: Les Editions de Minuit.

Dirèche, Karima. 2017. "La vulgate historique berbère en Algérie: savoirs, usages et projections." In *Les revendications amazighes dans la tourmente des 'printemps arabes'*, ed. by Mohand Tilmatine and Thierry Desrues, 67–89. Rabat: Centre Jacques-Berque.

Elbaz, Robert and Martine Mathieu-Job. 2001. *Mouloud Feraoun ou l'émergence d'une littérature*. Paris: Karthala.

El-Zein, Amira. 2015. "Mythological Tuareg Gods in Ibrahim al-Koni's Work." *Alif: Journal of Comparative Poetics*, 35: 200–216.

Études et Documents Berbères. 2016 (35–36). [Special volume on Berber manuscripts].

Farès, Nabil. 1987. "Civilisation berbère et langue française au Maghreb." *Revue de l'Occident Musulman et de la Méditerranée*, 2(44): 92–96.

Galand-Pernet, Paulette. 1998. *Littératures berbères, des voix, des lettres*. Paris: PUF.

Gans-Guinoune, Anne-Marie. 2010. "Autobiographie et Francophonie: cache-cache entre 'nous' et 'je'." *Relief*, 3(1): 61–76.

Genevois, Henri. 1974. *Légende des rois de Koukou* (Le Fichier périodique 121). Alger: Le Fichier Périodique.

Ghouirgate, Mehdi. 2015. "Le berbère au Moyen Âge. Une culture linguistique en cours de reconstitu-tion." *Annales. Histoire, Sciences Sociales*, 70(3): 577–605.

Goodman, Jane E. 2005. *Berber Culture on World Stage, from Village to Video*. Bloomington: Indiana University Press.

Haines, Daniel. 2015. "From Deleuze and Guattari's Words to a Deleuzian Theory of Reading." *Deleuze and Guattari Studies*, 9(4): 529–557.

Hanoteau, Adolphe. 1867. *Poésies populaires de la Kabylie du Jurjura*. Paris: Imprimerie Impériale.

Hindi Zahra. 2009. "J'ai envie de promouvoir l'amazigh à travers mon chant." [Interview]. *Aujourd'hui le Maroc*, 29 January. www.aujourdhui.ma/maroc-actualite/magazine/zahra-hindi-j-ai-envie-de-promou voir-l-amazigh-a-travers-mon-chant-61657.html

Hindi Zahra. 2010. "Oursoul." *Handmade* (music). CD. Label EMI/Blue Note (UK/US).

Hindi Zahra. 2011. "Discovery: Hindi Zahra." *Interview*, 29 August. https://www.interviewmagazine. com/?s=hindi+zahra

Igli n tlelli [Horizon of Freedom, pseud.]. 2004. *Lwerd n tayri* (The Rose of Love) nd.

Ilikoud, Ouali. 2006. "FFS et RCD: partis nationaux ou partis kabyles?" *Revue des mondes musulmans et de la Méditerranée*, 111–112: 163–182. http://journals.openedition.org/remmm/2870

Irele, F. Abiola and Simon Gikandi (eds.). 2004. *The Cambridge History of African and Caribbean Literature*. Cambridge: Cambridge University Press.

JanMohamed, Abdul R. and David Lloyd. 1987. "Introduction: Minority Discourse: What Is to Be Done?" *Cultural Critique*, 7: 5–17. doi:10.2307/1354148.

Jay, Cleo. 2016. "Playing the 'Berber': The Performance of Amazigh Identities in Contemporary Morocco." *The Journal of North African Studies*, 21(1): 68–80.

Kateb, Kamel. 2004. "Les séparations scolaires dans l'Algérie coloniale." *Insaniyat*, 25–26: 65–100.

Khadda, Naget. 1991. "Autobiographie et structuration du sujet acculturé dans Le Fils du Pauvre de Mouloud Feraoun." In *Itinéraires et contacts de cultures*, 13: 79–85. Paris: L'Harmattan.

Khaïr-Eddine, Mohammed. 1984. *Légende et vie d'Agoun'chich*. Paris: Seuil.

Kizzi, Akila. 2019. *Marie-Louise-Taos Amrouche Passion et déchirement identitaire*. Paris: Michalon.

Knibiehler, Yvonne. 1994. "L'enseignement au Maroc pendant le protectorat (1912–1956). Les fils de notables." *Revue d'histoire moderne et contemporaine*, 41(3): 489–498.

Kossmann, Maarten. 2000. *A Study of Eastern Moroccan Fairy Tales*. Helsinki: Academia Scientiarum Fennica.

Koudache, Lynda. 2009. *Adecciw n tmes* [The Fire Hut]. Tizi-Ouzou: Tiẓrigin Tasekla (Éditions Littérature).

Lacheraf, Mostefa. 1953. "La Colline oubliée ou la conscience anachronique." *Le Jeune Musulman*, 15, 13 February: 4–6.

Lacoste-Dujardin, Camille. 1970. *Le conte kabyle, étude ethnologique*. Paris: Maspéro.

Lahlou, Abdelhak. 2017. *Poésie orale kabyle ancienne: histoire sociale, mémoire orale et création poétique*. Dissertation. Direction: Tassadit Yacine. *École des hautes études en sciences sociales*, Paris.

Laurie, Timothy and Rimi Khan. 2017. "The Concept of Minority for the Study of Culture." *Continuum*, 31(1): 1–12.

Lee, Benjamin Todd, Finkelpearl, Ellen and Luca Graverini (eds.). 2014. *Apuleius and Africa*. New York: Routledge.

Le Rouzic, Maurice. 1996. "Écritures autobiographiques chez Mouloud Feraoun." In *Littératures autobiographiques de la francophonie*, ed. by Martine Mathieu-Job, 45–55. Paris: l'Harmattan.

Maddy-Weitzman, Bruce. 2011. *The Berber Identity Movement and the Challenge to North African States*. Austin: University of Texas Press.

Maddy-Weitzman, Bruce. 2017. "Insécurité à la périphérie: les griefs socio-économiques et le mouvement amazigh au Maroc." In *Les revendications amazighes dans la tourmente des "printemps arabes"*, ed. by Mohand Tilmatine and Thierry Desrues, 195–213. Rabat: Centre Jacques-Berque.

Magdelaine-Andrianjafitrimo, Valérie. 2006. "Champs et espaces littéraires: le cas des romans mauriciens." In *Qu'est-ce qu'un espace littéraire?*, ed. by Xavier Garnier and Pierre Zoberman, 137–156. Saint-Denis: Presses Universitaires de Vincennes.

"Mali Tuareg Rebels' Call for Independence Rejected." *BBC News*, 3 June 2012. www.bbc.co.uk/news/world-africa-17640223

Mammeri, Mouloud. 1969. *Les Isefra. Poèmes de Si Mohand-ou-Mhand*. Paris: Maspéro.

Masbah, Mohammed. 2017. "A New Generation of Protests in Morocco? How Hirak al-Rif Endures." *Policy Alternatives, Arab Reform Initiative*, November.

Merabti, Fatima. 1997 and 1998. *Yir Tagmat* [Bad Brotherhood]. *Tizir*, November: 36–40 and January: 35–38.

Merolla, Daniela. 1995. "Peut-on parler d'un espace littéraire kabyle?" *Études et Documents Berbères*, 13: 5–25.

Merolla, Daniela. 2006. *De l'art de la narration tamazight (berbère). 200 ans d'études: état des lieux et perspectives*. Paris and Louvain: Peeters.

Merolla, Daniela. 2014. "Intersections: Amazigh (Berber) Literary Space (Intersections: l'espace littéraire amazighe–berbère)." In *Vitality and Dinamism: Interstitial Dialogues of Language, Politics, and religion in Morocco's Literary Tradition*, ed. by Kirstin R. Bratt, Youness Elbousty, and Devin J. Steward, 47–72. Leiden: Leiden University Press.

Mezdad, Amar. 1990. *Id d wass* [Day and Night]. Alger: Azar and Asalu.

Millar, Fergus. 1968. "Local Cultures in the Roman Empire: Libyan, Punic, and Latin in Roman Africa." *Journal of Roman Studies*, 58: 129–130, 133.

Modéran, Yves. 2003. *Les Maures et l'Afrique Romaine (IVe–VIIe siècle)*. Rome: École Française de Rome.

Morgan, Andy. 2007. "Tinariwen: Sons of the Desert." *Songlines*, 29. Online in *Andy Morgan Writes . . .*, Website, 6 January, 2011. www.andymorganwrites.com/tinariwen-sons-of-the-desert/

Mouline, Nabil. 2016. "Qui sera l'état? Le soulèvement du Rif reconsidéré (1958–1959)." *Le Carnet du Centre Jacques Berque*, December. https://cjb.hypotheses.org/186

Mouralis, Bernard. 2001. "Pertinence de la notion de champ littéraire en littérature africaine." In *Les champs littéraires africains*, ed. by Romuald Fonkoua, Pierre Halen, and Katharina Städtler, 57–71. Paris: Karthala.

Oiry-Varacca, Mari. 2012–2013. "Le 'printemps arabe' à l'épreuve des revendications amazighes au Maroc. Analyse des enjeux territoriaux et politiques des discours sur l'identité." *L'Espace Politique*, 18. http://espacepolitique.rev. ues.org/2504.

Ould-Amar, Tahar. 2006. *Bururu* [Owl]. Bejaia: Azur.

Pennel, C. Richard. 2017. "How and Why to Remember the Rif War (1921–2021)." *The Journal of North African Studies*, 22(5): 798–820.

Plantade, Emmanuel and Nedjima Plantade. 2014. "Libyca Psyche, Apuleius: Narrative and Berber Folktales." In *Apuleius and Africa*, ed. by Benjamin Todd Lee, Ellen Finkelpearl, and Luca Graverini, 174–202. New York: Routledge.

Ponzanesi, Sandra. 2004. *Paradoxes of Post-Colonial Culture: Contemporary Women Writers of the Indian and Afro-Italian Diaspora*. Albany: State University of New York Press.

Roberts, Hugh. 1982. "The Unforseen Development of the Kabyle Question in Algeria." *Government and Opposition*, 16(3): 312–334.

Roberts, Hugh. 2014. *Berber Government: The Kabyle Polity in Pre-Colonial Algeria*. London and New York: IBTauris.

Rouighi, Ramzi. 2011. "The Berbers of the Arabs." *Studia Islamica* (new series), 1: 67–101.

Sadi, Said. 1983. *Askuti* [Boy Scout]. Paris: Imedyazen.

Sahli, Mohammed Cherif. 1953. "La Colline oubliée ou la colline du reniement." *Le Jeune Musulman*, 12(3), 2 January.

Salhi, Mohand Akli. 2005. "La nouvelle littérature kabyle et ses rapports à l'oralité traditionnelle." In *La littérature amazighe: oralité et écriture, spécificité et perspectives. Actes du colloque international (. . .) Rabat, 23, 24 et 25 octobre 2003*, ed. by Aziz Kich, 103–121. Rabat: IRCAM.

Salhi, Mohand Akli. 2011. *Études de littérature kabyle*. Alger: ENAG.

Salhi, Mohand Akli. 2014. "Quelle grille d'analyse pour le (sous) champ littéraire kabyle." In *Champs littéraires et stratégies d'écrivains*, ed. by Mohamed Daoud and Faouzia Bendjelid, 145–154. Oran: CRASC.

Salhi, Mohand Akli and Nabila Sadi. 2016. "Le Roman Maghrebin en Berbère." *Contemporary French and Francophone Studies*, 20(1): 27–36.

Schipper, Mineke, Merolla, Daniela and Inge Brinkman. 2019. *Afrikaanse Letterkunde. Tradities, genres, auteurs en ontwikkelingen* [African Literatures: Traditions, Genres, Authors and Developments]. Amsterdam: Amsterdam University Press.

Tanti, Samriddhi. 2011. "Hindi Zahra: Music for the Soul." *EF News International*, 21 September. www.efi-news.com/2011/09/hindi-zahra-music-for-soul.html

Tazaghart, Brahim. 2003. *Salas d Nuja* [Salas and Nuja]. Bejaia: Privately Printed.

Tilmatine, Mohand. 2017. "Des revendications linguistiques aux projets d'autodétermination: le cas de la Kabylie (Algérie)." In *Les revendications amazighes dans la tourmente des printemps arabes: Trajectoires historiques et évolutions récentes des mouvements identitaires en Afrique du Nord*, ed. by Mohand Tilmatine and Thierry Desrues, 125–160. Rabat: Centre Jacques-Berque.

Wolf, Anne. 2018. "Morocco's Hirak Movement and Legacies of Contention in the Rif." *The Journal of North African Studies*: 1–6. doi: 10.1080/13629387.2018.1538188

Yacine, Tassadit. 1995. "Femmes et création en Kabylie." *Awal*, 12: 23–27.

Yedjis n Idura n Arrif, Samira. 2001. *Tasrit n weẓru* [The Bride of the Rock]. Oujda: Anakhla.

Zaheur, Lahacem. 2008. *Amussu n umalu* [The Movement of the Shadow]. Agadir: Aqlam.

Zénia, Salem. 1995. *Tafrara* [Dawn]. Paris: L'Harmat

Zouggari, Ahmed. 2005. "Le système d'enseignement sous le protectorat français et espagnol." In *50 ans de développement humain au Maroc et perspectives 2025*, 453–469. http://www.rdh50.ma/fr/index.asp

4

NEGOTIATING THE GLOBAL LITERARY MARKET

Chimamanda Ngozi Adichie's short fiction

Maximilian Feldner

In the early twenty-first century, English-language literature from Africa has been remarkably successful. Many writers from across the Anglophone parts of the African continent have published notable novels, including the Ghanaian Ayesha Harruna Attah, the Sierra Leonean Ismael Beah, the Sierra Leonean Aminatta Forna, the Cameroonian Imbolo Mbue, the Zimbabwean NoViolet Bulawayo, the Zimbabwean Brian Chikwava, and the Ethiopian Dinaw Mengestu. By far the largest literary output comes from Nigerian writers, such as Chimamanda Ngozi Adichie, probably the most famous contemporary Nigerian novelist, but also Chris Abani, Sefi Atta, A. Igoni Barrett, Helon Habila, Okey Ndibe, Adaobi Tricia Nwaubani, Chigozie Obioma, Chinelo Okparanta, Chibundu Onuzo, and many more. These writers have certainly left their mark on the global literary scene.

A closer look at their novels reveals that their literature shares a number of similar thematic concerns. Among the most dominant of these are the focus on migration, diasporicity, and transnationalism and the engagement with the sociopolitical situation in the writers' home countries. In other words, many examples of current African writing either deal with issues of migration and movement or with their characters' lives in their African home, where they have to cope with issues such as corruption, political mismanagement, and serious conflicts such as Civil Wars and authoritarian leaderships.[1]

As a result, African fiction appears to be rather homogeneous, which, considering the broad sample of novelists, is quite surprising and striking. The shared focus of the literature is generally comprehensible, of course, as it is an outcome of the writers' own diasporic experiences, considering that most of them are themselves migrants who have left Africa to live in the United States, United Kingdom, or other parts of the world. Likewise, it is a result of their placement in the literary tradition of the Anglophone African novel that started in the 1950s as part of the decolonisation processes in many countries. Perhaps to an even greater extent, however, the literature's relative homogeneity is a consequence of the demands of the global literary market and its impact on postcolonial African writing. It comes as an effect of processes of commodification and the pressures and demands of literary markets, which influence the kind of literature that is produced and published.

Literature from Africa can be considered a minority discourse in several regards. This chapter proceeds from the assumption that 'African literature' is a category primarily defined by the literary institutions of the global North. Its minority status thus comes, first, as a result of the

African countries' subordinated economic position to Europe and the United States. Second, what is considered 'African literature' on the global literary market is, in fact, only a fraction of literary production in Africa and therefore forms a minority discourse in the context of actual African literature. Third, this literature is constructed as a minority discourse on the global literary market and marketed as such, as African writers are classified according to the component elements of 'African literature', which include cultural difference, anthropology, political engagement, and migration and movement.

In a literary analysis of Chimamanda Ngozi Adichie's short story collection *The Thing Around Your Neck* (2009), particularly the stories "The Headstrong Historian", "The Arrangers of Marriage", and "Jumping Monkey Hill", the chapter shows how these features manifest themselves in her fiction. It aims to illustrate the ways in which Adichie's fiction adheres to and activates the requirements of the global literary market but also to demonstrate the literary possibilities a writer like her has to undermine and criticise the market's mechanisms. As she offers stories of quiet but powerful female resistance, Adichie thus both emphasises and resists the placement of her literature in a position of minority.

'African literature' on the global literary market

In the wake of globalisation, the market for literature, particularly English-language literature, has become a global one in which literatures from all kinds of backgrounds need to assert themselves. In the "global literary marketplace" (Brouillette), books "are no longer imagined to exist in a single literary system but may exist, now and in the future, in several literary systems, through various and uneven practices of world circulation" (Walkowitz 528). The problem for African writers in this respect is that the instances where their works are ascribed meaning are predominantly located in the global North. Only a few companies in England and the United States are in control of most of global publishing (Brouillette 53), and this is also where most of the agents of legitimization – publishers, reviewers, academics, booksellers, and readers – can be found and where decisions as to which novels get read, reviewed, and taught are made.[2] This means that internationally accessible African literature is "classified and given social purpose" (Walkowitz 527) not so much on the African continent but in the global North. This situation illustrates "the disproportionate influence of the West as cultural forum, in all three senses of that word: as place of public exhibition and discussion, as place of judgement, and as market place" (Bhabha 31).

On the global literary market, writers from Africa are placed in a category that can be termed 'African literature'. In a publishing situation characterised by competition for attention, where a lot of emphasis is put on "stratified and specialized 'niche' marketing" (Apter 141), a placement in a visible, recognisable, and attractive category can be valuable. At the same time, it allows only for a restricted range of literary expression and might therefore prove limiting and oppressive to the individual author. Regarding African writing more generally, such classifications have a homogenising effect, flattening potentially diverse, complex, and rich literary cultures and allowing only for a fraction of their expressive potential. Because 'African literature' is typically used to refer only to the writings of black authors from sub-Saharan countries, it suggests a very specific and exclusive notion of what can constitute literature from Africa and is therefore itself conceptually highly problematic. Furthermore, it is a category that produces stereotypical visions of Africa, visions that result particularly from "foreign publishers bringing out texts that conform to their notion of 'African' literature, which is usually a distorted Western view of Africa" (Ojaide 15).[3]

The writings grouped under 'African literature' are typically expected to represent 'Africa', an expectation that is problematic and unrealistic enough by itself. What is more, the category assembles literature that is certainly not representative regarding Africa's literary output. It not only erases the individual traits of and the differences between the manifold forms of literary expression produced in the various countries and cultures on the continent but also excludes and ignores oral story-telling, the literature produced in the numerous African languages, and the popular fiction sold in cheap editions on the streets. In Nigeria, fiction that is internationally read is predominantly written by novelists from Igbo or Yoruba backgrounds, by writers who are informed by European influences and a Christian background and come from the South and South East of Nigeria. Writings in other languages such as Arabic, Hausa, Yoruba, and Igbo do not play a role, not even in translation. In addition, writers of 'African literature' typically write and live outside the continent. Because it is the members of the African diaspora who are noticed and acknowledged abroad, they are not only considered the primary exemplars of African writing but are also seen by a non-African readership as representatives for Africa at large. As Tanure Ojaide remarks, however, it is contestable whether their literature can be assumed to "represent African experience, since the content and style of their works are geared towards foreign markets and readers" (16).

Ojaide's objection indicates that his conception of African literature considerably differs from that of the global literary market. For Ojaide, African literature will "remain that literature that responds to the concerns and expresses the sensibility and aspirations and ideals of African people in a form and manner that they see as part of their living reality" (18). It is for this reason that he aims to formulate the parameters for a canon of African literature. Attempts by African critics to define and classify literature from Africa are important and relevant because they contribute to the overcoming of the distorted and distorting perspectives on African writing that are transported in categories such as 'African literature'. So far, however, "the African literary canon is suffering the inability of the cultural home (Africa) to define itself and so surrenders its identity to others to define in the editorial rooms of Western publishers" (Ojaide 17). A major problem is that very little African and Africanist literary criticism can actually be found in Africa but takes "place essentially in institutions situated outside the continent" (Kom 431) and that there are "practically no scholarly literary journals of repute publishing from the continent" (Adesanmi 111).[4]

In addition to an intellectual climate that cannot offer much support, the inadequate infrastructure of the domestic cultural markets is a major reason for African writers to seek their fortunes abroad. Ojaide points out that "many of the writers in the continent are helpless and desperate for good-quality publishers and often send their works outside to be considered for publication in the West" (Ojaide 17). The publishing situation in Nigeria, for example, is characterised by a literary complex that can only provide a weak and restricted infrastructure.[5] This state is the consequence of a number of factors, including current misgovernment and corruption, the legacy of colonialism, and the general economic imbalance between African countries and the global North. Since their beginnings, African literatures in English have been firmly in the hands of metropolitan publishers located especially in the media centres of London and New York. This has resulted in limited possibilities for distribution and marketing, having led to "poor editorial staff, poor quality of books, and the weak distribution network of the African publishers" (Ojaide, 2009, 17). A reading culture defined by low literacy rates, a lack of purchasing power, and the collapse of public libraries (see Griswold 88–120) further compounds the problem and has enticed Nigerian novelists to publish their literature abroad.

If African writers on the global literary market are subsumed under 'African literature', this necessitates a closer look at this category's features. Graham Huggan's concept of the 'postcolonial exotic' serves as a useful starting point in this regard. As part of the global commodification of cultural difference, "exoticism describes a particular mode of aesthetic *perception* – one which renders people, objects and places strange even as it domesticates them, and which effectively manufactures otherness even as it claims to surrender to its immanent mystery" (13, original emphasis). The term 'postcolonial exotic' thus describes the process of taking literature from the margins and recuperating it for mainstream markets by rewriting the unfamiliar in terms of the familiar and packaging it as new and exotic (22). Therefore, one central expectation for literature from Africa is that it be accessible and comprehensible to a metropolitan readership while presenting cultural difference and safe visions of marginality. Huggan notes that cultural difference has been imbued with aesthetic value in order to serve the readers' interest in the exotic and that "the fetishisation of cultural otherness . . . allows metropolitan readers to exercise fantasies of unrestricted movement and free will" (10). Like cultural difference, marginality has become a valuable intellectual commodity, but only in aesthetical terms, where it is "deprived of its subversive implications by being rerouted into safe assertions of a fetishized cultural difference" (24).

In the context of 'African literature', one main way this cultural difference is expressed is by offering insights into African cultures which are considered 'foreign' and 'other' by the readers in the global North. African novels are especially often read as a source of knowledge about exotic worlds and cultures and for ethnographic or anthropological insights into the culture they claim to represent. Huggan calls this the 'anthropological exotic', meaning "a reading of African literature as the more or less transparent window onto a richly detailed and culturally specific, but still somehow homogenous – and of course readily marketable – African world" (37; see also Pucherová 17). However, this does not imply "empirical documentation, but . . . the elaboration of a world of difference that conforms to often crudely stereotypical Western exoticist paradigms and myths ('primitive culture', 'unbounded nature', 'magical practices', 'noble savagery', and so on)" (Huggan 37).

Writers need to be perceived as authentic in order to be considered "not just . . . *representers* of culture but . . . bona fide cultural *representatives*" (26; original emphasis). Since authenticity is vital for the plausibility of the writers' problematic role as cultural representatives, in the marketing of 'African literature' – and postcolonial literature more generally – the connections between authors and their work are highlighted. Sarah Brouillette argues that the "author's name and attached personae have become key focal points for the marketing of literary texts, such that one could argue that the current industry brands literature more by authorship than by other aspects of or ways of approaching a given work's meaning" (66). It increases the supposed authenticity if novelists can be closely identified with the stories they tell, while the focus on authenticity also unduly disregards the fictionality and aesthetic complexity of a literary text.

The prominence of postcolonial studies in academia has led to a focus on political activism and anticolonial resistance in its various shapes. As a result, the "politics of postcolonial stories" (Adesokan 1) are important, in the sense of overtly political concerns regarding issues such as anticolonialism, nation building, and the repudiation of racism and stereotyping. As 'African literature' is specifically geared towards the American academy, which forms a potent target group where an inclusion on reading lists and course syllabi can provide a decisive boost for novelists, its anthological and political content is of particular interest. Informing and educating about foreign cultures, the novels allow for an extension of imaginative scopes beyond the United States (see Appiah 70). Brouillette notes that "readers want to be educated to a certain degree about 'other' realities [and] the texts that fulfil that interest most often accord with a broadly anti-imperialist political liberalism" (60).

Similarly, due to the focus of postcolonial studies on forms of migration and diasporic formations, depictions of mobility and migration are also sought for in 'African literature'. In other words, "diasporic, migrant textualities . . . are the prized features of Western diversity/multicultural syllabi" (Adesanmi 111). Paul Tiyambe Zeleza calls this the "the boon and bane of postcolonial criticism": African literature might be more present in the Euro-American academy than ever before, but only at the cost of being "increasingly decentred and filtered through the formulaic focus on transnational and migrant subjectivities and textualities" (14). A related issue is that only particular forms of migration, typically comparatively privileged, are emphasised, while other less auspicious migratory movements are overlooked. This results in idealised versions of migration that are celebrated in academic discourses, ignoring the fates of many real-life migrants (see Parry 73). On the basis of these elements, a preliminary framework of criteria that African writers have to meet in order to be selected for publication and dissemination can be argued to include the features of cultural difference, marginality, anthropology, authenticity, politics and resistance, and mobility and migration.

Writing 'African literature'

Chimamanda Ngozi Adichie serves as a useful example to illustrate the ways the criteria of the global literary market manifest themselves in the works of diasporic African writers. Among the most famous African novelists, Adichie is certainly a very successful writer whose works have achieved a high degree of international visibility. Her three novels, *Purple Hibiscus* (2003), *Half of a Yellow Sun* (2006), and *Americanah* (2013) were all published to great acclaim, and her essays and talks have proven influential and are often quoted, particularly the TED Talks "The Danger of a Single Story" and "We Should All be Feminists". Her popularity with a wide reading public has been accompanied by many prizes, including a MacArthur Foundation "Genius" Fellowship in 2008, the Commonwealth Writers' Prize for Best First Book for *Purple Hibiscus*, the Orange Prize for Fiction for *Half of a Yellow Sun*, and the National Book Critics Circle Award for fiction for *Americanah*.

While Adichie's high profile is the result of her exceptionally engaging writing style, it is also due to her ability to cannily activate for her purposes the criteria of 'African literature'. Her fiction and her authorial persona are characterised by a high degree of authenticity.[6] She is a diasporic writer, dealing with experiences of migration, and in the global North, her status as an African woman places her in a position of marginality and cultural difference. She also fulfils the criteria of political engagement and resistance, as she repeatedly criticises and highlights racism, sexism, and the workings of the literary field she positions herself in. Analysing several short stories from her collection *The Thing Around Your Neck* (2009), the following discussion will demonstrate the ways her literature is informed by the requirements of the global literary market.

Adichie's fiction is typically written in a realist mode using a literary style that is accessible, non-experimental, and seemingly simple and transparent. The readability and translatability of her writing facilitates wide circulation. Nevertheless, although her fiction does not exhibit a lot of generic experimentation and linguistic adventurousness, in most of her stories, "there are traces of an alternative signifying system to that of novelistic realism, however obscured and however tangential" (Bryce 53), bearing traces "of preexisting nonrealist modes of expression and belief, however deeply buried" (54). These traces, which can be seen as an element of "ornamenting" (Julien 679), contribute to the perception of Adichie's literature as exotic and therefore interesting for the global literary market.

Among the most obvious ways in which Adichie writes 'African literature' is by rewriting *the* classic and defining text of African literary history: Chinua Achebe's *Things Fall Apart* (1959). Like no other piece of writing, this novel has determined the look of the African novel, to the extent that it has almost become a template for African fiction. Achebe, in the words of Elleke Boehmer, "offered a way of writing Africa that would prove influential, not to say path-breaking" and has become "a dominant point of origin, a hyper-precursor one might say, in whose aftermath virtually every African author self-consciously writes" (141–142). Similarly, Simon Gikandi points out that "Achebe is the person who invented African culture as it is now circulated within the institutions of interpretation" and that his novels have "become an essential referent for the African cultural text" (6–7).[7] For better or worse, Achebe has become a viable model for 'African literature' which many African writers consciously follow.

Achebe's legacy and influence not only on Adichie but also on other contemporary Nigerian writers have been well documented.[8] In *The Thing Around Your Neck*, *Things Fall Apart* is most directly addressed in the story "The Headstrong Historian". The correspondences between both texts are obvious, as the former is basically a rewriting of the latter.[9] Like Achebe's novel, "The Headstrong Historian" depicts precolonial Igbo society just before the arrival of the missionaries and the changes they bring. Both narratives use the backdrop of the Igbo community and provide detailed pictures of the villagers' everyday lives, their social, political, and religious rules, customs, norms, beliefs, and cultural practices.

Where Achebe's novel tells the story of protagonist Okonkwo's rise and fall from grace in his community, Adichie's story focuses on the "headstrong" Nwamgba, a widow who has to defend her possessions and her son from her late husband's avaricious cousins. Thus, Adichie reframes Achebe's story, presenting a female perspective that is largely missing from *Things Fall Apart* (see Uko 84; Doherty 188). As her short story "recounts a particular story of Igbo female agency in the more general historical narrative of African encroachment and colonization" (VanZanten 93), Adichie adds to Achebe's vision by expressing "her own convictions on gender, religion, historiography and literature" (Tunca, "Appropriating Achebe" 234).

In terms of 'African literature', both texts fulfil at least two functions on the global literary market. First, they provide an exotic setting unfamiliar to readers in the global North offering glimpses of the Igbo culture that correspond to Huggan's 'anthropological exotic'.[10] However, they do not idealise their ancestors' lives. Achebe renders negative aspects, such as the killing of twins, human sacrifice, or the ostracising of certain groups, and Adichie highlights other internal reasons for the collapse of the community. Second, they are expressively political as they stage the onset of colonisation and the arrival of the white missionaries. *Things Fall Apart* shows the disintegration of the village when the colonisers slowly work their way into the heart of the community, undermining traditional rules and converting parts of the population. Because of the reduced scope of her short story and her different focus, Adichie does not make the destruction of the clan as explicit as Achebe. The corrosive changes are nevertheless rendered as the white man's schools divide not only individual families but the whole village community.

Although she is sceptical of the missionaries' teachings, Adichie's protagonist Nwamgba sends her son to their school, because she recognises the future advantages he will have from an English education. Warily she notices the way he changes in the process, wondering if she has made a mistake. She finally loses him, as he leaves to become a teacher and is "appointed catechist at the new mission" (Adichie 211).[11] A generation later, in the 1950s, Nwamgba's granddaughter, whom she named Afamefuna ("My Name Will Not Be Lost"), studies history in order to become a historian of her people. Having begun "to rethink her own schooling" (216), she sets out to write a history of her ancestors. She "would become haunted by the image of a destroyed village and would go to London and to Paris and to Onicha, sifting through moldy files in archives, reimagining the lives and smells of her grandmother's world for the book she would write called *Pacifying with Bullets: A Reclaimed History of Southern Nigeria*" (217). This title is a direct response to the District Commissioner whose perspective ends *Things Fall Apart* and who intends to write about his efforts "to bring civilization to different parts of Africa" (Achebe, *Things* 208) in a book named "*The Pacification of the Primitive Tribes of the Lower Niger*" (209).

Thus, Adichie adds to *Things Fall Apart*'s two-generational narrative a third generation which is concerned with the recovery of their grandparents' past. A contemporary of Achebe's, the fictional Afamefuna assumes a role similar to his own, embodying his wish to provide a counter-narrative to European representations of Africa. Achebe not only attempted to teach African readers that "their past – with all its imperfections – was not one long night of savagery from which the first Europeans acting on God's behalf delivered them" (Achebe, *Hopes* 45) but also addressed an international audience. His use of the English language, as Daria Tunca remarks, "points to a wish to reach an international audience" ("Appropriating Achebe" 230) in order to rectify the one-dimensional representations of Africa in colonial discourses.

With her fiction, Adichie similarly provides a strong counter-discourse to stereotypical images of Africa. Her short story collection offers insightful as well as critical and complex perspectives of life in Nigeria. The stories deal with corruption and embezzlement ("Cell One"; "Ghosts"), the political situation in 1990s Nigeria ("The American Embassy"), and religio-ethnic conflicts ("A Private Experience") and thus meet certain expectations for stories about Nigeria while providing plenty of 'exotic' subject matter. On the surface, the stories confirm the trope of Africa as a place of catastrophe and disorder. Viewed unfavourably, it can be argued that they tap into notions of African countries as places of violence, trauma, and war, constituting a "residue of racist images of the 'dark continent'" (Adesokan 13). This shows the tightrope walk African writers have to perform if they want to meet the market requirements without falling into the trap of perpetuating racist stereotypes. However, Adichie's stories avoid this problem by undermining expectations and by refusing to lend themselves to simple and straightforward readings that elide the complexities involved. A story like "Ghosts", for example, a narrative about the wounds of the Biafran War, does not stage the war directly but approaches it through the memory of the protagonist forty years later. Instead of presenting glorified accounts of chaos, danger, and war, it shows the civil war's long-lasting impact on the characters' humanity.

Throughout her work, Adichie's themes are anticolonialism, empowerment, and nation building, and she consistently attacks racism and sexism. Thus, her writings satisfy the requirement of resistance and political engagement. But her approach to these issues is complex and detailed enough to meet the market criteria without succumbing to them. One example where she complicates the idea of activism in a Nigerian context is her short story "The American Embassy". A woman stands in line to apply for asylum after her son was killed by soldiers. The soldiers were actually looking for her husband, an investigative journalist responsible for several articles criticising General Abacha's ruthless and corrupt military government. Public opinion considers him a person who "fights repression with a pen, he gives a voice to the voiceless, he makes the world know" (Adichie 137). Other characters in the story praise him, holding him up as an example for "the kind of people Nigeria needs. They risk their lives to tell us the truth. Truly brave men. If only we had more people with that kind of courage" (135). In short, he is the perfect postcolonial hero. As the story presents his wife's figural perspective, however, his heroism is offset by the duties as a husband and father he failed to satisfy, which considerably reduces his appeal. Numbed by the medication that should help her to forget the loss of her son, the woman thinks that his behaviour "was not courage, it was simply an exaggerated selfishness" (136). Highlighting that political activism can endanger and harm a family, Adichie indicates that there are also circumstances where political participation and activism can have severe downsides which are often enough ignored in the search for stories of political emancipation and enfranchisement.

Migration to America

Much of Adichie's fiction deals with issues of migration and diaspora. This is a major focus in her novel *Americanah* and several of the stories assembled in *The Thing Around Your Neck*. As these stories depict the movement of Nigerians to the United States, they render the characters' culture shock, their difficulties with getting used to the new place and with coming to terms with the changed circumstances, and their attempts of building a new life. They predominantly narrativise the early stages of the process of migrating to the United States and so address, among other things, the realisation of the hollow promises of the American Dream.[12] The characters have to realise that their high expectations of immediate financial success, a big car and house, and generally an easy life prove delusory. Having to adjust their outlook, they need to adapt to the situation and find their way in the new country.

One typical example for this kind of narrative can be found in Adichie's short story "The Arrangers of Marriage". Its protagonist, Chinaza, a Nigerian woman, arrives in New York after having married an American-Nigerian man, whom her uncle and aunt, the eponymous "arrangers of marriage", found for her. Although they presented the husband as a win in the lottery, Chinaza soon realises that the marriage is far from a lottery win. Instead of the expected house, a "house like those of the white newlyweds in the American films that NTA showed on Saturday nights" (Adichie 167), her new home turns out to be in a brownstone in Flatbush, with "a flight of brooding stairs" and "an airless hallway with frayed carpeting" (167). Their flat is small and bare and lacks "a sense of space, as though the walls had become uncomfortable with each other, with so little between them" (167–168). Also, Chinaza's new husband is not a doctor as promised, but a badly paid intern, albeit with the intention to climb the social ladder at all costs (175). To fit in better, he changes his name from Ofodile Emeka Udenwa to Dave Bell and without his wife's consent renames her from Chinaza Agatha Okafor to Agatha Bell (172).[13] He urges Chinaza "to be as mainstream as possible" (172) in order to adapt to what he perceives as the right American way of life: "I got used to the way things are done here a long time ago. You will too, baby" (171).

Part of becoming American for Chinaza's husband involves the use of language. Chinaza notices how his speaking style has changed: "He sounded different when he spoke to Americans: his *r* was overpronounced and his *t* was underpronounced. And he smiled, the eager smile of a person who wanted to be liked" (176). He corrects her when she does not use the American expression for a word – "Americans say busy, not engaged" (170); "It's an elevator, not a lift. Americans say elevator" (177); "Pitcher. Americans say pitcher, not jug" (183) – and urges her to "Speak English" (177) when she uses Igbo words and phrases, such as "*Ike agwum*" (168) to state that she is tired, and "*Ezi okwu?*" (169) to express amazement.

Chinaza's use of Igbo serves a narrative purpose but is also an example of how Adichie's characters frequently intersperse their conversations with Igbo expressions. This can be seen as a strategy to show authenticity and to exoticise the story. From the perspective of the global North, such language use can be viewed as a marker of cultural difference. This is illustrated, for instance, in a passage where Chinaza's luggage is inspected at the airport. The customs officer:

> had examined my foodstuffs as if they were spiders, her gloved fingers poking at the waterproof bags of ground *egusi* and dried *onugbu* leaves and *uziza* seeds, until she seized my *uziza* seeds. She feared I would grow them on American soil. It didn't matter that the seeds had been sun-dried for weeks and were as hard as a bicycle helmet.
>
> *(168)*

These Igbo words signal cultural difference for European or American readers while simultaneously expressing Chinaza's cultural background, which is constitutive to her identity. It is not a coincidence that cultural difference is indicated with words for food. Tunca points out that "metaphors related to language and food are central in Adichie's examination of themes such as belonging, adaptation and discrimination, and they form a consistent pattern in the author's work" (Tunca, "French Fries and Cookies" 296).

Since "The Arrangers of Marriage" is narrated from Chinaza's first-person perspective, it is she who experiences the United States as culturally different, not the other way around. When shopping for food, for example, Chinaza is "wary when [her husband] put a beef pack in the cart. I wished I could touch the meat, to examine its redness, as I often did at Ogbete Market, where the butcher held up fresh-cut slabs buzzing with flies" (Adichie 173). From the American point of view that the husband has adopted, the apparent backwardness of Nigeria is emphasised. At one point he explains something, "sneering, as though he was the one who had invented the superior American system" (173). By contrast, for Chinaza, whose perspective dominates the story, the United States is perceived as foreign, strange, and lacking. The food especially does not meet her standards. The frozen pancakes are limp and "so much thinner than the chewy slabs I made at home" (171). When she complains that the tomatoes on a pizza are not cooked well, her husband responds that "We overcook food back home and that is why we lose all the nutrients. Americans cook things right. See how healthy they all look?" (176) Considering the quality of typical fast food, his earnest affirmation comes across as ironic and ridiculous.

In this vein, Chinaza's narration consistently subverts expectations. The neighbourhood she lives in is described in terms one would expect for a Nigerian city and not New York: "Our neighborhood was called Flatbush, my new husband told me, as we walked, hot and sweaty, down a noisy street that smelled of fish left out too long before refrigeration" (173). As the direction of the perceived cultural difference is reversed, readers perceive not Nigeria as the exotic and unfamiliar place but America. This strategy of deliberately catering to the demands for cultural difference is a form of what Huggan calls 'strategic exoticism' (x), a way of employing the codes of exoticism to the writer's advantage as she is working "toward dismantling self-privileging Western modes of vision and thought" (40). This also involves the knowledge that their criticism can always be recuperated by the system and turned into "a means of reconfirming an exoticising imperial gaze" (Huggan, 2001, 81).

Resistance and criticism

On an international level, it is not possible for African writers to escape the processes of commodification and avoid being measured against the construct of 'African literature'. In this respect, it is not surprising that Adichie's stories present anthropological insights into Nigerian lives, deal with cultural difference and migration, and are distinctly political on several levels. At the same time, her fiction proves that writers can retain the possibility for resistance and criticism. Resorting to self-reflexivity, they can comment on their position on the global literary market and the contradicting and complementing forces at work there. Laying open the tendencies of exoticising inherent in this field, they can reveal the constructedness of the literary categories applied (see Huggan 26; Brouillette 68). In this way, they can work from within dominant systems of representation in order to challenge them.

This is exactly what Adichie does in her short story "Jumping Monkey Hill", where she narrativises the situation of African literature on the global literary market.[14] The story depicts a workshop for African writers held in South Africa, with participants from different African countries.[15] The workshop leader is Edward, "an Oxford-trained Africanist" (Adichie 108), who is able to get them published: "Edward was connected and could find them a London agent; there was no need to antagonize the man, no need to close doors to opportunity" (113). Personifying the institutions involved in the mediation of literature, he judges and evaluates the participants' contributions to the workshop.

Edward claims that he is "keen on the 'real' Africa and not the imposing of Western ideas on African venues" (108). His critiques of the participants' short stories show, however, that imposing Western ideas on African venues is exactly what he does. He clearly favours stories about conflicts, war, and violence, praising, for example, a story about civil unrest in the Congo for being "urgent and relevant" and for bringing "news" (109). Then, he dismisses a story by a Zimbabwean woman about religious beliefs linked to pregnancy as irrelevant "when one considered all the other things happening in Zimbabwe under the horrible Mugabe" (107). His views are in line with perceptions of African countries as places where nothing but conflict, violence, and war is possible – the "representation of contemporary Africa as a site of perennial political and humanitarian emergencies" (Adesokan 11). Edward is clearly depicted as reducing Africa to its problems and political troubles and accepting only literature dealing with these issues as relevant and truly 'African'.

The story operates on two levels and in this way exposes Edward's posturing and self-declared expertise about Africa. On the story level, he dominates the scene; his comments remain mostly uncontradicted by the workshop participants. But he does not go unchallenged on the discourse level, as the events are filtered through protagonist Ujunwa's third-person perspective. The figural narration, which presents her thoughts and feelings, provides a running commentary on Edward's statements and thus offers a different view of the workshopped stories. For instance, to her, the story about the Congo reads "like a piece from *The Economist* with cartoon characters painted in" (Adichie 109). Also, regarding the story by the Zimbabwean woman, she wonders how Edward can find a story passé that she believes is "a story so true" (107) as well as "familiar and funny" (106).

By contrasting Edward's views with those of Ujunwa, the story reveals and criticises Edward's racist opinions. It highlights how he dismisses stories about the everyday realities of Africans, when, regarding a story in which a homosexual Senegalese woman processes her experiences, he claims that "homosexual stories of this sort [are not] reflective of Africa, really" (108). His ignorance becomes most apparent when Ujunwa presents her own contribution, a story about the sexism and resultant indignities women like her are exposed to in the Lagosian banking sector. He grandly declares that it is "never quite like that in real life, is it? Women are never victims in that sort of crude way and certainly not in Nigeria. Nigeria has women in high positions" (113). He further argues that her story is implausible and "agenda writing, it isn't a real story of real people" (114). As readers are aware, Ujunwa has based her contribution on her own previous experiences. Thus, Edward's comments strike as especially ridiculous. They are not surprising when one considers the misogyny he exhibits throughout the story. The critically foregrounded sexism in Ujunwa's story mirrors Edward's sexist behaviour towards her and shows that women can certainly be "victims in that sort of crude way" (113).

For Tunca, Edward incarnates "both European condescension towards Africa *and* sexism" and thus "suggests a parallel between two forms of domination inherited, respectively, from colonialism and patriarchy" ("Danger of a Single Short Story" 74, original emphasis). As an African woman and participant of the workshop, Ujunwa is silenced, wondering why "we say nothing? . . . Why do we always say nothing?" (Adichie 112). Once, when she contradicts Edward, he looks at her "in the way one would look at a child who refuses to keep still in church" (108). Yet, the story renders her perspective and the direction of the readers' sympathy certainly works in her favour. As readers get the impression of having direct access to Ujunwa's consciousness, it is her voice that dominates the story, which reflects the potential of literature to empower silenced groups and to transport minority discourses. Adichie's story therefore fictionalises the unequal positions of power in the global literary marketplace and serves as a critical account of how this hierarchical relationship renders a distorted view on literature from Africa: if only a specific and limited set of topics and issues is deemed suitable while countless possible stories are elided, its narrative and expressive potential is considerably reduced.

It is clear that "Jumping Monkey Hill" is a story about resistance in many forms. It depicts Ujunwa's opposition to Edward's sexism and racism. As she struggles against Edward's, and, by extension, the global literary market's expectations for African writing, it is also about postcolonial resistance. Perhaps most forcefully, the story deals with resistance against being silenced, as a woman, as African, and as an African woman. Resistance is generally a thread that connects the stories from *The Thing Around Your Neck* discussed in this chapter. In "The Headstrong Historian", Nwamgba is a strong-willed woman who grapples with the pressures of a patriarchal society. She is a "sharp-tongued, headstrong" (199) girl who is able to defeat her brother in wrestling and grows up to become a strong and tough woman who stands up to her late husband's greedy cousins. She also confronts the missionaries who beat her son in school and for whom there is "something troublingly assertive about her" (209). Eventually, she passes on her defiance to her granddaughter. The protagonist of "The Arrangers of Marriage" is also a quiet but strong-willed woman, who, by the end of the story, is about to leave her domineering husband in order to start her own life in the United States. Before that, she shows her own mind in quiet defiance; she may assent to his demands to speak English at home but does not tell him that she is speaking Igbo to herself while cooking. The female protagonists of "The Headstrong Historian", "The Arrangers of Marriage", "Jumping Monkey Hill", and "The American Embassy" all struggle against the overbearing men in their lives.

Through Adichie's stories runs a current of quiet but defiant female opposition against the demands of their patriarchal surroundings, an opposition that could be symbolically extended to include her own grappling with the market pressures. This argument's focus on resistance may run the risk of partaking in the same operations that this chapter aims to critique, namely reducing African writing to functions such as expressing political engagement and resistance. While complicity can hardly be avoided anyway as soon as one enters the discursive arena around the phenomenon of 'African literature', the very point of this analysis is to show that both affirmation and rejection are inherent in Adichie's work. She is aware that the success of an African novel is often determined by its faithfulness to the expectations for 'African literature', and her work accordingly at the same time assents to and struggles with the market demands for African writers. Even though this category may prove limiting to the individual author, avoiding it is difficult and heightens the risk of not being published at all and thus being excluded from the market altogether.

As a consequence, Adichie consciously caters to market demands, but not without using her position and high profile to criticise the conditions under which African writers are judged. With her fiction, she exposes and, to some extent, dismantles the exoticising market logic and shows the limitations of a category such as 'African literature'. Her literature demonstrates the way postcolonial authors can negotiate the demands of the global literary market for their purposes without submitting to them completely. As a result, *The Thing Around Your Neck* emerges as a fascinating document of simultaneous adherence and resistance to the mechanisms of the global literary market.

Notes

1 For a detailed analysis of the recurrent tendencies in contemporary Nigerian literature, see *Narrating the New African Diaspora* (Feldner, 2019). This book includes an early version of this chapter's argument, however, without backing it up with concrete analyses of literary texts.

2 This argument is based on Pierre Bourdieu's sociology of literature, which provides a useful theoretical and terminological framework to understand cultural markets (see Bourdieu, *Field of Cultural Production*; *Rules of Art*; and Huggan, *Postcolonial Exotic*).

3 Indeed, sometimes works by African writers are made "publishable", that is, they are made to "conform more closely to an educated reader's expectations of the novel form", which means "not only correcting grammar and syntax, but restructuring and rewriting" (Bryce 57).

4 Connected to this situation is the process of "reversed extraversion" (Adesokan 16), which describes the phenomenon of African novelists only getting attention at home after having found success abroad. Because 'African literature' is directed at international audiences, it is not surprising that its representatives are better known abroad than at home.

5 Wendy Griswold has suggested the term 'Nigerian literary complex' to indicate a complex "consisting of multiple parts that do not fit together very well", instead of 'Nigerian literary system', which "would imply a smoothly functioning interrelationship of components, something distinctly absent in the Nigerian case" (25).

6 Due to the obvious parallels between Adichie's biography and her narratives, it is easy to identify or even confuse her with several of her fictional characters. It is tempting to read *Americanah*, for example, a novel about a young woman moving to the United States to get an education, as an autobiographical account of her own experiences there. The possible conflation of her biography and her fiction certainly helps to increase her perceived authenticity.

7 The fact that Achebe dominates the image of African fiction to this degree can also be seen critically. First, because he wrote in and for a particular moment in time, just before independence and the end of formal colonisation, as a contribution to the then prevalent attempts of shaping an African cultural identity, and his work cannot be seen as unconnected from this moment. Second, because the notion of one person's work forming the definitive image of a whole continent is reductive, even if originally "his project has indeed valorized the idea of culture in the thinking of African worlds" (Gikandi 7). Daria Tunca notes that "one can easily imagine how reading *Things Fall Apart* as the unique narrative of the continent might flatten the perspective which Achebe was trying to enhance, and thus give rise to further pre- and misconceptions" ("Appropriating Achebe" 231). Third, if his influence leads to writers being expected to imitate his formula in order to be considered properly African and thus have a chance to get published, this considerably limits the possible diversity of African literature and creates a rather homogenous set of texts.

8 See Hewett, Boehmer, Andrade, Tunca, Highfield, Doherty, VanZanten, Wenske, Akpome, and Anyanwu. This wealth of scholarly responses to the connections between Achebe and contemporary Nigerian literature is in itself a significant illustration of Achebe's importance in conceptions of African literature.

9 For a detailed look at the manifold links between Achebe's and Adichie's texts, see Tunca ("Appropriating Achebe"). As she astutely notes, the connections between "The Headstrong Historian" and Achebe's work are not limited to *Things Fall Apart* but extend to all three novels of his African trilogy (237).

10 This example also reveals how questionable and tenuous the notion of the African writer's perceived authenticity actually is: neither Achebe nor Adichie need to have had direct experience with the culture they depict in order to be regarded as authorities on their subject matter.

11 This and all subsequence quotations of Adichie refer to her short story collection, *The Thing Around Your Neck* (2009).

12 Disappointment with the American Dream is a staple in diasporic African fiction. For Nigerian examples of the disappointing arrival in the United States, see Sefi Atta's short story "News from Home" from the collection *News from Home* (2010), Ike Oguine's *A Squatter's Tale* (2000), and Okey Ndibe's *Foreign Gods, Inc.* (2014).

13 The identity change that such a renaming implies also plays a role in "The Headstrong Historian", where the characters also get new names when they join the missionaries' Christian church. The protagonist's son's Igbo name, Anikwenwa, is changed to Michael, while her granddaughter, whom she calls Afamefuna, is baptised Grace.

14 "Jumping Monkey Hill" is also an example of the way Adichie plays with and lampoons expectations concerning literature from Africa. The story's title alludes to exoticist ideas about Africa, namely that a story set in South Africa must include monkeys. Accordingly, Ujunwa looks for "lurking monkeys" but quickly realizes that there are "none, unfortunately" (Adichie 95). Instead, "Jumping Monkey Hill" is the name of a resort that also caters to certain expectations, with its thatched-roofed cabins and names like "Baboon Lodge" and "Porcupine Place". It is a place where "affluent foreign tourists would dart around taking pictures of lizards and then return home still mostly unaware that there were more black people than red-capped lizards in South Africa" (Adichie 95). It does not contradict the story's critical

thrust to assume that it is in fact the workshop participants who are supposed to be the jumping monkeys (see Tunca, "Danger of a Single Short Story" 72).

15 The workshop appears to be a fictionalised version of the annual workshop organized by the Caine Prize for African Writing, for which Adichie was shortlisted in 2002 (see Pucherová 22; Tunca, "Danger of a Single Short Story" 71).

Works cited

Achebe, Chinua. *Hopes and Impediments*. New York, Anchor Books, 1990.

Achebe, Chinua. *Things Fall Apart*. 1958. New York, Anchor Books, 1994.

Adesanmi, Pius. "Third Generation African Literatures and Contemporary Theorising." *The Study of Africa, Vol I: Disciplinary and Interdisciplinary Encounters*, edited by Paul Tiyambe Zeleza. Dakar, Senegal, CODESRIA, 2006, pp. 105–116.

Adesokan, Akin. "New African Writing and the Question of Audience." *Research in African Literatures*, vol. 43, no. 3, 2012, pp. 1–20.

Adichie, Chimamanda Ngozi. *Purple Hibiscus*. New York, Anchor Books, 2003.

Adichie, Chimamanda Ngozi. *Half of a Yellow Sun*. 2006. London, Harper Perennial, 2009.

Adichie, Chimamanda Ngozi. *The Thing around Your Neck*. London, Fourth Estate, 2009.

Adichie, Chimamanda Ngozi. *Americanah*. 2013. London, Fourth Estate, 2014.

Akpome, Aghogho. "Intertextuality and Influence: Chinua Achebe's *Anthills of the Savannah* (1987) and Chimamanda Ngozi Adichie's *Half of a Yellow Sun* (2006)." *Journal of Postcolonial Writing*, vol. 53, no. 5, 2017, pp. 530–542. doi: 10.1080/17449855.2017.1333449.

Andrade, Susan. "Adichie's Genealogies: National and Feminine Novels." *Research in African Literatures*, vol. 42, no. 2, 2011, pp. 91–101.

Anyanwu, Chikwendu Paschalkizito. "Corruption in Post-Independence Politics: *Half of a Yellow Sun* as a Reflection of *A Man of the People*." *A Companion to Chimamanda Ngozi Adichie*, edited by Ernest N. Emenyonu. Woodbridge, James Currey, 2017, pp. 139–151.

Appiah, Kwame Anthony. *In My Father's House: Africa in the Philosophy of Culture*. Oxford, Oxford University Press, 1992.

Apter, Emily. "'Untranslatable' Algeria: The Politics of Linguicide." *Literature and Globalization*, edited by Liam Connell and Nicky Marsh, New York, Routledge, 2011, pp. 140–146.

Atta, Sefi. *News from Home*. Northampton, MA, Interlink Books, 2010.

Bhabha, Homi K. *The Location of Culture*. 1994. London and New York, Routledge, 2004.

Boehmer, Elleke. "Achebe and His Influence in Some Contemporary African Writing." *Interventions: International Journal of Postcolonial Studies*, vol. 11, no. 2, 2009, pp. 141–153.

Bourdieu, Pierre. *The Field of Cultural Production*. Cambridge, Polity Press, 1993.

Bourdieu, Pierre. *The Rules of Art: Genesis and Structure of the Literary Field*. Translated by Susan Emanuel. Stanford, CA, Stanford University Press, 1996.

Brouillette, Sarah. *Postcolonial Writers in the Global Literary Marketplace*. New York, Palgrave Macmillan, 2007.

Bryce, Jane. "'Half and Half Children': Third-Generation Women Writers and the New Nigerian Novel." *Research in African Literatures*, vol. 39, no. 2, 2008, pp. 49–67.

Doherty, Brian. "Writing Back with a Difference: Chimamanda Ngozi Adichie's 'the Headstrong Historian' as a Response to Chinua Achebe's *Things Fall Apart*." *Matatu*, vol. 45, 2014, pp. 187–201.

Feldner, Maximilian. *Narrating the New African Diaspora: 21st Century Nigerian Literature in Context*. Cham, Palgrave Macmillan, 2019.

Gikandi, Simon. "Chinua Achebe and the Invention of African Culture." *Research in African Literatures*, vol. 32, no. 3, 2001, pp. 3–8.

Griswold, Wendy. *Bearing Witness: Readers, Writers, and the Novel in Nigeria*. Princeton, NJ, Princeton University Press, 2000.

Hewett, Heather. "Coming of Age: Chimamanda Ngozi Adichie and the Voice of the Third Generation." *English in Africa*, vol. 32, no. 1, 2005, pp. 73–97.

Highfield, Jonathan. "Obscured by History: Language, Culture, and Conflict in Chinua Achebe's *Things Fall Apart* and Chimamanda Ngozi Adichie's *Half of a Yellow Sun*." *Cultural Encounters*, edited by Nicholas Birns. Ipswich, MA, Salem Press, 2013, pp. 262–280.

Huggan, Graham. *The Postcolonial Exotic: Marketing the Margins*. London, Routledge, 2001.

Julien, Eileen. "The Extroverted African Novel." *The Novel, Volume 1: History, Geography, and Culture*, edited by Franco Moretti. Princeton and Oxford, Princeton University Press, 2006, pp. 667–700.

Kom, Ambroise. "African Absence, a Literature without a Voice." *African Literature: An Anthology of Criticism and Theory*, edited by Tejumola Olaniyan and Ato Quayson. Malden and Oxford, Blackwell Publishing, 2007, pp. 427–431.

Ndibe, Okey. *Foreign Gods, Inc.* New York, Soho, 2014.

Oguine, Ike. *A Squatter's Tale*. Oxford, Heinemann, 2000.

Ojaide, Tanure. "Examining Canonisation in Modern African Literature." *Asiatic*, vol. 3, no. 1, 2009, pp. 1–20.

Parry, Benita. "The Institutionalization of Postcolonial Studies." *The Cambridge Companion to Postcolonial Literary Studies*, edited by Neil Lazarus. Cambridge, Cambridge University Press, 2004, pp. 66–80.

Pucherová, Dobrota. "'A Continent Learns to Tell Its Story at Last': Notes on the Caine Prize'." *Journal of Postcolonial Writing*, vol. 48, no. 1, 2011, pp. 13–25.

Tunca, Daria. "Of French Fries and Cookies: Chimamanda Ngozi Adichie's Diasporic Short Fiction." *Présence africaine en Europe et au-delà/African Presence in Europe and Beyond*, edited by Kathleen Gyssels and Bénédicte Ledent. Paris, L'Harmattan, 2010, pp. 291–309.

Tunca, Daria. "Appropriating Achebe: Chimamanda Ngozi Adichie's *Purple Hibiscus* and 'the Headstrong Historian'." *Adaptation and Cultural Appropriation: Literature, Film, and the Arts*, edited by Pascal Nicklas and Oliver Lindner. Berlin, De Gruyter, 2012, pp. 230–250.

Tunca, Daria. "The Danger of a Single Short Story: Reality, Fiction and Metafiction in Chimamanda Ngozi Adichie's 'Jumping Monkey Hill'." *Journal of Postcolonial Writing*, vol. 54, no. 1, 2018, pp. 69–82. doi: 10.1080/17449855.2017.1419833.

Uko, Iniobong. "Transcending the Margins: New Directions in Women's Writing." *New Directions in African Literature*, edited by Ernest N. Emenyonu. Oxford, James Currey, 2006, pp. 82–93.

VanZanten, Susan. "'The Headstrong Historian': Writing with *Things Fall Apart*." *Research in African Literatures*, vol. 46, no. 2, 2015, pp. 85–103.

Walkowitz, Rebecca. "The Location of Literature: The Transnational Book and the Migrant Writer." *Contemporary Literature*, vol. 47, no. 4, 2006, pp. 527–545.

Wenske, Ruth. "Adichie in Dialogue with Achebe: Balancing Dualities in *Half of a Yellow Sun*." *Research in African Literatures*, vol. 47, no. 3, 2016, pp. 70–87. doi: 10.2979/reseafrilite.47.3.05.

Zeleza, Paul Tiyambe. "Introduction: The Disciplining of Africa." *The Study of Africa, Vol I: Disciplinary and Interdisciplinary Encounters*, edited by Paul Tiyambe Zeleza. Dakar, Senegal, CODESRIA, 1–35.

5

ANGLOPHONE CAMEROON LITERATURE

Writing from the margins of the margin

Joyce Ashuntantang

Introduction

November 11, 2018, marked the 100th anniversary of the Armistice that ended Word War I. It can be argued that this date also marks the beginning of what is now known as the "Anglophone problem" which is leading Cameroon to the brink of civil war today. After the defeat of Germany in World War I, Germany lost its hold over Kamerun, and Cameroon/Cameroun was born, a trust territory administered by Britain and France, with France gaining 4/5 of the territory. The British territories named Southern Cameroons and Northern Cameroons were administered as part of another British colony, Nigeria. French Cameroon and Nigeria gained independence in 1960. Wedged between these two larger geographical entities, Southern and Northern Cameroonians were asked to decide their fate in a United Nations–sanctioned plebiscite in 1961. They were to choose between joining French Cameroon, which became La Republique du Cameroun (LRC) at independence, or Nigeria. Northern Cameroons voted to join Nigeria, and Southern Cameroons voted to join La Republique du Cameroun. Southern Cameroons morphed into the Federated State of West Cameroon, while LRC became the Federated State of East Cameroon in the new Federal Republic of Cameroon. Southern Cameroons's move to join LRC compounded the problem of language that confronted postcolonial nations. Although the new federal government established English and French as the official languages, a "diaglossic" situation quickly became apparent, with English being the language of the minority and thereby having a lesser status. The marginalized position of English within the new nation-state translated to an inferior position for the English-speaking minority. However, positioning the minority problem within the praxis of language conjures up binaries that present a complex problem. First, there is the position of the English language in the world. According to Seth Mydans:

> scholars say that about one-fourth of the world's population can communicate to some degree in English.
>
> It is the common language in almost every endeavor, from science to air traffic control to the global jihad, where it is apparently the means of communication between speakers of Arabic and other languages.
>
> It has consolidated its dominance as the language of the Internet, where 80 percent of the world's electronically stored information is in English, according to David Graddol, a linguist and researcher.

There may be more native speakers of Chinese, Spanish or Hindi, but it is English they speak when they talk across cultures, and English they teach their children to help them become citizens of an increasingly intertwined world.

At telephone call centers around the world, the emblem of a globalized workplace, the language spoken is, naturally, English. On the radio, pop music carries the sounds of English to almost every corner of the earth.

("Across cultures, English is the word." New York Times, April 9, 2007)

Thus, it is inconceivable to some that Anglophone Cameroonians can claim a minority status in a world where knowing the English language is coveted in the global marketplace. It is also inconceivable to others that fifty-five years after independence, Cameroon is experiencing a civil war because of a fight over two colonial languages. These assumptions do not take into consideration the nature of English in Cameroon, which has imbued the term "Anglophone" with a highly connotative meaning nonexistent in other countries in Africa where English is spoken like Ghana, Liberia, Sierra Leone, Nigeria or Kenya.

The Anglophone identity in Cameroon

The term "Anglophone" in Cameroon "lives" in opposition to the word "Francophone," with "Francophone" wielding power. While the term "Anglophone" certainly alludes to the speaking of English, in Cameroon, it is tied to an identity that goes beyond language. This begs the question: Who is an Anglophone in Cameroon? The Anglophone Cameroon educator Tambo Leke defines an Anglophone as "A person whose first official language, in the context of the Cameroon constitution is English. Although Cameroonian Anglophones by this definition may hail from any part of the country, their base is mainly in the South-West and North-West Provinces" (Tambo 36). Alobwede d'Epie, another Anglophone Cameroon scholar and professor of English, explained that "Anglophones should see themselves as a people of varied ethnic languages and cultures but whose individual identities have been made to merge and function in a union of thought moulded by the English Language" (57). However, the definition of the term "Anglophone" that best captures its meaning in the Cameroon context is that proffered by the linguist Simo Bobda in "Varying Perceptions of English in Cameroon: A Diachronic and Synchronic Analyses":

> The term Anglophone, as is understood in Cameroon, has mostly an ethnic connotation. It refers to a member of an ethnic group in North West and South West Provinces which were formally part of British Cameroons . . . the term Anglophone has very little to do with knowledge of the English Language; indeed, an Anglophone in the Cameroon sense does not need to know a word of English.

Consequently, despite the ninety-five ethnic languages spoken in the North West and South West regions, Anglophones rally around their historical heritage, which binds them socioculturally, including the English language. Anglophones have become an "ethnic group." This is the same sentiment captured by JanMohamed and Lloyd when they opine, "Cultures designated as minorities have certain shared experiences by virtue of their similar antagonistic relationship to the dominant culture which seeks to marginalize them all" (1).

The marginal position of Anglophones in the Republic of Cameroon is what binds them together. The education and legal system inherited from Britain is markedly different from what is practiced in the Francophone region. In fact, a Francophone fluent in both oral and written English is not considered an Anglophone because he or she does not carry the sociocultural-political burden of being Anglophone. Consequently, the value of English as an official language carries an important signifier akin to skin color in places where racial difference leads to discrimination. Not surprisingly, Francophones do not rally around the French language as an identity marker the way Anglophones do. They are more inclined to declare Cameroon "one and indivisible," oblivious to the second-class status of Anglophones. As JanMohamed and Lloyd posit, "The semblance of pluralism disguises the perpetuation of exclusion insofar as it is enjoyed only by those who have already assimilated the values of the dominant culture" (8).

This marginal status of English was ingrained right at the inception of the union. Article 59 of the constitution of the Federal Republic of Cameroon clearly stated that:

> The present provisions, by which the constitution of the Republic adopted on 21 Feb-ruary 1960 by the Cameroonian people is revised, shall enter into force on 1 October 1961. The revised constitution shall be published in French and English, *the French text being authentic.*

The outcome of this provision created a situation where government documents are usually released in French, and an English translation may or may not follow. Equally, public signs are done with French in big fonts and the English translation, where it exists, in smaller fonts under-neath the French version. Even in government offices or public spaces like the airport, English is not acceptable. It is normal for a government employee to declare that he or she does not understand English so the Anglophone must speak in French to be understood. This situation constantly creates humiliating moments for Anglophones, who permanently find themselves being treated as outsiders in their own country once they start speaking in English.

This derogatory position ascribed to English in the federal constitution did not go unno-ticed. According to the Anglophone Cameroon political activist, Albert Mukong, "We had even before the 1st October 1961 questioned the concept that only the French text was authentic but got no answer. Then we hoped that as this article came in the section for transitional and special Provisions it would be the transitional period" (The Case for the Southern Cameroons, 24). Nevertheless, this provision stayed in the constitution even after the Federal Republic gave way to the United Republic of Cameroon in 1972. Consequently, fighting for the status of English in Cameroon in relation to the French language translates to fighting for the rights of Anglophones in the nation-state Cameroon.

As Han-Georg Wolf makes clear:

> It is the imbalance in every part of Cameroon life, intertwined with the feeling of being losers in the historical processes that have created considerable discontent among the Anglophones. As underdogs, Anglophones rally around English as a common ref-erence point. English is a form of protest against the de facto dominance of French.
>
> *(233)*

This quest for recognition of a sovereign identity reached a boiling point in the 1990s. The end of the Cold War and the creation of more democratic governments in the Communist nations of Eastern Europe served as a launching pad for Africans to make demands for reforms. In Cameroon, these demands included a clamor for a return to multiparty politics, which had been abolished in 1966 with the establishment of the one-party state. Within the general demands of Cameroonians, the Anglophones as a subgroup clamored for a recognition of their identity and independence within the nation state called Cameroon. This led to the formation of pressure groups, including the Cameroon Anglophone Movement (CAM), Southern Cameroons National Council (SCNC), Free West Cameroon Movement (FWCM), and Confederation of Anglophone Parents-Teacher's Association (CAPTAC) in the early 1990s.

Amid all the tension heightened by the demands of these various groups, John Fru Ndi, an Anglophone, launched the Social Democratic party on May 26, 1990. Government gendarmes tried to disperse the 30,000–40,000 supporters who had gathered, and when they failed to do so, they opened fire, killing six young supporters (Takougang and Kreiger). The deaths of these young people, Fidelis Chosi (corn mill operator), Tifuh Mathias Teboh (student), AsanjiChristopher Fombi (student), Nfon Edwin Jatop (tailor), Julliete Sikod, (student), and Toje Evaristus (student), who became known as the "Bamenda Six," stunned Anglophones. This incident became a watershed moment, as it eventually paved the way for the reinstitution of multipartyism in December 1990 and the legalization of the SDF as a political party in 1991. It also catapulted the nation into a period of massive civil unrest.

In reaction to the deaths of the "Bamenda Six," John Ngu Foncha, the Southern Cameroons prime minister who was instrumental in Southern Cameroons joining LRC in 1961 and who was the vice president of the ruling party, resigned from his position. It was a monumental moment considering his parting letter to the president. In that resignation letter, he lamented that,

> the Anglophone Cameroonians whom I brought into the union have been ridiculed and referred to as 'Les Biafrais,' 'Les enemies dans la maison,' 'les traitres,'[1] etc. and the constitutional provisions which protected this Anglophone minority have been suppressed, their voice drowned while the rule of the gun has replaced the dialogue which Anglophones cherish very much.
>
> *(155)*

In 1993, the Anglophones mounted another fierce fight to protect their system of education. This was the culmination of a ten-year struggle against the government that had systematically tried to Francophonize the Anglophone educational system. In 1983, the Ministry of Education reformed the General Certificate of Education (GCE) ordinary and advanced levels into a group certificate exam structured along the lines of the Francophone baccalaureate exam. The reaction of the Anglophone students at the University of Yaoundé was swift. They organized student strikes that echoed in major cities in the Anglophone region. These student-led protests forced the government to cancel the reform. Nevertheless, the proposed reforms had the effect of reminding the English-speaking students of their marginal status in Cameroon. As a result, the leaders of the organized protests sent a letter titled, "Open Letter to all English-Speaking Parents of Cameroon from the English-Speaking students of the North-West and South West Provinces," drawn up on August 20, 1985. This letter included a compilation of examples of Anglophone marginalization in Cameroon and centered on the domination of the French system of education, particularly in higher education. This letter called on Anglophone parents to intervene to stop these actions, which they felt would inevitably lead to bloodshed. The letter ominously stated:

> If there is no permanent solution to the sectorial injustice and economic deprivation that we witness today, if there is no end to the assimilation destined towards

us in the guise of integration; we your children, assure you that eventually we shall have to smear the homes, streets and gardens of this nation with blood. We won't accept to be eternally stigmatized as second-class citizens, nor shall we want to be shorn of the cultural heritage, which is ours, and which we recognize is of greater significance around the globe. So we shall fight for the justice we cannot otherwise have.

(The Case for Southern Cameroon, 116)

Four years later, another attempt was made by the then minister of education, Georges Ngango, to change the structure of Anglophone secondary and high school by imposing the Francophone structure of four years for the first cycle and three years for secondary education. As with the 1983 reform, the result was violent opposition and popular demonstrations by Anglophone students and their parents, which culminated in the dismissal of the minister and a termination of the reform package.

Therefore, it was with determination to protect the Anglophone system of education that the Teachers Association of Cameroon was born. Top on its agenda was the creation of the GCE board. Frustrated by the government's deliberate sluggishness in creating a GCE board, the members set up the Cameroon Examination Board in Buea on April 16, 1992. Among their pledges, the one subsequently captured their identity.

Let us all realize once and for all that the greatest bond that binds:

1 South-Westerners with South-Westerners or
2 North-Westerners, or
3 South-Westerners with North-Westerners is our common *Anglo-Saxon*[2] *heritage* exemplified through our common educational, legal, cultural and social values which differ very much and are superior to the same values on the other side of the Mungo. (Francophone Cameroon)

(Cameroon post No. 160, April 29, 1993, 12, qtd. In Nyamnjoh 75)

In addition, parents and teachers of Anglophone schools came together and formed the Confederation of Anglophone Parents-Teacher's Association of Cameroon. A top item on its agenda was the creation of the GCE board. Although the government made continuous attempts to repress these organizations, the Anglophone parents and teachers persisted, enduring water cannons and tear gas during demonstrations. Finally, on October 12, 1993, the government signed the text of application for the Cameroon GCE board (Nyamnjoh 1996) While Anglophone parents and teachers were fighting for the creation of the GCE board, another historic milestone in the fight for Anglophone identity happened. Despite the intimidation and prospect of arrest by the military of Cameroon, the All-Anglophone Conference (AACI) took place in Buea in April 1993, with about 5000 persons in attendance. In a widely circulated document titled "The Buea declaration," it was stated that the conference was convened "For the purpose of adopting a common Anglophone stand on constitutional reform and of examining other matters related to the welfare of ourselves, our prosperity and our territory." The conference also requested Cameroon to return to the federal state to protect their cultural heritage.

The following year, another All Anglophone Conference (AACII) took place in Bamenda on April 29 to May 1, 1994. An important outcome of this conference was the "Bamenda Declaration," which stated, should the government either persist in its refusal to engage in meaningful constitutional talks or fail to engage in such talks within a reasonable time, the Anglophone leadership would proclaim the revival of the independence and sovereignty of the Anglophone territory and take all measures necessary to secure, defend and preserve the independence, sovereignty and integrity of the said country.

(Konings & Nyamnjoh 1997: 218–220)

The continuous refusal of Biya's government to enter into negotiations with Anglophone pressure groups led to the increasing radicalization of the Anglophone movements. On December 30, 1999, Justice Fredrick Alobwede Ebong, a member of the Southern Cameroon National Council, briefly took over the government radio station in Buea, where he announced the restoration of the former Southern Cameroons. Following this action, a provisional government was announced, along with a coat of arms, flag, and anthem (Konings & Nyamnjoh 2003).

In fact, SCNC promoted the use of the name Southern Cameroons because it wanted to make "it clear that our struggles are neither of an essentially linguistic character nor in defence of an alien colonial culture . . . but are aimed at the restoration of the autonomy of the former Southern Cameroons which has been annexed by the Republic of Cameroon" (SCNC Press Release *Cameroon Post*, 16–23 August 1994, 3). These landmark events served as a catalyst for a number of organized movements, some of which gained momentum abroad as some key activists went into exile in Nigeria, the United States, and Britain.

There was a reemergence of Anglophone nationalism in 2016 like that of the 1990s when the Cameroon Anglophone Civil Society Consortium, composed mostly of lawyers and teacher trade unions, organized protest marches in the Anglophone regions to decry the Francophonization of the Anglophone legal and educational system. They called for a return to the two-state federation that existed prior to 1972 which gave Anglophones significant autonomy over their own affairs. The government's brutal crackdown of the pro-federalist movement and the arrest of Consortium leaders in January 2017 led to the rise of a separatist movement, which called for the establishment of an independent state known as Ambazonia consisting of the two Anglophone regions.

The separatists symbolically declared the independence of Ambazonia on October 1, 2017. The government crackdown on these separatists has given rise to an armed struggle between the pro-Ambazonia fighters and the government. Because of this ongoing war, "200 villages have been partly or completely destroyed forcing hundreds of thousands of people to flee. The rate of attacks on villages has increased steadily, usually causing significant damage. Between 450,000 and 550,000 people have been displaced as a result of the crisis" (Center for Human Rights and Democracy in Africa).

It is therefore evident that, contrary to what some observers outside Cameroon may think, the problems of the Anglophone minority in Cameroon are real and not just superficially tied to the English language. The African Commission on Human Rights, an organ of the African Union, after deliberating on the petition by Anglophone Cameroon, states that:

The people of Southern Cameroon can legitimately claim to be a "people." Besides the individual rights due to Southern Cameroon, they have a distinct identity, which attracts certain collective rights . . . the Commission finds that "the people of Southern Cameroon" qualify to be referred to as a "people" because they manifest numerous characteristics and affinities, which include a common history, linguistic tradition, territorial connection, and political outlook. More importantly, they identify themselves as a people with a separate and distinct identity. Identity is an innate characteristic within a people. It is up to other external people to recognise such existence, but not to deny it.

(266/03: Kevin Mgwanga Gunme et al. vs Cameroon. *African Commission on Human and Peoples' Rights. www.achpr.org/sessions/descions?id=189)*

Anglophone Cameroonians want to be recognized as a "people." The literature produced by writers from this region has for the most part mirrored the political realities on the ground, from independence until today.

The beginning: Cameroon literature in English

The peculiar nature of Anglophone Cameroon and its minority status also had an effect on its literature since Anglophone Cameroon was virtually "erased" in "postcolonial" Africa. Steve Arnold, who was one of the first to document this literature, argued enthusiastically for its existence in an article titled "Preface to Cameroon Literature in English" published in 1983 in the journal *Research in African Literature*. Refuting Sam Kubam's complaint that there was paucity of Anglophone Cameroon literature (Abbia 1978), Arnold argued that Sam Kubam's position became the dominant view even among Anglophone writers because "In spite of its existence, anglophone Cameroon writing was conscious of itself only in fragments, having been isolated from the mainstream literature on the continent, and even within its own national boundaries by Cameroon's unique historical circumstances" (p. 498).

In 1986, the first anthology of Cameroon literature in English was published by Longman and edited by Genevieve de La Taille, Kristine Werner, and Victor Tarkang. It was divided into five sections, The Novel, The Short Story, Poetry, Drama, and Essays. The novel section displayed excerpts of Peter Nsanda Eba's *The Good Foot*, Joseph Ngongwikuo's *Taboo Love*, and Kenjo Jumbam's *The White Man of God*, published by Heinemann's African Writer's Series. The short story section had vibrant pieces by Peter Abety, Bole Butake, and Ndely Mokoso. The poetry section, on the other hand, had poetry by Takere Mesack Fongang, Kitts Mbeboh, and Victor Tarkang. In addition, Sankie Maimo, Victor Elame Musinga, and Princess Rabiatou Njoya made up the Drama section. For Essays, Bernard Fonlon, Tala Kashim, and Ojong Ayuk led the way. All the essays focused on cultural integration and how it could be done effectively. This was not a topic being discussed in a vacuum; the unification of the Francophone and Anglophone territories meant the merging of two cultures, and Cameroon scholars debated the best ways to go about it

In fact, the essays provide a framework for the texts in this anthology. These literary pieces did not strive to stake out an Anglophone identity in their writings. Among the editors, only one was Cameroonian. Even the name of the anthology, *Balafon*, an instrument mostly found among the Fang-Beti ethnic groups in the Francophone region of the country, shows that no "Anglophone identity consciousness" framed this volume. In addition, one of the writers in the volume, Rabiatou Njoya, is from the royal family in Foumban, which is part of the Francophone region. She would not be considered "Anglophone," although she is fluent in English.

Two important writers missing from the group in the anthology are Asong Linus and Jedida Asheri, the pen name of Prudencia Hene Chilla. Asong had written four novels by this time, including his celebrated *Crown of Thorns*, which elicited serious interest from Heinemann and Fotana but no publishing contract (Ashuntantang 2009). Asong's *Crown of Thorns* succinctly captures some of what Anglophone Cameroonians lost by joining French Cameroon, first as part of a federal state and later as part of a unified state. This novel is set in Nkokonoko Small Monje, in Anglophone Cameroon in the late 1960s and early 1970s. The story is divided into three parts. Part One opens with a realization by the people of Nkokonoko that their God is stolen, rooted from its stump. Immediately, the people suspect their master carver and the chief. Part Two creates suspense by taking the reader through a revealing flashback which shows that the present chief of Nkokonoko, Achiebefuo, was never groomed to be chief. His brother Nkoaleck was the one chosen by the leaders and groomed for the job. However, the government-appointed district officer thwarts the will of the elders by imposing the reluctant Chief Achiebefuo as chief of the village. Part Three returns to plot of the stolen God, and investigations reveal that the theft was masterminded by the district officer with the complicity of the chief and a few elders. This novel captures some of the challenges of Anglophones in the new nation of Cameroon dominated by Francophones who had been groomed under the French system of assimilation. The British employed indirect rule in their colonies, ruling indigenes through the Native Administration (N.A.) and House of Chiefs. As I explain in *Landscaping Postcoloniality: A Dissemination of Anglophone Cameroon Literature:*

> After Anglophone Cameroon gained independence by joining French Cameroon, the new nation state adopted a system of direct control and the Native Administration was not only replaced by a D.O., but the House of Chiefs was dissolved. The territory was divided into administrative units with a government-appointed official responsible for each unit. The chiefdoms now came under government control. Consequently communities found themselves answering not only to government officials that knew nothing about their customs and traditions, but to remnants of French colonialism practiced by francophone officials who were often arrogant in dealing with the local population, leading to a breakdown in communication between the administration and the ruled. In the case of the people of Nkokonoko Small Monje, this led to the theft of their god.
>
> *(89)*

The people of Nkokonoko Small Monje are aware of the debilitating changes that threaten to change their daily lives in cataclysmic proportions. As the narrator explains:

> The coming of the missionaries was not the people's worry; nevertheless, they found that fact alone unbearable. The Government too had arrived. Small Monje needed a District Officer to replace the defunct N. A. Office, the administrative body that had governed the tribes for generations. It was merely a more elevated title for the Council of Elders.
>
> *(65)*

Unfortunately, Crown of Thorns was published in 1990, twenty years after the novel was written, due to the lack of publishing opportunities.

Another important writer missing from the Balafon Anthology is Jedida Asheri, the pen name of Prudencia Hene Chila. *Promise*, the first novel by an Anglophone Cameroon woman, is set in the 1930s and 40s in Banso in the North West region of Cameroon. This novel gives a rare glimpse into Anglophone Cameroon under British rule. The story captures the life of the narrator from the age of seven to her early twenties. The novel ends with the narrator leaving for a teacher's college in Nigeria. This is a reflection of the lack of post-primary educational opportunities in British Cameroon. Indeed, there were no secondary schools in British Cameroon during the first seventeen years of British rule in Cameroon (Ashuntantang 2009). The autobiographical stance of Asheri's novel confirms Yvonne Vera's assertion that "the woman writer in Africa is a witness; forgiving the evidence of the eyes, pronouncing her experience with insight, artistry and fertile dexterity." Viewed within the framework of postcolonial womanist discourse, *Promise* takes its place as one of the early pieces of literary resistance to female oppression by an African woman. Although this novel was written three years after Flora Nwapa's *Efuru* and three years before Buchi Emecheta's first novel *In the Ditch*, it remains largely invisible in the pantheon of early novels by African women.

The invisibility of Anglophone Cameroon literature has always been a challenge to overcome. When Albert Gerard was editing *European Language Writing in Sub-Saharan Africa*, Anglophone Cameroon was omitted since it was not an independent political entity. Stephen Arnold came to the rescue by updating his earlier introductory account of Anglophone Cameroon literature, which he now titled "Emergent English Writing in Cameroon," and it was included in the collection as an appendix to Nigerian Literature! As heroic as Arnold's efforts were, this placement of Anglophone Cameroon literature underscores the subservient position Anglophone Cameroon continues to endure. Richard Bjornson's seminal work on Cameroon, *The African Quest for Freedom and Identity: Cameroonian Writing and the National Experience*, published in 1991, also revealed the marginalization of Anglophone Cameroon literature. This work barely makes mention of writers from Anglophone Cameroon. Although the book is 528 pages and Bjornson's research references are up to 1988, Bjornson only devotes less than twenty pages to Anglophone Cameroon Literature as a whole.

Anglophone Cameroon writing: a minority writes back!

The term "Anglophone" gained more currency in the 1990s with growing Anglophone nationalism. A workshop on Anglophone Cameroon writing sponsored by the Goethe Institute in Yaoundé, Cameroon, captured the mood of the times with regard to literature. According to the organizers, the purpose of the workshop was to assess "the important role of Anglophone Cameroon writing in the 'Anglophone movements,' and to redefine [their] sociocultural political status within the national and international arena" (Lyonga, Breitinger, and Butake, "Foreword" 9). In addition, the workshop was meant "to take stock of the corpus and volume of Anglophone Cameroon writing, assess its standing, evaluate and redefine its status and its functions in the present situation" (Lyonga, Breitinger, and Butake, "Foreword" 9).

The keynote speaker at the conference, Bate Besong, made this call to Anglophone writers:

> The Anglophone Cameroon writer at home and in the Diaspora must tell the outside world the story of his tragic land from the point of view of its hostage minority. In addition, such a literature, fellow writers, can only be written by you: Anglophone Cameroon writers, in Anglophone Cameroonian Language and on Anglophone Cameroonian subjects.
>
> *(18)*

Bate Besong's call fell on very receptive ears. Most of the writers, like Butake, Besong, Epie Ngome, and Eyoh, were already engaged in writing literature that galvanized the people because it "rejected the claims of the center to exclusivity" (Ashcroft, Griffiths, and Tiffin, 17). During this period, drama was the genre of choice. The plays protested what Emmanuel Doh has aptly termed "horizontal colonialism" from Francophone leaders who have victimized Anglophones due to their minority status, and the Anglophone leaders who are complicit in the second-class citizen status meted out to their kind. As Bate Besong explains, "With the wave of democracy that preceded multi-party politics in Cameroon, Anglophone dramatists found themselves face to face with theater audience of thousands seeking answers to political questions" (14). The questions arose from many decades of being subjected to what JanMohamed and Lloyd call, "'Institutional forgetting' which as a form of control of one's memory and history is one of the gravest forms of damage done to minority cultures" (6).

The dramatists, while writing to the center, had to write and produce plays that acted as a "form of counter-memory," which JanMohamed and Lloyd identify as crucial to minority discourse. Two plays exemplify this, Victor Epie Ngome's *What God Has Put Asunder* and Bate Besong's *Beasts of No Nation*.

Victor Epie Ngome's play *What God Has Put Asunder* could be said to be the play that defined that period. On the surface, it was an all-too-familiar story of domestic abuse. Weka, a young orphan girl, has two suitors who want to marry her, Miche Garba and Emeka, who also grew up in the same orphanage. Weka is not ready to marry any of these suitors and would rather remain single. However, she is pressured by Rev. Gordon and Sister Sabeth, administrators of the orphanage, to decide because she is too old to remain in the orphanage. She reluctantly agrees to marry the overbearing Garba as the lesser of two evils. During the marriage ceremony, Emeka objects to the marriage, Garba deliberately refuses to repeat the portions of the marriage vows that say "to honor and obey," and Weka voices her discomfort in marrying Garba. Due to these irregularities, the presiding priest, Rev. Unor, grants the couple a conditional marriage for ten years, after which they can renew their relationship if they so choose. In spite of the fact that in marrying Weka, Garba inherits Weka's property, including reach forests and farmlands, Garba does not maltreat her. In fact, it is revealed that he has many other wives, and when he makes decisions, their voices drown out Weka's voice. At the end, Weka decides to leave the marriage. Fortunately for her, the decision to leave the marriage is supported by the Rev. Unor, who solemnized the marriage. In fact, Rev. Gordon comes back to see Weka when he hears of all her trouble. He comes along with his friend, the gun-selling Jim Rican from Memphis, Tennessee, who is ready to help Weka rebuild her father's homestead. The court grants Weka the right to live separately from Garba based on the irregularities that took place during the marriage and the fact that Garba did not keep to the terms of the marriage. This is a fascinating story of an underdog getting justice. However, what endeared this play to Anglophone Cameroon audiences was the allegorical dimension of the play. The play was performed by the Flame Players several times in Yaounde and in Buea in 1993. As a member of the cast, I witnessed the euphoria of the audience as they immediately recognized Weka as "West Kamerun," Epie Ngome masking the "C" with a "K," which also gave a nod to the history of "Kamerun" under German rule. In fact, Epie Ngome uses names as a dramatic technique to explore meaning. Adaku Ankumah points out, "Literary onomastics, therefore is not quite so simple; for a name carries with it culture and heritage, character and aspirations, plot and theme. Authors, therefore spend more time choosing character names" (xiv).

The names chosen by Epie Ngome reveal the allegory because of a shared history and culture. Thus, from the sound of the name, ethnic origin of the name, costumes, or actions of the characters, the audience can tell who or what is being represented. These metonymic references embedded in the names are discovered to the satisfaction of the Anglophone audiences. Garba is a name from Northern Cameroons, the birthplace of Amadou Ahidjo, the first President of Cameroon, so Garba is not just representative of Ahidjo in this play; he is a representation of Francophone Cameroon. Rev. Gordon and Sister Sabeth represent Great Britain, and the orphanage is Britain's colonial empire. Jim Rican from Memphis, Tennessee, is seen as the United States, especially with his stereotypical interest in selling guns. Emeka's obvious Ibo name gives him away as representing Nigeria, and Rev. Unor, who solemnizes the marriage, is the United Nations Organization. By using the metaphor of marriage, Epie Ngome creates a plot that can be easily understood by everyone in the audience.

However, Epie Ngome uses the medium of a play to bring out certain salient points in the political history of Cameroon that have contributed to the woes of Anglophone Cameroonians as a minority group. As Ndumbe Eyoh argues, many of these playwrights,

> See themselves in a role of developing the critical consciousness of their society, of mobilizing people for change through the destruction of the "culture of silence", which has so far subjected them to years of oppression. Their role seems to be that of building the foundation of a new society in which social justice and a sense of communal belonging can prevail.
>
> *(10)*

Consequently, Epie Ngome's play helps revive parts of the history that have been suppressed in order to "fabricate" an alternative reality that gives agency to those controlling power. The role played by Rev. Gordon and Sister Sabeth in coercing Weka to get married shows that Anglophone Cameroon had little or no say in how it gained independence. Weka wanted to remain single, which translates to Anglophone Cameroon's interest in becoming an independent country, but the United Nations did not make that option available. Garba's disregard for the terms of the probational marriage point to the disregard for any agreements made between French Cameroon and Anglophone Cameroon. However, Epie Ngome goes beyond creating history to creating possibilities. Weka is able to leave the marriage and stand up to Garba. Weka's agency is revolutionary. For a quiet, meek orphan, she is able to project her identity and voice to argue for her rights. She is articulate when she explains her abuse at the hands of Garba, especially after the probation period:

> Once the festivities were over, he brought a fleet of trucks and bundled all my children and me out of our house. His drivers gathered all our staff trampling and damaging many things and so he forced me to settle in with him. Since then, he has been forcing my children to learn his own mother tongue and to forget mine with which they grew up; I must abide by the customs of his clan, not mine, and . . . in short he has simply been breathing down my neck since then.
>
> *(53)*

This is what forces Weka to abandon the marriage and take her children back to her home (West Cameroon). Her desire is "build this place back to a respectable home." Rev. Gordon shows up at the right time when Weka needs help. He even apologizes for marrying her off the way he did and not maintaining a "dissuasive presence . . . to deter him [Garba] from his excesses" (39). Anglophones watching the play were thus encouraged to stand up to the Francophone government and fight for their rights the way Weka does. Their hope to see Britain come to their aid is satisfied by seeing Rev. Gordon show up and even apologize to Weka for not sticking around like Louis (France). These plays, to use Abiola Irele's phrase, created a "new realism," which reflected the disillusionment that had invaded Cameroonian minds while also promoting the wishes of the people. When the court at the end of the play upholds the terms of the marriage, as stipulated on marriage number 001/UN of Feb. 11, 1961, which allows the couple to live in physical separation in a "simulated wedlock," the audience jubilates. Thus, Victor Epie Ngome's play provides a return to federation as a possible solution to the Anglophone problem in Cameroon. In addition, the marriage registration date is the actual date of the plebiscite when West Cameroon gained independence by joining La République du Cameroun. This date is important because it proves that West Cameroon was a separate autonomous entity before the federation. To mask the importance of this date for Anglophones, the Francophone-led government celebrates this national holiday as youth day instead of "Plebiscite Day."

Another important play during this period is Bate Besong's *Beasts of No Nation*. Set in Ednouye, an obvious anagram for Yaounde to the perceptive eye, *Beasts of No Nation* presents the predicament of night-soil men who work long hours transporting huge amounts of "shit" while the narrator instigates them into action. Unlike Femi Osofisan's *Aringindin and the Night Watchmen* (see Ashuntantang 2009), where the two voices of conscience in the play, Ayinde and Teacher, die, Besong gives agency to the night-soil men who storm the office of the supreme commander of Ewawa to demand their identity cards. On March 26, 1991, the Yaounde University theater gave a landmark performance of *Beasts of No Nation* at the Amphi 700 Theater, directed by Bole Butake. Although there is no plot in this play and the dialogue is bare and fragmented, the stage props of three wooden toilet bowls filled the theater with stench from the metaphoric fetid waste, and it becomes clear that the night-soil men want their freedom. The narrator's constant refrain of a "hero goes to war to die" underscores the determination that frames the narrator's actions and his self-sacrifice. As Lyonga points out, Besong's images of filth "constitute his views of Cameroon, as a country in a state of advanced degeneracy instead of the officially declared 'advanced democracy'" (162). The night-soil men are representative of Anglophones who have no identity in Cameroon. They are lost in "shit" and dehumanized. The identification papers become a metaphor for their identity as full members of the Cameroonian nation. For Besong, Anglophones are night-soil men performing moribund drudgery. The "Narrator," labeled "professor" by the night-soil men, seems to be a mouthpiece for the playwright as he pursues liberty. The narrator prods the night-soil men into thinking. He announces, "O most venerable Anglo . . . my co-workers in the field of shitology don't have their independence and freedom. It appears that you'll soon have to decide to fight or run" (39).

The political references in this play were not lost on the audience. The government agent, Mr. Biatcha, who watched the play, not only wrote a now-notorious letter accusing Bole Butake and Bate Besong of subversion, Bate Besong was subsequently arbitrarily arrested. The Yaoundé University Theater (which caters to Anglophone student actors) was also "taken out" of business by cutting off all funds to the program. The university's Amphi Theaters were also no longer available for performances. For the next ten years, Butake was intimidated and courted at the same time to join the ruling party if he was to get any funds. In spite of this, Butake refused.

It should be noted that while the Anglophone male writer during this time was concerned with the predicament of Anglophones in Cameroon, women writers had to deal with their double marginalization as women and Anglophones. Anne Tanyi-Tang wrote and published *Ewa and Other Plays*, which touched on themes affecting womanhood, dealing with early marriages, childlessness, and the importance of education for women. Furthermore, Makuchi also published *Your Madness Not Mine*, a collection of short stories dealing with a wide range of themes, but each story invariably presents a central character who is a woman ready to fight for survival.

Anglophone Cameroon writing in the global market

After the charged nationalistic atmosphere of the 1990s, the fervor for plays that engaged with the Anglophone problem died down amid intimidation and constant threats of censorship and arrests. However, the recent crisis has ushered in another heightened sense of nationalism, which is bound to affect the literature being produced now. Nevertheless, post-1990s, Anglophone writers continued writing prose, poetry, and drama that carry their aspirations for self-determination, but the themes have become very varied as Anglophone writers straddle the global stage. Writers like Francis Nyamnjoh, Rosemary Ekosso, Tande Dibussi, Joyce Ashuntantang, Barbara Gwanmesia, Yenika Agbaw, Bannavti Joseph, Lloney Monono, Peter Vakunta, Bertrand Fote, Bill Ndi, Emmauel Doh, Labang Oscar, Kebuma Langmia, Kangson Wakai, and Eric Ngalle who live in the diaspora have published multiple volumes of prose, poetry, or plays. On the home front, writers like Alobwede D'Epie, Nol Alembong, Jane Ekaney, Nkemkong Nkengasong, Monique Kwachou, Nsah Mala, Patricia Nkweteyim, Mathew Takwi, Douglas Achingale, Ekpe Inyang, Babila Mutia, Jong Ngongkum, and a host of emerging writers are making their voices heard. The establishment of publishing houses owned by Anglophone Cameroonians like Design Publishers, Miraclaire, Langaa, Spears Media, and so on has also increased publications by Anglophone writers. One can also not discount the role played by social media in the dissemination of Anglophone Cameroon writing. In the past, writers needed to be published in print to be read, but this is no longer the case. Anglophone Cameroon writers are using the social media space effectively to promote their works. Poets like Nsah Mala and Ekpe Inyang frequently post new poems on Facebook. To add, the United States-based Imbolo Mbue, award-winning author of *Behold the Dreamers*, who is originally from Anglophone Cameroon, is leading literary historians to find out about Anglophone Cameroon Literature. Her second novel *How Beautiful We Were* has been announced.

The present crisis and the literary response

The Anglophone Cameroon crisis is slowly gaining international attention as the death toll spirals over 3000. Early this year, Joyce Ashuntantang, Dibussi Tande, and Adjani Opku-Egbe made a call "for submissions of poetry, artwork, short stories and creative non-fiction that respond to the Cameroon Anglophone Crisis/Ambazonia Conflict from 2016–present." Writers were asked to submit "poetry, prose and artwork that encapsulate the themes of alienation, despair, displacement, disability, loss, imprisonment, trauma, torture, as well as courage, hope, heroism, justice, resilience, resistance, rebellion, survival, among others." This anthology of literature is tentatively titled *Bearing Witness: Voices from Southern Cameroons*. The response has been overwhelming. We received 76 individual poetry submissions with 205 poems, 14 nonfiction pieces, and 10 short stories. The contributors include budding writers and known Anglophone Cameroon writers like Makuchi, Nol Alembong, Victor Epie Ngome, Douglas Achingale, Dibussi Tande, Tangyie Suh-Nfor, NkweteyimNsah Mala, John, Ngonkum, Monique Kwachou, Eunice Ngonkum, Eric Ngalle Charles, and Christmas Ebini. The themes are varied, but the pervading tone is that of despair and frustration, as the world seems to have abandoned Anglophone Cameroonians to the mercy of the Francophone-dominated government of 86-year-old president Paul Biya, who has been in power for 37 years.

As Bate Besong reflects, it is an irony:

> of the Cameroon situation that the British Southern Cameroons after achieving independence as the state of West Cameroon with an elected parliament, a lively opposition, a vibrant economy thus signifying for many the quintessence of the new Africa where freedom and equality would hold sway, came to unwittingly enmesh herself in the throes of a wholly assimilated neo-colonial French Cameroon.
>
> *("Ontogenesis" 1–2)*

This irony is still the reality today, and Anglophone Cameroon literature is on task to capture that reality in all its dimensions.

Notes

1 "Biafrans (from Nigeria)," "enemies in the house," and "traitors."
2 My italics for emphasis.

Works cited

Ankumah, T. Adaku. "Introduction." *Nomenclature, Poetization and Globalization*. Bamenda: Langaa Publishers, 2014.

Arnold, Stephen. "Preface to Cameroon Literature in English." *Research in African Literatures*. Winter 14 (1983): 498–515.

Arnold, Stephen. "Orphans of the Commonwealth: An Account of the 1978 Guinness Cameroon Great Writers Contest." *Signs and Signals: Popular Culture in Africa*. ed. Raoul Granquist. Umea: Umea University, 1990. 35–47.

Ashcroft, Bill, Gareth Griffiths and Helen Tiffin. *The Empire Writes Back*. London: Routledge, 1989.

Asheri, Jedida. *Promise*. Lagos: African Universities Press, 1969.

Ashuntantang, Joyce. *Landscaping Postcoloniality: The Dissemination of Cameroon Anglophone Literature*. Bamenda: Langaa Publishers, 2009.

Asong, Linus. *The Crown of Thorns*. Limbe: Cosmos Educational Publishers, 1990.

Besong, Bate. *Beasts of No Nation*. Limbe: Nooremac Press, 1990.

Besong, Bate. "Literature in the Season of the Diaspora: Notes to the Anglophone Cameroonian Writer." *Anglophone Cameroon Writing*. eds. Nalova Lyonga, Eckhard Breitinger, and Bole Butake, Bayreuth African Studies Ser. 30. Bayreuth: Bayreuth University, 1993. 15–18.

Besong, Bate. "Ontogeneis of Modern Anglophone Cameroon Drama & Its Criticism: Excursus." *Voices*. Spring 5 (2002): 1–9.

D'Epie, Alobwede C. "The Concept of Anglophone Literature." *Anglophone Cameroon Writing*. eds. Nalova Lyonga, Eckhard Breitinger, and Bole Butake, Bayreuth African Studies Ser. 30. Bayreuth: Bayreuth University, 1993.

Doh, Emmanuel. "Anglophone Cameroon Literature: Is There Such a Thing?" *Anglophone Cameroon Writing*. eds. Nalova Lyonga, Eckhard Breitinger, and Bole Butake. Bayreuth: University of Bayreuth, 1993. 76–83.

Epie-Ngome, Victor. *What God Has Put Asunder*. Yaounde: Pitcher Books, 1992.

Eyoh, Hansel Ndumbe. "Historicity and New Anglophone Cameroon Drama." *Anglophone Cameroon Writing*. eds. Nalova Lyonga, Bole Butake, and Eckhard Breitinger. Bayreuth: University of Bayreuth, 1993. 101–109.

Foncha, John Ngu. "Dr. J.N. Foncha's Letter of Resignation from the CPDM." *The Case for Southern Cameroons*. ed. Albert Mukong. Maryland: CAMFECO, 1990.

JanMohamed, Abdul R. and David Lloyd (eds.). *The Nature and Context of Minority Discourse*. New York: Oxford University Press, 1990.

Konings, Piet and Francis Nyamnjoh. "The Anglophone Problem." *Journal of Modern African Studies*. 35 (1997): 207–229.

Konings, Piet and Francis Nyamnjoh. *Negotiating an Anglophone Identity. A Study of the Politics of Recognition and Representation in Cameroon*. Vol. 1. Leiden–Boston: Brill (Afrika-Studiecentrum Series), 2003.

Krieger, Milton. *Language in Cameroon: Bilingual Policy, Multi-Lingual Practice: Issues in Language and Education*. Vol. 6. Boston: Boston University, 1991.

Lyonga, Nalova. "Le degre Zero . . . Deconstructing Victimhood." *Anglophone Cameroon Writing*. eds. Nalova Lyonga, Bole Butake, and Eckhard Breitinger. Bayreuth: University of Bayreuth, 1993. 159–162.

Lyonga, Nalova, Bole Butake and Eckhard Breitinger. "Foreword." *Anglophone Cameroon Writing*. eds. Nalova Lyonga, Bole Butake, and Eckhard Breitinger. Bayreuth: University of Bayreuth, 1993. 9–12.

Mukong, Albert (ed.). *The Case for Southern Cameroons*. Maryland: CAMFECO, 1990.

Mydans, Seth. "Across Cultures, English Is the Word." *New York Times*, April 9, 2007. www.nytimes.com/2007/04/09/world/asia/09iht-englede.1.5198685.html. Accessed October 1, 2019.

Nfah-Abbenyi, Juliana Makuchi. *Your Madness Not Mine*. Ohio: Ohio University Press, 1999.

Nyamnjoh, Francis. *The Cameroon GCE Crisis: A Test of Anglophone Solidarity*. Limbe: Nooremac Press, 1996.

Sam-Kubam, Patrick. "The Paucity of Literary Creativity in English speaking Cameroon." *Abbia*. 9 (1978): 203–206.

Takougang, Joseph and Milton Kreiger. *African State and Society in the 1990's: Cameroon's Political Crossroads*. Boulder: Westview Press, 1998.

Tambo, Leke. "Anglophone Cameroon Writing in Relation to Textbooks in Cameroon Schools." *Anglophone Cameroon Writing*. eds. Nalova Lyonga, Eckhard Breitinger, and Bole Butake, Bayreuth African Studies Ser. 30. Bayreuth: Bayreuth University, 1993.

Tanyi-Tang, Anne. *Ewa and Other Plays*. Yaounde: Edition CLE, 1999.

Vera, Yvonne. "Preface." *Anthology of African Women's Writing*. ed. Yvonne Vera. Oxford: Heinemann Educational Books, 1999.

Wolf, Hans-Georg. "Transcendence of Ethnic Boundaries: The Case of Anglophones in Cameroon." *Journal of Sociolinguistics*. 1.3 (1997): 419–426.

Wolf, Hans-Georg. *English in Cameroon*. New York: Mouton de Gruyter, 2001.

6

NIGER DELTA AND ITS MINORITY CONDITION IN NIGERIAN WRITING

Obari Gomba

Introduction

What is the factor that has made the Niger Delta immanent in Nigeria's writing? It is the history of the region. It makes it possible to engage the writing on the basis of New Historicism, which has "a combined interest in 'the textuality of history' [and] 'the historicity of texts'" (Barry 173). The ethnic nationalities that populate that region of Nigeria were once self governing and largely self sufficient until they were dragged willy-nilly under European suzerainty through colonial conquest. That region which cartographically stretches around the triangular delta from the Calabar River to the Benin River was at different times called the Oil Rivers Protectorate and the Niger Delta Protectorate as the British tightened their stranglehold on the territory they later named Nigeria.

If some of the ethnic nationalities ever viewed themselves as minorities in precolonial times in relation to their neighbours, postcolonial Nigeria is a dire amplification of the suffering of ethnic minorities in a manner that has hardly been known in that deltaic area. Thus, the minority condition that troubles the region today is precisely a postcolonial problem in a poorly integrated nation-state that has modelled its power-structure after the failings of colonial hegemony. The ethnic nationalities of the region are without question the minorities of Nigeria. As the region was a hub of palm oil production in the colonial era, it is today a terribly dispossessed hub of crude oil production in postcolonial Nigeria.

The politics of the Nigerian state has ensured the subjugation of ethnic minorities. This situation is particularly obvious in the Niger Delta region, where resources have provoked contention since remembered time. Present-day experiences are built on a history that goes far back into time. The history of the region has been impacted by the slave trade, colonialism, independence and colonial hangovers, local hegemonies, majority domination, multinational profiteering, resource dispossession, environment despoliation, civil war and displacement, state-sponsored violence and terror, resistance, complicity and implosions, and so on. At every stage of this history, resource extraction has been a major crisis factor.

There are diverse narratives from diverse fields of learning that attest to a continuum of control and dispossession in the region, and literary narratives (across the genres) have commanded particular attention due to their mimetic capacity for verisimilitude. There are two major categories of writing on the Niger Delta. There are works written by writers of Niger

Delta extraction about the condition of the region, and there are works written by writers from other regions and countries about the Niger Delta condition. The first category qualifies as "the literature of the Niger Delta"; the second category is relevant as "literature on/about the Niger Delta." There is no doubt that cross-currents and contestations within the Nigerian nation-state create a link between both categories of narratives. It should also be noted that although works in the second category can be as insightful as those in the first (depending on the depth of authorial perception and/or empathy), the works in the first category tend to deserve particular focus because the "nativity" of the authors positions the texts as insider narratives on a lived experience.

There has been a legion of writers from the Niger Delta region: Gabriel Okara, JP Clark, Elechi Amadi, Okogbule Wonodi, Ken Saro-Wiwa, Tanure Ojaide, Odia Ofeimun, Festus Iyayi, Isidore Okpewho, Miesoinuma Minima, Ibiwari Ikiriko, Joe Ushie, Nnimmo Bassey, G. 'Ébinyo Ogbowei, Ogaga Ifowodo, Ebi Yeibo, Vincent Egbuson, Nengi Ilagha, Bina Ilagha, Chimeka Garricks, Kaine Agary, Sophia Obi-Apoko, and Ekaete George, to name but a few. Given the large corpus of writing from the region, this chapter is a survey of the depiction of the Niger Delta's minority condition through selected Nigerian writings by writers of Niger Delta extraction. Rather than present detailed explication of individual literary texts, the survey will "locate" each text in the material history that has provoked it. The equal weighting of literary and historical texts is consistent with the praxis of New Historicism which historicizes the text and textualizes history to the extent that a reading of literary and non-literary texts is achieved (Barry 173). Thus, the terms "text" or "writing" are ascribed to poems, novels, plays, memoirs, historical and political documents, and so on. The aim is to reveal the major issues that have made postcolonial Niger Delta immanent in Nigerian writing and to link appropriate history to appropriate texts in a manner that may perhaps help pedagogically should anyone be willing to study the discourse further.

To understand the "minority-tenor" of such texts, it is important to pay attention to their historical contexts. The works depict all aspects of the human condition; the works reflect different styles and textures; the works evoke many tonalities. But the one motif that exemplifies the minority condition (the most) is oil production and the politics of resource transfer. A lot has been written about this subject matter. However, in this chapter, the discourse around resource-related politics and conflicts is presented in five sections: "Minority Fears on the Threshold of Independence"; "Boro and the Resistance"; "The Nigerian Civil War"; "Environmental Despoliation, Dispossession and Militancy"; and "Saro-Wiwa and Ogoni Uprising". The five topics are crucial to the Niger Delta's discourse.

Minority fears on the threshold of independence

Anyone who will compile a worthy anthology of writings on the Niger Delta discourse cannot ignore the "Manifesto of the Niger Delta Congress" (NDC) for the 1959 federal elections. It was a precursor to both the "Ogoni Bill of Rights" and the "Kaiama Declaration," two equally nuanced and purposeful texts that have been produced by the minority condition of the region. The said "Manifesto" expressed fears about possible troubles ahead in the postcolonial future of Nigeria. As a political text, it was clear in its intent, which was to mobilize the region against the hegemony of ethnic majorities and to protect the resources of the region from maladministration. That text stands as a forerunner at the bridgehead of all postcolonial writing on the region.

Long before JP Clark, Ken Saro-Wiwa, Tanure Ojaide, and many more began to write and to publish texts on the challenges of the region, a "small" political party published a political text (perhaps widely unpopular then as it is today) on the issues that have now become a conflagration. Was there a cause then for minority fears? Yes. As the colonial state grew, the Niger Delta found its halves in the Western Region and the Eastern Region (1939), and they were outnumbered in each by the Yoruba and the Igbo, respectively. It placed the region at a disadvantage in the era's untoward democracy of numbers. This gave rise to the cry of marginalization which heralded postcolonial Nigeria.

In the buildup to Nigeria's independence, the agitation for self-determination/state creation by the nations of the Niger Delta reached an intensity that warranted the Willink Commission in 1957. The commission, which was urged to determine the veracity of minority fears, acknowledged the grounds for such fears but did not offer redress. The most the British and the ethnic majorities could concede in the report (1958) was the establishment of a Niger Delta Development Board, to be jointly funded by the central and regional governments, to cater for the development needs of the Niger Delta. Some commentators have held the ethnic majorities squarely responsible for that decision. Kole Omotoso, to cite but one example, puts it succinctly: "the British colonial government did attempt to resolve the position of the minorities within the Nigerian federation before the granting of independence" and a "minority rights commission . . . was set up in 1957. This was scuttled by the politicking of the major ethnic nationalities," which argued "that they would rather have independence and then deal with the issue of minorities after" (101). As devious and culpable as the ethnic majorities were, the British did not have a strong commitment to solving the problem. They had nothing to lose and everything to gain by setting Nigeria on a false start. Crude oil had already been discovered in the Niger Delta in 1956. There was the prospect for greater finds all over the Niger Delta, and the exploratory concession was already under the control of Shell-BP. This meant that the British had already secured the next wave of accumulation in the Niger Delta given that petroleum security was a crucial index of post-World War II reality in Europe. The British also secured the complicity of the emergent political class in Nigeria, who by their actions held that it would be better if the nationalities whose soil held the black gold had no political control. This raised the heat in the polity, from the days leading to independence, especially in the Eastern Region which controlled the early oil fields of the Niger Delta.

Crude oil was found in commercial quantity in Oloibiri (riverine Ijo in the Eastern Region) in 1956. The find ended years of fruitless exploration by a band of wildcatters who had established their presence in Nigeria starting in 1937. Shell D'Archy had also started exploratory activities in 1937, and they got an Exploration License on 4th November 1938. Exploration was suspended in 1941 because of World War II, and it resumed the year after the war (1946). By 1951, Nigeria's colonial government had given full endorsement to exploratory activities, and Shell D'Archy drilled the first well at Iho, northwest of Owerri. It was a futile effort. But it was that drive which culminated in the Oloibiri find in 1956. From Oloibiri Well No.1, the Shell-BP party proceeded to sink seventeen more wells in their days of business there.

The historic shipment of oil was made in 1958. *Hemifusus*, the eighteen-ton sea tanker, moved "from the Port Harcourt dockside half full," navigated "its way through the shallows of the Bonny River", and "a shuttle tanker accompanied [it] to Bonny Bar" to pump more "9000 tons . . . into the hold" (Watts 36). Probably the additional tons were sourced from elsewhere, perhaps from Afam, perhaps from the giant Bomu oil field in Ogoni, which had been discovered in 1958. The oil was "shipped to the Shell Haven refinery at the mouth of the River Thames," and in just weeks, Nigerian oil "was fueling Austins, Triumphs, Fords, and Sunbeams in London, the new icons of a much-heralded post-war British prosperity" (Watts 36). In 1959, Shell-BP signed an Oil Profits Agreement with Nigeria's colonial government in Mosaic House, Tinubu Square, Lagos.

In the year 1959, on the threshold of independence, it became clear that oil would be a problematic subject in postcolonial Nigeria. The sign was shown in the said manifesto of the grassroots political party, the Niger Delta Congress, for the federal elections of 12th December 1959. The cardinal points were self-determination and resource control, depicted as inseparable factors, crucial to the well-being of the Niger Delta nationalities. There was also a strong swipe at the government of the Eastern Region, which controlled 50% of derived revenue from oil. The fiscal arrangement at the time gave 50% of oil proceeds to "the region of origin; 20% to the federal government; and 30% to a distributable pool for all units of the federation"(Etekpe et al., 210), and the federal government also received company tax profits from oil exploration. Nothing was set aside for the oil-bearing communities of the Niger Delta. To this end, the NDC position was loud and clear: if a region or a state was created for the nationalities of the Niger Delta, they would be entitled by law to retain 50% of revenue derived from oil, as against the situation where such revenue was controlled by the Igbo-dominated regional government in Enugu. The NDC argued that Enugu always got hold of the money and "burnt it up" without showing concern for the development needs of the Niger Delta (Etekpe et al. 210).

The NDC hoped to achieve two things from the elections of 12th December 1959. First, to dislodge the Igbo-dominated National Council of Nigerian Citizens (NCNC) from the Niger Delta. The NDC saw the NCNC as the instrument for Igbo hegemony, and believed the NCNC had enabled the Igbo to take possession of oil resources. Second, the NDC hoped to win sufficient seats in the federal parliament so as to have the clout that would enable it push for the self-determination of the Niger Delta in parliament. So the NDC courted the Hausa-Fulani–dominated Nigerian Peoples' Congress (NPC) for an alliance.

It was ironic that the Niger Delta politicians did not see the similarities in the politics of the Northern Region and the Eastern Region. The former had kept a rein on the Middle Belt nationalities just like the latter had done to the Niger Delta. It was really naïve of the Niger Delta politicians to have considered the so-called Northern solidarity genuine. The North was up to sheer politicking – to stoke discontent in a rival political enclave, only there were genuine grounds for discontent.

The NDC lost its scheme. It could not dislodge the NCNC in the Niger Delta. It was only in Oloibiri that the NDC got "its only parliamentary seat in the 1959 federal elections" (Ukiwo 73), and as such, NDC could not form an alliance with the NPC. It was the NCNC and NPC that formed an alliance, and the Niger Delta had no foothold in the independence government, which was inaugurated in 1960.

The nations of the Niger Delta in the Western Region had a similar experience until 1963. They were split by the Action Group (AG) and the NCNC. The only uniting factor was the clamour of marginalization which ripped through the axis, and it grew as crude oil production increased in the area. In 1963, the government of the Western Region was benign to letting go of the Niger Delta. The Midwestern Region was created to calm the agitations for self-determination and resource control. The irony of ironies was that the NCNC championed the self-determination crusade of the Midwestern Region, and it also became the ruling party in the region. It appeared that the NCNC championed the birth of the Midwestern Region in order to expand its own sphere of influence and to reduce the size of the Western Region. For what else would have prompted the NCNC to secure for the western Niger Delta what it had denied the nations of the Niger Delta in the East where it controlled the government?

The new Midwestern Region had the right to retain 50% of revenue derived from oil. There might have been a series of intraregional tensions between the component units of the new region, but the situation was far better than they experienced in the Western Region and far better than the experience of the Niger Delta nations in the East, who grew more and more agitated. The creation of the Midwestern Region fuelled the agitation by the eastern Niger Delta for self-determination.

The first five years after independence saw a massive growth in Nigeria's oil infrastructure and production. For example, twelve giant oil fields came on-stream with the very first discovery of oil offshore, at Okan (near Escravos), in 1964. The Trans-Niger Pipeline was also built in 1965 to link the oil fields in the Ughelli axis to the Bonny terminal. And there was also the construction of the premiere refinery at Alesa Eleme. The process for building the refinery began with the signing of "the Refinery Agreement" in July 1962. The facility came into operation on 7th June 1965.

Boro and the resistance

Isaac Adaka Boro was largely misunderstood and underrated until he fought and died for the liberation of the Niger Delta during the Nigerian civil war. Ken Saro-Wiwa has remarked, in *On a Darkling Plain*, on Boro's exploits and death: "In the morning of 17th May, a Lieutenant Duke . . . walked into my office to inform me that Major Isaac Adaka Boro had been shot dead on his way to Bodo from Okrika, which he had just liberated in his usual classic style. I was deeply touched by the news" (170). Boro, as Saro-Wiwa further notes, was an inspiring and courageous officer:

> Later, six members of Boro's 19 Brigade joined us in my office and regaled me with stories of the brave exploits of their Commander. He it was who, alone, had volunteered to make the dangerous crossing from Egwanga to Kono. He had taken Opobo, Nkoro, Kono and Okrika, with the loss of but two men. Loved by his men, he was accessible to them.
>
> *(170)*

Boro left behind a memoir, *The Twelve-Day Revolution*. It gives an account of his development, struggles, and imprisonment. It does not cover his civil war exploits. Because he is known as a revolutionary and soldier, many tend to ignore the significance of that text in the narratives/discourse of the region. His person has grown over time to overshadow the text. But the new waves of agitators, who have come to see him as a symbol of the region's struggle, do so precisely because of the incidents that are recorded in that memoir. In the postcolonial era, he was the first to pursue self-determination for the region through violent means. For that reason, JP Clark has written an "Epitaph for Boro" in *State of the Union*, and Tanure Ojaide, in "Wails" (*Delta Blues and Home Songs*), sees Boro as Saro-Wiwa's peer in the struggle of the region, even though the two figures are known to have adopted different approaches to resistance.

The sentiments expressed by both Clark and Ojaide are rooted in their knowledge of history. The nations of the Niger Delta in the Eastern Region became more restive as the oil industry grew. In February 1966, Boro raised a rag-tag army of secessionists, named the Niger Delta Volunteer Service (NDVS), against the Nigerian state. He declared the Niger Delta Republic. Boro's action was beclouded by conflicting interpretations. The NCNC loyalists interpreted it as a plan which had been sponsored by Sir Tafawa Balewa and his party to destabilize the East and cripple the NCNC. They held that Boro had gone ahead with the plan even though it had been overtaken by the coup of 15th January 1966 in which Sir Balewa was killed. They made this case by counting on Boro's avowal of love for the slain Sir Balewa and his party. Boro did not hide his disaffection for what he perceived to be Igbo hegemony in the East. He felt piqued that whereas the Sir Balewa–led federal government, which held 20% of oil proceeds, made contributions to the Niger Delta Development Board formed in 1962, the regional government, which held 50%, had refused to contribute to the Board (Boro 56).

The Igbo were not the only ones who were displeased with Boro's rebellion. Some people from the Niger Delta also saw Boro's action as "farcical recklessness" (Tebekami 6). However, the logic of his argument for self-determination and resource control remained strongly cogent, much more cogent than his firepower. Boro's army held its ground for twelve days. It was a war in which Shell BP was said to have allied with the federal government. Boro says: "we saw a Shell Company pontoon . . . loaded with . . . troops and police" (134–135). It would appear that given Shell BP's exploratory knowledge of the Niger Delta, the federal forces depended on the company to lead them into the crevices of the Niger Delta. Boro lost. He was captured, tried, and sentenced to death (for treason) by Gen. JTU Aguyi-Ironsi's government. He was later released by Gen. Yakubu Gowon.

The Nigerian Civil War

Boro's foiled secession was a prelude to the civil war which began the following year, 1967. Texts by Niger Delta writers, such as Elechi Amadi and Ken Saro-Wiwa, reveal why the centre could hold. Amadi has captured the impact of the war in *Sunset in Biafra* (a memoir), *The Road to Ibadan* (a play), and *Estrangement* (a novel). Saro-Wiwa has written about the war in *Sozaboy* (a novel), *On a Darkling Plain* (a memoir), and some poems in *Songs in a Time of War*. The texts tell their stories from a Niger Delta perspective. Many minority communities suffered from mass death and displacement even before the war raged in Igbo land. The sacrifices made by minorities in support of both sides of the conflict are often discounted by both sides. Too often, the minorities are vilified by some Igbo narrators for supporting the federal side in the civil war, and Yoruba and Hausa Fulani narrators would rather present the federal side as an altruistic agency that liberated the minorities. It is proper that Amadi and Saro-Wiwa are unafraid to state their motives and involvement as they also show how minority communities were caught in the crossfire between Biafra and Nigeria.

Nigeria has not acknowledged the faith that minorities had in the country when the ethnic majorities were eager to tear it apart. Whereas other sections of Nigeria (including the North, which called for Araba) had lost faith in the country in 1966 and sought to break up the country along regional lines, the western fringe of the Niger Delta (the Midwestern Region) pushed for unity (Ikime 306–311) at the Conference of the Leaders of Thought. The irony is that, in the days leading to 1966, the Niger Delta had been the loudest on the subject of self-determination. When the opportunity came for the balkanization of Nigeria, the Niger Delta pushed for the federation of states. In the end, only Col. Chukwuemeka Ojukwu and the East differed, and Col. Ojukwu was at the receiving end of Anthony Enahoro's butt. Enahoro, a leading member of the western Niger Delta delegation, had taken his argument to Kingsway London on 17th July 1967. He has been quoted to have said: "If secession by Ojukwu and his group is accomplished, Nigeria would most probably disintegrate. Once fractionalization starts, it certainly would result in the further disintegration of the former Eastern Region of Nigeria. Neighbouring states with ethnic and other problems will in due course also disintegrate" (Ibrahim 14).

Were Enahoro and his group right? Did they unwittingly mortgage the future of the Niger Delta by that decision? Would it not have been better if the Niger Delta had stood on its own? It appears that the decision of the Western Niger Delta delegation was, besides JS Tarka's influence (Ikime 310), also conditioned by concern for the lot of the Eastern Niger Delta peoples who would most probably not have been favoured by secession. The eastern flank of the Niger Delta was bound to have been incorporated into Biafra willy-nilly. Years of conflict between the Igbo and the Niger Delta peoples had meant that the latter would be disadvantaged if the Eastern Region was allowed to take the eastern flank of the Niger Delta into a new country. This is why the creation of Rivers State was an exciting experience for many Niger Delta elite and a stimulus for Boro, who died in the civil war while defending Nigeria's claim on Rivers State.

The Niger Delta was indeed a bride at the centre of that conflict. Oil was once again a factor in the war. Of course, there were other factors like electoral failures, ethnic bigotry, two coups d'état, and waves of genocidal pogrom. But oil was no less crucial in the conflict. Wole Soyinka has said that the "discovery of oil in huge reserve in the East, largely in the Niger estuary, played a role, unquestionably, in the propulsion of Biafra leaders towards secession" (120). Soyinka, however, adds that "it would be a distortion of history, and an attempt to trivialize the trauma that the Igbo had undergone, to suggest" – as some analysts have been wont to do – "that it was [only] the lure of the oil wealth that drove the Igbo to seek a separate existence" (120). Soyinka's position runs contrary to that of David Yergin, who says that the war broke out when the "Eastern Region . . . wanted a bigger share of government oil revenues" (537). Given that the revenue formula was never a subject of conflict between the Igbo and the central government, Yergin's point is an example of the misreading of history which Soyinka speaks against. But – even so – Soyinka himself does not deny the role of oil in the conflict.

It is a fact that Nigeria and its foreign partners lurched into the civil war in order to take control of the oil fields in the Niger Delta area. The Nigerian government knew that the leadership of Biafra had factored the oil fields and facilities into Biafra's viability plan. To counter this, the Nigerian government took a number of steps in the early days of the conflict. One, Rivers State was "created," right on the threshold of the war, to assuage the age-long agitation of the peoples of the eastern Niger Delta, and this polarized their support for Biafra. Two, the Nigerian forces captured Bonny, the oil export terminal, on 28th July 1967, even before the war got earnest. Three, the Nigerian air force bombed the premiere oil refinery in Alesa Eleme to prevent Biafra from making use of the facility. Four, right in the heat of the war, the Nigerian government promulgated the Petroleum Act and the Petroleum (Drilling and Production) Regulations in 1969, both of which vested oil rights on the central government. In all these, Soyinka says that Nigeria's military leaders were guided in no small measure by the British intelligence network (124, 150). This point has been corroborated by Michael Peel.

The British did not see the war on the basis of rights and wrongs. Britain, as Peel states, saw the war as a "defining episode in the unfolding conquest of Nigeria's crude" (48). Britain armed the Nigerian government because it saw the federal side "as a better bet to protect British access and the interests of the oil companies, Shell and BP" (Peel 48). Peel has confessed to seeing some documents in Britain's National Archives which prove that Harold Wilson's government had been resolute "about the ruthlessness with which Britain planned to protect and increase its profits from Nigeria's nascent oil industry" (55). The Biafran leader Col. (later Gen.) Ojukwu is said to have also revealed, many years after the war, that "he believed the question of oil was crucial to understanding British policy during the civil war" (Peel 52). British support for Nigeria might have grown intense when France and Portugal began to court Biafra over the oilfields of the Niger Delta. If Biafra had not lost Bonny's oil terminal and the oilfields too early in the conflict, the war would most likely have ended differently.

Of all the actions taken by the Nigerian government, the loss of Bonny seemed to have piqued Biafra's leadership the most: "Bonny was a real prize . . . its capture came at . . . a time when there was a tussle over oil royalty payments" (Saro-Wiwa, *Darkling* 98). Biafra lost the royalty to Nigeria (which had possession of the terminal). Biafra would react by arresting Mr. Stanley Gray (the general manager of Shell BP) for a while, by seizing a few oil installations, and by establishing a Petroleum Management Committee under the headship of Prof. Eni Njoku. It has also been said that Biafra captured and killed some "oil men who were caught drilling for oil in the Midwest" (Amadi 49). This brought Biafra under intense diplomatic pressure until the captives were released to Rome after a month of captivity.

No doubt, Bonny pained Biafra, and the Biafra army fought very hard to regain Bonny, perhaps more than it fought to keep Enugu, which was its seat of power. In the battle for Bonny, Biafran troops bombed Shell's loading terminal off the coast of Bonny, but it could not reclaim the terminal.

Environmental despoliation, state terror, and militancy

The dispossession of the region has been made possible through the nation-state's mechanism of environmental degradation, violence, and terror. As expected, repression begets resistance. Thus, the aforementioned themes have been depicted in Isidore Okpewho's *Tides*, which, though first published in 1993, has been largely prophetic in its enunciation of a violent response to state violence.

The previously listed themes are also significantly shown in novels like Tanure Ojaide's *The Activist*, Kaine Agary's *Yellow-Yellow*, and Chimeka Garricks' *Tomorrow Died Yesterday*. There are poems on the subject in many of Ojaide's poetry collections such as *Delta Blues and Home Songs*, *The Tale of the Harmattan*, *Waiting for the Hatching of the Cockerel*, *The Beauty I Have Seen*, *Songs of Myself: Quartet*, and so on. Other poets have also written on the themes. There are clear examples in Ibiwari Ikiriko's *Oily Tears of the Delta*, Nnimmo Bassey's *We Thought It Was Oil but It Was Blood*, Ogaga Ifowodo's *The Oil Lamp*, and G. 'Ebinyo Ogbowei's *Song of a Dying River* and *Marsh Boy and Other Poems*. The writers have been driven to write about a condition that has become increasingly painful since the end of the civil war.

By the end of the civil war in 1970, the Niger Delta woke up to "Shell's first major oil spillage" (Omoweh x) on a trunkline linking Ejamaa Ebubu (in Eleme) and Bonny. The spillage lasted for "three weeks," and it left severe impact on the environment (Omoweh x). And this occurred at a time when the displaced survivors from the affected area were returning to rebuild their lives and homes. Over the years, environment despoliation has become a recurrent pattern across the minority communities of the region.

After the war, another wave of discontent started in the Niger Delta. The modest autonomy (at the level of state creation) which the region gained from the jaws of war was made hollow by the fiscal policy which was introduced by the military government. As Saro-Wiwa has argued: "Nothing drove home this fact more than the decree modifying the system of revenue allocation which became effective on April 1, 1970. Under the new decree, a sizable chunk of oil revenue of Midwestern and Rivers States was seized from them and transferred to the Federal Government" (*Darkling* 238). He adds that "as revenue allocation lies very much at the heart of the Federal system of government," the policy launched by "the dictatorial action of General Gowon was seen in Rivers State as striking at the very essence of the life of the minorities and as an attempt to nullify whatever gains may have accrued to the Rivers people from the dreadful war" (*Darkling* 238). Even the nations of the Western Niger Delta, who had secured 50% derivation (on their status as a region in 1963), lost it in the postwar formula of resource allocation.

It appeared that whereas the nations of the Niger Delta earned a degree of political autonomy from the jaws of the civil war, the Nigerian state had been quick to undercut their economic advantage, as evident in the change of the revenue formula. It was the beginning of a consistent pattern of transfer of oil revenue from the Niger Delta states to the centre, which was dominated by the ethnic majorities. Kole Omotoso has argued that the ethnic majorities manipulated the revenue formula to their favour. He notes that, "because of the manipulation of the process . . ., the creation of states has not benefited the minority ethnic nationalities as it would have been expected to do" (101–102). "Put simply," he says, "the creation of new states became a means of cornering for each ethnic nationality more and more of already over-exploited national cake, especially after the concentrated exploitation of petroleum products" (102).

The new formula was the scheme of hegemony. Before then, federal fiscal policy stated that places of derivation of any economic product would be the major beneficiary (Omotoso 102). Omotoso corroborates the position of Saro-Wiwa on the scams of state creation and revenue adjustments. He notes that with "the coming of the Petrol Dollar after the civil war, fiscal policy shifted to 'equitable' distribution of available financial resources. This arrangement favoured the three big ones and the sources of these resources suffered" (102). The federal government continued, through brazen legality, to tighten its control of oil revenue until the proceeds accruing to the producing states fell as low as 1.5% in the 1980s. It was raised to 13% in 1999, but the increase has not led to improvement in the region, nor has it stemmed the tide of discontent.

The political climate from the 1980s to the 1990s was downright repressive. And the nations of the Niger Delta suffered, but they were toughened by experience. Decades of repression gave rise to the resolve of the communities to confront the state continually. When Saro-Wiwa and Ogoni began their protest in 1990, they knew that they were up against a crass system. Saro-Wiwa himself knew of the government's repressive strategies against oil-related dissidence. Saro-Wiwa knew the dangers inherent in challenging the status quo. He knew there was a slick alliance between the Nigerian state and the transnationals. He knew of Umuechem, which was reduced to rubble for daring to hold Shell accountable (to its corporate responsibility).

On 30th October 1990, Umuechem had protested against the operations of Shell in their area. The Anglo-Dutch giant had in turn raised a false alarm against Umuechem and had instigated security forces to swoop in on the community. Umuechem was attacked. Several lives and property were lost. The public outcry forced the government to set up a ritual commission of enquiry, but the commission could not gloss over the weight of evidence against Shell and state security. The commission could not find "a single thread of evidence of violence or threat of violence on the part of the villagers and censured the police for displaying 'reckless disregard for lives and property'" (Okonta and Douglas 139). But a swipe, no matter how strong, at the police, did not translate to a new dawn for Umuechem. They nursed their losses, as the Ogoni were to do some months later.

The tragedies in Umuechem and Ogoni, where peaceful protests were met with violent state action, have led to a wave of violent resistance in the Niger Delta. Groups such as the Egbesu Boys, the Movement for the Emancipation of the Niger Delta (MEND), and Niger Delta People's Volunteer Force (NDPVF) are known to have launched attacks on oil infrastructure and the military and taken oil workers hostage. It is important to note that Saro-Wiwa had predicted at the tribunal (before he was later executed with his compatriots) that the state's disregard for peaceful redress would give rise to violent resistance. He made that statement from a place of insight. No wonder he stands to date as the clearest articulator of the minority condition in the Niger Delta and the rest of Nigeria.

Saro-Wiwa and the Ogoni uprising

The two foremost narratives from the region on the Ogoni resistance are Ken Saro-Wiwa's *A Month and a Day* and Ken Wiwa's *In the Shadow of a Saint*. The first is Saro-Wiwa's prison memoir, which captures the struggle and suffering of the Ogoni; the second is Saro-Wiwa's son's effort to find the essence of his father's activism and the place of the Ogoni nation in a tragedy that appears too far from a resolution. It is not surprising that both authors knew the value of documentation/writing to a resistance movement. When a people choose to rise against oppression, they must also be willing to tell their story in texts that will endure. As William Boyd notes, Saro-Wiwa declares in one of his letters (from prison) that: "the most important thing for me is that I [have] used my talents as a writer to enable the Ogoni people to confront their tormentors" (xv).

The enormity of the engagement and sacrifice of the Ogoni people has caused other men and women of letters to write about their struggle. For instance, Kaine Agary's *Yellow-Yellow* has a telling portrayal of the impact of the struggle on the psyche of the region: "It was the year after the government hanged Ken Saro-Wiwa, along with nine other Ogonis, for inciting an insurrection that led to the deaths of four elders in Ogoni land. Every young boy had visions of dying valiantly for the cause, as Ken Saro-Wiwa just had and Isaac Adaka Boro done nearly thirty years before him" (34). Even though Agary is wrong about the number of men that were hanged on 10th November, 1995, she is right in her depiction of mood of the region. This mood has not only been expressed by those who are willing to fight for rights, it has also been expressed by poets in the region and beyond who have committed their art to the concerns of the struggle. Unarguably, Tanure Ojaide deserves to be acknowledged for that.

Besides dedicating his novel (*The Activist*) to Saro-Wiwa, Ojaide has also dedicated *Waiting for the Hatching of a Cockerel* to Saro-Wiwa, and the first part of Ojaide's *Delta Blues and Home Songs*, comprising twenty-eight poems, is committed to Saro-Wiwa and the Ogoni struggle. There are mentions of the struggle in many other poems in other collections by Ojaide. Similarly, other poets have also written on Saro-Wiwa and the struggle: two parts of Ogaga Ifowodo's *The Oil Lamp*, entitled "Ogoni" and "The Agonist"; three poems ("For Ken," "Remembering Saro-Wiwa," and "Ogoni Agony") in Ibiwari Ikiriko's *Oily Tears of the Delta*; and a poem entitled "Ken" in Odia Ofeimun's *Go Tell the Generals*, to name but a few. One can safely say that no other resistance figure in the region has attracted as much attention as Saro-Wiwa.

In the very year of the Umuechem saga, Saro-Wiwa and Ogoni presented a Bill of Rights to the government of Nigeria. The launch of the Ogoni Bill of Rights and the formation of the Movement for the Survival of Ogoni People (MOSOP) gave fresh impetus and vitality to the Niger Delta crusade. The government reacted in character. Repression. But the blood of Saro-Wiwa and his kinsmen, killed in 1995, was just the fuel the Niger Delta needed. There has been a conflagration ever since, as Saro-Wiwa himself predicted.

Although the steps towards self-determination and resource control since 1995 are not all free of flaws, the Niger Delta has come to the realization that, as Obaro Ikime has put it, "the soul of the Nigerian nation has . . . little place" for the communities which bear the black gold (220). They have come to know that they have carried the burden of oil from colonialism to postcolonialism. They have come to view Nigeria's independence as a mere change of guards – a view that has credence when matched against the imperial framework that gave birth to the independence. Come to think of it, has the eminent Chinua Achebe not suggested that Nigeria is an extended colonialism? Has Achebe not said that the British on the eve of their departure made sure that power got in the hands of those who would protect the status quo? (Omotoso 109). Even those, like Omotoso, who query Achebe's statement for its Biafran perspective (109), cannot deny that the nature of Nigeria's independence and its ruling circles is rapaciously neocolonial.

Conclusion

The texts that have been mentioned do not in any way exhaust the range and number of writings on the Niger Delta condition. But they are significant enough to call attention to the ongoing discourse of minorities emanating from the region. The political environment was already colonially programmed before independence. Nigeria and its ruling circles stepped into a pattern which has ensured the dispossession and domination of the weak components of the Federal Project. This has made leadership not only a programme of ethnic bigotry but also "a fierce defend[ing]" of the interests of the ruling circles and "the ex-colonial companies," as Fanon would say (133–134).

Those who give credit to our nationalist movements for securing independence may not have understood the imperial stimulus that prompted the British to concede self-government to colonized peoples. The pressures from the colonies did not count as much as the demands of the post-war reality in the Western world. Independence was a tactical change of strategy. Independence was structured as an advanced type of indirect rule: a strategy adopted to safeguard the continuity of wealth transfer from resource-bearing peoples. Britain knew it had finished the groundwork and stepped behind the scenes with the faith that Nigeria would not break the pattern. Those who took over power from the British, whether politicians or soldiers, have shown – by their enterprise of plunder, repression of resource owners, "materialistic woolliness and self-centred pedestrianism" (Achebe 13) – that Nigeria is capable of terrifying fidelity to colonial/imperial character. For that, the Niger Delta has continued to bear the brunt of history.

The Niger Delta lost its footing long before independence. As Hoogvelt succinctly states, long-term "concessions for mineral exploration and exploitation had been granted" to colonial firms before independence (30). And Nigeria was hooked on technology dependence in the oil industry. All that was left was to hand over power to a local political order which was poised to protect, exploit, and profit from the colonial legacy. And the British knew that "formal colonialism had the indirect effect of laying the foundations for continuous control and domination over colonial resources even in the absence of direct political overlordship and administration" (Hoogvelt 29–30). This is how the Niger Delta has come to be in resource bondage in Nigeria's postcolonial polity. The success of neocolonialism as, to quote Hoogvelt again, "the survival and continuation of the colonial system in spite of formal recognition of political independence" (30) in Nigeria has ensured the continuous transfer of oil wealth from the Niger Delta to both the imperial circles of the West and the complicit local circles in ethnic drapes. This gives credence to Saro-Wiwa's avowal: "Any nation which can do to the weak and disadvantaged what the Nigerian nation has done to the Ogoni," and to the Niger Delta in general, "loses a claim to independence and to freedom from outside influence" ("Testimonial" 44).

In this neocolonial system, all is fair as long as the local circles are able to deploy petroleum security to the service of powerful personal agenda, ethnic agenda, class agenda, and transnational agenda, all linked by a connective of profiteering by the pain of oil-bearing communities. This is the scheme of what Saro-Wiwa has called the "slick alliance" (Watts 37).

The slick alliance depends on colonialism's ability to adapt to times, undergo mutations, replicate itself in diverse forms and places, take on local colour, and recruit agents/foot soldiers even amongst its victims. The slick alliance has accomplices in the Niger Delta who, like Chief Dore Numa in the age of palm oil, help in the subjugation and dispossession of the long-suffering peoples. The imprints of the Dore Numa type can be found in the account books of the defunct Oil Mineral Producing Areas Development Commission (OMPADEC), the Niger Delta Development Commission (NDDC), local government councils, state governments, and so on. This is a recurrent index of the Niger Delta situation. It is one out of the many indices that show that resource-related conflict in the Niger Delta is truly the doom of repetition.

The gravity of this repetitive doom has caught the attention of scholars from diverse fields of activity – politics, economics, sociology, environmental studies, and literature, to name but a few. The boundaries of analyses are always fluid because of the interdisciplinarity of oil and its related conflicts in the Niger Delta. It is usual to see perspectives that are political, economical, sociological, and environmental woven – as provoked by the situation in the Niger Delta – into the matrix of literature. Nigerian writing has been able to represent the problems of the Niger Delta through the sense of commitment and the tropes of craft.

Works cited

Achebe, Chinua. *The Trouble with Nigeria*. Enugu: Fourth Dimension, 1983.

Agary, Kaine. *Yellow-Yellow*. Lagos: Dtalkshop, 2006.

Amadi, Elechi. *Sunset in Biafra*. London: Heinemann, 1973.

Barry, Peter. *Beginning Theory: An Introduction to Literary and Cultural Theory*. Manchester: Manchester UP, 2002.

Boro, Isaac Jasper Adaka. *The Twelve-Day Revolution*. Ed. Tony Tebekaemi. Benin City: Idodo Umeh, 1982.

Boyd, William. Introduction. *A Month and a Day: A Detention Diary*. By Ken Saro-Wiwa, Channel Islands: Safari Books, 1995. vii–xv.

Fanon, Frantz. *The Wretched of the Earth*. Middlesex: Penguin, 1967.

Hoogvelt, Ankie. *Globalisation and the Postcolonial World: The New Political Economy of Development*. 2nd ed. Maryland: The Johns Hopkins UP, 2001.

Ibrahim, Jibrin. "Enahoro, Federalism and Nigerian Nation(s)". *Next on Sunday*. 19 Dec. 2010. 2.103. 14.

Ikime, Obaro. *History, the Historian and the Nation: The Voice of a Nigerian Historian*. Ibadan: HEBN, 2006.

Niger Delta Congress. "Niger Delta Congress Manifesto for the Federal Election of 12 December 1959". Appendix IV. *Harold Dappa-Biriye: His Contribution to Politics in Nigeria*. By Ambily Etekpe et al. Port Harcourt: Onyoma, 2004. 195–226.

Okonta, Ike and Oronto Douglas. *Where Vultures Feast: Shell, Human Rights and Oil in the Niger Delta*. San Francisco: Sierra Club Books, 2001.

Omotoso, Kole. *Achebe or Soyinka: A Study in Contrasts*. Ibadan: Bookcraft, 2009.

Omoweh, Daniel A. *Shell Petroleum Development Company, the State and Underdevelopment of Nigeria's Niger Delta: A Study in Environmental Degradation*. Trenton, NJ: African World Press, 2005.

Peel, Michael. *A Swamp Full of Dollars: Pipelines and Paramilitaries at Nigeria's Oil Frontier*. London: IB Tauris & Co., 2009.

Saro-Wiwa, Ken. *A Month and a Day: A Detention Diary*. Channel Islands: Safari Books, 1995.

Saro-Wiwa, Ken. *On a Darkling Plain: An Account of the Nigerian Civil War*. Port Harcourt: Saros, 1989.

Saro-Wiwa, Ken. "The Testimonial, the Foresight". *If I Live to Tell the Tale*. 10 Nov. 2005: 44.

Soyinka, Wole. *You Must Set Forth at Dawn*. Hardback Edition. Ibadan: Bookcraft, 2008.

Tebekaemi, Tony. Foreword. *The Twelve-Day Revolution*. By Isaac Jasper Adaka Boro, Ed. Tony Tebekaemi. Benin City: Idodo Umeh, 1982. 5–6.

Ukiwo, Ukoha. "Empire of Commodities." *Curse of the Black Gold: 50 Years of Oil in the Niger Delta*. Ed. Michael Watts. New York: PowerHouse Books, 2008. 71–73.

Watts, Michael, ed. *Curse of the Black Gold: 50 Years of Oil in the Niger Delta*. New York: PowerHouse Books, 2008.

Yergin, David. *The Prize: The Epic Quest for Oil, Money and Power*. 1991. New York: Free Press, 2009.

7

JOLA VERBAL ARTS OF CASAMANCE, SENEGAL, AND THE GAMBIA

A question in search of a literature

Tijan M. Sallah

Introduction

The Jola ("Diola" in French) peoples of the Casamance, Senegal, and The Gambia are among the most resistant to the forces of Westernization (and thereby Christianization) and Arabization (and thereby Islamization) in the Senegambian region. The Jola are the dominant ethnic group in the Casamance region of Senegal and the Fogni region of The Gambia. In both Senegal and The Gambia, the Jola are a marginalized people, with very little voice in the central government. Their entrenched immersion in African traditional religions and their resistance to Westernization and Arabization has tended to compound their isolation and marginalization, especially in the modern order where these two forces confer advantages in terms of a broadening of alliances. The only major symbol of Jola empowerment came with the military seizure of presidential power in July 1994 by Yahya Jammeh in The Gambia, who came from an ethnic minority, the Jola, and who sought to reinvent history by trying to alter the social order to privilege the Jola, with only transient success. This chapter will explore the verbal arts of the Jola, collections of which are scant, and whether there is a Jola literature and/or orature and how that links with the Jola culture of marginality.

This chapter thus looks into the following questions: Who are the Jola people of West Africa? How have past narratives, mostly colonial in nature, treated them? How do the Jola see themselves? Given the paucity of written material on them, especially in English, do the Jola have any tradition of literature or orature? And how has the political status of the Jola in The Gambia and Senegal reflected a position of marginality, which in turn is reflected in their narratives? For that, we will look at the poems of the Jola woman prophet, Aline Sitoe Jatta of Kabrousse, Casamance, and her verses of resistance against French colonialism.

Perspectives on the Jola: who are they?

The Jola ("Diola" in French) peoples of Casamance (Senegal), Fogni (The Gambia), and Guinea Bissau are among the least studied ethnic groups of Africa. The Jola today number about 1.1 million people and constitute about 5 percent of the population of Senegal (about 810,000); 11 percent of the population of The Gambia (about 224,700), and 2 percent of the population of Guinea Bissau (38,000). The Jola should not be confused with the "Dyula" or "Jula" peoples of West Africa, who are Mande-speaking peoples who engage in petty trading across West Africa. The Jola, on the other hand, are predominantly farmers, mostly swamp-land rice cultivators, and now also include peanut farmers. Although relatively small in number, the Jola are internally a diverse ethnic group, comprising about 16 mutually unintelligible dialects. These include *Jola Fogni* (or *Filham*), *Jola Kombo, Jola Casa, Jola Huluf, Jola Kuwataye, Jola Er* or *Her, Jola Esulalu, Jola Banjial, Jola Jiamat* or *Feloup, Jola Calequisse, Jola Hulon, Jola Fogni Buluf, Jola Blis, Jola Karon (Karoninka), Jola Bayot,* and *Jola Bainunka* (David Sapir, *Grammar,* xiv–xv; 1–2).

In colonial narratives, the ancestors of the Jolas are usually described as "Feloups" or "Flups" or "Banyons." Colonial narratives about the Jola have been uncongratulatory. In narrative after narrative, they view the Jola with tainted binoculars, with an implicit bias that is patently self congratulating, that involves measuring the Jola against their own externally imposed colonial metric. Their narratives represent attempts, perhaps unwittingly, to "put down" an entire people and not see and understand them within their own context. The colonial syllogism went like this: the British wear suits. Suits are marks of civilization. But the Jola wear only a piece of cloth to cover their private parts, so the Jola are a significant standard deviation from the British or French norm; hence, they must then be "uncivilized." This way of reasoning, of course, is problematic because the British and French live in countries where there is cold weather, but the Jola live in a generally hot climate. In narrative after narrative, colonial writers portray the Jola as a meagerly clothed, primitive people without kings or queens and without any system of hierarchic government. In fact, in many narratives, the Jola are described as "acephalous," as without a hierarchic leader or head. Francis Moore, in his *Travels Into the Inland Parts of Africa (1723)*, described the Jola (in this case, the Feloups) in condescending detail. He noted that the Jola did not have any institutions of centralized rule and were therefore difficult to pacify:

> On the South-side of this River (*i.e., River Gambia, italics mine*), over against James Fort, in the Empire of Fonia (*a reference to Fogni, italics mine*) and but a little Way inland, are a Sort of People called Floops, who are in a manner wild. They border close to the Mundigoes (*i.e., Mandingoes, italics mine*), and are bitter Enemies to each other. Their Country is of a vast Extent, but they have no King among them, each of their Towns being fortified with Sticks drove all round, and filled up with Clay. They are independent of each other, and under the Government of no one Chief, notwithstanding which, they unite fo firmly, that all the Force of the Mandingoes (tho' fo very numerous) cannot get the better of them.
>
> *(25)*

Francis Moore's colonial narrative is heavily influenced by the colonial agenda of *divide and rule.* The narrative is blatantly suspect, for why should the enmity between the Jola and Mandingo be of interest, except that it reflects the colonial propensity to find differences so that they can be exploited to sow division and gain advantage? Moore goes on further to give a psychological assessment of the Jola, describing them as practicing retributive justice but as compassionate if treated kindly. He noted, "These Floops have the Character never to forgive, or let the least Injury go unrevenged, but then, to make amends, the least good Office done them is always repaid by them with a grateful Acknowledgement" (*Travels,* 26).

Henry Fenwick Reeve, colonial governor of The Gambia from 1900–1911, in his book, *The Gambia: Its History, Ancient, Medieval and Modern*, also offers a non-flattering perspective of the Jola:

> The Flups . . . Those who inhabit the mouth of the river Zamanee (the Kazamansa) on the northside (the country towards the Gambia) are extremely savage, with whom no nation have any commerce. Everyone has his own god, according to his particular fancy; one worships a bullock's horn; another a beast, or a tree, to whom they sacrifice in their manner.
>
> (The Gambia, *190*)

The Jola are described here as "savage" and practicing various forms of animism. Reeves gives a further description of the Jola:

> Their dress is like the negroes of Cape de Verde and the inhabitants of the river Gambia, which consists in a piece of cloth, striped according to the custom of the country, which barely covers their privities. They have no succession of kings, the most absolute and powerful amongst them bearing sway. They cultivate their land in pretty good order, which they sow with millet and rice. Their riches consist of bullocks, cows and goats, of which many of them have great droves. Their villages are well peopled, distant from each other about a quarter of a league.
>
> *(190)*

Here again, we learn from Reeves' description that the Jola ran primitive, independent, populous, and acephalous communities that were geographically dispersed, where the law of survival of the strongest prevailed. This was buttressed by the fact that the Jola were good farmers and self-sufficient, lived in harmony with their ecosystem, and had abundant natural wealth.

Reeves goes on to give a description of the physical and attitudinal characteristics of the Jola in lurid, if not graphic, condescending detail:

> The Felupp negroes, who occupy . . . on the banks of the Cazamance, and on the upper part of the river Vintam, retain all the rudeness of savage life, in which they delight to live and remain, without, however, being of a ferocious character. The country they inhabit is well covered, and fertile: they rear cattle, which they defend with great courage against lions, leopards and bears, which are common in their forests.
>
> The Felupps go almost naked; they wear only a little apron passed between the thighs . . .; they bind the upper arms, wrists, upper parts of thighs, above the knees, and the upper and lower parts of the legs, with leather laces, so that the intervals between the parts of their limbs thus bound are much larger than in the natural state.
>
> They cicatrise their face and body, and engrave on them all sorts of irregular and ludicrous figures.
>
> These negroes have very wooly and curled hair, but longer that of negroes in general. They collect it on top of their head, and over their forehead, where they form it into a sort of queue, or aigrette, which stands erect to the height of five or six inches; they let their beard grow, which they collect and tie, so that it forms a point projecting several inches from the chin.
>
> They cover themselves with Gri-gris (charms); their colour is deep black; their skin is rough, their features tolerably regular, and resemble those of the blacks of India rather than that of the negroes.

The Felupps are small and chubby, but strong and active; their physiognomy is downcast, and they are reserved. They have but little communication with their neighbors, and they are very jealous of their women, who nevertheless are not pretty.

Their arms were bows and poisoned arrows, with four or five lances held in the same hand as the bow, while their arrows were swung in two quivers over their back, one at each shoulder, by which one would conclude they were ambidextrous.

. . . Although, they are savage, melancholy, and not very communicative, their neighbors do not complain of them, and the Felupps pass for good people; they are, however, warlike, and when offended, they avenge themselves with ferocity.

It would be curious to inquire into the origin of this horde, whose characteristic features, forms, manners and customs differ considerably from those of the nations by which they are surrounded.

(191–192)

The direct descendants of the Floops of former chroniclers still exist in a nation called by us the Jolahs, the Banyons, a branch of the Floops occupying Combo.

(191–193)

Reeves' reference to "CaZamance" is today's "Casamance," and "Vintam" is today's "Bintang Creek" – a tributary of the River Gambia. Although Reeves' description is tinged with colonial condescension, it opens us to aspects of the Jola past which have been carried into the present: that the Jola are hardworking, agricultural peoples who practice traditional African religions; who are peaceful until offended (after which they can be ferocious fighters); who are reserved, not garrulous and therefore guardedly secretive; who in the past carried body tattoos or skin scarring and had hairdos resembling the African American TV character Mr. T; who are jealously protective of their women; and who seem to live apart from their other ethnic neighbors.

Fenwick Reeves, in a later description of the Jola, notes:

the Banyons still exist in small communities, and are mostly employed in the collection of palm oil, palm wine, and kernels, with other forest products. The Jolahs, however, are still a distinct people occupying the same territory as in the time of the Portuguese, still known as Fogni. They are comparatively short in stature, plump and well formed, with pleasant dreamy faces, round heads, with the tuft of hair like a Red Indian's scalp lock still in evidence. They still despise clothing to a degree, even in the streets of Bathurst (*i.e., colonial name for Banjul, Gambia's capital, italics mine*), and wear ligatures round their limbs and bodies.

(193)

These colonial narratives are self-servingly amusing, if not self aggrandizing; they reflected the asymmetric power of the colonial monologue in their encounter with the "native" other; they reflect a problematic imperial pattern – that only the bowler-hatted colonial intruder "knows" and "speaks," but the "native" has to be silent. The self-apprehension of the "native" is never factored into the narrative. To get a balanced and contrasting perspective, however, it is important to explore in the next section how the Jola see themselves, to ask the question – Do the Jola have any literature or orature? One needs to also ask: How do their self-apprehension and narratives relate to their own marginality?

Although it is difficult to point to any distinct text that represents the existence of a Jola literature, the Jola do have a rich orature (the vast majority of which is not yet recorded) which characterizes and enriches Jola life and attitude to the world. It is important to place this orature within the broader self-affirming narratives of how the Jola see themselves – outside of the condescending, biased gaze, the intermittent cultural voyeurism, of the colonial intruder. It is important to note that Jola life is defined by work and leisure in the form of rituals and ceremonies which characterize different rites of passage.

Jola life and the Jola cultural self-apprehension

Every Jola belongs to an extended family household that lives in a compound known as *"fank."* The *fank*, by the principle of subsidiarity, is the lowest level of decision-making in Jola society, headed by the father. The Jola are patriarchal (Momodou Kolley, *Personal Interview*, January 2019).

Jola life is defined by birth, circumcision, marriage, religion, and death. The Jola do not celebrate birthdays as a significant ceremony. When a baby is born, on the eighth day, a naming ceremony is held which is called *"kuliye"* (which resembles the Mandinka word of *"kuliyoo"* – used for a naming ceremony in which there is cutting of the baby's hair). Every member of the community shares in the joy of the new arrival. (It is possible that this ceremony is borrowed from the Mandinka – as the Jola have had a long history of interactions with the Mandinka, in which the Mandinka tried to subjugate and convert them to Islam but often met with fierce resistance. They have fought interethnic wars and made peace and sometimes even intermarried.) If the family has means, they may slaughter a ruminant, such as a bull, sheep, or goat, or even another animal such as a pig or chicken (depending on the means of a family) may be killed and its meat cooked to entertain guests at the naming celebration. If, however, a family is totally without means, they may hold a "small" naming ceremony but will call it a *"nyambuwe,"* which should lower the expectations of guests, implying that the event will be a very modest one. (*Personal Interview*)

Another important rite of passage that a Jola boy or young man goes through is known as *"futampaf."* A *futampaf* is held every 15 to 30 years for young men and it is a ceremony in which young men are taken to the bush for two weeks and taught lessons about what it means to be responsible men. Young men are taught about how to handle themselves well in society and the role of an adult. Usually, the oldest men speak and share wisdom about life based on events, issues, and/or disputes that have risen in the past and how they were resolved by their forefathers. At the *futampaf*, there is a reliance on learning from precedence and age-old practices.

In a *futampaf*, all the Jolas in the various communities are invited. Uncles and aunts of the young men going through the *futampaf* are also invited and given special accommodation and treatment. For every young man participating, a bull is slaughtered and the meat cooked to entertain the guests during the festivities. A bull is also killed for every uncle and aunt participating. This makes the *futampaf* a very expensive ceremony, and families participating have to plan and save resources for it in advance. (*Personal Interview*)

An important ceremony for women is *"ebunee,"* which is a retreat held annually or biannually to work on a particular topic (*waaf*). A woman is chosen to be in charge of a project and to provide progress report and feedback. Jola women from far and near attend the retreat, which usually lasts from one to two weeks, and there are discussions on various self-help activities and enterprises, and there are also festivities of song and dance. In an *ebunee*, the women gathered also choose one woman as "queen," but this queen is only ceremonial and has no royal powers. The queen chosen is only for recognition and reigns for only one or two years until the next *ebunee*. (*Personal Interview*)

The Jola are very insular in their marriage choices – a Jola should marry only a Jola once young men and women reach puberty or marriage age. Men can marry their nieces and women their nephews. This is done to strengthen ethnic cultural ties and to ensure that differences during marriage can be easily mediated. As a result, Jolas have very few divorces. Marriage choices are usually made by the father of the suitor. Jolas do not allow dating. Generally, young men follow their father's wishes and pose few challenges to their father's authority. For the young women, virginity is a premium. The Jola guard virginity seriously. A promiscuous young woman is deemed to bring shame to her family. (*Personal Interview*)

When a marriage is proposed, usually the dad of the suitor gives a bull or cow as bride price, as well as other livestock to be used to buy special dress for the bride's mother, father, and brothers. When the marriage takes place, all the elders in the village gather to pray for the newly married couple. The young men in the village are advised to stay away from the newly married woman, since she has a husband now. (*Personal Interview*)

The Jola traditionally practice polygamy. Marriage is based on socioeconomic status, and so the larger the farms and livestock men possess, the more they are inclined to marry more wives to bear them children to help them with farm labor. In earlier days, when there was little mechanized farming, having more family labor was particularly handy. With a large family, they are able to cultivate foodcrops such as rice, maize, millet, sorghum, and some peanuts, which they can sell to get money to buy manufactured goods and pay taxes. (*Personal Interview*)

The Jola celebrate with a wide range of masquerades and musical performances – one of the most popular masquerades being the "*ekumpai.*" The *ekumpai* is a masked dancer, usually dressed with dried palm leaves in the shape of a spruce with a sharp projectile protruding from its head. Usually, it will be accompanied by a crowd of drummers, dancers, and singers. The *ekumpai* would then dance by sticking its projectile into the earth and swirling its head and the rest of the body in a roundabout manner in a circle, like a leafy porcupine. The name "*ekumpa*" derives from "*kumpo,*" which literally means "one does not know who the individual is"; in short, it points to a rite of secrecy, a cryptic ritual. (*Personal Interview*)

The other Jola masquerade is the "*samai.*" The *samai* is a masked dancer that is dressed with discarded rice bags or gunny sacks. Like the *ekumpai*, the *samai* is accompanied by drummers, dancers, and singers. Another Jola masked dancer is the "*kankurang,*" which is dressed with the red bark of tree, head to knee, and barks are also tied into rings around the leg of the masked dancer. Usually, the *kankurang* will dance with a cutlass in one hand and stamp the feet on the ground in several fast repetitive motions, accompanied by a rhythmic drum, singers, and clappers. (*Personal Interview*)

One of the activities that accompanies festivities is communal street drumming called *bugaraab* or *bukarabu*. Usually, in a *bugaraab*, a skilled drummer (*ajaalao*) will play multiple drums, usually three, simultaneously. The drums will be made from hollowed-out tree trunks and animal skin and will be of different sizes so that they give different sounds. The bigger the trunk of the tree, the bigger the sound. In a *bugaraab*, the Jola community dances and makes merry for up to six hours non-stop. Through it, children run around and have fun, and elders – men and women – interact, dance, and make gestures, sometimes carrying freshly cut palm leaves or mango tree branches, daintily waving them toward the sky. (*Personal Interview*)

In addition to entertainment activities, the Jola also celebrate funerals as a sad chapter in a person's life. When a person dies, before the person is buried, an old person is brought from within the family to "talk to the dead person." In that conversation, the dead person is asked to tell them about what happened in the person's life to result in their death. Because the Jola believe in witchcraft, the conversation with the dead is believed to reveal whether the person died of natural causes or perished from the spell of a witch. (*Personal Interview*)

Before the dead person is buried, the Jola usually have a three-day ceremony. During that period, the dead body is embalmed with traditional herbs to prevent it from rotting and smelling. The body is then transported on a stretcher by six strong men to each home in the community to say goodbye. If there is a home the dead body does not want to enter, the spirit of the dead body will enter the six men carrying the stretcher, and they will be seen struggling, and the body carriers will then ignore that home. If it is a home that the dead body wants to go to, the body carriers will proceed smoothly to that home. After the processions and a three-day festival, the dead person is buried with some of their artifacts of greatest value, such as their gun, spear, arrows, and sword. (*Personal Interview*)

During funeral ceremony, there are special people or helpers called "*assempulao*" who are usually the niece or nephew of the dead person. The *assempulao* has a special place in Jola society, as they are given broad degrees of freedom to act. They do the domestic chores, mediate family matters, can slaughter chicken in the compound and cook them to entertain guests, and generally have broad latitude to act to entertain guests. They can be resourceful with any assets in the compound and use them as they wish to entertain guests without anyone complaining. (*Personal Interview*)

Jola life aside, do the Jola have a literature and/or orature? From the available evidence, there does not seem to exist any distinctive text that one can point to suggest that they have a literature; however, there is a rich existing orature. In terms of their orature, there are three strands of oral narratives that can be identified: (i) stories (singular, *kerigeg*; plural *uregawu*), (ii) poems/songs (*kechimak*), and (iii) proverbs (*mansali*). In storytelling, usually by older folk, children gather at their feet and the storyteller holds them spellbound with stories about animals and their hair-raising adventures. Various animals are identified with particular traits, such as cunning with rabbits/hares and greed with hyenas. Often the motif is to teach a moral, such as greed does not pay or lying can result in punishment. The children are then taught good principles about how to live well in society. The storyteller among the Jola is called "*arigawo*." The singer is called "*uchimao*." (*Personal Interview*)

A few examples of Jola stories (*uregawu*) are as follows. The first story is "The Hyena and the Rabbit." The story goes:

> A farmer working on his farm saw a rabbit and set a trap. He caught the rabbit alive and took it home. At his home, he tied the rabbit to a tree near his goat, and went out to work. A hyena came wanting to eat the goat and asked the rabbit, "Can we trade places?" The rabbit agreed. The hyena untied the rabbit, and the rabbit tied the hyena near the goat. The hyena ate the goat, but was unable to untie himself. When the farmer came, he found the hyena and was outraged at what he did. He killed the hyena.
>
> (Personal Interview)

The motif of the story is that excessive greed is bad for you. It could even kill you.

Another *kerigeg* (story) of the Jola, titled "Jealousy Does Not Pay," goes like this:

> There were two women married to one man and each had a son. One son was very successful. He had left the village and gone very far and worked to make something for himself. He came back to the village with bags full of money and plenty of goods. The mother of the other son saw this and was jealous. He saw that her son had stayed home and was playful. He had no focus and no direction. So one day, he ordered her son. "Don't bring disgrace to me. Please go as far as you can and do as well as your

step brother did!" The young man listened to his mother's orders and left without any plan or preparation. He ended up being killed at his new destination to the anguish of his distraught mother.

(*Personal Interview*)

The moral of this story is that whatever one does in life, one should plan and prepare for it. Following other's successes wildly could lead to one's own peril.

The second strand of Jola oratures are poems/songs (*kechimak*). Poems/songs are used for both sacred and secular rituals. To understand their use in the context of the sacred, it is important to note that Jola religion is decentralized into several spirit shrines and fetishes to which a family or families owe their devotion. Usually, the spirit shrine is a sacred grove in the bush where the family engages the mysteries of nature. In engagement with spirits, the Jola use poetry to implore the spirits to bring peace, rain, and natural prosperity to their farms. Perhaps one of the most engaging narratives about Jola religion is one presented by Robert M. Baum in his ritually rich book on the Jola woman prophet, Aline Sitoe Jatta (in French, Alinesitowe Diatta), titled *West Africa's Women of God* (2016). Aline Sitoe was born in 1920 in Kabrousse, Lower Casamance, and passed away on May 22, 1944, in Timbuktu, Mali (Simone Schwarz-Bart, *In Praise of Black Women*, 68–72). She was born as an orphan among the Esulalu Jolas and raised by her uncle, Elubaliin Jatta (*In Praise of Black*, 60). She was a symbol of Senegalese resistance against French colonial authority, which resulted in her exile to Timbuktu, Mali. Her short but truly consequential life earned her the heroic sobriquet the Senegalese Jola Joan of Arc (*West Africa's Women*, 2).

In her youth, Aline Sitoe left her village of Kabrousse for the French seat of "white power" in Ziguinchor, Senegal. When she discovered Ziguinchor as only a marginal colonial outpost, she proceeded to the real seat of colonial power in Dakar and was exposed to several unfamiliar landscapes along the way (*In Praise of Black*, 60). In Dakar, she dwelled in the Medina (the squatter settlements by migrants from all over Senegal) that had developed outside the white seat of power (*In Praise of Black*, 62). Although illiterate, she experienced in Dakar the humiliations and frustrations suffered by the natives under colonialism. Her experiences magnified her boldness to join the resistance and seek redress (*In Praise of Black*, 63). Dakar, in short, proved to be a source of education to Aline Sitoe about what was wrong with colonialism.

When Alinsitowe returned to her home region of Casamance, she had a revelation, a calling from the ancestors. Schwarz-Bart (64) noted:

> On her way home, approaching Cassamance, she heard a vague call and hurried her step. Once in Kabrousse, her mouth suddenly opened to speak with the voices of the ancestors, the *Boekin*, who spoke through her the truth about humanity's problems and the world's problems, but then began to speak about the problems of the Diola people./These words healed the sick and desperate; these words told the future. Day and night, coming from all corners of Cassamance, people flocked to her to witness this miracle. Already her reputation was growing and crossing borders. People came to see her from Kaolack, Saint Louis, Guinea Bissau, and even from far off Mauretania. They may have sought healing from an obsolete illness or from an ill spirit possessing the body. Above all, they wanted to hear from the very mouth of the prophet the words that foretold the future.

Aline Sitoe Jatta became a Jola "prophet" whose fame spread far and wide in the immediate West Africa region. Her shrine of "*Houssahara*" became a popular site of pilgrimage to the

Jola supreme deity, "*Emitai*." Although the Jolas have an enduring tradition of "prophets" or "messengers of God" – for which they use the epithet "*Emitai dabognol*" – prophetic tradition used to be confined only to men (*West Africa's Women*, 1–5). After colonialism, this shifted to mostly women, and Aline Sitoe became a pioneer in that regard among the esulalu Jolas. Her teachings about Jola religion (the "*Awasena path*") involved instructions from *Emitai* and the rituals that needed to be performed to placate the desires of the deities and appease the supreme deity. The rituals often involved sacrifice of a black bull, some pigs, and chickens, which the entire community ate together over several days, accompanied by songs or poems honoring the ancestors. The prophetic tradition continued as other women followed Aline Sitoe's steps by developing privileged communication with the supreme deity and engaging in the "*kasila*" ritual, a community ritual seeking rain from the supreme deity (*West Africa's Women*, 1–2).

When the French, in 1937, prohibited the Jola from cultivation of upland rice (a drought-resilient food crop) in the Lower Casamance region and instead promoted its replacement with peanuts (a cash crop), Aline Sitoe challenged the French and encouraged the Jola to continue to grow rice, the staple. Besides, she saw in French policy a pernicious motivation, which was purely to serve their industrial interests while simultaneously ignoring the immediate food security and welfare needs of the Jola community. Although Aline Sitoe was aware of the metropolitan power of the French against the Jola's marginal situation, she was also conscious of the power of populist resistance. She saw in peanut cultivation destructive tendencies which degraded forests and also led to the loss of biodiversity, such as of important sources of palm products and wild fruits, herbal medicine, and game (*West Africa's Women*, 145). A poem (*West Africa's Women*, 144) by a significant Jola priest of Ehugna captures this local dilemma:

> The young Balibah (*a title for Alinesitoe*)
> The young Balibah and her child.
> *Ohoway, Ohoway.*
> Who is looking for upland rice.
> Young Balibah, who gave us our rice

The poem or song is simple but it captures the vigor of Aline Sitoe and her advocacy of the Jola's survival interest in growing rice.

The populist, spiritual power of Aline Sitoe grew, as large numbers of Jola pilgrims came to Kabrousse to hear her teachings and carry back to their places of origin the charity and rites of *Kasila*. Alinsitowe greeted them and provided them with accommodation and fed the pilgrims with the meat from past sacrifices for almost a week. They would eat all the meat outside, for it was forbidden to bring the sacrificed meat inside. Aline Sitoe would take various gifts brought by pilgrims – baskets of rice and fruit as well as black chickens and black bulls and palmwine – and perform the *huasene* at her shrine in Houssahara, asking *Emitai* to provide them with help (*West Africa's Women*, 146–147), and it appeared *Emitai* would answer her prayers in the form of rainfall for their farms and cures of various ailments. Her prayers for the pilgrims were followed by the ritual of the *Nyakul* and the *djigum*, which were dances for the women's fertility shrine (*West Africa's Women*, 147). Usually, when they did the *Kasila* ritual and had the communal meals, the gathering would perform a dance and sing the songs of Aline Sitoe until late at night. The song or poem (*West Africa's Women*, 147) goes:

> Kasila ho!
> Ata-Emit ho!

We are tired.
Emitai will send rain.

After the pilgrimage, the Jola pilgrims carried cows' horns stuffed with the sacred soil from Aline Sitoe's shrine, which they carried home to start their own shrines (*West Africa's Women*, 147)

In addition to being a "prophet," Aline Sitoe was a social change agent and a poet. She challenged hierarchy and advocated egalitarian ideals across gender and age (*West Africa's Women*, 166). In a poignantly resonant poem, which illustrates her struggle for social justice against the domineering forces of the French, she proclaimed an egalitarian spirituality:

All the women of the family have said
That an idiot has taken charge of the fetish
There it is, very happy
All of a sudden, we hear the thunder high in the sky.
We are all in a great hurry to take our canoe.
The French are approaching.
There it is that the rice is thrown all over the place
There is the bird that flew high up between the clouds and the sky.
Oh! God! Pardon us.
Give us water, thanks to our "charity"
Because the French have plunged us
into famine.

The village republican spirit of the religion of Aline Sitoe is reflected in the lines that "an idiot has taken charge of the fetish." The fetish did not need "priests" – but even a member of the "laity" – even an "idiot," an ordinary person, can perform the ritual. Baum (166) describes it well that, "Even an idiot can carry their prayers to Emitai, and Emitai will respond with life-giving rain."

Another poem by Aline Sitoe postulates the revolutionary resistance of the Jola "natives" against the coercive machinations of the French empire (*West Africa's Women*, 170). As peanut farming spread, Aline Sitoe saw this as a trap that the French had set for her people which would destroy Jola lives and make them dependent on the colonial economy. She saw peanut farming, according to Father Diamacoune Senghor, as the "farming of people who are not free" (*West Africa's Women*,168). In a sense, Aline Sitoe's own poetry was beginning to reflect her struggles between the colonial intrusion and reordering of local priorities and the native resistance to such agenda setting. Her poem (*West Africa's Women*, 170) captures these sentiments:

I am very happy to show how you must take it,
To cut the neck of a steer
Because I regret to see the Europeans kill people with their long rifles.
A day will come when God will inflict a harsh punishment upon Them.
Because that which they do is not good
And God does not like evil-doers.

During the Second World War years, the Vichy Administration of the French intensified their imperial efforts in the Esulalu and throughout the Casamance region. The Jola experienced a social crisis characterized by proselytization to join the Catholic Church, as well as "taxation, conscription, . . . and drought" (*West Africa's Women*, 171). The French intensified efforts not only to conquer the minds and the territorial space of the Jola but also to win their hearts to Catholicism. As a result, Jola society was divided – between those that staunchly defended the old religion of *awassena* and those who aligned with French Catholic belief. Aline Sitoe, a devout advocate of the old religion, was seen as a threat to French interests, so she was arrested on November 11, 1942 (*In Praise of Black*, 70). The administrator of Casamance at the time was Commander Sajous, who was based in Zinguinchor and commanded the Jolas to hand over their rice reserves as a contribution to the war effort. Aline Sitoe resisted and publicly recited the following song/poem (*In Praise of Black*, 70):

> Here comes the French
> Watch out, get ready, watch out
> Diolas, get out your rifles
> Do as the whites do
> What did we ever do to them?
> Why do they treat us this way?

Asking very legitimate questions in her poem, this, however, did not win sympathies for her cause among the colonial administrators, who were unprepared to grant horizontal relations and dialogue with the "native." The Vichy regime was heavy-handed and rapacious, and their local tentacles, in the form of Commander Sajous, fetched Aline Sitoe immediate arrest. During her arrest, she was injured and taken for confinement at a camp in the Kayes region in Eastern Senegal and condemned to ten years in jail (*In Praise of Black*, 71). The charge against her was that she "led the population into systematic disobedience, and was at the origin of the Diola revolt" (*In Praise of Black*, 71). Later, however, the French recognized that by keeping her in confinement near Casamance, this was a bad idea, for if nothing else, it amplified her heroism. Therefore, they secretly exiled her to Timbuktu, Mali, where she was socially cut off from contact with her community and followers. She tragically died there in prison on May 22, 1944, at the young age of 24 (*In Praise of Black*, 71–72).

The third strand of Jola orature are proverbs (*mansali*). Proverbs among the Jola are like language lubricants, speech-appetizers, or speech-slime that facilitate or invigorate speech and storytelling. In fact, many Jola songs and poems are a piecing together of proverbs into a grand tapestry, like the interweaving of grass in a thatched hut. Among the Jola, the proverb can be used to praise, remember, educate, or insult. J. David Sapir captured some funeral verses (*bunansanab*) in a song that was performed by Anara Suleman Jeme of Jila Kunda at the funeral of Jaan Badjie obtained in 1965 from the town of Jirem in Casamance, Senegal. The verses were provided by Sapir's informant, Kalilu Badjie (Sapir website). A few subsequent proverbs from Anara Jeme's *bunansan*, all obtained in Sapir's website, will suffice as illustrations.

One of the proverbial lines in the *bunansan* was, "*Abili binab busibsab jiwu kabasa, ban le bo mukuluje*" translating as "Abili, the corpse is questioned and changes to a mat. And then there are no bad words." Since, as noted earlier, in Jola tradition, when a person dies, the corpse is questioned for cause of death, the good humor in this proverbial verse is that this dead person becomes "welcoming", that is, "changes to a mat," and so what follows then is only "good words," or "a eulogy." A second Jola proverb goes, "*Batan buloe nawunen bo*," or "Bullets fall, and he turns and farts" or "Bullets fall and he shows his ass (as if to fart); i.e., defies the bullet." This proverb has a dual meaning, suggesting either courage or timidity. When bullets are fired and a person turns and farts, it can either be interpreted that the person is courageous and makes mockery of the act by "farting" or that the person is timid and the experience is so frightening that they lose all sense of control to the extent of "farting." A third Jola proverb goes, "*Busanay bati Abantan o kone, inayool api manaiko mapinco banomer*," or "They say that his mother always put him in danger, for prettiness is bought with a heifer." This criticizes the custom of the "bride price for women" in which the "value" of a bride is reduced to a "bride price," when in fact other considerations should matter more both to the bride and the suitor, such as compatibility, shared values and beliefs, and shared goals in life. A fourth Jola proverb goes, "*Ajaneni nen kawonk ebeoo*," or "He is as known as his cow's call." This conflates the "owner" with his "mobile property" and suggests perhaps the popularity and familiarity of a person. A fifth Jola proverb goes, "*Bukoji bunuli ujuk nen jisond*," or "Ugliness is woven when you see a thatched roof" or "Observe a thatched roof and see how ugliness is woven." This is a complex proverb and perhaps points to the intricacies of "ugliness" when one peels its tangled branches and leaves. A sixth Jola proverb, provided by Momodou Kolley, is that, "A dog surveys its environment first before lying down," which suggests that people should not be careless about the safety of their environment. Considering the three different strands of orature discussed previously, the Jola do have a rich and untapped body of orature that perhaps needs more investigation and recording.

Marginality and the scramble to the center

Reflecting on the issue of "marginality," how does the Jola's peripheral position in Senegalese and Gambian society contribute to the relegation of their narratives to the margin and therefore to their own marginality? It could be argued that the Jola have been latecomers to accepting Christianity and Islam and have therefore been disadvantaged in getting the privileges conferred by reading and writing in European languages and Arabic, which has given other Senegambian ethnic groups a global advantage in being part of a larger world co-fraternity. The empires and states built by the Arabic and Western intrusion tended to confer privileges to those local agents who have assimilated or adapted to the missionaries' languages, technical skills, and values of those power intrusions.

This adverse dynamic on the Jola has, however, been increasingly changing in the past fifty years, as more Jola became Moslem or Christian and sent their children to Moslem and Western schools. Successes, particularly in Western schools, have made the Jola successful professionals and in some cases helped them contest political power at the central governments of The Gambia and Senegal. In recent years, there has been a Jola president, Jola ministers, Jola doctors, engineers, and other professionals. The association of "Jola" with the work of "housemaids" in the households of other ethnic groups (to the extent that the word "Jola" became an epithet for "housemaid") is drastically and justifiably disappearing. This is all for the good. There is little reason to justify the subjugation of an entire ethnic group simply because they initially preferred keeping their traditions and were resistant to modernizing forces.

Already in agriculture, the Jola as an ethnic group contribute a lot to the Senegalese and Gambian economy. They are also already contributing and will contribute more to other areas of Senegambian society. One of Senegal's most famous architects, Pierre Goudiaby Atepa, is a Jola, who was born in Baila, Casamance, and studied engineering at Rensselaer Polytechnic Institute. He is credited with designing major architectural marvels, such as the African Renaissance Monument in Dakar; the Central Bank of West African States headquarters; the Yundum National Airport of the Gambia; the ECOWAS Head office in Lome, Togo; Place de La Nation in Chad; and many of the African continent's most significant architectural landmarks (Nduka Waweru, "*Meet Pierre Atepa Goudiaby*").

Another significant Jola personality of world repute – though in this case adverse – is The Gambia's former president, Yahya Jemus Junkung Jammeh. Jammeh was born in Kanilai in 1965 in the Fogny region in the Gambia of a career wrestler father and trader mother. He joined the army after completing high school, had a year's military training at Fort McClellan in the US, and was at the rank of sergeant when he carried out a military coup against the democratic government of Sir Dawda Kairaba Jawara on July 22, 1994. In his initial years, Jammeh became the Chairman of the Armed Forces Provisional Ruling Council (AFPRC), broke relations with mainland China, and aligned the country with and received money from Taiwan and used this and other resources to pursue a number of ambitious infrastructure projects to gain public credibility (built the national airport, started the first university, built a monument in the form of an arch as one enters Banjul – the capital city – and expanded the road network and hospitals significantly). However, these positive initial moves were short lived and overshadowed by his negatives as he outmaneuvered and removed his other four junior army coup co-conspirators, eliminated political opponents, undermined inherited political institutions, muzzled the political opposition, persecuted the press, and perpetuated a regime of terror and fear. He carried out elections amidst a paralyzed opposition and crowned himself president in successive national elections and perpetuated a culture of patronage and a personality cult throughout the country, with large pictures of himself posted on billboards in main thoroughfares and even in non-public buildings. He also had antics of claiming he could cure HIV-AIDS and performing therapies on patients (when the international scientific consensus had not found a cure yet) and of giving anti-colonial and anti-imperialist rants. Most damaging to the country, he became rapaciously corrupt, seizing local properties and appropriating some for himself and plundering the country's resources to acquire a vast wealth alleged to be over $1 billion, with properties in the Middle East, North Africa, the US, Europe and elsewhere (Stuart A. Reid, "The Dictators Who Love America," *The Atlantic*; Lamin Jahateh, "Recovery of Jammeh's Stolen Assets Would Take Years," *The Point*, July 14, 2017; Saine, *The Paradox*).

During his rule, Jammeh tried to change The Gambia's social and cultural order by privileging the Jola with key political appointments and key positions in business. This perhaps may have been justified as restitution for historical disadvantages suffered by the Jola. He hosted an annual International Roots Festival in his hometown of Kanilai, cleverly exploiting the celebration of the African American author, Alex Haley's, genealogical trace of his Gambian "Roots" and used that global platform to feature Jola musical and dance arts and the *futampaf* ceremony prominently. The attempt to popularize the *futampaf* and other Jola celebratory rituals reflected how culture can be reinvented and reordered when political power rests in the hands of marginalized ethnic groups.

Conclusion

This chapter has explored the question of whether the Jola have a literature and/or orature and concluded that, on the basis of the available evidence, one could not point to any example of a corpus of literature, but one could point, undoubtedly, to a rich and widely undocumented orature, which needs further exploration and recording. This chapter explored those oral "literary" forms and provided examples, including the poetry of that hero of Jola resistance against French colonialism, the prophet Aline Sitoe Jatta of Kabrousse, Casamance. We have also explored in this chapter colonial derogatory perceptions of the Jola, using their own externally imposed biased metric, and juxtaposed that with the Jola's own affirmative self-apprehension. We have argued that the Jola position of marginality in the modern order in The Gambia and Senegal was linked to their resistance to Westernization and Arabization and their strong loyalty to their indigenous culture. This situation is, however, changing, as more Jola acquire Western Christian and Arabo-Islamic schooling and values and reap the benefits of modernity conferred by those encounters. We discussed two famous Jola personalities in the modern era who have reaped these benefits of modernity, Pierre Goudiaby Atepa, a continentally acclaimed architect from Senegal, and Yahya Jammeh, The Gambia's former authoritarian president.

References

Baum, Robert M., *West Africa's Women of God*, Bloomington and Indianapolis: Indiana University Press, 2016.

Jahateh, Lamin, "Recovery of Jammeh's 'Stolen Assets' Would Take Years," *The Point, Banjul*, July 14, 2017.

Kolley, Momodou, *Personal Interview by Phone on the Jola*, January 2019.

Moore, Francis, *Travels into the Inland Parts of Africa*, London: Printed by Henry and R. Cave, 1730.

Reeve, Henry Fenwick, *The Gambia: Its History, Ancient, Medieval and Modern*, New York: Negro Universities Press, 1969.

Reid, Stuart A., "The Dictators Who Love America," *The Atlantic*, February 8, 2016.

Saine, Abdoulaye, *The Paradox of Third-Wave Democratization in Africa*, Lanham, MD: Lexington Books, 2009.

Sapir, J. David, *A Grammar of Diola-Fogny*, Cambridge: Cambridge University Press, 1965.

Sapir, J. David, University of Virginia, College of Arts and Sciences, Department of Anthropology, J. David Sapir, Professor Emeritus, Professional Website, *Kujamaat Language and Folklore Materials*.

Schwarz-Bart, Simone, *In Praise of Black Women*, Madison: The University of Wisconsin Press, 2003.

Waweru, Nduta, "Meet Pierre Atepa Goudiaby, the Senegalese Architect Behind the Most Prolific Landmarks in Africa," *Face2Face Africa*, September 3, 2018 (Internet).

PART III

Culture and language

8

NEGATING HEGEMONY

Linguistic and rhetorical formations as discursive praxis of resistance in Yulisa Amadu Maddy's *Obasai and Other Plays*

Ernest Cole

Theoretical construct

Abdul JanMohamed and David Lloyd's *The Nature and Context of Minority Discourse* provides the theoretical foundations for this chapter. In this book, they assert that intellectuals involved in ethnic and feminist studies have enabled fresh examinations of a variety of minority voices. Through this process, they suggest that minority discourse studies strive to establish relations between nonhegemonic cultures and communities in academic as well as other spheres and that it is tasked with describing and defining the common denominators that link various minority cultures. The two editors further note that "cultures designated as minorities have certain shared experiences by virtue of their similar antagonistic relationship to the dominant culture, which seeks to marginalize them all" (1). From this recognition of hegemony and marginalization, they stress that writers, critics, and scholars of minority studies should strive to "collectively examine the nature and context of their common marginalization and to develop strategies for their reempowerment" (2).

In the corpus of Sierra Leone literature, Pat Amadu Maddy (later Yulisa Amadu Maddy) is one such writer who employs linguistic and rhetorical constructs as discursive praxis of resistance to Western hegemony. Maddy uses local languages to break free from reinforcing Western intellectual and political hegemony by creating a Sierra Leonean linguistic form of expression that borders on transliteration, hybridization, or creolization of the English language. Maddy adopts these linguistic tools as praxis to deconstruct hegemony in the use of standard English and to foreground the vernacular as cultural and communicative medium that initiates resistance to the domination of minority culture in Sierra Leone.

Obasai and Other Plays reflects the attempt of the playwright to expose the destructive effects of Western humanistic ideologies as embodied in education and religion on traditional African societies and their values. Maddy creates religious characters in juxtaposition with local spiritual figures to show the "damage more or less systematically inflicted on cultures produced as minorities by the dominant culture" (4). As JanMohamed and Lloyd further contend in their Introduction, in time "with this material destruction, the cultural formations, languages, and diverse modes of identity of the "minoritized peoples" are irreversibly affected, if not eradicated, by the effects of their material deracination from the historically developed social and economic structures in terms of which alone they "made sense" (4). The contrast between the values of the Reverend JJT and the local spiritual figure, Daddy Jebu, as I later explore in this chapter, lends credence to the threat of destruction posed to both cultural values and psyche of society by the legacies of Western hegemonic discourse.

In my analysis of the character and role of the Reverend, I postulate that Maddy's scrutiny of the practice of Western religion in traditional society indicates one of the foremost tasks of minority discourse – displacing the legitimacy of marginalizing indigenous cultures. This act of resistance constitutes a praxis of Maddy as he challenges the role of the dominant culture in instituting "a single model of historical development within which other cultures can only be envisaged as underdeveloped, imperfect, child-like, or – when already deracinated by material domination – inauthentic, perverse, or criminal" (4–5). It is this regard that JanMohamed and Lloyd further express that "[a]ttending to minority cultural forms requires accordingly a double vigilance, both with respect to their availability for hegemonic recuperation and to their strategies of resistance" (5). For Maddy, this resistance involves the need to demonstrate the power and valor of traditional forms and possibilities of advancing their place in society as well as a recognition of the need to resist the ideology of inferiority with which they are defined by Western humanistic discourse.

Josaphat Kubayanda's essay "Minority Discourse and the African Collective: Some Examples from Latin American and Caribbean Literature" is also critical to my analysis of language as discursive praxis of resistance. In it, Kubayanda notes: "Language itself contains the world, and minority discourse borrows the language of the dominant world, which in its purely dominant form negates or diminishes the minority subject. What, then, does the minority literature do with such a dominant tongue?" (117). He suggests that one way of contesting and reformulating this capacity of the dominant language to diminish the subject is to "deterritorialize" its boundaries and re-appropriate it in the indigenous context in which it operates. Citing Caliban as the "supreme example in the Western literature of the minority subject crushed by the language of the majority," he further asserts the power of Caliban to save himself "through a counter-discourse which 'deterritorializes' the borrowed English tongue with curses" (117). In subsequent sections of this chapter, I analyze Maddy's re-appropriation of the English language by infusing it with Krio words and phrases, wise sayings and proverbs, and skillfully configuring it to obey the nuances and rhythms of the vernacular as strategy of re-empowerment of the minority culture.

From this premise, I develop a set of critical formations to analyze Maddy's plays. These include irony, sarcasm, paradox, substitution, creolization and hybridization of language, transliteration, deconstruction, negation, affirmation, linguistic encoding, contrast, and imagery and symbolism. I argue that Maddy uses these elements of language to condemn the stereotypes with which indigenous practices, languages, customs have been characterized by the dominant culture and to celebrate traditional values such as the "awujor" and divination ceremonies in *Obasai*. Maddy's praxis gestures to his theoretical positioning that clearly "involves a critical-discursive articulation of alternative practices and values that are embedded in the often damaged, fragmentary, hampered, or occluded work of minorities" (8). In the words of JanMohamed and Lloyd, this positioning is necessary in asserting that "even the very differences that have always been assumptions of inadequacy can be reread transformatively as indications and figurations of values radically opposed to those of the dominant culture" (8).

Apart from his focus on linguistic and rhetorical forms as strategies of resistance, Maddy uses characterization to articulate alternative points of view and perceptions of societal values. I contend that creating characters that resist Western supremacy by challenging the efficacy and relevance of western hegemonic discourse constitutes perhaps Maddy's biggest contribution to minority discourse. As JanMohamed and Lloyd note, "[t]he most crucial aspect of resisting hegemony consists in struggling against its attempt to form one's subjectivity, for it is through the construction of the minority subject that the dominant culture can elicit the individual's own help in his/her oppression" (104). In *Obasai and Other Plays*, Maddy creates characters that resist stereotypical construction by the dominant culture by refusing to be defined by the decadent and reactionary societal norms. Their resistance constitutes a negation of hegemony, an assertion of the value of minority culture, and articulation of the voice of the subaltern.

Critical analysis

If I am alone in my choice, it is because I appreciate the values in the vices. That means that I am different. Like a Judas, I cheat and lie and perhaps will regret. For now, I create sensation for a static society. I am the unusual surprise; the once in a while abnegator who upsets societies, established order and systems. Yes, I dared to cross into the camps of the under-trodden dogs, the unprivileged. Here in this cell I grace their company by finding out how it feels to be within and yet without – to drift.

(Yulisa Maddy, *Allah Gbah*)

Language itself contains the world, and minority discourse borrows the language of the dominant world, which in its purely dominant form negates or diminishes the minority subject. What, then, does the minority literature do with such a dominant tongue?

(Josaphat Kubayanda, *The Nature and Context of Minority Discourse*)

The excerpts provide two platforms as entry points for exploring minority discourse: the marginalized in society and the possibility of language reformulation as praxis of resistance. In presenting a critical analysis of the process by which linguistic and rhetorical devices negate Western hegemony in indigenous drama from Sierra Leone, I structure my chapter into three sections: an introductory background on the development of indigenous drama, Maddy's characterization as index of marginalization, and his creolization of the English language as an act of resistance to the dominant culture in society.

For an understanding of Maddy's plays in the context of minority discourse, it is important to begin with a brief history of the growth and development of drama and the theater in Sierra Leone. Indigenous drama in its earliest forms could be traced to dramatic rites and rituals within cultural groups and traditional practices. These groups or secret societies, as they came to be known, celebrate certain rites of passage and initiation ceremonies via public performances. These performances are theatrical to the degree to which they dramatize certain aspects of traditional society.

Another significant influence in the development of drama in Sierra Leone is the establishment of the church and organizations within it. These organizations dramatize liturgical aspects of the Gospel for specific occasions such as the Nativity, Crucifixion, and Resurrection. However, the development of secular drama is entirely credited to the school system, where plays written by European writers form an integral part of the school curriculum. These plays were performed as part of school educational and public function.

The establishment of the British Council Dramatic Society in 1948 gave added impetus to drama, but, unfortunately, most of the plays performed were written in English, for an educated audience, and by European dramatists. The history of the theater in Sierra Leone reveals the domination of local plays by a preponderance of British drawing-room–style comedies. These plays constitute and reflect Western hegemony and cultural values that threaten to occlude or destroy traditional ones. Moreover, they provide the context within which society and its people were constructed; more often than not, as inferior and subservient to the dominant culture. The British-style plays provide the context for local playwrights to contest the superiority of Western culture and its representation of indigenous people and their values, as well as a reformulation of the minority culture and its empowerment.

However, it was not until 1962 that the society performed its first play written by an indigenous writer, Raymond Sarif Easmon, titled *Dear Parent and Ogre*. This play in many ways represents the beginnings of indigenous drama in Sierra Leone, but it also has a lot of room for improvement: it is written in English and is reminiscent of 18th-century British drawing-room comedies with its emphasis on affectation, rigid morality, and sterile codes of conduct.

Notwithstanding, the seeds of indigenous drama were sown, and so by 1952, the Brunswick Social and Cultural Circle produced two plays in Krio – *E yay de shine leke puss yay* and *Morenike de pan wahala*. It was in the late '60s and the beginning of the '70s that indigenous drama reached its apogee with the creation of dramatic groups that wrote and performed plays in the vernacular. These include Tabule Experimental Theatre (1968), Gbakanda Tiata Club (1968), Songhai Theatre (1973), and Balangi Dramatic Group (1974). Tabule Theatre performed plays like *Ofori comot na do*, *Ambas Geda*, and *The Blood of a Stranger*. Gbakanda Tiata Club produced plays like *Big Breese Blow*, *Gbana-Bendu*, *Big Berin*, and *Dar Pikin Dae*. Songhai Theatre performed plays including *Rayday Rahoon*, *Ibosio*, and *Poyo Tong Wahala*, while Balangi Dramatic Group produced plays such as *Ipocrit Modenloh*, *God pas consibul*, and *Mista Big Waite Fawl*. These are all comedies in Krio with strong social comments and criticisms.

Eustace Palmer contends that "[t]he tremendous transformation in the Sierra Leonean literary and cultural scene in the 1960s, 1970s, and 1980s was largely due to the rise of plays in the vernacular written by a group of young indigenous dramatists who wished to change not only the nature of the local theatre but also that of the theatre audience" (55). He cites the woks of playwrights like Dele Charley, John Kolosa Kargbo, Julius Spencer, Tonie French, and Mohamed Sheriff as representative of this phase of development in indigenous drama and asserts that "[m]ost of [Kargbo's] extremely well-crafted plays were written in the vernacular, Krio, and warmly received when staged in Freetown. They were popular because they addressed some of the fundamental ills that seemed to be endemic to Sierra Leone society" (56). Linguistic experimentation with language is crucial to the success of the plays and, as Palmer further notes of Kargbo, it "[d]emonstrat[es] that he could flawlessly deploy the resources of the English language to maximum effect and yet, like Achebe and Soyinka, introduce ingredients from the indigenous Mende language and thus create a genuine African environment" (57). In so doing, Kargbo's works avert to the use of language as context of minority discourse in indigenous drama in Sierra Leone.

Two major influences on the rise of indigenous theater in Sierra Leone are the negritude movement and the rise of pan-Africanism and nationalism. The plays are concerned with social commentary, the beauty of the African past and its culture and traditions, the clash of cultures between traditionalism and Westernization, exploitation of the working class by a corrupt elite, bribery, social prejudice, juvenile delinquency, and class distinction. Juliana John's *Na Mami born am*, Raymond De'Sousa George's *Apikrismes* and *Bobo Lef*, and Dele Charley's *Titi Shain Shain* are examples of such plays. Yulisa Maddy's *Obasai and Other Plays* expands upon and amplifies these themes earlier explored by these writers. His use of drama as a means of social commentary, his concerns for the downtrodden in society, and his abhorrence of religious hypocrisy, cultural discontent, post-independence disillusionment, and social stratification recall the early writers and illustrate a significant aspect of representation of minority culture.

In this section of my chapter, I show how Maddy's characterization reflects his preoccupation with the marginalized and their resistance through isolation. I analyze the characters and their roles to illustrate their interrogation of the social malaise and their reaffirmation of traditional values. Published in 1971, *Obasai* is a social satire that explores ethical and moral degeneration in society. It tells the story of two young men, Isaac and Majekudume, who, disgusted by the moral turpitude and economic strangulation that permeate their society, embrace isolation as acts of resistance to conformity to and invalidation of the social ethos. Given the record of youth unemployment, hardship and juvenile delinquency, class distinction, and snobbery, Isaac and Majekudume represent the subaltern, and their actions are indicative of the voice on the margins.

PC Gbep, of long-standing service to the police, captures the state of oppression in unveiling the corruption that permeates the conditions of service in the police force. In spite of 25 years of service, he is yet to receive a promotion, and his monthly salary is **a** pittance. He tells us that he is "still stripeless," his wage is "twenty-one pounds, thirteen shillings and nine pence," and his family constitutes "a wife and eight children" (26). PC Gbep's predicament is part of a broader narrative of corruption and the lack of upward mobility in professional circles. His being "stripeless" after 25 years is indicative of the fact that upward mobility is not based on merit and hard work but rather on nepotism and corruption. By juxtaposing his family commitment with his wage, Maddy nods to the inequities in the workplace that motivate corruption in the rank and file of the police force. The exploitation of the minority and their lack of agency to contest their oppression constitute a significant aspect of minority discourse and Maddy's commitment to unveiling it.

The plight of the oppressed is further revealed in the repressive social structure. PC Gbep's career underscores the absence of dignity of labor in the workplace and, as Maddy tells us, his disclosure that "one should always remember that you are not one of the chosen few" is crucial to understanding society (27). The notion of the selective elite points to privilege and class distinction, but, more importantly, it conveys a sense of otherness, exclusion, and marginalization. PC Gbep, like Majekudume and Isaac, are Other and by implication inferior not because they lack intellect or capacity for transformation but rather because they are held captive by a repressive social system that privileges the elites and stifles growth in the masses. The social and economic constructs create the subaltern and highlight their exploitation by the dominant group.

Majekudume explains the plight of the oppressed when he tells us:

> No matter how hard you will try P.C. Gbep, you should always remember that you are not one of the chosen few . . . or should I ask with impertinence, what efforts have you made to pave your way to get in? How do you intend to get to the top? . . . You must pay your way?
>
> *(27)*

The contrast in the parallel syntactic structures "pave your way" and "pay your way" is biting in its sarcastic substitution of "pay" for "pave." The substitution reveals inversion of values and validation of corruption. As he further tells us, to be promoted one must consider how to:

> deliver [his] wage to [his] immediate boss who would be too pleased to help bring your files up-to-date. Or to be a little faster in the move, try to be much more tolerance fellow and allow your wife, if she is chick and prim, to be exquisitely indulgent.
>
> *(27)*

When bribery is compounded with sexual degeneracy, Maddy holds up his society to scrutiny and chastizes it for its objectification and dehumanization of women. In "delivering" one's wife to his boss, as he would his wage, Maddy captures the objectification of women in their use as pawns for social and material aggrandizement.

Significantly, the construct of otherness is used as a rhetorical device for irony and resistance in the play. The title of the play itself draws attention to and introduces the notion of otherness and its appropriation as strategy of resistance by the characters. In Krio, "Obasai" connotes difference that emanates from a sense of distance. It indicates a disconnect between two sets of values, one of which is inferior and based on difference. The Obasai community accordingly constitutes people and places that deviate from the norm and are therefore perceived as deviants and miscreants. Because of this perceived difference, they operate on the margins of society and are relegated to a lower status in the social order. Otherness is chiefly characterized by class distinction and exclusion.

In this play, as with others, Maddy mocks the affectation and snobbery of the elites by not only creating deviants but by empowering them with insight, creativity, and empathy which the so-called sophisticated elites and cultured society lack. Through irony and sarcasm, the supposed miscreants are the custodians of the truth, morality, and virtue. It is on their shoulders that society's transformation lies. By transcending the social divide and the binaries of core and periphery that define otherness, the social outcasts paradoxically become the bringers of the truth, the mirror through which the social malaise is depicted, and the instruments of social transformation.

However, in order to be the touchstone of truth, the outcasts must first embrace their otherness and exclusion. By appropriating the state of isolation unto themselves, they create a space outside of the norm from which they operate and a canvas to engender acts of resistance. In effect, they are using society's tools to bring down the very society. Hence, if they are outcasts, it is not because society has condemned them rightfully to a life of exclusion but inherently because they chose to reject society and its oppressive institutions. Their rejection of Obasai society is based on choice and predicated on their perception of the vices. Daddy Jebu, Isaac, and Majekudume fall within this category and in many ways constitute typologies of the life of Maddy. It is in their rejection that the act of resistance is located.

Daddy Jebu, perhaps more than any of the other characters in this play, reveals Maddy's preoccupation with the struggles of minority groups. Daddy Jebu is positioned to embody and reveal the ironic inversion of values as strategy of resistance. Marginalized by society and insulted by the local pastor as a "child of satan," Daddy Jebu is regarded as Other and a symbol of moral turpitude. He is perceived as a bad example to the young generation, a lowlife who is not only socially ostracized but religiously damned.

Interestingly, and ironically, Daddy Jebu is a loving, caring, and progressive individual. He understands the needs of the young generation and works toward assisting rather than condemning them. Unlike the society that passes moral judgment on them, he gives them opportunities to maximize their potentials and carve out a future for themselves. In establishing the fishing project for Majekudume, Isaac, and Jokutor, Daddy Jebu registers his belief in the youths and provides the motivation for success in the fulfillment of their dreams. In so doing, he embodies Maddy's message that the social rejects or miscreants are ironically the custodians of moral values in the society. By providing a space for the young men to thrive, Daddy Jebu is resisting the repressive social structure that condemns and stifles the growth of the young generation. Through this act of resistance, he is calling for an overhaul of the social ethos and a reconfiguration of the system that thrives on religious hypocrisy, moral degeneracy, and economic disparities. Majekudume's advice, to "hold fast, to fight, sustain and keep it," reflects the spirit of resistance. His proclamation that "we, as from today, refuse to accept any more dictates of decadence with which Obasai reeks" constitutes a deliberate act of resistance to a reactionary status quo (28).

A quick look at the characters that constitute the elites in Obasai society reveals that Daddy Jebu's, and by implication, Majekudume, Isaac, and Jokutor's, decision to reject society is valid. Social prejudice and class snobbery characterize the actions of characters. Big Miss BK epitomizes affectation and bias. She aspires to elitism not because of an admiration for or an adherence to moral values but rather from a warped vision of sophistication and culture that equates success with family name. In her world, respect for individuals should stem from their ancestry and cultural heritage rather than hard work and moral uprightness. She values humanity exclusively on the basis of heritage and believes the elites are superior because they are descendants of "a good and respectable family," preferably one with such British-oriented last names as "Mason-Cole," "Tobias Streeter," and "Lewis-Scott." In recalling their colonial origins, Maddy gestures to the mimic men in post-independent societies whose belief in Western superiority threatens indigenous identities and gravitates towards erasing traditional values. In the eyes of Big Miss BK, to be successful is to mimic Western values, because to be Western, or to appear to be, is considered to be cultured, educated, and civilized. Here lie not only the roots of social division and repression but also tribalism and ethnic prejudice.

Religious hypocrisy also constitutes an aspect of social degeneration in the play and an instrument of oppression of minority groups. Revren JJT epitomizes Maddy's satire on religion in the practice of Christianity. In the portrait of the local preacher, Maddy calls attention to the discrepancies between doctrine and its practice. Revren JJT preaches on the Christian concept of brotherly love, yet by all indications, he is bereft of love. He condemns Daddy Jebu as damned, yet he, as the saved, can only offer "motical promises" to the degenerate youths. He fails to fulfill the most important commandment of "loving your neighbor as yourself," and Daddy Jebu, the "child of satan," becomes the Christ-like figure in the play. Revren JJT espouses the Old Testament God of fire and brimstone: essentially, the punitive God, and excludes the redemptive glory of Christ through forgiveness and the manifestations of the fruit of the spirit – mercy, grace, peace, love, and reconciliation. As Majekudume rightly tells his mother:

> It is good Mother, that you prefer to satisfy a man of God and neglect me, your son. I hope you will all go to heaven. Don't worry, I won't hold onto your skirt, or even your Cassock Revren, for you to save me from the everlasting Dungeon where fire and brimstone will roast and burn My insides out.
>
> *(33)*

This hypocritical and death-directed form of Christianity is further explored in *Allah Gbah*, where Pastor George uses religion as cover for moral degeneracy.

Religious commentary also constitutes acts of resistance, and in this regard Revren JJT epitomizes religious hypocrisy. Alafi expresses one of the most salient commentaries on religion in the play:

> Revren' J.J.T., you surprise me. You mean to say, sah, that after all these years, it has not yet come to your notice that some of your staunch members who go to church every Sunday, receive Holy Communion and pay their collections and sing hallelujah and hosanna . . . After they have prayed to their maker with all their hypocritical reverence

they can muster, they also go to daddy Jebu to hold the 'Thunder hammer' in readiness to strike their neighbour and shout 'crucify'.

(18)

Alafi expresses the contrast between praise and worship of God signified by Holy Communion, songs, and regular church attendance, on the one hand, and adoration for the devil through the practice of divination and sorcery, on the other. The contrast between "hosanna" and "crucify" illustrates the struggle between appearance and reality, good and evil.

It is in realization of the power of social institutions to suppress minorities and exclude them from society that characters like Isaac and Majekudume reject the reactionary and decadent practices associated with the status quo. For Isaac and others, the rejection constitutes the revolt of the marginalized and gestures to the need for social reform. Embracing the social outcast, the downtrodden, and the destitute, all made vulnerable by society, constitutes for Isaac the ultimate act of resistance of the minority. He tells PC Gbep:

Tell them that we have got our strength and courage from the worst of the despised rejects. Now we are prepared to disown our good and blessed homes and parents. Daddy-Jebu, the reject of the church, state, society and morals, is now our saviour. We, as young rejects from the good old society, have now realized how best to judge the respectable human kind. In short we have now teamed up with the reject. The heathen they accuse of bowing down to wood and stone.

(28)

Laced with irony and sarcasm, Isaac's speech reveals a deliberate rejection of the vices of society by embracing paradoxically what society perceives and condemns as vice, which in reality demonstrates the opposite. If anything, the so-called rejects are depicted as more humane, empathetic, kind, and compassionate than the religious leaders or elites. The problem is that the leaders are blind to their faults. Until there is a realization of their moral decadence, which in part will imply a recognition of the inversion of values, society will continue to degenerate.

Allah Gbah extends the conversation on Western religion as domination of minority culture earlier started in *Obasai* through Maddy's exploration of religious hypocrisy in the character of Pastor George. The play tells the story of Joko Campbell, begotten from a forbidden and clandestine relationship between the local pastor and his mother, Mama Ola. Frustrated by the constraints of being an illegitimate child, and angry over his mother's complicity in the relationship and in keeping the identity of his father a secret, Joko seeks love and refuge in the arms of an aging prostitute, Mrs. Manly. When he later discovers Mrs. Manly in bed with another man, his world of succor comes crashing down, and he kills her out of desperation.

At the opening of the play, Joko Campbell is a condemned man awaiting execution over his murder of Mrs. Manly. As he sits in his cell pondering the events of the past, the play takes the form of a memory play where, through a series of flashbacks, the reader comes to understand the motives for his crime, his mother's complicity, the pastor's adultery, and society's guilt and responsibility. In the nightmare he experiences at the opening scene, depicted as an interview with his Id in the form of a fellow student, the play ventures into psychoanalysis as Maddy lays bare the inner thoughts, fears, and hopes of a condemned man. From a psychoanalytic standpoint, Joko is having a conversation with himself, as he searches his mind for evidence to justify or rationalize his action. In the process, Maddy reveals the hypocrisy, moral degeneration, and inversion of values in the society. Joko goes through a psychological process of self-examination through which both self and society are scrutinized. It is through his thoughts and reflections that the reader comes to engage with the society and understand the reasons for him rejecting its values. The memory scenes constitute the majority of the play.

The use of the psychoanalytic approach sets up two interrelated but contrasting lenses with which to read society – Joko's claim of exclusion and marginalization and society's perception of delinquency and crime. The murder of Mrs. Manly becomes the linchpin that connects both claims and serves as the canvas against which both narratives are tested and either validated or rejected. A small but equally important section of the play depicts the reactions of Joko's parents and the larger society to Joko's crime and resulting fate. It is largely in this section of the play that Maddy demonstrates his aversion to the dominant discourse of oppression and advocates for reform. The satire is more biting and palpable in these sections of the play.

The reflections of Joko's parents and the gossip in society create two meta-narratives that compete for the reader's attention and moral sympathy. A crime has been committed by a young, desperate, and hopeless youth who is angry and bitter at the fact that his father, the local pastor, refuses to publicly acknowledge him as son. Immediately, the discourse of exclusion and marginalization which Maddy introduces in *Obasai* is recalled and amplified. Here, Joko is an outcast and rejects society not out of choice, as Majekudume, Daddy Jebu, Isaac, and Jokutor do, but because he is disowned by his parents out of fear of exposure and the stigma that comes with forbidden love. On the level of resistance, the murder shows Joko's desire for freedom and the possibilities of self-transformation. However, one also realizes that a homicide is committed and that Joko deserves some form of punishment, even as he uses crime as an act of resistance. Joko's oppression and action indicate the "limitations and possibilities" of minority discourse as the narrative competes for the reader's moral sympathy for or condemnation of Joko.

From the outset, Joko is constructed by society as a child of sin, begotten out of an illegitimate relationship and forced into silence for the sins of his parents. In killing Mrs. Manly, I argue that Maddy invites the reader not to judge him but rather to participate in and experience his moral dilemma. Through this, the reader will then wrestle with the prospect of sympathy for him, which, by extension, indicates recognition of the plight of the marginalized. Given the fact that a crime has been committed and a man stands to lose his life, Maddy is also asking society a number of crucial questions – On whose behalf should sympathy lie? Should sympathy be reserved for Joko Campbell? Should judgment be reserved for his parents and society? What should society learn from the tragedy? Is it individual or is it a societal tragedy? Is society responsible for the predicament of its youths?

Maddy's revulsion at society constitutes another aspect of minority discourse. The title of the play calls attention to his satirical intent. In the culture of Sierra Leone, "Allah Gbah" refers to a man of wealth and social standing; a "big man," as the vernacular connotatively affirms. He is usually a man of power and occupies a position of moral authority in society. He is supposed to be a role model, and it is here that the irony undermines his stature for, in spite of his wealth and position, he lacks the moral fiber or authority to lead and be a shining example to his people. An expression usually reserved for corrupt politicians who become wealthy by siphoning state resources into private foreign accounts, it could also be leveled at any figure of authority who compromises their moral stature in the execution of their duties for personal gains. In this instance, the local pastor is "Allah Gbah;" the morally bankrupt preacher who compromises the principles of his calling by having an illegitimate child with a member of his church.

It is out of this realization of moral bankruptcy and the hypocrisy and double standards that come with it that Joko rejects society and his parents and embraces Mrs. Manly as an act of resistance. Expressing his opposition to an oppressive, discriminatory, and exploitative system, Joko states:

> If I am alone in my choice, it is because I appreciate the values in the vices. That means I am different. Like a Judas, I cheat and lie and perhaps will regret. For Now, I create a sensation for a static society. I am the unusual surprise, the once in a while abnega-tor who upsets societies, established orders and systems. Yes, I dared to cross into the camps of the under-trodden dogs, the underprivileged. Here in this cell I grace their company by finding out how it feels to be within and yet without . . . to drift.
>
> *(49)*

In "dar[ing] to cross into the camps of the under-trodden dogs, the underprivileged," Maddy expresses his concern for the subaltern, the downtrodden, and the need for resistance if they are to overcome the marginalization of living "within and yet without" society. Joko registers the pains of minority groups and articulates the discourse of Otherness, the burden of exclusion, and the struggle to belong. In his utterance, Maddy reminds us of the irony of the miscreant and social reject becoming the reformer and bearer of the truth. Even though he is isolated and marginalized, he is perceptive and shows tremendous powers of discernment in his isolation. It is almost as if his alienation sharpens his perception and sets him apart from the corruption and decadence in society. In this way, Maddy's characters negate hegemony by contesting sterile codes of conduct and affirming the dignity of the marginalized through isolation and defiance of societal norms.

Indeed, Joko's exclusion is heightened by his mother's apparent complicity in the silence of his father and rejection of him. He brands her a hypocrite and liar:

> My mother, she is a liar. An artist of deception . . . It is forbidden for me to talk to my father. To address him as father. To look upon him as a father and expect him to treat me as his son. I carry my mother's maiden name. Not my real Father's name.
>
> *(50)*

The excerpt is scathing in its revelation that the pastor's actions contradict the dictates of his vocation, while his mother's clandestine love and silence interrogate the values of motherhood. In labeling his mother "an artist of deception," Joko recalls Hamlet's dilemma and anger over his mother's marriage to his uncle and apparent complicity in his father's death. The intertextual reference is effective in conveying both Joko and Hamlet's resentment of their mother's actions and the loss of the father-figure as a direct result of those actions. The psychological torture is complete. The shame that comes with the child "carry[ing] [his] mother's maiden name" is real and illustrates the social binaries between legitimacy and illegitimacy and accentuates the ten-sions between acceptance and rejection.

It is evident that the psychological torture pushes Joko to distance himself from his mother and to seek a mother-figure in his life. The choice of the aging Mrs. Manly is not by happenstance – it registers a deep-seated desire for association with a mother-figure as well as the physical attractions to womanhood, love, and sex. The emotional stress creates in Joko a state of delusion that is anchored in escapism. In this way, he comes to perceive his relationship with Mrs. Manly in grandiose terms – "the trinity of a perfect unity." He refers to it as "not a philosophy," but rather "a feeling and genuine one at that" (51). In his conception of the love relationship and his desire for escapism, Joko describes Mrs. Manly as his "Madonna." In so doing, he conflates two contrasting images of the woman – the redemptive woman characterized by spiritual love, the virgin Mary, and the sinful woman that epitomizes carnal love, the prostitute. In this attempt to unify two dialectical images, what I loosely described earlier as the "limitations and possibilities" of minority discourse, Joko confuses love and lust, the spiritual and the material, and the redemptive and the sinful.

Equally, his attempts to paint her in noble images are overblown, and the reader gets the impression that fantasy has its limitations. He says:

> It is sacrilegious to compare her to the world of girls who lack feelings. They are faithless, passionless, devoid of affection. She was my Madonna. That unique inexpressible beauty and love which transforms everything. That which gives life, new life, purpose and hope and meaning to the fallen.
>
> *(46)*

Joko's diction reinforces his delusion and expresses a tormented soul whose distorted view of womanhood clouds his perception of the world. His mother's complicity creates a warped view of women so that love and lust are being conflated and expressed as sacred in the images of the Trinity and the Madonna. What the excerpt reveals is the workings of a troubled mind, of suffering under the weight of exclusion, and of struggling to belong. Society's contribution is foregrounded as crucial to Joko's predicament, and Aunty Lulu, the local gossip, reminds us of the treachery, hate, and selfishness that the subaltern has to contend with. Characters like Aunty Lulu and the guitarist whose song celebrates Joko's tragedy are indicative of the broader narrative of oppression that constitutes minority discourse.

In the final analysis, Maddy endorses the view of Neighbour towards capital punishment and societal reform. The neighbor clearly identifies the cause of Joko's predicament and the solution to the malaise. Assuming the position of the moral voice in the play, she says:

> This capital punishment belongs to the decadent, distant, ruthless generations of the past. I am a reformer, Aunty Lulu. I believe that Joko needs help. Your help and my Help and everybody's help in the neighbourhood. It Was up to you all to have helped him into making a decent and better citizen. Your interest in him would have helped to reassure him. To cure his mind's malady.
>
> *(62)*

Neighbour brings in another dimension to crime in society – its connections to mental health. As reformer, she emphasizes the need for reform of criminal law and for access to quality mental health facilities to victims. Society needs to care for its citizens, to create opportunities for growth, and to rethink the role of institutions – legal, mental, and educational – in the lives of its people.

Maddy's *Obasai and Other Plays* is published in English. Its greatest claim to indigenous drama in Sierra Leone and engagement of minority discourse is its use of transliteration. The playwright adopts a blend of standard English and the vernacular, Krio, that gives the plays a distinct African flavor. He draws extensively from the syntactic structures and diction of Krio to construct phrases and sentences that reflect a hybrid of both languages.

The names of the characters in *Obasai* demonstrates symbolism of diction. For the purpose of illustration, I will take each character in turn. Lagbaja is nameless, and in this sense, he could be any one of the residents in the town. The name is used in situations where the speaker intends to keep the identity of the person spoken about anonymous. However, by a witty reference to an aspect of their character, most times derogatory, the audience has a sense of who is being referred to despite the fact that the speaker chooses to not name them. The appellation is reserved for characters with deep-seated flaws, and so, in *Obasai*, Lagbaja represents the town gossip. Since he is Everyman, Maddy hints that every character in the town is a gossip, and this further illustrates the moral decadence in the society.

Workhog is a representation of the exploited worker. Typically, he is the domestic help or least favored sibling who bears the family burden. He is the prototype of the workaholic, though in this instance, he is compelled to work and is exploited from his ceaseless labors. Workhog also appeals to a broader discourse – the working class exploited by society and unaccomplished in spite of their labors.

Tokumbo and Daddy Jebu connote deception. Tokumbo is second-hand material and therefore inauthentic, while Jebu is deceit with the connotation that the character is a thief, swindler, or villain. Maddy uses symbolism drawn from the vernacular to point out social degeneration in the community.

Titty Shine Shine completes the picture of moral and social degeneration. The image is one of insatiable desire for prominence or material acquisition regardless of means. It is predicated on feminine vice; the woman who aspires to material wealth without moral scruples and uses her body as means to an end. Titty Shine Shine is the symbol of the prostitute or loose woman. Together, Maddy creates a society of rejects and miscreants.

The third aspect of negation, as earlier mentioned, is Maddy's re-appropriation of the English language to suit the nuances and rhythms of the vernacular. This act represents one of the major tasks of minority discourse and his discursive strategy of resistance to Western hegemony. I use this section of my paper to analyze the role of the vernacular in contesting the cultural and communicative import of the English language. I also focus on Maddy's characterization of Yon-Kon, in his final play, as index of the marginalized.

As Kubayanda remarks in his essay,

> the minority writer eventually must attempt to cast away the cultural burden that the language of the majority . . . imposes. This can be done . . . through a rebellious don de sabotage or through a recontextualizing, reframing, or destruction of, in Guillen's words, "the purity of academe/the purity of grammarians/the purity of those who insist they have to be pure, pure, pure." Should a new grammar be created? Can it be done, the perceptive reader wonders, when dominant discourse seems indestructible, when language, despite its apparent neutrality and innocence is . . . the pillar that supports dominant power and behavior.
>
> *(117)*

Maddy adopts this strategy of reframing and re-contextualizing the grammar of English to resist the control and behavior the dominant language exerts on the minority or indigenous languages. In the plays, diction and syntax are also directly drawn from the vernacular. The following examples illustrate this: "Open for me," "How for do . . .," "He beats records . . .," "Let go my balls or I'll strangle you," "Shut your trap and listen," "Come touch me again. I'll beat you with this stick like a snake. Come, come and I'll wager you like a top," and "We are glad God's breeze took you away and brought you back safe to us, Logan." Other examples include, "I am the one who is spared no peace nor rest," "they were busy playing 'Winnie and Lossie' card gambling," "Majekudume is the boss and Isaac his peggy-boy," "People get easily carried away these days and as such they easily add pepper and salt to make other people's stories seem more spicy than it should normally taste," "womanizing, money grabbin' and pianoing," "To cut long story short," "People who do things and not just keep talking and promising motically," and "You were born the day when death struck shame."

Some of the expressions are drawn from Krio proverbs, wise sayings, and witty statements to shed light on the situation. These include: "You should never let them use your eyes to sleep," "things are jagra-ja," "Our elders used to say 'Nar eye for look eye an' feel sorry for each other,'" "The Lord that split our mouths . . . will always provide," "Like his wife, he comes with fas-mot gossips," ". . . a patient dog always get the fattest bone at the end," "What have I said that you should blaze on me like a noonday fire being blown all over the place by wild winds . . .?," "It's no surprise that as soon as people see you or your wife approaching, if they are messing up themselves, they sooner sit and hide their mess rather than to ask the likes of you for help of any kind," "He's a real punk. Look how he's running to meet the bitch. She wears his trousers and he wears her frock," "Go Mr. Big Man Big Fool," and "Fas-Mot Lagbaja you are good as an information passer."

At other times Maddy uses words and phrases directly from Krio. These include: "Maybe someday Daddy Jebu will Jagae-butu, Jagae-tinap for PC Constable," (will use divination with cowrie shells to contact the spirit of the ancestors on behalf of the constable), "Chai," (an expression of disgust), and "Awujor" (a traditional ceremony commemorating the anniversary of the dead). As Kubayanda contends, and as these examples show, "[m]inority discourse is circumstantially a counter-hegemonic discourse [and] it thrives on a counter-hegemonic vision also" (118).

Allah Gbah also depicts Maddy's attempt at creolization of the English language. These include the use of Krio proverbs such as, "it is like our people will say, 'The herb that tempts the appetite of a goat, always exposes the poor animal to a disgraceful diarrhoea'," (unbridled ambition leads to tragedy); "Mama Ola if you look to the noise of the market you won't buy fish," (do not be distracted by gossip); and ". . . if you play with God, Jesus Christ will make you shit," (every decision attracts a consequence). The use of diction taken directly from Krio as "Take suru" (an expression of sympathy) is also noted.

Perhaps it is in the song of the guitarist that Maddy most effectively uses Krio to articulate plot and meaning in the play. The song highlights the theme of decisions and consequences and the need to take responsibility for one's actions. It points out that Joko's indiscretion, stubbornness, and lust are the causes of his predicament. The moral judgment is that Joko's downfall is self imposed and that society is better off without him. However, the note of rejoicing and celebration that permeate the song undercuts the moral of the guitarist's message. Without embracing moral turpitude and providing an excuse for murder, Maddy questions the kind of society that rejoices over the murder of an innocent woman and eventual execution by hanging of a 21-year-old student. Even though Joko is blamed for the murder, society is recognized as co-conspirator, if not complicit, in his predicament. Failure to recognize this accentuates the need for reform and the need to address the flaws of both Joko and the larger society. Joko is a product of his environment, and not to see him as indicative of the vices is to miss society's oppression of minorities and the need for change.

The song of the guitarist also provides examples of direct translation of words and phrases from the vernacular. These include: "Tranga yaase" (stubbornness), "big-sisi" (elderly woman who sleeps with younger men like Mrs. Manly), "rope go eat you wase" (you will bear the consequences of your indiscretion), "big 'oman pillar" and "big 'oman lappa" (situations that are out of one's league), "Joko Campbell don krais for Mrs. Manly" (he is head over heels in love with Mrs. Manly), "Mrs. Manly dat sabie how for bahyo-bahyo" (she knows how to seduce and comfort men), ". . . turn Joko loose en mass 'im mole" (knocked his wits out of him), and "go disgrace lek chek-chek foll" (his shame will not be hidden and can be easily noticed like the featherless chicken).

Maddy's final play in this collection is *Yon-Kon*, a one-act play centered on a criminal in prison. My analysis of *Yon-Kon* in the light of deconstruction of Western hegemony lies in Maddy's characterization in depicting the struggles of the marginalized to resist oppression and re-assert dignity in society. Yon-Kon, the protagonist, has been serving prison sentences since the tender age of 16 years. He has been in and out of prison for 40 years running. His long association with Pademba prison, the maximum-security prison in Freetown, earns him the office of chief prisoner and the responsibility of taking his fellow prisoners for routine exercises. He is well respected, feared, obeyed, and liked in prison. Prison offers him the space to be in control, productive, and give meaning to his life and existence. On this level, prison symbolizes the corrective dimension of social institutions in its capacity to transform minds and re-shape individual desires and actions in line with the codes of good behavior that govern citizenship.

However, Maddy undercuts this notion of transformation by alerting the reader to the fact that Yon-Kon's claim to authority rests entirely on his repeated incarceration and knowledge of prison life. We are informed that, for Yon-Kon, incarceration is a choice and deliberate act of defiance and resistance to society. The focus shifts from Yon-Kon's authority to his motivations for incarceration. Maddy tells us that he "has been in and out of Pademba Road prison for 40 years and has been going in and out since he was 16 years" (167). The question becomes: What is it about society that makes incarceration attractive to Yon-Kon? To understand the playwright's message, it is essential to shed light on his technique of reversal or inversion of values earlier depicted in *Obasai* and *Allah Gbah*.

Yon-Kon represents the minority in society. He, like Joko, Isaac, and Majekudume, is ostracized by society. Again, like the other characters, Yon-Kon comes to reject the social and moral degeneration in his society. However, unlike Joko, who seeks comfort in the arms of a prostitute, or Isaac and Majekudume, who choose to be isolated, Yon-Kon opts for the seclusion of prison life. There is a sense in which Isaac, Majekudume, and Yon-Kon intentionally choose to be isolated. What makes Yon-Kon's situation a bit more alarming is that he rejects the world of social interaction for the restrictions of incarceration. That Yon-Kon prefers restriction over freedom and liberty is indicative of the extent of rottenness in society and the need to reject its decadence. Yon-Kon's choice of prison existence constitutes an act of resistance to society.

The world of the prison paradoxically depicts the freedom and liberty that should constitute the realities of the outside world. Maddy employs this technique of inversion to show the oppressive nature of society and its institutions. In prison, Yon-Kon is described as a "good man" and "boss" of the inmates. In his relationship with the other prisoners, he is respected, and he achieves a level of self-fulfillment and self-realization that the outside world of normal existence would never accord him.

Further, Maddy shows continuities between life in prison and life in the outside world. Clearly, life in prison can be dangerous. The vicious fights that break out from time to time, the lack of proper medical facilities, and the psychological challenges of isolation are made manifest in the death of Pa Gbaratae and the depression of Pagu. However, normal life outside the walls of the prison reflects the same violence and threats to human life and existence. Life outside of prison is defined by a sense of aimlessness and emptiness, such as the robbery, heavy drinking, and debauchery of Agba Saiteiny and his merry band. The difference between the world of the prison and the world of incarceration is hard to tell. In fact, for people like Yon-Kon, life behind bars is more productive and fulfilling. Thus, it makes little difference whether he is in or outside of prison.

The title of the play is drawn directly from Krio. It symbolizes the kleptomaniac, the individual with compulsive, obsessive stealing impulses. Born to parents who died before and shortly after he was born, brought up by a foster mother, Yon–Kon lacks the necessary knowledge and skills to succeed. Without opportunities for education or access to vocational training, the only option open to him is stealing. Raised with livestock, he develops a strange but strong bond with and emotional connection to them. He develops a compulsion to protect them, and so he steals them and is caught and sent to prison.

At the start of the play, Yon–Kon has served his term of sentence and would be released the following morning. He conducts the usual physical exercise and gets the prisoners to recite the "code of good behaviour" (165). On the eve of his departure, Yon–Kon vows never to return to prison. He plans to make his exit in grand style. In making the case for continuities between the prison and society, Maddy focuses on the death of Pa Gbaratae and the role of the prison doctor. Even though the crime is committed inadvertently and Pagu acted in self-defense, he is charged with murder and stands to lose his life. Yon–Kon suggests a way out of the debacle by having Pagu bribe the prison doctor to write a false autopsy. The law is here satirized, and the prison cell becomes an extension of the lack of professionalism with which the law is practiced on the outside.

It is without doubt, then, that Maddy views society both in terms of the outside world and the prison as synonymous. The prison becomes an extension of the vices of society, and the jail yard is a microcosm of society. The vices prevalent in society are also noticeable in the prison cells. It then becomes unfair for prisoners to be held behind bars for such crimes when these atrocities are being perpetrated in society by the very people who decide the fate of the prisoners. In effect, the question becomes: Why should the lawyer live in freedom and the prisoner behind bars when both are guilty of the same offences? It then becomes difficult to distinguish between the innocent and the guilty in society.

The world of *Yon-Kon* depicts a situation where the convicted prisoners and the state authorities are hard to distinguish. They are all criminals – some are hiding behind their professional status and privileges, while others are apprehended and incarcerated. The point Maddy is making here is that prisons are reflective of the nature of societies and that prisoners are products of their environments. If the inmates are products of their societies, then it stands to reason that the crimes for which they are incarcerated define the nature of the societies they come from.

In explaining his own experience to Pagu, bribing the prison doctor and getting away with stabbing a fellow inmate, Yon-Kon reminds us of the inequities of law enforcement. He tells us, "I got away with it by spending the last/penny I had. 'See to see,' by 'see to see'" (175). He advises Pagu to "see the doctor and talk to him" professing that he is a "good man. That is if you'll spend 200 pounds, of course" (175) – a suggestion Pagu refuses to commit to. In juxtaposing Yon-Kon's prison experience and Pagu's innocence, Maddy further demonstrates inversion of values. However, the point is well made – even though the reader finds Yon-Kon's suggestion of bribery appalling, he flinches at Pagu's naivety. The reader sympathizes with him but also recognizes that he has a lot to learn from the sordid realities of life. At the end of the case, he is found guilty of manslaughter and sentenced to seven years imprisonment. Even though we find Yon-Kon's advice repulsive, we are aware of its validity in the context of a corrupt society. It is in creating such a moral conundrum that Maddy highlights the rationale for Yon-Kon's rejection of society and embrace of prison.

Maddy presents a society in disarray. He seems to be looking at society through a convex lens in which the front and back ends of an object are inverted so that the values of the society are mixed up inextricably. The images are themselves presented inside out. The mirror image offers a lopsided vision of society, but it is a lopsidedness that is in reality true. A prison that symbolizes a barrier to life, a denial of one's personal freedom, and a violation of civil rights as a citizen becomes the symbol of freedom, happiness and contentment.

In contrast to the outside world, the world of Pademba Road prison is a more ordered and fulfilling environment. Hence, Yon-Kon rejects the freedom of the outside world and repeatedly goes back to prison. His rejection of society is a pointer to how futile life can be for the downtrodden and vulnerable in society. Social and economic disparities not only breed social misfits and miscreants such as Yon-Kon and Joko Campbell, capital punishments and jail sentences transform them and cause them to reject society. It is through their rejection that the sordid realities of society are exposed.

In conclusion, Maddy succeeds in creating five major characters, all outcasts of society, who totally reject society's values: Joko Campbell in *Allah Gbah*; Majekudume, Jokutor, and Isaac in *Obasai*; and Yon-Kon in *Yon-Kon*. They all share a common feeling of disgust for their societies. In using language as act of resistance, Maddy embraces Kubayanda's concept of deterritorialization of language by adopting linguistic and rhetorical constructions that:

> raise and nurture a combative consciousness through linguistic subversiveness . . . introduce a new set of discursive features, which include the cohesive and symbiotic relationships of oral and written discourses, the presence in print of paralinguistic cues usually denied to the writer in the formal linear traditions of Europe, the use of "irregularities" and other sociolinguistic patterns from the African continuum rather than the standard reservoir of the culturally and historically dominant discourse.
>
> *(119)*

Works cited

JanMohamed, Abdul R. & David Lloyd (eds.). *The Nature and Context of Minority Discourse*. New York: Oxford University Press, 1990.

Kubayanda, Josaphat. "Minority Discourse and the African Collective: Some Examples from Latin American and Caribbean Literature" in *The Nature and Context of Minority Discourse*. New York: Oxford University Press, 1990.

Maddy, Pat Amadu. *Obasai and Other Plays*. London: Heinemann, 1971.

Palmer, Eustace. "The Agony and the Ecstasy: Sierra Leonean Dramatists' Confrontation with the Sierra Leonean Landscape" in *African Literatures and Beyond* (eds.) Bernth Lindfors & Geoffrey V. Davis, *Cross/Cultures: Readings in Post/Colonial Literatures and Cultures*. Amsterdam-New York: Rodopi 2013.

9

OF PIDGIN, NIGERIAN PIDGIN POETRY, AND MINORITY DISCOURSES

The pidgin poems of Ezenwa-Ohaeto

Chike Okoye

Introduction: the concept of pidgin and the Nigerian case

Pidgin, for the layman, is a language formed from a mixture of several languages as the only option for communication among people from diverse and mutually unintelligible linguistic backgrounds. This mixture that necessitates the emergence of a pidgin is as a result of contact. Brian Tiffen describes it cryptically as "the language of the market place" (9), and Bolander et al. define it as "any mixed language spoken usually in trade, which uses the vocabulary of two or more languages and a simplified form of the grammar of one of them" (760). The issue of contact is reinforced with J.E. Reinecke's position that "a minimum or makeshift language" comes into being "when men of different speech are thrown into contact and must reach an understanding" (534), while the context of trade is underscored further with De Camp's position that pidgin is "used in trading or in any situation requiring communication between persons who do not speak other's languages" (Elugbe and Omamor, 1). Loreto Todd is more elaborate:

> (Pidgin is) a communication system that develops among people who do not share a common language. In early stages of contact, such as the first encounter between British sailors and Coastal West Africans or between American Soldiers and the Vietnamese, a make shift system emerges involving a few simple structures – mostly commands – and a limited number of words, drawn almost entirely from the language of the dominant group.
>
> *(3)*

At this point, a clear picture emerges: pidgin is a language that arises as a result of a necessary contact between people of diverse linguistic backgrounds, a language made up of elements in varying degrees of all the contact languages involved. Many a time, though, pidgin's nature as a minimum or makeshift language is put to the test. According to Elugbe and Omamor, a pidgin is likely to "disappear if the condition which gave rise to it ceased to exist" (2), but then if it develops beyond that, it transforms into a creole. A creole is described as a language that evolved from a pidgin but becomes more relevant, as it then serves as a native language of a speech community.

Elugbe and Omamor describe it aptly thus: "creolization simply means the acquisition of first language speakers by a pidgin" (3).

Further clarification is needed regarding the status and meaning of lingua franca in respect of the creole and pidgin. In the simplest of terms, a lingua franca is a language that is used among people who speak various different languages. In relation to this discourse, Ferguson and De Bose clarify: "a pidgin can become a recognized language while retaining only a lingua franca status and thus being without a community of first language speakers" (11). Therefore, a pidgin could be a lingua franca without being a creole but, of course, with the right and favorable conditions, later metamorphose into a creole and maybe aspire toward official language status. Again, the expressions "broken" and "broken English" are not the same as pidgin. Broken English or any other language in question refers to a mixture (mostly varied and personal according to the source of speakers) of pidgin and imperfect English or any other language.

Some of the most popular pidgins around the world are all based on a European language, most commonly English, French, Italian, Portuguese, and Spanish. The contact context that gives rise to a pidgin cuts across all the languages involved in the development of a pidgin regardless of the contact spots (Africa, the New World, Asia). In Sierra Leone, there is a creolized pidgin that is both used as a first and a second language known as Krio and, according to Elugbe and Omamor, is "fully developed and has a sizable volume of literature in and on it" (16). Another notable one is found in Papua New Guinea and its surrounding islands. It is known as Tok Pisin and is regarded highly, having attained the status of "the main language for deliberation in the national legislature of Papua New Guinea" (Valdman, xvi). In West Africa again, there is the "Ewondo Populaire . . . an African-based pidgin spoken over a large area of Eastern Cameroon" (Elugbe and Omamor, 17). The Barikanci, meaning "language of the barracks," is an example of pidgin Hausa, which is spoken in the military barracks of Northern Nigeria, mostly among the lower ranks. Its development was due to the large influx of Hausa speakers recruited into the Nigerian army as a result of the civil war battlefront shortages of personnel. According to Elugbe and Omamor, "majority of such recruits – i.e., of those who could not speak English – were Hausa speaking" (18). In East Africa, Kiswahili and Kisettla, which are made up of Arabic and Bantu and then pidginized Swahili, respectively, are in varying degrees of pidgin and creolized pidgin.

An interesting and contentious case, however, involves the claim that the Sierra Leonean Krio actually gave rise to Nigerian Pidgin because of the instance(s) of freed and about-to-be resettled slaves who landed first in Freetown and had already developed a pidgin (Krio). Some were subsequently sent to places such as Nigeria to relocate, thereby exporting the Krio pidgin. Countering this stance is this position by Elugbe and Omamor concerning the dating of Krio in Freetown:

> The dating of this event is in the second half of the nineteenth century (see Jones 1971). On the other hand, by our account, based on the historical facts, NP arose from sixteenth and seventeenth century contact between West Africans and their English-speaking trading partners. In fact even Antera Duke's Dairy predates the return of slaves to Freetown.
>
> *(20)*

Antera Duke's diary is historically the first document discovered to have been written in Nigerian pidgin. Krio most possibly influenced Nigerian Pidgin, but it was much later – because, according to the account, "a pidgin English would already have existed for two centuries before the founding of Freetown" (Elugbe and Omamor, 20).

Historically speaking, a Portuguese-based pidgin would have blossomed in Nigeria. This is because the Portuguese first landed in 1469 along the coastal region of Niger Delta in their bid to fulfill the slave needs of the gold-mining Akan tribes with whom they were trading. These coastal regions of the Niger Delta had communities even further inland along the myriad of tributaries that emptied into the ocean. It was with these people that the Portuguese made contact in the 15th century. It is natural to assume that a pidgin Portuguese developed in order for trade negotiations to occur. But this did not last. According to Elugbe and Omamor, "As it turned out, the French, the Dutch, and finally, the English competed with and ousted the Portuguese" (4); this logically put an end to Portuguese presence, and the "condition which gave rise to a 'jargonized' Portuguese ceased to exist" (4). But, importantly, this does not deny or negate "the contribution of Portuguese to NP (Nigerian Pidgin)" (5). Actually, the Portuguese stayed for only about 70 years (1469–1539) before being replaced by the Dutch as the principal trading partners of the coastal communities of Nigeria. But even before the Dutch, the French had come around 1539 to the Benin coast, when the Portuguese had attempted missionary work with the Benin kingdom. Nevertheless, "the Portuguese did not stay long enough to leave a permanent legacy in the form of language – standard or otherwise" (Elugbe and Omamor, 7).

We have seen that pidgins arise as a result of contact, and, in the Nigerian case, between coastal communities and different European groups, culminating with the British. Ultimately, what we have today is aptly designated Nigeria Pidgin (NP), having Nigerian properties. Eyo Mensah, in "Grammaticalization in Nigerian Pidgin," opines that "NP is a variety of West African creole . . . traced to the 15th century along the coastal regions of Calabar, Port-Harcourt, Sapele, Warri, and Badagry among others" (168). Theresa Heyd adds that its rise was "in the 15th century along the slave coast through Portuguese contact" (672). Ugot et al. also contribute thoughts on the origin of NP: "Historical sources of the origin of (Nigerian) Pidgin point towards Calabar, . . . where first contact with Portuguese trading merchants brought about a Portuguese based pidgin" (225). Mensah adds that "The first recorded form of NP was documented by the famous Antera Duke, a prominent Chief and trader in old Calabar" (168) and reminds us that, despite its later expansions, "NP started off as a language of business and communication" (168). The process of developing a pidgin, as noted earlier, is rooted in contact, and the most feasible hypothesis or theory is in the form of a scenario: European and local peoples of different languages meet, and communication is needed, a rudimentary form at least that will cover the basics of (a) fruitful transaction(s). After halting starts, attempts improve over time, and gradually a marginal makeshift mixture (with input from all) that later grows into a pidgin is formed.

Nigerian Pidgin, according to Nicholas Faraclas, "is the most widely spoken creole language in the world and the African language (aside from Arabic) with the largest speech community" (417). It occupies this position alongside others such as Gambian Krio, Sierra Leone Krio, Ghanaian Pidgin, and Cameroonian and Equatorial Guinean Pidgins and is "a dialect of West African English lexifier Creole which itself is a dialect of Afro-Caribbean English-lexifier Creole" (417). Faraclas considers Nigerian Pidgin a creole for the mere fact that it has a first language status for millions of people, but still maintains that it occupies a "fuzzy border between Pidgin and Creole." He is of this somewhat confused view because, according to him, "the majority of NigP speakers, however, speak it as a second language" (417). He finally avers: "I consider NigP to be a creole language, others do not" (417). However, this clarification between NP and PE by Eyo Mensah in his "Lexicalization in Nigerian Pidgin" helps:

> There have been a lot of misconceptions about the status of NP (Nigerian Pidgin) and PE (Pidgin English). Most references . . . combine the two varieties and refer generally

to them as Nigerian Pidgin English (NPE). NP is a language with its unique linguistic structure and identity. Some of the known varieties of NP include Ikom, Calabar, Warri, Port-Harcourt, Onitsha, and Ajegunle . . . PE on the other hand, is ". . . a substandard attempt by a large proportion of ill-equipped, illiterate Nigerians to manipulate the English language . . ." While NP is a descriptively adequate grammar, PE is grammatically aberrant and defective . . . I refer to PE as a language that looks like a pidgin but does not have the full-fledged character of Pidgin.

(214–216)

Nigerian pidgin has a home base – a continually expanding source area of concentration where it first developed and diffused outward. This base is at the coastal regions of Nigeria – the Bights of Benin and Biafra. Faraclas confirms this: "NigP has been spoken as an ancestral/ mother tongue for several generations by millions in Warri, Sapele, and other Delta towns" (417). Meanwhile, Mercy Ugot et al. have their own view: "Historical sources of the origin of pidgin and its evolution point towards Calabar" (225). Interestingly, a lot of literature toes both lines: many people speak it in the Warri-Sapele area; the oldest historical sources trace it to Calabar, but this does not change the narrative much, as they are all located at the coastal regions of Nigeria's Niger Delta. A more engaging issue is the present status of Nigerian Pidgin. Despite it being spoken by millions for so many years and being a creole, lingua franca, and pidgin in varying degrees in diverse parts of Nigeria, it has yet to achieve a formal status and official approval in spite of its linguistic spread, usage, and strength. For Herbert Igboanusi, "it does not enjoy official recognition as a Nigerian language and is excluded from the education system" (68). This is despite the fact that "The use of Nigerian Pidgin is widespread across Nigeria, especially in informal situations. All classes of Nigerians have been noted to use NP in both formal and informal conversations" (Osoba, "Discourse" 132). Charles Mann supports this:

> it remains, possibly, and, at least in the urban south, the most used inter ethnic *lingua franca*, a vital means of public market trading, and, . . . *the* language of peer communication between Nigerian youths on university campuses, i.e. – even between youths, who have the same mother tongue.
>
> *(465)*

Yet it has no official recognition like the three major local languages of Nigeria. Faraclas adds this: 'Unlike Hausa, Yoruba, Igbo and StE (Standard English), NigP has no official recognition or role in education, no overt prestige, few public advocates, no standardized orthography or grammar, and little written literature" (418). The previous observations make Nigerian Pidgin a minority discourse, and the situation is further reinforced by Igboanusi's observation: "It lacks prestige because it is often perceived as a bad form of English, and is associated with *non-literate persons and a socioeconomically deprived group*" (68). The deliberately emphasized lines in italics are the ingredients for a perfect minority whose discourse does not measure up. Nevertheless, its bleak posture as a minority and unofficial discourse does nothing to its widespread and accepted utilitarian status as Nigeria's arguably most effective and permeative language. These formidable qualities of Nigerian Pidgin have made it a veritable medium – one with prospects.

The Nigerian Pidgin medium

Dagmar Deuber and Lars Hinrichs documented the general usage of the NP medium and captured it thus: "There has for quite some time been a growing trend towards the use of these varieties in a set of special written genres . . . literary texts (poetry, drama, in prose . . . news-paper columns and cartoons, radio scripts" (24). Mensah espies a "renewed role of NP," saying: "A number of literary genres such as drama, poem [sic] and prose have been published in NP" ("Lexicalization" 213–214). Mann supports the observation thus: "It [NP] is now sometimes employed in news casting and broadcasting, especially in popular comic soaps and advertising, in certain states in the Pidgin zone" (465). On a semi-formal basis, NP has been very useful even from the days of the Nigerian civil war, as radio stations used it for propaganda purposes. Cur-rently, its place in the advertising world is indispensable. Its reach to different classes of people over wide distances that cut across all ethnicities in Nigeria make it a highly formidable medium. In strictly informal contexts, it occupies a very important position again, as it helps diffuse street lore, "songs, folktales, proverbs, work chants and the like" (Elugbe and Omamor, 123). An important classification and clarification is offered by Elugbe and Omamor concerning the use of NP in literature. They posit:

> There is the question of literature *in* NP. For example, if a novel were written in NP; or the Bible were translated into NP; or a government release were translated into or published in NP, all that would be literature (put out) in NP. However, if, for example, a novelist were to resort to NP through some of his characters, this would be one use of NP in literature.
>
> *(124)*

In the previous classification, some Nigerian writers belong to either sides of the coin. Cyprain Ekwensi and Chinua Achebe and even Wole Soyinka have created works in which their characters use pidgin to communicate, for example, *Jagua Nana, No Longer at Ease* (1960), *A Man of the People* (1966), *Anthills of the Savannah* (1986), and *The Road*, respectively. In these examples, characters of city dwellers with low education and exposure mostly talk in pidgin. A clear departure from this practice is Frank Aig-Imokhuede in his work *Pidgin Stew and Sufferhead* (1982), a collection of poems in formal English and NP, with roughly two-thirds written in NP. Ken Saro-Wiwa's *Soza Boy* is another interesting piece, though not written in the strictest sense of NP but rather in the author's own description: "rotten English". There are many other examples of literature written in NP, and they will be given more mention later. In entertain-ment, some periodicals like the obscene *Ikebe*, a publication of Daily Times of Nigeria, some characters in the Nigerian Television Authority (NTA) series "Village Headmaster," the popular comedy series "Hotel de Jordan," the late Fela Anikulapo-Kuti, and so on all use NP. Mann says of Fela: "one of Nigeria's most popular musicians, recognizing its potency as a direct medium to reach the greater mass of the people, sang his lyrics in ANP [Anglo-Nigerian Pidgin; NP] – unusual for a Yoruba since this ethnic group is not commonly associated with ANP [NP]" (468). These show the reach and effect of NP.

NP is making inroads in the formal education world. The progression from sparse use to more suffusion of NP in literary works (e.g. from Achebe's *No Longer at Ease* to *A Man of the People* and *Anthills of the Savannah*; and from Cyprain Ekwensi's *People of the City* to *Jagua Nana*) and to even more recent works, especially poems – as we will see later – written completely in NP seems to suggest brighter prospects for NP's possible use as a formal medium of instruction. Elugbe and Omamor support this view:

> The fact that NP has been used in all the ways indicated above leaves one in no doubt that, if given the chance, NP can easily function as a medium of instruction.
>
> *(134)*

Instruction, here, is a reference to classroom usage in Nigerian schools. In fact, there have been numerous cases of the use of NP in primary schools of Benin City where communication becomes difficult or downright breaks down between pupil and teacher. This is possible in many other cities in Nigeria, though there are no available data to support this. Nevertheless, adequate education cannot take place without effective communication. Given that a large number of Nigeria's primary school–age children have a relatively poor grasp of the official English language, it will only be practical if occasional use of NP is encouraged for teachers' use with pupils – a major step toward greater prospects for NP – in order to enhance proper communication for effective education. Presently, NP's influence and reach are solid. The recent pervasive permeation of the social media has revived and helped diffuse NP globally to people in the Diaspora. The connection and recourse to NP between the Diaspora, migrants, and the home base is worthy of note and gives NP a new and more formidable pride of place, thereby re-interrogating its erstwhile subaltern identity as a minority discourse. This is because of the numerical strength of interlocutors. Theresa Heyd comments:

> the large-scale global migration and the emergence of a new African Diaspora have paved the way for the deterritorialized and diasporic usage of NgP [NP]. Finally, the digitized usage of NgP [NP] . . ., both by local Nigerian speakers and users across the global diaspora, is nowadays a significant factor in the sociocultural profile of the repertoire. The leap from the streets of Lagos and its media outlets, to the global urban settings of the new African Diaspora, to Twitter and Tumbler is simply a logical one in the mediasphere of the early 21st century.
>
> *(672)*

NP's internet and Diaspora spread and wide interlocutor base in Nigeria are enough to call for it to be made a national language. One of the reasons for its peculiar position includes what Joseph Osoba has observed: "[that it] has more communication power, is far more entertaining and definitely more far reaching" (111). Nigerians accept this and appreciate its power. Rudolf Gaudio puts it this way: "Nigerians of all class backgrounds often express great appreciation for what they perceive to be pidgin's capacity to convey genuine emotions and trenchant social truths" (236). In fact, many Nigerians who speak English are also very competent in the different varieties of Nigerian Pidgin and are found to easily code-switch depending on need. Its use, as has been shown earlier, now transcends and dominates what erstwhile was the exclusive preserve of English, Hausa, Igbo, and Yoruba, especially in advertising, politics, media, and so on. Osoba makes a very germane observation about NP's special qualities, one that will validate our argument in the next part:

> There are feelings, emotions, ideas . . . captured in NP conversations that are almost impossible to express in standard dialects. Thus nastier, sharper, more basal, and more naturally unobtrusive conceptions and inclinations towards a brutally lower level of emotion laden acquaintance can be observed to feature more prominently in NP than any other language in Nigeria.
>
> *("Discourse" 138)*

As clear as the root-based acceptance of NP is one of the points raised by Osoba previously, which also points out the cause of the segregation that NP is facing today – upper-class and lower-class society sequestration. This trend is even captured in literary works. The idea is that persons that people the lower-class society are home to the use of "a brutally lower level of emotion laden (language)"; therefore you find in "Soyinka's *The Trials of Brother Jero*, . . . Saro-Wiwa's *Soza Boy*, Chinua Achebe's *A Man of the People* or *Anthills of the Savannah*, . . . (that) low class characters speak NP while those of high class speak impeccable English" (Osoba, "Discourse" 138). Nevertheless, it is indeed in the other half of NP's characteristics that the greater power of utilitarian uniqueness is found – the power to depict and express things more poignantly and succinctly than any other dialect or language available to the Nigerian. But the major problems that face the promotion of NP as arrayed by Igboanusi cannot be over-looked because they are clear:

> The first problem relates to its perceived lack of economic value . . . (it) suffers from low social prestige . . . and from prejudices . . . The second problem is the fear that any expansion of NP will have adverse effects on indigenous language development . . . since speakers of such languages may perceive the inclusion of NP in the struggle for supremacy as a threat . . . (and) the main speakers of NP lack the power base to influence policies. The third problem is the perceived effect of NP on English language proficiency.
>
> *(75–76)*

Despite these fears, however, NP's empowerment case is valid. According to Mensah, linguists such as "(Essien 1993; Egbokhare 2003; Emenanjo 1985, etc) have called for the adoption of NP as the national language in Nigeria" (213); while others "(Marchese and Schnukal 1982) have called for its recognition as an indigenous Nigerian language as a result of its popularity, simplicity and neutrality" (213). Deuber supports this in her *Nigerian Pidgin in Lagos: Language Contact, Variation and Change in an African Urban Setting*: "NigP [NP] is as desirable a candidate for the status of a national language, and a considerably more realistic one, than the trilingual option" (188–189). Mensah caps it up thus: "The rivalry among the three dominant languages places NP at an advantage as a better alternative and indispensable favorite in the quest for a lingua franca of Nigeria" (213). This quest, long overdue, has recorded better successes by other countries and societies with similar peculiarities. Igboanusi's research shows that, "in Simo Bobda (2006:75), Kriolu is the national language in the Cape Verde Islands . . . while Creole is now co-official with French in Haiti. Sandred (1996:527) reveals that Krio is officially recognized as a national language of Sierra Leone" (75), among others.

As has been noted earlier, there has been a progression from the marginal use of NP in media and literature to more functional, widespread, and representational application of the same. Radio, TV, and other media outlets, especially social (internet), billboards, and literature (creative) are growing in their dedication to the propagation of NP. Of special interest here, resting on the backdrop of what Frank Aig-Imokhuede, Ken Saro-Wiwa, and Mamman Vatsa have done in the literary world using NP, is the twin-barrelled effort of Ezenwa-Ohaeto with his pidgin collections *If to Say I Bi Soja* and, to a large extent, *I Wan Bi President*. However, the position of NP with its wide acceptance and usage still remains a minority discourse medium, albeit a powerful one. This minority discourse remains because official, policy-backed endorsement is still lacking.

Meanwhile, the concept of minority discourse(s) that straddles the fields of sociology, postcolonialism, and cultural studies forms the crux of this treatise. In sociology, a minority group is a category of persons and/or a community who are subject to or experience certain disadvantages when compared to other members or dominant social groups. In this case, from the ongoing discussions, certain lacks and class segregation automatically place major speakers of NP in a minority position as against the formally accepted English, Hausa, Igbo, and Yoruba language speakers in Nigeria. The linguistic elements, cultural appurtenances, existential and ontological nuances, and indeed the fabric of being of these NP speakers, as it is their cultural identity, is placed in a marginalized position. This essentially positions NP in the minority discourse category as a less privileged but powerful medium. The speakers and "owners" of this medium are, for the purposes of this treatise, what we will regard as educational and social strata minority as distinct from other minorities of the same ilk, such as ethnic, racial, age based, involuntary, voluntary, gender and sexual, people with disabilities, political, religious, and women as a minority, and so on. Nevertheless, NP still remains an indispensable medium despite its minority discourse status as long as more writers toe the line of the likes of Ezenwa-Ohaeto and continue producing literature in the medium to ensure reach, versatility, and upgrade.

The case for pidgin literature, pidgin poetry, and Ezenwa-Ohaeto's pidgin poems

Certain questions and problems set the stage for appropriate replies and solutions. If colonial writers did not paint derogatory images of Africa (notably Joyce Cary's *Mister Johnson* and Joseph Conrad's *Heart of Darkness*), cultural nationalism as described by Emmanuel Obiechina would not have reckoning forces exemplified by Chinua Achebe's charge to let the world know, through his novels, that Africans are and were never savages who were saved by divinely appointed colonial masters. Allwell Onukaogu and Ezechi Onyerionwu put it thus: "Perhaps one of the first sociopolitical tasks which challenged the Nigerian writer of the pre-independence era was the need to counter the derogatory images of Nigeria and . . . Africa painted by colonial writers" (59). The "cultural renaissance" and "literary nationalism," as Onukaogu and Onyerionwu tag them, have Achebe, T.M. Aluko, Onuora Nzekwu, John Munonye, Chukwuemeka Ike, Gabriel Okara, and Adebayo Babalola as the proponents (60). With the fledgling Nigerian republic of the sixties teetering toward the war debacle, the atmosphere necessitated works such as Okara's *The Voice*, Wole Soyinka's *The Interpreters* and *Kongi's Harvest*, Achebe's *A Man of the People*, and Christopher Okigbo's *Labyrinths (with Path of Thunder)*, these being prophecies against the impending doom. When the war itself inevitably drew blood and wreaked carnage, literature again captured it as a peculiarity, with corresponding paragraphs and verses ranging from Soyinka's *Season of Anomy*, Festus Iyayi's *Heroes*, Ike's *Sunset at Dawn*, and Isidore Okpewho's *The Last Duty*, to Soyinka's *A Shuttle in the Crypt*, *Idanre and Other Poems*, Achebe's *Beware Soul Brother*, J.P. Clark's *A Decade of Tongues*, and others. This trend continued through the military era. Onukaogu and Onyerionwu comment:

> Nigerian writers once again swooped on the . . . major themes of the day, which bordered on a socioeconomic, political and cultural tragedy. Writers like Chinua Achebe, in *Anthills of the Savannah*, queried the rationale behind persistent military domination of the Nigerian nation . . . Others like the Poet Ezenwa-Ohaeto in the . . . pidgin poems, *If to Say I bi Soja* and *I Wan bi President*, satirized the high-handedness of the . . . men in uniform.
>
> *(65)*

Ezenwa-Ohaeto, in *Subject, Context and the Contours of Nigerian Fiction*, relates to the issue of societal responses such as the Onukaogu and Onyerionwu take: "This development is not unexpected, considering the fact that African literature is informed by social affairs as well as the culture, politics, economy, and religious activities prevalent on the continent" (1). From a sure-footed critic's standpoint, Ezenwa-Ohaeto defends the use of pidgin for literature and at the same time defensively preempts future attacks by restructuring Achebe's warning during the controversies concerning African literature:

> The European critic of African literature must cultivate the habit of humility appropriate to his limited experience of the African world and purged of the superiority and arrogance which history so insidiously makes him heir to.
>
> *(6)*

Achebe's previous quote forms the structure and tenor for Ezenwa-Ohaeto's defense of the use of pidgin as a special tool appropriate for the peculiar times in need of the conscientious writers' radical intervention(s):

> The *elitist* critic of African literature must cultivate the habit of humility appropriate to his limited experience of the *pidgin* world and purged of the superiority and arrogance which history so insidiously makes him heir to.
>
> *(10)*

Ezenwa-Ohaeto's stance is that there is more to be learned and re-learned in this postcolonial dispensation for a rigid critic who has refused to embrace the dynamics of a society in perpetual flux and therefore in constant need and production of appropriate accessories and apparatuses and who will therefore will be lost and ineffectual. For priggish critics and naysayers, he advises that they should embrace the fact that there is always the possibility of originality in patterns or constructs that are unconventional and that all "theories inevitably converge in African litera-ture . . . (in) the zone of *relevance* because African literature has not imbibed . . . art for art's sake" (12) (Emphasis mine). Literature in NP is, in all ramifications, relevant.

The growth of literature written in NP was not a sudden occurrence – it snowballed into a sizable avalanche. First is Frank Aig-imokhuede's "One Wife for One Man" of which Tony Afejuku reports: "Aig-Imokhuede – can rightly be said to have popularized the use of Pidgin as a medium . . . with . . . his highly successful Pidgin poem, 'one wife for one man' . . . in the for-ties" (69). This was followed by Abigail Ukpabi's feminist-toned rejoinder, "one man, one wife (a wife's rejoinder)." The eighties saw an upsurge in NP poetry, for example, "I Bi Somebody" by Tanure Ojaide appears in his *The Eagle's Vision*; Tunde Fatunde's "Woman Dey Suffer" and "Bad Belle Too Much" both appear in *Okike* and *The Anthill Annual*, respectively. Chronicling the poems of the era, Diribe Amaechi writes and comments:

> In *Voices from the Fringe*, we have A. Ajakaiye's "Common Wealth" just as Haj Bello's "Haba! Father" appeared in Uche Nduka and Osita Ike's "Poets in Their Youth" . . . Anthony Ogunlowo's "Dem Dey Kill Dem Self" which is a ridicule of soldiers who through treachery and conspiracy, exterminate other soldiers; Godwin Erupi's "Chop-ping Freedom" which is an attack on military dictatorship; Onuorah Udenwa's "Who Send You?", which declaims the idea of "Civilized Soldiers".
>
> *(9)*

NP poems have not only appeared in magazines, journals, and anthologies, poets have also featured them in their personal collections. Frank Aig-Imokuede's *Pidgin Stew and Suffer Head* (1982) ranks as the first to appear in such a manner. It is a mixture of poems in both English (formal) and NP, totaling 21 poems in NP. The soldier Mamman Vatsa also came out with his 1985 collection, *Tori For Geti Bow Leg*, a collection of poems in NP. According to Amaechi,

Ezenwa-Ohaeto came out in 1986 with *Songs of a Traveller*, which contains "one pidgin poem", "If to Say I Bi Soja," while his next collection, *I Wan Bi President* (1988) is made up of poems in formal and NP, with NP poems dominating (9). His NP only poetry collection, *If to Say I Bi Soja*, was published in 1998.

In addition to the earlier stance of this treatise on peculiar social issues requiring unique responses such as NP is Ralph Uzoezie's musings on Nigerians' natural proficiency in NP as against English:

> It is perhaps the . . . awareness of these contradictions that have led new-generation Nigerian writers such as Ezenwa-Ohaeto, . . . to explore new linguistic models which can combine elements of both indigenous languages and the English language to teach a broader local audience without sacrificing their international listeners.
>
> *(367)*

Uzozie's stance may possibly be an outcrop of the position of the *bolekaja* troika, Chinweizu et al., on the ease of poetic comprehension as opposed to the obscurantism of the Euromodernist poets – J. P. Clark, Christopher Okigbo, M.J.C. Echeruo, and Wole Soyinka. Their charge against the Euromodernists is that their poems have:

> Glaring faults e.g. old fashioned, craggy, unmusical language, a plethora of imported imagery; a divorce from African oral poetic tradition, tempered only by lifeless attempts at revivalism.
>
> *(165)*

The African oral cadences the troika preaches are to be found in NP, as it represents the masses and the grassroots fabric of Nigerian society and above all appeals to them, allowing easy access. Ezenwa-Ohaeto's NP poems provide what society can easily relate to, which also gives them a sense of belonging.

According to Amaechi, Ezenwa-Ohaeto has been variously described as "'a restless spirit' (Nwachukwu-Agbada 1987), a 'poet-president' Omoife 1988), 'a dreaming Jacobin' (Okezie 1987), 'a rebel' (Uzoezie 1997) and so on" (12), but, in summary, the late professor was a teacher, scholar, critic, poet, and short story writer. He obtained his B.A. and M.A. degrees from the University of Nigeria, Nsukka, and his Ph.D. at the University of Benin; he also taught literature and English at various higher institutions in Nigeria and Germany. A prolific writer, his works include the poetry collections: *Songs of a Traveller, I Wan Bi President, Bullets for Buntings, If to Say I Bi Soja, Voice of the Night Masquerade, Chants of a Minstrel*, and so on. He also wrote the seminal *Chinua Achebe: A Biography*. Ezenwa-Ohaeto won several poetry prizes, including a BBC Arts and Africa Poetry Prize; Best Poem Orphic Lute Prize; a University of Nigeria, Nsukka prize; and the prestigious Humboldt Research Fellowship in Germany. Shortly before his death in 2005, he was joint winner of the $25,000 NNLG (Nigerian Natural Liquefied Gas) Award for Literature.

Ezenwa-Ohaeto's poetry shows him for what he is: an angry agitator for social justice. His satire spares none on the subjugation of the masses as he continually rails against the culprits. The privileged class and unscrupulous rulers, especially the military, are the targets of his barbed jibes. In Amaechi's words: "Ezenwa-Ohaeto's poems are a missile directed at the oppressors of the masses"; he continues: "it is in his Pidgin poems that his best colour as an angry poet, a revolutionist, a 'rebel' personified, blooms" (14). This is Uzoezie's observation:

[the] first two volumes catalogue the iniquities in the human social systems in a part-pleading and part-angry tone. In the later volume(s), the poet has become a fearless mouth piece, . . . of an anonymous and faceless majority whose apparent inconscience [sic], insensitivity and passivity against its oppressors and tormentors who systematically dehumanize it frustrate the poet and turn him into a rebel using poetry as bullets to effect a speedy revolution and change the status quo.

(373)

The real tenor of a charged minority discourse medium is effective with Ezenwa-Ohaeto's NP poems. His persona as a fighter for the subjugated in the ever-poignant garb of poet, delivering in bare-knuckled, hard-hitting language of the masses – Nigerian Pidgin – becomes through his verses the quintessential subaltern who must speak despite the minority status of the class strata he represents. Our interest in the NP poems is born out of the fact that they are couched in a language that despite its grassroots reach, base, and structure has no official backing for development. It continues to be neglected despite all the positivity it promises and harbors, its predicament very akin to the plight of almost all minority constructs and discourses. Nevertheless, its message and punching power in the hands of Ezenwa-Ohaeto are true, real, and pungent.

In *If to Say I Bi Soja* (1998), a collection of 30 NP poems in five sections, the first, "Only me no Get Mouth", opens as he stubbornly prepares himself to speak out in the midst of hardship, even if everyone else is cowed into silence. In lines 15–17, he says "No bi only me get mouth/But I go dey talk true/My power pass all dem weapon" in order to register his defiance. He demonstrates the strength in and behind his venture in "De Poem Go Talk," where he shows that a strong voice is needed through strong poetry to speak the truth: "I wan poem wey go kill/. . ./I wan poem wey strong . . ./I wan poem wey go bite . . ./We wan poem wey go kill." In "How I go Believe You?", he tackles the untrustworthy, dishonest, and lying nature of the wealthy and powerful. His questions: "You say you no get kobo/But your dress dey expensive . . ./You say Kontri no rich/ Oil money you carry alone . . ./How I go believe you?/ You say you be honest man/Public property you don steal . . ./ You say you get better plan/All bad people na your friend . . ./How I go believe you?"

"We no Get Cook" is a satire on Nigerian leaders and their incompetent, inconclusive, and clueless regimes, likening the leaders and rulers who succeed each other to incompetent cooks that mismanage the resources and produce tasteless trash as food. "Messiah Don Come" chronicles Nigeria's history, civil war, and the trademark incompetent military and civilian interchanging rulership failures. In "Fire Game," the poet satirically comments on convenient 'fires' that take care of fraud cases, shoddy investigative panels, and the culture of "unknown" everything. Hear him: "Kalakuta house burn to ashes/Na unknown soldier,/Smuggler load miss for border/Na unknown customs,/Student wey bullet kill/No be unknown policemen?" (lines 61–66). "Politician na Wind" and "As One General Pray" expose politicians' dishonesty and empty promises and a general's greedy and unconscionable prayer to amass ill-gotten wealth, respectively.

The title poem, "If to Say I Bi Soja," is a satirical litany of corrupt, inept, and greedy wishes that corrupt soldiers are actually known for in Nigeria. Lines 21–31 of the poem summarize the whole idea:

If to say I be soja
My stomach for don big
My cheeks for don fat

Who for dey pass for road
If to say I bi soja
Who for talk for my face
I no for dey take examination
Weder I pass or no pass
I for dey get plenty promotion
And small time I go become
One big better General so,

These "wishes" present the actual ills of a non-professional, greedy, and power-hungry military that aspire to gluttony, high-handedness, corruption, and other vices. In "Wetin Dis Generation Do?", the poet laments the disadvantaged and hopeless conditions of the present generation: "For dis generation/Dem no see employment/. . . Dey look for even labourer work/But labourer work no reach dem,/. . . Dem no see house live/Dem no see land buy" (Lines 13–20). In "Blood don Soak de Land" and "Africa Get Problem," Ezenwa-Ohaeto tackles the blood-letting in apartheid South Africa and Africa's woes as a dumping ground for the West, coupled with its incessant internecine wars, respectively.

The NP poems in *I Wan Bi President* (1998) present a more eclectic array of themes. In "Catch Naira for Me," the love for money, including the weakened and inflationary naira, is satirized, and the need for workplace respect for all co-workers, especially the low placed, is emphasized. He closes it with this admonitory advice for office superiors: "Oga as you get promotion/ . . . /I greet you well well/Make you remember say/Na right hand dey wash left hand" (lines 29–33). The disgust of helplessness in the fight against societal anomalies is the subject matter of "De Thing Wey My Eye See" as it ends with the worst scenario saved for the unwritten last because he addresses the listener: "Make you wait small stranger/E get de thing de mouth no fit talk" (lines 41–42). The poem ends with the poet's assumed inability to chronicle further. "Fingers no Equal" features the issue of capitalism and the stark contrast between the haves and the have-nots and all other undesirable opposites. The need to be logical and practical when it is needed is aptly juxtaposed with the misplaced religiosity of religious resignation in the philosophical "Where God Dey?", while the backwardness of African countries is "celebrated" in "My Life Don Spoil." In this poem, the terrorists in Angola and Namibia and the apartheid police brutality of South Africa are compared to the West's moon voyages and other ground-breaking technological feats.

"Water no Get Enemy" is the lament of the common man, the poor and ordinary. The poem is put in the construct of water: it can serve anybody and suffer from anybody; it has no enemy. It is captured in this stanza:

You take money slap me
I turn make I open mouth
You take power box me
I fall for ground begin get up
You take money kick me for head
I begin dey cry small small
You take power hit me for eye
De only question wey I begin ask
Na to know wetin I do you
You sabi say water no get enemy
                    (lines 55–64)

The title poem, "I Wan Bi President," is a scathing satire on African and Nigerian leaders from the perspective of a helpless and dreaming commoner. The rulers in Nigeria and Africa bask in ill-gotten opulence at the expense of their subjects. The poet comments on the fact that the president never goes hungry or thirsty, he answers to no police, is served round the clock, motorcade sirens clear the roads for him only, his servants are well fed, some never lose elections – they rule forever; they have no worries, least of all the plight of the populace. They are unlike working leaders burdened with ideology; they have no need for that. Do not question them or you will die: "Some president dem dey/Wey dey kill person like dem be flies/ If you frown face na firing squad/If you say you no see food chop/Na bullet you go see chop one time" (77–81). These presidents live life to the hilt; they get choice girls, do whatever they like, and bag all kinds of titles, and he (the poet) really wants to be like them. Of course, this is tongue-in-cheek, but Ezenwa-Ohaeto pulls the perfect self-effacing punch line when he reminds us that this is a dream: "My broder/I wan bi President/Even for my Papa House/But na dream I dey dream" (146–149).

Ezenwa-Ohaeto's NP poems, as we can see, have the voice and quality of the lowly and suffering. They are earthy and unpretentious; they communicate directly without ornamentation, and the satire is both biting and amusing. He chose the medium the common man can afford, the one at his disposal as a minority, and has spoken to power.

Conclusion

Pidgin has been treated in this discourse – its meaning, concept, and the beginnings – and, in the Nigerian case, the role of the coastal communities and the European visitors. Again, the widespread popularity of the emergent and systematized Nigerian Pidgin is weighed, and it is sad that, despite all its qualities, the government of Nigeria has yet to give it a befitting and utilitarian official status. Nevertheless, other agencies, persons, businesses, and the literati who know the value of NP have been using it to great success and advantage in passing messages across to desired audiences, its minority discourse status notwithstanding.

Literature, in its peculiar manner, continues to move alongside society in its twists and turns, serving and representing as the contexts morph and aggregate. NP, from its modest and trickling beginnings, has in the hands of Ezenwa-Ohaeto shown that despite all the shortcomings and obstacles of approval and the stigma of minority unapproved status, it remains a formidable medium that has been used variously to speak truth to power. This, done in the most pungent of manners, has left few or none in doubt that indeed Nigerian Pidgin has all it takes to build positivity up and also pull negativity down – it only needs the right craftsman to weave thoughts, hopes, and worlds out of its words.

Works cited

Achebe, Chinua. *Morning Yet on Creation Day: Essays.* London: Heinemann, 1975.

Afejuku, Tony. "Towards a Nigerian Standard Pidgin Literature". *Okike.* 34 (October, 1996): 65–73.

Amaechi, Diribe. "Poetry in Pidgin English: A Study of Ezenwa Ohaeto's *I Wan Bi President* and *If to Say I Bi Soja*". Unpublished MA Thesis, 2000. Abia State University, Uturu, Nigeria.

Bolander, Donald, et al. Eds. *The New Lexicon Webster's Dictionary of the English Language.* Danbury: Lexicon Publications, 1995.

Chinweizu, et al. *Toward the Decolonization of African Literature I.* Enugu: Fourth Dimension, 1980.

Dauber, Dagmar. *Nigerian Pidgin in Lagos: Language Contact, Variation and Change in an African Urban Setting.* London: Battlebridge, 2005.

Dauber, Dagmar and Lars Hinrichs. "Dynamics of Orthographic Standardization in Jamaican Creole and Nigerian Pidgin". *World Englishes.* 26.1 (2007): 22–47.

Elugbe, Ben and Augusta Omamor. *Nigerian Pidgin: Background and Prospects*. Ibadan: Heinemann, 1991.

Ezenwa-Ohaeto. *If to Say I Be Soja*. Enugu: Delta, 1998.

Ezenwa-Ohaeto. *I Wan Bi President*. Enugu: Delta, 1988.

Ezenwa-Ohaeto. *Subject, Context and the Contours of Nigerian Fiction*. Eckersdorf: Bayreuth Africa Studies Series, 2007.

Faraclas, Nicholas. "Nigerian Pidgin". *The Mouton World Atlas of Variation in English*. Eds. Bernd Kortmann and Kerstin Lukenheimer. De Gruyter, 2012. 417–432.

Ferguson, C.E. and C.A. de Bose. "Simplified Registers, Broken Language, and *Pidginization*". *Pidgin and Creole Linguistics*. Ed. A. Valdman. London: Indiana University Press, 1977. 99–125.

Gaudio, Rudolf. "The Blackening of 'Broken English'". *Journal of Linguistic Anthropology*. 23.2 (2011): 230–246.

Heyd, Theresa. "The Metacommunicative Lexicon of Nigerian Pidgin". *World Englishes*. 34.4 (2015): 669–687.

Igboanusi, Herbert. "Empowering Nigerian Pidgin: A Challenge for Status Planning?". *World Englishes*. 27.1 (2008): 68–82.

Mann, Charles. "Reviewing Ethnolinguistic Vitality: The Case of Anglo Nigerian Pidgin". *Journal of Sociolinguistics*. 4.3 (2000): 458–474.

Mensah, Eyo. "Grammaticalization in Nigerian Pidgin". *Ikala*. 17.2 (2012): 167–179.

Mensah, Eyo. "Lexicalization in Nigerian Pidgin". *Concentric: Studies in Linguistics*. 37.2 (2011): 209–240.

Onukaogu, Allwell and Ezechi Onyerionwu. *21st Century Nigerian Literature: An Introductory Text*. Ibadan: Kraft Books, 2009.

Osoba, Joseph. "Analysis of Discourse in Nigerian Pidgin". *Journal of Universal Language*. 16.1 (2015): 131–159.

Osoba, Joseph. "The Use of Nigerian Pidgin in Political Jingles". *Journal of Universal Language*. 15.1 (2014): 105–127.

Reneicke, J.E. "Trade Jargons and Creole Dialects as Marginal Languages". *Language in Culture and Society*. Ed. Dell Hymes. New York: Harper and Row, 1964. 534–546.

Tiffen, Brian. "The Position of English in African Education". *A Language in Common*. Ed. Brian Tiffen. Essex: Longman, 1969. 7–13.

Todd, Loreto. *Modern Englishes: Pidgins and Creoles*. Lexford/London: Stockwell/Andre Deutsch, 1984.

Ugot, Mercy, et al. "Nigerian Pidgin Variations in the Ikom-Ogoja Axis of Cross River State, Nigeria". *International Journal of Applied Linguistics and English Literature*. 2.2 (2013): 223–231.

Uzoezie, Ralph. "Old Songs in a New Flute: Theme, Language and Audience in Ezenwa-Ohaeto's Poetry". *Neohelicon*. 24.1 (1997): 363–383.

10

THREE MOMENTS OF MINOR AFRIKAANS LITERARY EXPRESSION

Hein Willemse

دان اس نودخ اك موت سكريجو مت دي تال وت ميري دويدلك اس توسن هولل لات هولل كن ويت اكام
مت خماكاك اب دي رختي منري
(Abu Bakr Effendi, *Bayān-al-Dīn* [1869/1877])[1]

Afrikaans is 'n witmanstaal, 'n suiwer Germaanse taal, een van suiwerheid, een-voudigheid, bondigheid en kragtigheid.

(S. J. du Toit in *De Zuid-Afrikaan* [1874])[2]

[ons] digkuns wil die kuns wees wat die swartman direk aanspreek [. . .] totdat ons vry sal wees [. . .] die afrikaans wat [hier] bedryf word, word 'n krag van afrika tot bevryding.

(Patrick J. Petersen, *amandla ngawethu* [1985])[3]

Introduction

Afrikaans literature is a major South African literature, as is the Afrikaans language. It was not always the case. Its fortunes have fluctuated with changes in the political, economic, and social position of its speakers. The case of Afrikaans is highly instructive since the language was elevated from being a "variant of a major language" to a major regional language; its literature, once a "minor literature", evinces in the latter half of the 20th century the characteristics of a dominant (regional) literature. Using Gilles Deleuze and Felix Guattari's observations on "minor literature" as a point of departure, three moments of minor literary expression are discussed in the second half of this chapter.[4]

First, when Muslim teachers and writers (mostly former slaves) in the mid-19th century used Afrikaans, or more precisely, Cape Dutch, the patois of the lower classes, in their teaching, writings and translations amid a colonial environment where formally Dutch and later English were the dominant languages. The Afrikaans language and emerging literature in Deleuze and Guattari's formulation was "deterritorialized", dislocated, as in the second instance when (white) Afrikaner activists around the same time adopted the language as their vehicle for linguistic and social empowerment.[5] In the three decades following, they and their fellow nationalists embarked on a concerted drive to secure their cultural-politico and economic aims. The position of Afrikaans was reterritorialized as a language of power when it became an official language in 1925 and especially after 1948 when the vanguard of Afrikaner nationalism, the National Party, won a parliamentary election. A third moment of minor literary expression can be identified when black Afrikaans writers in the mid-1970s associated themselves with Black Consciousness and engaged in overt anti-apartheid writing and activism. They experienced Afrikaans and their varieties of Afrikaans as deterritorialized, dislocated from the government's language of power or the "generally civilized" language of the dominant version of Afrikaans culture.

Preceding the discussion of these three moments of minor literary expression, two key factors informing Afrikaans literary history are explored. It is necessary to provide a background to the development of Afrikaans, especially since the mid-19th century up to the mid-20th century, when it became reterritorialized as an official and increasingly dominant language. It is also important to note that access to education fundamentally shaped the nature of South African society and, in the present instance, the production of literature in South African languages.

On terminology: minority and majority

In a lengthy diary entry on Christmas Day, 1911, Franz Kafka (206–213; Brod 191–197) made notes on the notion of *kleiner literaturen* along with observations about his own family history, Jewish life in Russia and the dominant impact of Goethe on German literature. In the extensive introductory sentence, he enumerates the many gains of literary labor *(dass viele Vorteile der literarischen Arbeit)* – an outline of his thoughts on Czech literature and his discussions with a friend on Jewish literature in Austro-Hungarian Warsaw. He advances several gains that an "own literature" apparently bestows on "a nation". With their publication *Kafka. Pour une littérature mineure* in 1975 and its English translation *Kafka, Toward a Minor Literature* in 1986, Deleuze and Guattari developed from these and other Kafka writings their concept of *littérature mineure* ("minor literature"), thereby bequeathing to literary historiography a layered concept, hinting at once at its literary evaluative, tonal, psychoanalytical, sociocultural and political undertones.[6]

In a 1991 interview, Deleuze remarks on the distinction between "majority" and "minority":

> The difference between minorities and majorities isn't their size. A minority may be bigger than a majority. What defines the majority is a model you have to conform to. . . . A minority, on the other hand, has no model, it's a becoming, a process. One might say the majority is nobody. Everybody's caught, one way or another, in a minority becoming that would lead them into unknown paths if they opted to follow it through.

Deleuze and Guattari (18) regard the three features of a minor literature as "the deterritorialization of language, the connection of the individual to a political immediacy, and the collective assemblage of enunciation". Deterritorialization in this sense marks the dislocation of people, place and language, where, to use their example, the Czech majority and Jewish minority in Bohemia speak German, the region's prestige language, with "a withered vocabulary, an incorrect syntax", "appropriate for strange and minor uses" (22, 17). It is within this context of "a language . . . affected with a high coefficient of deterritorialization" that a minor literature ("a minor practice", 18) comes about, constructed by a minority "within a major language" (16). Such moments of deterritorialization would lead to vitality and new forms of expression, resulting in the "revival of regionalisms, with a reterritorialization through dialect or patois" (24).

Kafka explicitly references the political in his diary entry, while Deleuze and Guattari (17) state that "everything" in a minor literature is "political". In this sense, individual concerns and individual intrigues "connect immediately to politics" (17). The defense of a "small" people's identity and the rise of national consciousness are plainly treated in Kafka's notes. Literature, he posits, "is less a matter of literary history than a matter of the people" and everyone is implored "to defend and champion" the literature that "belongs to him", even if he does not know or support it *(wenn er ihn auch nicht kennt und trägt)* (Kafka 208). The third characteristic of a minor literature is the collective nature of it: that it is not dominated by (a) major writer(s). Literature functions as an expression of the "national consciousness" while the political has "contaminated every statement" (Deleuze and Guattari 17). Within this realm of the collective, literature's revolutionary potential comes to the fore, producing "an active solidarity" (17). Deterritorialized language can lead to an enrichment of language, vibrating with new intensity (18).

An overview of selected factors informing Afrikaans literary history

From a language of becoming to a monologic symbol

As early as the 15th century, several North Atlantic European seafaring merchant companies attempted to settle outposts on the southern west coast of Africa. It was the Dutch Vereenigde Oostindische Compagnie (East India Company; VOC) that eventually built "an earth fort in the vicinity of an abandoned Danish fort" in 1652 (Mlambo and Parsons, 64). During the next two centuries, the economic, sociopolitical and cultural power relations of the inhabitants of the place that the indigenes called Camissa, the place of sweet waters, and the seafarers called the Cape of Good Hope, would change fundamentally. The VOC's outpost became a permanent settlement with domesticated local labor, imported slaves and an assortment of European settlers – a greatly divergent community of people deterritorialized through colonial capitalism not only from their original localities but also from their languages and cultures (Davids 51–56, 59–63). The geopolitical influence of successive Dutch (1652–1795), Batavian (1803–1806) and British colonial administrations (1795–1803; 1806–1910) in this region would eventually reach the Great River, the Eyn or Gei-Gariep (later renamed the Orange). During the mid-19th century, offspring of the European settlers breached the colony's boundaries, embarking on a wave of northward migrations, some of them reaching the Limpopo River and beyond.

For about 150 years, Dutch was the administrative language of the Cape, the language of commercial, economic, judicial and political power or in Deleuze and Guattari's sense (following Henri Gobard 23–24) the vehicular language that is "everywhere". In consequence, an indigenous contact language with Dutch as its lexifier developed among the local disparate underclass population. The deterritorialized speakers of this evolving language were mostly remnants of dispersed indigenous communities, newly colonized laborers, imported and locally born slaves, hybridized communities and locally born farmers.

This creolized patois (or stated otherwise: this vibrancy of "minor practices") evolved into the first language of a sizable lower-class speech community. Cape Dutch, as it became known, was "welded from different tongues by white, brown and black people" and became the lingua franca of the Cape Colony (Giliomee 216). In visitors' travelogues or comedies and farces produced for the local colonial Dutch-English elite or in letters to the local English-medium newspapers and in editorials, their speech was ridiculed and lampooned as "Hotnots-Hollands" (Hottentot Dutch) or "Kitchen Dutch" (Davids 62; Giliomee 216). By the beginning of the 19th century, there was a clear distinction between metropolitan Dutch and Cape Dutch, that is, between the normative major expression and the "withered" speech of the patois (see Davids 50; Deleuze and Guattari 22). During the upsurge of Afrikaner centeredness by the end of the 19th century, local linguists were at pains to identify several stratified racialized varieties of Cape Dutch often reduced to the nationalist-inspired binary pair "White" or "Citizens' Afrikaans" and "Hottentot Afrikaans" (Van der Merwe and Posthumus 69). Despite these seemingly static social (and linguistic) categorizations, there is clear evidence of significant linguistic cross-pollination in 19th century Cape Dutch across all social indices. Eventually, by the beginning of the 20th century, it became known as "Afrikaa" or "Afrikaans" (i.e. literally "from Africa") (Davids 139).

The first extensive usage of Cape Dutch as a medium of instruction probably occurred in the madāris, the Muslim religious schools. Since the early to mid-19th century, imams, often former slaves, taught Islam through Cape Dutch written in Arabic script and contributed to creating a local Muslim scribal tradition (Davids 36, 64–75, 84). Although similar processes of Cape Dutch literacy were taking place in several 19th-century Moravian mission stations, this form of Cape Dutch/Afrikaa/Afrikaans in Arabic script developed into a distinctive form of Islamic instruction. Later, this format of Afrikaans was Latinized and continued until the late 1950s, when English became the prevalent language of madrassah instruction (Davids 33).

Towards the turn of the 19th century, especially among the locally born, Cape Dutch-speaking offspring of the European settlers, a sense of resistance developed against the imposition of the English language and imperial rule, exacerbated by the defeat in the South African War (also called the Anglo-Boer War, 1899–1902) of the independent regions across the Caledon (Mohokare) and Vaal (Tky-Gariep) Rivers, respectively: the Oranje Vrystaat (OVS) and the Zuid-Afrikaansche Republiek (ZAR). Claiming the descriptor "Afrikaner", successive nationalist leaders – political and cultural – expressed a sense of Christian predestination and exclusivity while campaigning for political self-determination; the equal use of Afrikaans instruction in educational, business and judicial institutions and the elevation of it to official status.

The South African War at the turn of the century unleashed hitherto unimagined economic and political forces and ethnic and social ordering that would shape the country for the rest of the 20th century. The country experienced profound political transformation, early industrialization, a succession of regional migrations, inward migration to southern Africa, internal conflict and increased ethnic and social class stratification, among others. For the African and Coloured minorities, in Deleuzian terms, the prospects of integration in the mainstream economy and social life were foreclosed (Marks 144). In the aftermath of the war, after an initial period of diminished fervor, a wave of renewed Afrikaner nationalist activism followed which strengthened the position of Afrikaans in a variety of ways. Alongside Dutch and English, Afrikaans became the third official language of the Union of South Africa in 1925. Even if this and other "successes were hard won" (see Steyn, *Tuiste in eie taal* 230), they were predicated on the rigid racial demarcation of those of "European descent" and the "non-Europeans" who were largely precluded from participating as citizens in the Union.

English supremacist detractors often ridiculed early 20th-century Afrikaans for its perceived limited lexicon and its lack of a long literary tradition, unlike English (Steyn, *Tuiste in eie taal* 213). It was in the north where the designs of an emerging Afrikaner intelligentsia – clergymen, journalists and writers – were taking shape, closely linked to the methodical "redutchification" of Afrikaans, the establishment of language and cultural institutions, agitation for the equal treatment of Afrikaans in education, the setting up of Afrikaner businesses and the shoring up of an ethnic nationalism. Redutchification was aimed at reterritorialization, that is, making Afrikaans respectable in the eyes and to the ears of its speakers but especially at pitting it against the cultural dominance of English. In a narrow sense, it meant the standardization of the written language along the lines of *Algemeen Beschaafde Nederlands* (Generally Civilized Dutch); the excision of its lower-class variants associated with the indigene, Cape Muslims and lower-class white speakers and the weeding out of anglicism from everyday speech (see Uys 154–170; 177ff; Van der Merwe, "Taalbeïnvloeding en taalvermenging" 264).[7]

Over the first half of the 20th century, the scope and function of Afrikaans, its reterritorialization as a *kultuurtaal*, that is, a language of literature, culture, education and bureaucracy, took shape. In terms of Gobard's tetralinguistic model (in Deleuze and Guattari 23–24), Afrikaans at once filled at least three of his four spheres of language use with its attendant centers of power: as territorial vernacular; as vehicular language of government and bureaucracy, in practice, even replacing English and as referential language, "the language of sense and of culture". (The role of Gobard's fourth sphere, that is, as a language of myth, in this instance was fulfilled by the 17th-century High Dutch of the *Statenbijbel*, States Bible). From being a "minor practice", a language of becoming, Afrikaans became a symbol of the Deleuzian majority, the homogenous, standardized linguistic norm, the expression of government power, control and dominance. The reterritorialized, totalizing Afrikaans of Afrikaner nationalist governance and culture created *Algemeen-beskaafde Afrikaans* (Generally Civilized Afrikaans) as its monologic symbol.

Following their epoch-defining parliamentary election in 1948, the whites-only National Party, the standard bearer of Afrikaner nationalism, spawned a slew of policies that had lasting impact on South Africa and its people. Customary segregationist practices coalesced into fixed ethnic categorization and enforced political, social, educational and spatial separation. In response, black protest movements were galvanized in the first mass uprisings of the 1950s. Non-white South Africans increasingly felt discriminated against, while generations of white South Africans benefitted from the government's affirmative policies that included privileged schooling, job reservation and economic entitlement. These measures were followed by the balkanization of the country into separate ethnic authorities and Bantustans, mounting internal tensions within the ruling party and attempts at reform and pragmatism. With the nationwide uprisings of 1976, the National Party experienced an increased loss of legitimacy, an escalation in anti-apartheid resistance and intensified state repression in response.

By the mid-1970s, the government embarked on a policy that enforced the use of Afrikaans, alongside English, as a language of instruction in schools under the control of the separate Department of Bantu Education. The imposition itself had little educational justification, for it was chiefly a demonstration of Afrikaner nationalist dominance. Opponents to the policy called Afrikaans "the language of the oppressor". The policy was an overreach, and resistance protests broke out in June 1976 in Soweto, Johannesburg, on the central plateau and rapidly spread across the country, setting in motion an unsettled period eventually leading to the democratization of the country in the mid-1990s.

Reading, writing and printing: creating social difference

The anthropologist Sheila Patterson (90) observes insightfully that:

> The ruling class . . . uses education as a means for supplying itself with a docile labour force, sufficiently instructed and trained to perform its allotted tasks, but not to hanker after further knowledge or intellectual speculation. Where there is more than one subordinate class or group, the ruling group may use education and other devices to perpetuate the difference between those groups, and to allocate a different, though always subordinate status to each. In its own group it is able, by means of segregated education, to inculcate the principles of superiority and separateness from an early age, and thereby to perpetuate its own existence as a ruling group.

Patterson's statement made in 1953 may well serve as a characterization of the history of education in southern Africa since the beginning of European settlement. For the first two centuries, education was precarious, generally haphazard and, despite some colonial authority interventions, largely administered by under-resourced missionary societies. The notion of education, that is, arithmetic, reading and writing, in the 17th to 19th centuries needs some clarification. Although both the Dutch and British colonial powers provided some basic and structured education to the offspring of the colonial elite, the education of the indigenous Khoekhoen and the slaves was at best lamentable. Their education served as a tool of social differentiation, to inculcate a compliant work ethnic and to propagate Christianity. The purpose was mainly to teach slaves "a smattering of the Dutch language" (or English later on), often enticed with a tot of alcohol (Patterson 82, 91, 254). As late as 1805, missionaries were instructed "to teach only reading and the scriptures, and prohibited them from teaching the Hottentots to write" (Patterson 92; see also Davids 65, Marais 171).

Under these circumstances, the history of Muslim education is somewhat different. For almost 180 years of European settlement, the Cape was a slave-importing and slave-holding society, functioning at times as a Dutch penal colony. Besides the thousands of slaves imported from Southeast Asia, a number of Islamic resistance leaders and members of their families were exiled to the Cape (Giliomee and Mbenga 69; Kähler 101; Ross 194; see also Yunis and Reinders). An undetermined number of the slaves and the exiled were literates who had the ability to read and write Arabic and Austronesian languages such as Buginese, Javanese, Malayu and Sunda (Davids 51ff, 75ff). With time and language displacement in the Cape, these capabilities lessened, and fewer adherents had access to their religious texts. Nevertheless, among the leaders of the Muslim community a strong sense of loss of their "original language", "books" and "religion" remained, so that some of the key skills were retained and even transferred (see Gençoğlu 63).

The Dutch colonial authorities promoted Christianity as the language of civilization and actively prohibited the practice of Islam. Despite this prohibition (only lifted following British occupation), many slaves were attracted to Islam, since Muslims enjoyed "a high standing among them by reason of their sobriety, self-respect and civilisation" (Marais 173, see also Davids 64–65). It was in this community's informal madāris that the Islam faithful and converts were taught the reading and writing skills, even if in Arabic, that their forebears were denied in the colonial schooling system. Today, the *ajami* literary tradition of the Cape can be traced back to the 17th century with texts written in Arabic, *jawi* (Arabic-Malay) and Arabic-Afrikaans (Jappie 58; Kähler 101; see also Yunis and Reinders).[8]

In 1910, with the formation of the Union of South Africa, the nature and scope of education were influenced by the terms of unification. During the first half of the 20th century and under successive apartheid governments, the education of white and non-white children diverged greatly. The Union bequeathed on children of "European descent", including white Afrikaans speakers, compulsory, free public education, while the education of non-white children was mostly administered by religious denominations with insufficient resources.[9] The education of non-white Afrikaans speakers, primarily classified as "Coloureds", was beset by adverse social circumstances, restrictive syllabi, poorly trained instructors and limited vocational or career possibilities (Patterson 90ff). Prior to the 1950s, very few Coloured children ever reached the secondary school level, and some earlier observers deemed the nature and quality of their education to be "training for helotry" (quoted in Patterson 104).

This divergence in education had a direct bearing on the production of literature in South Africa, seen most clearly in the production of Afrikaans literature. In comparison to other South African languages, the production and growth of Afrikaans literature and publishing were spectacular. Numerous Afrikaans writers of "European descent" were published, and by the 1960s,

Afrikaans literary critics had constructed a comprehensive literary canon, created a literary history stretching back centuries, identified several literary greats and enabled a well-supported award system. In contrast, by the 1960s, less than ten non-white Afrikaans writers had published with established publishers.

Printing and literary production in South Africa can be traced to the importation of the first printing press towards the end of Dutch rule in the 18th century. The first printers were mostly missionaries who invariably produced religious tracts, books and translations of the Bible (Crocombe 2; Woeber 204–206). In the instance of Arabic script printing, Cape Dutch Islamic texts were initially printed in Turkey, Egypt or India and later during the 20th century even in Cape Town (Davids 89, 65; Kähler 102). Regardless of the colonial government's initial control and monopolistic tendencies, English printers, publishers and newspapers became fairly established in the major coastal towns, although the output was small and limited. South African English writers, mostly white up to the mid-20th century, actively sought the patronage of British and American metropolitan publishers and readers. Gradually, over the next century, among the broader public and among second and third English language writers, deterritorialized forms of English evolved, again marked by the practices of "minor", "creative", revitalized expression.

During the first decades of the 20th century, Afrikaans printers and publishers set themselves up in Cape Town and the Northern provinces. Afrikaans publishing was a nascent industry, but its output advanced in scope, volume and quality after mid-century, often benefitting from government printing and publishing contracts. By the 1980s, more Afrikaans books were published and distributed than in any other indigenous literature, even rivaling the internationally connected local English publishing industry. The growth of indigenous language literatures (in e.g. the Nguni, Sotho, Tshivenda and Tsonga languages) was constrained by illiteracy, lack of demand and elite suspicion that the National Party government was using indigenous language publishing for its apartheid ends.

Three moments of minor literary expression in Afrikaans literature

The Cape Muslim Afrikaans scribal tradition: دی تال وت میری دوبدلك اس

The first stirring of the conscious use of Cape Dutch in the 19th century was religious, initially with the Afrikaans Islamic scribal tradition and later with the suggestion that the Bible be translated for the benefit of the impoverished Coloured population (Steyn, *Tuiste in eie taal* 136–137).[10] Several years after slave emancipation (which happened in 1834), Muslim adherents formed at least one third of the inhabitants of Cape Town (Dangor 123; Davids 36). In a letter, Shaykh Abu Bakr Effendi al Amjadi (1814–1880),[11] a venerable Kurdish theologian, observed around the mid-19th century: "Muslim people were abused under Dutch rule and therefore Muslims have a strong dislike for the Dutch" (in Gençoğlu 62). Notwithstanding these antagonistic sentiments, the language of the Muslim community remained Cape Dutch, the lingua franca, while a small number could also express themselves in Malayu and Arabic (Davids 36, 84). Davids avers that although the local form of creolized Dutch was derided as the language of the uncivilized lower classes (*onbeschaafde volksklasse*), that is, the broader population consisting of Khoekhoen and other servants, former slaves, and the under-educated offspring of the settlers, Cape Muslims did not view it as inferior (Davids 61). "They saw Afrikaans as an inherent part of their psyche and were prepared to transmit it in writing, using their sacred script" (Davids 86).

In spite of being a sizable community, the Muslims were clearly a minority in the Deleuzian sense. Economically, they were impoverished, culturally marginalized and politically subservient to the former Dutch and from 1806 onwards to the ruling British colonial élite. The imams had produced religious tracts and publications for their learners and congregations since 1845. These bore the imprint of minor practice, that is, marginalized, vernacularized and written in a non-dominant orthography. In addition, these texts were excluded from broader social recognition and excluded from institutional protection and record-keeping. The unavailability of lithographers conversant with the Arabic script and presses that "could handle the printing of Arabic letters" prevented the mass distribution of early Arabic writing and translations (Davids 89). As early as 1830, a local English-medium newspaper reported that *Hidayutool Islaam* (Divine Guidance of Islam), written in the vernacular, could not be published due to these circumstances. One of the first published books to be written in Cape Dutch, Abu Bakr's *Bayān al-Din* (Explanation of the Religion), circulated for twelve years "as loose pages of study notes" before it was eventually printed in Constantinople in 1877 as "a gift from the Sublime Porte of the Ottoman Empire" to the Cape Muslim community (Davids 89–90; see also Dekker 8).

Texts produced in this scribal tradition, also called Arabic-Afrikaans, deal mainly with doctrinal matters and practices. Researchers have identified three broad categories, namely didactic religious texts, talismanic texts and sociohistorical texts, such as personal correspondences (Jappie 59; Dangor 125). As with Abu Bakr, some of the early prominent writers in the Cape Muslim scribal tradition were immigrants. Achmat Davids (137) regards the immigrant Shaykh Abdurahim ibn Muhammed al Iraki as one of the most influential and prolific writers in this tradition. Among his translations of religious texts and commentaries on social matters is his five-language travel glossary, *Vaif talige woordelais en kort sinnetjies in Arab, Farsi, Hindistani, Afrikaa en Engels* (Five language glossary and short sentences in Arabic, Farsi, Hindi, Afrikaa and English, 1905). Locally born writers such as Hisham Neamatullah Effendi, the son of Abu Bakr, and Abdurahman Kassiem Gamieldien wrote children's books toward the end of the 19th century and promoted their distribution to various madāris, as far north as Kimberley and as far southeast as the coastal town of Port Elizabeth. In 1898, Imam Abdurakib ibn Abdul Kahaar wrote the first Latinized Afrikaans text, *Kitāb Tarjamah al-Riyād al Badī'ah fi Usul al-Din wa ba'd furū al-Shañ-ah* (The Book explaining the Wonderful Garden relating to the Principles of the Faith and some Branches of Islamic Law), making Islam instruction available to converts who were not schooled in Arabic reading. Among the formidable contributors to this new direction was Shaykh Ganief Edwards, who wrote eighteen publications in Arabic-scripted Afrikaans but also played an important role in latinizing Afrikaans (Davids 136; see also Stell 94ff).

Some texts classified within the first category have been archived in South African public libraries, but the majority of texts within the second and third categories "are kept in private family collections" with people "wary of disclosing their *kietaabs* [books] . . . to outsiders" (Jappie 59, 60). Leading Arabic-Afrikaans scholars have compiled several inventories totaling about eighty texts falling within these broad categories (Davids 92–95). These, however, may not even be the fullest extent of texts in existence. In a recent search of a prominent imam's estate, several instances that have not been "recorded or mentioned" in the literature on Cape *ajami* texts were found among his books (Jappie 60). A researcher found that people's unwillingness to disclose their heirlooms may also be caused by "beliefs about the mystical nature of some of the *kietaabs*" (Jappie 60; see also Yunis and Reinders; Dangor 125).

If the Cape Muslim Afrikaans scribal tradition was practically invisible to the uninitiated, their expressive culture, that is, oral storytelling, folk music, festivals and carnivals, was there for all to see and experience. Tales and legends infused with the remnants of their lands of origin and their lived experiences were told after work, often accompanied by music (Du Plessis 53). It was in the Cape Muslim expressive culture, be it public choir and musical performances, that local, European and Southeast Asian influences commingled, not only in the use of musical instruments or genres but also in the use of their language idiom (see P. R. Kirby in Du Plessis

65–66). These popular texts, unlike the formality of religious textuality, expressed a practice of independent narrativity relating to historical longing, contemporaneous events and perspectives on the narrators' social, economic and political place in society. For example, Davids (142) cites a folksong called "Suid-Afrikaanse Lied" (South African Song), which pays homage to the British colonial authorities who emancipated the slaves and offered their services on the British side against the Northern republics whose forebears they associated with their subjugation:

> Suid-Afrika ons niem 'n eed om vry vir jou te veg.
> Om saam te woon en saam te dra vir vryheid en vir reg.
> Met majesteit en plegten trots, met hart en met verstand.
> Al wiet ons niets, ons bly steeds, met volk en vaderland.
> South Africa we take an oath to freely fight for you.
> To live together and together bear freedom and justice.
> With dignity and solemn pride, with heart and mind
> Although we know nothing, we still remain with the people and the fatherland.

Their minority status lies in their subject positionality, their differentiation and their distance from the colonial elite. While their expressive culture sets them apart from the dominant order, it also draws them together as a community:

> In Cape Town the folk-song flourishes because of these simple people who are the city's hewers of wood and drawers of water. At night they are transported to another world, when almost within a stone's throw of Adderley Street [the city's main street] old troubadours nod approvingly while youngsters sing the songs of other days.
>
> (Du Plessis 67)

While the Cape Muslim community has undergone significant anglicization in the latter half of the 20th century, aspects of Cape Muslim Afrikaans expressive culture persist as public performances in the present.

Making words and books: early Afrikaner print nationalism

During the latter half of the 19th century, a sense of discontent developed among some young Afrikaners against the growing imposition of English as the sole official language of the Cape Colony, even within private domains such as the church. Initial requests came forth from evangelists for a suitable Cape Dutch translation of the Bible, but very soon it was clear that "a movement for Afrikaans as a religious medium [turned] into one with classic nationalist aims": "we stand for our language, our nation and our country" (Giliomee 218). In a town outside Cape Town, a group of eight young men founded an activist group, the *Genootskap van Regte Afrikaanders* (GRA, the Society of True Afrikaners, est. 1875) and called themselves Afrikaners, signifying a distinct community of people of European descent, laying claim to the language as an expression of their people's character and their "most precious possession". Even if others thought this language to be identical to the patois of the "Hottentots" or the slaves, their leading intellectual drew a clear distinction: "Afrikaans was a white man's tongue, 'a pure Germanic language', one of purity, simplicity, brevity and vigor" (S. J. du Toit quoted in Giliomee 217).

The early Afrikaner nationalists would have recognized in Kafka's Christmas Day, 1911, diary entry resonances of their own minor literature vis-à-vis metropolitan Dutch writing or local

English prejudice, for example, the creation of a sense of consistent cohesion *(das einheitliche Zusammenhalten)* of a national consciousness in an often fragmented public life, the transmission of pride and support *(der Stolz und der Rückhalt)* in a hostile world, the recording of a nation's life *(dieses Tagebuchführen einer Nation)*, the bringing together *(Bindung)* of people who were disaffected *(unzufriedener Elemente)*, the integration of the "whole structure" of a people *(das ganze angewiesene Gliederung des Volkes)*, the tightening of attention *(die Einschränkung der Aufmerksamkeit)* of the nation on itself, the subsequent awakening of higher aspirations among the young, the politicizing of literary events, the refinement and resolution of disagreements between fathers and sons *(die Veredlung und Besprechungsmöglihkeit des Gegensatzes zwischen Vätern und Söhnen)*, the painful recognition and working through of national faults towards forgiveness and liberation and the development of a lively book trade (Kafka 210).

Early Afrikaans literary practices and practitioners remind one also of many of the traits that Deleuze and Guattari define as "minor literature": its collectivity, its sense of being politicized, its sense of sociocultural resistance and the absence of dominant literary masters. It is clear from the introduction of the first editorial of their newspaper *Die Afrikaanse Patriot* (The Afrikaans Patriot, est. 1876) that they had to persuade their readers – the newly interpellated – to the nationalist cause. Many members of the activists' putative community did not associate themselves with these ideas, but they were set on mobilizing them: "Afrikaners must be taught that Afrikaans was their mother tongue, and their duty was to develop Afrikaans as a *landstaal* (national language), along with Dutch" (Giliomee 217). The paper became the standard bearer of an Afrikaner proto-nationalism, reporting local and regional news that affected people they identified as fellow Afrikaners with a consistent demand for the equal treatment of Afrikaans in the public sector, the empowerment of Afrikaner education and businesses and a strident anti-imperial/anti-English orientation (see Steyn, *Tuiste in eie taal* 139–141).

The GRA activists also published a magazine, *Ons Klyntji* (Our Little One, 1896–1905), and literary and children's publications. The editors of *Ons Klyntji* in their first foreword envisaged the creation of a literary tradition: "We want to cultivate Afrikaans writers and therefore an Afrikaans literature". They actively created a counternarrative to British imperial history by writing their own Christian National history entitled *Die Geskiedenis van ons land in die taal van ons Volk* (The History of our Land in the Language of our People, 1877) and supported the standardization of written Afrikaans with *Di eerste beginsels van di Afrikaanse taal* (The First Principles of the Afrikaans Language) (see Giliomee 219). The leading figures of the movement and a band of supporters produced cookbooks, literary translations, poetry, plays and prose for the edification of the mostly poor and under-educated Afrikaners in the Cape and elsewhere espousing the virtues of rural life, Christianity, social mores, language and nationalism.

Novellas, poetry and plays, often biblically inspired, cultivated a readership with basic needs while forging a sense of collective history, Christian morality and ethnic association. The titles of some of these works capture their didactic or humoristic aims, like C. P. Hoogenhout's *Catharina, die dogter van die Advokaat* (Catharina, the Advocate's daughter, 1879); M. N. Neser's *Wat geld kan doen* (What money can do, 1879); Jan Lion Cachet's *Sewe duiwels en wat hulle gedoen het* (Seven devils and what they have done, 1882); G. R. von Wielligh's *Jakob Platji: Egte karaktersketse uit die volkslewe van Hotnots, Korannas en Boesmans* (Jakob Platji: True character sketches from the folk life of Hottentots, Korannas and Bushmen, 1896) and the prolific writer and primary intellectual figure, S. J. du Toit's *Di koningin fan Skeba* (The queen of Sheba, 1898) and *Magrita Prinslo, of, Liifde getrou tot in di dood: 'n historiese toneelstuk uit di tyd fan di grote trek* (Magrita Prinslo, or, Love until death: a historical play from the time of the Great Trek, 1897). By 1900, these writers and others had published about eighty works in Afrikaans (Steyn, *'Ons gaan 'n taal maak'* 34). Generally, literary scholars regard these publications as "thematically limited", "propaganda and didactic" and "weak sources of artistic inspiration" (Dekker 24; Kannemeyer 58–59). Yet these texts became the precursors of an expanding pan-Afrikaner print nationalism, creating a secular literary tradition and a sense of group cohesion and political solidarity exclusively aimed at those who identified as white Afrikaners in the Cape and in the OVS and ZAR (see also Steyn, *Tuiste in eie taal* 139).

From the 1930s onward, Afrikaner nationalists had positioned themselves as influential power-brokers while linguists wrote spelling rules, standardized and "redutchified" the Afrikaans language and literary critics actively fashioned a literary canon with its own literary masters, traditions and movements. With a few exceptions, the majority of early Afrikaans writers were white, and their thematic interests and envisaged readership tended to be ethno-nationalistic rather than broadly national. In concert with Afrikaans' institutionalization in the first half of the 20th century, cohorts of young intellectuals and scholars came to the fore contributing to its intellectualization, that is, the translation of the Bible; the development of general, bilingual and subject dictionaries; the writing of primers and dissertations and Afrikaans versions of textbooks in all subject areas from primary school to university level.

The Afrikaans writers and poets were revered. They gave Afrikaans "the status of a fully developed literary language", assisted in creating "a positive self-image of the Afrikaner" and "indirectly contributed to the national [election] victory" of 1948 (Steyn, *Tuiste in eie taal* 226). Although these poets closely associated themselves with the travails of the war and a nascent nationalism, some more closely than others, contemporaneous literary critics were keen on recognizing the first "real poets of our literature". In the collections of Eugène N. Marais (1872–1936), Jan F. E. Celliers (1865–1940), J. D. "Totius" du Toit (1877–1953) and C. Louis Leipoldt (1880–1947), they recognized "real poetry", involved themes, refined poetic form and "aesthetic beauty" (Dekker 57, 60ff). Marais' poems, including the iconic "Winter Nag" (Winter night), were hailed as portents of Afrikaans as a sophisticated literary language: "With one leap our poetry is elevated above what is only of concern to a people and their time. These poems would be prized possessions in any other language" (Steyn, '*Ons gaan 'n taal maak*' 86–87; Dekker 62).

As with many traditions, Afrikaans literary critics and young professionals regarded poetry as the most esteemed genre. Very soon they identified figures and works to canonize and invented eras of distinct decadal periodization, similar to Dutch literary history. They distinguished a second generation of "real poets", the poets of the 1920s ("Die Twintigers"), followed by the poets of the 1930s ("Die Dertigers"), "Die Veertigers" and so on. Being mostly trained in the Netherlands, these critics created an early comparative (and sustained) literary discourse with Dutch literary history and its established figures, some even suggesting continuities. They used the Dutch literary tradition as a buttress for an emerging Afrikaans literary tradition.

The first generation of professional literary critics identified N. P. van Wyk Louw (1906–1970) and D. J. Opperman (1914–1985) as the outstanding poets of their time: "Afrikaans was fortunate that it had early on in its history as a language of culture two [such] poets of stature. . . . Both created work of the highest order and both were nationalist oriented" (Steyn, *Tuiste in eie taal* 215; see also Olivier 308; Voss 339, 341). Of Louw, the premier poet of the 1930s, it was said: "He is one of the most outstanding living poets of the whole of the Dutch speaking world", "the greatest personality in Afrikaans literature" (W. A. P. Smit in Steyn, *Tuiste in eie taal* 215; Kannemeyer 386). The discourse of Afrikaner nationalism construed Louw as its most revered poet-intellectual, its most erudite literary critic and its most incisive sociocultural commentator.

A nationalism fueled by activist reactions to social derision, a bitter humiliating aftermath of a devastating war and a struggle for respectability found in Louw the epitome of the urbane nationalist who was knowledgeable about the world of letters and philosophy and whose writings could be measured "against the best world literature could offer" (Olivier 310; see also Voss 355). The nationalist orientation was clear: only a developed language as the symbol of a developed people could bring forth accomplished poetry, and, in turn, only the talented few of a people could produce accomplished poetry. Cultural bodies duly recognized the Dertigers' writing, written mostly in the now-established norm of *Algemeen-beskaafde Afrikaans*, ridding itself of its perceived backwardness. The writers were fêted for the "excellence of [their] literature and other cultural expressions that would endow the nation with the right to exist" (Olivier 310).

Within less than a century, a minor literature had gained the allure of a literature written in a major South African language. As with the Afrikaans language, it was reterritorialized as "our literature", the "white man's literature", "the Afrikaner's literature". Not all poets were on first appearance worthy of the emerging pantheon of Afrikaans literature. For various reasons, difference marked the authorships of Elisabeth Eybers (1915–2007), Olga Kirsch (1924–1997), S. V. Petersen (1914–1987) and P. J. Philander (1921–2006). As a woman, Eybers was denied membership of an Afrikaans literary society, while Kirsch, as a Jew, and Petersen and Philander, as non-white authors, were considered outsiders to the Afrikaner nationalist cause. In time, Eybers would be celebrated as Afrikaans' first significant woman writer.

The accomplished modernist poetry of the Dertigers was a harbinger of the ultimate political success of Afrikaner nationalism when the National Party won the elections of 1948 and thereafter for the following couple of decades systematically implemented their apartheid policy and the institutionalization of standardized Afrikaans in the civil service. As stated earlier, this policy eventually led to the implementation of the 50–50 Afrikaans-English language policy in the Department of Bantu Education, triggering the 1976 protests.

Reclaiming Afrikaans: black anti-apartheid writing

It was considered exceptional at the time that with the rise of an ethno-centered Afrikaans literary system, establishment publishing houses published non-white writers such as Petersen and Philander, the poet-playwright Adam Small (1936–2016), the playwright Paul Roubaix (ps. Isaac Pfaff, 1920–2005) and the novelist Arthur Fula (1908–1966). However, the impact of this ethnic-centeredness was soon clear: by the beginning of the 1960s, debuts of non-white Afrikaans writers had all but dried up (see Gerwel 17–18). With the forceful declamation of *Algemeen-beskaafde* Afrikaans as a written and official language, non-white first-language speakers had systematically been reduced to second-order participants. In the new hegemonic language and literary histories, their role, place and presence as Afrikaans speakers had been minimized and for much of the 20th century, their regional varieties were exoticized or treated as deficient.

Yet, counter-intuitively, in the wake of the 1976 uprisings, more black Afrikaans writers than ever before were self-published, published with small publishers or contributed to journals and publications associated with anti-apartheid organizations (Willemse, *Aan die ander kant* 154). For a variety of reasons, ranging from literary aesthetic to overt political considerations, they were excluded from the mainstream Afrikaans publishing houses (Petersen, "Digter van 'bevryde Afrikaans'" 19–20). In turn, they set up their independent publishing concerns and magazines, both rather ephemeral (Willemse, *Aan die ander kant* 164). The majority of these writers came from rural backgrounds working in occupations ranging from clergymen, teachers, bookkeepers and journalists to writers with working-class occupations. Many engaged in anti-apartheid activism as students or in their civil society organizations.

Among young non-white students and intellectuals, Black Consciousness emerged as the prevailing political orientation. They grew up under segregation and were schooled in enforced ethnic homogeneous institutions. They called themselves "black", and the term itself became a symbol of resistance, self-reliance and a way of reaching across the fissures that apartheid social engineering created (Coetzee 42–45). Most of these writers were classified Coloured and were based in the southern and southwestern regions, where Afrikaans, unlike in the center and the northern parts of the country, is the first language of people across ethnic and social backgrounds. In these regions, anti-apartheid political and civil society organizations and cultural bodies, including religious denominations, used Afrikaans as a lingua franca and as a medium of resistance and protest.

The slogan "Afrikaans is the language of the oppressor" may have had a ring of truth to it in the north; however, in the south, first-language Afrikaans speakers were primarily non-white, impoverished and as subjugated to apartheid rule as anywhere else. The Cape region is considered the cradle of the Afrikaans language and had been firmly established notwithstanding earlier non-white elite attempts at anglicization (Willemse, *Aan die ander kant* 158–159). In comparison to earlier administrations, the National Party government broadened access to secondary education and introduced first-language instruction, which further entrenched the language, especially in Coloured schools. However, the presentation of an Afrikaans curriculum heavily influenced by Christian National Education and the hegemonic narrative of its genesis and literary practices meant that even these first-language speakers felt alienated from it (Coetzee 40). It is from this background that the post-1976 generation of black Afrikaans writers emerged.

Some of the leading figures firmly associated themselves with the identity-affirming tendencies of Black Consciousness, while others regarded themselves as the representatives of underrepresented sections of the South African population (Willemse, "Die vooruitsig van oopheid" 11–13). The poet Patrick J. Petersen (1951–1997), a Dutch Reformed clergyman, declared that he came to Black Consciousness through Black and Liberation Theology: "It had a far-reaching impact on me. It made me feel part of this country. Black Consciousness brought political awareness. . . . Through Black Consciousness, as a shy man I simply became a different person" ("Digter van 'bevryde Afrikaans'" 20). Within a broader context, "shy" functions as a euphemism for the sense of alienation, inadequacy and inferiority that colonialism, white supremacy and apartheid passed on to generations of non-white South Africans.

Petersen breaks with this history of subjugation. He declares his poetry to be "a mighty weapon", "a bearer of the message of the people", "a weapon of a fighting voice where black cannot be a duplicate of white" (*amandla ngawethu* vii). The title of his debut volume, *amandla ngawethu* (The Power is Ours, 1985) is rendered in Xhosa rather than in Afrikaans, in itself a gesture pointing toward black solidarity across the ethnic divide that apartheid ideologues promoted. In a series of poems on South African women in his second volume *Advent* (1988), he refuses to celebrate only the women of "his kind" but deliberately crosses the divide of the apartheid separatist gaze. A tendentious, even militant, poetry of resistance emerged as well. Frank Anthony (1940–) writes of this incarceration as a political prisoner on Robben Island in *Robbeneiland, my huis, my kruis* (Robben Island, My House, My Cross 1983), while Kenneth de Bruin (1957–), in his poem "swart kind" (Black Child), references the violence that marked apartheid repression in the 1980s: "that is what your life is worth/black child/a deadly shot from a firearm" (Willemse, *Aan die ander kant* 192).

A second, somewhat controversial, tendency among some of this generation of poets is the activist reclamation of the Afrikaans language and particularly its Cape Vernacular variety (also called *Kaaps*), the contemporary scion of 19th century Cape Dutch. With the march of reterritorialization of *Algemeen-beskaafde* Afrikaans, the working classes of the Cape Peninsula region continued to speak and practice their culture in *Kaaps*. Adam Small, in several of his plays and collections of poetry in the early 1960s, valorized this stigmatized variety. Among the post-1976 generation of poets, Peter Snyders (197, 199) is its most prominent advocate, proclaiming it to be "a language in its own right": "*Kaaps* is a complex language . . . we're not lazy or slothful; we do not speak Afrikaans. We speak *Kaaps* and when we use our own language, we always speak it correctly, obeying its rules".

This development in Afrikaans literary history has been acknowledged as its most explicit occurrence of a "minor literature" in the Deleuzian sense (see Coetzee, Viljoen). These poets directly pit themselves against the canonized standards of Afrikaans language and literature, exploring quotidian practices and language variety. As with Deleuze and Guattari's theorization, much of what was written during this period was explicitly political, drawing these marginalized writers together, most notably in the Black Afrikaans Writers symposium, launched in 1985 and thereafter held at ten-year intervals until 2015 and the publication of several prose and poetry anthologies, including the notably titled *Aankoms uit die skemer* (*Arrival from the Dusk*, 1988) and *Optog* (March, 1990).

Conclusion

This chapter demonstrated that the trajectory of the Afrikaans language and literature over a period of about 150 years has a lot to do with its immediate sociopolitical context and the fluctuating fortunes of its speakers. In the mid-19th century, Muslim clergy established an Arabic-Afrikaans scribal tradition to address the spiritual needs of their flock, mostly recently emancipated, impoverished and illiterate slaves. Although the extant texts deal primarily with doctrinal matters, writers also produced talismanic and sociohistorical texts, which are under-represented in the public record. In addition to the religious features of the Cape Muslim scribal tradition, the Afrikaans expressive culture of the Cape Muslims presents us with a form of independent narrativity on social, political and cultural events. The *Genootskap van Regte Afri-kaanders* was established at about the same time. Its literature was initially deterritorialized and minor. However, within half a century, Afrikaner activists had established a literary culture that exhibits the characteristics of a dominant tradition. Since the mid-20th century, the Afrikaans language in its standardized form as *Algemeen-beskaafde Afrikaans*, to its detriment, has gained symbolic association with Afrikaner nationalism and political dominance. The third moment of minor literary expression that this chapter covered is the literature of the Black Afrikaans writers of the mid-1970s and 1980s. They resisted Afrikaans' association with the apartheid policies of the National Party government and created a vibrant anti-apartheid literary tradition produced through alternative outlets, publications and publishers. It should be said that the political, economic and social changes that are afoot in South Africa will continue to impact the place and status of the Afrikaans language and its cultural expressions.

Notes

1 "dan es noedigh ik moet skrijwe met die taal wat miere daidelik es tussen hulle, laat hulle kan wiet *agaama* met ghamaakelik op die righte maniere" ("Then it is necessary that I must write in the language that is clearer to you, so that you can do (practice) the religion *(agaama > agāma)* in the right manner") (Abu Bakr Effendi [iii], the original is unvocalized; see Kähler 106; Van Selms [vii] for alternative trans-literations). All translations are mine, unless stated otherwise.
2 "Afrikaans is a white man's language, 'a pure Germanic language', one of purity, simplicity, brevity and vigor" (translated and quoted in Giliomee 217).
3 "[our] poetry wants to be the art form that directly addresses the black man . . . until we are free . . . the afrikaans that is practiced here, becomes a force of africa for freedom" (Petersen, *amandla ngawethu* [vii]).
4 These are not the only moments of minor literary expression in Afrikaans literature. For instance, the early Afrikaans oral tradition, the Afrikaans writing of the women of the Garment Workers Union or

even the writings of individual writers could be identified as such (see Anker; Pakendorf; and Willemse, "'n Inleiding tot buitekanonieke Afrikaanse kulturele praktyke" 79–86).

5 A number of unavoidable South African ethnic descriptors are used in this chapter. These terms are often controversial, imprecise and confusing. They therefore need closer definition. All these terms are used for analytical purposes without prejudice. The term "white" people has been constructed through colonial differentiation. From as early as the mid-17th century, a term that suggested phenotype variance gained defined cultural connotations. The Dutch settlers differentiated themselves from the Khoekhoen as "Christians", "Europeans" and "whites". By the late 18th century, these terms became synonymous and were associated with superiority and education, while the indigenes and slaves were associated with inferior status, "colour and heathendom" (Patterson 91). The overarching term "Khoekhoen" refers to the indigenous pastoralists, consisting of a number of smaller communities. In colonial times, they were referred to as Hottentots. "Hottentot" is said to have derived from a distortion of *hette hie* or *hautitou,* a repetitive phrase used during Khoekhoen ceremonial dances. Since click sounds characterized their speech, the early Dutch travel writers often associated these with "stuttering". Hence Hottentot gained the secondary meaning of "stutterer" (Nienaber 76). In the main, the indigenes resisted the settlers' life of labor, with the result that the colonial authorities, up to the end of the 18th century, imported slaves to augment their labor needs. The slaves originated from the Asian archipelago, the coasts of the Indian subcontinent, the Mascarene Islands, Madagascar and Southeast and West Africa. The term "Coloured" originated in the 18th century to delineate people of color and later became a catch-all phrase denoting the offspring of liaisons between the indigenes, slaves, free blacks and colonists. Sections of the population so defined reject the term from the 1950s onwards, while others reclaim it in the post-1994 period. A term with a similar earlier connotation to Coloured is "Afrikaner" (African). In the 19th century, Cape Muslims called themselves "Afferkaners", as did the |Hôa-|aran, an Oorlams-Khoekhoen group, led by Jonker and Jager Afrikaner (see Davids 139; Willemse 42–43). From the late 19th century onwards, the term is used almost exclusively to refer to Afrikaans-speaking people of "European descent" (a term of difference used at the beginning of the 20th century), that is, white people. The nationalist leader S. J. du Toit glossed the word as follows in 1908: "Afrikaner or Afrikaander, a name we call ourselves, well with some presumptuousness, as if we are the only true owners of the whole of Africa!" (in Van der Merwe, *Vroeë Afrikaanse woordelyste* 230). The term "Cape Muslims" refers to adherents of Islam who are the progeny of the slaves imported from the archipelago or accepted into that community. Under colonial and apartheid legislation, they were defined as "Cape Malay" and classified under the broad rubric "Coloured". The term "African" in South African parlance is generally used to refer to Bantu-speaking people, indigenous to the country, excluding the Khoekhoen and the San or Bushmen people. "Black people" is used as an overarching term in the binary pair "white/black". The term, when used here, is intended as a more positive rendition of the colonial and apartheid negations "non-white" or "other than white". When the official terms "non-European" and "non-white" are employed, the usage should suggest enforced subordination or limited agency.

6 An alternative translation of Kafka's original concept is "small" rather than "minor" literatures. Joseph Kresh (Brod 194), in his translation of Kafka's diaries, prefers "the literature of small people", thereby underplaying the literary focal point in favor of foregrounding its political intent.

7 In 1959, with the 50th anniversary of the Academy of Science and the Arts, some intellectuals tended to mythologize the formation of the language, as the "miracle of Afrikaans", perhaps most memorably when the poet doyen of Afrikaans literature, N. P. van Wyk Louw, declared that the language "was given to us; we did not make it. . . . Our task lies in how we use and will use this shining vehicle" (Louw quoted in Steyn, *Tuiste in eie taal* 230).

8 The term *ajami* refers to non-Arabic texts and languages written in Arabic orthography. Among the many African languages written in Arabic script are Hausa, Mandinka, Longhanda, Oromo, Songhoy/Zarma, Somalian, Tamasheq, Wolof and Yoruba (see Chtatou; Haron).

9 Charles Simkins (499) notes that in 1885, white children had on average eight years of schooling, which increased by 1970 to twelve years. The comparative figures for non-white children were less than two years of schooling in 1885 and between eight and nine years in 1970; in the case of children of Indian descent, the relevant figure in 1970 was eleven years.

10 In early language histories, the Islamic scribal tradition or broadly non-Afrikaner traditions are minimized or simply ignored (see Van der Merwe, "Taalbeïnvloeding en taalvermenging"; Van der Merwe and Posthumus). In later, more recent writings greater, if still limited, attention is paid to the history of Afrikaans within these communities (see Steyn, *Tuiste in eie taal* 136–137; Steyn, *'Ons gaan 'n taal maak'* 39–40).

11 Traditionally, "Effendi" is a Turkish title of social eminence or nobility similar to the British "Sir". The South African offspring of Abu Bakr have adopted it as their family name.

Bibliography

Abu Bakr Effendi. *Bayān al-Din*. Constantinople, 1877.

Anker, Willem. "'Spanner in die wat?' – Wopko Jensma en die mineurletterkunde van Deleuze en Guattari." *LitNet Akademies*, vol. 8, no. 3, 2011, pp. 168–195.

Brod, Max, editor. *The Diaries of Franz Kafka, 1910–1913*, translated by Joseph Kresh. London: Martin Secker & Warburg, 1948.

Chtatou, Mohamed. "Using Arabic Script in Writing African Languages, Revisiting Isesco's Experience 25 Years Later: Field Successes and Shortcomings." www.academia.edu/11834406/USING_ARABIC_SCRIPT_IN_WRITING_AFRICAN_LANGUAGES. Accessed 15 Mar. 2019.

Coetzee, Ampie. "Swart Afrikaanse Skrywers: 'n diskursiewe praktyk van die verlede." *'n Vlag aan die tong. Gedenkbundel van die derde Swart Afrikaanse Skrywerssimposium*, edited by Hein Willemse & Steward van Wyk. Wilderness: Abrile Doman; Pretoria: Hond, 2015, pp. 38–52.

Crocombe, Jeff. "Hubertus Elffers (1858–1931) and the Dutch-English Tensions in the Developing South African Seventh-Day Adventist Church." Association of Seventh-Day Adventist Historians Conference, Maryland, 2010. www.researchgate.net/publication/274139981_Hubertus_Elffers_1858-1931_and_the_Dutch-English_Tensions_in_the_Developing_South_African_Seventh-day_Adventist_Church. Accessed 1 Mar. 2019.

Dangor, Suleman Essop. "Arabic-Afrikaans Literature at the Cape." *Tydskrif vir Letterkunde*, vol. 45, no. 1, 2008, pp. 123–132. www.scielo.org.za/scielo.php?script=sci_arttext&pid=S0041-476X2008000100007. Accessed 15 Mar. 2019.

Davids, Achmat. *The Afrikaans of the Cape Muslims*, edited by Hein Willemse & Suleman E. Dangor. Pretoria: Protea Book House, 2011.

Dekker, Gerrit. *Afrikaanse Literatuurgeskiedenis*. 7th expanded edition. Cape Town: Nasou, s.d.

Deleuze, Gilles & Felix Guattari. *Kafka, toward a Minor Literature*, translated by Dana Polan. Minneapolis; London: University of Minnesota Press, 1986.

Deleuze, Gilles & Antonio Negri. "Control and Becoming, Gilles Deleuze in Conversation with Antonio Negri." Translated by Martin Joughin. *Generation-Online.org*. www.uib.no/sites/ w3.uib.no/files/attachments/6._deleuze-control_and_becoming_0.pdf. Accessed 1 Mar. 2019.

Du Plessis, Izak David. *The Cape Malays*. Cape Town: Maskew Miller, 1944.

Gençoğlu, Halim. Abu Bakr Effendi: A Report on the Activities and Challenges of an Ottoman Muslim Theologian in the Cape of Good Hope. M.Phil diss., University of Cape Town, 2013.

Gerwel, Gert Johannes. "Van Petersen tot die hede: 'n kritiese bestekopname." *Swart Afrikaanse Skrywers. Verslag van 'n simposium gehou by die Universiteit van Wes-Kaapland op 26–27 April 1985*, edited by Julian F. Smith, Alwyn van Gensen & Hein Willemse. Bellville: University of the Western Cape, 1986. 11–22.

Giliomee, Hermann. *The Afrikaners: Biography of a People*. Cape Town: Tafelberg; Charlottesville: University of Virginia Press, 2003.

Giliomee, Hermann & Bernard Mbenga. *Nuwe Geskiedenis van Suid-Afrika*. Cape Town: Tafelberg, 2007.

Haron, Muhammed. "The Making, Preservation and Study of South African Ajami Mss and Texts." *Sudanic Africa*, vol. 3, no. 12, 2001, pp. 1–14.

Jappie, Saarah. "Taking a Local Turn: The Tombouctou Manuscripts Project Explores the Ajami Tradition at the Cape." *Annual Review of Islam in Africa*, vol. 10, 2008–2009, pp. 58–61. http://www.cci.uct.ac.za/usr/cci/news/Saarah_Jappie.pdf. Accessed 15 Mar. 2019.

Kafka, Franz. *Gesammelte Werke*, edited by Max Brod. New York: Von Schocken Books, 1951.

Kähler, Hans. "Studien zur arabisch-afrikaansen Literatur." *Der Islam*, vol. 36, no. 1–2, Oct. 1960, pp. 101–121.

Kannemeyer, John Christoffel. *Geskiedenis van die Afrikaanse Literatuur Band 1*. 2nd revised edition, Cape Town, Pretoria: Academica, 1984.

Marais, Johannes Stephanus. *The Cape Coloured People 1652–1937*. Witwatersrand University Press, 1968.

Marks, Shula. "Class, Culture, and Consciousness in South Africa, 1880–1899." *The Cambridge History of South Africa, Volume 2, 1885–1994*, edited by Robert Ross, Anne Kelk Mager & Bill Nasson. Cambridge: Cambridge University Press, 2012, pp. 102–156.

Mlambo, Alois & Neil Parsons. *A History of Southern Africa*. London: Red Globe Press, 2019.

Nienaber, Gabriël Stephanus. *Oor Afrikaans 2*. Johannesburg: Afrikaanse Pers-boekhandel, 1953.

Olivier, Gerrit. "The Dertigers and the *Plaasroman*: Two Brief Perspectives on Afrikaans Literature." *The Cambridge History of South African Literature*, edited by David Attwell & Derek Attridge. Cambridge: Cambridge University Press, 2012, pp. 308–324.

Pakendorf, Gunther. "Kafka, en die saak vir 'n 'klein letterkunde'." *Stilet*, vol. 5, no. 1, 1993, pp. 99–106.

Patterson, Sheila. *Colour and Culture in South Africa: A Study of the Status of the Cape Coloured People within the Social Structure of the Union of South Africa*. London: Routledge and Kegan Paul, 1953.

Petersen, Patrick J. *amandla ngawethu*. Genadendalse Drukkery, 1985.

Petersen, Patrick J. "Digter van 'bevryde Afrikaans." Interview with Hein Willemse. *Karring*, no. 2, 1991, pp. 19–21.

Ross, Robert. "Khoesan and Immigrants: The Emergence of Colonial Society in the Cape, 1500–1800." *The Cambridge History of South Africa, Volume 1: From Early Times to 1885*, edited by Carolyn Hamilton, Bernard K. Mbenga & Robert Ross. Cambridge: Cambridge University Press, 2012, pp. 168–210.

Simkins, Charles. "The Evolution of the South African Population in the Twentieth Century." *The Cambridge History of South Africa, Volume 2, 1885–1994*, edited by Robert Ross, Anne Kelk Mager & Bill Nasson. Cambridge: Cambridge University Press, 2012, pp. 492–517.

Snyders, Peter. "My Moedertaal is Kaaps." *'n Vlag aan die tong. Gedenkbundel van die derde Swart Afrikaanse Skrywerssimposium*, edited by Hein Willemse & Steward van Wyk. Wilderness: Abrile Doman; Pretoria: Hond, 2015, pp. 197–199.

Stell, Gerald. "From Kitaab-Hollandsch to Kitaab-Afrikaans: The Evolution of a Non-White Literary Variety at the Cape (1856–1940)." *Stellenbosch Papers in Linguistics*, no. 37, 2007, pp. 89–127, doi: 10.5774/37-0-16. Accessed 30 Feb. 2019.

Steyn, Jacob Cornelius. *Tuiste in eie taal. Die behoud en bestaan van Afrikaans*. Cape Town: Tafelberg, 1980.

Steyn, Jacob Cornelius. *'Ons gaan 'n taal maak', Afrikaans sedert die Patriot-jare*. Pretoria: Kraal, 2014.

Uys, Mariette. Deleen. Die vernederlandsing van Afrikaans. D. Litt diss., University of Pretoria, Pretoria, 1983.

Van der Merwe, Henderik J. J. M. "Taalbeïnvloeding en taalvermenging." *Afrikaans – sy aard en ontwikkeling*. Pretoria: J. L. van Schaik, 1968, pp. 240–264.

Van der Merwe, Henderik J. J. M. *Vroeë Afrikaanse woordelyste*. Pretoria: J. L. van Schaik for the Patriot Society for Afrikaans text edition of the S.A. Akademie vir Wetenskap en Kuns, 1971.

Van der Merwe, Henderik J. J. M. & M. J. Posthumus. "Die opkoms van Afrikaans as Kultuurtaal." *Afrikaans – sy aard en ontwikkeling*. Pretoria: J. L. van Schaik, 1968, pp. 67–97.

Van Selms, Adrianus. *Abu Bakr se 'Uiteensetting van die godsdiens*. Amsterdam: North-Holland, 1979.

Viljoen, Louise. "Displacement in the Literary Texts of Black Afrikaans Writers in South Africa." *JLS/TLW*, vol. 21, no. 1/2, 2005, pp. 93–118. Accessed 9 Mar. 2019.

Voss, Tony. "Refracted Modernisms: Roy Campbell, Herbert Dhlomo, N. P. Van Wyk Louw." *The Cambridge History of South African Literature*, edited by David Attwell & Derek Attridge. Cambridge: Cambridge University Press, 2012, pp. 339–359.

Willemse, Hein. "Textual Production and Contested Histories in a Performance of the Namibian Storyteller." *Research in African Literatures*, vol. 34, no. 3, Autumn, 2003, pp. 27–45. https:// www.jstor.org/ stable/3821248. Accessed 15 Mar. 2019.

Willemse, Hein. *Aan die ander kant. Swart Afrikaanse skrywers in die Afrikaanse letterkunde*. Pretoria: Protea, 2007.

Willemse, Hein. "Die vooruitsig van oopheid." *'n Vlag aan die tong. Gedenkbundel van die derde Swart Afrikaanse Skrywerssimposium*, edited by Hein Willemse & Steward van Wyk. Wilderness: Abrile Doman; Pretoria: Hond, 2015, pp. 9–19.

Willemse, Hein. "'n Inleiding tot buitekanonieke Afrikaanse kulturele praktyke." *Perspektief en profile. 'n Afrikaanse Literatuurgeskiedenis 1*. 2nd edition, edited by Hendrik P. van Coller. Pretoria: Van Schaik, 2015, pp. 73–91.

Woeber, Catherine. "The Mission Presses and the Rise of Black Journalism." *The Cambridge History of South African Literature*, edited by David Attwell & Derek Attridge. Cambridge: Cambridge University Press, 2012, pp. 204–225.

Yunis, Alia & Samantha Reinders. "The Handwritten Heritage of South Africa's Kitabs." *AramcoWorld*, March/April 2019. www.aramcoworld.com/en-US/Articles/March-2019/The-Handwritten-Heritage-of-South-Africa-s-Kitabs. Accessed 3 Mar. 2019.

11

SWAHILI LITERATURE AS A MINORITY DISCOURSE IN AFRICAN LITERATURES

Mwenda Mbatiah

Swahili literature refers to the body of writing comprising fiction, biography, autobiography, travelogue, drama, and poetry expressed in the Swahili language, which is widely spoken in East and Central Africa. This literature can be termed a minority discourse in the African context where literature is predominantly produced in European languages such as English, French, and Portuguese. This is a result of the colonial experience. Even after the end of formal colonization, the colonial system remained. Apart from European colonization, the East African coast, where Swahili language originated, also experienced colonization by Omani Arabs. This is the historical and cultural context in which Swahili literature germinated and developed. This chapter seeks to demonstrate that Swahili literature is a hybrid derived from traditional African, Arabic, and European models. This hybrid is also a postcolonial literature that continues to be used to respond to the East African situation as an aftermath of colonization.

Swahili language and its literature originated from the East Coast of Africa and spread to the hinterland as far as Central and Southern Africa. Among other scholars, Chimerah (73–78) has noted that the historical factors that accelerated the spontaneous but spectacular spread of the language over such a vast region were trade, religion, and politics. According to Massamba, Kihore, and Hokororo (14–15), the first phase of the diffusion of Swahili from the coast to the interior took place long before the arrival of Oriental and European visitors. The Swahili, a Bantu people of the East African coast, had traditionally conducted trade with their neighbours from the interior such as the Miji Kenda (the nine communities). Since the various interior communities had their own languages, a common language to facilitate trade between them and the Swahili people had to be found. Swahili turned out to be the language that was acceptable to all.

There is ample historical evidence to show that contact between the Swahili people and foreigners started as early as the 10th century A.D. Initially, the visitors came for purposes of trade, but with time, this changed into immigration. The earliest groups of immigrants came from the Arab world and Persia. This contact with people from the Orient changed Swahili language and culture, making it significantly different from the cultures of other Bantu communities in the interior. The greatest impact was that of Islam and the Arabic language. The Swahili people adopted Islam and infused their language with Arabic words and expressions. Nevertheless, Swahili language retained its Bantu identity. The adoption of the Arabic script, which was Swahilized to some extent, laid the foundation for the development of written Swahili literature.

Thus, the bulk of classical Swahili literature (mostly poetry) produced before the 20th century was written in Arabic script. We use the term "classical" to refer to literature that is written using traditional conventions, especially prosodic rules of versification.

The establishment of Islam as the religion of the Swahili people led to accelerated literacy due to the fact that the religion was taught using written material. Swahili language also benefitted from the translation of the Koran and other religious writings from Arabic. It is necessary to point out at this juncture that Oriental immigrants to the coast were assimilated into Swahili culture through intermarriage. This led to a cultural exchange whereby the two sides willingly adopted elements of each other's culture. There is no evidence of forced acculturation whatsoever. Nevertheless, the immigrants gradually took over control of the economic and political activities of the coastal city states such as Mombasa, Malindi, Pate, Zanzibar, and Kilwa. As William Ochieng states: "By the thirteenth century, these Asiatics had settled as far south as Kilwa, establishing ruling dynasties and introducing the elements of Islamic civilization" (50).

Although the coastal city states had generally been under the control of Omani Arabs since the 18th century, it was not until 1840 that the Omanis effectively took control of the entire coast, including all the main islands. That year, the Sultan of Oman, Seyyid Said, moved his headquarters to Zanzibar. His action was driven by the desire to be in firm control of the entire coast so as to realize his commercial ambitions of enriching himself from the long-distance trade. The most valuable goods in this trade were ivory, beads, cloth, weapons such as guns, and slaves. Zanzibar became the centre of this trade and, as a result, gained considerable wealth. As Assa Okoth rightly points out, "Zanzibari wealth was due not to its own resources, but to the rapid and deep penetration of the hinterland by the Arabs" (24). The Arabs could not have made a success of the long-distance trade without the collaboration of their Swahili subjects. This collaboration was instrumental in spreading Swahili language, which had become the trading lingua franca, from the coast and the East African hinterland to Central and Southern Africa.

The Omani Arabs were replaced by the German and British colonial powers who became the new overlords of not only the coast but the entire East African region, from the second half of the nineteenth century onwards. During the German and British colonial rules, the spread and modernization of Swahili language was accelerated. As a result of the historical dynamics mentioned previously, the colonialists found that Swahili was the most widely spoken language. They therefore had no choice but to start using it in their educational, commercial, and political activities. In order to make the language serve their interests better, they replaced the Arabic script (that had traditionally been used to write in Swahili) with the Roman one and took the initial steps in standardizing the language. In 1930, the British – who had replaced the Germans as the rulers of Tanganyika after the First World War – established the Inter-Territorial Language Committee to spearhead standardization efforts. This resulted in a form of the language that was used in the entire region for all official business. The Committee was tasked with developing not only the language but also its literature, in order to produce books for use in schools.

On the whole, the entire period of European colonial rule, up to the decade of independence in the 1960s, was a turning point in the development of Swahili literature. This was the time when classical Swahili literature began to lose its dominance. However, it is important to make clear from the outset that European colonizers were not interested in developing Swahili language and literature to replace their own as the languages of high culture. Swahili and other African languages continued to be regarded as inferior. In East Africa, English retained its status as the language of higher education and a symbol of elitism. No wonder, the products of the colonial education system were more proficient in English than in their first languages. Those among them, like Ngugi wa Thiong'o (Kenya), Robert Serumaga (Uganda), and Gabriel Ruhumbika (Tanzania), produced their initial works, from the 1960s onwards, in English. Thus they established a writing tradition in the colonial language that eventually dominated the East African literary scene. The same trend was replicated in West Africa, where writers in some of the countries used English, while others used French, depending on the language of the former colonial master. The same happened in Southern Africa, where the former Portuguese colonies of Mozambique and Angola used the colonial language to develop their national literatures. English was dominant in the rest of the countries of the region.

Generally, therefore, colonial languages became the media of the dominant discourse during colonial rule and even after independence. Nevertheless, even before the invasion and colonization of Africa by the West, significant amounts of art were produced in African languages. Most of this was orature, except in a few cases like Northern, Western, and Eastern Africa, where Islamic civilization had led to the establishment of written literature in African languages. In East Africa, classical Swahili literature in Arabic script emerged and prospered in the city states along the coast. It is important, at this juncture, to discuss briefly, the main features of this literature, which remains an important component of the entire Swahili letters.

Classical Swahili literature is almost entirely in verse form, and most of it that is known outside Swahililand is embodied in manuscripts in Arabic script that are preserved in university libraries across the world, such as the School of Oriental and African Studies of the University of London, University of Dar es Salaam, and Humboldt University. A small percentage of those works have been transliterated, edited, translated, and published for wider circulation by various researchers. Examples are: *Tendi*, compiled by J.W.T. Allen, which is a collection of six long poems, or *tendi* (plural of *utendi*) in Swahili and *Diwani ya Muyaka Bin Haji al-Ghasainy. Swahili Poems of Muyaka* by William Hichens, which is a collection of short verses or *mashairi* (plural of *shairi*) in Swahili, composed by Muyaka, the great poet from Mombasa. We also have examples of single works such as *Al-Inkishafi. The Soul's Awakening*, also by William Hichens.

In Standard Swahili, the poetic genre, referred to previously as *utendi*, is called *utenzi*, while the term *utendi* is reserved for the equivalent of an epic in the Western world. In modern Swahili literary terminology, *utenzi* is a long narrative poem ranging in length from a few dozen to thousands of stanzas and can deal with religious, historical, or political themes. The exact dates when the pioneering *tenzi* were composed are unknown, but the oldest Swahili manuscript, the *Hamziyya* by Sayyid Aidarus, is, according to Jan Knappert, dated AD 1652 (103). Other scholars, such as Euphrase Kezilahabi (147), suggest that the *Hamziyya*, which is centred on the life of Prophet Muhammad, was written in 1690 or 1749. Other early *tenzi* include *Utenzi wa Tambuka/Chuo cha Herekali* (epic of Tabuk/the book of Herakleois), composed by Mwengo bin Athumani in 1728 and *Al-Inkishafi. The Soul's Awakening*, written by Sayyid Abdalla bin Nasir between 1810–1820, according to William Hichens (19).

In a chapter like this one, it is not possible to discuss in detail the form and content of the early *tenzi*, but a general observation that can be made that they reflect an Arab-Islamic civilization to such a high degree that it is difficult to know whether they were original compositions of Swahili poets or translations/adaptations of Arabic works. Nevertheless, *tenzi* that were written during European colonial rule and afterwards are centred on the sociohistorical and cultural circumstances of the new East African states. A good example is the *Utenzi wa Vita vya Uhuru:1939 hata 1945* (an epic of the liberation war: 1939 to 1945) written by the foremost Swahili writer, Shaaban Robert. It is 3,000 stanzas long and is a narrative of the outbreak, progress, and conclusion of the Second World War. This is the longest of the over twenty books that Robert wrote, most of which were published posthumously (he died in 1962). It is "in this work that Shaaban Robert's ideas on peace, and its antithesis war, are most strongly articulated" (Mbatiah, 58).

The *shairi* is another verse form that was established during the classical period. Like the *utenzi*, the *shairi* had a fixed prosodic structure, albeit different from that of the former. The most widespread type was the *tarbia* (quatrain) of four-line stanzas, with each line or *mshororo* having sixteen syllables, or *mizani*. Each *mshororo* had two hemistiches and a mid-caesura, and the first three lines had a mid and final rhyming pattern. The metrical and rhyme system of the quatrain can be represented thus:

8a 8b
8a 8b
8a 8b
8b 8c

These prosodic conventions are reflected in the following one-stanza *shairi* by Mathias Mnyampala (1), which is typical of the type of verse we are talking about in terms of both form and content:

Uungwana

Atiwe ndole puani, na kumtemea mate
Wamwambie punguani, hayawani wamuite
Yeye hana kisirani, huyavumilia yote
Muungwana hushinda kite, ule uchungu mkali.

Civility

Poke a finger in his nose and spit at him
Tell him he's an idiot and call him a beast
He'll never become a nuisance, he endures all
A thoroughbred defeats grief, however painful

The rhyme (*kina* in Swahili) of the first hemistich (*ukwapi ni Swahili*) is *–ni*, and that of the second hemistich (*utao* in Swahili) is *–te*. This is replicated in the first three lines, but in the last line it changes to *–te*and *–li*, respectively. In terms of length, this *shairi* is not typical because it is too short (most *mashairi* tend to have an average length of four to six stanzas), but it is typical in terms of form and content. As we have seen, it conforms to the classical rules of prosody. Second, it is a didactic verse that uses hyperbole to extol the virtues of civility. This is a common trend in Swahili *mashairi*, having been popularized by Shaaban Robert, the undisputed craftsman of Swahili verse in general, and the *shairi* form in particular, in the 20th century.

In his *Muyaka: 19th Century Swahili Popular Poetry*, Mohamed Abdulaziz has done a comprehensive study of this type of *shairi* during its classical phase, including a collection of Muyaka's poetry, which can be taken as a representation of the *shairi* genius of that period. According to Abdulaziz, "This verse form has dominated popular Swahili verse since at least the beginning of the 19th century, and is still widely regarded as the most suitable medium for short themes" (50). While *tenzi* can be book-length compositions with thousands of stanzas, as pointed out previously, a *shairi* can be the size of only one stanza – as we have seen.

Shaaban Robert and other notable poets such as K.A. Abedi, Mwinyihatibu Mohamed, Ahmad Nassir, Hassan, M. Mbega, Mathias Mnyampala, Abdilatif Abdalla, Saadan Kandoro, Jumanne Mayoka, and Boukheit Amana continued following the conventions of the classical tradition with varying degrees of fidelity. There is consensus among critics of Swahili literature that Shaaban Robert made some innovations in the rules of traditional Swahili prosody, but on the whole, they were minimal. His conservative stance is reflected in his description of Swahili poetry, which basically asserts the classical conventions. He says: "*Ushairi ni sanaa ya vina inayo-pambanuliwa kama nyimbo, mashairi na tenzi.*"/Poetry is an art of rhymes which distinguishes itself as songs, short poems and long poems. This is echoed by K.A Abedi in his Aristotelian treatise on Swahili poetry entitled *Sheria za Kutunga Mashairi na Diwani ya Amri/ The Laws of Versification and Amri's Anthology*. He says: "*Shairi au utenzi ni wimbo. Hivyo, kama haliimbiki, halina maana.*"/A short poem or a long poem is a song. Therefore, if it cannot be sung, it is useless.

A momentous literary happening of the 1970s changed the trajectory of Swahili poetry, leading to the birth of a new verse form that deliberately rebelled against the classical prosodic and other conventions. In Swahili scholarship, this movement is referred to as *mgogoro katika ushairi wa Kiswahili*/conflict in Swahili poetry. It was a long, raging quarrel involving Swahili poets, critics, and scholars, with one side supporting the continuation of the classical modes of verse, while the other side fought for free verse that was not tied to the conventions of traditional poetry. The protagonists used the mass media such as radio and newspapers, journals, and books to articulate their respective positions. Alamin Mazrui, who has discussed the phenomenon in question at length, has characterized it thus:

> There was a sense in which the introduction of free verse in Swahili poetry was projected as a liberating force from the "fetters" of rigid prosodic formalism. Breaking away from this Swahili poetic tradition was regarded as a bold and revolutionary pioneering act intended to liberate the full potential of the Swahili creative genius.
>
> *(47)*

The *avant-garde* champions of free verse were university-educated people who were poets, critics, or both. Prominent names in this group were Euphrase Kezilahabi, Kulikoyela Kahigi, and Mugyabuso Mulokozi – all writers and notable Swahili scholars at the University of Dar es Salaam. On the conservative side, there were poets like Jumanne Mayoka, Abdilatiff Abdalla, Ibrahim Noor Shariff, and Saadan Kandoro. These were mostly ethnic Swahili poets and cultural nationalists. On both sides, there were many others who did not directly participate in the raging debate but demonstrated their stance by either composing free verse or following the path of classical poetry.

It is beyond the scope of this chapter to deal comprehensively with the causes and impact of the revolutionary change that took place in Swahili poetry in the 1970s. However, two pertinent points need to be made. First, the hostility towards the introduction of free verse fizzled out as more Swahili poets chose to express themselves in this mode, leading to the publication of several anthologies (including Alamin Mazrui's *Chembe cha Moyo*) of high-quality free verse poetry. Second, Alamin Mazrui (54) makes an insightful observation in his commentary referred to previously when he says that free verse was inspired by English poetry in East Africa.

Mazrui's observation is germane to the treatment of Swahili literature as a minority discourse as well as a hybrid art in this chapter. First, it is an affirmation of the reality that literature in English dominates the scene in East Africa – as postulated from the outset. This is the reality all over postcolonial Africa. Second, it follows that consciously or unconsciously, the minority discourse imitates the genres and forms of the dominant discourse – for better or for worse. By drawing their inspiration from East African writers of poetry in English, free verse poets in Swahili want to respond to their postcolonial situation using the same genres as their counterparts in English – free of the "fetters" of traditional forms. In this sense, it is not just Swahili poets who are forced to conform, in varying degrees, to the dominant literary discourse in English. Swahili writers of fiction, drama, and biography find themselves in the same situation. No serious writer wants to find themselves in such a predicament, but so long as the postcolonial situation of East Africa persists, this reality will remain.

The fact of Swahili literature being a minority discourse has debilitating consequences to the art and its practitioners. This is because the colonial ideology that African culture, including language and literature, is inferior to Western culture remains intact in the postcolony, especially among the elite. Writers and scholars of Swahili literature suffer in various ways under these circumstances. First, there is the tendency to ignore Swahili literature when talking about East African literature, because in the minds of most literary scholars, literature means literature in English and the two are inseparable.

Second, there is the reluctance or inability of most scholars to appraise Swahili literature in its own right rather than as an appendage of literature in English. Thus most commentaries on this writer's Swahili novel *Wimbo Mpya/The New Song* by English-oriented critics tend to rush to the conclusion that it is following Ngugi wa Thiong'o. This is because the latter pioneered writing novels in English on the Mau Mau. Bearing in mind that the Kenyan liberation war, also referred to as the Mau Mau War, was an historical event, this is like saying that Ngugi wrote everything that needs to be written about this momentous event. Any other writer, such as P.M. Kareithi, who wrote *Kaburi bila Msalaba/The Grave without a Cross*, and Peter Ngare, who wrote *Kikulacho ki Nguoni Mwako/That Which Bites You Is in Your Clothes*, must be following Ngugi.

The failure to recognize the unique contribution of Swahili letters is sheer critical incompetence. This argument might seem to contradict what has been said previously about Swahili writers imitating their counterparts in English. However, there is absolutely no contradiction, because the imitation referred to previously is that of genres and forms. This is different from negative mimicry. Moreover, we should remember that writers in English did not invent the forms and genres they write in. They appropriated them (in the postcolonial sense) from the English literature they read in colonial schools.

At this juncture, it is opportune to turn to the other forms and genres that writers in Swahili have used to respond to the postcolonial situation in East Africa. While poetry is the oldest form of written Swahili literature, and while it is true that it dominated the literary scene for centuries, it is no longer the dominant literary form. The Westernization of East African intellectual culture which resulted from European colonization and the spread of Christianity led to the emergence of new literary forms. The Swahili-speaking East African world no longer found poetry an adequate means of engaging the postcolony. Swahili writers appropriated European forms such as drama, the novella, short story, and biography and started producing works that reflected the aspirations of East Africans.

Drama was one of the new art forms that were the result of the Westernization of East African literary culture. The authors of *Outline of Swahili Literature: Prose Fiction and Drama* emphasize both the newness of Swahili drama and how it continued to exhibit the influence of European theatre (Zubkova et al. 171–175). The pioneering plays were published in the 1950s (Wafula vii). This early Swahili drama was the handiwork of Graham Hyslop, a British expatriate teacher, who published two plays: *Afadhali Mchawi/A Wizard Is Better* and *Mgeni Karibu/Welcome, Visitor*. Both works are didactic and immature in terms of form, but they nevertheless inspired Hyslop's student, Henry Kuria, to write a more mature play entitled *Nakupenda Lakini . . . /I Love You but . . .* This play is set during the liberation war in Kenya, and though it is not an historical work, it portrays a changing society where traditional values are disappearing and being replaced by materialism. This is one of the negative effects of Westernization.

After independence, Swahili drama became more Africanized and more immersed in the cultural lives of East Africans. It was during the early years of independence that *ngonjera*, a dramatic form derived from orature, was developed. It started in Tanzania and became popular across the Swahili-speaking world. It is a fusion of drama and poetry, consisting of two characters that argue or debate about a pertinent social issue. *Ngonjera* are normally didactic and geared toward solving social problems. This became an important tool in the reconstruction of Tanzania under the *ujamaa* (African socialism) policies introduced by the first president, Mwalimu Julius Nyerere. At that time, this dramatic form was used to spread progressive messages about the importance of embracing *ujamaa*. *Ngonjera* became popular even among poets, as we see in many anthologies that were published after independence. In the 1970s, we have examples such as *"Mwanafuu na Mkufuu"/Teacher and Student* in Ahmad Nassir's *Malenga wa Mvita* and *"Mnazi: Vuta N'kuvute"/Coconut Palm: You Pull and I Pull* in Abdilatif Abdalla's *Sauti ya Dhiki/A Cry of Distress.*

Swahili drama developed rapidly and attained maturity in about two decades. This was partly because published plays became part of the curriculum in schools and institutions of higher learning. Performing arts, including staging of plays, were also popularized in schools and colleges. Moreover, playwrights such as Ebrahim Hussein, Penina Muhando, Emmanuel Mbogo, and Chacha Nyaigotti emerged in East African universities and produced high-quality plays which put Swahili drama at the same level as the best that was written anywhere else in Africa. Some of these artists were experts in theatre arts. They not only wrote plays but organized performances.

With the publication of plays like *Wakati Ukuta/Time Is a Solid Wall* and *Kinjeketile* (published simultaneously with an English translation bearing the same title) at the end of the 1960s, Ebrahim Hussein emerged as the most outstanding playwright. The first book is centred on the theme of cultural conflict between the traditional way of life and the modern lifestyle brought about by Western education, which has had a great impact on the youth. It is a clash between children who want to discard the traditional way of life and their parents who want to cling to it. The second one is an historical play based on the Maji Maji war of 1805–1807. *Kinjeketile* dramatizes the bloody conflict between the German colonialists and the Africans around River Rufiji in Southern Tanzania, united under Prophet Kinjeketile Ngwale. Though the African fighters were eventually defeated, as happened in similar wars across the continent, it demonstrated their rejection of colonial domination.

After that initial phase of Hussein's writing career, he published more accomplished plays, including the highly sophisticated *Mashetani/Demons*, which portrays the social tensions that arose from the introduction of *ujamaa* in Tanzania after the Arusha Declaration of 1967. On the whole, Hussein's plays raise serious sociopolitical issues that engage the audience intellectually but avoid providing answers. His compatriot, Penina Muhando, is the only outstanding female playwright whose works started appearing in the 1970s. Her first play, published in 1974, is *Heshima Yangu/My Dignity* and is centred on the lives of two young village lovers who face the stumbling block of traditional taboos. The chief's daughter, who wants to marry an illegitimate son, puts his father in a predicament because such a marriage would be against the custom. *Hatia/Guilt*, is Muhando's second play, which also explores a social problem: that of girls getting impregnated by wily city men who subsequently dodge their responsibility, thus causing the girls serious problems. Cheja is a rural girl who goes to work in Dar es Salaam and gets into a love relationship with Juma, who eventually impregnates her and persuades her to lie to her parents that it is her employer, Sembuli, who is responsible for the pregnancy. After causing serious conflict in the village, Cheja eventually reveals the truth about her condition. Henceforth, the community is faced with the daunting task of healing the rift that has occurred.

Muhando's subsequent plays are *Tambueni Haki Zetu/Respect Our Rights*, *Pambo/Adornment*, *NguzoMama/Mother Pillar*, and *Lina Ubani/There Is a Remedy*. In general, "Muhando's plays have depth in their portrayal of characters, many of whom achieve quite complex dimensions" (Zubkova, 209). Another important quality of her works is the deliberate effort to use ora-ture, including songs and oral narratives, thus giving them an authentic African flavour. It can be argued that the axis of Penina Muhando's career, including teaching and writing scholarly works, is the Africanization of Swahili theatre.

Apart from plays written in Swahili such as the ones mentioned previously, translations, mainly from English, have made a major contribution to the development of Swahili drama. The pioneering translations are those of the first president of Tanzania, Mwalimu Julius Nyerere, who rendered Shakespeare's two plays *Julius Caesar* and *The Merchant of Venice* into Swahili as *Juliasi Kaizari* and *Mabepari wa Venisi*, respectively. Subsequently, Shakespeare's other plays such as *The Tempest* and *Macbeth* were translated as *Tufani* and *Makbeth*, respectively, by Samuel Mushi. This effort to make Shakespearian plays available to Swahili readers continues, as is evidenced by the translation of *Othello* in 2012 by Ayub Mukhwana and Patrick Iribemwangi, Swahili scholars at the University of Nairobi. Apart from Shakespeare's works, the plays of major African writers in English such as Wole Soyinka, John Ruganda, Francis Imbuga, and Ngugi wa Thiong'o have been translated.

We now turn our attention to Swahili prose, which has dominated Swahili literature since the second half of the twentieth century. We can only give an overview of the main trends, since a detailed treatment is not possible within the limited space that is available in this chapter. We begin by looking at the contribution of Shaaban Robert. While this giant of Swahili letters championed classical poetry and became its greatest writer in the twentieth century, it is in the development of Swahili prose that he played a pioneering and pivotal role. He pioneered the Swahili biography when his *Maisha Yangu/My Life* was published in 1949. He later enlarged the book, and it was published posthumously as *Maisha Yangu na Baada ya Miaka Hamsini/My Life and after the Age of 50*, in 1966. His other book within this genre is *Wasifu wa Siti Binti Saad/The Biography of Siti Binti Saad*, first published during the author's lifetime in 1958.

Robert's love for poetry is evidenced by the fact that nearly half of his autobiography is made up of verse. First there is the six-stanza *shairi* (5) entitled "Amina," which eulogizes his departed wife and expresses the Islamic belief that the dead will be resurrected and meet God in heaven, and that he will meet her there. It is a tearful, prayerful composition in which the author pours out his emotions of deep love and sadness. This is followed closely by two *tenzi* or long poems (7–36), for each of his two children, intended to advise them on how to lead virtuous and God-fearing lives, especially in the absence of their mother. There are several other *mashairi* scattered in various parts of the text. The author talks about his private life, particularly the challenge of bringing up his two children in the absence of their mother. He also talks about his second mar-riage, five years after the death of his first wife of ten years.

About his public life, the author narrates his experiences as a clerk in the colonial civil ser-vice. It is clear that though he was a diligent and hard-working servant of the government, he was not rewarded with promotions or good pay. This was because, in the colonial system, senior positions were reserved for whites only. The author does not articulate this discrimination, but it is implicit in what he says. Moreover, he complains about disruptive transfers from one depart-ment to another. The struggle for independence was underway at this time. Africans had started organizing themselves and forming political parties as they agitated for the end of colonial rule. Shaaban Robert talks about his involvement thus:

Nilitekwa na uzalendo kama alivyotekwa mtu yeyote mwingine. Sikutaka kuwa mgeni katika nchi ya asili na uzazi wangu. Sikutaka kuwa mtazamaji wakati wananchi wengine

walipokuwa wachezaji nikajiunga na chama. Chama cha siasa katika wakati ule kili-
kuwa Chama cha Waafrika kilicho-undwa na kuanzishwa katika mwaka wa 1929.

(76)

I was seized by patriotism like any other person. I did not want to be a stranger in the
country of my birth. I did not want to be a spectator while other citizens were players,
so I joined a political party. The political party of that time was the Tanganyika African
Association which was formed in 1929.

According to Assa Okoth, the Tanganyika African Association (TAA) reorganized itself into
TANU (Tanganyika African National Union) under Julius Nyerere in 1958. This was the party
that led Tanganyika into independence. Okoth summarizes this process in the following
words: "Then, on December, 9, 1961, Tanganyika regained its full independence, and Nyerere
became the new nation's first prime minister. A year later, December 1962, Tanganyika became
a republic. In 1964 Zanzibar and Tanganyika joined in a Union to form the republic of Tanzania" (53).

Shaaban Robert the writer complains bitterly about consistently being short-changed by
his publishers. He received meagre payment as royalties, and this was after following up on the
payments for lengthy periods of time. It is clear that the publishers were dishonest and unfair,
but there was nothing the author could do to change the situation. Like all true artists, Shaaban
Robert did not give up writing even in the face of being grossly underpaid by his publishers.
Writing for him was like breathing, which he could not do without.

Wasifu wa Siti Binti Saad, which first appeared as supplement to no. 28/1of the *East African
Swahili Committee Journal*, 1958, was one of the few books that was published during the author's
lifetime. This is the story of a Zanzibari woman, Siti, who rebels against the enslaving customs
and traditions of her community and runs away from the village to the city where she develops her talent as a musician and performer. This is a revolutionary move in a community where
a career in music and entertainment in general is out of bounds for women. Siti proves herself
to be a bold, highly disciplined, and diligent person. She gradually develops her talent as a singer
of the popular Swahili *Taarab* music. Within a short time, she emerges as the best and the most
popular *Taarab* performer in the whole of Zanzibar. Her fame spreads beyond Zanzibar, and she
gets invitations to perform and record her music abroad. Siti grows rich and becomes an international pop star. With great emphasis, the author makes it clear that Siti becomes successful
after overcoming seemingly insurmountable obstacles because of her exemplary character. Her
positive qualities constitute the central theme of the book.

In a nutshell, the author tells us that Siti was successful because of the following qualities:
(a) "*Alikuwa na moyo wa kuhifadhi mambo upesi kama umeme.*"/She had the ability to learn and
commit things to memory as fast as lightning. (b) "*Siti alikuwa mwanamke mcha Mungu wa sala na
saumu*"/Siti was a God-fearing woman who prayed and fasted. (c) "*Alikuwa na adabu na mlahaka
kwa watu wote.*"/She was courteous and able to get along with everyone. Moreover, she did not
allow money and success to go to her head. All these qualities are repeated in various parts of
the book with so much emphasis that the reader feels that they are exaggerated. In other words,
there is an imbalance between the positive and negative qualities of the character in question.

In terms of form, Shaaban Robert's prose is presented in rich Standard Swahili that is abundant with idiomatic expressions and rhetorical figures. The language is figurative to such a high
degree that the reader feels as though he/she is reading a fictional narrative rather than a story
about real people. One quality that runs through both works is that the author highlights the
positive side of his main characters with the aim of making them paragons of integrity that East

Africans ought to emulate. In the first book, the central character emerges as the perfect father, husband, and civil servant. In the second book, Siti is the perfect example of a progressive woman who should inspire fellow women to play an active role in liberating themselves from the shackles of the patriarchal society.

The moralistic tendency in Shaaban Robert's non-fictional prose also pervades his fictional works such as *Adili na Nduguze/Adili and His Brothers*, *Kusadikika/Believable Country*, *Kufikirika/Imaginary Country*, *Utubora Mkulima/Utubora the Farmer*, and *Siku ya Watenzi wote/The Day of All Actors*. In the first three books, the author uses stories of fantasy akin to folktales of the oral tradition to explore themes such as evil and goodness in human nature, conservatism versus reformism in society, justice, and good governance. In all the stories, the positive side or the side of morality always wins. The bad are punished and the good are rewarded. While the first three books lack the qualities of the mainstream modern novel, the last two can be categorized as true novels. They have realistic sociohistorical and geographical settings, plausible characters, and narratives. They also deal with concrete social problems and attempt to provide solutions.

Bearing in mind the historical circumstances in which Shaaban Roert was writing, it is evident that he was using fiction to respond to the evils of colonialism in such a manner that his safety was ensured and his books had a chance of getting published. The colonial authorities controlled the publishing industry, and they would not have allowed the publication of any materials that were even mildly critical of the status quo, especially touching on evils such as racial discrimination and oppression. In such circumstances, a writer is forced to go the extra mile to avoid censorship. The flip side of it is that art suffers when a writer is forced to express himself in unnatural ways. Thus many of the formal flaws in the novels of Shaaban Robert could be attributed to the restrictions imposed by the colonial administration. It was after Shaaban Robert, especially in the 1970s, that Swahili writers were able to use the novel form to respond to the postcolony in ways that their forerunner could not have done.

From the 1970s onwards, the novel emerged as the dominant fictional form, though there were other genres such as the novella and the short story. The novel became the most suitable means of exploring the devastating effects of colonial rule that continued to determine the lives of East Africans even after the end of direct colonial occupation. First, there were novelists who looked back in time and created stories about the process of the liberation struggle, highlighting the heroic deeds of the African fighters who were daring enough to face the mighty colonial rulers and their well-armed troops. Examples are P.M. Kareithi's *Kaburi bila Msalaba/The Grave without a Cross*, Peter Ngare's *Kikulacho ki Nguoni Mwako/That Which Eats You Is in Your Clothes*, and Mwenda Mbatiah's *Wimbo Mpya/The New Song*. All three novels focus on various aspects of the armed struggle waged by the guerrilla Mau Mau fighters against the British colonial forces in Kenya.

Kareithi's novel is set in Kikuyuland (Central Kenya), and this is authenticated by references to physical features such as Mount Kenya and forests and rivers around the Mountain. It also evokes aspects of Kikuyu culture such as the language, beliefs, and oathing, which was used by the Mau Mau fighters to maintain discipline, secrecy, and unity. The main focus of the book is the motivation behind the decision by Africans to take up arms against the British and the devastating consequences of the war. One of the main grievances of the Africans was the loss of land, which was forcefully taken away from them and given to white settlers. Since the social and economic life of the community was tied up with land, taking it away was tantamount to dispossessing them of their sole source of livelihood. To make matters worse, Africans were engaged as forced labourers to work in the same land from which they had been driven out. Another grievance was the betrayal of young people, like Meja Blue, the main character, who were recruited to join British forces that were fighting on various fronts during the Second World War. After the War, those who survived were neglected, while their white counterparts were supported by the government to rebuild their lives. The embittered African youth were left with no alternative but to join the Mau Mau guerrilla fighters in the forests.

Apart from the betrayal of the African survivors of the Second World War, many others perished. For instance, we are told that Mumbi's father left the village and joined the war in Burma when she was about two years old, and he never returned. Mumbi is the central female character in the novel. One of the consequences of the liberation war was that the villages in the Kikuyu countryside were left desolate. Able-bodied men and women had either joined the fighters in the forest or had been arrested and put in detention camps. We see how Mumbi is arrested by the chief's guards and detained on suspicion that she had taken the Mau Mau oath. She leaves her sick and elderly mother without anyone to take care of her. The powerful symbol of the grave without a cross is used to represent the large numbers of Africans who died under various circumstances during the war and disappeared without leaving any mark of their existence. Mumbi herself dies from the complications of her pregnancy after being raped by the chief. Without any able-bodied men to bury her, this role is performed by old men.

Like Kareithi's novel, Peter Ngare's work is socially and geographically set in Kikuyuland during the Mau Mau war. There are a number of similarities between the two historical novels, but they also differ in significant ways. Both dwell on the brutality of colonial rule, the inevitability of the liberation war, and the patriotism of the Mau Mau fighters. Nevertheless, Ngare's novel touches on a number of different themes. First, there is the theme of the introduction of Christianity and its impact, which went hand in hand with colonization. We see that some Africans, such as Yohana and his family, embrace the new religion, while others, like Mwai and his family, reject it. The two are neighbours but they become bitter enemies because of their differences over conversion to Christianity.

Thus the new religion is portrayed as a divisive factor that weakened Africans and prevented them from forging a common front against their common enemy. Christianity is also portrayed as the religion of traitors. Yohana is recruited into the colonial administration as a chief, while Mwai and his family join the freedom fighters. The dominant theme of betrayal emerges towards the end of the novel, when the erstwhile collaborators and traitors like Yohana are rewarded by the new African government after *uhuru* (by getting appointed to senior positions), while the surviving patriots like Nunga are neglected. The message we get here is that the new administration is made up of traitors who cannot be expected to bring about real change for the benefit of their fellow Africans (Mbatiah 308).

While *Wimbo Mpya* touches on some of the issues raised in the earlier novels mentioned previously, its main contribution is in the exploration of the positive and negative consequences of the liberation war. The novel's title captures the new orientation of politics and social life after *uhuru*. *Wimbo Mpya* also deethnicizes the Mau Mau war by showing that, apart from the Kikuyu, there were other Kenyan communities that were involved. As Yenjela says:

> Mwenda Mbatiah's *Wimbo Mpya* engages Mau Mau fighters' plight after independence; and contests the ethnicisation of Mau Mau memory mostly attributed to the Kikuyu in literary and public memory. Mbatiah shows that Meru and Embu people actively participated in the Mau Mau liberation war and the building of post-independence Kenya.
>
> *(70)*

We know from history that even among those countries that were ruled by the British, the colonial situation was not uniform across Africa. In East Africa, for instance, there were initial

162

wars of resistance against external aggression such as the Maji Maji War in Tanzania which was referred to earlier. Other examples are the Bunyoro Campaign of 1893 (Uganda) and the Nandi Resistance of 1895–1905 (Kenya). All these resistance wars were won by the British, who went on to establish colonial rule. The struggle to dislodge the colonial system differed from one country to another. On the whole, independence in Uganda and Tanzania was attained through the struggles of nationalist movements. In Kenya, the nationalist movement was almost overshadowed by the armed struggle. While Swahili historical literature from Kenya fictionalized the armed struggle, such literature from Tanzania dwelt on the nationalist movement.

A good example of an historical novel based on the nationalist movement in Tanzania is Gabriel Ruhumbika's *Miradi Bubu ya Wazalendo/Deceitful Projects of the Patriots*. It narrates, with consistent fidelity to history, the struggle for independence spearheaded by TANU under Mwalimu Nyerere and portrays the nationalist leader as an astute politician, a patriot, and a truly popular figure. He was an orator with a brilliant command of Swahili, which enabled him to mobilize the masses to agitate for independence. All these qualities of Nyerere enabled him to use TANU to secure independence for Tanzania. The novel goes on to examine Nyerere's rule from the time he ascended to power up to 1985 when he voluntarily stepped down as president. The story "ends with Nyerere's farewell messages to the people and media reports of his praise for an exceptionally patriotic messenger" (Mbatiah 153).

On the whole, Ruhumbika's novel is a satirical indictment of the leadership of Tanzania for failing to fulfil the promises of *ujamaa* to create an equitable and just society. The failure of the whole experiment is symbolized by the exit of Nyerere, who was its architect. Part of the reason the experiment failed is alluded to in the foregoing quotation. The messenger referred to is Saidi Jabiri/Ndugu Saidi, a diligent and faithful servant of TANU who made a tremendous contribution to the liberation struggle. In the end, after serving TANU since its formative stages, Saidi works as a messenger in one of the state corporations. He retires into abject poverty and tries, in vain, to present his problem to Nyerere during the farewell ceremony. Saidi's fate is painfully ironic, and it illustrates how the real patriots ended up in misery, while the hypocrites like Nzoka Mwanakulanga/Ndugu Nzoka (the other main character) use their leadership positions to enrich themselves, at the expense of the poor.

Nyerere is portrayed as a virtuous intellectual, a philosopher king, who made an honest attempt to dismantle the colonial system and replace it with a humane system rooted in the African traditional society. However, he failed because all the high-ranking officials who surrounded him were hypocrites, exemplified by Ndugu Nzoka. They pretended to be faithful to the ideology of *ujamaa*, while secretly they were using public resources to feather their own nests. Meanwhile, they used all manner of tricks to ensure that Nyerere never got to know the truth.

The controversy surrounding the implementation of *ujamaa* in Tanzania is one of the favourite themes in the works of historical novelists from that country. Writers such as Euphrase Kezilahabi in *Gamba la Nyoka/The Snake's Skin*, C.G. Mung'ong'o in *Njozi Iliyopotea/The Vision That Went Astray*, and George Liwenga in *Nyota ya Huzuni/A Sorrowful Star* deal with the challenge in question. All of them exonerate Nyerere and blame the corrupt leaders under him for the tottering and eventual collapse of *ujamaa*.

Tanzanian literature naturally classifies itself geographically into Mainland and Island literatures. This is because the two regions, Mainland and Island Tanzania, that constitute the United Republic of Tanzania were separate countries before the historic union of 1964. The regions are therefore different in many ways, and their literatures attest to this fact. For instance, while the historical novels of the Mainland writers we have mentioned previously responded to the postcolonial situation of Tanzania by examining Nyerere's failed attempt to break away from it, those from the Island were preoccupied with a different matter altogether.

Zanzibari writers such as M.S. Mohamed in *Nyota ya Rehema/Rehema's Star*, Adam Shafi in *Kasri ya Mwinyi Fuad/Mwinyi Fuad's Mansion*, and S.A. Mohamed in *Asali Chungu/Bitter Honey* fictionalize the causes and effects of the Zanzibar Revolution of 1964. It was the same year the revolution happened, ushering in a socialist regime, that the union with the Mainland took place. M.S. Mohamed, Adam Shafi, and S.A. Mohamed all paint a picture of an oppressive, exploitative, and racist Arab-controlled feudal system as the root cause of the revolution. The marginalized African majority population rose up in arms and overthrew the tiny Arab ruling class.

In conclusion, it is ironic that in East Africa, Swahili literature predates literature in English, yet it remains a minority discourse in the African context. This is because the postcolonial situation is itself ironic in the sense that it generally refers to stalled decolonization. Even as a minority discourse, the literature in question has continued to use forms appropriated from East Africa's literature in English, such as free verse, biography, and the novel, to engage the postcolony. Swahili literature is enriched not only by incorporating elements of Oriental and European literary culture but also by drawing from the rich African orature.

Works cited

Abdulaziz, Mohamed H. *Muyaka: 19th Century Swahili Popular Poetry*. Nairobi: Kenya Literature Bureau, 1979.

Abedi, Kaluta A. *Sheria za Kutunga Mashairi na Diwani ya Amri*. Nairobi: Kenya Literature Bureau, 1954.

Allen, John W.T. *Tendi*. London: Heinemann Educational Books, 1971.

Chimerah, Rocha M. *Kiswahili: Past Present and Future Horizons*. Nairobi, Nairobi University Press, 2000.

Hichens, William ed. *Al-Inkishafi: The Soul's Awakening*. Nairobi: Oxford University Press, 1972.

Kezilahabi, Euphrase. "Uchunguzi katika Ushairi wa Kiswahili." *Fasihi* (144–151), 1993.

Knappert, Jan. *Four Centuries of Swahili Verse: A Literary History and Anthology*. London: Heinemann, 1979.

Massamba, David, Kihore Yared and Hokororo Joseph. *Sarufi Miundo ya Kiswahili Sanifu (SAMIKISA)*. Dar es Salaam: TUKI, 1979.

Mazrui, Alamin. *Swahili beyond the Boundaries*. Athens: Ohio University Press, 2000.

Mbatiah, Mwenda. *Riwaya ya Kiswahili: Chimbuko na Maendeleo Yake* (The Swahili Novel: Its Origin and Development). Nairobi: Jomo Kenyatta Foundation, 2016.

Mbatiah, Mwenda. "Satire and the Theme of Victims and Culprits in *Miradi Bubu ya Wazalendo*." *Kiswahili* Vol. 77 (149–159), 2014.

Mbatiah, Mwenda. "Shaaban Robert as a Champion of Peace." *Daisaku Ikeda and Voices of Peace from Africa* (57–64), 2008.

Mnyampala, Mathias. *Waadhi wa Ushairi* (Sermon on Poetry). Nairobi: East African Literature Bureau, 1966.

Ochieng, William R. *A History of Kenya*. Nairobi: Macmillan, 1985.

Okoth, Assa. *A History of Africa* Vol. 1. Nairobi: East African Educational Publishers, 2006.

Robert, Shaaban. "Hotuba juu ya Ushairi." *Journal of East African Swahili Committee* (28/1), 1958.

Robert, Shaaban. *Utenzi wa Vita vya Uhuru: 1939 hata 1945*. Nairobi: Oxford University Press, 1967.

Wafula, Richard M. *Uhakiki wa Tamthilia: Historia na Maendeleo Yake* (A Critique of the Play: Its History and Development). Nairobi: Jomo Kenyatta Foundation, 1999.

Yenjela, David W. "Narrated Histories in Selected Kenyan Novels, 1963–2013." Diss. Stellenbosch: Stellenbosch University, 2017.

Zubkova, Elena B., et al. *Outline of Swahili Literature: Prose Fiction and Drama*. Leiden: Koninlikje Brill NV, 2009.

12

BECOMING-MINORITARIAN

Constructions of coloured identities in creative writing projects at the University of the Western Cape, South Africa

F. Fiona Moolla

Bereft as they are of a prelapsarian (that is, precolonial) or European past, coloureds are completely grounded in South Africa. Unlike the autochthonous Africans, they belong only to the site of that first encounter between the colonizer and the colonized. . . . Unlike the European colonialists, they are rooted in this part of Africa, without connections to the metropole. . . . Paradoxical as it might seem, it is not surprising that these quintessential "South Africans" have not had their national identity endorsed either by whites or by blacks, nor have they themselves embraced it; marginality has been accepted, transformed into the dominant coloured subject position, as much as it has been imposed from without. Hybridity is a sign of difference, of racial, cultural, and ideological impurity; a marker of alienation, hybridity is not read as a measure of integration into (and centrality to) the nation. . . . Racial impurity does not so much disqualify as it signifies a perpetual symbolic disenfranchisement, a marginalization that cannot be transcended. No South African community is better versed in the vagaries and contradictions of the politics of the impure than coloureds.

(Farred, G Midfielder's Moment 8)

He was a milk and coffee man in a milk and coffee world.
He was both and neither, too mixed to be either.
He was too milk to live a coffee life.
Coffee knew only black bitterness.
. . .
He was too coffee to live a milk life.
Milk in tall white holders.
The milk coffee man lived a milk coffee life.
The cup was short with chips but had no holes.
And life was sweet as Canderel.

(Williams, S. "Milk and Coffee" 46)

The epigraphs to this chapter, the one taken from a scholarly work by Grant Farred, a University of the Western Cape (UWC) alumnus and now Professor of Africana Studies and English at Cornell University, and the second a poem by Shirwileta Williams, a recent creative writing student in the English Department at UWC, underscore the deep and proliferating paradoxes out of which coloured identity is conceived. "Coloured" in the context of South African apartheid racial classification and sociocultural lived experience means something different to the use of "coloured" internationally and in the United States in particular. "Coloured," used as it is by Henry Louis Gates, Jr. in *Colored People*, a memoir for his daughters whom he suspects in their lifetime will go from identifying as "African Americans, to 'people of color,' to being, once again 'colored people'" (xvi), refers to any person of any degree of black African descent. In the South African context, a concise definition is hard, as we shall see, given the complexities of the historical, political, social and cultural constructions (and their constant transformation) that form the alembic out of which coloured identity comes into amorphous but persistent being.

A sociopolitical history of South African coloured identity

The salient features of this most shape-shifting of South African cultural identities as outlined by Mohamed Adhikari, doyen of the study of coloured history, politics and identity, include the following: First, coloured identity is culturally marginal in popular conceptions; second, it is an identity strongly associated with Western culture "in opposition to African equivalents", but which, in a racist South Africa, was largely repudiated by white, European culture; and, third, it is an identity that, in racial terms, is intermediate, winning it advantages and disadvantages in relation to the black-white racial polarities between which it gets constituted. Racial intermediacy grants the bearers of coloured identity an affiliation with dominant white culture which, paradoxically, by the same racial thinking, is conceptualised as miscegenation where "racial mixture" is considered to be "pejorative" and will lead to "degeneration and weakness" (Adhikari, *Burdened by Race* viii). Adhikari adduces evidence of the racist belief in black communities also that coloured people are "mixed-breeds" without a cultural or national identity (Adhikari, *Not White Enough, Not Black Enough* 24). Thus, coloured identity is constituted not as purity and "fullness" but as taint and "lack" between polarised black and white identities, which are conceived as racially and culturally unadulterated. Adhikari tracks the origins of the conception of coloured identity to the early period of Dutch rule of the Cape, with a clearer sense of cultural community arising in the period of British colonisation "after the emancipation of the Khoisan in 1828, and other slaves in 1838 . . . [where] various components of the heterogeneous black laboring class in the Cape Colony started integrating more rapidly and developing an incipient shared identity" (Adhikari, *Not White Enough, Not Black Enough* 2). The Khoisan are an autochthonous Southern African ethnicity, a "first people" contrasted with other Bantu-speaking groups that historically migrated southward from central Africa.

Coloured identity is consolidated, however, in the period after large-scale mining of gold and diamonds transformed the South African economic landscape generally, resulting in large numbers of black African people moving to the Western Cape from the 1870s. As Adhikari observes, "[t]hese developments drove acculturated colonial blacks [in the Cape] to assert a separate identity as Coloured people, in order to claim a position of relative privilege in relation to [incoming] Africans on the basis of their closer assimilation to Western culture and being partly descended from European colonists" (*Not White Enough, Not Black Enough* 3). Thus coloured identity is an identity that in its origins and in various historical periods is claimed by its bearers.

Fluid constructions of identity from below, as it were, in the late nineteenth century and the first half of the twentieth century became rigidly defined in the context of apartheid social engineering after 1948, when a raft of racist legislation effected an imposition of racial identities from above. Most significant was the Population Registration Act of 1950 (and its various subsequent and very complicated and confusing amendments) that sought to classify all South Africans according to apartheid categorisations of race, namely (in order of hierarchy) White, Coloured and Black, to which other subcategories were later added as needed, including, in racist desperation, Chinese South Africans as coloured. This period saw phenotypically white coloured people abandoning their darker-skinned kin to be legally classified white – with the attendant privileges – and a small minority of black African people seeking to be classified coloured. People of Indian descent also, mainly in the Cape, tried to be classified coloured in order to continue to live and trade in mixed areas. The former move, where coloured people "played white", is the popularly more familiar one and the one that is fictionally explored in Zoë Wicomb's novel, *Playing in the Light*, and in Rayda Jacobs's short story collection, *The Middle Children*. "Coloured" thus, in the apartheid period, was a "catch-all" categorisation into which anyone who did not fit one of the other more clearly defined groups was slotted. People from the same family, connected by blood, could thus end up being differently classified by phenotype and cultural association. Coloured identity was also significantly impacted by the Group Areas Act, also of 1950, which attempted geographically to separate a racially classified population (Trotter, Field). The romantic idealisation of District 6, a poor, crime-ridden slum near central Cape Town (Adhikari *Not White Enough* 118) but an area which was also vibrant, multicultural and open, both in the popular imagination and in literature, has been central to the constitution of coloured identity (Soudien). Fiction which has celebrated District 6 and has memorialised the displacement of its residents to various coloured townships on the Cape Flats includes Richard Rive's *"Buckingham Palace", District Six*, Alex la Guma's *A Walk in the Night and Other Stories* and Rozena Maart's *Rosa's District 6*.

Viscerally responding to crude apartheid racism and capitalism, the concept of "coloured" became contentious in the twentieth century. From the mid-1930s, many coloured people and coloured political organisations consciously identified with a universal humanism, which, in the later 1970s context of heightened anti-apartheid resistance, was subsumed into the identification "black" that forged political unity across racially divided groups. Intellectual, educationist and one-time political prisoner on Robben Island, the late Neville Alexander was one of the most significant rejectionists of all racial classifications, especially the label "Coloured" applied to him based on his appearance, as he anecdotally recounts in the collection of essays, *Thoughts on the New South Africa* (159). He suggests that redress in the post-Apartheid "rainbow nation" has paradoxically entrenched racial thinking and that the "rainbow metaphor['s] . . . emphasis on coexisting colour groups . . . reinforces beliefs in racial categories" (130). Alexander's conviction that class identity is more significant than cultural identity is a position that was, and continues to be, widely held pre- and after the end of formal apartheid.

But coloured identity has been contested from non-Marxist positions also, related centrally to the question of (and questioning of) shame. Professor of sociology Zimitri Erasmus confirms the social position of coloured identity determined by hierarchical racial architecture: "For me, growing up coloured meant knowing that I was *not only* not white, but *less than white*; *not only* not black, but *better than black*" (13). Coloured identity is riven, furthermore, by two consequences of "miscegenation" to which racial conceptualisations lead. The one is the idea of "lack" in relation to "pure" races, referred to earlier; the other is the gendered notion of (sexual) shame attached to coloured identity. Erasmus recalls the expressions she often heard growing up: "*Hou jou linne binne* (Keep your linen hidden). *Hou jou koek in jou broek* (Keep your fanny in your panties). *Vroeg ryp, Vroeg vrot* (Early to ripen, early to rot)", which "stipulate[d] the bounds of sexual behaviour for young coloured women" (13). The South African language, Afrikaans, to whose vivid expressions Erasmus refers, with sources in Dutch, Khoisan and Melayu (Da Costa and Davids 67–68) languages, is equally linked with coloured identity as it is with white Afrikaner identity. Debunking the myth of Afrikaner cultural purity, Achmat Davids, scholar of Muslim history at the Cape, has fully studied in *The Afrikaans of the Cape Muslims* the earliest Afrikaans written in the Arabic script of East Indian slaves, identified as "Arabic-Afrikaans" by Adrianus van Selms, scholar of Semitic languages and theology. The Afrikaans expressions referred to by Erasmus originate in the idea of shame attached to coloured identity as a consequence of sexual relations between colonising men and indigenous and enslaved women. These unequal and exploitative sexual relations are captured in a well-known joke that the coloured race was born nine months after Jan Van Riebeeck, the first Dutch governor, arrived at the Cape in 1652. The context, nuances and consequences of the assumptions of this crude joke are analysed by Adhikari in *Not White Enough*, 19–32. It is this conception of coloured shame, gendered female, that lies at the heart of Wicomb's essay, "Shame and Identity: The Case of the Coloured in South Africa". Wicomb constructs her essay around the figure of Saartje Baartman, the "Khoi/coloured woman", also known as the "Hottentot Venus, who was exhibited [near naked] in London and Paris from 1810 to her death in 1815" (91). (Khoi/Hottentot, San/Bushman, Griquas, Namas and Basters are all groups who have been regarded, and regarded themselves, at one time or another, as coloured.) Wicomb suggests that she adopts Baartman as "icon precisely because of the nasty, unspoken question of concupiscence that haunts coloured identity" (93). The ghosts of this haunting wander the pages of much of the relevant fiction that engages this identity.

"Shame" means something slightly different, however, for South African former Oxford philosophy scholar and well-known media personality Eusebius McKaiser. Interestingly reversing the historical trend for coloured people to "play white", iterated in much of the relevant published literature, McKaiser is open about his stronger identification with black culture ("Racial Baggage" 31–32). McKaiser admits to feeling shame about being coloured for all of the stereotypes and realities created from the particular conjunction of oppressions suffered by this group. These include alcoholism, foetal alcohol syndrome and gangsterism ("Cape Town's Dirty, Coloured Secrets" 41–47 and "For Coloured People Only" 172). He suggests: "My grappling with being coloured and my emotional reaction . . . is, – sadly – not mere embarrassment. Embarrassment is not strong enough to capture the depth of my anxiety, my grappling, my guilt – and more. *Shame* feels like the label that just about gets it right" (emphasis in original, "Cape Town's Dirty, Coloured Secrets" 45). In a flagellating self-reflexive move, McKaiser also confesses to feeling ashamed of his conflicted neglect of the interests of his community because of the shame of identification with them. McKaiser writes: "I do not find coloured people interesting. I do not know how to write about coloured people. I do not know what to say about coloured people. And I feel bad about feeling this way"("For Coloured People Only" 165). In this way, McKaiser signals a paradoxical disconnect borne out of the deepest sense of connection.

Despite political challenges to the concept of coloured identity, the period after the advent of parliamentary democracy in South Africa has seen a resurgence of what Adhikari terms a "newfound creativity in the manifestation of coloured identities" (*Burdened by Race* xv). The exploration of post-apartheid fashioning of coloured identity is most cogently presented by Zimitri Erasmus's edited volume, referred to earlier. Erasmus acknowledges the specificities of coloured identity and compellingly reinvents coloured identity out of "hybridised" presence rather than "lack", forcing the need to "move beyond the notion that coloured identities are 'mixed race' identities" (21). Erasmus identifies, in particular, some of the dangers of the complete subsumption of coloured identity into black identity, a move justified in the context of the ideal of unity of the oppressed in anti-apartheid resistance but which post-1994 may bolster the "emergent discourse of African essentialism" (20) and hides historical coloured collusion in racialised injustice:

> For me it is a "truth" which defies the safe prison of the dominant ideology: that I ought to identify only as black and not coloured; that coloured identity is an illusion from which I need to be saved by my black sisters who promise to put me on the right road and confer my "true" blackness upon me; that the former aspect of my identity is best discarded as a relic of the past. I refuse the safety of identifying only as "black" because . . . identifying only as "black" denies the "better than black" element of coloured identity formation. It denies complicity. . . . Identifying only as black further expresses a desire for political authenticity . . . [where] black political identities are themselves constructions, they too are multiple and marked by internal contradictions. There is no "pure" black politics. There are no "pure" black identities. There is no authentic black self.
>
> *(25)*

Based on the previous contentions, Erasmus, much like Farred quoted in the epigraph, proposes a conception of coloured identity theorised as hybrid or "creolized", the term she prefers given its theoretical origins in studies of slavery. The implication is that coloured identity as creole identity may illuminate a South African political discourse in which a complex minority identity may signpost the path to a more productive, less divisive national majority politics. But Erasmus's position is not the only one, as made clear by Adhikari's analysis of post-1994 resurgences of coloured identity politics. Adhikari suggests that: "The new democratic dispensation has brought with it a degree of freedom of association and possibilities for ethnic mobilization that were inconceivable under white domination" (*Not White Enough* 175). Even as some of the most basic racialised assumptions of coloured identity were undermined, for example, the value of its proximity to whiteness, nevertheless "varied and creative responses to the nature of Coloured identity and its role in South African society" (Adhikari *Not White Enough* 175) have sprung forth. Among these is a politically astute reinterpretation of interstitiality, summed up in the idea that "first we were not white enough and now we are not black enough" (Adhikari *Not White Enough* 176). Other positions include the "mobilization of coloured opinion primarily through identification with a slave past, [while] others trace or invent a Khoisan ethnic identity, and yet others retreat into a laager of Coloured exclusivism" (Adhikari *Not White Enough* 176). Adhikari sums up that "[s]ince 1994, a motley marketplace with distinctly idiosyncratic elements has developed for ideas and movements related to Coloured identity" (Adhikari *Not White Enough* 176). The term coloured would appear to have more valence post-1994 than pre-1994, when the terms "brown people" and "first nation" are also claimed.

Bush College: the "coloured" university and its transformations

The institutional history of the University of the Western Cape in some ways mirrors the paradoxes, ambiguities, absurdities, contradictions and possibilities – in short, the complexities – of the concept "coloured". The university was created by fiat of the apartheid state in 1960 as a constituent college for "Coloureds" of the University of South Africa (UNISA). The University College of the Western Cape was granted the status of a university ten years later. In one of many apartheid ironies, the college exclusively for "Coloureds", racially defined, was legally constituted by the Extension of Universities Act of 1959. Premesh Lalu, director of the UWC Centre for Humanities Research and one of the editors of *Becoming UWC*, a volume reflecting on fifty years of the university's history, notes the observation of prominent black writer and intellectual A.C. Jordan that "[w]hile [the Extension of Universities Act] claimed to be extending higher education, making it presumably more accessible, it in fact foreclosed access by indicating racial and ethnic identification as the basis for entrance" (Lalu "Campus: A Discourse on the Grounds of an Apartheid University" 39).

The University College of the Western Cape was quite literally built in a clearing in the *fynbos*, the heathland vegetation unique to the region, a small endangered section of which now is cautiously conserved in the Cape Flats Nature Reserve, which forms part of the campus. The bush out of which the university arose generates a range of unintended connotations, all of which have been played upon by generations of students. Zoë Wicomb, one of the most well-known alumnae of the university, graduating with a BA degree in the late 1960s, alludes to the racial origins of the institution in her short story "A Clearing in the Bush" (Wicomb *You Can't Get Lost in Cape Town* 37–62). The story uses the occasion of the commemoration at the university of the assassination of Hendrik Verwoerd, notorious architect of apartheid, to reflect on the contained South African racial, but also gender and class, tensions for which the institution was a microcosm. Wicomb's "A Clearing in the Bush" is not the only work by a notable alumnus of the university where the university itself comes under scrutiny. The poet Arthur Nortje is described by Grant Farred, whose work on coloured literature has been cited as an epigraph to this chapter, as a writer who "'accepts,' in the most contorted and even disabling sense of the term, colouredness as an identity" (16). Where Wicomb is able to clear the ground and address the contradictions of the university directly, Nortje, by contrast, in the three poems about UWC collected by English Lecturer Mark Espin for the volume *Becoming UWC*, literally lingers about the university – on its threshold. The first poem, "Thumbing a Lift", describes the angst-filled attempt to reach the college; the second, "Scene Near an Ethnic College", suggests zones of alienation, culminating in the alienation of the campus itself; and the third poem, "Operation Clean-up", intimates the disillusionments at the end of a UWC academic year when "old poetry drafts and examination notes" are destroyed (Nortje *Becoming UWC* 134–136). The bush, referred to in the title of Wicomb's short story, and the angst of the coloured student at the university expressed in the poems by Nortje, are presently being reimagined. "Bush" in the short story title "A Clearing in the Bush" alludes also to the contested identity of the Bushman (or San), on whose social genocide and "disposability" the formation of the South African nation, in part, depended (Baderoon "Surplus, Excess, Dirt" 257–272). The term "Bushman" has a history of complexity that comes close to the complexities of the term "coloured", being historically both rejected and accepted. The term "Bushman" and its variations, "*Bushy*" or "*Boesie*", has been used as a racial slur (Adhikari, *Not White Enough* 28), but the identifier "Bushman" has also been claimed. Coloured identity as Bushman identity in the evolving self-reflection of UWC, or "Bush College", as it was known, currently is playfully and ironically re-inscribed on campus lifestyle merchandise: "Back your Bushie" proclaim the supporters' club t-shirts worn by coloured students and students of all other cultural backgrounds to whom the university now is open.

Transcending its origins in apartheid racial segregation, the university has, in succeeding decades, actively and consciously transformed itself and has been continuously made, un-made and re-made by buffeting forces of politics, (globalised) economics and history. Moving out of its origins in apartheid racist social categories, and ignited by the student protests of 1976, UWC made the political shift under the "unifying force of Black Consciousness that would shake the foundations of the racial logic of a university created to function as an instrument of apartheid" (Lalu "Constituting Community at the Intellectual Home of the Left" 111). The university increasingly came to be regarded as a black university as a consequence of its alignment through student struggle and protest with broader regional and national communities and resistances, as this extract from a pamphlet issued by UWC students after the 1976 Soweto uprising shows:

> We as students at the University of the Western Cape . . . find a type of education that forces us to believe that we are Coloureds and hereby making us believe that we do not have anything in common with the rest of the country and specifically those who are suffering with us . . . We maintain that Black people all over the country **suffer** in the same manner and feel the **pains of oppression** in a common way . . . *BLACK PEOPLE [SHOULD] STAND TOGETHER.*
>
> *(emphasis in original, in Thomas ed. Finding*
> *Freedom in the Bush of Books 87–88)*

The early 1980s saw the university challenging apartheid segregation "by opening its doors to all South Africans" regardless of colour, with "[l]arge numbers of black students from the north flock[ing] to the institution" (O'Connell x). The vice-chancellorship of former UWC student and lecturer Jakes Gerwel, who hailed the university as the intellectual home of the left, marked further the shift of the university, where the mutual imbrication of academic and political projects became clearer. The university thus had moved full circle from what Marxist writer Alex la Guma had disparagingly referred to as its position at the centre of a "Colouredstan" created by the Nationalist Party (Lalu "Campus: A Discourse on the Grounds of an Apartheid University" 42). In the post-1994 era, UWC has fallen "into the category of the historically black university . . . caught in a conundrum . . . of seeking access to claims of universality while increasingly being interpellated into a predetermined structure of hierarchy" (Lalu "Constituting Community at the Intellectual Home of the Left" 118). The coloured university thus, in the contemporary period of high-velocity internationalisation and globalisation, is required to contest equally, eliding the historically specific constraints attendant on its origins and development. In this sense also, institutional tensions reflect the tensions of historical impacts on coloured social identity as it negotiates contemporary national and postnational forces.

Of minorities and the marginal

Coloured as a sociocultural and political concept in South African discourse, as channelled through the institutional history of UWC, established as a coloured university, furthermore, is a discourse of marginality of a group that throughout the twentieth century "never formed more than about 9 percent of the South African population" (Adhikari *Not White Enough* 17). Throughout its history, discourses of coloured identity have sought to overcome marginality through racial identification with a dominant majority. In the apartheid period, these discourses pursued identification with a dominant white political and cultural majority, a tendency Erasmus terms "complicity" (24). Discourses of coloured identity have also sought political affiliation with a dominant politically black majority as part of anti-apartheid resistance. Post-1994, discourses of coloured identity have generally eschewed political and cultural affiliation with a now dominant black political, but not cultural, majority. Black identities are "major" in the sense that they enjoy political dominance and since they can lay claim to an authenticity denied coloured identity. However, cultural and epistemological "majority" belong to varying white identities both pre- and post-1994. New sociopolitical constructions of coloured identity, paradoxically, have found a voice through connections with even more marginal historical and ethnic subgroups than the marginality represented by catch-all coloured identity. These identity discourses claim origin from and connection with slavery and Khoisan cultures. Thus the one

feature that remains constant in coloured identity constructions is the conception of marginality, a marginality which primes it for consideration through the lens of theoretical articulations
of minority discourses generally and minority literature in particular when one considers the
fiction-writing by and about coloured communities.[1]

Theorisation of minority discourses may be tracked back to Gilles Deleuze and Félix Guattari's reflections in *Kafka: Toward a Minor Literature* on the work of Franz Kafka, as a member of a
Jewish minority in Prague, writing in the majority language of German. In the chapter, "What
Is a Minor Literature?", three key features are identified. These are, first, the idea that a "minor
literature doesn't come from a minor language; it is rather that which a minority constructs in a
major language" (16). The second characteristic of minor literatures is that "everything in them
is political" (17). What is meant is that while major literatures foreground the individual through
the Oedipal "intrigues" of the family, with the social milieu as a backdrop, minor literature, by
contrast, foregrounds the socioeconomic and political contexts of individual concerns and experiences. The third, and somewhat critically contentious, point is that "in [minority literatures]
everything takes on a collective value" (17). The authors go on to suggest that:

> Indeed, precisely because talent isn't abundant in a minor literature, there are no possi-
> bilities for an individual enunciation that would belong to this or that "master" and that
> could be separated from a collective enunciation. Indeed, scarcity of talent is in fact
> beneficial and allows the conception of something other than a literature of masters;
> what each author says individually already constitutes a common action, and what he
> or she says or does is necessarily political, even if others aren't in agreement.
>
> *(Deleuze and Guattari 17)*

Implying a "paucity of talent" among minor writers has been the object of critique (Rosaldo
124), which may be disputed by Deleuze and Guattari's general anti-hierarchical bent, privileging the "becoming-minoritarian" of all discourses, in particular discourses seeking fascist mastery. Thus, the delineation of a "standard" and the canonisation of masters of this standard would
constitute precisely the majoritarianism of which Deleuze and Guattari are critical. Minority,
therefore, is not a claim to an authentic identity, nor a status linked to an empirically adduced
numerical minority. Instead, philosophical minority may be read as a condition or a constant
potentiality (often held by numerical minorities) whose discourse allows it "to take flight along
creative lines of escape" (Deleuze and Guattari 26), "deterritorialising" majority discourses.

Deleuze and Guattari's philosophical observations regarding minor literatures were given
broader application to minorities, popularly construed, through a conference and its proceedings
published as *The Nature and Context of Minority Discourse*, edited by Abdul R. JanMohamed and
David Lloyd. Here, the concept is linked more practically to minority groups, identifying "the
political and cultural structures that connect different minority cultures in their subjugation and
opposition to the dominant culture" (JanMohamed and Lloyd ix). The project was, furthermore,
conceived as a way to marginalise the centre through articulations of minority discourses that
did not have to pass through hegemonic culture. Despite this more practical approach, the tension in Deleuze and Guattari between an outright deterritorialisation of minority identity and
the need for strategic articulations of identity is maintained – as JanMohamed and Lloyd express
it, "the physical survival of minority groups depends on the recognition of its culture as viable" (6).
Deleuze and Guattari's concept of minority discourse also refracts unitary notions of nationhood in many of the essays in the well-known volume *Nation and Narration* but perhaps is most
clearly articulated in Homi Bhabha's "DissemiNation: Time, Narrative, and the Margins of the
Modern Nation". For Bhabha,

[m]inority discourse sets the act of emergence in the antagonistic in-between of image and sign, the accumulative and the adjunct, presence and proxy. It contests genealogies of "origin" that leads to claims of cultural supremacy and historical priority. Minority discourse acknowledges the status of national culture – and the people – as a contentious, performative space of the perplexity of living in the pedagogical representations of the fullness of life.

(307)

In its theoretical genesis and development, thus, the idea of minority discourse is precariously balanced between its representation of both identity and non-identity. To latch onto Bhabha's striking expression, let us turn now to the performative space of (possible) perplexity in the figuring of the following minoritarian "concepts": first, coloured identity as a national minority discourse in, second, creative writing, which may be construed a minority "discipline", third, at UWC as a "minority", historically disadvantaged institution. (In the Western Cape, UWC may be contrasted with formerly white institutions which include the University of Cape Town, the historically English university, and Stellenbosch University, the historically Afrikaans university.)

In the landscape of writing in the public domain, creative writing produced in an academic setting occupies an interstitial place, almost as interesting as the interstitiality of coloured identity. As Tim Mayers's "manifesto" on the establishment of the *Journal of Creative Writing* suggests, creative writing courses may better be regarded as constituting a field of "issues, texts, theorists, and practitioners on a plane of immanence – on a flat, non-hierarchical surface" (Mayers quoting Byron Hawk 2). The discomfort with the institutionalisation, or the "becoming-major", of creative writing is echoed by Antjie Krog, supervisor and facilitator of UWC Creates workshops who, on the cusp of a conundrum, suggests that "I don't believe it is possible to teach somebody to write literature" (interview with author). Mayers suggests further that while creative writing studies has arrived in "force" since 2005 (2), its roots stretch further back in institutions of higher learning (mainly in the global north). As a "non-discipline", where disciplines are hierarchical and prescriptive, creative writing, as the marginal "outsider" study that in numerous ways challenges the majoritarian norms and conventions of academia, may inherently constitute a minority discourse pursuing the "lines of escape" described by Deleuze and Guattari. The fact, furthermore, that creative writing, by and large, exists in the marginal media of the thesis and the small self-publications of university departments and minor funded projects makes creative writing a minority form in the regional and national publishing landscape.

Creative constructions of coloured identity at UWC

Almost inescapably, questions of identity have been central to the writing produced by participants in the creative writing programmes at UWC. There are good reasons for this, and the focus on social identities does not preclude literary quality and aesthetic concerns, as rigorous examination standards and often-successful publication in print and online journals and collections confirm. The origins of creative writing at UWC may be tracked back to both extra-curricular projects and credit-bearing courses, which prioritised access to participants who otherwise would be excluded. UWC Creates is a multilingual project established in 2009 (Brown and Vandermerwe, Preface to *This is My Land* 5), outside of formal study programmes, which provides a supportive context through workshops and other opportunities for the creativity of mainly marginalised participants, who, in most cases, do not have formal literary training and lack the cultural capital and access to networks of influence that open doors to publication. The credit-bearing courses, started in 2010 (Moolman Introduction to *Cutting*

Carrots 9), include undergraduate semester options, courses at Honour's level, a structured Master's in Creative Writing, the full-thesis master's and a newly offered full-thesis PhD. Although all of the writing produced through UWC may potentially be multilingual, given institutional flexibility that encourages multi- and trans-linguality, it is mainly writing in English, which often incorporates Afrikaans, that has been focused on here. Meg Vandermerwe, a significant actor in the establishment of the programmes, suggests that the UWC projects give voice to writers who are unlikely, for financial or academic reasons, to be able to access creative writing courses at universities of privilege in the region. She suggests further that while questions of social identity are not explicitly foregrounded, the encouragement to "identify story roots", where participants creatively reinterpret a story told to them by the oldest member of their family or community, has the consequence of foregrounding sociohistorical impacts and local culture on identity (Interview). This methodology is clearly visible in the anthology of ghost stories, *Constant Companions*, whose artistic reinterpretations of informant interviews nevertheless bear strong imprints of local culture and language and where apartheid trauma experienced in coloured communities remains a ghostly presence. Antjie Krog, referred to previously, as facilitator of UWC Creates workshops and projects and thesis supervisor, observes that programme participants are often fairly new to writing and that, in practice, "first efforts are usually autobiographical", where "avoidance of cultural identity is not easily possible". Krog adds: "One's culture, the one in which one has functioned as a child and young adult is what one knows best, is what one could write an authentic voice for . . . so there is immediately a confidence in the writing that would not necessarily be there when a UWC student imagines herself a Viking". She stresses, however, that "[t]he story comes first. Only later one can see, oh yes, there is also a specific identity. But if the identity is very specific and very typical, then the story or poem usually suffers – it becomes a kind of propaganda, instead of a sensitively lived-through text . . . nobody, absolutely nobody came with a wish to talk about identity . . . everyone had a story to tell" (Interview with author).

More recently appointed creative writing lecturer Kobus Moolman confirms Krog's observations when he says that "[i]ssues of cultural identity thus form a natural and seamless part of the material selected" but continues "[h]owever, I am also serious on moving students from what they know (their own cultural and historical milieu) to that which is outside them – particularly because as writers I feel that they owe it to themselves to explore work as widely as possible" (Interview with author). It is thus clear that in creative writing programmes at UWC, coloured identity gets foregrounded as a consequence of the social and cultural backgrounds of participants, the fact that they are novice writers for whom a certain amount of autobiographical ground-clearing is necessary and because the methodologies employed focus on artistically reworking compelling stories from people who would not otherwise have a voice in broader national discourses.

Conversations with a significant number of programme participants[2] suggest that these methods have been positively taken up and often have had successful outcomes in producing well-received publications that have launched careers in arts and culture spheres. But it has also generated tension that reinforces the tensions in the conception of coloured identity. In a few cases among students, coloured identity is acknowledged without conflict. Former master's student Saaligh Gabier, whose family was part of the South African diaspora escaping apartheid by emigrating to Canada, identifies himself as a "Muslim Coloured/Cape Malay South African living in a majority Christian White Canadian city" (Interview with author). It is fascinating that even though Gabier's novella, *The Wedding Interviews*, explores intra-Muslim cultural differences in Canada, it nevertheless incorporates a pre-history in which many of the motifs identifiable in fiction representing coloured identity are discernible. For Gabier in the post-9/11 North

American context, the more contentious identity is Muslim identity. Another former master's student, Janine Lange, also uses the term comfortably in acknowledgement of what, for her, is its cultural reality. As the mother of a daughter with a white father, she makes clear that her daughter is not coloured but mixed-race since she is an outsider to the culture in which Lange herself grew up. Lange feels it is important, even post-1994, to highlight coloured experience through the possibilities presented by fiction since racist stereotypes of coloured people and communities persist post-apartheid. She qualifies this observation by saying that in writing her thesis, she had to re-learn the coloured culture of her community since hegemonic white culture had forced an alienation on her from her roots. Lange's PhD continues this exploration since it involves the collection of the oral traditions of coloured communities of the Northern Cape, which, apart from the Western Cape, is most strongly associated with coloured culture and identity. Similarly, current master's student Lisa Julie, in acknowledgement of the almost abyssal hybridity of her background and affiliations, accepts coloured as the only term that encompasses the complexity of her experience.

However, engagement of the work of and exchanges with the greater number of students suggests a complex use of the term "coloured", with transformations in attitudes to the use over time. Creative writing theses at UWC consist of a creative component and a reflective essay, which in some ways undermines New Critical orthodoxies regarding the absolute self-containment of the work of art, where authorial intention plays no role. Asked to reflect on their creative work and their artistic journeys, most students quite unproblematically use the term coloured, often included in the keywords of the thesis. In many cases, however, this use is explained or rejected in subsequent interviews in favour of a more general black political identity. In the case of master's student Hayley Rodkin, who was deeply involved in the anti-apartheid resistance movement, there is a self-critique implied in all her references to the term "coloured", even as the social realities of such communities and their political struggles are represented. Rodkin rhetorically asks the question of identity in the post-1994 period, in particular: "When did I become coloured?" The double bind is lucidly articulated by Llewellin Jegels, whose degree was made possible by UWC's special admissions policy designed to give access to people whom apartheid disadvantaged directly and indirectly: "Initially . . . I avoided dealing with racial/cultural themes because of the 'burden' and obligation that writers of colour feel of writing the (often unspeakable) truths of their pasts. However as a multi-ethnic writer, I could not ignore the weight of my context as a writer. It began to feel as if the voices of the past, both the silent and silenced voices clamored for expression" (interview with author).

These are not, however, the only responses to the question of identity as it emerges in UWC creative writing projects. Former student Chad Brevis is critical of the ways in which the story-root methodology of creative writing teaching encourages stereotypical representations of the "Cape Coloured community". He feels that his own voice, as a "modern, information aged, secularised and globalised youth" was "colonis[ed]" to reinforce a stereotype. Brevis's contention is a new one that is not encountered elsewhere in the sociology of coloured identity, where rejection of the term most often is associated with enlightenment universal humanist affiliations or conceptions of political blackness.

If published writers of coloured identity are a minority in the South African literature landscape, as a glance at the lists of most South African publishers suggests, where the literary conversation is mainly between white and black, the creative writing student is an interesting minority within that minority. Jolyn Phillips, part of the first cohort to graduate from the UWC creative writing programmes, has had her work published and nationally distributed. Like Tiresias, she has experience of both worlds. Her work has also garnered a number of major South African literary awards. Her success has made her a frequent guest on the South African literary festival and book fair circuit, where she acknowledges a pigeonholing based on social identity. Phillips deftly deflects anthropological appreciation of her work by contesting that coloured identities are "characters" in her art. With experience in both camps, she confirms the ways in which marginal cultural identity is made to pass through, and thus be moulded by, hegemonic culture generally in the publication process and in the circuits where books are marketed, sold and celebrated. This idea is iterated by Maxine Case, author of two novels and a biography, who suggests: "I think that the politics of cultural representation definitely does influence the politics of publication, specifically in terms of the gatekeepers – who are the readers and key decision makers and how integrated the general publishing industry is" (interview with author). Similarly, Kobus Moolman, creative writing lecturer mentioned earlier and well-published author, wryly responds to a question about the role of identity in the South African publishing industry by saying, "[c]ynically I feel that the publishing world often encourages and actively searches out [such] work" (interview with author). Phillips, however, goes on cannily and realistically to note that these are constraints imposed on publishers in a capitalist marketplace, which she, as author, necessarily is also forced to negotiate and where she sometimes also has to make strategic compromises. Phillips's first book, *Tjieng Tjang Tjerries*, a collection of short stories, was published by feminist press Modjaji Books. Managing Editor Colleen Higgs clarifies Modjaji's niche interest in opening up new "places" in the South African literary landscape. Place, Higgs suggests, is an important consideration in the context of a manuscript that tells a good story well (interview with author). Phillips, whose stories are set in the fishing village of Gansbaai, opens up a voice that is not the voice of urban coloured identities. Based on Phillips's experience of the publishing industry after her first publication and the networks into which she has subsequently been drawn, it becomes apparent that creative writing students as a minority, contrasted with published authors, may have a latitude in the representation or non-representation of social identities that dependence on publishing and its circuits curtails. In theory, a UWC student could write about life as "a Viking", but this is a possibility no UWC student has to date considered in the context of the continued urgency of the experience and expression of sociohistorically shaped identities.

Almost without exception, creative writing at UWC[3] explores the margins of the margin. The following short story collections, Jolyn Phillips's *Let's Go Home*, Bronwyn Douman's *The Marginal Grey*, Hilda Andrews' *Visklippie*, Janine Lange's *We Dare Not Say*, Hayley Rodkin's *Of Flowers and Tears* and the novel *The Girl with the Red Flower* by Waghied Misbach each foreground the experience of marginal groups within coloured communities in highly distinctive ways (see endnote 3 for full bibliographic details of the theses). Many of the stories zero in on female characters that stay afloat in challenging circumstances at the confluence of racial and gender discrimination, fictionally represented in unique ways. Many of the stories also are focalised through children whose literal minority and vulnerabilities are impacted by forms of patriarchal authority and violence, often constituted by the historically specific ways in which communities have been shaped by apartheid. The concept of intergenerational trauma comes up again and again in the stories and glosses on stories in reflective essays. Abuse, neglect, molestation, incest, femicide and dysfunctional families are themes that are treated in striking, often highly experimental ways. In this respect, creative writing at UWC reflects the interest in the margin of many published works also, where focalisation occurs through female characters. It is interesting that while the older generation of relevant writers were mainly male, for example, Alex la Guma, Richard Rive and the poet James Matthews, the newer generation is mainly female, reflected also in UWC creative writing, where most of the student-writers of coloured identity are female. But UWC creative writing goes further in its exploration of marginality or interprets marginality in different ways to much of the relevant published prose. The stories by

Hilda Andrews, for example, intersect coloured identity with marginal black identity and marginal white identities, namely the white elderly and white socially deviant, in a different take on the "rainbow" nation, as post-1994 South Africa has memorably been named by Desmond Tutu. One of the short stories by Hayley Rodkin considers the "majoritarianism" of heteronormativity in the anti-apartheid resistance movement through a complex homosexual male character who does not encourage sympathy. Inverting the norm, Bronwyn Douman's entire collection, *The Marginal Grey*, is about inserting the experience of the coloured middle class into a literary canvas which has foregrounded working class, especially "skollie" or gangster stories. Here Douman plays on "grey" as the interstitial shade between white and black and also plays on the distinction between grey and "brown" as coloured people are more conventionally referred to in the South African context. The Afrikaans, "*bruinmens*", literally, "brown person" is often translated into English as "coloured". Interpreting "minor" in an unexpected literary sense, Waghied Misbach's novel, *The Girl with the Red Flower*, is a bracing exercise in "minor character elaboration", which takes the incidental character, Soraya, the prostitute in J.M. Coetzee's *Disgrace*, and constructs a compelling life which overturns all of the assumptions of submission and victimhood expected of the Muslim/Cape Malay/coloured woman, constituted in this case around violent "perpetrating agency".

Fiction representing coloured experience has generally highlighted the proximity of coloured identity to white identity. This comes across strongly in the "play white" or white-aspirational motif that is iterated across the greater majority of the texts considered, even where it may not be the central focus. Where the intersection of white and black subjectivity is explored, it is done mainly through the figure of the black domestic worker, whose position in the coloured household is charged with ironies. In this context, Jerome Cornelius's novella, *What Lies* (see endnote 3 for full bibliographic details), is path breaking in its acknowledgement of possibilities of relationships between coloured and black people beyond the domestic worker scenario encouraged by economic and social histories of apartheid. Here, a central middle-aged, married coloured male character is presented as marginal in terms of pre- and post-1994 racial hierarchies and the victim of the emasculation of his wife, whose cloistered, conservative and traumatic past makes her treat him in a demeaning and cruel way. Conflict in the novella is created by his overwhelming love for a young, black UWC student, who is obliged to engage in sex work to support herself as a student. Cornelius's novella, written in 2011–2013, is one of the first works of fiction to explore crossing racial borders in the opposite direction, so to speak. In published work, the engagement of coloured identity with black identity is considered in the debut 2018 novel by Kharnita Mohamed, titled *Called to Song*. This novel of development narrates the self-realisation of a Muslim female protagonist from Mitchell's Plain, one of the largest coloured townships in which the residents of District 6 were resettled, who discovers that her husband has a fulfilling relationship and a stable family with a black woman, denied to her in her own troubled relationship with him. Rehana Rossouw, journalist and author of *What Will People Say* and *New Times*, identifies the need "in a country like South Africa [for] writers [to] grapple with changes in identity rather than retaining apartheid's twisted racial categorisations" (interview with author). It is possible that the freedom of exploration permitted the creative writing student, curtailed in writing for the trade, may give creative writing an avant-gardist position on questions of the transformations of social identity.

Perhaps what is most unique about the UWC creative writing programmes is the way in which they have fostered a "becoming-minoritarian" in respect of language, through the multi- and trans-linguality encouraged by cross-faculty collaborations, bringing in disciplinary expertise from Afrikaans, English and Xhosa, the Nguni language most commonly spoken in the Western Cape. The Xhosa-English component of the programmes also makes for interesting study, but this would be outside of the focus of this chapter. Most of the creative writing that articulates questions of coloured identity necessarily needs elaborate Afrikaans in the dialogue. Afrikaans in this context is linked in the South African cultural hierarchy with low-class expression, where English is the language of status. These forms of Afrikaans have been linked predominantly with the Western Cape, giving this dialect the identifier "Kaaps", which is the Afrikaans word for "Cape." So ubiquitous a language of communication is Kaaps in the Cape Town communities represented that even Douman, whose short stories were referred to previously, needs to include Kaaps in stories representing aspirational middle-class characters.

The student in whose work language is most foregrounded, however, is Jolyn Phillips, mentioned earlier. Kafka's dilemma (or possibility) is Phillips' dilemma (or possibility). In writing the stories of the Blompark fishing community of Gansbaai, the natural language of expression is the minority language of Afrikaans, specifically the even more minority Overberg variety of Afrikaans. Kaaps and the Overberg variety are two of seventy-six varieties of Afrikaans. However, strategically recognising the dominance of the majority language of English, Phillips felt she would "defy the purpose of introducing Blompark to a diverse reading audience" (Reflective Essay 83) if she wrote in Afrikaans. In writing what she understands to be a "bilingual" text, Phillips, in fact, does much more. Phillips writes in Afrikaans and then translates her own text into English, retaining distinctive expressions in Afrikaans. But through this method, Phillips also ends up doing violence to English at the level of syntax and expression. As the author describes her style, it is one of "fighting with" English. A close reading, which is not possible in the survey nature of this chapter, would reveal the "lines of escape" which may be traced in the linguistic forms of these stories.

To conclude, what does a "middle distance reading" of creative writing at UWC suggest about coloured identity as a minority discourse? Most significantly, creative writing suggests the continued overwhelming need to reflect on questions of coloured identity even more than two decades after the dismantling of formal apartheid. It is mainly the ways in which historico-political trauma shapes individual and domestic trauma that are teased out in narratives of uniquely distinctive style. Nowhere in the narratives is coloured identity approached through racial discourse or the biological essentialisms implied in miscegenation. The creative writing narratives stress instead the construction and continuous reconstruction of coloured identity as an experienced matrix of social and cultural reality – or, as Wicomb pithily expresses the idea, "[identity] simply exists, whether we like it or not, so no need to fetishise it" (interview with author). These fictional discourses of coloured identity also suggest that there is not one coloured identity, rather that there are multiple coloured identities that are constantly shape-shifting. The dynamic driving the narratives is the recognition of the discourses of the marginal or the minorities even within coloured identity as a minority discourse. These minorities include women, children, homosexual characters, the coloured middle class and male characters who transgress social norms. The foregrounding of South African coloured identity as possibly the most identifiably constructed, hybrid, fluid, flexible, incorporative, creolised and encompassing of all identities, both claimed and imposed, makes it a fragmented mirror which could productively be used to refract and disturb the self-reflexive certainties of identity politics generally. In this sense, coloured may be the new black – but with a built-in self-reflexivity. This is the insight articulated in the work of Farred, Erasmus and Wicomb. However, what theoretical articulations of minority discourse alerts one to are the possibilities contained also in the position of coloured identity in the South African national sociopolitical landscape. Forever borderline, and on the margins of power, interstitial coloured identity has the inherent structural potential always to track new lines of escape from majoritarian political identity discourses. Constructed on the knife-edge of complexity and contradiction, when it comes to conundrums of identity, coloured identity may be, to roughly quote Claude Lévi-Strauss, "good to think with".

Acknowledgements

Thanks to Mark Snyders of the UWC Library Institutional Repository and Digital Scholarship Office, who ensured that all theses consulted are available on the publicly accessible dissertation portal. The study was further facilitated by Villeen Beerwinkel, UWC arts faculty officer, who provided administrative information regarding creative writing theses and students. Heartfelt appreciation to colleagues and students who shared their time and material that was not easily accessible. Finally, thank you for the recommendations of pre-reader Rajendra Chetty. Thank you to the A. W. Mellon funded project, Rethinking South African Literature(s), housed in the Centre for Multilingualism and Diversities Research at the University of the Western Cape, for generously facilitating the completion of this article.

Notes

1 Questions of coloured identity in prose fiction in English frequently come up in relation to the work of the following established authors, even though among earlier writers, the term "coloured" is rejected in favour of other non-racial, purportedly universal forms of identification or is entirely deconstructed: Bessie Head, Richard Rive, Alex la Guma, Arthur Nortje and Zoë Wicomb. More recent or less well-established writing that foregrounds coloured identities includes the short fiction and novels of Achmat Dangor and Rayda Jacobs; Rozena Maart's *Rosa's District 6*; Maxine Case's *All We Have Left Unsaid* and *Softness of the Lime*; C.A. Davids's *The Blacks of Cape Town*; Mary Watson's collection of short stories, *Moss*; Rehana Rossouw's *What Will People Say* and *New Times*; Nadia Davids's *An Imperfect Blessing*; Yvette Christiansë's *Unconfessed*; Kharnita Mohamed's *Called to Song* and Simon Bruinders's *A Handful of Earth*.

2 Of a possible fifteen students whose work fits the profile, ten students were interviewed: Hilda Andrews, Chad Brevis, Llewellin Jegels, Connie Fick, Hayley Rodkin, Waghied Misbach, Saaligh Gabier, Janine Lange, Jolyn Phillips and Lisa Julie. Creative writing lecturers and supervisors consulted include Meg Vandermerwe, Jacobus Moolman and Antje Krog. The following authors participated in the project: Rehana Rossouw, Zoë Wicomb and Maxine Case. Of the handful of publishers with relevant titles on their lists, an interview was conducted with Colleen Higgs of Modjaji Books.

3 The relevant published outputs of the UWC creative writing programmes, the UWC Creates projects and other UWC initiatives include print publications and dissertations available through the UWC Library Dissertation Portal, listed subsequently. Poetry and short fiction consulted, but which may not have been directly cited in the essay, may be found in the following anthologies: *This Is My Land: Writing from the UWC Creates Programme* (UWC publication, no date), *Harvest: The University of the Western Cape Masters in Creative Writing Poetry Anthology 2016* (Department of English, 2016), *Constant Companions: South African Tales of the Supernatural* (edited by postdoctoral fellow Annel Pieterse, UWC Creates and the Stellenbosch Literary Project, 2017), *Cutting Carrots the Wrong Way: Poetry and Prose about Food from the University of the Western Cape Creative Writing Programme* (collected and edited by Kobus Moolman, University of the Western Cape/Uhlanga, 2017). Theses consulted include the following: Jerome Cornelius, *What Lies*, MA mini-thesis (novella), 2014, http://hdl.handle.net/11394/6486; Jolyn Phillips, *Let's Go Home: Stories and Portraits*, MA mini-thesis, 2014, http://hdl.handle.net/11394/6485; Bronwyn Douman, *The Marginal Grey: A Collection of Short Stories*, MA mini-thesis, 2015, http://hdl.handle.net/11394/6484; Hilda Andrews, *Visklippie and Other Cape Town Stories*, MA mini-thesis, 2016, http://hdl.handle.net/11394/5715; Muhammad Saaligh Gabier, *The Wedding Interviews: A Novella*, MA mini-thesis, 2016, http://hdl.handle.net/11394/6524; Janine Carol Lange, *We Dare Not Say*, MA mini-thesis (short stories), 2016, http://hdl.handle.net/11394/5538; A.W. Misbach, *The Girl with the Red Flower*, MA full-thesis (novel), 2017, http://hdl.handle.net/11394/5884; Hayley Rodkin, *Of Flowers and Tears: Collection of Short Stories*, MA full-thesis, 2019, http://hdl.handle.net/11394/6645.

Works cited

Adhikari, Mohamed, editor. *Burdened by Race: Coloured Identities in Southern Africa*. Lansdowne, Cape Town: UCT Press, 2009.

Adhikari, Mohamed, editor. *Not White Enough, Not Black Enough: Racial Identity in the South African Coloured Community*. Athens, OH: Ohio University Press, 2005.

Alexander, Neville. *Thoughts on the New South Africa*, edited by Kindle. Johannesburg: Jacana, 2013.

Baderoon, Gabeba. *Regarding Muslims: From Slavery to Post-Apartheid*. Johannesburg: Wits University Press, 2014.

Baderoon, Gabeba. "Surplus, Excess, Dirt: Slavery and the Production of Disposability in South Africa." *Social Dynamics*, vol. 44, no. 2, 2018, pp. 257–272.

Da Costa, Yusuf and Achmat Davids. *Pages from Cape Muslim History*. Pietermaritzburg, South Africa: Shuter and Shooter (Pty) Ltd, 1994.

Davids, Achmat. *The Afrikaans of the Cape Muslims from 1815–1915*. Pretoria, South Africa: Protea, 2011.

Erasmus, Zimitri, editor. *Coloured by History, Shaped by Place: New Perspectives on Coloured Identities in Cape Town*. Cape Town: Kwela Books, 2001.

Deleuze, Gilles and Felix Guattari. *Toward a Minor Literature*. Trans. Dana Polan. Minneapolis, MN: University of Minnesota Press, 1986.

Farred, Grant. *Midfielder's Moment: Coloured Literature and Culture in Contemporary South Africa*. Boulder: CO: Westview Press, 2000.

Field, Sean. "Fragile Identities: Memory, Emotion and Coloured Residents of Windermere." *Coloured by History, Shaped by Place: New Perspectives on Coloured Identities in Cape Town*, edited by Zimitri Erasmus. Cape Town: Kwela Books, 2001, pp. 97–113.

Gates, Henry Louis, Jr. *Colored People: A Memoir*. New York: Alfred A. Knopf, 1994.

Hendricks, Frank and Charlyn Dyers. *Kaaps in Fokus*. Stellenbosch, South Africa: SUN MeDIA, 2016.

Jacobs, Rayda. *The Middle Children*. Toronto: Second Story Press, 1994.

JanMohamed, Abdul R. and David Lloyd. *The Nature and Context of Minority Discourse*. New York: Oxford University Press, 1990.

La Guma, Alex. *A Walk in the Night: Seven Stories from the Streets of Cape Town*. 1962. London: Heinemann, 1968.

Lalu, Premesh and Noëleen Murray, editors. *Becoming UWC: Reflections, Pathways and Unmaking Apartheid's Legacy*. Bellville: Centre for Humanities Research Publication, 2012.

Maart, Rozena. *Rosa's District 6*. 2004. Claremont: David Phillip, 2006.

Mayers, Tim. "Creative Writing Studies: The Past Decade (and the Next)." *Journal of Creative Writing Studies*, vol. 1, no. 1, 2016, pp. 1–7. http://scholarworks.rit.edu/jcws/vol1/iss1/4

McKaiser, Eusebius. "Cape Town's Dirty, Coloured Secrets." *A Bantu in My Bathroom! Debating Race, Sexuality, and Other Uncomfortable South African Topics*. Johannesburg: Bookstorm and Pan Macmillan, 2012, pp. 41–48.

McKaiser, Eusebius. "For Coloured People Only." *Run Racist Run*. Kindle ed. Johannesburg: Bookstorm, 2015, pp. 164–181.

McKaiser, Eusebius. "Racial Baggage." *A Bantu in My Bathroom! Debating Race, Sexuality, and Other Uncomfortable South African Topics*. Johannesburg: Bookstorm and Pan Macmillan, 2012, pp. 31–38.

Mohamed, Kharnita. *Called to Song: A Novel*. Cape Town: Kwela, 2018.

Moolman, Kobus, editor. *Cutting Carrots the Wrong Way: Poetry and Prose about Food from the University of the Western Cape Creative Writing Programme*. Bellville: University of the Western Cape and uHlanga, 2017.

O'Connell, Brian. "Foreword." *Finding Freedom in the Bush of Books: The UWC Experience and Spirit*, edited by Cornelius Thomas. Wendy's Book Lounge, 2010, pp. ix–xi.

Phillips, Jolyn. *Tjieng Tjang Tjerries & Other Stories*. Rondebosch, Cape Town: Modjaji Books, 2016.

Rive, Richard. *"Buckingham Palace", District Six*. Cape Town: David Phillip, 1986.

Rive, Richard. *Selected Writings: Stories, Essays, Plays*. Johannesburg: A.D. Jonker, 1977.

Rossouw, Rehana. *New Times*. Kindle ed. Johannesburg: Jacana, 2017.

Rossouw, Rehana. *What Will People Say?* Kindle ed. Johannesburg: Jacana, 2015.

Soudien, Crain. "District Six and Its Uses in the Discussion about Non-Racialism." *Coloured by History, Shaped by Place: New Perspectives on Coloured Identities in Cape Town*, edited by Zimitri Erasmus. Cape Town: Kwela Books, 2001, pp. 114–130.

Thomas, Cornelius. *Finding Freedom in the Bush of Books: The UWC Experience and Spirit*. East London, South Africa: Wendy's Book Lounge, 2010.

Trotter, Henry. "Trauma and Memory: The Impact of Apartheid-Era Forced Removals on Coloured Identity in Cape Town." *Burdened by Race: Coloured Identities in Southern Africa*, edited by Mohamed Adhikari. Lansdowne, Cape Town: UCT Press, 2009, pp. 49–78.

Wicomb, Zoë. *Playing in the Light*. Houghton, Johannesburg: Umuzi, 2006.

Wicomb, Zoë. "Shame and Identity: The Case of the Coloured in South Africa." *Writing South Africa: Literature, Apartheid, and Democracy, 1970–1995*, edited by Derek Attridge and Rosemary Jolly. Cambridge: Cambridge University Press, 1998, pp. 91–107.

Wicomb, Zoë. *You Can't Get Lost in Cape Town*. London: Virago, 1987.

PART IV

Patriarchal domination, gender, sexuality, and other sociocultural "minorities"

13

A REFLECTION ON GENDER AND SEXUALITY AS TRANSNATIONAL ARCHIVE OF AFRICAN MODERNITY

Frieda Ekotto

> To my great delight and surprise, however, people there knew how to listen to my silences in all complexities and subtleties, and I learned that this mute language could be effectively shared. In their silences, I returned home.
>
> (Trinh T. Minh-ha, "Walls of Silence")

> One cannot ask, "Who is Venus?" because it would be impossible to answer such a question. There are hundreds of thousands of other girls who share her circumstances and these circumstances have generated few stories. And the stories that exist are not about them, but rather about the violence, excess, mendacity, and reason that seized hold of their lives, transformed them into commodities and corpses, and identified them with names tossed-off as insults and crass jokes. The archive is, in this case, a death sentence, a tomb, a display of the violated body, an inventory of property, a medical treatise on gonorrhea, a few lines about a whore's life, an asterisk in the grand narrative of history.
>
> (Saidiya Hartman, "Venus in Two Acts")

As a consequence of globalization, with better access to information and a stronger involvement of the international community, the visibility of African LGBTQ+ communities has increased. Yet, in part due to this enhanced visibility, voices oppositional to the recognition and protection of LGBTQ+ rights have also grown louder and more pronounced. These forces proclaim same-sex sexuality to be deviating from traditional African values or to be a "bad habit" imported from the West. Nevertheless, despite the opposition's denouncements and violence, it is clear that sexual diversity on the African continent can no longer be ignored. We cannot pretend to understand Africa's modernity if we do not recognize diversity in sexuality and gender to be part of the lived experience of individuals across the continent and its diaspora. With a focus on silence, the colonial past, and salvaging memory, this chapter will discuss how to both recognize and theorize lived experiences of sexual and gender diversity on the African continent and its diaspora, ultimately making the argument that we cannot reckon with the colonial past and its continuing traces in Africa and its diaspora until we reclaim sexual and gender diversity as part of the continent and its diaspora's present.

As we rethink questions of gender and sexuality on the African continent and its diaspora and examine how their representational practices continue to define "Africa" and the "West," we must not lose sight of the effect anti-sodomy laws continue to have on African LGBTQ+ individuals. Same-sex sexuality was criminalized in many parts of Africa as part of the colonial project. Since that time, many countries have toughened their laws, engendering a societal backlash against LGBTQ+ people. For example, in Cameroon, Senegal, Ghana, and Nigeria, both female and male homosexuality is currently illegal. Although punishments vary, to be a convicted homosexual can mean prison or fines. In addition, gay men and women are subject to prejudices that lead to ostracism and disownment; their relationships are often denied or condemned, as official and familial discourses refuse to speak of or acknowledge love between two people of the same sex. Additionally, gay men and women are frequent targets of violence, including beatings, rape, and murder (Dougueli 2014).

Considering the political climate, it is ironic that lesbian women are the subjects of many films produced in Nigeria today. The booming film industry – named Nollywood for its provenance in Southern Nigeria – is the second largest in the world based on "the sheer number of films it produces each year" (Green-Simms 34). It finds its audience in sub-Saharan Africans both on the continent and its diaspora as well as throughout the world. In her article on these films, Lindsey Green-Simms shows that although films depicting lesbianism have increased in the past decade, these films inevitably use lesbianism to depict pathology and social deviance and refuse to speak of the love between women as anything but perversion. As one Nigerian director states, he made his film to "call attention to the 'social menace' of lesbianism that is secretly infecting and destroying society" (45). This is true in films made outside of Nigeria as well. As I have shown in my work on the Senegalese film *Karmen Gei* (2001), which depicts a love relationship between two women, the taboo of lesbian love is almost always silenced by the death or conversion of the lesbian character. Unsurprisingly, lesbian women in sub-Saharan Africa object to these depictions and offer compelling critiques of the fact that these films refuse to call the women "lesbians" or even "women loving women." As one woman put it, people refuse to "'say what is' when every-one, of course, knew what was going on" (46).

While this example underlines how it is crucial to stress the cultural factors that lead to widespread suffering of individuals who are subject to the power of this silencing, silence cannot always be considered a convenient tool of oppression controlled by those in power. This is why it is imperative that we understand silence and silencing to be a choice in language, one that allows for a diversity of experiences. As Michel Foucault reminds us in *The History of Sexuality* (1978), sexuality has to do with the impossibility of naming, it marks silence, or, more accu-rately, it *silences*:

> Silence itself – the things one declines to say, or is forbidden to name, the discretion that is required between different speakers – is less the absolute limit of discourse, the other side from which it is separated by a strict boundary, than an element that functions alongside the things said, with them and in relation to them within over-all strategies. There is no binary division to be made between what one says and what one does not say; we must try to determine the different ways of not saying such things, how those who can and those who cannot speak of them are distributed, which type of discourse is authorized, or which form of discretion is required in either case. There is not one but many silences, and they are an integral part of the strategies that underlie and permeate discourses.
>
> (27)

Neither the counter-discursive ideal of silence, which leads to simplified, triumphalist narratives of resistance, nor the notion of lost voices, in particular lesbian voices, allows for the reality of sexual and gender diverse experiences, and one should remain skeptical of the notion that silence is passivity. In fact, there are oppositional practices that suggest this kind of imposed silence is not merely a reduced performance of human agency.[1] We might use, for example, Maryse Condé's term "disorderly,"[2] which suggests that we disrupt cultural narratives that silence experiences through a deconstructive reworking of traditional ideas. This approach destabilizes the traditional and historical ways of understanding gender and lesbian sexuality in sub-Saharan Africa and its diaspora, even as it complicates our understanding of African modernity by accentuating tensions and dynamics involved in rethinking it. To begin to read for this displaced sensibility, I would like to argue that when approaching literary and cinematic texts by African and its diasporic writers and directors, one has to be sensitive to how coded language is used to talk about homosexuality. In the section that follows, I would like to consider the many silences about women loving women that permeate cinematic and literary texts from the continent and its diaspora. Then, I will consider how pre-emptive "naming," as a means of expunging the identities of those who do not fit into heteronormative categories, has created an environment of unidirectional cultural narratives that silences discourse about the possibilities of same-sex relationships. So, even as my purpose is to reclaim narratives of desire and love, my discussion must begin by considering the vulnerability spaces – which I am terming "damage zones."

In her book *Writing the Feminine Body* (2009), Nathalie Etoke analyzes homosexual desire in three sub-Saharan novels: *The Little Peul* by Mariama Barry, *Riwan ou le chemin de sable* by Ken Bugul, and *Because the Sun Hath Burnt Me* by Calixthe Beyala. Etoke questions why authors simultaneously allude to desire between women and yet do not develop it beyond a suggestion. For example, *The Little Peul* by Mariam Barry starts with a description of female genital mutilation, and throughout the narrative, there are no discussions of heterosexual relationships. Indeed, although her desires are never consummated, Little Peul, the main character, appears to desire women:

> To reach my father's native village, it was necessary to cross a beautiful river by means of huge rocks lined up by nature in the middle of the water. Some women were standing there bathing. They had long, beautiful hair that sparkled with the reflection of the sun; hanging carelessly down their body, it made them look feline. Some of them were rubbing their feet to remove calluses; others, seated, were massaging each other's backs. I threw an envious and sustained glance at their lovely, pointed breasts. I passed my hand first on one, then the other, as if I were imploring them to appear. I got a pleasant sensation from it.
>
> *(137)*

This is a typical example of an author suggesting attraction between women but not fully developing the possibilities – or the implications – of that attraction. Just having brushed up against the subject, the gaze of the woman protagonist shifts, and we quickly move away.

This kind of silencing – in which the desires are presented, but the author refuses to consummate them – is frequently found in literature from the continent and its diaspora. In her collection of short stories *The Thing around Your Neck* (2009), Chimamanda Adichie has several stories in which the issue of homosexuality is brought up, only to disappear. There is, for instance, the Senegalese woman in "Jumping Monkey Hill," who briefly suggests her love of women, but the other characters act as if they do not want to hear it. Moreover, Kamara, in "On Monday of Last Week," is interested in Tracy's interest in her . . . but again nothing transpires. Adichie, like Barry, alludes to love between women and then stops short of narrating it. The texts fall silent.

Another example of this "present absence" can be found in the work of Cameroonian novelist Calixthe Beyala, who writes sympathetically of her heroine's lesbian yearnings in *C'est le soleil qui m'a brûlée* (*Because the Sun Hath Burnt Me* 1997): Ayesha (the heroine) embodies a need for tenderness and love in a corrupt and brutal society; however, the context of the story suggests that these yearnings are no more than a "mental escape, imperfect, sympathetic *faute de mieux*" (Dunton) – there being no, if you wish, truly "phallocratic alternative." This approach is essentially a *silencing* of ways to conceptualize relationships between women. The relationship in the novel seems to occur only as a reaction to sexual violence and/or conditions of marginalization, which leads to the implication that if the world had treated her differently, Ayesha would prefer relationships with men.

These examples all manifest "a silencing in plain sight" reminiscent of Trinh T. Minh-ha's description of the chador in her essay "Walls of Silence." In Minh-ha's words, the chador is "a portable wall, the garment that shrouds female bodies from lustful male inquisition" (3). Similarly, in Beyala's story, language silences the intimacy and choices made by these women, even as it amplifies and sexualizes their interactions.

Thus far, I have focused upon how different kinds of silences surround the subject of women loving women in literary and cinematic representations. I have argued that instead of looking for violence, approaching the topic through the silences that surround it allows one to be sensitive to signs of damage that otherwise could pass unseen – or unheard. Let me now turn to another popular notion about same-sex sexuality in Africa: that it is a bad habit imported from the West. While this may be true on a discursive and epistemological level (given that homosexuality as a concept is a sexological product), this is not the case on the level of lived experience. Part of the work this "blaming" does, however, is silence the cultural memory about the historical diversity of sexuality and gender on the continent and its diaspora. To discuss questions of gender and sexuality in the politics of African memory, it is crucial to begin with significant moments such as slavery and colonialism, which are global events that have entered our consciousness as historical narratives. Our understanding of events is directly shaped by how events are told and retold, who tells of them, to whom the events are addressed, and in what order they are represented. As Mudimbe teaches us, the Colonial Library is the archive of knowledge on Africa from which knowledge is drawn whenever a person speaks, writes or thinks about the continent. To create a *de-colonialized* archive, Africans need to first excavate historical silence and the forms of violence that it entails. This work is essential to the articulation of contemporary epistemologies of African sexualities and subjectivities that are not inflected or framed by the colonial past.

Ayo Coly's 2013 groundbreaking collection for the *African Studies Review* begins this project by addressing homophobia in Africa. In bringing together diverse disciplines and geographic locations, the collection engages discourses that continue to impact LGBTQ+ individuals across the continent. In her introduction, Coly clearly indicates that "homophobic Africa is in fact a Euro-American-African co-production," in which homosexuality is often articulated as "non-African." She writes:

> This *ASR* Forum, entitled "Homophobia Africa?" – a deliberate echo of Marc Epprecht's Heterosexual Africa? (2008) – is concerned with the concept of African homophobia, as it prevails in non-African but also African engagements with LGBTI rights on the continent. In the columns of *The Guardian*, Keguro Macharia has critiqued the discourses on homophobia in Africa, contending that "homophobia in Africa is not [the] single story" that some analysts are making it out to be. "Homophobia in

Africa is a problem," he writes, "but not as African homophobia, a special class that requires special interventions. And certainly not the kinds of special interventions that reconsolidate old, ongoing and boring oppositions between a progressive west and an atavistic Africa (2010)."

(22)

Coly's critique is related to the pervasive discourse that links homophobia in Africa to the racist characterization of Africa as an uncivilized continent. In a similar vein, discursive tropes such as "homophobia" and "uncivilized" can be understood as Eurocentric inventions that assign structural colonial violence to individual or cultural phenomena.

To specifically consider gender and sexuality as a rewriting of lost memory, one must first do what I consider to be the work of "salvaging." Quite often, we find that people of diverse sexual identities are "territorialized," a term that reveals how identities are structured and produced by power relations and interactions that often map out on regional organizations of culture. Such framing of territorialization allows us to understand that sexual subjects are not just (re)inventions of the self in alliance with a group but that they are also fabricated in and through signs never far removed from constellations of hegemonic discourses. Salvaging lost memory here, then, has two meanings: first, a power to put together the pieces, so as to understand their constellations in a new way, and second, an attempt to recall and revisit slavery and colonialism, whose representational practices are defined, legitimized, and valorized via cultural production.

Using the concept "territorialization" in relation to Deleuze and Guattari's critique of psychoanalysis and its politics of memory, I argue that this theoretical lens allows one to juxtapose remembering and salvaging and reframe them as territorial events. If remembering can be understood through the metaphors of space, then its territorial boundaries can well be reconfigured and redrawn. The moment we try to remember something, we create a box into which we fit our memory. In order to place it within that box, we leave out many details and often end up sanitizing the messiness of our memories. We create a so-called coherent territory (read memory). But coherent according to whose maps/configurations? Within the purview of what (colonial) logics/legacies? In my work on memory and salvaging, I intend to subvert that box, to deterritorialize its cartographies. My reading of memory resists territorializing impulses of remembering by challenging the assumed naturality/neutrality of its coordinates. I stress that this work of deterritorialization does not aim at producing a sanitized or disciplined narrative. When I make an argument in favor of salvaging, I do not argue that salvaging does the work of translating the messy discourses and constellations into an intelligible framework. In other words, my politics of memory and deterritorializing act of salvaging do not reinforce the psychoanalytic (Eurocentric) frames of Intelligibility. Rather, salvaging reveals the often concealed Eurocentric ideology that confers coherence and intelligibility on some memories at the expense of others.

Jasbir Puar's use of assemblage to critique the territorializing impulse of intersectionality is important here. She writes:

> Therefore, to dismiss assemblages in favor of retaining intersectional identitarian frameworks is to dismiss how societies of control tweak and modulate bodies as matter, not predominantly through signification or identity interpellation but rather through affective capacities and tendencies. It is also to miss that assemblages encompass not only ongoing attempts to destabilize identities and grids, but also the forces that continue to mandate and enforce them. That is to say, grid making is a recognized process of agencement. But to render intersectionality as an archaic relic of identity politics bypasses entirely the possibility that for some bodies – we can call them statistical

outliers, or those consigned to premature death, or those once formerly considered useless bodies or bodies of excess – discipline and punish may well still be a primary apparatus of power. There are different conceptual problems posed by each; intersectionality attempts to comprehend political institutions and their attendant forms of social normativity and disciplinary administration, while assemblages, in an effort to reintroduce politics into the political, asks what is prior to and beyond what gets established. So one of the big payoffs for thinking through the intertwined relations of intersectionality and assemblages is that it can help us produce more roadmaps of precisely these not quite fully understood relations between discipline and control.

(63)

In similar vein, I am not suggesting a stable LGBTQ+ identity in Africa (however intersectional it might be) but rather thinking about the gendered and sexualized identifications as events that unfolded and continue to unfold in the (post-)colonial African time and space. Salvaging memory is an act of assemblage, a temporal and spatial reordering that deterritorializes the colonial bibliography and the Western archival modernity. In a sense, my use of memory is a strategy to avoid the archival re-inscription of the colonial normative subject and rethink the eventness of the identifications enabled/disabled by the (post-/neo-)colonial violence in Africa.

One act of salvaging that I find essential is an articulation of the genealogy of naming in sexual diversity. This work can confront disturbing ways in which racial violence that manifests itself through categorical inclusivity is repeated in the cultural imaginary despite the efforts of black subjects to speak out against domination. For example, we must fundamentally reconsider sexual diversity by concentrating on the category of "queerness" in a postcolonial African context. The term *queer* is an Anglophone concept that *is not* universal. In an article entitled "Baldwin, Homosexuality and Plural Identities: An Encounter with the Avant-Garde," Jean-Paul Rocchi defines the word "queer" this way:

> Developed in the United States, but strongly inspired by the work of Michel Foucault, *queer*, which means bizarre, strange and "gay," examines notions of normality and abnormality. Although its original context was sexualities and gender identities, it reaches toward the political and universal and thus also examines notions of race, class, desire and forms of discourse. Transdisciplinary, focusing on the normative power of psychoanalysis as well as on literary and linguistic structuralism and history, *queer* theory is the epitome of decompartmentalized knowledge. Its essential, transversal quality aims to break apart monolithic systems and reestablish a multiplicity of significations. This is indeed inscribed within its etymology, for at its origins, *queer* means "oblique" or "perverse."

> *(11, translation is mine)*

In other words, if we are talking about blackness, for instance, everything that is not white is in fact other, even *queer*. We need to reconfigure existing notions of gender and sexuality so as to kiln them more effectively to understandings of power, resistance, and emancipation as well as in the politics of memory in Africa.

Gender and sexuality are inescapable dimensions of differential power relations, and cultural memory is always about the distribution of and contested claims to power. What a culture remembers and what it chooses to forget are intricately bound up with issues of power and hegemony and thus with gender and sexuality. But, as we consider memory – as we put together its pieces – we must remain cognizant of the fact that gender, along with race and class, marks identities in specific ways. This allows us to place cultural memory in specific contexts rather than allow it be subsumed into monolithic and essentialist categories. Any historiographical work that does not incorporate gender and sexuality as categories of historical analysis would be incomplete in its capacity to theorize African modernity.

Knowledge production emerging from, processed through, and validated by Western academia is often constructed and understood as the sole source of "real," "authentic," and "legitimate" knowledge. This is largely a legacy of academia's empiricist and positivist foundations, a topic which has been heavily discussed by scholars in the humanities and social sciences. This dynamic simultaneously obscures and erases the very existence of other forms of knowledge production such as movement knowledge, poetic knowledge, experiential/tacit knowledge, cultural knowledge, and so on, while also delegitimizing and under-cutting their authenticity and legitimacy (Moraga 23, Lorde 355). This occurs in the service of protecting the representational hegemony of an Enlightenment-era conception of heteromasculinist, rationalist knowledge and knowledge production as well as conceptualizing it as the most appropriate way of approaching and representing a singular, universal, and discoverable "truth" about a matter. Established by and rooted in Western philosophical thought, this approach has also been the basis by which non-Western forms of knowledge and, by extension, non-Western peoples have been deemed inferior and disposable.

It is imperative that we continue to create our own spaces for self-reflexive engagement in knowledge production. As I dwell on how to rethink gender as a useful analytical category of historical analysis, I would like to offer some insights into how to think about silence and gender by drawing on the short story "Rock" by Lindiwe Nkutha, published in *Queer Africa: New and Collected Fiction*. In particular, I would like to highlight a reconsideration of gender fluidity as an emerging theme in African literature. The narrator, who goes by the nickname Rock, is a perspicacious youth who, from her wheelchair view, shares neighborhood gossip with pathos and a large dose of humor. This includes the story of how she lost her own legs: "I lost both my legs to hunger. Thanks to the ravenous appetite of our neighbour's dog, which had not been fed for over a week, my legs were mistaken for lamb shank" (185).

It is in this tone that Rock recounts the return of his mother's lover:

> My gift for remembering faces was useful for purposes of spotting newcomers, a service which I offered my mother for free. For her it was important because she used it to hustle those whose defenses had not been solidly built up yet. We also kept a close eye on anyone new, and treated him or her with lavish suspicion until they proved themselves differently. This is why, on this Thursday, I could not release my gaze from the picture of the bizarre that was gradually taking shape right in front of my eyes. Even in my transfixion I could sense a lingering feeling that I had seen this apparition before. Perhaps not in this life, but seen it I had.
>
> It was wearing a purple hat with two quail feathers on either side, and a brown corduroy jacket that looked as if it had not been washed since 1994.
>
> *(190–191)*

Here Rock uses the pronoun "it" to talk about a human because she is unsure about the gender and therefore unwilling to mark the person male or female. After this strange person speaks to her, Rock continues:

> Caught in a moment of shock, I could not answer for a while, my silence possibility confirming in his head that physically disabled people are also mentally challenged.

He spoke again, this time more slowly. Only at this point I was beginning to change my mind about him. He was increasingly becoming both in demeanour and decorum more and more a woman. My mind and I almost agreed that he was as she.

(194)

This quote dwells on the politics of memory/salvaging, particularly on the politics of classifying and naming, which are indeed colonial practices. So what does it mean for Rock to classify Dan as a woman? Is this a violent act? This narrative/fictional imposition of gender is reminiscent of the colonial imposition of gender/sexual system on the colonized. What would it mean for us to have access to Dan's subjectivity before the act of classifying? Can we remember (or perhaps salvage) Dan?

This is clearly a new grammar in our understanding of African gender and sexuality, an invitation to open up the reading of gender in different directions. Rock's curiosity is unguarded, unafraid, and unaffected by the many discourses about homosexuality on the African continent. If Dan is a woman, then Rock's mother loves a woman, but this is incidental to the fact that Dan brings both joy and peace to Rock, her mother, and their extended family. As such, Rock's understanding of Dan's appearance forces us to rethink the archive, to confront silence, erasure, and epistemic violence, in short, to make room for alterity, to dig deeper in the search for new meanings and possibilities. After all, our humanity depends on understanding and accepting that Africans are as complex as any other human beings on earth.

Although there is still a long way to go before LGBTQ+ experiences and contributions in African cultural contexts are given proper space and respect, it is clear that Africans are producing cultural work that addresses and confirms sexual diversity. We now have narratives and visual art produced by Africans within the continent and in the diaspora, including Jim Chuchu's film *The Stories of Our Lives* (2014), Wanuri Kahiu's award-winning film *Rafiki* (2018), Razinat Talatu Mohammed's novel *Habiba* (2013), Karen Martin and Makhosazana Xaba's *Queer Africa: New and Collected Fictions* (2013), Uzodinma Iweala's novel *Speak No Evil* (2018), and Frieda Ekotto's French-language novel and short stories *Don't Whisper Too Much* and *Portrait of A Young Artiste from Bona Mbella*, translated by Corine Tachtiris (2019). This burgeoning cultural production on LGBTQ+ individuals by African and diasporic writers/filmmakers is beginning to disrupt the existing hegemonic frameworks that read sexual diversity only in terms of scandals, silences, and violence.

In Western academic discussions of African LGBTQ+ cultural production, the discourse has begun to shift from violence and oppression to love and a diversity of experiences. Within African and diasporic studies, there is a growing recognition of the need to offer a diverse range of readings to better understand the terrain of knowledge about LGBTQ+ individuals. Academic spaces, as we traditionally understand them, largely exist within Western contexts and are often characterized by their inability to avoid elitism and reach the broader public. Despite these limitations, however, they still have the potential to address discursive and material landscapes and contest hegemonic representations. Mobilizing resources to center the representational autonomy and self-determination of Africans both on the continent and in the diaspora should not be regarded as a battle to shift the contours of inclusion and representation. Rather it represents an attempt to destabilize and disrupt hegemonic power networks more broadly, forcefully, and sustainably. Representational autonomy and self-determination serve as means of countering the dehumanizing construction of the LGBTQ+ subjects in Africa. These alternative representations, often referred to as "counter-narratives," challenge the established ongoing discourse that the continent is homophobic. More importantly, however, representational autonomy and self-determination for LGBTQ+ subjects in Africa is a means of disrupting the underlying structural relationships of power.

In closing, I would like to note that such challenges can be seen as a threat to the representational bases by which the West comes to define and understand itself as the morally superior global force. Given that these bases are often presented as carrying a civilizational force and thus construct the African continent as backwards, ahistorical, and pre-modern, any attempt to challenge their ideological pillars poses, in a way, a radical threat to the Western representational dominance. Hence, in thinking about sexual and gender diversity on the African continent and in the diaspora, it is imperative to fundamentally reconstruct historical and cultural knowledge and to transform that potential epistemological threat into a material outcome. This should be done through a radical rethinking of silence and the genealogy of naming in sexual diversity that is informed by African experiences that are often obscured in dominant archives. In such work, engaging the transnational archive occupies a particularly important place to make decolonial epistemological interventions in the definition of African modernity. There is an urgent need to rethink the Eurocentric spatial and temporal logic of the archive in order to create opportunities for representational power that enables and sustains African and diasporic self-determination. We cannot liberate Africans from the colonial past and its ongoing hegemonic representations until we fundamentally reconceptualize – and welcome and embrace – sexual and gender diversity on the continent.

Notes

1 I would like to emphasize here that agency is a very complex concept that has been problematized by many feminist thinkers. Although I am aware of these debates, I do not have the space to discuss the implications here.
2 See Maryse Condé, "Order, Disorder, Freedom, and the West Indian Writer," *Yale French Studies*, no. 97 (2000).

Selected bibliography

Anzaldúa, Gloria and AnaLouise Keating. Eds. *This Bridge We Call Home: Radical Visions for Transformation*. New York: Routledge, 2002.
Ayo Coly, Guest Editor. "Introduction." *African Studies Review, Special Issue: Homophobic Africa?*, vol. 56, no. 2, 2013, pp. 21–30
Barry, Mariam. *The Little Peul*. Translated by Carrol F. Coates, Afterword by Assiba D'Almeida. Charlottesville: University of Virginia Press, 2010. pp. 173.
Dougueli, Georges. "Homophobie: vox populi, vox diaboli." *Jeune Afrique*, 11 février, 2014.
Dunton, Chris. "Whetying be dat." *Research in African Literatures*, vol. 20, no. 3, 1989, pp. 423–447.
Foucault, Michel. *The History of Sexuality Volume 1: An Introduction*. London: Allen Lane, 1979 [1976]. pp. 27.
Green-Simms, Lindsey and Unoma Azuah. "The Video Closet: Nollywood's Gay-Themed Movies." In *Transition*. Bloomington: Indiana University Press, Issue 107, 2012, pp. 34.
Ibid. 45.
Ibid. 46.
Hartman, Saidiya. "Venus in Two Acts." *Small Axe*, vol. 12, no. 2, ser. 26, 2008, pp. 8.
Lorde, Audre. "Poetry Is Not a Luxury." *Poetry and Cultural Studies: A Reader*, 2009, pp. 355.
Martin, Karen and Makhosazana Xaba. *Queer Africa: New and Collected Fictions*. Johannesburg: MaThoko's Books, 2013. pp. 185.
Ibid. 194.
Minh-ha, Trinh. "Walls of Silence." *International Journal of Okinawan Studies*, vol. 2, no. 2, Special Issue on Women and Globalization, pp. 3.

Moraga, Cherríe. "Theory in the Flesh." *This Bridge Called My Back: Writings by Radical Women of Color.* Vol. 23. SUNY Press, 2015.

Puar, Jasbir K. *Terrorist Assemblages: Homonationalism in Queer Times.* Durham, NC: Duke University Press, 2007. pp. 63.

Rocchi, Jean-Paul. "Baldwin, *l'homotextualité* et les identités plurielles: une rencontre à l'avant-garde." *Revue LISA/LISA e-journal* [Online], Writers, writings, Homage to James Baldwin (Dossier by Benoît Depardieu), Online since 1 January, 2004 connection on 27 February 2016. http://lisa.revues.org/611; DOI: 10.4000/lisa.611

14

"WHO DO YOU THINK YOU ARE, WOMAN?" WANGARI MAATHAI ANSWERS IN *UNBOWED*

Gĩchingiri Ndĩgĩrĩgĩ

At the height of the clamor to save Karura Forest from deforestation following the patrimonial state's unconscionable allotment of government-protected forest land to reward its political clients, Wangari Maathai led a group of Green Belt Movement protestors into the forest, where they attempted to plant symbolic traditional trees as a gesture of reclaiming the forest for the Kenyan people. A group of rowdy young men armed with crude weapons confronted the Green Belt Movement (GBM) protestors, telling them to get out of the forest in order to allow a construction project to proceed. When she did not back off, they asked her, "Who do you think you are, woman?" (268) In the asymmetrical meeting of armed young men – who obviously enjoyed police protection – and mostly female tree-plant-carrying protestors, the question was inherently rhetorical. Even then, it spoke to the ways Wangari was "hailed" by the prevailing discourses regarding women, as I show shortly. The Kenyan state's dismissal of her earlier protests against the building of the tallest tower in Africa at Uhuru Park, the only open public space in the middle of Nairobi, and the deforestation of Karura Forest itself played on a shallow nationalist but misogynistic discourse that marginalized her as just a woman, and a divorced one at that. However, as I show, the success of her protest movement led to the grudging acceptance that she was "the only man left" (204), a perverted re-gendering of the public sphere as masculine. I probe Wangari's yoking of environmental concerns to women's and human rights, and the greater push for democratic space progressively, in ways that answer the coercive patriarchal state. Having been denied a voice in the public sphere, she reverts to memoir, whose narrative voice generally serves a tripartite function: "as participant, witness and reflective/reflexive consciousness" (Buss 16).

Before proceeding to the recovery of her voice and the centering of her subjectivity in narrative, it is important to unpack the question "Who do you think you are, woman?" which describes Wangari in problematic ways informed by the prevailing gender codes. The unsaid assumption in the question was that Kenya had its "owners" who were entitled to expropriate national forests and also speak, and women were obviously excluded. If the inquirers merely wanted to know who she was, they would have asked that, and Wangari would probably have rattled off a string of personal and professional identifiers that legitimized her presence at Karura forest. But the inquirers were apparently foregrounding the disconnect between what the objectively verifiable bodily and professional Wangari-self was, and the questionable – to them – rights those layers of identity/identification guaranteed her. Tagging her as a woman went further to remind her of her supplementarity and incompleteness as a self-articulating subject and suggest that, being a woman, her image of herself and her thinking were misinformed and irrational. The other unsaid was that her interruption of the construction project was a feminized privileging of the natural over the cultural, or "development" sponsored by the rational patriarchal forces. This gendering of the public sphere speaks to the marginalization of women and the clashing narratives of national environmental degradation and development that I amplify in this chapter.

Wangari's environmental activism invites a productive engagement with the central ideas in ecofeminism and Frantz Fanon's premonitions about the marginalization of women as a symptom of the pitfalls of national consciousness in the newly decolonized African states. I build up to that discussion by foregrounding three facets in her narrative that best illuminate her central concerns: an evocation of an ecological balance that is then lost, followed by a reading of two incidents in which she clashes with the state, raising questions about the marginalization of women and environmental issues in the modernizing economy. An interrogation of the ways marginalized groups complicate the romantic narrative of nationalism – out of many, one, turning chance into destiny, and so on – clarifies the ways the patriarchal state hijacked the women's movement to advance its masculine symbolic content. The discussion then loops back to the mobilization of memoir as the genre through which Wangari chose to speak back to power and amplify her melancholic voice and closes with some reflections on the significance of her melancholic oppositionality.

To fully appreciate the emergence of the melancholic voice, it is appropriate to dive into Wangari's life story, with a focus on three principal vignettes: her maturation in a setting where ecological balance was maintained, her growing awareness of the effects of deforestation and her efforts to do something about it through reforestation, and the third phase of confrontation with the patriarchal state as she mobilized opposition to the degradation of a public park and a natural forest. She progressively became aware of the connections between deforestation, lost soil cover, silting of rivers, and the recurrence of landslides and decided to do something about it, though she was an elite woman who could afford to be oblivious to these realities. By so doing, she ran afoul of the master narratives that aligned women with the bodily, the non-rational, and the domestic. As I show, when her activism successfully blocked government-supported projects that had adverse environmental impact, she was marginalized as just a woman. I go back to her home at Ihithe and then loop back to Nairobi, where Wangari would block the building of the 60-story monument of concrete and stone in Uhuru Park, the only recreational green space in the Central Business District, and then amplify her opposition to the grabbing of Karura Forest, which Wangari describes as Nairobi's lung.

Wangari recounts memories of growing up in the pristine environment of the central Kenya highlands surrounded by bountiful nature, in a landscape traversed by youth-stage rivers that roared, and becoming riveted by a revered fig tree whose roots reached deep into the earth's core, becoming the source of a spring that was filled with tadpoles and ridged with arrow roots in days past. She powerfully evokes the Ihithe imprinted in her memory when she was seven years old:

> a landscape full of different shades of green, all springing from soil the color of deep terra cotta – smooth and dark and richly fertile, but mostly hidden behind the mass of wet, fresh vegetation. . . . It rained frequently, but the rivers were always clear and clean because the land and the riverbanks were covered by vegetation. Hailstorms, too, were frequent. . . . One hailstorm was so intense it turned the landscape white for a week.
>
> (32–33)

The description is suffused with color – the green landscapes, the smooth/dark/richly fertile soil that invites the desire to turn it over to marvel at the worms it likely contains – and smell, as one is invited to picture the rejuvenating raindrops landing on the fertile soil, and the sight of clear rivers in which one could see tadpoles, in addition to the spectacle of a hailstone-covered landscape. These images linger, but as we already know from the first chapter, that pristine world had been irredeemably lost. As she tells us, nonnative trees were soon introduced: "pines from the northern hemisphere, and eucalyptus and black wattle from the southern hemisphere. . . . Farmers appreciated their commercial value and planted them enthusiastically at the expense of local species" (39). The trees "eliminated local plants and animals, destroying the natural ecosystem that helped gather and retain rainwater. When rains fell, much of the water ran downstream. Over the subsequent decades, underground water levels decreased markedly and, eventually, rivers and streams either dried up or were greatly reduced" (39). Her recollection of the fate of a particular fig tree that was connected to the Gĩkũyũ sacred is particularly riveting:

> This tree's canopy was probably sixty feet in diameter and it produced numerous fruits that birds loved. When the fruit was ready you would find hundreds of birds feeding on them. The undergrowth of the tree was very fertile because people did not cut anything near those trees but allowed the undergrowth to flourish. All this added to the tree's mystery . . . [as her mother warned her] . . . 'that's a tree of God' 'We don't use it. We don't cut it. We don't burn it'.
>
> *(44–45)*

The interdependence between the soil, tree life and undergrowth, and birds illuminates the symbiosis found in the natural world. In addition, the connection of the natural to the Gĩkũyũ sacred speaks to the way that the natural and the human could co-exist in a non-hierarchical and non-extractive relationship. Wangari reports that a stream arose not far from the fig tree and it had:

> water so clean and fresh that we drank it straight from the stream. As a child I used to visit the point where the water bubbled from the belly of the earth to form a stream. . . . I can envision that stream now: . . . I can see the life in that water and the shrubs, reeds, and ferns along the banks. . . . I later learnt that there was a connection between the fig tree's root system and the underground water reservoirs. The roots burrowed deep into the ground, breaking through the rocks beneath the surface soil and diving into the underground water table. The water traveled up along the roots until it hit a depression or weak place in the ground and gushed out as a spring. . . . The reverence the community had for the fig tree helped preserve the stream and the tadpoles that so captivated me. The trees also held the soil together, reducing erosion and landslides. In such ways, without conscious or deliberate effort, these cultural and spiritual practices contributed to the conservation of biodiversity.
>
> *(45)*

I use this long quote because it is important to hear Wangari speak in her own voice about a world that would be soon lost. The evocative description of life-filled self-purifying rivers fed through natural hydraulics and devoid of human contamination, tree cover and roots that protected the soil, and the connection of the natural to the cultural and spiritual is captivating. Wangari celebrates the beauty of the environment in which she grew up and her closeness to the soil: "I knew that the soil should remain on the land and painfully recognized the destruction of the land when I saw the silt in rivers, especially after the rains" (48). Elsewhere around Kenya, she started noticing in the 1970s "that the rivers would rush down the hillsides and along paths and roads when it rained, and they were muddy with silt" (121). Her own natal home in Nyeri was no different: "I saw rivers silted with topsoil, much of which was coming from the forest where plantations of commercial trees had replaced indigenous forest. I noticed that much of the land that had been covered by trees, bushes, and grasses when I was growing up had been replaced by tea and coffee" (121). These exotic crops may have done well in some of the local soils, but they were not necessarily good for replenishing or covering these soils. Later she learns that somebody had acquired the piece of land on which:

> the fig tree I was in awe of as a child stood. The new owner perceived the tree to be a nuisance because it took up too much space and he felled it to make room to grow tea . . . it did not surprise me that when the fig tree was cut down, the stream where I had played with tadpoles dried up. My children would never be able to play with the frogs' eggs as I had or simply to enjoy the cool, clear water of that stream. I mourned the loss of that tree. . . . Ironically, the area where the fig tree of my childhood once stood always remained a patch of bare ground where nothing grew.
>
> *(122)*

Wangari uses the word "mourning" to describe the loss of the tree, but like the melancholic subject, she keeps it alive and kills it simultaneously. Later she explains the connection between traditional sacred spaces and environmental protections that were now lost:

> Before Europeans arrived, the people of Kenya did not look at trees and see timber, or at elephants and see commercial ivory stock . . . cheetahs beautiful skins for sale. But when Kenya was colonized and we encountered Europeans, with their knowledge, technology, understanding, religion, and culture – all of it new – we converted our values into a cash economy like theirs. Everything was now perceived as having monetary value.
>
> *(175)*

That perception had to be changed drastically. The unsaid is that, like the concrete jungles she would be fighting against later in life, the commodification of the environment was largely a male project, whether during the colonial or the neo-colonial phase. Paradoxically, even though men were the major beneficiaries of the new cash crop economy centered on agricultural and forest cultivation, women paid the heaviest price, being the first to be affected when food sources produced less and they had to walk farther to find firewood or water.

Wangari chose to re-educate local communities to recognize that the symptoms of environmental degradation and their causes – deforestation, devegetation, unsustainable agriculture, and soil loss are linked. She came up with the idea of tree planting that eventually led to the birth of the Green Belt Movement:

> The trees would provide a supply of wood that would enable women to cook nutritious foods. They would also have wood for fencing and fodder for cattle and goats. The trees would offer shade for humans and animals, protect watersheds and bind the soil, and, if they were fruit trees, provide food. They would also heal the land by bringing back birds and small animals and regenerate the vitality of the earth.
>
> *(125)*

Through the Green Belt Movement, Wangari empowered local women's groups to band together to establish tree nurseries for traditional trees that helped in the restoration of native tree cover around Kenya in a reversal of the investment in fast-growing but environmentally unfriendly exotic commercially grown trees. The women were motivated to establish tree nurseries for local trees and local transplanting for which they were compensated if the seedlings survived past six months, thus creating an army of "foresters without diplomas" who were eventually able to plant over 30 million trees over the next twenty years. Increasingly, GBM mounted environmental education seminars that incorporated civic education that illuminated connections between democracy, human rights, gender, and power (174). GBM also resisted the subordination of women's issues to political agendas advanced by the government. By emphasizing environmental, women's, and human rights, GBM pushed for greater democratic space progressively. This interpenetration of rights advocacy explains Wangari's role in the Uhuru Park and Karura Forest crises.

Chapter Nine of Wangari's memoir is titled "Fighting for Freedom," and in it, she details the fight to preserve the 34-acre Uhuru Park as a green space, which she describes as "a large green swath amid the bustle of crowds and the concrete and steel of the metropolis. Its lawns, paths, boating lake and stands of trees provide millions of people in Nairobi with a natural environment for recreation, gatherings, quiet walks or simply a breath of fresh air" (184). Using the developmentalist narrative, the government argued that the tower "would be a prestigious project, look magnificent, and . . . would provide spectacular views of Nairobi and the surrounding area" (190), provided, of course, that one could avoid seeing the urban slums of Kibera and Mathare, some of the largest in Africa. In a 45-minute "emergency" session specifically marshaled to discuss Wangari on November 8, 1989, parliamentarians called GBM "a bogus organization," questioned its "unelected" leader's mandate to speak for the people, and wondered why "a bunch of divorcees [were] coming out to criticize such a complex" (191). To cap it all, the then president used the Independence Day speech on December 12 – at Uhuru Park, ironically – to berate Wangari, suggesting that "if I was to be a proper woman in 'the African tradition' – I should respect men and be quiet" (196), thus inadvertently resituating the conflict within an ecofeminist context. Ironically, the supposedly rational, public sphere was the preserve of the intellectually challenged men. But Wangari framed the issue in terms of the larger fight for freedom, in which cause the right to open space for the underprivileged was enmeshed. She foregrounds the intellectual and political labor that produced her triumph against great odds. She worked with a network of pro-democracy campaigners, philanthropists, and environmental activists in Canada, the United States, the United Kingdom, and West Germany, who put pressure on investors from their own countries who had been tapped to supplement the government's meager resources available for the project. She therefore mobilized support globally while organizing the resistance locally in ways that illuminate the limitations of national boundaries to contain dissent by marginalized groups within the territorial space. These marginalized groups are able to mobilize international networks as a sort of insurance for their activist work. For stopping a project backed by the powers-that-be, a man from central Kenya apparently hailed her: "You are the only man left standing" (204). Before interrogating the gender codes mobilized by the state, it pays to consider how this re-gendering is ironically inverted in the Karura Forest crisis.

In the 1990s, the Kenya government degazetted numerous forests in order to make land available to reward political clients. Ngong, South Western Mau, and Karura forests were the most blatant settings for the land-grabbing. The GBM found the grabbing of Karura Forest particularly egregious. As Wangari says,

> I was outraged. For generations, Karura Forest had acted as a break between the winds
> off the savanna to the south and those descending from the highlands to the west and

north. Its 2,500 acres of natural forest serve as a catchment area for four major rivers, while its dense undergrowth and canopy are home to many rare species of flora and fauna, including *mĩhũgũ* trees, Sykes monkeys, bush pigs, antelopes, and hundreds of species of birds. Situated on the edge of Nairobi, Karura Forest serves as the lung of the congested metropolis.

(262)

There is some pointed irony that the United Nations Environmental Program (UNEP) head-quarters and the American Embassy were built on land hived off from Karura Forest, but we need not dwell on that point in order to paint the larger picture. As the dubious owners of the degazetted forest plots were cutting down trees and moving construction equipment into the for-est, GBM mobilized sympathizers to plant trees in the deforested areas. The first time they did that, hired thugs "descended on us with machetes . . . [and] uprooted all the trees we planted . . . we were saved from being hurt by the arrival of the construction workers . . . [who] calmed the young men down, telling them not to beat the women but only to force us out of the forest." (263) Aside from the suggestion of gender discrimination in the mobilization of violence, we may remark the political undertones to the confrontation: the violence was being deployed not by construction workers who stood to lose if the construction was stopped but by an amorphous gang of agitated young men who were obviously serving different masters. While attempts to convince the construction workers that they, too, stood to lose if Karura Forest was degraded worked temporarily, they too joined the assault on the GBM tree planters soon afterwards. The police were mobilized to keep the protestors out of the grabbed part of forest that was subse-quently fenced off and its entrance sign-posted "PRIVATE PROPERTY" (264–265). Even though the UNEP executive director issued a strong statement supporting the GBM cause and saying that Karura Forest was "'a precious natural resource that the city cannot afford to lose'" (266), the government escalated the confrontations. When GBM supporters arrived at the forest to plant tree seedlings in January 1999, they were "confronted by two hundred guards armed with machetes, clubs, whips, pangas, and bows and arrows. Some even had swords" (268). Wan-gari was told that the GBM could not plant trees on "private" land, but when she resisted and started digging a hole, "the men got aggressive and began hurling abuse and obscenities at us. 'Who do you think you are, woman?'" (269). The men descended on the tree planters, hurting many of them, including Wangari who got a big gash on her head. Even though they could plainly see the evidence of blood streaming down her neck, as captured in a picture that was widely circulated globally, the police would not do anything to the violent gang. At the hospital, a doctor told her that had she been hit again, she might not have survived the trauma (269).

I find the gender codes deployed against Wangari and GBM in both the Uhuru Park and Karura Forest sagas intriguing. In both cases, the rhetoric dispossessed her from her own space by constructing her as an interloper who lacked the mandate to speak for other Kenyans, least of all because she was a divorcee – and arguably not under the control of "rational" male facul-ties. She was also labeled an "improper" woman in 'the African tradition' who should respect men, be quiet, and retreat into the private sphere. Even the well-meaning man who compli-mented her for being "the last man standing" was oblivious of her agency as an empowered woman. At Karura, violence was not deployed against her at first specifically because she was a woman, even though the men accompanying GBM activists were not so lucky. When she did not back off, she was reminded of her incompleteness as a self-articulating subject with the question "Who do you think you are, woman?" In order to speak, she had to be verifiably recognizable as a member of the propertied political elite with the ability to call the shots, and as a woman, she could not conceivably expect to be heard. There is an element of excess in the violence deployed against her in ways that remind us of Foucault's monarch breaking down the body of a defiant subject in a spectacle of punishment that reactivated male power (49). And yet, all GBM was trying to do was to restore the degraded ecosystem in Karura Forest in ways that would ensure its continued ability to sustain non-human life at the same time that it sustained the human. However, in both instances, we encounter the clashing narratives of development: the patriarchal state sponsors the building of the concrete jungle urbanscapes as the underprivileged urban masses find inspiration in the women-inspired agitation for the preservation of natural landscapes.

Left unsaid in the description of the Uhuru Park conflict is that the propertied classes had enough open spaces in their suburban homes and golf clubs where they consumed leisure. The plight of lower-income people is well captured by a city resident who wrote in the daily press, "This is where I escape from the crowded [[housing]] estates over the weekend or during the holidays" (193). In yoking her environmental activism to the needs of marginalized groups in the emerging urbanscapes to that of women who bore the brunt of degraded soils, rivers drying up, and lack of firewood due to deforestation, Wangari appears to have been reading from a radical ecofeminist scorecard. She voices the anxieties over the lost ecological balance in Ihithe; destabilizes the hierarchies of men over women at Uhuru Park and Karura Forest; and defends an ecosystem that nurtures Sykes monkeys, *mĩhũgũ* trees, fig trees, tadpoles, hundreds of species of birds, and flora and fauna locally, in the Congo rainforest and beyond. Wangari appears to have been attempting to strike a balance between the human and the non-human in pursuit of a more egalitarian world devoid of the hierarchies of men over women. To appreciate her actions fully, it is helpful to read them through an ecofeminist frame.

By now, the connections Wangari makes between women and nature are already clear. The commitment to the environment and a recognition of the interdependence between the human and the natural world have also been amplified severally. The patriarchal discourses that, to borrow Althusser's term, "hail" Wangari as irrational and out of control and call on her to subject herself to male authority – presumably rational – has also been foregrounded. Implicit in the discussion so far is her push for a non-patriarchal and non-hierarchical ordering of the world in order to deprivilege the interests of men to the exclusion of women and nature itself. Also implicit in the argument so far is the congruence between the domination of women and nature by men and the degradation of the environment in Kenya in order to advance development that advances the interests of the patriarchal state and its male clients. The thread that we need to weave now is the push Wangari makes to enable women to recover some lost agency by empowering them to reject marginalization from the state and foreground their interests in redressing the lost ecological balance that affects them the most. By connecting their push to end their domination by men to the restoration of their environment that has been degraded principally by men, Wangari shows the interdependence between the marginalized women's struggle to end their domination and that of nature. There is a twinned emphasis between a commitment to the environment and the feminist investment in the equality of genders.

As Ruether reminds us, "[e]cofeminist hope for an alternative society calls for a double conversion or transformation" of social hierarchies of men over women, of "egalitarian societies which recognize the fullness of humanity in each person" (94), leading to:

> a major restructuring of the relations of human groups to each other and a transformation of the relation between humans and the non-human world. Humans need to recognize that they are one species among others within the ecosystems of earth. Humans need to embed their systems of production, consumption, and waste within

the ways that nature sustains itself in a way that recognizes their intimate partnership with non-human communities.

(Integrating Ecofeminism, Globalization and World Religions, *94*)

Ruether draws upon the work of Francoise d'Eaubonne, who coined the word "ecofeminism" in 1972, positing that "'the destruction of the planet is due to the profit motive inherent in male power.'" (91) We can immediately hear the echoes of Wangari's critique of the European profit-driven changes to her home environment and their perpetuation by the neo-colonial state mentioned earlier. If Francoise's 1974 book *Feminism or Death* saw women as central to bringing about an ecological revolution (Ruether 91), Wangari advances that recognition in the Kenyan cases and the larger African context. As Ruether argues, [radical] ecofeminism sees a connection between the domination of women and the domination of nature. On an ideological-cultural level, women are said to be closer to nature than men because of the master narratives aligning them with body, matter, emotions, the animal world, the spheres of reproduction, food preparation, and so on, realms that are devalued in relation to the public sphere of male power and culture. Further, Ruether says, "claiming that women are 'naturally' closer to the material world and lack the capacity for intellectual and leadership roles justifies locating them in the devalued sphere of material work and excluding them from higher education and public leadership" (91). Like most ecofeminists, Ruether rejects the essentializing of women "as more in tune with nature by virtue of their female body and maternity . . . [because this social construct] naturalizes women and feminizes non-human nature, making them appear more 'alike'" (93). As she states, women may suffer more due to the abuse of the natural world and hence become more aware of its abuse due to their experience "in their particular social location, not due to a different 'nature' than males . . . A peasant woman who has to struggle for the livelihood of her family in immediate relation to these realities [e.g. stripping of forests and the poisoning of water] is acutely aware of them. Such awareness, of course, does not translate directly into mobilization for change" (93–94). Wangari's story is an interesting study of a woman with roots in the peasantry who launches herself into the middle class but retains the keen awareness of the abuses her natural world has been subjected to by a patriarchal order and mobilizes others to change it. When she realizes that it is not enough to organize for women's and environmental causes from the margins, she enters the political arena and is able to make some difference. It is important to probe the disconnect between women's causes and the narrative of nationalist consolidation and its development cloak.

Frantz Fanon warned at the dawn of African independence that in the newly independent state, the national party soon collapses and becomes an instrument that is "objectively . . . the accomplice of the merchant bourgeoisie" (172). Given the imbrication of this merchant bourgeois in propping up undemocratic regimes and acting as conveyor belts for Western capital, Fanon suggested that in these underdeveloped countries, "the bourgeoisie should not be allowed to find the conditions necessary for its existence and its growth. In other words, the combined effort of the masses led by a party and of intellectuals who are highly conscious and armed with revolutionary principles ought to bar the way to this useless and harmful middle class" (175). Again and again, Fanon berates this class for its inability to think in terms of the nation as a whole, in ways that speak to the choristers and politicians who propped up the Moi state. He was insistent that a national government must take responsibility for the totality of the nation; raise the level of national consciousness in the people, especially the youth; detribalize and unite all citizens in the nation; and safeguard the rights of women (201–202). As he argued,

> in an underdeveloped country every effort is made to mobilize men and women as
> quickly as possible; it must guard against the danger of perpetuating the feudal tradition

which holds sacred the superiority of the masculine over the feminine. Women will have exactly the same place as men, not in the clauses of the constitution but in the life of every day.

(202)

Nationalism, Fanon said, "that magnificent song that made the people rise against their oppressors," must not be allowed to "die away on the day that independence is proclaimed" (203). However, as several studies by Lois West, Anthony D. Smith, Parker, Yaeger, and others have shown, the story of nationalism has a masculine symbolic content. As R. Radhakrishnan states, "the advent of the politics of nationalism signals the subordination if not the demise of women's politics" (Parker 78). Further, he wonders, "Why does the politics of the 'one' typically overwhelm the politics of the 'other'? Why could the two not be coordinated within an equal and dialogic relationship of mutual accountability?" (Parker 78).

Reading *Unbowed* forces one to see how the feudal traditions Fanon warned against are recycled in the independent state in order to marginalize women and subvert the popular will, all while subordinating women's politics to a thinly disguised politics of nationalism that advances the parasitic interests of a merchant property-owning class that converts state resources into the "private property" tagged in the Karura Forest incident. It is a far cry from the romantic narrative of nationalism that should have produced Anderson's "deep horizontal comradeship" held together by the "magic" of nationalism that would turn "chance into destiny" (*Imagined*, 11–12) and the ideal nation celebrated in the notion "out of many, one." As Bhabha argues, "the political unity of the nation consists in a continual displacement of its irredeemably plural modern space . . . [and] the boundary that secures the cohesive limits of the western nation" may paradoxically provide "a place from which to speak both of, and as, the minority, the exilic, the marginal, and the emergent" (300). Wangari destabilizes the deceptive political unity of the nation by emphasizing its plurality and speaking from within the boundaries of the modern state as the voice of the minority, of the internally exiled and marginalized. Her counter-narratives of women involved in environmental restoration as a counter to the extractive/destructive patriarchal state and its clientilist merchant class mirror Bhabha's "counter-narratives of the nation that continually evoke and erase its totalizing boundaries – both actual and conceptual – [and] disturb those ideological manoeuvres through which 'imagined communities' are given essentialist identities" (300). To modify Fanon's reading of the postcolony, Wangari disturbs the essentialist identities of the Kenyan state as a feudal space "which holds sacred the superiority of the masculine over the feminine" (202) and nature. Through her memoir, she speaks back to those who questioned her right to be in particular places/spaces, her right to speak, and her subordination based on gender.

As Helen Buss says in her authoritative study of memoir, the memoirist enjoys relative freedom to animate past experience in which the subject of memoir was a participant, to witness to the experience of others, and to engage in retrospective reflection on their past experience and include reflexive interludes that historicize the personal. The tripartite narrative voice in memoir is a participant and witness to the self (and others) and also acts as a reflective/reflexive consciousness. The narrator in memoir selects episodes that incrementally allow the performance of the self in relation to the larger society (16–25). The three facets of Wangari's story discussed in the paper illuminate the thing that was lost – the ecological balance at Ihithe and other places in Kenya; the greenspace at Uhuru Park that was about to be converted into a concrete monstrosity; and Karura Forest, the lung of the urban metropolis that was being degraded by "development." Wangari moves from the passive onlooker gazing at nature to an active agent mobilizing environmental restoration and respect for environmental and human rights.

With the foregoing context in mind, it is understandable that Wangari starts her memoir with a melancholic retrieval of a lost world, and she is anguished that those in power were attempting to silence her. To invoke Ross Chambers, the "sense of dispossession from one's 'own' space and this awareness of an exceedingly drifting self are among the symptoms of melancholia . . . whose oppositional function . . . [is] that the 'complaints' of melancholics are in reality 'accusations' . . . [there being] the etymological connection . . . between melancholy and anger." Further, he says, "Melancholy is . . . an oppositional text . . . but one that is necessarily also a social text" (*Room for Maneuver* 108). If melancholy requires reading as a social text, as the "place" – a deterritorialized place crisscrossed by a nomadic subject – where a political unconscious becomes readable, in and as the tension of the self and the self-constituting other(s) (*Room for Maneuver*, 108–109), Wangari's articulation of environmental grievance voiced the political unconscious nearly twenty years ahead of the pack. We may not remember much about the Moi state, but we do remember the melancholic voice speaking grievance and articulating the political unconscious. As a result of her activism, Uhuru Park is still a green space. Grabbing of Karura Forest stopped. As for undoing the environmental degradation around Nyeri, it may take a while. While some reforestation has been done successfully using more environmentally friendly trees, it takes at least thirty years for traditional trees to mature and restore the soil cover. Wangari inspired that work.

Wangari's environmental activism earned her the Nobel Peace Prize in 2004. She suggests that she won the prize because the Nobel Peace Prize Committee "had also heard the voice of nature" (293) and adds that the Nobel Committee made a connection "between peace, sustainable management of resources, and good governance" (294). The award gave her a louder megaphone to amplify her ideas and "empower the huge constituency that felt honored by the prize: the environmental movement, those who work on women's and gender issues, human rights advocates, those advocating for good governance, and peace movements" (293). As she asks rhetorically at the end of the memoir, "issues of good governance, respect for human rights, equity, and peace" are particularly pressing in Africa, a continent rich in resources: "The big question is, Who will access the resources? Who will be excluded? Can the minority have a say, even if the majority have their way?" (294). These observations and questions take us back to the question contained in this chapter's title, "Who do you think you are, woman?" In the end, having achieved agency by refusing to reproduce herself as Althusser's interpellated subject is supposed to, and having disrupted the compelled performances by the parodic repetition of gender codes, Wangari could comfortably answer back that her gender was not an appendage to her being, that there was no disjuncture between who she thought she was and who she was. In any case, others seemed to agree with what she thought was her role in checking environmental degradation and standing up for the marginalized, at the very least. Indeed, she could comfortably say, "I am what I am." Her mobilization of memoir enables her to construct an agentive subjectivity, to be the center of her story instead of being the object in the patriarchal state's misogynous discourses, to be a witness to the agency of other marginalized women and a despoiled environment, and through the reflective/reflexive consciousness, she shapes the way we interpret her story.

Works cited

Anderson, Benedict. *Imagined Communities: Reflections on the Origin and Spread of Nationalism*. London: Verso, 1991.

Bhabha, Homi. "Dissemination: Time, Narrative and the Margins of the Modern Nation." *Nation and Narration*. Ed. Homi Bhabha. London: Routledge, 1990.

Buss, Helen. *Repossessing the World: Reading Memoirs by Contemporary Women*. Toronto: Wilfrid Laurier University Press, 2002.

Chambers, Ross. *Room for Maneuver: Reading Oppositional Narrative.* Chicago: Chicago University Press, 1991.

Fanon, Frantz. *The Wretched of the Earth.* Trans. Constance Farrington. New York: Grove Press, 1963.

Foucault, Michel. *Discipline and Punish.* New York: Vintage, 1979.

Maathai, Wangari. *Unbowed: A Memoir.* New York: Alfred A. Knopf, 2006.

Radarkrishnan, Rajagopalanche. "Nationalism, Gender and the Narrative of Identity." *Nationalisms and Sexualities.* Eds. Parker Andrew, et al. New York: Routledge, 1992.

Ruether, Rosemary. *Integrating Ecofeminism Globalization and World Religions.* Lanham: Rowman & Littlefield, 2005.

Smith, Anthony. *Nationalism and Modernism: A Critical Survey of Recent Theories of Nations and Nationalism.* London: Routledge, 1998.

West, Lois. *Feminist Nationalism.* New York: Routledge, 1997.

15

REPRESENTATION OF WOMEN IN UDJE, AN URHOBO MEN'S-ONLY ORAL POETIC PERFORMANCE GENRE

Enajite Eseoghene Ojaruega

Introduction

Literature in Africa in oral, performative, or written forms has always addressed the experiences of culture and the people's living realties and conditions. Women as the female gender have always been represented in relation to male. Africa's traditional patriarchal sociocultural system has been an institution of power that oppresses, exploits, and often downgrades women at the expense of men. Age-old patriarchal values place the financial, physical, emotional, and social needs of the man above the woman's. Women are seen in patriarchal cultures such as the Urhobo one in Delta State of Nigeria as subordinate to men. They are hardly projected in many male-dominated spheres as politics, society, and the economy. The mere fact that Urhobo men, like many traditional African men, can marry as many wives as they desire or can afford to shows the subjection of women almost to the extent of being "owned" by men. Males are socialized to see themselves as superior to females in many of these patriarchal societies. However, the women sometimes react to the male treatment to affirm their own humanity. Often, men want to rub it in to women that they are in control and can get away with many things, such as denigrating women without the women having the opportunity or avenue to respond. *Udje* is one of the literary and performative spaces that men in Urhoboland often use to subject women to discriminatory treatment. Many udje songs often attack what the dominant males consider threats to their patriarchal society. In this chapter, I intend to discuss the Urhobo men's subjection of women to ridicule in their udje songs and how the attacks on women, unlike attacks on fellow men, reinforce the "minority" status of women in Urhobo traditional society.

By being treated as "minority" in the male-dominated patriarchy, Urhobo women fall into the minority discourse of Urhobo sociocultural tradition. They are a minority in the sense that they are treated as a collective group in their subjugation as a lower-class gender as compared to the male gender. Furthermore, in whatever situation they find themselves, they are presented as underlings whose voices may not be heard or, if heard, not as loud as men's. From a feminist perspective, Urhobo women suffer voiceless-ness in the highly articulate udje repertory of performance songs. They are present as objects and enablers of the songs and never as composers or main singers themselves. Urhobo women could be used to gather secrets to be used in the songs;

they are given subordinate roles of clapping and fanning the dominant *ebo-ile* (cantors); they dance outside the theatre of performance, but they are never the centre of the udje performance. From almost every aspect of their lives, Urhobo women are victims of male domination, and the udje songs only confirm the subjectivity and minority status of women to male dominance. Quoting Louis Wirth, Helen Hacker summarizes a minority group as:

> any group of people who because of their physical or cultural characteristics, are singled out from others in the society in which they live for differential and unequal treatment, and who therefore regard themselves as objects of collective discrimination.
>
> *(60)*

Women occupy a subaltern position in traditional Urhobo societies, the backdrop against which udje evolved, and therefore they can be regarded as a minority group or of minority status. This is essentially as a result of the fact that patriarchy, the sociocultural system practiced there, favours men as they wield power to enforce their sociocultural, political, and economic advantages at the expense of women in the community. Therefore, right from birth, the Urhobo woman is socialized to see and accept male dominance as normal within and outside her immediate environments (Regina Otite 12). Standards of values and ethics are set by and implemented from male perspectives. In this regard, the woman lives and operates under conditions that are culturally dictated and regulated by men. As a daughter, wife, and mother, her existence is closely tied to that of male acquaintances, where in most cases, she experiences unequal treatment or discrimination. As a girl-child, she grows up with the consciousness that the male child is valued over her because the latter perpetuates the family's lineage and therefore is treated as indispensible. She grows up and fulfils one of the societal expectations when she gets married. While married, she is treated as the collective property of the husband's family, commonly referred to as "our wife" and compelled to play her role as the position demands. If her spouse dies, she can be "inherited" by any of the younger male relatives of the late husband with or without her consent. Even as a long-serving wife, she has no rights to inheritance in a home she has helped build. As a mother, her worth is usually defined by her ability to bear male children; else she is disparaged. Sometimes, without any scientific proof, she is held responsible for being barren or unable to give birth to sons. Politically, she does not have the privileges to enable her attain the highest seat of traditional power or authority. While the men are privileged to high positions, Urhobo women are not even allowed to take chieftaincy titles in some clans, like in Agbarho, where the oldest chief eventually becomes king. The idea behind this deliberate exclusion from this cultural rite is to disenfranchise her and further consolidate the notion that women are second-class citizens.

Generally, the Urhobo woman's life is dogged by many taboos that conscript her person and take away fundamental rights and privileges. She is culturally enjoined to keep sexual relations only with her husband and is even forbidden from having close physical contact like handshakes and hugs with other men. Any act of adultery involving the Urhobo woman is not only strongly frowned upon but also accompanied by strict penalties, stigmatization, and even divorce. However, the men or husbands are not penalized for indulging in extra-marital relationships. Urhobo women in traditional times were relegated to the periphery and subjected to marginalization, oppression, and exploitation, thus confirming their minority or disadvantaged status. All of the previous contribute in establishing the fact that even though, statistically, women are not a minority, they qualify as such because they tend to have less power and fewer privileges than men based on observable sociocultural characteristics or practices. Though old or menopaused women are given limited access to male spaces, this is an inadequate good gesture in the minoritization of women in Urhobo land. And so, as if in reaction or protest against these series of discrimination by virtue of gender, "Omotejowho!!" is one of the popular names given to the Urhobo girl-child and meant to remind us as well as reiterate the often glossed-over fact that indeed, "a female is still a human being!"

Udje: an Urhobo oral poetic performance tradition

In his seminal book on udje, G.G. Darah asserts that "Udje was the classical song-poetry and dance form in the political divisions occupying most of the southern half of Urhobo terri-tory" (1). It is believed to have originated from the Ujevwe and Udu areas in Urhobo land of Nigeria's Delta state. This oral poetic performance art form comprises dance, poetry, and music and is performed against the backdrop of adversarial competitions akin to a battle of wits and acerbic words. It strongly attacks attitudes traditional society considers disagreeable in people with the aim of exposing and shaming violators of social ethics as well as upholding positive models. David T. Okpako regards it as "a tradition in which the singer gives voice to social cri-tique" (vii), while Tanure Ojaide says it is a "means of maintaining law and order" (42). Okpako further locates the importance and relevance of this genre when he declares that "It is an impor-tant source of information on Urhobo culture, history and ethics" (7). Indeed, it is through this oral poetic performance that we shall come to see some aspects of Urhobo patriarchal attitudes towards women.

In udje, rival or opposing groups privately compose abusive, satiric, and sometimes ele-giac songs in their respective workshops, which they later take turns to perform in public domains on appointed days or during festival occasions. Juxtaposition, exaggeration, sarcasm, humour, hyperbole, and masking are some of the techniques employed in creating the desired effect. The men carry out the compositions and other preparations towards public performances under some kind of oath of secrecy or strict rules of privacy and exclusion of non-members, as demanded by the competitive nature of the performance. This helps the group jealously guard against any form of external infiltration or ousting of the contents and nature of their songs. In fact, the all-male cast of composers and performers retreat to designated groves and sacred places, away from prying and public eyes during the period of gestation. These settings can be abodes of traditional deities that are also influential as sources of spirituality and inspiration but out of bounds for women, thus promoting male exclusivity. Uhaghwa, the Urhobo god of creativity and spectacular performance, is one of the patron gods of udje.

The surprise element is also quite important to this art. The rival wants to ensure that the materials and information gathered about the opposition's supposedly hidden secrets and skil-fully woven into the fabric of the songs are exposed in an unexpected and poignant manner. The aim is to leave a lasting impression in the minds of the witnesses to the performance and also demobilize the subject of attack without the opportunity for an immediate rejoinder. At the end of the outing, the audience leaves with a new and different, often negative, impression of the subjects of the songs. Therein lies the concept of shaming in the udje tradition and perhaps why Ojaide and Darah respectively aver that "the dominant temper in udje's oral poetic tradition is a censorious one" (*Theorizing African Oral Poetic Performance* . . . 73) and is "capable of causing the victims social and psychological discomfort. An Udje song that does not achieve this purpose is considered unsuccessful" (*Battles of Songs* . . . 19).

It is significant that women are most likely to suffer from social and psychological discomfort when attacked through these songs than men. They are emotionally and psychologically weaker than men in those aspects as far as the Urhobo experience attests to as a result of the udje songs. As Ojaide finds in his book, *Performance, and Art: Udje Dance Songs of the Urhobo People*, there are extant tales of women hiding after the festival of songs of which the udje performances are a part because they have been subjected to virulent attacks through the songs. Also, some women have left their marriages because they could not bear the insults and scandal that the songs subjected them to. Even though I will discuss the songs in great detail later, the case of a woman whose chest is described as "*phre rere*," to signify its flatness or equate it to a plain, is body shaming and quite derogatory. The breastless woman is made to feel that she is not a complete woman because of what men regard as a physical disadvantage, her very small breasts. Similarly, it appears men, through patriarchal constructs that suit them and their desires, determine a woman's perception of her beauty and sexuality.

The poetry/song aspect of udje entails joint compositions by members of a group, one of whom is the lead composer or *ororile* (thinker/maker of songs or poet), after which the final product is handed over to a lead singer known as *obo ile* (cantor or lead vocalist), who is considered the best person to render the song most aesthetically before an audience. The men dress in loincloths tied around their waists and with a string of small bells attached to it. Around their heads, they tie a thin piece of cloth or female scarf which has a piece of feather stuck in it. Some of them hold hand fans made from animal hides or wool. As they dance, they execute practiced dance steps in accompaniment of fast tempo and rhythmic drum beats and clapping. The movements are quite vigorous and athletic and include acrobatic displays like intermittent leaps into the air, twirling, and even back flips. In most cases, the male dancers are bare-chested, with flexible torso movements as if possessed by the passion and frenzy whipped up during the dance. No doubt, the dance pattern of udje is meant for the fit and able-bodied, from which the patriarchal culture excludes women.

By many of its features, the performance aspect of udje is structured in such a way as if to deliberately exclude women because of their feminine and more delicate structure. Urhobo women generally in traditional times tend to have small and middle-built bodies and to be of short or medium height. They do not have the huge and tall figures expected of male dancers. Women do not go about bare-chested or dance in that state of undress as men do in udje. Also, the masculinity meant to be part of the udje display of athleticism, such as the leaping into the air, twirling, and back flips earlier described are all male strokes, so to say. Udje does not make room for any female dancers, unlike some other patriarchal dances that men and women dance together, though with different movements, which J.H. Nketia describes as "angular" male dances and female "rounded" performances. Thus, the practice of udje oral poetic performance is emotionally, psychologically, and physically constructed to exclude women for men's-only participation. The most women do in udje is handclapping, fanning the dancers, and on rare occasions choral accompaniments of the male singers.

Udje songs and women as minority discourse

Udje is a predominantly male enterprise, as women are relegated to the fringes and only play minimal and minor roles as clappers and attendants to the men during the public performances. On rare occasions, a female member of the community known as *omotogbe* (usually a divorcee returned to her natal home or a woman who has menopaused) is allowed to "participate on equal status with men" (Darah 6) during the composition process. But, even if allowed into the workshop, the woman is neither the poet acknowledged as the poet or composer of the song, nor a cantor or a performer, so the issue of parity as Darah claims is invalidated. Sometimes, women married into a rival community are sent as spies by their people to gather information which will be incorporated into the text of the songs in order to pre-empt the opponents' moves and floor them during the competition. This smacks more of exploitation than a privilege!

Moreso, these token roles do not take away the minority status of women in udje, neither do they elevate the image of the generality of women.

Ironically, in spite of their deliberate exclusion, many udje songs have women as the subjects of abuses or the butt of their attacks. This further perpetuates the concepts of power and control prevalent in gender relationships in many African cultures, including Urhobo's. Along the line of patriarchal constructs, men are in charge of defining and deciding what should pass as acceptable social norms and behaviours. By extension, udje songs are composed by males, and the men use them as a mechanism of control of the women. Women who fail to live up to patriarchal expectations come under attack in udje songs and are ridiculed for not being role models as demanded by tradition. Society fails to understand that some of these deviant behaviours of women might just be ways of resisting or protesting the unfair and unequal social conditions foisted on them. It could also be that the women are just acting true to their individual character. What makes the women come under scrutiny in such satiric songs is that the men who have set the criteria for conventional social conduct in gender relations are the ones not at ease with the women's actions. As in most patriarchal situations, it is the men who construct and enforce the yardstick for what is acceptable behaviour. Consequently, they are also responsible for assessing what aspects of a woman's character or actions conform to expected social norms and values or not and should or should not become the object of satiric attacks. Let me quickly add that even when men are often at the other end as co-perpetrators of the act women are accused of, their roles are glossed over or not mentioned because men are the composers of these songs and tend to be more sympathetic to one another. This is why many "deviant" behaviours exhibited by men such as boastfulness, laziness, avarice, sexual immorality, and others are not roundly condemned in udje songs as they are when women are involved.

Women are therefore compelled to accept their identities through the prism of the male perspective. These subjective and discriminatory practices are what gives rise to women's minority status in this men's-only poetic genre and consequently enforces female silence, repression, misrepresentation, and misrecognition as gleaned from some of the songs. Aside from physically excluding women from the main processes of udje, these women do not have a commensurate or equally popular or public traditional performance platform for rebuttals or counter-attacks. Thus, the nature of the composition and performance of udje songs does not allow women the voice and space to respond to or refute the allegations heaped on them in such songs, thereby entrenching inequitable conditions. On the other hand, the men who are the butts of derision in Udje songs are given the opportunity to re-group and come back with their reprisals, which would in most cases cancel out some of the effects of or sting in the opponents' initial attack. It also affords them the opportunity to revoke false or negative impressions. In fact, many udje songs are rejoinders to a previous provocation or call out by a rival, as the words are overtly or covertly directed to a specific individual or community.

Representation of women in udje songs

The manner in which Urhobo women are portrayed in udje songs shows men's perception of them in a patriarchal society. It also reflects the realities of the lived experiences of these women. Women are usually presented in unflattering roles or positions in many of these songs. The idea behind this form of attack is to shame and stigmatize the female subjects and also discourage other young girls or women from emulating the so-called foibles outlined in the songs. Sometimes, too, women are attacked through these songs because of their associations or affiliations with male subjects or rivals whom the composers seek to ridicule or diminish. In fact, many of the songs attacking men invariably drag in women (mothers, wives, daughters, and mistresses) related to them in a bid to further deflate the men.

On a general note, some udje songs derisively attack women for what society perceives as bad behaviours and even personal defects. Some include ugliness, laziness, boastfulness, sexual immoderation, and witchcraft. Even rejecting the advances of a man could earn a woman such negative attention through udje songs! She is ridiculed; scorned; and described in scathing, contemptuous, scornful, and derogatory terms. This notion of pejorative name-calling and unwholesome exaggerations also falls into one of the mechanisms of udje songs used to blackmail women to conform because rarely are the men condemned for indulging in these same or similar practices, as we shall come to see later. Worse still is that these women are not provided the medium to respond to the accusations and stand the risk of being defamed because their character has been irreparably damaged in public. People rarely consider the emotional or psychological implications of these visceral attacks on the women despite the claims of promoting "good behaviour."

Udje songs are orally composed, but over the years and beginning with J.P. Clark's 1963 publication in *Nigerian Magazine*, some academic scholars have carried out ground-breaking research on this traditional Urhobo poetic genre. Today, we have as published documents or literary texts quite an impressive collection of udje songs in their Urhobo transcriptions alongside their English translations. Therefore, the bulk of udje songs I will be examining are taken from Ojaide's *Poetry, Performance, and Art: Udje Dance Songs of the Urhobo People* (2003); Darah's *Battles of Songs: Udje Tradition of the Urhobo* (2005); and Okpako's *Kpeha's Song: Ethics and Culture in Urhobo Udje Poetry* (2011). These distinguished scholars, through their individual and collective efforts, have examined udje as an art form. Ojaide in particular admits that udje has greatly influenced the content and style of his poetry (Ojaide 2015) and consequently many critics (Tayo Olafioye 2002; Onookome Okome 2002; Ogaga Okuyade 2012; Obari Gomba 2012; Enajite Eseoghene Ojaruega 2015; Mathias Orhero 2017; Tony Afejuku 2018; Kufre Usanga 2018) have also examined his poems using udje aesthetics. While we bear in mind the fact that udje generally satirizes deviant behaviours in humans, a major significance of this study is the writer's choice of women as subjects in these songs, especially since they are not active participants in the composition or performance, nor do they have the privilege of refuting or responding to attacks on their character. Many of the songs under this category even have the names of the female subjects as their titles, which seems like a direct call out!

Traditional Urhobo society is quite conservative in its outlook on issues pertaining to sexual etiquette in gender relationships. For the woman, especially, many strictures are culturally imposed to ensure she adheres to some rules or else be ready to face the consequences of her acts. A young Urhobo woman is expected to remain a virgin before marriage. She is also expected to accept being married off through arrangements made by her male relatives with little or no consultation. While married, she is also expected to be hardworking and responsible for keeping the domestic aspect of the home running smoothly. Even in a polygamous situation where two or more women are married to one man and probably live under the same roof, each woman is expected to accept and work with the "sharing" formula drawn up by the man. All of the previous expectations hardly take into consideration whether the women personally find them suitable. If for one reason or the other she eventually quits the marriage, she is expected to remain unmarried or accept being concubine to a married man. If she returns home after a divorce and has reached middle or menopausal age, then she is derisively referred to as an "omotogbe" and treated like a discarded object. Sexual delinquencies like promiscuity, prostitution, adultery, incest, and others are frowned upon and worse when committed by or involving women. All of the previous sociocultural issues and more form the themes in some udje songs with women as characters or subjects.

"Eyabure", "Ijiriemu," "Kowhiroro," and "Umukoro" (Ojaide's *Poetry, Performance, and Arts* . . .) are titles of songs where women are presented as indulging in sexual misbehaviours and thoroughly abused for violating sexual codes. We are told in "Eyabure" (108) that the fate she suffers now in her old age is a consequence of the choices she made, even probably before birth. This brings to light the Urhobo belief in the concept of pre-destiny and the existence in the spiritual realm of a place called *urhoro* where humans make life's choices which they later live out when they are born. Thus, the speaker of the poem is merciless in condemning Eyabure even when, clearly, her plight is pathetic. The opening lines of the song accuse her of having "wandered" through different cities away from home, plying her trade, "whoring . . . from her dawn to her dusk." Hence, when she decides to return home and settle down to have a family, it is too late because "she is now dry." Much as it is about the oldest profession in the world, the Urhobo patriarchal society does not condone an Urhobo woman's indulgence in prostitution. It is quite easy for people to ascribe any form of ill fate she suffers to this deviant act of hers. Therefore, going by patriarchal standards, Eyabure's inability to give birth to a child must be because she has misused her body! Hence, she deserves no sympathy, even though "Eyabure still weeps and weeps/ She exhausted herself in other lands,/and nobody here should pity her." Without any proven or scientific evidence, they arrive at this conclusion with which they justify their mockery of her childlessness. Nobody is concerned about her misery, hopelessness, and resignation when she laments "I will no longer ask for any god's favour . . ./*Mother is gone* will not be sung for me,/Wherever death meets me,/let me end there." She suffers from a double jeopardy, as she does not have a child of her own (something which the society places premium value on and defines a woman's identity through), and she is further disparaged in this condition.

Kowhiroro (Ojaide 162–164) is also tagged a prostitute who "night and day she rests not;/ her vagina covers the entire stomach space./She makes love in coven/and night and day she rests not." It appears the sexual libido of women offends men, as if women have no rights to satisfy their high sexual urges. It is common even in modern society to slut-shame a woman for this, while, on the other hand, the man vaunts his sexual prowess based on his active sexual life. It is rare to find udje songs censuring men's sexual infractions as strongly as they do women's. In a case like Okpoto's (Ojaide 109), who goes about sleeping with other people's wives even in public places such that women see him and "shut themselves in" for fear of being sexually assaulted, the most he is described as is a "sex maniac". Nobody ascribes his inability to settle down to family life or give birth to children as consequences for his errant lifestyle, as they are quick to do for women. Even when he commits incest by sleeping with his own mother under a tree, it is the mother that eventually dies as a result of this abominable act. This is proof that the men (and, by extension, society) accommodate and are more lenient with men's sexual violations, while they do not spare women for this same offences.

The central female character in the song "Ijiriemu" (128) is a married woman who does "the abominable,/barters her vagina over town." Adultery by a married woman in traditional Urhobo culture is considered a grievous offence and a sexual taboo. Some implications of this act for the woman include the possibilities of strange ailments or afflictions for her, her husband, and even children. So, she is expected to confess her transgressions to avoid incurring the wrath of the ancestors and attracting physical and spiritual calamities. In addition, she is penalized through a fine of money, hot drinks, or/and a goat to be used for cleansing. The notion of confessing her adulterous liaisons with other men is part of the punishment for going against cultural restrictions on sex and should be part of the signs of her repentance. But in Ijiriemu's case, after she makes "random confessions of adultery./she always entices young men into trouble" (Ojaide

129). By this, Ijiriemu again offends the sensibilities of cultural decorum or decency in gender relationships, as it is the man who usually initiates or proposes sex to the woman and not the other way round like Ijiriemu does. Worse still is the fact that her targets are young men or bachelors and she goes on to boast before other women "that she is strong." Her actions lead to a general stigmatization for her womenfolk and, as a deterrent, the song warns other men that "Ugbede women should not be married." Kenamiru, the wife of Umukoro, is also shamed as a prostitute who confesses but still continues in her adulterous act (Ojaide 157–158).

Women are also stigmatized and shamed on the suspicion that they are witches. This can be because they exhibit some bad character traits or possess some personal defects that men find disagreeable. Childlessness, ugliness in a woman, and rejecting a man's advances are reasons enough to tag a woman as a witch from what we find in udje songs. "Amonomeyararia" (124–126) explores the theme of the woes of a woman who is unable to bear children. Research has shown that this song is a mask which the renowned composer and performer Memerume of Edjophe used to sing about himself in the *iteh* (masking) tradition of udje. Even though married to several women and having concubines, he had no child, and knowing folks would laugh at him or use this weakness against him; he decided to compose a song about himself to take the sting out of the pain it would cause him. Thus, instead of using himself or a male, he employs a female character to carry his pain! Amonomeyararia is referred to as "an empty shell" because of her infertility and is variously described as "unripe," "barren," "sterile," "incomplete," and leading "a futile life." The sum total of these tags is that "The sterile woman is doubtless a witch/she is doubtless a witch" (125). The impression this accentuates is that because she is barren, she is subhuman and has no right to a self or any other form of personal identity because she has failed at motherhood. Rather she is referred to as a curse and "a water spirit/ that is stranded on land," "money lavished on her is wasted," and her marriage "a failure." Going by traditional precepts outlined in this udje song, "the life of a childless one is incomplete" ("Amonomeyararia" 124). Many udje songs never fail to underscore this view when dealing with affected women. Conversely, in some situations, they point accusatory fingers at the woman when she loses a child. They mock her grief, which they believe is forced or pretence saying "you have killed again./ After a witch has brought about death,/she weeps as if in earnest grief" (Arutere 144).

Some udje songs dwell on the physical appearances of women in a derogatory manner. Aruviere is a spinster who stubbornly rejects the advances of some men who only want to have sex with her. For this, she is viciously attacked as ugly and parts of her body subjected to ridicule. They claim that her ugliness is responsible for her spinsterhood, as she has been rejected by several suitors because of this. Even those who initially show interest on seeing her never come back again! According to the song, no matter the efforts she makes, "her ugliness couldn't diminish" (Ojaide 149). In fact, they recommend that she should be jailed for being this ugly! This poem, in keeping with the udje tradition of abuse, deploys many hyperbolic and disparaging words and expressions in describing Aruviere. She is referred to as "the gate-keeper at coven," "her face is swollen like a curse charm/she has overgrown in her backside- /everything disorderly in her body." At one point, her situation was so hopeless that "they are doing medicine to attract men for her!" (151). The song ends with the dismissal that "A young woman who . . . cannot have a man, that is really a tasteless dish!" This declaration emphasizes the patriarchal conceit that a woman's existence can only be validated through her associations with a man. In other words, an unmarried and/or childless woman has no self or social value!

Women's characters are also subject of criticism regarding their inability to function effectively within domesticity. An Urhobo woman is expected to be dexterous and hardworking. She should be responsive to her duties as a wife and mother and capable of multitasking. Of course, as usual, the parameters for fulfilling or falling short of all these are dictated and decided by men and how best or not it favours them. Thus, an Urhobo woman who has the knack for coping with marital challenges through a long-suffering nature has the praise name "*Ayayughe!*" On the other hand, the woman who is sloppy in her attitudes and actions towards her marital responsi- bilities according to patriarchal expectations is referred to as "*Ayada aye!*" Because she fails to fall in line, she becomes the subject of ridicule and shaming in udje songs. Itemi and Tuwevwire are women in udje songs that are censured for being indolent, quarrelsome, greedy, and unable to fulfil their marital obligations. They are thus regarded as burdens or liabilities to their husbands and families. In Itemi's case, her attitude is said to be capable of bringing her husband down or making life difficult for the man. Worse still is that she is lazy yet very greedy! In the same way, Tuwevwire is described as "a lazy woman . . . a chronic ache to her man" (100). She is further depicted as a shrew who sings songs to heckle her husband at home and broadcasts her matrimonial issues in public. She covets other people's property and steals and loafs about town while neglecting her duties as a wife. The impression these songs create is that these women's vices negate the true essence of traditional gender relationships in a patriarchal setting, as the man expects a wife to adeptly take care of his personal comfort as well as taking charge of the smooth running of the home. Anything short of these means she has not conformed and should therefore be shamed!

In all the previous examples of women as subjects, the criticism is direct. Almost all the titles of the songs are the names of the women, so there is no doubt as to who is being addressed in them. However, there are instances where the subject of the song is clearly a man, but a female relative of his, daughter, mistress, wife, or mother, is brought in and equally abused to further hurt or denigrate him. Darah's book has a series of songs composed by a rival of Oloya, one of the most famous poet-performers of udje. In the course of denigrating or deflating his person, the rival ridicules Oloya's women. "Oloya the Fugitive" (Darah 145–146) casts aspersions on Oloya's manhood when he marries a new wife. He achieves this through an allusion to the fact that he (Oloya) "did not share a night with her before she left." In Urhobo, when a young bride leaves her new home even on the first night, it then means she found something wrong with the man, and in this case, she must have discovered that he was not virile or sexually active. Generally, men are quite sensitive to an issue like this being made public knowledge. Their egos are bruised and their status diminished if such news about them goes out. Even though a man might seem accomplished in many areas, if he is unable to perform sexually, then he is deemed less than a man. Oloya's rival avoids directly calling him an impotent man, but uses the idea of a runaway bride to imply that he is one. In another song, Oloya is described as a pauper, thief, and indolent. He is taunted for subjecting his wife to hardships and his mother to mockery by his actions. A beautiful woman elopes with him, but in no time, "Palm oil is Revukperi's pomade," and soon she becomes "A filthy wife who buys on credit and cannot pay" (Oloya the Drifter 146–149). Both husband and wife are described as living on stolen goods from which they grow fat but still look unhealthy and unattractive.

From attacking Oloya's wife, the poet moves to his mother, Kpaenban. He uses her case as an example to upturn the popular notion that a mother of many children enjoys many benefits, as instead her children only cause her shame and grief. All her nine children "grew up to spe- cialise in crime./Developed taste for adultery with neighbours' wives"; thus, "Why wouldn't the mother grieve?" (Darah 153). Sadly, "Kpaenban had many children only to suffer"/What a great pity!" and he seals this impression when he declares "Barrenness is preferable to this kind of motherhood!" (164). Gbogidi is the subject of another reprisal udje song. While much of the attack is on his person, his wife and mother are also mentioned in abusive language. He is mocked for inheriting a wife "with bleached hands and feet/A wife worth fifteen kobo /The man thinks he has married a wife!" (Darah 173). When his mother dies, his abject poverty makes him leave the corpse until it "was now festering with worms" and the family had to arrange "to bury her secretly at night," such that "The corpse of Gbogidi's mother received a token burial/ Like a snake used for rituals" (175–176). This form of shaming does not end only with the man, but, by extension, the family's poverty is also the subject of criticism. Okpako's "Ekueivie" (92–93) is also a satire on a matriarch's kinsmen's inability to give her a befitting burial. There are dire social and spiritual implications in the previous case. M.Y. Nabofa explains that in such a state, the spirit of the deceased, known as *erhi* in Urhobo, is in "a restless situation" and "is said to be in serious agony" (*The Urhobo People*: 367). As a result, the family is taunted for being responsible for the restive spirit of the dead woman wandering aimlessly without a final resting abode.

In traditional Urhobo society, the woman, especially the married woman, is treated as if chattel or a transferable object even without her consent, the reason being the bride price paid, which makes her the man's and his family's property. One of the reasons a girl child is not reckoned with in her natal home is because she is seen as another man's or family's property, as she will eventually marry and leave home to contribute to the growth of her marital instead of her birth home. A husband is chosen for her by the men in her family when she is considered old enough to marry. The husband, as the head of the home, treats her like a second-class citizen and requires her to concentrate only on her duties as a wife and mother and leave almost if not all decision-making in the family to him. Urhobo culture and custom recognizes what Ojaide calls "levirate transfer," a situation where, at the death of her spouse, she can be "inherited" by a younger male relative of the husband. She is shared to another in much the same way his other personal possessions are. This can happen with or without her consent and is one of the mechanisms patriarchy has put in place to further subjugate the Urhobo woman. She is repressed and her right to make a personal choice conscripted. She allows this violation for fear of being cast out of the family fold or, in a situation where her children are still very young, to secure the family's assistance in helping with their upkeep.

The udje songs on this theme further present the intrigues that sometimes go with this practice where men for their selfish gains ensure they ultimately acquire the woman who perhaps has been an object of interest even before her husband's death. Ironically, sometimes a husband's male relative who all along has been bad-mouthing a woman, even branding her a witch, eventually allocates her to himself as a means to an end. "Tefue" (Darah 121–123), "Obiohun" (Ojaide 143–144), and "Noruayen" (Okpako 125–133) present women's predicaments as a result of this anti-women cultural practice. This practice is quite unfair to the woman, who loses a spouse and is almost immediately expected to move over to share the bed of a blood relative of the man. It also does not recognize the woman's right to choose her next partner. It is most likely that, under this type of arrangement, the inherited wife would be marginalized, as she might be the one living outside and often receive the least of the man's affection or care-giving. However, one of the wives in Okpako's "Noruayen" is bold enough to challenge this ill treatment, as she would rather return to her family than agree to be the wife of her "son's age grade" (129). In fact, there is a reversal of gender roles in "Tefue" as Rhupherien, the inherited wife, takes over as the bread-winner of Tefue's large family. This arrangement reveals Tefue's hypocrisy and deliberate subversion of cultural norms for personal benefits, as the woman he once accused of "witchcraft no longer kills/Rather Tefue's sustenance is assured" (123).

Apart from the subject matter and themes, udje is an art form rich in the poetics of language. The songs are transcribed in verse forms that alternate between long and short stanzas. There is also the use of mnemonic devices like repetition and refrain that provide musicality as well as allowing for memorability. The songs attacking women comprise rich imageries in form of descriptive epithets, parallels, axioms, metaphors, and simile through which the character traits or personality of the woman in question are juxtaposed negatively or greatly undermined.

Humour, the kind that is meant to further ridicule or shame the women, is achieved through the use of hyperbole, sarcasm, idiophones, and onomatopoeia. Traditional oral tropes such as proverbs and allusions are used to further deflate or paint an absurd picture of the subject of their attack.

Conclusion

Women have been examined as a minority discourse in udje songs, an Urhobo men's-only oral poetic performance genre. As a result of this, this chapter has been able to establish the fact that Urhobo women suffer relegation and other discriminatory practices that clearly place them in a minority status. The songs with women as subjects or characters show women being censured for sexual misbehaviours, indulging in bad habits, possessing personal defects or disabilities, and even because of their associations or relationships with men who have rivals. They are scorned for being renegades, prostitutes, sirens, witches, liabilities, and others. Women are also excluded from the spiritual rituals involved in udje as if their presence will desecrate the art. From the manner they have been portrayed, it is quite clear that "it is the person whom one can beat that one seeks a fight with!" After all, this genre deliberately excludes women from playing key roles during composition and performance yet consistently censors women's behaviour through the songs.

Many of the cultural and moral offences they accuse women of committing have their standards set and enforced by men. It is the men's expectations of women that determine what is right or wrong, that which is acceptable behaviour or a violation of cultural etiquette. Women are seen as having no expectations of men and are to merely conform to the patriarchal principles of social relationships. Similarly, there is a systematic form of gender discrimination and marginalization promoted by udje songs with women as subjects. This is because, for example, while men are praised for and boastful about their sexual prowess and conquests with no life-threatening physical or spiritual retribution credited to their indulgences, women are abused and made to feel not only ashamed, but whatever calamities they eventually suffer from are ascribed to their sexual indiscretions. Much as udje songs are meant to address threats to communal harmony, by often focusing on women who do not have an equal platform to respond to or defend their actions, they would continue to fall short of achieving one of their major objectives. Therefore, it is a single-sided poetic narrative and would remain a site for gender conflict instead of gender balance or complementarity.

Works cited

Afejuku, Tony. "Tanure Ojaide as a Poet for All Sorts and Kinds: A Reading of Songs of Myself: Quartet- Part 1." *The Guardian*, September 16, 2018. https://m.guardian.ng/art/tanure-ojaide-as-a-poet-for-all-sorts-and-kinds-a-reading-of-songs-of-myself-quartet-part-1/

Clark, John Pepper. "Poetry of the Urhobo Dance Udje." Reprinted in *Radical Essays on Nigerian Literatures*. Ed. G.G. Darah. Lagos: Malthouse, 2008, 105–117.

Darah, Godini Gabriel. *Battles of Songs: Udje Tradition of the Urhobo*. Lagos: Malthouse Press, Ltd., 2005.

Gomba, Obari. "To Oil the Songs: Tanure Ojaide's Dissemination and Udje Aesthetics" *Mgbakoigba: Journal of African Studies* 1, 2012. https://www.ajol.info/index.php/mja/article/view/117178

Hacker, Helen. "Women as a Minority Group." *Social Forces* 30, 1951, 60–69. http://media.pfeiffer.edu/lridener/courses/womminor.html. Accessed February 6, 2019.

Nabofa, Michael Young. "Erhi and Eschatology." *The Urhobo People* (3rd Edition). Ed. Onigu Otite. Ibadan: Gold Press Limited, 2011, 363–387.

Nketia, Joseph Hanson. *The Music of Africa*. New York: W. W. Norton & Company, 1974.

Ojaide, Tanure. *Poetry, Performance, and Art: Udje Dance Songs of the Urhobo People*. Durham: Carolina Academic Press, 2003.

Ojaide, Tanure. *Theorizing African Oral Poetic Performance and Aesthetics: Udje Dance Songs of the Urhobo People*. Trenton, NJ: Africa World Press, 2009.

Ojaide, Tanure. *Indigeneity, Globalization, and African Literature: Personally Speaking*. London: Palgrave Macmillan, 2015.

Ojaruega, Enajite Eseoghene. "The Place of Urhobo Folklore in Tanure Ojaide's Poetry." *Tydskrif vir Letterkunde* 52 (2), 2015, 138–158.

Ojaruega, Enajite Eseoghene. "Songs Only Women Sing: Female Struggles with Identities and Roles in Traditional and Modern Urhobo Poetry." *The Niger Delta Literary Review* 1 (1), 2017, 81–112.

Okome, Onookome. *Writing the Homeland: The Poetry and Politics of Tanure Ojaide*. Bayreuth: Eckhard Breitinger, 2002.

Okpako, David Tinakpoevwan. *Kpeha's Song: Ethics and Culture in Urhobo Udje Poetry*. Ibadan: Book Builders, 2011.

Okuyade, Ogaga. "Aesthetic Metamorphosis: Oral Rhetoric in the Poetry of Tanure Ojaide." *Matatu*, 40 (1), 2012, 33–50.

Olafioye, Tayo. *The Poetry of Tanure Ojaide: A Critical Appraisal*. Lagos: Malthouse Press Ltd., 2002.

Orhero, Mathias Iroro. "Urhobo Folklore and Udje Aesthetics in Tanure Ojaide's In the House of Words and Songs of Myself." *CLCWeb: Comparative Literature and Culture*, 19 (2), 2017, 1–10. https://doi.org/10.7771/1481-4374.3014

Otite, Regina. *The Urhobo Woman*. Ibadan: Gold Press Limited, 2006.

Usanga, Kufre. "Orature and Eco-Engagement in Tanure Ojaide's Songs of Myself." *International Journal of Humanities and Cultural Studies*, 4 (2), 2018, 245–257.

16

VOICES FROM THE MARGIN

Female protagonists navigating power geometries

Oumar Chérif Diop

I concur with Abdul JanMohamed and David Lloyd that minority discourse is a product of damage inflicted on socioeconomic formations and their cultural systems by a dominant power. Such destruction, they posit, results in either deracinating whole populations or decimating them (4). The corollary to the violent transformation of their world is a radical transformation of the populations' in-der-welt-sein (being-in-the-world), to use Heidegger's concept. In *Being and Time*, Heidegger wrote:

> What is meant by "Being-in"? Our proximal reaction is to round out this expression to "Being in the world," and we are inclined to understand this Being-in as "Being in something" as the water is "in" the glass, or the garment is "in" the cupboard. By this "in" we mean the relationship of Being which two entities extended "in" space have to each other with regard to their location in that space. . . . Being-present-at-hand-along-with in the sense of a definite location-relationship with something else, which has the same kind of Being, are ontological characteristics which we call "categorial."

Then, being needs to be conceived and analyzed in terms of the order and the relations it entails in a given space. In other words, to quote Alain Badiou, "A world is not an empirical totality of everything that exists. The world is always relative to the structure of order immanent to the world" (82). Relationality, which is co-substantial to space, also has to be viewed diachronically. To understand the nature, scope, and impact of the damage caused to the "in" by the changes in positions within spaces requires us to consider the time factor in our analysis. As Doreen Massey puts it in "Concepts of Space and Power in Theory and Political Practice," "if space is constantly being made, if it is the ongoing product of relationships and exchanges, then while it is most certainly a dimension that is different from time, it is certainly not a dimension with no temporality within it" (17–18). The destruction that JanMohamed and Lloyd theorize and the ensuing sociopolitical and economic transformations indicate that a sequence of events happened to subvert an order of things which Massey refers to as power-geometry, a product of relations, which are dynamic social, political, cultural, and economic processes:

> In that sense, power-geometries precisely exemplify the conceptualization of space as always under construction. The spatial as imbued with temporality There are

geometries of power in all instances of society. Moreover, they relate to each other and, if there is any general tendency, it is that they are likely to reinforce each other. For that reason, the real functioning of a power-geometry within the political will also depend on that within the economic that within the distribution of educational resources, that within the cultural sphere, and so on.

(22–23)

Thus, the aforementioned dismantling of socioeconomic formations is imbued with processes of reconfiguration of various relations of power within those formations. In different parts of Africa, the role of social groups in economic and political processes changed from the precolonial to the colonial era, for example, the ways in which colonial authorities have manipulated the relations between ethnic groups in African countries or how post-independence African leaders have managed such relations. Therefore, it is imperative to consider Heidegger's "being in the world" not just as ontological but rather as existential and in relation to positionality in a given power-geometry. What does that "being in the world" offer in terms of privilege? Of what does it deprive subjects? What alliances and conflicts are determined by that "being in the world?"

Taking into account all the previous, it appears that because of the collapse of their previously functional socioeconomic and cultural systems, populations that are victims of the aforementioned damages may be marginalized and their identities and languages adversely affected. Under such circumstances, the two options they have to choose from are either to accept their subjugation to the new rule of dominant forces or to strive to preserve their languages and identities. The history of the colonized in Africa, Asia, the Americas, and the Caribbean is replete with struggles and strategies to transform the negative subject position of the oppressed into a positive one.

Besides, minority discourse should not be used as a unitary concept without regard to internal divisions within subaltern communities along ethnic, caste, or gender lines. In precolonial Africa, where women's role was paramount in the predominantly agriculture-based labor pool, the dismantling of indigenous socioeconomic formations had an adverse impact on households' financial well-being. As a result, in Nigeria, for example, women's loss of their social, political, and economic status was far more severe than men's:

> The new colonial economic order favored men more than women. Men and boys were trained in skills needed to manage newly introduced technologies and were also employed in the Native Courts, the transport industry, in the mines, the Christian missions, and expatriate trading companies. Women's access to Western education – the gateway to modern employment – was limited by its dual-gender structure that emphasized domestic science training for girls and leadership and technical instructions for boys. Access to the newly introduced British money also favored men more than women through the male-dominated cash crop economy and the colonial gendered employment policy that discriminated against women. Colonial economic policy favored men more than women in access to land, extension services, high-yielding palm seedlings, fertilizer, demonstration farms, oil presses, kernel crackers, pioneer oil mills, cassava graters, loans, and other innovations and new technologies that put men in a position to dominate the export and local economies of the region. With the above advantages, men penetrated and controlled female economic spheres. As a result, most Igbo women were pushed to the informal and petty sector of the colonial economy.

> *(Chuku 88–89)*

To their systematic exclusion and marginalization, women responded with various forms of resistance: boycotts, strikes, and demonstrations against colonial authorities. Igbo women remained steadfast and undeterred by colonial violence and pursued the struggles that earned them both economic and political successes. Before the most publicized Igbo Women's War in 1929, women's rebellious stances included demonstrations over the colonial control of market-places in 1916 and the Nwaobiala Movement to restore societal order and preserve Igbo heritage in 1925. Following the 1929 Women's War, in the 1930s, they demonstrated against colonial taxation and against produce inspection in the 1940s–1950s.

Like the Igbo in Nigeria, among the Kikuyus in Kenya, women's dominant role in agriculture gave them power in their community. Thus, economic policies imposed by the English colonizers, while exploiting women's labor, eroded their power. The ensuing women's resistance led to the development of their political consciousness and, in some cases, to their oath of allegiance to the Mau Mau movement. The Kikuyu people of Kenya, like most Africans, were laborers, with the women doing the most work at home while the men found work across the country. Following World War II, the British mandated the vaccination of all cattle and the terracing of all hilly landscapes for better production. Running the risk of being severely punished, women resisted the increased workload:

> The punitive action of the English towards the resistant women was a representation of their interpretation of gender roles. The women's passive resistance, as seen by their defiance of new farming regulations, and their active resistance within the Mau Mau, a violent men's organization that was an expression of Kenyan nationalism, was treated as the English intended to view it and therefore, not necessarily recognized with the validity it deserved. The colonial reaction against the passive wing of the movement was a useful indicator of the way in which the colonial authorities conceived the involvement of women in Mau Mau. While the participation of women in the Mau Mau was a "demonstration of the maturity of these women's political consciousness," colonial governments saw the protest as "an instrument of men's political action." However, the women, as members of this nationalist, political movement, followed the same rules for inclusion as men which included taking part in the oath that came with Mau Mau involvement. The oath was shrouded in ritual and secrecy and inherently violent. Yet it appealed to these women because it represented "ethnic and cultural cohesion." The oath and the movement, though violent, represented a means to an end of restrictive and oppressive colonial policies that altered their role in society. The women, in taking this oath, gained new responsibilities in the struggle against colonial power in spite of the English's attempt to minimize their role both within the movement and within society.
>
> *(Flood)*

Based on their own Victorian concepts of gender roles, the colonizers failed to understand the degree of women's commitment and involvement in the Kikuyu liberation movement. More disconcerting was the fact that, in spite of their sacrifices in the struggles, women were marginalized, cast in the shadow after independence.

In Senegal, novelist and filmmaker Ousmane Sembène explored in his film *Emitai* the anti-colonial struggles of Jola women in the southern province of Senegal, Casamance, in the 1940s. In spite of colonial authorities' violent repression against those who stood against *l'effort de guerre* (the war effort) during WWII, Jola women remained undeterred. Jolas offer rice to the spirits; it is also their staple food. Thus, women's resistance to colonial tyranny has both religious and economic implications. Pfaff opines that, women's fecundity being embodied in the rice/milk she produces, her fight is both to maintain tradition as well as her own integrity (341). While protesting against taxation during WWII, the Jola community found a leader in the young priestess Aline Sitoe Diatta. After the successful women's boycott of the market, she was eventually arrested by French authorities and deported to a jail in Timbuktu, Mali, where she died in 1944.

Before Aline Sitoe, another anticolonial female spiritual leader, Nehanda, emerged in Rhodesia in the 1890s when the British tried to subjugate the natives. She was captured at the end of 1897, brought to trial in 1898, and summarily sentenced to death by hanging. Nehanda's dying words, "My bones will rise again," meant that after her death, other nationalists would pursue the anticolonial struggle.

In Algeria, during the 1954–1962 revolutionary war, female activists challenged their marginalization in male-dominated environments. In 1956, some of them joined their male counterparts in a series of terror bomb attacks launched by an anticolonial guerrilla network. However, women remain skeptical about men's commitment to ending patriarchal rule and promoting women's emancipation. In 1958, during a nationalist meeting at the Casablanca Labour Exchange, a group of Algerian women spoke before hundreds of men, saying:

> You make a revolution, you fight colonialist oppression, but you maintain the oppression of women; beware, another revolution will certainly occur after Algeria's independence: a women's revolution!
>
> *(Nedjib Sidi Moussa)*

Given how patriarchy was entrenched in Algeria in 1959, female voices rose to indicate that the liberation of Algerian women could not be contingent on fighting colonialism. Recent events have proven them right. In 2016, Amira Merabet, a 34-year-old woman, was burned alive for refusing a man's advances. In the 1990s, Islamists assassinated women, including 17-year-old Katia Bengana, who refused to wear the hijab (Nedjib Sidi Moussa).

During the Arab Spring, Arab women played a central role in toppling dictators, but their dreams for expanded women's rights have been thwarted by perennial patriarchal structures and the rise of Islamists. In Egypt, for example, the rise of the Muslim Brotherhood to power signals the beginning of an era of declared war against women's rights activists. The Muslim brothers were staunch opponents to a UN declaration on women's rights. For their leader and former president of Egypt Mohamed Morsi, a woman's only legitimate aspiration is to be a mother devoting her life to her husband and children. Rampant gender violence, trafficking, and high rates of genital mutilation make Egypt the country with the worst women's rights records throughout the Arab world (Egypt "*Worst in Arab Women's Rights*"):

> The problem goes far beyond tongue-flicking, whispers, vulgar come-ons and groping. The gang rapes on Tahrir Square during the demonstrations for the ouster of President Hosni Mubarak and in support of his Islamist successor Mohamed Morsi sparked global outrage – but were only the tip of the iceberg.
>
> This type of mob violence against women has marred public gatherings for many years. The culprits often include state-sponsored provocateurs who, regardless of who happens to be in power, are hired to infiltrate and disrupt protests, discredit the opposition and, through systematic scaremongering, exclude women from the political process. According to a report by the International Federation for Human Rights (FIDH),

the so-called Baltagiya – thugs and gangs employed by the government – have existed since the 1990s. The report says that sexual violence is a "historic weapon of the Egyptian authorities," regardless of who happens to be in power.

(Violence Against Women)

Thus, violence against women is fundamentally a political weapon used by men in their fight for control. It is also a ghastly signifier of the exclusion of women from the public, political sphere, hence the indiscriminate use of Baltagiva and sexual violence as a weapon of war by men, regardless of their political or ideological affiliations. However, women were resolute and brave enough to ride the tidal waves of change that ousted dictators like Ben Ali in Tunisia and Hosni Mubarak in Egypt. In her article "On Egyptian Women after the Arab Spring," Nesreen Salem writes:

When history books reflect on modern Egypt, we will read the "official" version of the story but we will never read the stories that matter: her stories. We will not hear the voices of millions of women who stood shoulder to shoulder, together, on 25 January 2011. Yet the revolution diary is filled with pages upon pages of the tribulations of Egyptian women.

Our previous remarks on space and power-geometry and Salem's reflections on the Arab Spring remind us of Spivak's pronouncement about woman as a subaltern. She posits in "Can the Subaltern Speak?":

Within the effaced itinerary of the subaltern subject, the track of sexual difference is doubly effaced. The question is not of female participation in the insurgency, or the ground rules of the sexual division of labor, for both of which there is "evidence." It is, rather, that, both as an object of colonialist historiography and as the subject of insurgency, the ideological construction of gender keeps the male dominant. If, in the context of colonial production, the subaltern has no history and cannot speak, the subaltern as female is even more deeply in shadow. As such, the woman is doubly in shadow.

(287–288)

The previous examples from Nigeria, Kenya, and the Arab world prove women's involvement in productive economic activities and their participation in insurgent movements. The examples also show that male-dominant ideological constructions of gender run through precolonial, colonial, postcolonial socioeconomic formations. Most importantly, they underscore the fact that, in spite of their contributions to economic production or liberation movements, women are coerced to remain doubly in the shadow. The subsequent section focuses on female protagonists in a few African works of fiction to prove that point. Central to our study are the ways in which those protagonists respond to silencing strategies.

La Vie et Demie

La Vie et Demie takes place in an imaginary country, Katamalanasie, ruled by a ruthless, bloodthirsty tyrant. Despite all his power, he cannot subjugate his fiercest opponent, the rebel Martial. When he eventually captures and kills Martial, the latter refuses to die the way the despot wants him to die. Martial's ghost continuously torments the tyrant, who ultimately commits suicide.

To avenge Martial's death, his daughter Chaidana lures the regime's dignitaries with her body, and kills them.

In *La Vie et Demie*, Sony Labou Tansi seems to suggest that violence as a means to impose a hegemonic discourse is quite often met with resistance. The main protagonist Martial is not alone in challenging tyranny. Chaidana invents efficacious alternative ways to fight against despotism:

> Elle acheta la peinture noire pour trois millions, engagea un gérant avec fausse mission de revendre la peinture, en réalité elle organisa une véritable campagne d'écritures. Elle recruta trois mille garçons chargés d'écrirepour la nuit de Noël toutes les portes la célèbre phrase de son père: "Je ne veux pas mourir cette mort."
>
> *(44)*

> She bought black paint for three million, hired a manager with a false mission to sell the painting, in fact she organized a real writing campaign. She recruited three thousand boys charged to write on Christmas night on all the doors her father's famous sentence: "I do not want to die this death."

This battalion of fearless "pistolegraphers" was able to write graffiti on gates inside the presidential palace and, even more daring, on the bodies of high-ranking army officials.

As a strategist, Chaidana shows that she does not need her father's interventions to chart the course of her actions, reminding us of Scheherazade defying her father to deploy her strategy with the sultan. For Chaidana, as long as the insurgency is dependent on a messianic figure like Martial, it cannot capitalize on the wisdom of marginal, minority voices. When Martial realizes that Chaidana is escaping his overbearing omnipresence to chart new courses, he assaults her, and rapes her.

This is a clear demonstration that minority discourse cannot be used as a unitary concept. Moreover, a minority leader who represses other minority voices is not fit to chart an emancipatory path to oppressed minorities; Martial's incestuous act disqualifies him as a leader and redefines the emancipation agenda. Through her father's monstrous violation of her body, Chaidana learns that when the emerging minority heroes stifle the voices of their constituents, processes of change either reach a stalemate or are eventually betrayed. In that regard, Chaidana's initiatives remind us of the predicament of Arab women activists, who were assaulted and raped during the Arab Spring because they dared to join the movements for political change and to uphold the banner of women's rights.

When the rebellion marginalizes minority voices, it loses the capacity to capture all relevant aspects of people's lives and aspirations; it also shuns sources of rejuvenating vigor. The solutions to the oppression of minorities are to be found in the polyphony of all marginalized voices. Martial's ghostly presence in the past years may have had an enduring impact on the minds of the despotic ruler to a point of emasculating him. It might also have had an adverse psychological impact on those dreaming of a Martial-led emancipation. Chaidana's initiatives underscore the fact that neither Martial's charisma nor the collective trauma his assassination caused is sufficient to design winning strategies. Such an endeavor calls for fresh living ideas, not an aura of a martyr, who can certainly galvanize the people but may also lead them to an impasse. After being raped by Martial, Chaidana is gang-raped by the militia. Her ensuing pregnancy signals a bastardization of the cause for which she has fiercely fought.

Martial's reprehensible betrayal of Chaidana is an instance of Labou Tansi's deconstruction of the myth of the messianic liberator and the silencing of those minorities cast into the shadow, like women. Through Chaidana's stand and predicament, *La Vie et Demie* suggests that freedom of oppressed minorities is a result of the convergence of all their emancipatory initiatives. In spite of her father's ignominious act, Chaidana pursues her fight against tyranny and leaves a body of works published posthumously: *Les Mots font Pitié (Words Make You Sad)*; *Mon Père s'appelait Martial (My Father's Name Was Martial)*. If, according to Jacques Lacan, the Name of the Father is what defines, structures, and regulates the symbolic/phallic order, Chaidana's book sounds like a proclamation of her emancipation from the phallocentric order.

Later in the novel, Chaidana-aux-gros-cheveux, Chaidana's daughter, spends years in the forests and is filled with its secrets. After those years, she makes a pledge to win the war her grandfather lost. She declares, "My grandfather had lost the war. He had lost a war. I will invent another one. Not the one my mother had lost. If I do not win, the earth will fall apart. These things come to me as if they were part of me long before I was born. My blood shouts it out. Go and win! Without thinking." Until the end, Chaidana-aux-gros-cheveux fights fiercely against injustice and tyranny. She becomes a staunch opponent to her son, who rules Yourma with an iron fist, and organizes the resistance against tyranny with thirty of her grandsons. In a four-hundred-page letter to her son the tyrant, Chaidana-aux-gros-cheveux writes,

> l'enfer, l'enfer. Les gens savent-ils que l'enfer correspond à la mort de la vie, qu'il cor-respond à la mort de la liberté? Les pères ont crée l'enfer, que les fils cherchent ailleurs. Trouver. Qui ne sait pas que trouver est un drame? Trouver c'est l'enfer, laisse nous chercher, papa. Et il y'aura un temps où chaque homme sera une forteresse, nous com-mençons ce siècle-là. . . . Il faut vaincre la mort de la vie, parce qu'elle est plus odieuse que la mort de l'être.
>
> *(152)*

> [Hell, hell. Do people know that hell is the death of life, that it corresponds to the death of freedom? The fathers created hell, which the sons look for elsewhere. To find. He who does not know what to find is a drama? Finding is hell, let us search, Dad. And there will be a time when every man will be a fortress, we begin this century. . . . We must defeat the death of life, because it is more odious than the death of being.]

For Chaidana-aux-gros-cheveux, freedom is quintessential to life. As such, she equates its absence to death. Most importantly, she points at the so-called fathers of the nations as the sole assassins, who deprive people of their lives/freedom. In the life trajectories of Chaidana and her daughter Chaidana-aux-gros-cheveux, Labou Tansi draws attention to non-unitary aspect of minority groups, which may cast into the shadow other subgroups. As discerning and politically conscious subjects, Chaidana and Chaidana-aux-gros-cheveux are able to identify and locate the oppressors from within. Furthermore, there are lessons to be learned from their resilience, their sagacity, and their pugnacity that have allowed them to hold the banner of social justice, undeterred.

I now turn to two other women, Isma and Hajila in *A Sister to Scheherazade*, to find out what their trajectories reveal about their emancipation strategies in another patriarchal setting.

A Sister to Scheherazade

In her article "Sisterhood and Rivalry In-between the Shadow and the Sultana: A Problematic of Representation in Ombre Sultane," Anjali Prabhu considers *A Sister to Scheherazade*, Assia Djebar's version of "The Thousand and One Nights" (81). After her divorce, Isma arranges via a matchmaker her former husband's marriage with Hajila. In alternate chapters, Isma, the first-person narrator of the novel, recounts her own story and Hajila's in the second person. Having lived all her life in crass poverty, Hajila is lured into the marriage by the prospect of a luxurious life; so is her mother, who wholeheartedly agrees to marry her daughter to a wealthy suitor. Touma's dream for a better future is further entertained by the husband's financial support and his promises to get his in-laws out of the shantytown. After the marriage, Hajila has to put with an uncaring husband/drunkard, and endures being raped by him:

> You fumble with your collar, you start to unbutton your blouse. He has got out of bed, he grabs you by the shoulders, the patch of light from the lamp seems to diminish his action, while casting long shadows into the four corners of the room, as in a dream. You clench your teeth.
>
> Rape! Is this rape? People assert he is your husband, your mother always refers to 'your master, your lord' . . . he has forced you down on the bed, you try to fight him off, finding unexpected sources of strength. You are crushed beneath his chest. You try to wriggle free from under the weight, you stiffen your arms convulsively against your sides, bracing yourself as he clasps you to him. The man's arms tighten around you, then relax their grip, you bend your legs, not daring to kick, not trying to escape. A battle fought on a mattress in a tangle of crumpled sheets. . . . When the man's penis ruptures you, with one rapid sword-thrust, you scream out in the silence, breaking your silence.
>
> *(57–58)*

The deitics "I" for Isma and "you" for Hajila first points to the fact that Hajila has no control over what is told about or done to her. Isma, on the other hand, the "I," has freed herself from the strictures of patriarchal matrimony. With an unconscious structured, among other things, by phrases and pronouncements like "your master," "your lord," it is not surprising that Hajila refrains from kicking her husband and instead surrenders to his brutal sexual assault. The violence germane to her conjugal life, the ominous silences that surround her, all day long, her monotonous existence in crippling powerlessness makes her feel like being in a jailhouse, and she envies the men,

> who can all go forth into the sunshine! Every morning, you splash water over your face, neck, and arms. These are not the ablutions preparatory to prostrating yourself in prayer; no, they are a preparation for the act of leaving the house. Oh, to be able to leave the house.
>
> *(9)*

Goaded by men's freedom, Hajila tries to break free from her stifling entrapment by roaming the streets every day after her husband and the children leave the house. Feeling nervous at first, she wears her veil and wanders around town. Once her burning desire for freedom dispels her apprehensions, she takes off her veil during her daily escapades. Her husband not only beats her when he eventually finds out; he also tried to blind her with a broken beer bottle. Leaving the apartment and unveiling herself are both expressions of Hajila's desire to reclaim her body entrapped in a patriarchal system. However, relying on surreptitious wanderings proves ineffective even after getting duplicate apartment keys from Isma. It is only after her abortion that she seems relieved of domestic and matrimonial duties. By terminating her pregnancy, she frees herself from patriarchal tyranny. However, she could not have done it without Isma's help.

Nada Elia, in her book, *Trances, Dances, and Vociferations: Agency and Resistance in Africana Women's Narratives*, argues that the novel "reinscribes the message that women's solidarity can help them escape patriarchal oppression, while their internecine rivalry aggravates it" (34). In her book *Assia Djebar in Dialogues with Feminisms*, Priscilla Ringrose opines that the novel underscores the imperative need for sisterhood and solidarity among women under patriarchal siege. I concur with her that the relationship between Isma and Hajila "begins in ambiguity and ends in solidarity" (24). I would further add that Isma's first motives when arranging Hajila's marriage are opportunistic, informed and framed by her knowledge of how patriarchy operates in this socioeconomic formation. After realizing that because of her selfish scheme, Hajila has been victimized, Isma decides to help Hajila escape. The knowledge of how patriarchy works should be used by women to raise awareness and bolster their resistance to it. I would also contend that the fight against patriarchy requires solidarity among both men and women.

The Forbidden Woman

The way solidarity helps women in the fight against patriarchal tyranny is central to Malika Mokkedem's novel *The Forbidden Woman*. It starts with the main protagonist Sultana's return to her native Aïn Nekla, the village where she had grown up, to attend the funeral of her former lover, Dr. Yacine Mediane. From the airport to the village, she is dismayed by the nosy taxi driver interrogating her and young boys yelling "whore" at her. At the village, Sultana meets Yacine's best friend, Salah Akli, an Algerian doctor practicing in Oran. Even though Salah is unhappy about the way Sultana abandoned his friend, he stands by her against the conservative Islamists who want to exclude her from the burial procession. Then, Sultana encounters Vincent Chauvet, a French professor of mathematics who fell in love with Algeria and vowed to visit it after being the recipient of the kidney of a young Algerian woman, who died in an accident. Vincent meets a young girl named Dalila, who has been helping her to navigate the sociocultural restrictions of the local community. She used to be very close to Yacine and became Sultana's friend. Both Vincent and Salah fall in love with Sultana, who does not seem to reciprocate their feelings.

The hostility Sultana experiences from the town leaders causes her to suffer from anorexia. Concomitantly, she is tormented by the tragic loss of her parents. While progressively recovering thanks to help from her male friends and the village women, the leaders set fire to Yacine's house. In the face of such violence, Sultana has to flee. However, given the aspirations of the children and the solidarity of the women, there are reasons to hope for a brighter future. The battery of questions the taxi-driver hurls at Sultana as soon as she enters his vehicle: "Whose daughter are you?" "So, whose place are you going to in Aïn Nekla?" are germane to a gender hierarchy Sultana refuses to be drawn into. Any man in her country believes he has the innate right to interrogate and control any local woman. She fends off the driver's rudeness either by remaining silent or with her non-committal reply: "No one." Sultana's terse replies and her staring at the driver in the rearview mirror make him lose his temper. "The man stares at me in the rearview mirror and yells 'No one' doesn't exist. And there's no hotel" (6).

Sultana is further startled when a young boy calls her "whore" to the driver's satisfaction as the taxi is driving off. And Sultana comments:

> Treacherous word, for a long time, I was able to write it only in capital letters, as if it were women's destiny, their only divinity, the lot of rejected women. With satisfied eyes, the man observes me in the rearview mirror. Our eyes are glued to each other, size each other up, confront each other. Mine defy him, tell him how vile he is. He's

first to lower his eyes. I know he'll hold this offense against me. I try to concentrate on the countryside.

(8)

Sultana uses silences; pithy, meaningless replies; and daring gazes to boldly defy the driver and the patriarchal system he represents. It is the representatives of that system, who want to exclude Sultana from burial procession:

> The fire in his eyes is unequivocal. He ends up retracing his steps and coming toward me.
> "Madam, you can't come it's forbidden!"
> Salah takes me by the arm. "Forbidden? Forbidden by whom?"
> "She can't come! Allah doesn't want her to!"
> Well it so happens that Allah told her she could! She came from very far away for this!"
> "You are profaning the name of God!"
> "No more than you are!"
> And pulling me by the arm, Salah drags me along with him. The man remains silent.
>
> (15)

Beside the irreconcilable ideological stands this tense exchange reveals, on one hand, it underscores the determination of Salah and Sultana to challenge the predominant Islamist discourse of exclusion spread by the Front Islamique du Salut (FIS)/Islamic Salvation Front. On the other hand, it suggests that to come to terms with Islamist patriarchal ideology, Algerian men and women should stand together. However, such a coalition has to overcome its internal contradictions that appear in the heated exchanges between Sultana and Salah, who scolds her for her defiant, risky, and provocative attitude, which triggers village men's persecution of her. The question is whether moderation is a winning strategy in the face of the Islamists' agenda to exclude or obliterate the Other. Salah's admonition infuriates Sultana, who perceives it as an attempt to contain and dampen her free spirit. Salah may have a point because the townswomen use efficiently silence and dissembling to fight against the Islamists' restrictions. In the fight against sexist fanaticism, the women of Ain Nekhla have been conspiring in silence to defend Sultana accused of moral turpitude by the Islamists. When the latter move to oust Sultana from her physician's position at the hospital, women make them retreat by aggressively confronting them. In so doing, the coalition of women thwarts the Islamist patriarchal discourse:

> Most of the women, their backs up against his (the mayor's) outrageous behavior, refused to leave the place. I didn't have time to react when they rose up and barred his passage to the hallway. "We're going to squish you, flea of our misery!" One of them screamed. He backed up.
> "We're going to make you drink all of your arrogance," cried out another woman.
> "They were moving forward one step. He was backing up two. They were seething with rage. Suddenly, he was pale and mute under the assault of their sarcasm . . .
> So martyring and throwing into the street your own women will never be enough for you? You still have to ogle the neighbors' women and expect to control those women who infinitely out of your reach?
>
> (139)

Sultana is doubly appreciative of this heroic showdown in which women shield her, and make her realize that, in actual fact, they are "a wall of silence cemented together in unity." In silence, they process what is going on in their community. As a result, their clear understanding of the working of the power geometries hostile to the minority they constitute allows them to design winning tactics in their fight against the mayor and his accomplices. When Khaled refers to them as "speechless and full of fury," he does not anticipate that with their male allies, they will torch the city hall after the mayor's mob sets Yacine's house alight. This is a protracted war against social injustice, which has cast women in the shadow for so long.

In the following section, I will look into how Assia Djebar returns to that theme in "The Woman in Pieces," published in her collection of short stories *The Tongue's Blood Does Not Run Dry*.

"The Woman in Pieces"

Assia Djebar's "The Woman in Pieces" takes place during the Black Decade,[1] the ten-year Algerian civil war that claimed an estimated 200,000 lives. Atyka, a young teacher, is recounting Scheherazade's story "One Thousand and One Nights" to her students. The tale starts with the discovery in Baghdad of a woman cut into pieces, wrapped in a barely blooded veil, folded in a precious carpet, kept in a coffin, which is locked in a trunk. Infuriated by the discovery of this odious crime, the caliph instructs his minister and childhood friend Djeffar to find the culprit or, in his stead, be killed with his forty cousins. Djeffar is temporarily saved from the gallows when the husband of the woman confesses, having committed the crime out of jealousy. However, the caliph finds the husband pardonable since he acted in reaction to the black braggart, who slandered the young woman. Consequently, Djeffar is ordered again to find the culprit or be hanged. Djeffar finds the culprit, who happens to be his eunuch, and proposes to tell a story to the king and only be sentenced to death if the story is not entertaining enough.

Assia Djebar's "The Woman in Pieces" ends with the assassination of the teacher and activist Atyka during the Algerian Black Decade.

The intertextual construction of Assia Djebar's "The Woman in Pieces" results in a multivocal narrative shifting from Scheherazade's autodiegetic voice to Djaffar's and Atyka's intradiegetic and extradiegetic voices, respectively. Scheherazade's voice rises for those dead women slain by the emir and for all women to be safe from blind, revengeful jealousy. Scheherazade does not step forward for self-preservation. Instead, she chooses to marry a psychopath, risking her life in order to save thousands of women. She only relies on her encyclopedic knowledge and her words of wisdom to restore the king's sense and dispel his prejudice against women. Armed with her stories, she eventually ends the kings' vindictive slaughter of women.

Through Djeffar, Scheherazade shows the king the extent of the abuses against women and the need for judicial procedures to protect them. However, Djeffar's story also underscores how worthless the life of a woman is under the patriarchal system. Djeffar is more concerned about the life of his slave and eunuch than seeking justice for the woman cut into pieces. Such brutality against women foreshadows the brutal slaying of Atyka by the Islamist patriarchal system. Both the Black Decade and the Arab Spring have shown that such a system is always ready to rape and kill women who dare tear their shroud of silence and walk out of the shadow. At the end of her stories, Scheherazade is free and helps save women in the kingdom. As for Atyka, she is caught at a point in Scheherazade's story when the king is still blinded by his warped view of women. At the very moment,

> One of the boys in the last row of seats whispers, "The gendarmes!" Later, he will say that he had the impression that they were all part of the scene in front of the caliphs Baghdad palace. "Yes," he will repeat, days later, "I really believe that the sultan Haroun

el Rachid, who I thought was so terrible, such a dictator, who I felt on the sidelines, menacing us, had sent his guards to punish us. But for what?

(122)

During Algeria's Black Decade, coordinated attacks against civilians: death squads, massacres, abductions, kidnappings, rape, and the murder of entire families claimed an estimated 200,000 lives. By the turn of the new millennium, the Algerian security apparatus had succeeded in infiltrating and dividing the insurgent groups. During those years of utter chaos, the gendarmes' license to kill is reminiscent of the psychopath king, who indiscriminately murdered women because of their gender. Even though the discriminating factors were fundamentally political, religious, and professional, each side was doubly merciless when it came to silencing female voices. As a group whose voice is doubly shrouded in silence, women were neither safe with the Islamists nor with the gendarmes.

In Scheherazade's voice, Atyka is able to draw her students' attention to the social injustice and the predicament of women. However, if her story were to emulate Scheherazade's, it would have to integrate lessons from the insurgencies that failed to truly emancipate women from patriarchal tyranny. After the gendarmes decapitated Atyka, she manages to end Scheherazade's tale, and start hers.

Later on, Atyka's student Omar says that Atyka's last words were not Scheherazade's; they were her own: "Each of our day is a night, a thousand and one days, here at home, at . . ." (124)

"The body; the head. But the voice? Where has Atyka's voice taken refuge?" (125) Atyka's voice survives her, and hopefully, as Nehanda predicts before her death, it will emerge from her refuge to enlighten and galvanize those in the shadow when the time is right.

In her novel *Woman at Point Zero*, Nawal el Sadaawi seems to argue that death cannot silence a dissenting voice. Let's look at how the main protagonist's voice outlives her.

Woman at Point Zero

Nawal El Sadaawi's *Woman at Point Zero* is another tale of resilience and pugnacity set against the backdrop of a patriarchal society. The novel is the saga of the stoic female protagonist Firdaus, who is doubly in the shadow. At the start of the novel, a psychiatrist researching inmates at a women's prison has tried in vain to have an interview with the main protagonist Firdaus, accused of murder and awaiting her execution. Firdaus rarely eats or sleeps; she never talks and never accepts visitors. As the psychiatrist is about to leave the prison, the warden comes to her with an urgent message that Firdaus has agreed to speak to her. Firdaus describes her poor childhood in a farming community, where she was circumcised and later molested by her uncle. Upon her graduation from high school, Firdaus's aunt convinces her uncle to arrange her marriage with old Sheikh Mahmoud. Firdaus runs away and experiences a string of abuses from her hosts, from pimps, from policemen, and so on. Eventually, Firdaus's success in the prostitution underworld attracts the attention of the pimp Marzouk, who repeatedly beats Firdaus and forces her to give him larger percentages of her earnings. Firdaus ends up killing him and is sentenced to death. As she is finishing her story, armed policemen come to escort her to the gallows:

J'ai traversé les siècles en silence, exclue du cercle du parlant, étouffée par le brouhaha du désir des hommes et de leur commandement. Je n'ai pu m'exprimer que par chuchotement et n'ai bénéficié de complicité que muette . . . Maintenant que je suis sortie je ne rentrerai pas, maintenant que j'ai parlé je ne me tairai pas.

I went through the centuries in silence, excluded from the circle of speaking, stifled by the hub-bub of the desire of men and their command. I was able to express myself only by chuckling and have benefited from complicity only dumb . . . Now that I have come out, I will not return, now that I have spoken I will not be silent.

(my translation)

This passage from Fazia Zouari's *Pour en finir avec Sharazad*, quoted by Jane Evans in his book *Tactical Silence in the Novels of Malika Mokeddem* (13), could be Firdaus's proclamation of con-quered freedom and agency. At the beginning of the novel, Firdaus's muteness is a calculated attitude to make sure that her story is entrusted to a trustworthy steward, who will later be her mouthpiece. Through her life journey, Firdaus grasps the dynamics of the exploitive patriarchal system and eventually confronts "the multiple manifestations of her culture-punishing mascu-linities" (Royer 292). Firdaus's life has been charted by the phallocentric script, which has made her submit to the dictum of patriarchal order and has coaxed her to always surrender to the will of her male counterparts.

In *Woman at Point Zero*, Firdaus's identity as a shadowy subaltern is defined and established through violence, rejections, and deprivations. The string of humiliations, abuses, and betray-als she goes through are meted out by parents and relatives, policemen, religious leaders, and political activists, thus incriminating institutions like family, religion, education, and the political system. However, Firdaus's trials, tribulations, and her encounters with various breeds of preda-tors make her aware of the dynamics of the patriarchal system, which allows her to proclaim her ideological emancipation.

Ultimately, the level of consciousness that Firdaus attains through her life journey leads to her killing of a pimp who is trying to control her. Firdaus is then sentenced to death and executed. Unfortunately, Firdaus's willful enactment of selfhood did not change the status of a woman as a double shadow subaltern. Instead, to a certain extent, a mutation process unfolds through the psychiatrist's telling of Firdaus's story. Alas, Firdaus's very act of speech only results in a partial triumph over the patriarchal system. Were it not because of the demise of women's activists during the Arab Spring, we might have posited that Firdaus's narrative might have contributed to the constitution of a true collective subject that can defeat patriarchy. The consolation is that beyond point zero, Firdaus's voice has joined the chorus of women and human rights activists that articulate messages of resilience and pugnacity, which are tearing the shroud of silence that maintains women in the shadow.

In Sony Labou Tansi's *La Vie et Demie*, Chaidana declares that "there will be a time when every man will be a fortress; we must defeat the death of life, because it is more odious than the death of being." For Firdaus, the death of life is to surrender to tyranny. By defying her oppres-sors, she manages to transform herself into the impregnable fortress where her arms open wide to embrace the night as her voice starts to hum her freedom song:

I hope for nothing
I want for nothing
I fear nothing
I am free.

Conclusion

After considering the origins of minority discourses, I have contended that it is imperative to look at them not as unitary but as multiplicities shaped by the hierarchies which structure the power-geometries that produce them. Taking into account precolonial, colonial, and post-colonial socioeconomic formations as well as recent historical upheavals such as the Arab Spring and the Black Decade in Algeria, I have drawn attention to the exclusion of women from discursive spaces. A study of female protagonists in selected African works of fiction has shown the dynamics of power within minorities and the chasm that exists between dominant and marginal groups. The chapter has also highlighted the ways in which those female protagonists have responded to the strategies deployed by tyrannical powers to subdue and silence them and how, in return, the protagonists and their allies initiate or envision processes of de-silencing.

Note

1 When Islamist parties were poised to win in the early 90s, the government canceled legislative elections. The Islamists launched a violent insurgency, initially targeting the army and police, and then civilians. In their attempts to quell the insurgency, state security forces often killed indiscriminately.

Bibliography

"Across the Arab World, a 'Women's Spring' Comes into View." *Christian Science Monitor*, Aug. 2017. www.csmonitor.com/World/Middle-East/2017/0809/Across-the-Arab-world-a-Women-s-Spring-comes-into-view

The Arab Spring in Egypt. https://rlp.hds.harvard.edu/faq/arab-spring-egypt. Accessed 24 Mar. 2019.

"The Arab Spring: What Did It Do for Women?" *Middle East Monitor*, 24 Jan. 2014. www.middleeastmonitor.com/20140124-the-arab-spring-what-did-it-do-for-women/.

Badiou, Alain. *The Subject of Change: Lessons from the European Graduate School*. Edited by Duane Rousselle. New York: Atropos Press, 2013.

Benramdane, Djamel. "Algeria: A Long and Dirty War." *Le Monde Diplomatique*, 1 Mar. 2004. https://mondediplo.com/2004/03/08algeriawar.

Chuku, Gloria. "Igbo Women and Political Participation in Nigeria, 1800s–2005." *The International Journal of African Historical Studies*, Vol. 42, No. 1, 2009, pp. 81–103.

Djebar, Assia. *A Sister to Scheherazade*. Portsmouth, NH: Heineman, 1993.

Djebar, Assia. *The Tongue's Blood Does not Run Dry*. Translated by Tegan Raleigh. New-York: Seven Stories Press, 2006.

Dreyfus, Hubdert. *Being-in-the-World: A Commentary on Heidegger's Being and Time, Division I*. Cambridge, MA: The MIT Press, 1991.

Egypt. "Worst in Arab Women's Rights." 12 Nov. 2013. www.bbc.com, www.bbc.com/news/world-middle-east-24908109.

Evans, Jane E. *Tactical Silence in the Novels of Malika Mokeddem*. Amsterdam-New York: Rodopi, 1994.

Flood, Cassidy. "African Women's Role in Resistance against Colonization." *The Classic Journal*. http://theclassicjournal.uga.edu/index.php/2016/03/23/african-womens-role-in-resistance-against-colonization/.

Foundation, Thomson Reuters. "FACTBOX-Women's Rights in the Arab World." *News.Trust.Org*. http://news.trust.org/item/20131111115632-hn9t2/. Accessed 18 Mar. 2019.

Hallward, Peter. *Badiou: A Subject to Truth*. 1st edition. Minneapolis: University of Minnesota Press, 2003.

Heidegger, Martin. "Being and Time: PDF Free Download." *Epdf.Tips*. https://epdf.tips/being-and-time 64c5819fc7078380463780223ac95ac731195.html. Accessed 24 Mar. 2019.

Hornsby, Roy. "What Heidegger Means by Being-in-the-World." http://royby.com/philosophy/pages/dasein.html. Accessed 23 July 2010.

JanMohamed, Abdul R. and David Lloyd. *The Nature and Context of Minority Discourse*. New York: Oxford University Press, 1990.

Labou Tansi Sony. *La Vie et Demie*. Paris: Éditions du Seuil, 1979.

Lia, Nada. *Trances, Dances, and Vociferations: Agency and Resistance in Women's Narratives*. New York and London: Garland Publishing, Inc., 2001.

Manzoor, Saima. "Crossing the Threshold: A Critical Analysis of Women's Subversion and Solidarity in Assia Djebar's *A Sister to Scheherazade*." *Journal of Research in Humanities and Social Science*, Vol. 5, No. 10, 2017, pp. 32–34.

Mokeddem, Malika. *The Forbidden Woman*. Translated by Karen Melissa Marcus. Lincoln and London: University of Nebraska Press, 1998.

Moussa, Nedjib Sidi. "Algerian Feminism and the Long Struggle for Women's Equality." *The Conversation*. http://theconversation.com/algerian-feminism-and-the-long-struggle-for-womens-equality-65130. Accessed 18 Mar. 2019.

Pfaff, Françoise. "Myths, Traditions and Colonialism in Ousmane Sembène's Emitai." *CLA Journal*, Vol. 24, No. 3, 1981, pp. 336–346.

Prabhu, Anjali. "Sisterhood and Rivalry in-between the Shadoe and the Sultana: A Problematic of Representation in Ombre Sultane." *Research in African Literatures*, Vol. 33, No. 3, Fall 2002, pp. 70–96.

Ringrose, Priscilla. "Assia Djebar in Dialogues with Feminism." *Rodopi, 2006 Reflections on Women in the Arab Spring*. www.wilsoncenter.org/sites/default/files/International%20Women%27s%20Day%20 2012_4.pdf.

Royer, Diana. *A Critical Study of the Works of Nawal El Saadawi, Egyptian Writer and Activist*. Lewiston, NY: Edwin Mellen, 2001.

Saadawi, Nawal El. *Woman at Point Zero*. Translated by Sherif Hetata. London: Zed Books, 1990.

Salem, Nesreen. "On Egyptian Women after the Arab Spring." *Daily News Egypt*, 1 Oct. 2013.

Sarr, Fatou. "De Ndaté Yalla à Aline Sitoé: un siècle de résistance." *Communication faite au Musée de la femme de Gorée le*, 3 février 2007.

Sexual Violence as a Weapon of War. www.unicef.org/sowc96pk/sexviol.htm. Accessed 24 Mar. 2019.

Shahrazad as a Feminist: 1457 Words | Bartleby. www.bartleby.com/essay/Shahrazad-as-a-Feminist-F35H UN4CDB6S. Accessed 24 Mar. 2019.

Spivak, Gayatri Chakravorty. "Can the Subaltern Speak?" *Marxism and the Interpretation of Culture*. Edited by Cary Nelson and Lawrence Grossberg. Urbana: University of Illinois Press, 1988, 271–313.

Steiner, George. *Heidegger*. Hemel Hempstead: The Harvester Press Limited, 1978.

Toliver-Diallo, Wilmetta J. "The Woman Who Was More Than a Man: Making Aline Sitoe Diatta into a National Heroine in Senegal." *Canadian Journal of African Studies/Revue Canadienne des Études Africaines*, Vol. 39, No. 2, 2005, pp. 338–360.

"Violence against Women: 'As an Egyptian Woman, You Spend Your Entire Life Dealing with Sexual Violence: Spiegel Online-International." *Spiegel Online*. www.spiegel.de/international/tomorrow/almost-every-egyptian-woman-is-subjected-to-sexual-harassment-a-1198328.html. Accessed 24 Mar. 2019.

Women and the Arab Spring | UN Chronicle. https://unchronicle.un.org/article/women-and-arab-spring. Accessed 24 Mar. 2019.

"The Years of Black Decade in Algeria." *About Algeria | Discover Algeria*. www.aboutalgeria.com/2018/07/the-years-of-black-decade-in-algeria.html. Accessed 23 Mar. 2019.

17

RESPONDING FROM THE FRINGE

Women, Islam, and patriarchy in Nigerian Muslim women's novels

Saeedat Bolajoko Aliyu

Introduction

Discourse on gender relations affirms that there are entrenched practices and beliefs in societies which restrict women and subvert opportunities open to them. These practices are more emphasized in many African societies, especially as the African woman's access to the agency of representation came decades after African literature was established and populated by male writers. This resulted in the foregrounding of many negative stereotypes about femaleness in early African literature. The African Muslim woman seems doubly challenged; her gender and the selective and oftentimes over-application or misapplication of the tenets of Islam in matters concerning her combine to reinforce her subjugation. The initial resistance to Western education and its inability to penetrate and make significant impact in the already established Islamic societies of Northern Nigeria may have added to the slower response of women writers who write in English to emerge and take ownership of the agency to depict themselves, especially when compared to their male counterparts or other female writers in the larger Nigerian society. A large number of Nigerian Muslim women writers come from the northern part of the country, and this is not by chance. The north of Nigeria is where the first contact with Islam happened before the religion spread to other parts of what is today called Nigeria. In fact, the religion and its teachings had been established in Kanem by the end of the 13th century before traders and scholars spread its reach to other parts of the north in the early part of the 14th century (Fafunwa 53). The 1804 Jihad of Uthman Dan Fodio further spread and consolidated Islamic culture to more parts of the north. There is therefore a dominance of Muslims in the region and a corresponding dominance of the influence of Islam on the people. It is worthy of note that Islam is not just a religion; it is a way of life that is complete with a system of education that is drawn from the Arabic language, a legal system based on Islamic jurisprudence (Sharia law), and a culture that is influenced by the Arab way of life. With the teachings of Islam covering all aspects of human life, it is inevitable that aspects of indigenous cultures will be integrated into the dominant Islamic culture, so much so that some of the integrated cultural practices are taken to be authentic precepts of Islam.

This chapter takes a religio-geographic perspective to the interrogation of the term "Northern Nigeria." The religious delineation is based on the fact that while the region spans a wide area that is inclusive of diverse ethnic groups and religions, the issues explored in this present work are done from the perspective of Islam, the dominant religion of that part of Nigeria. The geographic breadth of the study is also limited to the core Hausa/Fulani/Kanuri areas which, by virtue of the dominance of Islam, have practices which are influenced by the religion. The rise in the number of northern Nigerian Muslim women writers and the ways their works explore issues that affect women and girl-children, especially in settings that in the main have Islamic influences, prompt a conclusion that their response is akin to that coming from the fringe in a determined effort to write/right their stories. In her delineation of minority groups, Sarah Song describes as cultural minorities groups who "demand measures aimed at countering social and political marginalization and disrespect, including revaluing disrespected identities and transforming dominant patterns of communication and representation" (1). Northern Nigerian women writers fit this mode, as their works address issues that impact their femininity and existence. This chapter therefore considers northern Nigerian Muslim women writers as a minority group in the sense that they write against popular but discriminatory practices carried out on the female gender in their region. Their works can thus be categorized as writings from the fringe of popular cultural practices as they seek remedies for, and an end to, the disadvantages their gender encounters in the region. They are responding from the fringe given the fact that they write from a patriarchal society about turning the tide against patriarchy. The exploration of gender issues in the selected novels will thus focus on areas which reveal discriminatory relations between the male and female characters. These areas include education, marriage and marital relationships, divorce, economic rights, and access to justice.

There are growing numbers of female writers who have joined Zaynab Alkali's hitherto lone voice in the creative arena. It is therefore imperative that studies are carried out on how they are telling their stories. How are these contemporary northern female writers depicting issues that affect women in that region? How are the writers depicting Islam and women in their works? Are they conforming to or resisting patriarchal modes in their depictions of women and the roles assigned to female characters? If they are resisting patriarchy, what form is the resistance taking? Are there underlying ideological influences in the choices they make? The depictions by the selected women writers will be examined against the background of the dictates of Islamic law to reveal if they too are not selecting, over-applying, or misapplying the tenets of Islam in their bid to depict issues and characters. I will carry out this discussion with Razinat Talatu Mohammed's *The Travails of a First Wife*, Azizah Idris's *A Sackful of Wishes*, and Hadizah Isma El-Rufai's *An Abundance of Scorpions*. The methodology will be qualitative using the African feminist theory to explicate the gender-related matters that emerge from the texts. Interviews with two of the authors – Azizah Idris M. and Hadizah Isma El-Rufai – provide other biographical/ideological details which can be said to have contributed to the choices the authors made.

Conceptualizing womanhood in Islam

The religion of Islam is one which legislates on virtually every aspect of human life. The Holy Quran and the Hadith (the sayings and actions of the Prophet Mohammad) form the primary sources of legislations on all human activity and interaction among Muslims, while the consensus of learned scholars constitute the secondary source. In the Holy Quran, God is said to state that:

> O mankind! Reverence Your Guardian-Lord, who created you from a single Person, created, of like nature, His mate, and from twain scattered (like seeds) countless men and women; – Reverence God through Whom ye demand your mutual (rights), and reverence the wombs (that bore you): for God ever watches over you.
>
> *(Surah 4, verse 1)*

This verse indicates the absence of superiority of one sex over the other before God, as they both have the same origin and are conferred with rights and responsibilities. This is again reinforced by the enunciation of responsibilities assigned to both sexes:

> The Believers, men and women, are protectors, one of another: they enjoin what is just and forbid what is evil: they observe regular prayers, practice regular charity, and obey Allah and His Messenger. On them will Allah pour His Mercy: for Allah is Exalted in power, Wise.
>
> *(Surah 9:71)*

These two quotes from the Quran reveal the primary purpose of the sexes, which is to reverence God and what is right upon each other. However, cultural practices impinge upon this purpose, such that Muhammad Qutb, in his book *Islam the Misunderstood Religion*, describes women as "respectable being[s] and it was not permissible for anyone to find fault with her or backbite her . . . or hold her in contempt due to her functions as a woman" (183–184). That there is widespread disregard of this description, even in Muslim-dominated societies, is a function of both deliberate and inevitable erosion of the dictates of Islam by indigenous cultures and individual whims to facilitate the emergence of social orders which overtly privilege men. This is quite visible in the society this work centers on.

In an attempt to contextualize the rights of women in Islam as contained in Quran 2:228, a report on *Promoting Women's Rights through Sharia in Northern Nigeria* issued by the Centre for Islamic Legal Studies of the Ahmadu Bello University, Zaria, Nigeria, relates these rights within the precepts of "family relationships." The report highlights the concept of reciprocity as instrumental both in understanding and formulating a framework for protecting women's rights in Muslim societies, especially as the religion promotes familial ties. The reciprocity which the report advances promotes the conceptualization of women's rights in Islamic societies as:

> arising from a system of mutual rights and obligations guaranteed by both religion and law. Women's rights in general are not unreciprocated burdens placed on society, or gratuitous favours done them, but compensatory gestures arising from an equitable distribution of claims and burdens within the society,
>
> *(8)*

This understanding situates women's roles and responsibilities within the context of a system which recognizes them as functional and important members of societies. It is from the position that women's rights in Islam arise from a system which accords rights and conversely extracts obligations from them that this chapter examines how three selected northern Nigerian Muslim women authors depict the rights and responsibilities of their female characters. These three northern Nigerian Muslim women authors represent a selection of emerging northern Nigerian female novelists who write in the English language. This implies that there are other female writers, quite a significant number, actually, who write fiction and other genres of creative writing in the many indigenous languages of the northern region of Nigeria.

The selected novels all focus on women and the challenges they face in patriarchal societies. Mohammed's work *The Travails of a First Wife* chronicles the lived experiences of Zarah, a first wife in a polygamous marriage. It details her challenges in the hands of an insensitive husband and two co-wives who are also caught up in the intricate web of societal expectations and patriarchal institutions. Idris's novel, *A Sackful of Wishes*, focuses on a young girl's experience as a new wife to a man whose psyche is negatively affected by the toxic relationship between his parents.

235

El-Rufai, on the other hand, focuses in the novel *An Abundance of Scorpions* on the travails of a young woman who loses her husband and daughter in the same accident and is faced with the financial burden incurred by her late husband. These three stories, though varied in focus, are, however, related in the facts that the central characters are women who must find ways to survive either psychologically, emotionally, or financially in societies where they are considered appendages to their husbands or a male member of their family. Similarly, the religious identities of the central characters and the societies in which they are set indicate the presence and influence of a blend of Islamic and Hausa/Fulani/Kanuri cultural practices.

Womanhood in sexist society

Fatma Osman Ibnouf (11) avers that the particularity of a given culture influences women's rights and the gender relationships inherent in that culture. Northern Nigeria is inarguably an established patriarchal society that has so been conditioned "by culture and an over application of some tenets of the major religion" (Aliyu 60). This claim can only be argued against from the perspective that the region is neither mono-religious nor mono-cultural to warrant a blanket statement. However, given the delineation of the scope within which this concept is engaged in this paper, it is a claim that can be made. A significant number of creative works allude to the sexist nature of the region. Though women are more often the victims of sexist practices, female writers from the region are prominent in the depiction and condemnation of such practices which restrict women from enjoying rights accorded them, especially those accorded by the religion of Islam. Some of these works include Zaynab Alkali's *The Stillborn* and *The Virtuous Woman*, Asabe Usman Kabir's *Destinies of Life*, and Balarabe Ramat Yakubu's *Sin Is a Puppy That Follows You Home*. Access to agency is obviously a crucial and fundamental form of empowerment alongside enlightenment, as it enables the holder to express not just opinion and desire but, importantly, provides the tool to negotiate and demand for fair dealings.

Depiction of female characters in the selected novels

A survey of contemporary northern Nigerian female writings reveals a conscious ideological perspective in the ways female characters are portrayed. Female characters are usually rounded, with significant focus on their growth and development. They are strong willed in facing the challenges associated with their femininity. El-Rufai responds to an interview question on why she portrays her female characters the way she does that, "There is the stereotype of the Northern Nigerian Woman that some people believe applies to all. When we write and get our voices heard, the world will have an alternative view, and dare I say, a more authentic perspective" (interview conducted with Hadizah Isma El-Rufai). This implies that there is a conscious ideological engagement among contemporary northern Nigerian women writers to subvert the stereotypical depictions of the northern Nigerian Muslim woman as meek, weak, and totally unaware and unresponsive to contemporary happenings within the society.

The role of education and access to agency is a central motif in the ways these women writers depict their central characters. Education is central, as it is crucial to an individual gaining awareness of her rights and responsibilities. It must be noted here that education need not be the Western form but any means that will accord the woman access to knowledge of her rights and access to attaining such rights. Idris affirms this with the major protagonist Hadiza in *A Sackful of Wishes*. Hadiza's knowledge of Islam, which she acquires in an Islamic school, ingrains in her the realization that her husband – Abdulrasaq – is going beyond the bounds of the dictates of the religion in the way he treats her and his parents. Hadiza is so emphatic about her knowledge of her rights that she tells Abdulrasaq's friend on the eve of her wedding that "I'm also an ustaziya, he won't tell me how Islamic weddings are done" (Idris 88). Her declaration of being a female scholar distinguishes her as a character with full awareness of her rights and responsibilities. It is this awareness that she holds on to later in the plot to take a decisive move against the abusive marriage in which she finds herself. Mohammed's lead female character, Zarah, is a university graduate who in spite of her restrained personal character traits speaks out when the ill treatment from her husband comes to a head. She shows awareness of her rights as a wife in a polygamous marriage and states the risks her husband faces when he will stand in judgment before God should he persist in depriving her of her rights. Worthy of note also is the fact that Zarah's co-wives are educated. Kellu, the second wife, is studying for her postgraduate degree, and Fantare, the third, is an undergraduate in a Nigerian university. Both Kellu and Fantare are studying for these degrees as married women. Tambaya in El-Rufai's work is also a graduate from a Nigerian university who uses her university certificate as a tool to seek employment with the primary aim of paying off her husband's debts so as to rescue his soul from condemnation arising from his unpaid debts. That all the female lead characters show awareness of their rights and responsibilities as wives and daughters, including their readiness to carry out their responsibilities in spite of incidences where their rights are infringed upon, suggests the emergence and foregrounding of a strong northern Nigerian Muslim female identity. This is counteracting previous perceptions and depictions of an accepting and unchallenging women population. That these writers are not compromising on depicting educated female protagonists is also an indication that concerns over the "girl child" education may not be as prominent as it was earlier depicted in northern Nigeria. In the selected novels, none of the lead female characters is challenged by a lack of education, western or Islamic. This can be considered a subtle ideological conditioning that promotes the Islamic precept that commands all Muslims, irrespective of their sex, to seek knowledge as far as China. What the selected authors achieve with educating their protagonists is the creation of female characters that, in spite of the inhibitions of culture, are contributing to the development of the family and society. This is especially so in *An Abundance of Scorpions*, where Tambaya, with the aid of her university degree and exposure, rises above the constraints imposed on her femininity. To another degree, Hadiza in *A Sackful of Wishes* is depicted as proactive when she starts a hair-making business to care for herself and her children when her husband stops providing for her. She had agreed to marry Abdulrasaq before completing her Islamic education, which is not an entirely unlawful move. The Centre for Islamic Legal Studies report affirms that "removing the girl-child from school to marry is in itself not contrary to Sharia provided she is given the opportunity to continue from the husband's house" (9). However, in spite of Hadiza's request to her husband to allow her go back to school after the wedding, she never does have the opportunity. Irrespective of her limited formal education, Hadiza is portrayed as fully aware of her rights, roles, and responsibilities not just to her husband but, importantly, to herself.

Marital relations and gender challenges

Early marriage of girls was a prominent issue in older works about northern Nigeria, and it is a reflection of the Islamic prompting to mitigate the rate of immorality in the society by allowing mature girls to explore their sexualities within the anticipated safety of matrimony. The selected works in this study, however, do not engage with issues of early marriage. Idris in her novel has the youngest female protagonist. Hadiza is sixteen years old and in a senior secondary class as at the time of her marriage. Idris depicts Hadiza's father as being against early or forced marriages. Though Hadiza is old enough to be married under Islamic law, she has her father's assurances that there will not be any forced marriage; "I also know that Baba does not believe in forced or arranged marriage. He always tells us that we should choose someone we are ready to spend the rest of eternity with" (Idris 31). This is an authentic Islamic practice, as "[n]owhere does the Qur'an or the Prophet (SAW) speak with approval of coercive authority" ("The Center for Islamic Studies"). Idris thus succeeds in bringing to the fore the illegality of forced marriages, either early or late. Idris, like Mohammed and El-Rufai, shows the importance of the female's consent to a union in Islam. It is a rupturing of cultural precepts which overlook the consent of the female. In Mohammed's novel, *The Travails of a First Wife*, Kellu, the second wife, gets married in her late thirties just as her friend Bilki is thirty-five years old and unmarried. In Kellu's case, the author describes the situation thus:

> Kellu was the kind of girl that people referred to as having over stayed without a man to call her own . . . After her National Youth Service, her father had *waited patiently* for her to bring home someone ready to engage him in discussions for the hand of his dear daughter, but no one did.
>
> *(Mohammed 31–32, emphasis mine)*

This may be an indication that arranging and coercing an unwilling bride may no longer be a popular culture in contemporary northern Nigeria. The Center for Islamic Studies report confirms the reduction in the number of early marriages in urban centers (10). It may equally be ideological to push the Islamic position that the woman's consent is an ingredient to the legality of the union. The Sharia ruling on coercing a woman into marriage is that such a woman has the right or option to repudiate the union. However, societal pressures upon the female to get married may still be prominent given Mohammed's description of popular opinion about Kellu's unmarried state. It must be stated here, though, that societal pressure on unmarried females is not peculiar to northern Nigeria.

Audee T. Giwa's opinion that "concern with the girl education, early marriage and polygamy is by now tested and rested, even temporarily, as the society has since moved forward" (312) is, however, problematic. Giwa makes this assertion in relation to the works of the leading northern Nigerian female writer, Zainab Alkali. Although part of Giwa's position on girl education and early marriage can be corroborated through the selected novels for this study, the inclusion of polygamy in the mix underestimates the challenges inherent in the practice and the concern writers show about it. Both Idris and Mohammed focus on polygamy in their novels. This is a pointer that the issue and the challenges of its practice are anything but tested and rested. As a form of polygamy or plural marriage, polygyny is the practice of one man having more than one wife at a material time. In Islam, there is a prescribed maximum number of four wives at any given time. Ibnouf (6) notes, however, that polygyny is "neither required nor encouraged, but simply permitted under extraordinary circumstances." These circumstances for which polygyny is permitted include when there is a high rate of unmarried, divorced, or widowed women in the society who are desirous of the benefits of marriage and there is a lack of a corresponding number of men capable of marrying them; a wife's inability to conceive or bear children, especially when the husband is desirous of children; and a wife's ill health which restricts sexual relations or her inability to satiate her husband, among others. The verse of the Holy Qur'an which talks about polygyny is unequivocal about the condition under which a man is permitted to engage in the practice: "Marry women of your choice, two or three or four; but if ye fear that ye shall not be able to deal justly (with them), then only one" (Surah 4:3). This indicates an overriding injunction to regulate the number of wives permitted any man. Fairness and justice in handling the multiple women according to this verse limit that right to plural marriages. It is instructive that non-conformity to this regulation is more of the norm.

Mohammed in her novel is the most vocal of the selected novelists in her depiction of the culture of non-conformance to God's law on polygyny. The title of her novel, *The Travails of a First Wife*, is a give-away of the central concern of the story. She places emphasis on the practice of polygyny, highlighting the challenges women encounter in the practice. These challenges range from physical to psychological and sometimes financial injustices. Zarah, the principal character in the story, is subjected to all of these challenges. Her husband, quite insensitively, marries two women on the same day. While there may be no particular injunction on the number of wives a man can marry in a day, Islam encourages that in the light of the importance of maintaining familial love and tranquility, a man should discuss "with his wife and prove to her the necessity for remarriage, assure her that he will observe justice and equality among his wives, and obtain her consent in any fair manner possible" ("An Introduction to the Rights and Duties of Women"). The manner in which Zarah's husband – Ibrahim – informs her is expectedly traumatizing:

> "Zarah, I have come to rub pepper as it were, to your wounds at this time of night". He did not intend to waste any time on the matter . . . "In four days I will be getting married not to one woman but . . . two women", the last words came as a grunt from the back of his throat but it was direct and succinct.
>
> *(Mohammed 56)*

While recognizing the pain his words will cause Zarah, Ibrahim succinctly informs her of his intension to marry two more wives in one day but fails to give her any assurance that he will be fair in his treatment of all the women. The reactions of Kellu, one of the two women Ibrahim marries on the same day; her family; and other characters in the story reveal the extent of Ibrahim's insensitivity and highlight both the patriarchal nature of the society and the jettisoning of Islamic injunctions in favor of personal desires. Kellu's aunt, Hajia Danna's, words that:"Men are wont to do such things without knowing what the women involved feel" (Mohammed 46) captures the lack of empathy for the woman who is about to begin sharing her husband. Ibrahim's friends' admiration of his "show of manhood" (Mohammed 68) and the seemingly general acceptance of his simultaneous marriage to two women on the same day is an indication that "it is a man's world" (Mohammed 46).

Idris, on her part, explores polygyny as a secondary issue in her novel. She portrays it through her lead character's parents: Hadiza's father, Mallam Musa; his first wife, Mairo Lauje; and, her mother, Binta, also called Inna. Idris shows that the success or otherwise of polygyny lies in all parties concerned working in tandem. She depicts Mallam Musa as striving unsuccessfully to ensure peace and equality between his two wives, but the first wife, Mairo Lauje, resists and works against it. That the practice ends up causing physical, financial, and psychological trauma to most of the characters involved, including children, may be an indication that the practice is fraught with pitfalls in spite of obvious gains. Mairo Lauje, the crux of Mallam Musa's unsuccessful practice of polygyny, is a bitter woman who, despite all efforts to ease her distaste, still reacts violently. She goes as far as engaging diabolical means to break the union between her husband and the new wife. The author depicts Mallam Musa as a man who wishes to practice polygyny within the ambit of the injunctions from God when he replies to Mairo Lauje's slave-binding conditions of accepting a co-wife that "Binta also has an equal right to this house as much as you do. She is someone else's daughter. I refuse to agree to your conditions" (Idris 9). Mallam Musa marries a second wife when Mairo Lauje fails in performing her duties of companionship to him. The novelist affirms in an interview with this writer that "sometimes women are the nemesis of other women . . . But just like in real life the men are not always the villains likewise in the story world" (Interview with Aziza Idris M.). This is an obvious strength in the way contemporary women writers characterize women. There is no overtly romantic depiction of womanhood in positive lights without a corresponding awareness that not all women can be good or progressive.

In El-Rufai's novel, reference to the practice of polygyny is not central. The protagonist, Tambaya, is propositioned to by her late husband's brother Suleiman in a way that emphasizes the permissive nature of the society which allows men contract marriages without considering the feelings of the women:

> "I'm happy you've decided to stay with us", he said . . . "We can make it permanent, you know" . . . "Maryam likes you, and she is not the jealous type," he said, and then winked at me. "Her father also has two wives." That was when I realised that this was, in fact, a marriage proposal.
>
> *(El-Rufai 26)*

Suleiman's assumption that Maryam, his wife, would not be jealous, especially given her pedigree, attests to the insensitivity in the ways men acquire more wives. Tambaya eventually accepts the proposal of another married man – Alhaji Surajo – who woos her and convinces her that he and his wife have grown apart (El-Rufai 314).

That the three novelists write about the practice of polygyny, albeit in differing degrees, makes it topical even without any significant attempt to shift popular perception about its acceptability. This is indicative of the general acceptance of the practice, and this can be explained in view of the fact that polygyny is one of the permissible acts in Islam. What is, however, significant is that there are no incidences where that type of marriage is depicted as working. All participants in plural marriages in the selected novels are depicted as enmeshed in psychological turmoil. This may also be ideological as a way to show that its practice is fraught with pitfalls. Of all the female characters involved in polygyny in the selected works, only Mairo Lauje in Idris's novel is depicted as decisively and openly rejecting the practice. In view of the challenges of maintaining justice and fairness within the practice of polygyny, Mairo Lauje's negative and diabolical traits, however, take away from her crucial points in rejecting a plural marriage where neither justice not fairness can be emphatically achieved.

Perspectives on divorce

Divorce in Islam is considered "the most detestable of the permissible things in the sight of God" (Centre for Islamic Legal Studies Report 18). The right to repudiate a marriage belongs to both sexes, though the form of repudiation differs. While men may divorce their wives by proclaiming it thrice on separate occasions, women need the intervention of a court for the dissolution. Dissolution under Islamic law is allowed when there is failure in the achievement of the objectives of the union. Some of these include loss of affection, incompatibility, unfulfilled sexual relations, and inability to procreate, among others. The prolonged process in attaining divorce is an indication of the abhorrence of the act and the expectation that there might be a rethink and reconciliation before the legal separation. Islamic law also prescribes a humane manner in the proclamation and execution of divorce by a man on his wife. In the selected novels, Mohammed and Idris provide insights into the ways divorce is carried out by both sexes, and these depictions allow perspectives into the ways gender relations implicate women in divorce situations in northern Nigeria. In Mohammed's novel, it is the man who initiates the process. Acts of disobedience are pitched as capable of invoking a proclamation of divorce, as the author notes:

He called her back and requested that she sat on the table with him. It was impossible for her to refuse him that because they both knew the consequences could cost her the marriage if she did not at least, obey some of his demands. She could refuse him her body only if she was unwell but she could not refuse to obey his other demands. He was the man and head of the home.

(Mohammed 51)

In another situation, Ibrahim threatens her by attempting to write out the divorce proclamation when she insists that their illegitimate son, Babagana, stay with them (Mohammed 133). Eventually, Ibrahim does make the first proclamation when Zarah refuses to sell her house:

"I asked what your decision on the sale of the house was!" She took her time before responding. "I should not sell the house Ibrahim", "I should not or I will not, Zarah?" "The house stays." "In that case, this marriage is over" . . . Finally, Ibrahim uncoiled his over six feet frame and looked down from that exalted height at the crumpled woman on the floor. He threw a sealed envelope towards her head and the paper fell on her back as she was crouched on the floor on her two hands.

(Mohammed 201)

Mohammed's depiction of Zarah as helpless and resisting divorce stems from the religious nature of northern Nigeria, which prescribes that a woman should always be under the authority of a man, either her husband or a male member of her family. This is why the author describes Zarah as "scared because the society was a conservative one that still did not recognize a woman if she was not appended to a man, as wife" (Mohammed 220). The appending of women to men inevitably limits women's capability to strike out on their own. At the death of her husband, Tambaya in El-Rufai's novel is depicted as restricted to either staying with her in-laws or going to her brother in Ghana; "To maintain her respectability in the eyes of society, a woman had to live under the protection of a husband or male relative, even an in-law" (El-Rufai 24). Tambaya eventually defies cultural and religious expectations when she is unable to secure employment in Accra. The debt of her husband needs to be paid and she realizes that "living with a guardian could be very complicated. At forty-one years of age, it was time to throw away my crutches" (El-Rufai 93). El-Rufai's analogy of crutches to describe the effect of appending women indicates a radical break with established practice, especially given the fact that it is a known precept in Islam. This particular author is emphatic in her stance about what and why she writes what she does when she says in the interview that: "As for censorship, I always try to be honest in what I write. A writer has to be courageous. At the end of the day, I am not looking for anyone's approval. I just want to tell my own truth. So I don't self-censor" (Interview with El-Rufai). El-Rufai's depiction of her lead character striking out despite religious inhibitions is to facilitate the greater good of rescuing her late husband's soul and saving her father-in-law's property. This is why she describes the strength her lead character exhibits as coming from a need to create strong female characters "because I want them to serve as role models to my female readers. When a woman sees another woman from the same culture as her, a woman whom she can relate to, occupying a position of authority, it can serve as an inspiration" (Interview with El-Rufai).

Hadiza in Idris's novel takes a different turn; she initiates the process of divorcing her husband when she can no longer take the psychological turmoil, lack of care, and insensitivity he shows to her. She leaves for her grandmother's home and declares that since Abdulrasaq has refused to divorce her, she will take him to court. Her grounds for seeking annulment are "ill-treatment, a threat to her health and rape" (Idris 194). Her success in divorcing Abdulrasaq opens her to other forms of psychological turmoil as he continues to threaten her. Her cousin, Ya Muzakhir, steps in by taking her to another state.

The three female protagonists in the selected novels are depicted as having peculiar strengths in the face of the varying challenges they face. Zarah in Mohammed's *The Travails of a First Wife* initially comes off as timid and accepting of all her husband does to her. She would have fit the stereotypical northern Nigerian Muslim woman, especially in the ways she meekly allows Ibrahim to deprive her of her rights, in the way she resists divorce, in accepting the other wives' bullying, and even in relinquishing her conjugal rights to the other wives. However, her actions can be defined as acts of revolt which show her as strong in the face of patriarchal social expectations. For instance, she stays on in the marriage with Ibrahim not because she cannot live without him but for a number of reasons. The first is to guard the secret of her illegitimate son, Babagana, who would lose all respectability should his illegitimacy be publicly known. She also agrees to limit Babagana's visits to the house to forestall any connection of his paternity being made to Ibrahim. Her continued marriage to Ibrahim also provides a platform for her to operate unhindered in the sexist society in which she exists. Mohammed depicts her as knowing that she needs the protection "that only marriage could provide" and "in her head, she had plans to establish herself as an estate owner, starting with the house in Damaturu" (Mohammed 220). Zarah relinquishes her claims to sleep in their husband's room, reconditioning "her mind to forget that she was a married woman whose body also needed male companionship" (Mohammed 192). All of these show Zarah as a character who assesses situations and exploits loopholes for the attainment of her goals despite the fact that she suffers for them. She learns invaluable lessons from an elderly woman – Hajjia Saudatu Waziri, who had married eight different men – that society would judge a woman on her failures, not on the factors that led to her failing (Mohammed 149).

Tambaya in El-Rufai's *An Abundance of Scorpions* is challenged by the need to pay off her late husband's debt. She decidedly seeks for and secures employment away from where she will come under the authority of male relatives. This is to allow her to fulfill the financial responsibility on her. She goes against cultural expectations by living on her own in an orphanage in Abuja and works assiduously to gather funds to pay off the debts. El-Rufai does not allow Tambaya's break with religious/cultural regulations to compromise her depiction of Tambaya as an upright woman who is facing contemporary challenges of unemployment, financial instability, and even advances from men. Rather, what the author succeeds in doing is creating a character that refuses to be handicapped by customs and religion. Tambaya therefore becomes the epitome of a contemporary woman who, in spite of limitations, rises above them without compromising her status as an upright woman.

For the character of Hadiza, she is depicted right from the start as knowledgeable. In spite of her young age, she is painfully aware of her mother's status in her father's home, especially in the eyes of her father's first wife, Mairo Lauje. Her depiction as an observant, kind, and thoughtful young girl sees her marrying Abdulrasaq despite her awareness that it will be a difficult marriage. She agrees to marry him when he offers to loan her father a significant amount of money to pay off her father's debt, a debt incurred when Mairo Lauje's son sells off caps he had been commissioned to make. Hadiza suffers for eight years, risking induced abortion from Abdulrasaq's cruel machinations, the loss of a child from neglect, hunger, rape, emotional turmoil, and financial instability. She takes the initiative to return to her home and seeks and obtains a court injunction dissolving the union that has brought her so much pain.

Economic empowerment plays a significant role in the ways these female characters carry out their rights and responsibilities. Hadiza takes up hair-making when Abdulrasaq stops providing for her. He in turn tries to stop her when he discovers that she is not as pliant from starvation as he would have her. Zarah in Mohammed's novel attains a status which her husband, Ibrahim, is uncomfortable with. Zarah is a civil servant and owns an apartment house, both of which have the capacity of conferring on her some degree of economic independence. Ibrahim insists she sells the house or he will divorce her. Tambaya, though spared the intrigues of an overbearing husband, voluntarily leaves her nursing job to care for her newborn daughter. She, however steps into the role of salvaging her late husband's soul when she determines to pay off the debts he incurred.

In all these, the recreation of a new image of the northern Nigerian Muslim woman is inevitably emerging from women's writings from northern Nigeria. Islam is also becoming a conscious tool used by contemporary women authors to challenge culture-established practices that are inimical to the growth of female characters. Rather than misapplying the precepts of the religion, there is the conscious and appropriate deployment of the precepts of the religion in their application. This, in more ways, grants authenticity to their portrayals, as they are verifiable facts.

Conclusion

The agitation for the rights of women the world over is similar to those championed by the selected authors, who are doing so under Islamic law. The subjugation of women's rights in societies that function under Sharia law has had an unnecessarily negative impact on the religion. Nawal El Saadawi, the vocal Egyptian feminist, is notable for her condemnation of the patriarchal Arab society. This condemnation is reflected in her depiction of women as servants and appendages to their husbands who in turn are portrayed in her works as "heartless, selfish and cruel, they are morally depraved" (Alkali 14–15). However, historical events in the time of the Prophet of Islam, even in the early years of the introduction of Islam to northern Nigeria, do not support the perception that the culture of Islam oppresses, subjugates, or discriminates against women in the ways that are recorded in contemporary times. There are clear indications that the education of women in particular was considered important by the vanguard of the 1804 Jihad, Uthman Dan Fodio (Abdul Raheem 28). Zaynab Alkali identifies a list of notable and formidable women in pre-colonial, colonial, and postcolonial times in northern Nigeria who were not only excellent in their domestic roles but also functioned as princesses, military generals, diplomats, teachers, merchants, warriors, and political and religious leaders and who played key roles in nation building (17). Some of them are Queen Amina of Zazzau, Nana Amau Dan Fodio, Ya Gumsu of Borno, Daurama of Daura, Inkipi of Igala, Laila Dogonyaro, the Miller Sister, and Gambo Sawaba, among others.

The selected authors in this study show concern for issues northern Nigerian Muslim women face in contemporary times. The contemporary settings of the novels attest to this, as do the recurring issues in the three novels. These issues can be broadly categorized into two realms: marital and financial. Both are concerns which Islamic legislation weighs in on. The fact that women are expected to be under the authority of a man, first as a daughter, then a wife and/or a divorcee or widow, confers some restrictions upon them. These restrictions do not come from the Islamic rulings but from of the actions and demands of the men they are related to. Except in the case of Tambaya in El-Rufai's novel, who breaks tradition by going to live and work without any male patron, both Hadiza and Zarah in Idris's and Mohammed's novels live lives that are inhibited by the actions of their husbands. This foregrounds that the patriarchal system of northern Nigerian society is still in force except in instances where the females, like Tambaya and Hadiza, take steps which emancipate them. In what Idris calls "cultural Islam," a "concept that was brought about by abiding by the (indigenous) culture so much so that it has merged with religion and the thin lines separating them has disappeared . . . Whereas it has no essence and is not even in line with the deen," there is the unfortunate legitimization of acts inimical to the well-being of women and contrary to the dictates of Islam. That the selected writers still foreground Islam – especially the injunctions that promote the rights of women – is indicative of their quest to challenge patriarchal stereotypes which inhibit women. Hadiza's bold move to start a business in spite of her husband's orders and her decision to speak up and end the marriage portray her as rising above the shackles in which her husband places her. However, the inability to depict significant advantages of polygyny and the apportioning of blame for its failure upon both men and women in instances where it is depicted show that these writers, as Muslims, accept God's injunction on the permissibility but are, however, concerned about the ways the characters involved carry out the rulings. All three authors depict their lead characters as resisting elements of patriarchy, especially when it inhibits their financial and psychological well-being: Tambaya strikes out by herself, Zarah forfeits both her sexual and motherly needs, and Hadiza defies popular expectations by divorcing her husband. In all three situations, the characters are essentially cast as being on the path of psychological peace. The emphases on marital and economic matters that inflect upon the lead female characters are carefully balanced against what Islamic law allows. The authors seem very aware of these laws and craft their stories in ways such that the lead characters do not overtly transgress the lines of propriety.

Works cited

Abdul Raheem, Hamza. "Promoting Women Education through Historical Antecedents: An Analysis of the Flyting of Ghoni and Dan Fodio as Contained in *Tazyin-ul-waraqat*." *Gender Politics: Women's Writings and Film in Northern Nigeria*, edited by Yerimah, Ahmed, and Saeedat Aliyu. Ibadan: Kraftbooks, 2012, pp. 28–39.

Aliyu, Saeedat B. "Constraints to Womanhood in Northern Nigeria: A Feminist Reading of Hilary Rouse-Amadi's *Amina*." *Gender Politics: Women's Writings and Film in Northern Nigeria*, edited by Yerimah, Ahmed, and Saeedat Aliyu. Ibadan: Kraftbooks, 2012, pp. 60–68.

Alkali, Zaynab. "Gender Politics and Sexual Dynamics, Imaging Men in African Women's Writings: The Quest for Identity and Integrity." *Gender Politics: Women's Writings and Film in Northern Nigeria*, edited by Yerimah, Ahmed, and Saeedat Aliyu. Ibadan: Kraftbooks, 2012, pp. 11–20.

Alkali, Zaynab. *The Stillborn*. Lagos: Esio Printers, 1984.

Alkali, Zaynab. *The Virtuous Woman*. Lagos: Longman, 1986.

"An Introduction to the Rights and Duties of Women in Islam." www.al-islam.org/introduction-rights-and-duties-women-islam-ayatullah-ibrahim-amini/islam-and-polygamy. Accessed Jan. 15, 2019.

Centre for Islamic Legal Studies of the Ahmadu Bello University, Zaria. *Promoting Women's Rights through Sharia in Northern Nigeria*. British Council, 2005.

El-Rufai, Hadiza Isma. *An Abundance of Scorpions*. Lagos: Ouida, 2017.

Fafunwa, Aliu Babatunde. *New Perspectives in Education*. London: Macmillan, 1971.

Giwa, Audee T. "In Search of Identity: The Emerging Male and the Emergent Female in Zaynab Alkali's *The Initiates*." *Literature, History and Identity in Northern Nigeria*, edited by Tsiga, Ismaila A. and Mohammed Bhadmus. Ibadan: Safari, 2016, pp. 311–340.

Holy Qur'an. *Surah 4 An-Nisa, Surah 9 At-Taubah, and Surah 2 Al-Baqara*. Trans. Abdullah Yusuf Ali. Riyadh: Ministry of Islamic Affairs, 2008.

Ibnouf, Fatma Osman. "The Gender Equality and Women's Human Rights in Islamic Texts (Quran and Hadith)." *Researchgate*, April 2015. www.researchgate.net/.../274899721_The_Gender_Equality_and_Women's_H. Accessed Jan. 15, 2019.

Idris, Azizah M. *A Sackful of Wishes*. Lagos: Parresia, 2018.

Interview with Azizah Idris M. via e-mail on February 18, 2019.

Interview with Hadizah Isma Idris via e-mail on February 20, 2019.

Mohammed, Razinat T. *The Travails of a First Wife*. Lagos: Perresia, 2015.

Qutb, Muhammed. *Islam the Misunderstood Religion*. 6th ed. Kuwait: Ministry of Awqaf $ Islamic Affairs, State of Kuwait, 1964.

Song, Sarah. *Justice, Gender and the Politics of Multiculturalism*. Cambridge: Cambridge University Press, 2007.

Usman, K.A. *Destinies of Life*. Ibadan: Caltop, 2005.

Yakubu, Ramat B. *Sin Is a Puppy That Follows You Home*. Chennai: Blaft, 2012.

PART V

Intranational, national, and international marginalization/conflict

18

THE ODDS AGAINST ERITREAN LITERATURE

Charles Cantalupo

A Google search of "North Korea of Africa" to describe Eritrea produces over 20,000 results. "Hermit Kingdom" is another popular epithet applied to Eritrea. No other African nation has a more marginalizing epithet, much less two, so widely circulated. Sharing a thousand-mile border with the three African nations of Sudan, Ethiopia, and Djibouti, along with a seven hundred-mile coast line on the Red Sea, Eritrea is hardly Asian, and it's over five thousand miles away from North Korea. While various kingdoms have ruled Eritrea, it has never been a kingdom on its own and is currently a single-party presidential republic. Furthermore, as anyone with familiarity of the Horn of Africa knows, while it has a tradition of religious hermits, Djibouti, Eritrea, Ethiopia, and Somalia are hardly countries of solitude and isolation. On the contrary, neither the region's politics nor its populations seem to abide such limitations, notwithstanding the many occasions when they have been imposed. Frankly, the history is long of their minding each other's business.

Isolating Eritrea internationally, terms like "North Korea of Africa" and "hermit kingdom" would further isolate Eritrea in Africa as well as in the Horn itself: in short, making Eritrea a minority of one. Moreover, if this perception or, what all too many consider, this reality prevails with regard to Eritrea as a nation, the odds might seem impossible against Eritrean literature breaking through such a dominant cultural and political mindset as anything other than a minority discourse.

Eritrea's marginalization as a nation is inseparable from the marginalization of its literature, although the reasons for the former are more familiar than the latter. Nor are they exactly the same. Yet not all of the reasons are unique to Eritrea. On the contrary, they exemplify many of the reasons for the historical marginalization of Africa, African literature, and, what is particularly important here, African-language literature. Thus, as a minority discourse in African literature, Eritrean literature is subject to different kinds or many layers of marginalization. While most of them originate externally from Eritrea, some are internal, and the marginalizing of Eritrean literature can also be attributed to some self-marginalization, too. Colonial repression of education and of African languages (from in- and outside Africa), geopolitical dictates, a long history of censorship, a necessary and indomitable dependence on self-reliance, a lot of literature focusing on war, and more factor into Eritrea's literary isolation. Yet the fact remains that Eritrean literature has a rich and long history and not only survives but continues in unprecedented ways so that the days of its characterization as a minority discourse may be numbered.

Eritrean literature might best be conceived by the Eritrean poet Tesfamariam Woldemariam, in his poem, "Our Village." Asked by an outsider about his village, the poet responds,

> You say, our village.
> Do you mean our exact village,
> The one we saw at dawn,
> Where we watched the sunrise
> And spent the morning,
> The afternoon,
> And the evening,
> And where we stayed?
>
> If you really mean
> This village,
> It has a village underneath,
> And a village under that
>
> Before the modern one you see:
> A village before Islam;
> Another village before Christianity;
> Yet another before the kingdom
> Of the Jews;
> And one before the worship of the sun;
> Yet another
> Before the deities of anyone.

He elaborates further,

> You say, our village, but
> In relation to what?
> The village has a village
> Behind it and before;
> To the right, in the middle,
> On the left, and more
> Villages beyond.
> Our village runs the range:
> From traditional, to hidebound,
> To life in balance, and to change.

Finally he concludes,

> So, you say, our village.
> Exactly which one?
> Our village of the past,
> Our village here, today,
> The modern wannabe,
> Or the village you cannot see,
> And the village that will really be
> Modern, even postmodern?

To substitute "Eritrean literature" for the word "village" in this poem is to begin to grapple not only with what the term "Eritrean literature" might mean but also with its repeated and longstanding repression if its status is no more than a minority literary discourse. The poet states this more harshly. Majority literary discourse – African or otherwise – relegates Eritrean literature to a "modern wannabe." Still other minority discourses in African literature might allow for a similar observation in their case if they are still in the minority, too.

To substitute "Eritrean literature" for the word "village" in Tesfamariam Woldemariam's poem also suggests the long history and the centrality in Eritrean culture of Eritrean literature. It is:

> One massive ladder
> With endless rungs
> Through vast and countless
> Levels upon levels
> Outspreading up and down,
> Set deeply in eternity
> To rise
> Beyond the skies.[1]

Eritrea's literary culture is readily apparent in the present, too, See Figure 18.1. My introduction to it came in 1998 when, finding myself swept in a vast crowd moving towards a performance space, I was surprised to learn it was for a poetry reading, which marked the first time I encountered the Eritrean poet Reesom Haile.[2] In subsequent years, I have witnessed and been a part of many more readings and book launches that always attract many hundreds of people. In the case of the poetry of Tesfamariam Woldemariam, who died in 2015, Eritrean literary culture is at a high point. After years of scrupulous editing, Hdri Publishers in Asmara has recently issued an all-Tigrinya, over 300-page collection of his poems that includes a lengthy essay on his unique poetics and language: an unprecedented literary edition in the history of Eritrean publishing. With a print run of ten thousand copies and reprinting expected, the book launch attracted five hundred people.[3]

No one knows more or writes more eloquently about Eritrea's marginalization as a nation – which is the primary although not the only reason for the marginalization of Eritrean literature – than Eritrea's greatest historian, who is also one of its greatest writers, Alemseged Tesfai. When he first started to write about Eritrea in 1971, a defining moment in its modern history had taken place two decades before. Writing in *The Atlantic*, Robert Kaplan recounts that after World War II, "The British occupied Eritrea until September of 1952. By the time they left, the Western powers had imposed a United Nations mandate on the region and made Eritrea a semi-autonomous territory under the sovereignty of Ethiopia." With this, as Kaplan adds, "The U.S. Secretary of State, John Foster Dulles, explained: 'From the point of view of justice, the opinions of the Eritrean people must receive consideration. Nevertheless, the strategic interest of the United States . . . [makes] it necessary that the country has to be linked with our ally, Ethiopia'."

Eritrea's United Nations-mandated federation with Eritrea in 1952 lasted only ten years before Ethiopia annexed it in 1962. A bloody and horrific thirty-year struggle for Eritrean independence ensued. Eritrea fought a war "Against All Odds," as Dan Connell has memorialized it in the most widely read account of Eritrea's epic combat, overcoming Africa's largest standing army backed at different times by the United States and the Soviet Union and their respective allies. The war also exacerbated political instability in Ethiopia and led to the overthrow of the

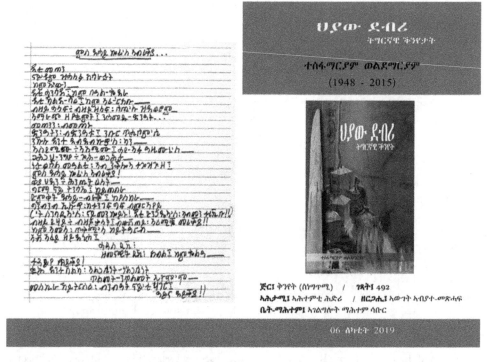

Figure 18.1 The odds against Eritrean literature.

Ethiopian emperor, Haileslassie, in 1974. Eritrean military forces also occasioned the fall of the Marxist regime, which replaced Haileslassie, known as the Derg, in 1991.

The extent of the violence consecutively inflicted on the Eritrean people by both regimes can now be better known and understood than ever before with the publication of *Gfi Gezati Ethiopia ab Etra*, literally meaning "Atrocities by Ethiopian Rulers in Eritrea." The English translation is *Untold Massacres of Eritreans: Making Peace from Memory*. It contains forty-three stories of untold, unprecedented, and unforgettable power:

- "untold" because until now, they have been largely unknown and concern unimaginable horrors that took place in Eritrea from the 1960s to the 1990s;
- "unprecedented" because such stories from Eritrea have never been published;
- "unforgettable" because the stories are so striking as to leave an indelible impression on a reader.

They recount the extraordinary, all but limitless capacity of human beings to terrorize, torture, and slaughter other human beings. The contrast between human savagery and human innocence is absolute and stark, including unprovoked, unjustifiable, sometimes random and sometimes planned massacres of people (including children, the sick, the elderly, pregnant women, and whole families); destruction of houses, property, livestock, whole villages, historical heritage, and the desecration of corpses; violent separation of families, rape, physical and psychological terrorism, and the weaponization of sexual abuse; and certainly more, which remains unspeakable. No account of Eritrea's marginalization more graphically and powerfully recounts the overwhelming trauma of war that Eritrea and Eritrean writers – both established and those to come – had to suffer. For a people to be subjected to so much terror and violence, they had to be considered marginal to the extreme.

For the last twenty-five years, I've been going to Eritrea, including many of the places that these stories mention: from Asmara to Agordat, Nefasit to Nakfa, Adi Keyh to Keren, Mendefera to Massawa, and many a village along the way. I've written several books about Eritrea and translated many of its poets, and I've read many good books about the Eritrean revolution, by Eritreans themselves and non-Eritrean observers, journalists, and scholars. In Eritrea: the remnants of war, disabled veterans, and martyrs' cemeteries I always saw. But Eritrean people going about the dailiness of life and largely at peace in a land of stark yet varying beauty were what I saw much more. So much so that I never could have imagined the horrors these people went through: which, going back to the stories and trying to read them again, after the first time when I barely could, I wouldn't have to imagine. I would know as I never did before, and as I had to know, if I really wanted to know Eritrea.

Yet by the same measure, to know Eritrea still requires a knowledge of its literature.

In his poem, "Believe It or Not," Reesom Haile not only sums up Eritrea's political geopolitical marginalization, he pinpoints its ultimate purpose through a catalogue of different foreign armies that have invaded:

> Believe it or not,
> They want to kill us.
>
> Remember the Italians
> Who invaded and said
> *Eat but don't speak?*
>
> Remember the English
> Who invaded and said
> *Speak but don't eat?*
>
> Remember the Amharas
> Who invaded and said
> *Don't speak and don't eat?*
>
> Still we're shocked
> The Weyanes invaded
> And said *You should be dead.*
>
> Believe it or not
> They want to kill us.[4]
>
>   (154)

Roughly twenty years after Ethiopia's calamitous federation with Eritrea, Alemseged Tesfai experienced his own personal crucible over Eritrean history. He writes,

> Imagine my own frustration in 1971, when I ventured into research for my Master's thesis on the Four Power-UN role on Eritrea's federation with Ethiopia. I could not find one single learned source written by Eritreans on their country's history. No Eritrean version or interpretation of their past and claims to nationhood could stand up to portrayals of them by outside sources – Italian, British, Ethiopian, Egyptian, etc.

As a result, according to Alemseged, "[n]o Eritrean version or interpretation of . . . [its] past and claims to nationhood" could exist but only its "portrayal . . . by outside sources" with "big power strategic interests:" the biggest being Eritrea's federation with rather than its independence from Ethiopia. Thus, as Alemseged continues,

> Eritrean historiography had to be sacrificed. Eritrean studies thus subsided into more or less insignificance, not figuring even as a regional area of focus within "Africa Orientale Italiana" (or Italian East Africa) and still less under the Ethiopian Empire, which equally aspired to centralism and grandeur. In the 1960s and 70s in fact, historicizing Eritrea became a taboo, the breach of which was dangerous for Ethiopians as well as Eritreans and unamenable to foreigners.

Alemseged further suggests that that a widespread inability or unwillingness to recognize a distinctly Eritrean historiography and all that it includes is contemporary and current, too, and, as I had suggested, the thousands of references to Eritrea as "North Korea of Africa" and "hermit kingdom" readily confirm this. Seeing the problem from a more thoughtful and scholarly perspective, as Alemseged observes,

> Ethiopian scholarship has also been an effective machine, aided by a host of British, American, Swedish . . . Ethiopianists who have been working hard to establish that discipline as the leading and dominant historiography in the Horn. International scholarship on the subject has been so influenced by their voluminous productions that no other version of history is acceptable to them.

Is it any wonder that if "Eritrean historiography had to be sacrificed," then Eritrean literature would fare no better?

Still, the greater wonder is that precisely such an historical precondition is what motivated Alemseged's desire to challenge the claim that Eritrea had no history of its own that was different or separate from what would be externally imposed on it. Nor was he alone. He had a guerilla army behind him that he would also join. The Eritrean revolution and thirty-year armed struggle for independence from Ethiopia that began in 1961 was the most direct and comprehensive challenge there could be against the prevailing narrative that Eritrea didn't exist. The war embodied "Eritrean history" as, as Alemseged recounts in the film documentary *Against All Odds*, "a struggle between forces that . . . [had] been trying to write off Eritrea as a nation, to simply ignore it as something that did not exist, and the heart of Eritreans that refused to bend to these forces of destruction" (23:33–24:44). The history of Eritrea has been a war between forces that have been trying to deny that it is even a nation and Eritreans themselves, including its writers, who have fought, on the battlefield but also in their writing, for the voices of Eritrea to be heard.

Ironically, perhaps, this prolonged, existential challenge to Eritrea's veritable status as a nation and not a mere minority territory within a larger federation of Ethiopia begot and inspired a generation of Eritrea's writers to be not only as distinctive as any African nation's or region's but also uniquely powerful for always writing in their own, indigenous African languages. Not only Eritrea but Eritrea's writers have had to struggle "against all odds" to be heard. This historical and literary achievement of Alemseged's writing is inseparable from Eritrean history because Eritrean literature is inseparable from Eritrean history. Deny one and you deny the other. Despite the denial, Alemseged has written *Aynfelale* ("Let Us Not Separate," 2001), *Kab Matienzo ksab Tedla Bairou* ("Eritrean Federation with Ethiopia: From Matenzo to Tedla,"

2005), and *Ertra kab FedereSn nab GobeTan Sewran* ("Eritrea – From Federation to Annexation and Revolution," 2016). Also despite the denial, a tradition of Eritrean literature reaches as far back as an inscription on a pre-Axumite stele, the Bible, and the Koran; a tradition that includes a 250-year-old legacy of poets or *getemti* in their poems called *massé* and *melkes*; a tradition anthologized in early 20th-century collections by scholars like Carlo Conti Rossini, Nefa'e Ethman, Enno Littmann, Jacques Faitlovitch, and Johannes Kolmodin; a tradition of literature that continued and was renewed for three decades in the field of battle during Eritrea's war of independence; a tradition after the war was won in 1991; a tradition that has continued since and yet even after three decades is still either denied or, to be realistic, a minority discourse in Africa and the world.

While international and inter-African geopolitical efforts "to write off Eritrea as a nation, to simply ignore it as something that did not exist" would, of course, also "write off" and "ignore" its literature "as something that did not exist," Eritrean literature not only continued to exist, but lived, as it always had, in African languages, particularly in Eritrea's languages. As Ngũgĩ wa Thiong'o has testified, commenting on the anthology of contemporary Eritrean poetry *Who Needs a Story*, "For at least four thousand years – from the ancient stele in Belew Kelew to the 20th century battlefields of Eritrea's heroic struggle for independence – into the 21st century, Eritrean[s] . . . have never given up writing in their own languages" (back cover).

Yet the way that Ngũgĩ came to this realization is telling. He shocked the international and African literary establishment in 1986 with his formal "Statement" in *Decolonising the Mind* that it was his "farewell to English as a vehicle for . . . [his] writings" and "From now on it is Gĩkũyũ and Kiswahili all the way" (xiv). Moreover, Ngũgĩ's arguing for African languages and his writing in them subsequently increased exponentially from then on. Yet mention of Eritrea's longtime and current African-language literature as well as the all but ubiquitous use of African, Eritrean languages in every aspect of life and governance in Eritrea goes unmentioned in Ngũgĩ's critical writings. Not until he travels there in the late 1990s and co-chairs the historic conference in Asmara in 2000, Against All Odds: African Languages and Literatures into the 21st Century, does he fully recognize the Eritrean African language paradigm and articulate its profound effect upon him:

> The key and cause for hope is that despite hundreds of years of imperial and neo-colonial repression, African languages have refused to die. The conference we had in Eritrea, where we produced the Asmara Declaration in African Languages and Literatures: even for me, an advocate of literature in African languages – I was totally amazed by the number of writers in African languages. I didn't know where they all came from . . . They came from Ghana, Ivory Coast, North Africa, South Africa, East Africa. We were all there, in Eritrea – writers who primarily wrote in African languages. I could make that claim, too. I was editing the journal *Mũtiiri* in Gĩkũyũ and was now writing all my novels in Gĩkũyũ. It was a beautiful thing to see.
>
> *(Non-Native Speaker, 209)*

Ngũgĩ's saying "even for me, an advocate of literature in African languages" attests to how very effective Eritrea and Eritrean literature's marginalization had been. Reinforcing the irony that even Ngũgĩ was "amazed" by the preponderance of African language literature in Eritrea was the development strategy that the Against All Odds conference employed in the extensive fund-raising that would allow for such a large and millennial gathering to take place. The project's organizers depended on its potential benefactors first and foremost recognizing the name and authority of Ngũgĩ as one of Africa's premier writers along with his well-known, critical advocacy of African languages as the ultimate means of decolonizing Africa in mind and body, spirit and letter. Not the fact that the conference would take place in Eritrea but Ngũgĩ's name would attract the foundations, universities, nations, banks, NGOs, and other institutions to make the project a success. The thousands-of-years-long literary history of an entire nation had become so marginalized that that the African language writing and advocacy beginning in the 1980s of one man was far more widely known and recognized for its power.

But not all of the reasons for the marginalization of Eritrean literature can be attributed to geopolitical efforts to restrict or extinguish it. First, unlike African literature that has over-come African political marginalization by being written in colonial languages, Eritrean litera-ture exists primarily in African languages, with a few notable exceptions. As a result, Eritrean literature is rarely accessible without translation. This means, for example, that Eritrea's and one of Africa's greatest novelists, Beyene Haile, and Eritrea's and one of the Horn's greatest historians, Alemseged Tesfai, cannot be widely read and appreciated beyond their national borders. In the case of the latter, one could argue that until his three-volume history of Eritrea and the region is further translated – parts of it have been translated into Tigre and Arabic – any effort to resolve the problem of the political marginalization of Eritrea and its literature is seriously handicapped. Moreover, as both writers offer their work for an Eritrean voice finally to be heard after historic exclusion, it is only reinforced since their work is in their own language, Tigrinya. Thus, the marginalization of Eritrean literature seems to thrive in a vicious circle. Marginalization is a kind of geopolitical given or *a priori*, while the liter-ary struggle against it through written expression in Tigrinya without translation redoubles such marginalization.

Second, unlike most widely recognized African literature yet even most African-language literature that has any currency, Eritrean literature uses a script other than Latin: Ge'ez. Not that Eritrea is unique in this. Ethiopian-language literatures, for example, Amharic, also do so. Still, that a literature or literatures exist primarily in Ge'ez script does not make it immune to the use and abuse of political power, although any more or less so than it would be in Latin script would require additional investigation.

In the case of Eritrea, it has nine languages with many speakers, and the population is fairly evenly split between Christian and Muslims, which means that the Tigrinya language of the former and the latter's Arabic are the most widespread. Yet 30% of the population, accord-ing to *The World Factbook*, also speak the language of Tigre, with the local languages of Saho (4%), Kunama (2%), Belin (2%), Afar, Beja, and Nera in the mix. In addition, the languages of colonial occupation, Italian and English, are also widely known. Still another language of colonial occupation is also widely known, but it's the African, Ethiopian language of Amharic: the language of the Haile Selassie and the Derg regimes. Semitic languages written not only in Ge'ez script but descended from ancient Ge'ez language itself, Tigrinya and Tigre are relatively young as written languages. Nineteenth-century Swedish missionaries were among the first to introduce their writing and printing, but by the time of the Ethiopian federation with Eritrea in 1952, Tigrinya and Arabic had become national languages and Tigrinya was being taught in schools as well as being the language of newspapers.[5] With Ethiopia's annexation of Eritrea in 1962, Emperor Haile Selassie banned Tigrinya in schools and publications in addition to ban-ning all Eritrean languages and making his own language, Amharic, the official language not only of Ethiopia but of Eritrea, too. The long history of writing in Amharic as well as its propaga-tion, to the point of vengeance, by the political power of the Ethiopian regime might have been expected to overwhelm Eritrean writing in its own languages, but on the contrary. Writing in Tigrinya and Arabic became identified with Eritrean nationalism and its opposition to merely becoming a part of Ethiopia instead of an independent nation. Acquiescing to African-language

Amharic linguistic hegemony was no more acceptable to Eritrea than defaulting to writing in European colonial-language Italian or English. Eritrea had its own languages and, whatever the odds against them, spoke in Eritrean, wrote in them, and never stopped speaking and writing in them: before, during, and after the Eritrean revolution, and the same applies for now, despite the continuing marginalization of the nation and of its literature.

Ethiopia's suppression of Eritrea's languages had an historical precedent. Before Ethiopia's internationally mandated federation with Eritrea and, ten years later, its annexation, Eritrea was an Italian colony. Extending officially from 1890 to 1947, Italian rule began in the early 1880s and ended in the early 1940s. Alemseged Tesfai testifies to the root causes for not only the sacrifice of Eritrean historiography but also Eritrean literature's marginalization. Italy forbade written Eritrean expression and allowed Eritreans no education beyond fourth grade. Writing in Tigrinya had to stop until the end of Italian repression and the interregnum of British rule, which began in 1941 (*History*, 114), when, in Alemseged's words "a crop of refined writers, especially in Tigrinya, rose out of the ashes to enrich the pages of the newspapers that the British allowed them to publish." In *A History of Tigrinya Literature in Eritrea*, Ghirmai Negash calls the 1940s "The years of revival" that followed "The years of stillness," and "The first years of the 1940s marked a revival in Tigrinya literature due to two related crucial developments in Eritrea. Firstly, Italian colonialism ended in 1941 and the administration of Eritrea was taken over by British." Negash also attributes "The years of revival" to the establishment of "the Tigrinya newspaper" called ናይ ኤርትራ ሰሙናዊ ጋዜጣ (*nay Ertra sämunawi gazetta*), *The Eritrean Weekly News*. "[F]ounded in 1942," according to Negash, "this provided a golden opportunity for the general reading public as well as the learned elite to debate and air their views about important issues concerning the country, including language and literature. The newspaper had a circulation of ca. 5000 copies. It was sold at 5 cents E.A. (East African currency)" (115). Cited by Negash, Edward Ullendorff, a founding editor, totals *The Eritrean Weekly News* "running to some 520 issues over ten years, each of four (occasionally six) pages of very large format. This represents a total of more than 2100 pages or some three million words." According to Alemseged Tesfai, the writing in Tigrinya of the paper's Eritrean editor and greatest essayist, Weldeab Weldemariam, "are yet to be surpassed." He joined the two causes of Eritrean languages and Eritrean independence together throughout his writing. Following Eritrea's annexation by Ethiopia, the Emperor, much like the Italians seventy years before, attacked and forbade Eritrean languages and literature in order to elevate his own, Amharic, as Eritrea's official language. Weldemariam went on using Tigrinya to energize and develop the Eritrean opposition – the literary as well as the armed struggle – against the annexation and, in consequence, to be widely considered as a father of the modern nation of Eritrea.

Thus, any consideration of the marginalization of Eritrean literature must take into account roughly sixty years of Italian rule that largely prohibited any written expression in indigenous Eritrean languages and, after a ten-year interim, thirty years of armed Ethiopian aggression aimed at anything that might question Amharic as Eritrea's official language.

Despite Eritrea's Italian-enforced "years of stillness," in Ghirmai Negash's phrase, when, as Alemseged Tesfai laments, "we have been left with no indigenous record of life under Italy," there is one notable exception: *The Conscript*, a novel written in Tigrinya by Gebreyesus Hailu, initially in 1927, and first published in 1950. The narrative's main character, Tuquabo, struggles against his conscription into the Italian army to travel to Libya and suppress a colonial uprising. He experiences the epiphany of realizing that he should not be fighting against but with Libya's Arab freedom fighters, since they are oppressed by the same colonial masters, the Italians, as he is. Hailu writes his novel in his own language thirty years before Chinua Achebe's *Things Fall Apart* and predates its publication by almost a decade.

A comparison between Hailu's Tuquabo in *The Conscript* and Achebe's Okonkwo in *Things Fall Apart* is revealing. Both of their respective cultures are under siege. Unlike Okonkwo, when Tuquabo must confront the evils of empire, he rebels and survives. He refuses to let his Tigrinya identity morph into a delusory if tragic form of macho exceptionalism. He is more Tigrinya everyman than hero manqué. Over half a century before Ngũgĩ wa Thiong'o's first African-language novel in Gĩkũyũ, *Caitaani mũtharaba-Inĩ* (1980) or *Devil on the Cross*, *The Conscript* is a timeless and unforgettable work of literary beauty for Eritrea, Africa, and the world.

However vain or doomed to being rhetorical, the question remains. How many other writers of the stature of Ghebreyesus Hailu in Tigrinya have been lost, prevented from writing, executed in the process of marginalizing Eritrea and its literature? Again, he is a lone survivor.

The first shots that were fired in the Eritrean revolution that began in September 1961 signaled there would be no more such lone exceptions. Until the 1980s, the Eritrean armed struggle consisted of two liberation armies: the Eritrean Liberation Front (ELF) and the Eritrean People's Liberation Front (EPLF). As Negash notes, both groups included literature in their publications (178), and many fighters were writers. In Tigrinya, they included Solomon Drar, Ghirmai Ghebremeskel, Beyene Haile, Angessom Isaak, Haregu Keleta, Saba Kidane, Fessahazion Michael, Meles Negusse, Ribka Sibhatu, Alemseged Tesfai, Isayas Tsegai, Solomon Tsehaye, Tesfamariam Woldemariam, Fessehaye Yohannes, Ghirmai Yohannes, and Zeineb Yassin. Eritrean fighters who were writers also wrote in Tigre, including Mussa Mohammed Adem, Paulos Netabay, and Mohammed Said Osman. Writing in Arabic had a long tradition, unlike Tigrinya and Tigre, but Eritrean Arabic writers who were fighters could also now publish their work in the name of a free and independent Eritrea, including Mohammed Osman Kajerai, Abdul Hakim Mahmoud-El-Sheik, Mohammed Mahmoud-El-Sheikh (Madani), Ahmed Mohammed Saad, and Ahmed Omer Sheik.[6] Eritrean writers in Eritrean languages, therefore, would certainly no longer be marginalized, at least in Eritrea.

I started translating Eritrean writers in February 1999, particularly the Tigrinya poet Reesom Haile. He wasn't a fighter but an expatriate who returned to his native country soon after Eritrea won its independence. By 1999, Reesom Haile and his poems had achieved near rock star status around the country. He was writing a poem almost every day and publishing it immediately on the internet. The website founded in 1992 by Menghis Samuel, called *Dehai.org*, which means "voice," was popular with readers in Eritrea but also with Eritreans around the world. Each poem appeared like a morsel of daily bread, eagerly grasped by a reading public who were caught up in a kind of communal ecstasy of building a free Eritrea. Celebrating independence from European colonialism, many an African nation could echo, or should I say, translate, William Wordsworth's famous words: "Bliss was it in that dawn to be alive,/But to be young was very heaven!" (10: 692–693). As the 1990s unfolded, Eritrea embodied it loud and clear. And Reesom Haile's spirit was always young. Living in Asmara, Eritrea's capital, he was constantly high-spirited, and his peers found it hard to keep up with him. His poems consistently exhibited a playful tone or, in his more serious lyrics, a playful edge. What could be more natural, I thought, than translating him into English so that his phenomenal work could be known and enjoyed worldwide? In the next three years, we published in dozens of journals and two books together. We gave many readings at leading American universities and international gatherings of scholars and writers. We had a two-volume CD. Appearing on BBC, CNN, Deutsche Welle, NPR, RAI, and VOA, the Eritrean poet Reesom Haile was anything but marginalized. Few poets from anywhere, much less Eritrea, ever got such coverage.

In 2002, I returned to Asmara to accept an invitation to translate and edit an anthology of contemporary Eritrean poets, including Reesom. Zemhret Yohannes, who was affiliated with Eritrea's Research and Documentation Center as well as with Hdri Publishers, and who also co-chaired the Against All Odds conference, initiated the anthology. Saying that it would allow more Eritrean poets in addition to Reesom to receive the attention they deserved, Zemhret added, "What they write needs to be heard, too." Since Reesom's poetry covered a myriad of topics, I wondered what Zemhret meant, and he explained. "These poets write a lot about the field and about war. And yet war isn't only about fighting. And it's not all about death. That's too restrictive. They write about friendship and the perennial issues of love and life. War has that, too" (*Joining Africa*, 243). He was right. Reesom didn't write about war. He left Eritrea just before its annexation and returned after the war was over.

At the time, I doubted whether war poetry could be any good, even if it included the other concerns that Zemhret mentioned. Like most Western readers, I had no appetite or tolerance for contemporary poetry about war and, frankly, I didn't know any I would want to read except translations of classical, biblical, or medieval epic. The famous line by Horace – *Dulce et decorum est pro patria mori*; to die for one's country is sweet and honorable – had been discredited and deconstructed so long ago, as in Wilfred Owen's eponymous poem in 1917, that its inclusion in a work of literature could only be heard as ironic.[7] Zemhret implied that the war poetry of Eritrea's fighter/writers was positive, straight, and sincere in praise of the Eritrean armed struggle. As Paul Fussell demonstrated in his book, *The Great War and Modern Memory*, war poetry like that in English had not only long ceased to exist, with the exception of some lines by Rudyard Kipling; it was impossible to write anymore or, by extension, to translate into English.

Translating hundreds of poems by Reesom Haile, I never even realized what I had now had to confront and fear. If few people or anyone wanted to read contemporary poetry about war, why should Eritrean poetry be an exception? Of course, I wanted my translations to be, but the subject of war for contemporary poetry was marginal from the start, whatever I could do, and war was the focus of half of the poems in the book. It was a book of historic literary firsts for Eritrea, Africa, and the world: the first anthology of contemporary Eritrean poetry ever published; the first book ever to present Eritrean poetry from three of Eritrea's major languages in the original, including their original scripts, and in translation; the first and only anthology of Eritrean available for a worldwide market. No book before *Who Needs a Story: Contemporary Eritrean Poetry in Tigrinya, Tigre, and Arabic* by an Eritrean publisher had ever even had an ISBN. While international journals published some of the war poetry, they published all of the other poems from the book. While it had wide circulation in Eritrea, international sales were small: certainly nowhere near the coverage and reception of Reesom Haile's work. It had become central, at least for a few years, to those who wanted an understanding of Eritrea and its literature. *Who Needs a Story*, however, never became more than a marginal text: marginal as Eritrea and its thirty year war for independence.

External factors of geopolitical expediency, colonial and neocolonial repression of African languages and education (from in and outside Africa), a history of censorship, and Western disenchantment with the glories of war (other than its own, perhaps) can account for the marginalization of Eritrea and its literature. And the Eritrean response or reaction? In the eyes of the Eritrean poet, dramatist, and filmmaker Isayas Tsegai, who was also a fighter,

> . . . I saw the world didn't care
> If I was stripped of everything,
> Even my dignity,
> And beaten like a slave
> Less than human. . . .
> I lost all sense of peace. . . .
> (*Who Needs a Story*, 9)

His response to, his way to survive such a condition of total abuse and abandonment, becomes his poem's refrain: "I am also a person. I'm an Eritrean." What else was there? The line epitomizes Eritrea's strategy of survival that after thirty years of war led to victory and an independent nation when, as another great writer/fighter, Angessom Isaak, recalls,

> I saw a color
> Unbelievably bright
> And like a power wind
> Encompassing the sky
> Mirrored across the sea
> And pouring freedom
> All around me.
> (*Who Needs a*
> *Story*, 23)

Eritrea's primary reaction against geopolitical disfavor and isolation was to depend on self-reliance or, as Simon Weldemichael has recently stated on the Eritrean Ministry of Information website, *Shabait.com*, "Starting from our revolution, self-reliance has become the gospel of Eritrea." Furthermore,

> reliance on others is a central source of abasement to the national and continental pride of Africa. . . . The history of Eritrea is based on unparalleled sacrifice for the promotion of self-reliance . . . if you believe in self-reliance you can survive any adversity. . . . [S]elf-reliance . . . define[s] Eritreans. We know very well that nobody can bring you change. . . . Eritrea's present and future is up to Eritreans. No more, no less. . . . In Eritrea, self-reliance is not a policy directive imposed by policymakers. Rather, it is . . . the foremost cultural component that shapes our society.

Notwithstanding all the citations that a Google search of negative epithets for Eritrea provides, a similar search for instances when the words "Eritrea" and "self-reliance" or its variants are used together produces abundant results, too. An epitome of Eritrea's hallowed self-reliance is in the Tigrinya word that became a popular motto during the revolution: *bgbri*. Literally meaning 'show by action' and connoting "do it yourself," *bgbri* became a kind of mantra repeated by Eritrean fighters in the field day in and day out. The one-word mandate produced results. To take an example: while Ethiopia was from the beginning to the end of war with Eritrea heavily equipped by the West and later by the Soviet Union with abundant and sophisticated weaponry and military hardware, Eritrea had no such supply of allies who provided military aid. Such a disparity had to change, or Eritrea would not have been successful, much less have persevered through thirty years of war. In a spirit of *bgbri*, however, Eritrea not only won its battles; it took its enemies' weapons: guns, tanks, armored vehicles, and other kinds of military hardware – 50% of Ethiopian weaponry, by some estimates. A matter of necessity, such self-reliance won the war not merely despite but because of successfully adapting to a strategy of isolation. Yet ironically, perhaps, it confirmed Eritrea's marginalization. As a problem, internally, it appeared to be overcome. Externally, however, few if any reasons became apparent for Eritrea not to remain marginalized, particularly if they were not coming from Eritrea itself.

Depending on self-reliance, Eritrea clearly had to turn inward and be alone with itself: a practice that can work for a writer as well as a small community, but only so far, since the writer ultimately must turn around and reach out to share his or her work. The issue becomes whether the writer and society or culture – political to social to family culture – agree about what the work can or should express and not only if it should be shared or published, much less with whom.

While the marginalization of Eritrea's literature also derives from a long history of censorship, going back to colonial Italian rule and continuing with the subsequent regimes of the emperor, Haileslassie, and the Marxist regime of the Derg, claims of continuing internal suppression of Eritrean literary expression are widespread, most importantly by Eritrean themselves, the most vocal of whom are out of the country. Most importantly, too, Eritrean writers and scholars are, nevertheless, still being heard more than they have ever been before – a basic fact, from whatever side that the question of the suppression of Eritrean literary expression is viewed. Open to question are both external claims that Eritrean writers from inside Eritrea are not being heard and internal assurances that they all are. Both sides provide credible exceptions, and both sides, inevitably, play a part in shaping their country's literary future, which includes the question of whether Eritrean literature will enter the mainstream of African literature or remain a minority discourse.

Obviously, since many of the writers whom this chapter includes are living and/or being discussed and published in Eritrea today, there is real and substantial literary work that is going on there. Yet epithets of expatriate discontent and pronouncements that would manage it by remote control seem no more likely to change the status quo of Eritrea and Eritrean literature's marginalization than the promotion of isolation as a timeless virtue instead of a timely necessity. Both sides, moreover, are in clear agreement about the highly aggressive marginalization that Eritrea and Eritrean literature have suffered at the hands of the pan-African and international community. The common enemy of Eritrean literature is the ignorance that is egregiously evident when a writer, Mark Tran, for a major Western news source like *The Guardian* recently reports on Eritrea under the headline, "What You Need to Know about Eritrea," without a word about its literature. Ultimately, the cure for such ignorance can only come from Eritrea itself and its own writers and scholars: first in their own languages and second in translation, including translation into international languages as well as African languages.

Eritrean writers must provide their own answers for their marginalization, be it in geopolitical discourse, the local political arena, or the international marketplace. Yet debates about suppression and the heavy hand of censorship are hardly unique to Eritrea, in the present or in the past. For example, observing the political turmoil in his native England in 1651, the philosopher Thomas Hobbes, at the beginning of his greatest work, *Leviathan*, confesses that he feels "beset with those that contend on one side for too great liberty, and on the other side for too much Authority," and "'tis hard to passe between the points of both unwounded" (75). Seven years earlier, in 1644, the poet John Milton, also amidst political turmoil, famously declares,

> I cannot praise a fugitive and cloistered virtue, unexercised and unbreathed, that never sallies out and sees her adversary, but slinks out of the race where that immortal garland is to be run for, not without dust and heat. Assuredly we bring not innocence into the world, we bring impurity much rather: that which purifies us is trial, and trial is by what is contrary.
>
> *(728)*

No Eritrean writer can be said not to have passed through the "trial" that Milton invokes, nor to have been, as Hobbes says, "unwounded."

Hobbes also writes, having reached the conclusion of *Leviathan*, "if there be not powerfull Eloquence, which procureth attention and Consent, the effect of Reason will be little" (717). That is, all the reason, or reasons, in the world for not marginalizing Eritrea cannot expect "attention," much less "Consent," unless the "powerfull Eloquence" of Eritrean literature is heard, as it is in Eritrea – and in the heart of Eritrea: in the oral poem, "Negusse, Negusse," the traditional poets that have been collected by Solomon Tsehaye, Woldedingel, Gebreyesus Hailu, Tesfamariam Woldemariam, Zeineb Yassin, Reesom Haile, Beyene Haile, Alemseged Tesfai, Isayas Tsegai, Mohammed Osman, Meles Negusse, and many more. Yet their "powerfull Eloquence" must be heard, if they are to avoid marginalization and to be recognized as more than minority discourse, beyond Eritrea, too. I've said it before, and I say it again: no nation can be known without its literature being known, ancient to modern. Examples are legion and all over the world. Furthermore, their literature being known is testimony to their own substantial political power. Again, examples are legion and all over the world. Yet further, testifying to their power, their literatures are in their own languages, which raises the question of how they can be known all over the world where they are not spoken, much less read and understood. Clearly, no nation can be known without its literature being translated. Geopolitical priorities, colonial and neocolonial repression of Eritrean education and languages, censorship, effects of protracted warfare, and national political turmoil have enforced and reinforced the marginalization of Eritrea and its literature. But so has its lack of translators, and even they are marginalized, too. I know. I also know the lines of Tesfamariam Woldemariam, from his poem, "A Tigrinya Nation," on how to keep going:

> Heed my advice.
> Go slow,
> And the power of your voice
> Will put your counterpart to shame.
> Eventually, the more you're heard,
> You'll find your reward
> In offering a few ironic words.
> Time is on your side.
> Your history cannot be denied,
> However bitter now must be.

Notes

1 See Charles Cantalupo, "Literature, Translation, and National Development in Eritrea," *Non-Native Speaker*, 110–111.

> The first entry in an anthology of Eritrean literature to mark a beginning of Eritrean literary history – be it oral or written – could be the inscription on a stele at least three thousand years old in a place called Belew Kelew in the southern part of the country. . . .
> From the time of the stele in Belew Kelew until now, how could the amount of literature, including orature or oral literature, not be voluminous, even if much of it, like Eritrea's archaeological heritage, remains to be discovered? Just because we do not know them, at least not yet, does not mean that we do not search for them. Yet subsequently we find them, and we find more and more. Fiction, nonfiction, poetry, drama – how could Eritrea not have it all? Even though I only know the literature, for the most part, through translation, how can I not ask such rhetorical questions? How can they not be a given for any contemporary national literature with an ancient tradition? Greece? China? Egypt? India? Where

there is language, there is literature. Where there are nine languages or more, there are nine literatures or more.

As a result, the opportunities for writers and scholars in Eritrean languages and literatures are innumerable. A literary tradition reaching as far back as the stele of Belew Kelew, as the Bible, and as the Koran demands and deserves more. This is the challenge.

2 Cf. Charles Cantalupo, "Reesom Haile, *Getamay*," *Non-Native Speaker*, 13–14 and passim.
3 Tesfamariam Woldemariam (1950–2015) attended the University of Asmara in the early 70s, where he was president of the student union, after which he joined the Eritrean nationalist independence movement. He was one of its leading intellectuals, writing in Tigrinya and establishing a number of Tigrinya journals. His political essays were particularly admired and influential and, according to the Eritrean literary scholar Ghirmai Negash, they "embodied the values of the revolution mixed with personal insight, and he fashioned a new style of Tigrinya writing characterized by complex sentences and many newly fangled words which he consciously and successfully coined in order to enrich the language so that it can carry the weight of the then evolving modernist ideals of the revolution and emergent Eritrea." He immigrated to the United States in the early 90s and lived in Atlanta. The first-ever collection of his poetry in Tigrinya was published in Asmara, Eritrea, in February 2019. Titled ህያው ደብሪ (*Hiyaw Debri*), which translates as "The Lost Monastery," here is the program cover, including a facsimile of the manuscript of one of the poems and the cover of the book itself.
4 "The Italians" ruled in Eritrea from the 1880s until ca. 1942, when "the English" took over. In 1952, when Eritrea's federation with Ethiopia took place, the ruling ethnic group of the Emperor Haileslassie was "the Amharas." "The Weyenes" refers to the post-Derg regime who came from Ethiopia's Tigre ethnic group.
5 Cf. Ghirmai Negash, *A History of Tigrinya Literature*, passim. Leiden: Research School of Asian, African and Amerindian Studies (CNWS), Universiteit Leiden, 1999.
6 Poems by many of these writers are included in *Who Needs a Story? Contemporary Eritrean Poetry in Tigrinya, Tigre, and Arabic*.
7 Cf. Charles Cantalupo, "The Reluctant Translator," *Non-Native Speaker*, 67–82, passim.

Works cited

Achebe, Chinua. *Things Fall Apart*. Edited by Francis Abiola Irele. 1958. New York City: W. W. Norton & Co., 2008.

Against All Odds: African Languages and Literatures into the 21st Century. Directed and written by Charles Cantalupo. Audio Visual Institute of Eritrea, 2007.

Berhe, S., Tesfaburuk, H., and Yemane, T. *Gfi Gezati Ethiopia ab Ertra* (Atrocities by Ethiopian Rulers in Eritrea). *Untold Massacres of Eritreans: Making Peace from Memory*. English translation by Charles Cantalupo, Rediet Kifle Taddese, and Menghis Samuel. Unpublished manuscript.

Cantalupo, Charles, and Negash, Ghirmai. *Who Needs a Story? Contemporary Eritrean Poetry in Tigrinya, Tigre, and Arabic*. Asmara: Hdri Publishers, 2005.

Cantalupo, Charles, and Negash, Ghirmai. *Joining Africa: From Anthills to Asmara*. Lansing: Michigan State University Press, 2012.

Cantalupo, Charles, and Negash, Ghirmai. *Non-Native Speaker*. Trenton: Africa World Press, 2017.

Central Intelligence Agency. *The World Factbook*. www.cia.gov/library/publications/the-world-factbook/geos/print_er.htm. Accessed 17 May 2019.

Connell, Dan. *Against All Odds: A Chronicle of the Eritrean Revolution*. Red Sea Press, 1997.

Fussell, Paul. *The Great War and Modern Memory*. Oxford University Press, 1975.

Haile, Reesom. *We Invented the Wheel*. Trenton: Red Sea Press, 2002.

Hailu, Gebreyesus. *Hadde Zanta*. Pietro Silla Printing Press, 1950. *The Conscript*. Translated by Ghirmai Negash. Athens: Ohio University Press, 2012.

Hobbes, Thomas. *Leviathan* (1651). Edited by C. B. Macpherson. London: Penguin Books, 1968.

Kaplan, Robert. "The Loneliest War." *The Atlantic*, July 1988. www.theatlantic.com/magazine/archive/1988/07/the-loneliest-war/518085/. Accessed 17 May 2019.

Milton, John. "Areopagitica" (1644). *John Milton: Complete Poems and Major Prose*. Edited by Merritt Y. Hughes. Indianapolis, 1957. Bobbs-Merril, and New York: Odyssey Press, 1957.

Negash, Ghirmai. A History of Tigrinya Literature. Leiden: CWS Publications, 1999.

Shabait.com. Eritrea. *Ministry of Information*. www.shabait.com.

Tesfai, Alemseged. "Marginalization." Received by Charles Cantalupo, 6 April 2019.

Tran, Mark. "What You Need to Know about Eritrea." *The Guardian*, 17 August 2015. www.theguardian.com/world/2015/aug/17/inside-eritrea-migrant-crisis-guardian-briefing. Accessed 17 May 2019.

wa Thiong'o, Ngũgĩ. "Caitaani mũtharaba-Inĩ" (1980). *Devil on the Cross*. London: Heinemann Publishers, 1982.

wa Thiong'o, Ngũgĩ. *Decolonising the Mind*. London: James Currey, 1986.

Weldemichael, Simon. "Self-Reliance Key to Eritrea's Independence and Development." www.shabait.com/categoryblog/24691-self-reliance-key-to-eritreas-independence-and-development. Accessed 17 May 2019.

Woldemarim, Tesfamariam. *ህያው ደብሪ* (*Hiyaw Debri*). Hdri Publishers, 2018. "The Lost Monastery." English translation by Charles Cantalupo and Menghis Samuel. Unpublished manuscript.

Wordsworth, William. *The Prelude: 1799, 1805, 1850*. Edited by Jonathan Wordsworth, M. H. Abrams, and Stephen Gill. New York: W. W. Norton, 1979.

19

MINORITY DISCOURSES AND THE CONSTRUCTION OF ILLICIT VERSIONS OF ZIMBABWEAN NATION-NESS IN NDEBELE FICTION IN ENGLISH

Maurice Taonezvi Vambe

Introduction: minority discourses and strategic ambiguity

The current fascination with engaging minority discourses in African cultural studies appears to have given rise to or even thrown up for public scrutiny more than perhaps what critics might have intellectually bargained for. A critical appetite by minority literary discourses to question the moral authority of the dominant discourses' exclusive claim to manufacturing, ordering and circulating certain subjectivities is emerging. Creative narrative and the diverse range of discursive paroles they authorise are socially constructed. As such, they are not beyond contestations from other discourses that seek to assert themselves as being based on a firmer epistemology. This chapter engages some notions of minority discourses constituted through selected Ndebele literary output in the English language. It is important to establish whether minority discourses 'know' or voluntarily name themselves as minority or in the 'minority.' This is crucial because what and how minority literary discourses create their cultural practices and tropes by which they distinguish or seek to differentiate themselves from dominant literary discourses is not a political given, for the very premise that a discourse can be minority or in the minority appears a tacit admission that there must be somewhere a majority, dominant or hegemonic discourse elsewhere with some authority to order and reorder the contents of minority discourses. Minoritisation of some literary discourses seems to be a function of power politics expressed on the other end of the cultural spectrum as an expression of a dominant cultural hegemon supported by canonical texts (Gates 32).

As a conceptual framework through which to make senses of certain experiences that might not have been included or that have been included under a subordinate status, the idea of minority discourses creates a binary. The assumptions of this binary work might not always favour or promote the discursive practices of minority discourses. The range of identities that the term minority discourse conjures can be of any number. However, in this chapter, minority discourses come close to self-inscriptions of certain narratives as constituting the subaltern, the vulnerable and in most cases a countercultural discourse (Gilroy 1). How to negotiate the semantic striations of a 'minority discourse' seems not always easy. This tends to be so because both a minority discourse and its imagined contender in the form of a dominant one may aspire and even project themselves as unified, organic and stabilised discourses when in reality they are not. In addition, if the issue of a 'minority' or a majority happens to be reduced to a game of numbers, the fragility of such conceptualisations becomes apparent. Colonialism was more economic/political and cultural institutions sustained by forms of certain grammar, perspectives and vocabulary through which to name itself as the authority. This despite the fact that the actual people who operated it on the ground were quite few compared to the natives they ruled over. Furthermore, although colonialism claimed to know its singular objective as the exploitation of the native populations, sometimes the colonised people appropriated some of its values. In Rhodesia, amongst the Shona and Ndebele people, colonialism invented new traditions where there were none and reconfigured native cultures to suit its economic goals. In extreme cases, colonialism deliberately reinforced certain obscurantist beliefs based on ethnic and gender superiority whenever these did not clash with colonialism's aims. Therefore, a minority discourse might be an understatement if it is intended to refer to people who are in the minority but existing in a shared space of political and geographical contiguities with a majority group that sets itself apart through certain shared cultural beliefs and values. It is possible that a numerical minority might be a numerical majority in the control of the publishing industry. By the same logic, a numerical majority might be a numerical minority in the field of knowledge production, management and its dissemination.

Ngugi wa Thiongo (10) has argued that in Europe, African literary discourses are described as 'ethnic studies' and minority discourses. In this inscription, minority discourse comes across as an epithet "often used to legitimate their claims to academic attention"(Chennels, 109). This view is highlighted further by Gates (32), for whom it appears that black literature in America exists as an ethnic or minority discourse seemingly imbricated in culture wars with white Americans with dominant discourses. In this view, minority discourse might appear synonymous with powerlessness arising from the vulnerability of the minority community. Arguably, minority communities might view their cultural vulnerability differently. The conditions of ideological powerlessness can be manipulated by minority discourses to achieve what seems not to be possible in the contestations between dominant and minority cultures were there to be an all-out war. This means that a resistance ethic in an ethnic or minority discourse might spur it to aspire to become the canon. If this happens, a cultural discourse that initially projected itself as a minority view might emerge as a dominant narrative with its own "essential" text, the crucially central authors who shape what might, in some future, become the marrow of a new dominant tradition (Gates 32). However, where minority discourses manage to escape the lure of presenting themselves as stable narratives, a possibility exists for a subversive revision of the dominant version of history. The instabilities inherent in metaphors and images in the field of African studies might energise some minority literary discourses to give "voice to a text muted by dominant historical referents, and it makes possible an imaginative invention of a self beyond the limits of historical representations available to the ethnic or minority subject" (Palumbo-Liu, 211).

There is constant tracking of cultural resources through appropriated vocabularies and some values between dominant and minority discourses. This means that the relationship between dominant discourses and minority literary discourses can assume a different trajectory and even an unexpected co-existence based on mutual dependency and antagonism to each other (Gilroy, 48). In this view, a minority discourse does not exist in a hermetically sealed cultural context. Possibilities of cultural infiltration of the values of minority discourses by hegemonic discourses might be difficult to rule out. Different factors such as resistance, incorporation, infiltration and cultural obeisance define the relationship between dominant and minority discourses as force field where one-off struggles might be secured, rather as a "combination of force and consent which balance each other reciprocally without force predominating excessively over consent" (Gramsci 81) can and does influence the ways in which minority discourses might authorise their own vocabularies in the process of narrating the nation. In this view, neither the dominant nor the minority discourse might become the nation's sole and most important cultural determinant in the struggle and negotiate control of cultural symbols and political sources of power. Moreover, there are fissures anticipated and embedded in the symbolical structures of both minority discourses and dominant ideologies. A discourse of any sort is a cultural artefact whose raw materials have been picked, brought together from disparate cultural sources and then creatively and fictionally reworked into a narrative in the forge of the imagination. Thus, it is crucially important and appropriate to embrace a cultural perspective that acknowledges that minority discourses are in perpetual flux. There might also be smaller instances of minority discourses within some minority discourses. Ndebele literature in English provides some tentative evidence drawn from an analysis of selected novels which show that authors emerging from the same minority community command linguistic resources differently and that these differences might energise one narrative to reject being peripherised by another in the process of defining Zimbabwean nation-ness.

My analytic sample comprises *The Stone Virgins, They Are Coming, Running with Mother*, and *We Need New Names*. Arguably, these creative works of fiction appear to have imaginatively foregrounded the theme of genocide that has tended to be declared taboo by ZANU PF government officials in both the political and literary lives of the predominantly Shona Zimbabwean nation. Literature in the English language written by Shona people has tended to shy away from this sensitive theme. The chosen Ndebele novels have represented genocide openly. This essential diversity that appears absent in Shona-authored literary works constitutes what Chennels (112) describes as a permanent feature of postcolonial minority texts. Such texts tend to be sceptical and eschew the cultural politics of originary identities supported by ideologies of cultural purity and authenticity. Ndebele cultures are rich and manifest themselves in different languages and forms. Relative to Shona-authored literature, Ndebele literature has experimented with what has been described as "illicit versions of war" (Vera 53). Therefore, Ndebele minority literary discourses might be viewed as subverting the global by engaging with the local and the atypical where dogma is replaced by ambivalence, stability by instability and purity by hybridity (Chennels 116).

Vulnerability as formal strategy in Ndebele minority discourses

Ndebele minority literary discourses tend to embrace perspectives that emphasise vulnerability and powerlessness when representing cultural ambiguities given rise to by the existence of hotly contested themes. Mwangi (458) has also shown that in Africa, those minority literary discourses that adopt the perspective of the vulnerable do so in order to register the traumatic experiences that the people inhabiting the physical and cultural spaces of minority communities need to use to reorder their shattered lives. Ndebele literature in English appears to share with Shona-authored literature unfettered freedom to write about colonialism and its effects on Africans. In Vera's *The Stone Virgins*, two sisters, Thenjiwe and Sonceba, grew under the baleful eye of colonialism. As the two women reminisce on the swift entrenchment of colonial rule in Rhodesia, they remember that their cultural values also were infiltrated and then subordinated to colonial values. The physical geographical landscapes that used to be familiar to Ndebele people have been displaced by colonialism's cultural symbols in the novel. Bulawayo, which used to be the seat of King Lobengula and resonated with Ndebele cultural symbols, is in the 1950s depicted as barely recognisable to Ndebele people. New roads constructed by the colonial administration to syphon raw materials out of the country bear the names of white fortune seekers. So, in the novel, there is now Jameson Road, Grey Road Rhodes Street and Borrow Street decorated with lush Centenary Gardens with their fusion of different imported flowers ". . . in resplendent yellow cones, in June and July, then the temperature is at its lowest" (Vera 3). Rhodes, Jameson and Wilson are the symbols of the new authorities in power and whose colonial enterprise has displaced and destroyed the Ndebele monarch. A new pattern of human settlement predicated on racially discriminatory policies is introduced, and most Ndebele people have been pushed out of Bulawayo and settled in Thandabantu in Kezi. Some of the population of Kezi move between Kezi and Bulawayo, where they offer their labour to develop Bulawayo as a distinctly Whiteman's city (Vera 17). Colonialism has also brought new commercial products such as bottles of Shield deodorant, Tomesei Shampoo, cocoa butter, tubes of camphor cream targeted to reconfigure the bodies of African women in line with colonialism's standards of beauty and progress (ibid). In the new identities forged for Ndebele women by white colonialism, black women lose the few rights they had under a precolonial patriarchal Ndebele society. In the new dispensation, white men who raped black women were made to pay a fine, while black men who raped white women were executed or hanged. This narrative that underscores the vulnerability of Ndebele men and women at the same time constituted them as a minority that had to be subdued through the use of brutal force. *The Stone Virgins* popularises the minority Ndebele narrative discourse. Strategically, such a narrative is meant to present Ndebele authors as the delegates of the deprived. However, the ambiguity of accepting powerlessness as existential reality focalises Ndebele people as emerging with new forms of power that might be bent on reversing colonialism.

In Mlalazi's *They Are Coming*, colonialism is narrated as an invasive force; the system grabbed African land and turned Africans into casual or manual labourers on European farms. The novel shows the role of colonial violence in reorganising African lives. This is nothing new because dominant discourses on colonialism have actually represented colonialism as the source of every problem that Africans suffer even after independence. This perspective is questioned in the novel. An Ndebele minority literary discourse that refuses to be lured by the dominant Shona expressive mode undermines the narrative of a triumphant African resistance. In *Running with Mother*, colonialism and liberation narratives are indexed as historical footnotes. These are attempts to subvert nationalism's desire to project itself as the new centre of all cultural truths. However, *We Need New Names* is compelled to reference both the colonial encounter and its backstory constructed as the liberation struggle (NoViolet 66). A minority discourse that constructs and presents itself as vulnerable to a palimpsest of colonial and liberation discourses might appear ahistorical if it does not acknowledge that European colonial and African liberation concepts of time and values have to some extent influenced how the minority knows or names itself. Notwithstanding, this summary of four Ndebele novels reveals that there is no appetite to compete with dominant discourses in constructing linear narratives based on binaries of the white oppressors and black oppressed. These simplistic narratives favoured by the dominant colonial and liberation narratives leave them to appear intact, stable and unassailable. A minority literary discourse can be an alternative space where different values might be elaborated. This strategic position allows a vulnerable minority discourse to represent itself as the repository of things left out of dominant history, that the ethnic subject can challenge history. A minority literary discourse might manipulate its own stock of images when projecting itself as a counter history (Palimbo-Liu 211).

Minority discourses as counterculture

Writing in the context of the Black Atlantic, Paul Gilroy has popularised the view that black minority cultures under and after slavery developed a countercultural perspective against dominant slave cultures and their relics. However, the countercultures that emerged out of the antebellum period were paradoxical; they proclaimed an organic identity in the same breath they amplified fractures within the experiences of the people who had wished to construct a poetics of minority discourse unified by common experiences. Countercultures exist inside and outside colonial modernities and the certitudes expressed through the discourse of liberation struggle. Some countercultures imagine the possibilities of creating their own cultural contexts and political values projected as free from infiltration by their perceived cultural opponents. Other countercultures claim a certain authenticity that appears to suggest that only the minority populations might have access to certain subjectivities denied to those not belonging the minority group. Other minority discourses go so far as to suggest that only people from minority communities are able to give voice to minority concerns. This means that most counter narratives are manacled by a tendency to only struggle *against* a dominant discourse and fail to struggle *for* a new society. Minority literary discourses are never complete but inchoate and unfinished.

None of the Ndebele novels I read in this section as counterculture are allowed to stabilise and become arrogant to the extent of committing the sin of conflating self-determination with democracy (Southall 79). For example, in *The Stone Virgins*, a sense of a foreboding authoritarianism hangs because within the ZIPRA liberation movement, the roles of African men and women are asymmetrical. In addition, the post-independence Zimbabwe is not experienced in the same way within the Ndebele minority community of Zimbabwe. *The Stone Virgins* focuses on the incipient and malignant narrative of genocide or Gukurahundi in Matabeleland. The novel surfaces the experiences of Ndebele people that are dismissed as "illicit versions of war" (Vera 53) in Shona dominant discourses. These illicit versions of the war are the novels' inchoate but *probable* narratives that deny the dominant discourses some coercive forms of interpretive closure. When most parts of Mashonaland are in relative peace, civil war breaks out in 1981 in Matabeleland. When the officials in Harare fail to impose new forms of hegemony on the people of Kezi, the Fifth Brigade resorts to shooting. Named as dissidents, the people of Kezi are stripped of their human rights and "soldiers shoot them, without preamble – they walked in and raised Ak rifles: every shot was fatal" (Vera 121). Where in most parts of Mashonaland, development is occurring in the form of new schools, Kezi, which represents itself and Matabeleland, are in smoke and reduced to "a naked cemetery"(Vera 143). This is the new war that assumes genocidal proportions and consumes 20,000 people, most of them of Ndebele stock. A triumphalist ZANU liberation war narrative is predicated on the desecration of the cultural life of Thandabantu. The banality of the dominant Shona-led government is revealed by the soldiers who carry out systematic torture to "intimidate, to kill, to extract confessions, to resurrect the dead" (Vera 124). Ndebele women are forced to axe their husbands and sons (Vera 80), setting the members of the minority community against each other. The authority that minority discourses in *The Stone Virgins* command and use to subvert errant Shona cultural nationalism extends to a critique of canonical Shona texts such as *Feso*, used by nationalists to contest colonial hegemony (Vera 109).

The counter-narrative sensibility projected in *The Stone Virgins* also dismantles the certitude that it was only Shona soldiers who maimed Ndebele people. People that officials named as 'dissidents' like Sibaso who have been viciously brutalised by the Mugabe government take to the hills. However, Sibaso commits the violence of murder and rape on Ndebele women. Two sisters, Thenjiwe and Nonceba, meet a different fate in the hands of Ndebele dissidents. Thenjiwe

(73) is murdered and Nonceba (62) is raped by Sibaso. In characterisation of Sibaso, Ndebele patriarchy is denied the privilege to speak on behalf of every Ndebele person. However, Vera's narratives are characterised by ideological anxieties. First, the author's characters are all drawn from the Ndebele ethnic group, and this might suggest that there the genocidal war was pre-meditated by all Shona people. This reveals the entrapment of the minority literary discourses in the novel. *Running with Mother* frames the minoritisation of the discourse of genocide differently. The government soldiers tell Rudo Jamela, a form two girl from the village of Mbongolo borne of a Shona mother and Ndebele, that the soldiers were killing "all the Ndebele people" (Mlalazi 17). Violence is indexed differently in the text. Men, women and children are stripped naked. Some people break free and run away. The soldiers shoot them, and several fall to the ground (Mlalazi 41). Rudo describes "a mass of human bodies, burnt together: charred limbs, bones shining white in the moonlight and defaced skulls. The stench of burnt flesh was intense" (Mlalazi 27).

Further down the river, Rudo, Mother and Auntie witness naked bodies in the river floating towards them. As Rudo says: "A naked body was floating towards us. . . . I saw it did not have a head, only a neck with a big open wound at the top" (Mlalazi 70). A minority discourse deliberately constructs victimhood through the stockpiling of images of destroyed lives. This is meant to underline the vulnerability of the people of Ndebele stock. As Mother, Rudo and Auntie run towards the Phezulu mountains, they also come across the body of Miss Grant, one white woman who has been raped and shot (Mlalazi 130). Rudo's friends have been raped by soldiers, and her neighbours are forced to kill and rape their neighbours while their children are watching (Mlalazi 130). Other Ndebele men are forced to dig mass graves into which the Ndebele dead are thrown (Mlalazi 129). Some Ndebele people killed by the soldiers are dumped into Saphela mine (Mlalazi 131)." Mass killing is sanitised of its horrors and even 'dignified' that mass murder is described as necessary work to keep ". . . our country clean of weeds and trash" (Mlalazi 138). Comrade Finish further describes the atrocities in Mbongolo as patriotic national duty (Mlalazi 139). *Running with Mother* singles out Ndebele people as the victims of the failure of the postcolonial Zimbabwean state. Violence unleashed by the soldiers is committed on men, women and children. In this regard, the novel surfaces how a Shona-dominated and masculinised violent liberation war narrative is instrumental in creating a post-war gendered political power configuration bordering on political misogyny. To further complicate its own ideological constructed-ness, Uncle Ndoro, who is a Shona man in Matabeleland, is killed by Shona government soldiers during the violence (Vera 137). This means that in *Running with Mother*, the "historical representations available to the ethnic subject" are never entirely allowed to stabilise and sediment as the only narratives that the novel might imagine and authorise. Where Rudo, who is half Shona and half Ndebele, is spared by the government soldiers, Ndebele girls meet a horrifying fate. Nobuhle's hands are cut off, while others are stripped, raped and then murdered (Vera 10). This narrative of rape, murder and bombing of Ndebele girls contains different memories of how independence is experienced in Zimbabwe. Strategically, the stockpiling of images of the dead is how a minority literary discourse calls for attention to some parts of the world who can still feel something to intervene.

The gory nature of the genocidal war institutes imagery that rejects the romantic narratives of war and peace favoured by the dominant Shona narrative in politics as in Shona fiction. *Harvest of Thorns* creates a linear narrative that ends up in disappointment because the freedom fighters have not received their rewards for participating in the liberation struggle. Novels by Shona authors such as Hove's *Bones* (1988), Samupindi's *Pawns* (1992), Mutasa's *Sekai Minda Tave Nayo* and Mtizira's *The Chimurenga Protocol* (2008) show how dominant discourses have institutionalised the novel form as the platform to celebrate and defend the gains of the land reform. This sample of influential fiction in English and Shona language by predominantly Shona authors shies away from the theme of genocide. Therefore, for the Ndebele literary discourse to focalise the theme of genocide that is left out of the dominant literary discourse is to expose how, in a post-colony Zimbabwe, some creative texts canonised as the marrow of tradition participate in minoritisation of Ndebele communities.

In *Running with Mother*, a minority literary discourse chooses to remember the atrocities committed on the members of the community and refuses to celebrate the liberation struggle. Ndebele people with alternative perspectives of imagining a new Zimbabwe are killed so that Ndebele children would, when they grow old, come to see what soldiers do to dissidents and later would reform. The official discourse that names Ndebele people as throwaway people is contested by Auntie. She argues that her brothers, Genesis and Francis, "were not dissidents [but] just simple people looking after their families and their livestock" (Mlalazi 24). The complexity of *Running with Mother* reflects on itself and acknowledges that Shona women also suffered during the genocidal war. Mother has lost an Ndebele husband and relatives and neighbours and friends. In addition, Mother is self supporting and takes care of Auntie who is Ndebele, and Gift, who is an Ndebele baby. She is symbolically transformed into an archetypal image of reconciliation. Mother organises the kinds of food that the running women are to take with them to Phezulu Mountain. She maintains a semblance of community even in the most distressing context of a genocidal war. Mother renders possible the idea of an imagined nation composed of Ndebele and Shona characters emerging from Phezulu Mountain. Mother is the agent who would patch together a communal quilt of national consciousness with all its acknowledged contradictions. Mother is distinguished from other mortals by her familiar determination and firm decisions and reassuring presence (Mlalazi 21).

Mother appears not to approve of Ndebele men like Mr Mkandla, who attempts to construct a reverse identity when he accuses Mother of belonging to the Shona group killing Ndebele people "with the permission of the Prime Minister" (Mlalazi 32). This narrative pits Shona people against the Ndebele people. Auntie argues that Mother has become part of the Ndebele family. In this narrative of female sisterhood, Ndebele men are denied the right to monopolise the pain of the genocide and speak on behalf of women. For Mr. Mkandla, all Shona people are guilty by association because "Shona soldiers are killing our defenceless families" (RM, 132). Mother believes Zimbabwe is "for everybody: the Shona, the Ndebele, Kalanga, Venda, Tonga, Suthu and all the other tribes that live within our borders, even the whites, the Indians, the Italians, the Chinese, coloureds, everybody. Isn't this why we went to war"? (RM, 109). Mother's confidence and her love for life are infectious to Auntie. Mother might come from Chisara, somewhere from Mashonaland, or Manicaland or Masvingo. This means that a minority discourse would deprive itself the capacity to create a cultural context outside the regime of signifiers in dominant discourses. This would mean that a minority discourse might allow itself to be co-opted and dictated by colonial and ZANU PF dominant discourses. Therefore, a novel that criticises Shona soldiers for murdering Ndebele people and places the burden of reconciling inhabitants of a scarred nation on the shoulders of Mother, who is Shona, deconstructs the notion of a parochial mentality that mistakes regionalism for a nation-ness. In other words, minority discourses can revise dominant historical discourses by stepping outside their functional paradigms. The distinctive identity of *Running with Mother* as a minority discourse is that it warns of the dangers of promoting a single narrative based on unitary and authentic identities of war and the liberation struggle.

They Are Coming refuses to forget the violence on women in the genocidal war. The novel reveals ideological striations or unevenness in the embodiment of a national consciousness evinced by individual characters. For example, there are Africans who fight on the side of white people against the liberation forces (Mlalazi 80), just as there are ZIPRA forces that prey on ordinary Ndebele people in the struggle for the country's self-determination. The fractured nature of the consciousness that seeks to forge a new Zimbabwe nation is further underlined in the efforts to sell MaNdlovu to one Mbambo who worked as an informer for a white farmer called Phillips who owned Wildberg Farm (Mlalazi 79). The fragility of a Zimbabwean nation in this novel is amplified by Senzeni, who has abandoned her MaNdlovu, her Father Ngwenya and her brother, Ambition Senzini, to join a ZANU PF militia in post-independence Zimbabwe. This militia has a specific mandate to burn the houses and kill those Ndebele people who have joined a new party called the Movement for Democratic Change. Historically, this party came into being in 1999 and championed the need to introduce changes to the economic lives of the Zimbabwean masses. In the novel, the ruling party enlists a militia called the Green Bombers to frustrate this agenda for change. Members of the Green Bombers militia receive lessons from a Mrs Gumbo, and her propaganda rehearses patriotic history (Mlalazi 98). Patriotic history suppresses alternative discourses and any narratives that it does not understand or cannot live with (Ranger 257).

Furthermore, in *They Are Coming*, the ominous consequences of adherence to patriotic history are manifest in the murder of Mr Nkani, who has embraced the new discourse of change. Senzeni is part of the militia group that terrorises her community by burning the houses owned by Ndebele people who are found "singing anti-Mugabe song" (60). Green Bombers are sometimes pushed back by the people agitating for social change. However, in most cases, the Green Bombers have the upper hand because when they begin to beat people and break the windows of people's houses, the police do not arrest them. The polarisation of the subjectivities of the MaNdlovu and her daughter Senzeni might be the way a minority literary discourse represents the fractures that define the concept of Zimbabwean nation-ness. *They Are Coming* draws out the conflicts attendant to forging a discourse of national identity. The novel appears to suggest that the distinctive identities of the concept of Zimbabwean nation-ness are manifest in how this concept is lived differently by characters who might be bound to each other as a minority in relation to the numerical advantage of another social group. Thus, if we accept the premise that minority literary discourses are forms of experimental fiction, the significance of this disruptive experimental fiction is that it involves endless revisions of colonial, nationalist discourses and questions the truth claims that minority discourses also authorise. Nothing is allowed to settle in novels that reclaim for themselves the aesthetic of the transitory nature of human subjectivities.

'Minor' voices and subaltern resistance

Set in the period after 2000 when ZANU PF's hegemony is on the wane, discourses of colonialism and the liberation struggle are referenced as fading footnotes. The emphasis on the novel is on interrogating the cultural irrationalities embodied in the obsolete programmes of ZANU PF. Instead of providing more houses to those without, the Mugabe government found itself destroying forms of shelters and houses that the masses had built for themselves. The main narrators in *We Need New Names* are a group of young children between the ages of 10 and 13 years. The use of the child perspective provides irony that functions to destabilise not only the ZANU PF narrative of false progress, but the children's narratives also subvert the adult Ndebele people's views on the meaning of freedom. *We Need New Names* might therefore be best analysed thematically as a novel that introduces dissonance within the minority discourses promoted by adult perspectives that are constructed around cultural ennui, anomy and moral stagnation. The quest motif for a better life given rise by the moral outrage at how ZANU PF has mismanaged the economy of the country and deprived the young and adults of their human rights is undermined by threats to constitutionalism from a liberation movement that has outlived its usefulness (Southall 80). *They Are Coming, Running with Mother* and *We Need New Names* embrace the voices of child narrator strategies of transgression. Child narrators appear to embrace tropological discourses of minors. Minor or child narrators use excessive significations of negative experiences to index post-independence Zimbabwe. This approach to minority discourses might expand rather than "narrow the aesthetic possibilities of semiotic disobedience" (Vambe, 123).

Human subjectivities authorised by children as minors who narrate the stories of failure in a *kaka* country in *We Need New Names* are differentiated but individuated and nuanced. Creative narratives by minors deconstruct colonialism, ZANU PF's triumphant nationalism based on some liberation war believed to have been fought on some physical space spanning from what Darling describes as the "home before the white people came to steal the country, home before independence, Home after independence . . . home of things fall apart before Aunt Fostalina went to America" (Bulawayo 193–194). In addition, narratives by minors or child characters subvert the aspirations of adults within the context of Ndebele minority communities. The creative imagination that ropes in the spirit of creative disruption also complicates the voices of minors or child narrators in *We Need New Names*. Minor child-authorised literary narratives appear to create and allow readers to access certain imaginative worlds not apparent in adult narratives that tend to conform to linear versions of Zimbabwean nation-ness. In *We Need New Names*, minor or child narrative privileges fragmented, disjointed conception of time. The community of minors in the novel is made up of Godknows, Forgiveness, Darling, Chipo, Bastard, Sbho and Stina. The views of the minors are irreverent of adult perspectives, and child narrator's voices "hover within, between and outside of temporal, spatial" (Mwangi 454) conception of development and definitions of freedom preferred in dominant discourses. For the minors or child narrators, colonial privileges have continued in post-independence Zimbabwe. Whites own large tracts of land, live in Budapest, a place of ". . . big houses with satellite dishes on the roofs and neat graveled yards, trimmed lawns, and the tall fences, and the Durawalls and the flowers, and the big trees heavy with fruit that's waiting for us since nobody around here seems to know what to do with it" (Bulawayo, 4). The physical distance that separates Budapest from Paradise where the minors live is emphasised by Heavensgates, a graveyard. Paradise, into which the minors' parents have been driven by the government's violent programme of Operation Murambatsvina (Vambe 1) or drive out trash is a place of poverty, dirt, hunger and shacks of ". . . tin that stretch out in sun light a wet sheepskin nailed on the ground to dry; the shacks are the muddy color of dirty puddles after the rains" (Bulawayo 34).

Most inhabitants from Paradise have been left stranded by government's heavy-handed maltreatment of its people. Most of the ordinary people have left the country and dispersed into diaspora in countries such as Dubai, South Africa, Botswana and Tanzania. Those people pushed into exile, like Darling's father, seem not to find it easy in the newly adopted countries. Host countries are "not country-countries" (49) because they are war-torn and therefore "No body wants to be rags of countries like Congo, like Somalis, like Iraq, like Sudan, like Haiti, like Sri Lanka and not even this one we live in" which are places of "hunger and things falling apart" (49). The nationalist discourses that project independence as progressive underestimate how, in these countries, democratic systems have failed to take root. Most third world countries, including Zimbabwe, are failed states; their governments commit violence that gives rise to internal and external displacement. This undermines the potential of African countries to harness the talents of their people. The people who have remained trapped in Paradise have been immiserated by State-induced faminogenic policies and have to be fed by NGOs in order to survive

(Bulawayo 55). Darling's voice registers the irreverence that the children have against the insensitive adult world. In her view, the "old president who doesn't want to die" (179) monopolises the power to speak on behalf of the suffering masses of Paradise. This old president rants on TV that Zimbabwe cannot be ". . . a colony again and what-what" (192), yet there is no democracy and the respect of the rule of law in the country. Before the people of Paradise came to live in this place, they had built their own decent houses, but the government sent bulldozers to pull the houses down (Bulawayo 65). Impoverishing ordinary people is one of the government strategies to keep the masses in slavery. A hungry populace is meant to be loyal and dependent on the patronage that the dominant discourses can selectively dispense. Masses are transformed from citizens to subjects without voice. Violence is meted on local whites to intimidate them to give up their land. Those young people like Bornfree who decide to embrace new political parties that challenge the dominant classes are subjected to systematic torture, pounded and clobbered until they die (Bulawayo 114).

The response of minority adult communities to the reign of terror unleashed on the Ndebele adults by the new black government is also not beyond reproach and criticism by the child narrators. MaDube "suffered from madness after the old President's security agents killed her son" (Bulawayo 148). Darling's mother supplements her cross-border informal trade with selling sex to a strange man who comes in the ". . . dark like a ghost, leap onto bed with mother" (Bulawayo 64).

Father has abandoned the child narrator and does not send money from South Africa. The world of adults is rejected for accepting vulnerability and settling for less when they should openly stand up against a system that oppresses them. When the adult Ndebele people decide to change their lives, they choose to vote for the new political party spreading the gospel of change. However, in the eyes of minors or child narrators like Darling, the world of their parents lacks conviction about the eventuality or possibility of change. The language that minors use to describe the temporary wave of the winds of political change registers scepticism over the capacity of the adults to effect meaningful transformation of the inhabitants of the people of Paradise. Darling expresses this doubt that the adults have when she says that children have heard about "change, about new country, about democracy, about elections and what-what" (Bulawayo 59).

In a country where political institutions have been captured by ZANU PF, Darling feels that the Ndebele adults appear to be investing in the enemy territory in believing that the old guard of Zimbabwean leaders would respect the results of an election that might push them out of power. The adults underestimate the creativity of abuse. Even when the adults go to vote, they are unsure about the political consequences of their actions. When change does not come, adults retreat into a world of inebriation at Mother of Love's tavern. Prophet Revelations Bitchington Mborro's religious zeal also shows how he is ill equipped to deal with the arrogant and yet dominant discourses that have reduced the people of Paradise to adopt mystical approaches to problems given rise by material inequalities, bad governance and systemic corruption that has eroded the power of the state to feed its own people. Darling observes that when, "afterwards no change came, the voices of the worshippers folded like a butterfly's wings, and the worshippers trickled down Fambeki like broken bones and dragged themselves away, but now they are back like God didn't even ignore them that time" (Bulawayo 137).

The minor discourses use irony to confront and expose the inadequacies of adults' agency in challenging the dominant discourses of ZANU PF. However, the complexity of child narratives is also their capacity to test the limits of their own strengths. There are no easy collective identities that child narrators can forge and aspire to and hold on to with certainty. Chipo has been raped by her grandfather and she is pregnant by him (Bulawayo 10). Sbho is compassionate and does not like to see white people being harassed and dispossessed of their property by the new ruling black elites under a spurious land reform programme calculated to benefit a few powerful nationalist politicians. Bastard is a bully, hard-hearted and devoid of sentiments and dreams small. He is distinctive for his rough ways that include beating his childhood friends and pelting a woman dangling from a tree after committing suicide with stones. Darling is a dreamer who imagines going to America to live with Aunt Fostalina in Detroit, Michigan (Bulawayo 15). The minors are depicted as a bunch of small-time thieves who do not go to school but spend their time stealing guavas in Budapest. Darling and her girlfriends attempt to assist Chipo to abort her pregnancy using the most primitive instruments that most likely might have killed Chipo. The fragility of the child narrator is amplified further when Darling goes to live with Aunt Fostalina in America. Darling finds out that people in America have a stereotypical view of Africa as exotic, and as a shithole continent riven with disease and war (Bulawayo 175). Aunt Fostalina sleeps with her white boyfriend, although she stays with Uncle Kojo from Ghana. Aunt Fostalina cannot go back to Zimbabwe because she has no legal documents that would enable her to go back to America.

Despite the fact that there is dissonance between the America Darling imagined and the actual America, Darling's experiences in America open her up to new worlds that were not available in Zimbabwe. In America, she eats plenty of food, and she also discovers her sexuality with new friends. The walls of inhibitions that Paradise posed for Darling are also fast destroyed in America. Darling also learns how to use a cell phone to connect with Chipo in Zimbabwe. Darling also feels that, though a rich country with every conceivable form of pleasures, the America she experiences is not the one she dreamt of while in Zimbabwe (Bulawayo 188). Darling denies her own minor narrative any closure sealed with a sense of stable fulfilment of her dreams. She recognises that minority discourses cannot aspire to closure, as these discourses appear to reflect contradictory human experiences as lived in the several homes in one's head. As she notes, memories destabilise each other in the process of imagining different ways of conceptualising multiple identities of Zimbabwean nation-ness. For Darling, no matter how much food she eats in America, she remains hungry for her country. This country that needs fixing (Bulawayo 153). In imagining Zimbabwean nation-ness through the lens of minority literary discourses, one is bound to experience several and even contradictory identities of belonging to the Zimbabwean nations, the first of which is home:

> Before the white came to steal the country, and a king ruled; home when the white people came to steal the country and then there was war; home when black people got our stolen country back after independence; and then the home of now. Home, one, Home two, Home three, home four.
>
> *(Bulawayo 192)*

The uncanny irony is that in its quest for new values, identities, aspirational goals and names, *We Need New Names* deliberately undermines conceptions of home plotted on a linear historiography because this mode of reconceptualising Zimbabwean nation-ness is reductive and limiting and imposes essentialised identities. The power of minority discourses discussed in *The Stone Virgins, They Are Coming, Running with Mother* and *We Need New Names* appears to have derived from a willed choice to embrace cultural diversity and not ethnic absolutism. This political option challenges ideologies of cultural authenticity based on Othering, which is the symbolical processes by which dominant discourses establish themselves as the hegemon and proceed to act "as if that reality existed in the perception of everyone concerned" (Chennels, 112).

Conclusion

The aim of this chapter was to explore how the themes of colonialism, liberation struggle and freedom are treated in four novels selected from the minority Ndebele literary discourse. It was shown that creative art by Ndebele authors simultaneously depicts the theme of colonialism and the liberation struggle just as literature by Shona authors has done. However, Ndebele minority discourses tend to depict the themes differently. Ndebele literary discourses in IsiNdebele language and Ndebele oral genres have not been considered. This chapter argued that *The Stone Virgins, They Are Coming,* and *Running with Mother* introduced the theme of genocide in Zimbabwe literature. This theme is hardly depicted in literature by Shona authors. To this extent, the Ndebele minority discourse presented itself as bringing thematic novelty. The image of powerlessness through which Ndebele minority discourse makes itself known is a strategic tool used by the authors to stake out or clear space for elaborating their own alternative rationalities and values. In revising nationalist discourses of Zimbabwe, Ndebele minority discourses have also presented themselves as countercultural. This means that minority discourses identify themselves as discourses of resistances. *The Stone Virgins* criticises the marginalisation of the Ndebele women during colonialism and in the liberation struggle and attacks the rape and murder of African women by ZIPRA freedom fighters. *They Are Coming* complicates the idea that Ndebele minority discourses are organic and culturally authentic. In the novel, some members of the minority Ndebele community such as Senzeni have been co-opted by the dominant nationalist ideologies. Senzeni joins the militia group called the Green Bombers. This militia outfit is used by the new ruling elites to burn houses and kill people who challenge the dominant discourse authorised by ZANU PF.

Running with Mother depicts the atrocities perpetrated by the Mugabe soldiers in Matabeleland in the 1980s. However, the novel also questions the view that a minority literary discourse can present itself as stable. In the novel, Ndebele people suffer the most from the genocidal war. The novel also shows that Shona women married to Ndebele men might have been spared death, but the women suffered emotionally. In presenting a Shona woman as a potential model for post-war reconciliation in Matabeleland, the novel also questions certain trends in Ndebele minority literature which tend to collapse the conduct of the soldiers and that of the Shona people. *We Need New Names* innovates with the views of minor or child narrators. The perspective of minors up-ends adults' views. The novel reveals that African children have been bastardised by the dominant discourses in post-independence Zimbabwe. The construction of Ndebele minority literary discourses reveals that this literature resists being minoritised. The significance of an Ndebele minority discourse lies in how it interrogates colonialism and the liberation struggle and how nationalism constructs the subjectivities of African men and women.

Primary sources

Bulawayo, NoViolet. *We Need New Names*. London: Vintage Books, 2014.
Mlalazi, Christopher. *Running with Mother*. Harare: Weaver Press, 2012.
Mlalazi, Christopher, *They Are Coming*. Harare: Weaver Press, 2014.
Vera, Yvonne. *The Stone Virgins*. Harare: Weaver Press, 2002.

Secondary sources

Chennels, A. John. "Essential Diversity: Post-Colonial Theory and African Literatures." *Brno Studies in English*, 25, 1999, 109–126.
Gates, L. Henry Louis. *Loose Canons: Notes on the Culture Wars*. New York: Oxford University Press, 1992.

Gilroy, Paul. *The Black Atlantic: Modernity and Double Consciousness*. Cambridge: Harvard University Press, 1993.

Gramsci, Antonio. *Selections from the Prison Note Books*. New York: International Publishers, 1971.

Hove Chenjerai. *Bones*. Harare: Baobab Books, 1988.

Mtizira Nyaradzo. *The Chimurenga Protocol*. Harare: Botshelo Publishing, 2008.

Mwangi, Evans. "Experimental Fictions." Simon Gikandi Ed. *The Novel in Africa and the Caribbean since 1950*. Oxford: Oxford University Press, 2016, 443–460.

Palumbo-LIU, David. "The Politics of Memory: Remembering History in Alice Walker and Joy Kogawa." Amritjit Singh, Ed. *Memory & Cultural Politics: New Approaches to American Ethnic Literatures*. Boston: Northeastern University Pres, 1996, 211–226.

Ranger, Terence Osborne. "History Has a Ceiling: The Pressures of the Past in *The Stone Virgins*." R. Muponde & M. Taruvinga, Eds. *Sign and Taboo: Perspectives on the Poetic Fiction of Yvonne Vera*. Harare: Weaver Press, 2002, 203–216.

Samupindi Charles. *Pawns*. Harare: Baobab Books, 1992.

Southall, Roger. "Threats to Constitutionalism by Liberation Movements in Southern Africa." *Africa Spectrum*, 49, 1, 2014, 79–99.

Wa Thiongo, Ngugi. *Moving the Centre: The Struggle for Cultural Freedom*. London: James Curry, 1993.

20

THE MUSE OF HISTORY AND THE LITERATURE OF THE NIGERIA-BIAFRA WAR

Maik Nwosu

The historical accounts of the Nigeria–Biafra War include books on the circumstances leading up to the war, how the war was fought, and the consequences of the conflict. *Nigeria's Five Majors: Coup d'Etat of 15th January 1966, First Inside Account* by Ben Gbulie; *Why We Struck: The Story of the First Nigerian Coup* by Adewale Ademoyega; *The Nigerian Revolution and the Biafran War* by Alexander A. Madiebo; *Requiem Biafra* by Joe O. G. Achuzia; *Nigeria and Biafra: My Story* by Philip Efiong; *My Command: An Account of the Nigerian Civil War 1967–70* and *Nzeogwu* by Olusegun Obasanjo; *On a Darkling Plain: An Account of the Nigerian Civil War* by Ken Saro-Wiwa; *Biafra: The Making of an African Legend* and *Emeka* by Frederick Forsyth; *Let Truth Be Told* by D. J. M. Muffett; *The Brothers' War: Biafra and Nigeria* by John de St. Jorre; and *Blood on the Niger: An Untold Story of the Nigerian Civil War* by Emma Okocha are some well-known instances. These studies present "factual" or "inside" accounts of the circumstances and consequences of Nigeria's first military coup on January 15, 1966; the counter-coup on July 29, 1966; and the declaration of secession by Eastern Nigeria on May 30, 1967. Some contested accounts allege that the first coup was organized by Igbo or Eastern Nigerian military officers with the objective of eliminating major political figures from Northern Nigeria. The counter-coup was a revenge mission, as was the pogrom against Igbos or Eastern Nigerians resident in Northern Nigeria. The declaration of secession or the Republic of Biafra represented a failure of dialogue as well as the decimation of the idea of Nigeria.

For Alexander Madiebo, in *The Nigerian Revolution and the Biafran War*, the January 1966 coup was a revolution that could have corrected some of Nigeria's problems. He points out that "the political struggle and the consequent drifting apart of the various peoples of Nigeria went on over the years unchecked, to an extent that the Federal Parliament was reduced to an intertribal battlefield" (5) and states:

> The January coup was sufficiently successful for that regime to have rectified whatever was done badly and still retain power, discipline and respect. What happened was that Nigeria, which was being treated for an overdose of compromise by those who carried out the coup, was being administered with more doses of compromise by Ironsi's regime, which inherited power after the revolution.
>
> *(28)*

276

Ben Gbulie, who was one of the so-called "five majors" that organized the January 1966 coup, set out in *Nigeria's Five Majors* to correct "the impressions formed by the half-truths, fabrications and fallacies already in print on the subject" (vii). His account also signposts the mismanagement of the Nigerian promise, including within the military: "Standards of officer prerequisites had . . . dropped drastically. So had those of discipline. But tribalism had risen like a phoenix in the Nigerian Army" (13). He was "fully convinced that a coup d'état would go a long way to remedy the whole situation" (13). Ademoyega's *Why We Struck: The Story of the First Nigerian Coup* similarly highlights the rise of tribalism and the destruction of the Nigerian promise, going back to 1861 when the British took "over the rulership of the country . . . (with the cession of Lagos)" (1). He examines the political-military prelude to the coup and also sets forth the intention of the coupists – the correction of "the worst anomaly of the 1957 constitution" by erasing the existing four regions at the time and breaking the country into "fourteen states, each of which would be conterminous with two of the former twenty-six provinces of the federation, except Sokoto and Oyo states which were to be conterminous with one province each" (33).

Madiebo, Gbulie, and Ademoyega contextualize the January 1966 coup almost as an inevitable uprising, driven by ideas, to check the upsurge of tribalism and the hegemonic impulse in a Nigeria that they apparently believed was still redeemable. Obasanjo agrees with their evaluation regarding tribalism. In *Nzeogwu*, he details his closeness to a major figure of the January 1966 coup, Chukuwma Kaduna Nzeogwu, with whom he "discussed at length . . . events in the country but particularly in the Army, where tribalism, favouritism, double standards and general indiscipline had set in as a result of over-politicisation" (qtd in *My Watch* 168). In *My Command*, Obasanjo identifies the January 1966 coup and the July 1966 counter-coup, "which altered the political equation and destroyed the fragile trust existing among the major ethnic groups," as "the immediate cause of the civil war" (xi). He writes:

> As a means of holding the country together in the last resort, twelve states were created from the existing four regions in May 1967 by the Federal Government. The former Eastern Region under Ojukwu saw the act of the creation of States by decree 'without consultation' as the last straw, and declared the Region to be the independent State of "Biafra."
>
> *(xi)*

Obasanjo's constant reference to Biafra in quotation marks is significative. As he points out in *My Watch*, "I see people for what they are: as good or bad human beings. We all have different identities, but I use the identity of tribe or language only when it is absolutely necessary. The commonest and most important identity for me is *Nigerian*" (195).

Emeka Ojukwu, the military governor of Eastern Nigeria who declared the secession of the region in 1967, did not publish a book about the Nigeria-Biafra War before his death. His book, *Because I Am Involved*, only makes somewhat passing references to the January 1966 coup – such as his description of Emmanuel Ifeajuna (rather than Nzeogwu) as the leader of the coup: "He conceived the idea, hatched the plot, recruited the participants and launched the action. He also botched the plot" (157). Ojukwu also identifies tribalism as "perhaps the one single factor that has nullified all our efforts at evolving a national leadership capable of fulfilling our national aspirations" (20). On the contentious issue of state creation, he writes rather philosophically: "In the attempt to allay certain ethnic apprehensions, states were created, but somehow along the line we have converted the whole idea from a political into an economic concept" (176). If Ojukwu did not publish a book about the war, he did speak about it, such as during an interview with *The Source* newsmagazine in June 1997. Responding to a question about whether the problems accompanying the declaration of Biafra were not obvious before the proclamation, he said:

> When you look at these things, they look so straightforward. We had no arms, no ammunition. The pogroms took place in the north of Nigeria. Huge massacre, what I then called a genocidal attack on our people. How could I have ordered them to go back to the North or other parts of Nigeria . . . Till I die, I will never forget. And I keep remembering. I close my eyes and I see it. The headless corpse sent to me. A very strong man beheaded, and written on the coach: A PRESENT FOR OJUKWU.
>
> *(The Source 9)*

From Ojukwu's perspective, the declaration of Biafra was an act of survival, and the war was necessitated by political circumstances in Nigeria at the time as well as the genocidal attacks against Igbos or Eastern Nigerians. Ken Saro-Wiwa, who supported Nigeria during the war (although he was from Eastern Nigeria), disputes this perspective in *On a Darkling Plain*: "To the majority of the Ibo elite, the case looked too good to be lost. The brutal killings in the 'North' had given the Ibos the rationale for opting out of the Federation" (82). He questions Ojukwu's motivation, writing that it "remains a big blight on the Ibo elite that they did not see through the man" (83) and that "Ojukwu was out on a naked quest for power. There is truth in the continued assertion that he was only using the suffering of the Ibos to further his private ends" (84). This sort of contention instantiates the divergent muse of history in the context of war and memory.

Another example is the argument about the true intention of the "five majors" that planned the January 1966 coup, which set off a chain of events that led to the war. Were they idealists or tribalists? Focusing on Nzeogwu, Fredrick Forsyth (who reported the Nigeria-Biafra War as a British journalist) writes in *Emeka*:

> Major Nzeogwu was a left-wing radical, and a Marxist, but he was no racialist. Far from hating the North, he loved it, and the Northern soldiers he commanded. During his coup three senior Northern officers were killed, Brigadier Maimalari and Colonels Pam and Largema. Two Yoruba senior officers were killed and two Ibo majors. The two key Ibo officers in infantry posts, Johnson Ironsi and Emeka Odumegwu-Ojukwu, were marked for death.
>
> The myth became fashionable to "justify" the July coup, which beyond doubt had no particular political philosophy but was extremely racial. *All* those taking part, senior officers, junior officers and soldiers, were Northern and *all* the victims were Eastern, except Fajuyi the one Yoruba.
>
> *(69)*

D. J. M. Muffett, who worked in Northern Nigeria as a British colonial officer, utilizes a different approach in *Let Truth Be Told*:

> In neither the Eastern Region, nor in Benin in the Mid West, were any attacks made on the heads of government or any politicians killed. This fact is undeniable and can indicate only either:

1   A failure on the part of the plotters to execute the plan *in toto*, due to

(a) ineptitude, or
(b) cowardice.

2   A lack of firm intention from the first, or a change of plan at the last moment, or
3   That there had never been any intention to execute a plot in the East or the Mid West at all, and that those who thought there had been were duped.

This last possibility can by no means be ruled out. A considerable body of evidence in fact tends to point towards it.

(43)

Referencing the Federal Police Report (prepared by the Nigerian Special Branch after inter-rogating "200 officers and men, including all the ringleaders involved in the coup"), John de St. Jorre, a British journalist who covered the war, concludes in *The Brothers' War: Biafra and Nigeria*:

The January coup, therefore, was not part of a Machiavellian Ibo plot to take over the Federation. The young majors who planned and executed it genuinely felt they were performing a painful but necessary piece of surgery to restore Nigeria's failing health. But they bungled – none of them appeared to have given a thought to post-operative care – and almost killed the patient.

(47)

On the question of genocide, there appears to be less dissension. Michael J. C. Echeruo describes "the underlying motivation for the war" as "genocidal rather than political. Biafra should stand in the world's conscience as a monument to the possibility of successfully resisting 'final solutions'" ("Biafra, Civil War, and Genocide"). In his 2001 prologue to his 1969 book, *The Biafra Story: The Making of an African Legend*, Frederick Forsyth describes Biafra as "a mis-take [that] should and need never have happened" (vii). He notes: "But nothing can or ever will minimize the injustice and brutality perpetrated on the Biafran people, nor diminish the shamefulness of a British government's frantic, albeit indirect, participation" (ix). In Chapter 13, entitled "The Question of Genocide," he states: "About the massacres of 1966 enough has been said. It is generally admitted that the size and scope of the killings gave them 'genocidal proportions'" (258). His focus extends to the massacre of Igbos not only in Northern Nigeria but also in the Midwest: "The widespread killing of Biafran civilians and of Ibo inhabitants of the Midwest State is equally incontrovertible. After the withdrawal of the Biafran forces from the Midwest in late September 1967 after a six-week occupation, a series of massacres started against Ibo residents" (259). This aspect of the war is detailed in *Blood on the Niger: An Untold Story of the Nigerian Civil War* by Emma Okocha. Focusing on the massacre of civilians in Asaba (and some neighboring towns) after the failure of the Biafran invasion of the Midwest (and the retreat of Biafran soldiers), Okocha's account includes how "the execution of two prominent Asaba giants, Mr Leo Okogwu and Mr Michael Ugoh sent the whole inner town scampering in terror. . . . The people's morale sunk to the lowest ebb" (59). Other books accentuate the pogrom that precipitated the war. Martin Meredith gives a condensed account in *The Fortunes of Africa: A 5000-Year History of Wealth, Greed, and Endeavor*: "In July, a group of Northern officers struck back in a counter-coup, killing scores of Eastern officers and other ranks. In a savage onslaught, disgruntled Northerners attacked minority eastern communities living in segregated quarters – *sabon garis* – in their midst, killing and maiming thousands. As easterners sought to escape the violence, a massive exodus to the east began" (606). John Reader's *Africa: A Biography of the Continent* presents a similar assessment:

> This time the killing was on a far more terrible scale than before, and the purpose was not simply vengeance but to drive Easterners out of the North altogether . . . Disgruntled politicians, civil servants, and students urged the mobs on to the streets and the Northern army joined in. Thousands of Easterners were killed or maimed; thousands more fled – from the North and from other parts of Nigeria as the climate of fear touched Igbos everywhere.
>
> *(669–670)*

Besides the personal accounts and the interpretations of motives and methods, two documents in particular articulate the official position of the Biafran government. The first is the Declaration of Biafra proclamation on May 30, 1967. Its ten-point declaration includes:

> (i) all political ties between us and the Federal Republic of Nigeria are hereby totally dissolved; (ii) all subsisting contractual obligations entered into by the Government of the Federal Republic of Nigeria . . . relating to any matter or thing, within the Republic of Biafra, shall henceforth be deemed to entered into with the Military Governor of the Republic of Biafra.
>
> *(Kirk-Greene 452)*

The declaration foregrounds the Biafran minority discourse against Nigeria by citing both the belief "that you [Eastern Nigerians] are born free and have certain inalienable rights which can best be preserved by yourselves" (Kirk-Greene 451) and the unwillingness of Eastern Nigerians "to be unfree partners in any association of a political and economic nature" (Kirk-Greene 452). Four days before the declaration, Lt. Col. Emeka Odumegwu-Ojukwu had addressed the Eastern Consultative Assembly and complained that the Federal Military Government (led by Lt. Colonel Yakubu Gowon) had refused to implement decisions reached at Aburi, Ghana, in a bid to unite the country: "As far as the regions were concerned, it was decided that all the powers vested by the Nigerian Constitution in the Regions and which they exercised prior to 15th January, 1966, should be restored to the Regions" (Kirk-Greene 434). Gowon has a different interpretation of what was decided at Aburi. In his "factional" narrative, *Just Before Dawn*, Kole Omotoso writes about the then-Ghanaian head of state, Lt. General Joseph Ankrah, saying to Ojukwu and Gowon after they reached an agreement at Aburi: "'Both of you have got 56 million people to look after. If you keep to these agreements you will achieve peace; if you don't, then whatever comes is your fault. You have seen the way. It is up to you'" (278).

The second document, "The Ahiara Declaration (The Principles of the Biafran Revolution)," was originally a speech by Ojukwu at Ahiara on June 1, 1969. The Ahiara Declaration forcefully makes the case for the existence of Biafra, decries international conspiracies against Biafra, and projects its capabilities. It trumpets the successes of the Biafran army in holding back Nigerian offensives:

> In the Onitsha sector of the war, our gallant forces have kept the enemy confined in the town which they entered 15 months ago. Despite the fact that this sector has great

strategic attraction for the vandal hordes, being a gate-way, as it is, to the now famous jungle strip of Biafra, and the scene of the bloodiest encounters of this war, it is significant that the enemy has made no gains throughout this long period.

Ojukwu situates the Biafran struggle within the larger history of black revolts against hegemonic institutions and racial prejudice:

> Our struggle has far-reaching significance. It is the latest recrudescence in our time of the age-old struggle of the black man for his full stature as man. We are the latest victims of a wicked collusion between the three traditional scourges of the black man – racism, Arab-Muslim expansionism and white economic imperialism. Playing a subsidiary role is Bolshevik Russia seeking for a place in the African sun.

Describing Nigeria as one of Africa's "sworn enemies of the Negro," the document projects: "[W]e in Biafra are convinced that the Negro can never come to his own until he is able to build modern states (whether national or multi-national) based on a compelling African ideology, enjoying real rather than sham independence, able to give scope to the full development of the human spirit in the arts and sciences." The Ahiara Declaration is functionally a wartime document meant to rally the army, assure the people, and broaden the narrative about Biafra by connecting it to significant aspects of black history as well as positioning the new country as an important signifier. The Declaration is structured as a historicizing document responding to the march of a hegemonic army empowered by a corrupt and corruptive government.

In addition to the factual accounts and the official declarations, there is also a corpus of Nigerian civil war literature, including literary works signaling Nigeria's season of anomy (the title of Wole Soyinka's second novel, published in 1973) before the descent into war and those that reflect the fighting and its aftermath. One of these works, Chinua Achebe's *A Man of the People* (published in 1966), is often referenced as having prophesied the end of the civilian government. It does so almost in a similar manner as Nadine Gordimer's *July's People*, which imagines the end of the Apartheid regime in South Africa by applying the cause-and-consequence principle evident in human history. In Achebe's novel, the government is brought down not by a military coup but by a different sort of revolt: "No, the people had nothing to do with the fall of our government. What happened was simply that unruly mobs and private armies having tasted blood and power during the election had got out of hand and ruined their masters and employers" (162). If Achebe's novel only foretold the collapse of the government, Christopher Okigbo's poetry collection, *Labyrinths, with Path of Thunder* (published in 1971, after his death fighting as a Biafran soldier) prophesied war. The final section is entitled "Path of Thunder: Poems Prophesying War" and contains images of discord and destruction contextually or aesthetically cusped by the ominous presence of lightning and thunder:

> Now that the triumphant march has entered the last street corners,
> Remember, O dancers, the thunder among the clouds . . .
> Now that laughter, broken in two, hangs tremulous between the teeth,
> Remember, O dancers, the lightning beyond the earth . . .
> The smell of blood already floats in the lavender-mist of the afternoon.
> The death sentence lies in ambush along the corridors of power;
> And a great fearful thing already tugs at the cables of the open air
>
> (66)

Sunday O. Anozie writes knowingly in *Christopher Okigbo: Creative Rhetoric*: "By its theme and craft, *Path of Thunder* differs from the poetry written by Christopher Okigbo up to and includ-ing the first half of December 1965. This is so because in it Okigbo makes, for the first time ever, a forthright and direct political statement which itself undisguisedly defines the poet's own revolutionary option" (174).

Okigbo died on September 20, 1967, a few months after the beginning of the war, but his life and death figure significantly in the literature of the Nigeria-Biafra War. By some accounts, including that of Obi Nwakanma in *Christopher Okigbo, 1930–67: Thirsting for Sunlight*, Okigbo's friendship with Emmanuel Ifeajuna made him a marked person:

> The poet was on the Special Branch's list soon after the January 1966 coup which had toppled General Ironsi. Those who had killed Ironsi were on the lookout for Okigbo for his role in the events soon after the January 1966 coup. Okigbo's connection with Major Emmanuel Ifeajuna was enough to put him among the list of Eastern Nigerian intellectuals marked for liquidation.
>
> *(230)*

As a writer, Okigbo "never ceased to be an Igbo/African poet . . . unwilling to conceive of himself within a state of cultural-ideological closure" (Nwosu, *Markets of Memories: Between the Postcolonial and the Transnational* 78), but he was so touched by the events leading up to the war that he chose to fight as a soldier. Okigbo "played his own part in the Biafran struggle with the same passion that ruled all his life. At the height of the secessionist debate, [he] stormed loudly into Ojukwu's office one afternoon, dismissing all the protocol and saying, 'Where is Emeka? What is going on here? If you don't declare Biafra today, I'm going to do it myself!'" (Nwakanma 234).

Many of the fictional narratives about the Nigeria-Biafra War are by writers from Eastern Nigeria. Their works tend to present the horrors of the war and reflect solidarity with the Biaf-ran cause. The case against Nigeria is often evident in the brutal nature of the fighting as well as the discord and massacres that led to the war. As in many instances of war literature, the lessons of war – including its effect on the human spirit – are also underscored. As Buchi Emecheta states in the foreword to her "historical fiction," *Destination Biafra*, "it is time to forgive, though only a fool will forget" (vii). These narratives represent acts of remembrance, and what is remembered – and how – is often rooted in relatively specific experiences or perspectives. *Destination Biafra* begins with "The First Election" and ends with "The Holocaust," titles with obvious historical associations. In between, Emecheta tells the story of Debbie Ogedemgbe, the Oxford-educated daughter of a Nigerian minister who is unsurprisingly corrupt. She decides to enlist in the war, and her role as a soldier – what it could or should be – highlights the feminist perspective of the narrative. Emecheta's stated goal includes calling attention to a lesser-known story of the war: "Records and stories have shown that Ibuza, Asaba and other smaller places along the border area suffered most; but we are glossed over, not being what the media of the time called 'the Ibo heartland'" (vii). This perspective registers in the novel in the sometimes-comparative approach to the evaluation of pain and suffering: "The Ibo officers did exactly as they were ordered, but none of them lived to tell the tale. They were lucky that at least their agonies and humiliations ended within five days; not so for their brothers in places like the North, in Lagos, in the bushes of the surrounding Ibo heartland, in towns like Ibuza, Asaba, Okpanam" (83). Ojukwu's conduct is also critically assessed, especially his departure from Biafra before the end of the war. Debbie sets out to try and eliminate Abosi (the Biafran army leader in the novel) so that "millions of lives would be saved"; otherwise, "the war would go on, a war that had become his personal war and no longer the people's war" (255).

Ojukwu is also spotlighted in Chimamanda Ngozi Adichie's *Half of a Yellow Sun* (a title that references an iconic aspect of the Biafran flag). When he appears, "[e]verything about him sparkled, his groomed beard, his watch, his wide shoulders" and his "Oxford-accented voice was surprisingly soft" and "a little theatrical" (214). The enthusiasm of the people calling for war seems to encourage his statement: "Even the grass will fight for Biafra" (215). Later, Kainene recounts: "Madu told me today that the army has nothing, absolutely nothing. They thought Ojukwu had arms piled up somewhere, given the way he's been talking, 'No power in Black Africa can defeat us!' . . . But I do think he is terribly attractive: that beard alone" (229). Overall, Adichie signposts the argument for the Biafran cause. In this regard, Odenigbo's circle of intellectuals, who discuss or debate a range of Nigerian as well as other issues (including Mungo Park, Hegel, the Herero genocide), is particularly important. In one instance, Odenigbo, who is described as "a hopeless tribalist," reasons: "[My] point is that the only authentic identity for the African is the tribe . . . I am Nigerian because a white man created Nigeria and gave me that identity. I am black because the white man constructed *black* to be as different as possible from his *white*. But I was Igbo before the white man came" (25). Later, he asks: "What peace are we looking for? Gowon himself has said that a basis for unity does not exist, so what peace are we looking for?" (199). Adichie also uses humor to accentuate perspectives and position – as in the case where Odenigbo says to Ugwu: "They will teach you [in school] that a white man called Mungo Park discovered River Niger. That is rubbish. Our people fished in the Niger long before Mungo Park's grandfather was born" (14). Ugwu "wished that this person called Mungo Park had not offended Master so much" (14). *Half of a Yellow Sun* incorporates a book-in-progress entitled "The World Was Silent When We Died," which backgrounds the post-independence crisis in Nigeria – including how the British government "fixed the pre-independence election in favor of the North" (195). In 1960, when Nigeria became independent, it "was a collection of fragments held in a fragile clasp" (195). Not only is *Half of a Yellow Sun* detailed and broad in its coverage, including a range of discourses and tragedies (as well as instances of transcultural humanism, such as some Northerners helping Easterners to escape), its structure reflects the trajectory of the war – the first exodus, the reprisal attacks, the second exodus, "police action," the "win-the-war efforts," and the transformation from "police action" to war. The novel's aesthetic texture is enriched by its heteroglossic incorporation of multiple voices and contexts to create a multi-tiered narrative.

Other novels about the Nigeria-Biafra War explore related or other dimensions of the experience. Chukwuemeka Ike's *Sunset at Dawn* details the fighting, including the air raids, in a way that centralizes the suffering and the mass killings characteristic of war. Ike's story is specific and the accounts are linked to actual experiences. In his author's note, he acknowledges that "reference is made [in the novel] to some actual battles and a few other historical events." At the center of the story is Dr. Amilo Kanu, an academic who becomes a soldier, and his wife, Fatima, who is from Northern Nigeria but is transformed by her experience of the devastation of war:

> She was amazed at herself . . . amazed that she should reject the offer to return to Nigeria at a time when she was at liberty to go back home without hindrance. She had been taken aback the day she saw Emeka, her son, angrily spanking a playmate for abusing him by calling him a Nigerian. Had she too become so sold on Biafranism that she considered herself a Biafran rather than a Nigerian?
>
> *(230)*

Flora Nwapa's *Never Again* points up the importance of women in the prosecution of the war. During a meeting at a school hall, an argument ensues between someone who counsels that "[t]he young men can stay to defend Ugwuta. But please send the women and children to safety" and someone else who demands: "When we evacuate the women and children, who will cook for the soldiers? Who will fetch water for women to cook for the soldiers?" (11). *Never Again* is forceful both in its condemnation of war and its imaging of Nigerians as "Vandals": "We must continue fighting against them until we vanquish them. God is alive and God knows that our cause is just. They killed us in Lagos, they killed us in Zaria, in Kano, in Jos, in Kafanchan, in Ibadan, in Abeokuta. We said to them, it is enough" (8).

Eddie Iroh's three novels about Biafra — *Forty-Eight Guns for the General, Toads of War*, and *The Siren in the Night* — are thrillers about how the war was fought as well as how it privileged some and (further) disadvantaged others, thus creating minorities within minorities. *Forty-Eight Guns for the General* focuses on the activities of mercenaries, who mostly profited from the war. As Colonel Jacques Rudolf tells his "six selected Christian Brothers," "we came here to earn a living and help the General. In that order. Not to score a quick victory" (61). The mercenaries seem relatively well provisioned: "Colonel Jacques Rudolf and his men lived two to a caravan. They found to their delight that the homes on wheels were reasonably comfortable, with refrigerators that were generously filled with food and liquor, and frequently replenished by Michel" (37). The prologue to *Toads of War* is set on December 24, 1968, and entitled "The Beginning of the End." It presents an image of bleakness both because of "the merciless weather" and the war circumstances: "But the gloom and grimness existed not in the quarters of a few people – the war racketeers and profiteers, the disaster millionaires, the big shots, the toads of war, civilian and military, who fought their own war by proxy. Fresh crates of assorted liquor, precious salt, canned food and cigarettes had long since arrived for their yuletide delectation" (1–2). Iroh's novels are historical thrillers. Each one, *Forty-Eight Guns* in particular, "derives its huge success, credibility and forceful impact from its historical authenticity" (Ezeigbo, "War, History, Aesthetics, and the Thriller Tradition in Eddie Iroh's Novels" 70).

Sozaboy, Saro-Wiwa's fictional account of the war, is written in "rotten" or broken English. Although Ken Saro-Wiwa was from Eastern Nigeria, he worked as administrator of the oil port of Bonny during the war. In his introduction (or "Author's Note") to *On a Darkling Plain: An Account of the Nigerian Civil War*, he writes:

> Most Nigerian works on the war, both fictional and otherwise, have been produced by Ibos and have been concerned mainly with their suffering in the war. . . . My account shows this to be far from the truth; the world and posterity have to know that the real victims of the war were the eastern minorities who were in a no-win situation. They are the oppressed in Nigeria.
>
> *(10)*

Sozaboy is about the disillusionment of war. Saro-Wiwa's decision to use "rotten" English mirrors the cognitive and emotional disorder that Sozaboy experiences:

> Then the soza captain told us that we were there to stop enemy from formfooling. He said, as I hear am, that we must do as we are told. He said we must not make noise, we must do as our leader tell us. He said many things. But as you know, soza cannot listen to everything soza captain is saying. Even if he listen, he cannot understand everything.
>
> *(83–84)*

Sozaboy returns to his village, Dukana, at the end of the war and is mistaken for a "ghost [who] is moving round killing everybody because when you were killed in the war, they did not bury you proper" (180). He departs, more or less an outcast: "And as I was going, I was just thinking how the war have spoiled my town Dukana, uselessed many people, killed many others, killed my mama and my wife, Agnes, my beautiful young wife with J.J.C. and now it made me like porson wey get leprosy because I have no town again" (181). Miscomprehension, dislocation, and decimation combine in *Sozaboy* to illuminate the (wartime) suffering by non-Igbo or Eastern minority communities.

Some of the novels about the Nigeria-Biafra War – such as *The Last Duty* by Isidore Okpewho, *Heroes* by Festus Iyayi, and *The Combat* by Kole Omotoso – were written by writers from other parts of Nigeria. They tend to probe aspects of Nigerian history and to use the tragedy of war as a basis for the exploration of suffering and being. T. Akachi Ezeigbo points out in *Fact and Fiction in the Literature of the Nigerian Civil War* that such works utilize "the symbolic mode"; consequently, "[n]ew insights are thus given to reality and new perspectives are revealed, so that experience is seen in a new light" (124). Okpewho's *The Last Duty* is set after the war and deals, from the perspective of six character-narrators, with questions about honor, duty, pain, betrayal, survival, and the connections between them. Its theater of war is not the physical battlefield but the minds of its key characters, and Okpewho deftly handles psychological issues in a way that is relatable to the physical tragedies of war – such as the circumstances under which Aku turns to Toje, the same man who facilitated the imprisonment of her husband, to ensure the survival of herself and her son. The emotional torture that even the young son, Oghenovo, goes through is touching: "*i want to go home and tell onome that my father has come back from where he travelled to but why was my mother crying when the man came here. I do not like that man because he makes my mother cry*" (233). The novel also raises the question of whether humanity learns from war and tragedy. As Ali hands over his command to Isaac Okutubo, he thinks: "But – if I had the same chance, if I was to hold this bloody post again, *Allah*, I'd make the same mistakes all over!" (243).

Iyayi's *The Heroes* adopts a class perspective. It projects as "heroes" not those who precipitated the war but the common people and soldiers. The minority discourse in this case is shaped more by economic than cultural or ethnic considerations. As Osime argues:

> The impression is created that the Ibo man's enemy is the man from the other tribe. In Biafra, the Ibo man will be king. Any Ibo man who doubts the word is told to look over his shoulder, at the pogrom. No wonder the Ibo man celebrates the announce-ment of Biafra. But the whole thing is a swindle. It is a swindle because the decision to create Biafra is not made by the working Ibo man.
>
> (168)

Osime advances the idea that "the Ibo man's enemy is not the man from the other tribe. His enemies are there in his own tribe as they are in other tribes. The Ibo businessman is a greater enemy to the ordinary Ibo man than the ordinary Hausa or the ordinary Yoruba man" (168). Dialogue is a key messaging tool in *Heroes*, so much so that the novel sometimes tends to privilege content over form or message over style. The end of the novel anticipates a post-war reconstruction era when the true heroes will be properly recognized: "[A] movement is bound to emerge from this war and if not from this war, then after this war. A movement that will write the history of the war and give each man and woman his or her proper due" (247).

The Nigeria-Biafra War also provoked poetic reflections or refractions. Written before and after the Nigeria-Biafra War, Pol Ndu's *Songs for Seers* is both about the war and the Igbo/human experience. Michael Echeruo describes it in his introduction to the book as "a sad study in passion, politics and pain" by "one of the strongest voices in African poetry since Okigbo; and probably the most verbally exciting" (ii). Ndu himself describes the poetry collection as "an attempt at exploring the ambivalencies of an awakening creative spirit caught in the trauma of social disaster" (i). "July 66" images a state of disorder and mourning: "In Bloodflood,//a broken bell lay at Opi junction/a rising spark died at the tip of the Miliken:/a bereaved world missed the crystal smile:/in summary to the seer's [t]rip" (16–17). "Song for Seer" invokes Christopher Okigbo – a "razor-tongued weaver-bird,/heard but not quite understood" (34). "Biafra Revisited" suggests the way forward: "Take past events as the/repentant woman's past/always forgotten and always retold" (32). Overall, *Songs for Seers* explores the Igbo cultural signifying system, the war experience, memory, and motion. Gabriel Okara's *The Fisherman's Invocation* also includes poems about the Nigeria-Biafra War. "Suddenly the Air Cracks" is about an air raid and the ominous silence that it leaves behind. First, there is the "striking cracking rockets/guffaw of bofors stuttering LMGs" in the first stanza, then (in the second stanza): "Suddenly there's silence – /And a thick black smoke/rises sadly into the sky as the jets/fly away in gruesome glee – " (37). Okara considers the fighting and the physical casualties as well as the psychological consequences of the war. "Cancerous Growth," for instance, cautions that "today's wanton massacre/burns up tender words/and from the ashes/hate is growing" (41).

Odia Ofeimun's *The Poet Lied* includes at least two sections, "Where Bullets Have Spoken" and "The Poet Lied," about the war that range from "Exodus '67," which mourns and warns: "behold these senseless abattoirs/and this seed about to be earthed:/what unhealthy hate convulses us all" (23) to "The Poet Lied" – a poem about the failure of an unnamed writer (or an artistic sensibility) to rise up to the social challenge of being human: "He was not a guerrilla fighter,/he sniffed about, disdaining/those who hatched themselves out/of their ivory bunkers/to strike some blow/for the many helpless of the earth" (41). Contrastively, *The Poet Lied* names and salutes writers – such as Christopher Okigbo and Chinua Achebe – who did not conveniently turn their backs on the circumstances of the time. J. P. Clark also creatively reviews aspects of the war in *Casualties*. The title poem, "The Casualties," widens the circumference of pain: "The casualties are not only those who started/A fire and now cannot put it out. Thousands/Are burning that had no say in the matter" (37). The transformative nature of war is part of the poet's concern: "Because whether we know or/Do not know the extent of wrong on all sides,/We are characters now other than before" (38). The loss that the poet mourns is sometimes also personal, as in "Song": "I can look the sun in the face/But the friends that I have lost/I dare not look at any" (3). *Casualties* has engendered varied responses. S.O. Asein describes it as "a major landmark in Clark's development as a poet" (73). In Michael Echeruo's evaluation, "*Casualties* is a disaster. It's sheer journalism; there's absolutely nothing in it, nothing that's good enough as poetry" (*Dem-Say: Interviews with Eight Nigerian Writers* 14).

Memoirs or diaries constitute another dimension of writing produced in response to the Nigeria-Biafra War. Wole Soyinka's prison notes after he was imprisoned by the Nigerian government were published as *The Man Died* in 1971. Soyinka recalls that his arrest was prompted by his:

> denunciation of the war in the Nigerian papers, my visit to the East, my attempt to recruit the country's intellectuals within and outside the country for a pressure group which would work for a total ban on the supply of arms to all parts of Nigeria; creating a third force which would utilize the ensuing military stalemate to repudiate and end both the secession of Biafra, and the genocide-consolidated dictatorship of the Army which made both secession and war inevitable.
>
> *(18)*

As Soyinka famously writes in *The Man Died*, "The man dies in all who keep silent in the face of tyranny" (13). He was determined not to be silent, not to be like the poet in Ofeimun's "The Poet Lied" who "asked this much:/to be left alone/with his blank sheets on his lap/in some dug-out damp corner" (40). Soyinka was kept in solitary confinement for 22 months. The consequent memoir sometimes utilizes mental associations or stream of consciousness in relation to a variety of topics, including questions about being: "In the Beginning there was a Void. Nothing. And how does the mind grasp it? As waste? Desolation? Nothing is cheaply within grasp from what was. But as the fundamental nought, the positive, original nil?" (255). *The Man Died* reflects Soyinka's state of mind at the time: "At some point the games which I played with mathematics must have gone too far. I moved into greater absurdities and plunged at some point over the brink of rational principles into clearly unhealthy regions" (269). It was during his imprisonment that *Madmen and Specialists*, Soyinka's play about the war which also deals with "unhealthy" experiences, was conceived. The play is set in the specialist (Dr. Bero)'s home. It explores issues such as insanity, depravity, and trauma as the son (Dr. Bero) tortures the father (The Old Man). Its absurdist frame, which tends to deny or question "the assumptions that human beings are fairly rational creatures who live in an at least partially intelligible universe . . . and that they may be capable of heroism and dignity even in defeat" (Abrams and Harpham 1), is further evident when The Old Man speaks frenziedly toward the end:

> you cyst, you cyst, you splint in the arrow of arrogance, the dog in doma, tick of a heretic, the tick in politics, the mock of democracy, the mar of Marxism, a tic of the fanatic, the boo of Buddhism, the ham in Mohammed, the dash in the criss-cross of Christ, a dot on the I of ego an ass in the mass, the ash in ashram, a boot in kibbutz, the pee of priesthood, the peepee of perfect priesthood.
>
> *(76)*

This existentialist expression about the unfathomability and incompleteness of being contextually applies to the miscomprehension and disintegration associated with war.

Elechi Amadi's *Sunset in Biafra: A Civil War Diary* is a personal history that begins with his decision to leave the army (as Captain Amadi) in 1965 because he did not "want to be a career soldier" (1) and then covers the events leading up to the war and his experiences during the war. Amadi is astute in his interpretation of events, such as his recognition of the significance of Ojukwu's broadcast: "Suddenly, Owerri fell for the second time. That day, 11 January 1970, Ojukwu made his last broadcast. I listened to it in bed. The moment he said he was going out of the country 'in search of peace', I knew it was all over" (182). Amadi also discusses the socioeconomic beliefs and circumstances before (and after) the war: "Ours was, and still is, a tribal society. The herd instinct is strong, and most people feel far more at home among members of their own tribe than in any other company. . . . Poverty, with its concomitant low standard of living, lends strength to this herd instinct" (10). The experience of war apparently made a deep impact on Amadi, and he returned to the subject of culture and war in *Ethics in Nigerian Culture*, published 12 years after the Nigeria-Biafra War. It is possible that wars represent the manifestation of the "fearsome fighting instinct" of the human species; he suggests: "It becomes very difficult to dismiss the suggestion that man's pugnacity originates in instincts planted in him not merely to ensure survival but also to check his population" (41). In this sense, war highlights the animalistic instincts of the human self or collective. This heedlessness creates a repetitive pattern of potential and actual conflicts. As a novelist, Amadi employs the concept of the repeating past in the context of conflict and war in *The Great Ponds*, a novel in which two villages fight unrelentingly over a pond in part because of claims rooted in oral tradition and a prior conflict. As Eze Diali insists, "'[t]he Pond of Wagaba is ours. My fathers fought for it. I fought for it. My son fought and died for it" (92).

In 2012, Chinua Achebe published *There Was A Country: A Personal History of Biafra*. Before then, Achebe had written about the war in some of the stories in *Girls at War and Other Stories* and in *Beware, Soul Brother*, a poetry collection. The title story in *Girls at War* probes the personal transformations that war can cause. The story ends with an air raid – "another terrible whistle starting high up and ending in a monumental crash of the world" (129). An air raid was always of grave concern in Biafra. "Air Raid," a poem in Achebe's *Beware, Soul Brother* (first published in 1971, then republished in 1973 as *Christmas in Biafra and Other Poems*) foregrounds the swiftness and tragic nature of an air raid: "It comes so swiftly/the bird of death/from evil forests of Soviet technology" (15). Writing about *Beware, Soul Brother*, Donatus Nwoga assesses that "[t]he relaxed narrative movement, often prosaic, becomes the technique of mythopoeic imagination . . . the novelist in Achebe has not been completely submerged in the poet here" (qtd in Ohaeto, *Chinua Achebe: A Biography* 162). In his own analysis, Emmanuel Obiechina argues that "Achebe, like Brecht, chose the poetic mode with which to respond to the harsh and brutal Nigerian situation because, as a committed writer, he recognized the multi-faceted uses of poetry for making a statement, for bearing witness, for instigating a humane social and moral order" (529). *There Was a Country* further provides insights into the Nigeria-Biafra War. Its scope is extensive, beginning not in 1966 but with the birth of Achebe's father "in the last third of the nineteenth century" (7). Achebe then goes on to tell the story of his formative years and the writing of *Things Fall Apart* (published in 1958) against the background of the movement of Nigerian history. That movement was often choreographed by Nigeria's colonial master, Britain, to achieve desired results – such as "the rigging of Nigeria's first election 'so that [Britain's] compliant friends (in Northern Nigeria) would win power, dominate the country, and serve British interests after independence'" (50). Achebe recognizes that other interpretations of events are possible: "Looking back, the naively idealistic coup of January 15, 1966, proved a terrible disaster. It was interpreted with plausibility as a plot by the ambitious Igbo of the east to take control of Nigeria from the Hausa/Fulani North" (82). But this plausibility does not resolve questions about the ensuing pogrom: "[I]n this particular case a detailed plan for mass killings was implemented by the government – the army, the police – the very people who were there to protect life and property. Not a single person has been punished for these crimes" (82). Achebe describes the Nigeria-Biafra War as "arguably the first fully televised conflict in history" (199); consequently, "'Biafra' became synonymous with the tear-tugging imagery of starving babies with blown-out bellies, skulls with no subcutaneous fat harboring pale, sunken eyes in sockets that betrayed their suffering" (199).

Other literary discourses or narratives about the Nigeria-Biafra War include S. O. Mezu's *Behind the Rising Sun*, I. N. C. Aniebo's *The Anonymity of Sacrifice*, John Munonye's *A Wreath for the Maidens*, Kalu Okpi's *Biafra Testament*, Chinelo Okparanta's *Under the Udala Tree*, Andrew Ekwuru's *Songs of Steel*, Ossie Anekwe's *Come Thunder*, and Cyprian Ekwensi's *Divided We Stand* and *Survive the Peace*. Uzodinma Iweala's *Beasts of No Nation*, a narrative about war in an unnamed African country, is sometimes discussed in relation to Biafra, although the writer has stated that "the setting is not Nigeria, nor are my characters from any of Nigeria's numerous ethnicities" (P.S. 12). Both the "Christopher dreams" in *A Gecko's Farewell*, including an instance in which "the grave spewed out the dead, armed with spectacular guns" (97), and the arrival of Opio, in *Invisible Chapters*, "singing a war song in a booming voice" (189), somewhat signify the haunting of Nigerian history by echoes of the Nigeria-Biafra War. The tension of battle and the projection of cultural memory in Chimalum Nwankwo's *Feet of the Limping Dancers* – in lines such as "why is the quartermaster counting our guns?" (1) and "who will remember the clan's next hero?" (2) – is related or relatable to the Nigeria-Biafra War. As D. I. Nwoga explains (about Nwankwo's development as a writer): "It was . . . natural that having fought in the Nigerian Civil War and seen some of the horrors of human degeneration in crisis situations, his insights tended towards frustration and disillusionment" (v). The title poem in Obi Nwakanma's *The Horsemen* is dedicated to Christopher Okigbo, Emmanuel Ifeajuna, and Chukwuma Nzeogwu. It includes phrases and images – such as "Memories of a carnage" (2) and "the one that ordered the massacre" (4) – that register as "sly" references "to the massacres at Asaba during the Nigeria-Biafra civil war" (x). Chielozona Eze's *Survival Kit* is dedicated to "You who fought in defense of yourselves" (52) and is about various conflict or repression scenarios as well as the echoes that persist: "We knew the truth:/after the war/comes the war./Always" (35). But it is also about letting go so that the present is not overdetermined by the past: "Why should I gnash my teeth this late in the day?/Why should I grouse the evil that exists?/I fling to the seas the evil I saw/ and hold on to the good I hugged" (49).

As is evident in the consequent literature and its varied projection of a minority discourse, the Nigeria-Biafra War raised questions about the idea of Nigeria. History as a muse has in this instance inspired accounts and contentions that sometimes problematize supposedly transparent concepts such as "truth" and "objectivity." Wars are inherently divisive, and reconstruction leaves fractures nevertheless. While the works that constitute the literature of the Nigeria-Biafra War engage with history, they do not propose repeating it. Many of the accounts or narratives tend toward clarifying or contextualizing the circumstances of the war (in relation to the precipitative effect of the January 1966 coup and the July 1966 counter-coup as well as the collapse of the Aburi accord). They reflect destitution and doubt, but they also project hope or possibility. In *Reflections on the Nigerian Civil War: Facing the Future*, Ralph Uwechue writes that "Biafra's secession had the effect of uniting otherwise bitter enemies and sharply opposed interests in a struggle to preserve Nigeria's integrity. . . . The one question that remains is whether the disappearance of these differences is permanent or only temporary" (170). Uwechue recommends that "a supple federal union remains the safest course for keeping the country together in tolerable stability" (170). Joe Igbokwe argues in *Twenty Five Years after Biafra* that "unless the Igbos are completely rehabilitated and reintegrated as a collective entity within the mainstream society, they will not be able to release fully their energies and industry towards the development of a great nation that will benefit all Nigerians" (114). Published thirty years after the declaration of Biafra, Igbonekwu Ogazimorah's *New Roads to Biafra: The Igbo Man's Burden* concludes: "It is customarily accepted that there are usually mistakes in what men do but such mistakes must be corrected for us to move on. But move on we must" (175). Considered progression is more or less a post-civil war imperative. The literature of the Nigeria-Biafra War attempts, in different ways and with varying success, both Erich Maria Remarque's goal in *All Quiet on the Western Front* ("to tell of a generation of men who, even though they may have escaped its shells, were destroyed by the war") and the Faulknerian ideal ("to help man endure by lifting his heart"). But they are ultimately not Remarquean or Faulknerian. The works that make up the literature of the Nigeria-Biafra War are fundamentally connected to the movement of Nigerian history, to Nigeria's centripetal as well as centrifugal discourses, so they are arterially shaped by Nigerian or Biafran or Nigerian/Biafran perspectives that also reflect different – but not necessarily irreconcilable – ways of being human.

Works cited

Abrams, Meyer Howard and Geoffrey Galt Harpham. *A Glossary of Literary Terms*. 9th edition. Boston: Wadsworth Cengage Learning, 2005.

Achebe, Chinua. *A Man of the People*. London: Heinemann, 1966.

Achebe, Chinua. *Girls at War and Other Stories*. New York: Doubleday, 1973.

Achebe, Chinua. *Beware, Soul Brother: Poems*. London: Heinemann, 1977.

Achebe, Chinua. *There Was a Country: A Personal History of Biafra*. New York: Penguin, 2012.

Ademoyega, Adewale. *Why We Struck: The Story of the First Nigerian Coup*. Ibadan: Evans Brothers, 1981.

Adichie, Chimamanda. *Half of a Yellow Sun*. New York: Anchor-Random House, 2006.

Amadi, Elechi. *The Great Ponds*. Ibadan: Heinemann, 1969.

Amadi, Elechi. *Sunset in Biafra: A Civil War Diary*. London: Heinemann, 1973.

Amadi, Elechi. *Ethics in Nigerian Culture*. Ibadan: Heinemann, 1982.

Anozie, Sunday O. *Christopher Okigbo: Creative Rhetoric*. London: Evans Brothers, 1972.

Asein, Samuel O. "J. P. Clark's Poetry." Yemi Ogunbiyi, ed. *Perspectives on Nigerian Literature: 1700 to the Present*, Vo. 2. Lagos: Guardian Books, 1988.

Clark, John Pepper. *Casualties: Poems 1966/68*. New York: Africana Publishing Corporation, 1970.

Echeruo, Michael J. C. "Biafra, Civil War, and Genocide." https://academic.mu.edu/koriehc/documents/BiafraconferenceABSTRACTS.pdf Accessed 10 September 2019.

Echeruo, Michael J. C. "Interview." Bernth Lindfors, ed. *Dem-Say: Interviews with Eight Nigerian Writers*. Austin: African and Afro-American Studies and Research Center, The University of Texas, 1974.

Echeruo, Michael J. C. "Introduction." Pol Ndu, ed. *Song for Seers*. New York: Nok Publishers, 1974. ii.

Emecheta, Buchi. *Destination Biafra*. London: Allison and Busby, 1982.

Eze, Chielozona. *Survival Kit*. New York: Akashic Books, 2016.

Ezeigbo, T. Akachi. *Fact and Fiction in the Literature of the Nigerian Civil War*. Lagos: Unity Publishing, 1991.

Ezeigbo, Theodora Akachi. "War, History, Aesthetics, and the Thriller Tradition in Eddie Iroh's Novels." Theodora Akachi Ezeigbo and Liz Gunner, eds. *The Literatures of War*, Vo. 4, No, 1, 1991, *African Languages and Cultures*: 65–76. doi: 10.1080/09544169108717728

Faulkner, William. "Nobel Prize Banquet Speech." www.nobelprize.org/prizes/literature/1949/faulkner/speech/ Accessed 10 September 2019.

Forsyth, Frederick. *Emeka*. Ibadan: Spectrum Books, 1982.

Forsyth, Frederick. *The Biafra Story: The Making of an African Legend*. South Yorkshire, England: Pen & Sword, 2007.

Gbulie, Ben. *Nigeria's Five Majors: Coup d'Etat of 15th January 1966: First Inside Account*. Onitsha: Africana Educational Publishers, 1981.

Igbokwe, Joe. *Igbos: Twenty Five Years after Biafra*. Lagos: Advent Communications, 1995.

Ike, Chukwuemeka. *Sunset at Dawn*. London: Collins and Harvill Press, 1976.

Iroh, Eddie. *Forty-Eight Guns for the General*. London: Heinemann, 1979.

Iroh, Eddie. *Toads of War*. London: Heinemann, 1979.

Iweala, Uzodinma. *Beasts of No Nation*. New York: Harper, 2005.

Iyayi, Festus. *Heroes*. Essex, England: Longman, 1989.

Kirk-Greene, Anthony Hamilton Millard. *Crisis and Conflict in Nigeria: A Documentary Sourcebook, 1966–1969*. Vol. 1: January 1966–July 1967. London: Oxford University Press, 1971.

Madiebo, Alexander A. *The Nigerian Revolution and the Biafran War*. Enugu: Fourth Dimension Publishers, 1980.

Meredith, Martin. *The Fortunes of Africa: A 5000-Year History of Wealth, Greed, and Endeavor*. Philadelphia: Public Affairs – Perseus Books, 2014.

Muffet, D. J. M. *Let Truth Be Told*. Zaria: Hudahuda Publishing Company, 1983.

Ndu, Pol. *Songs for Seers (1960–1970)*. New York: Nok Publishers, 1974.

Nwakanma, Obi. *The Horsemen and Other Poems*. Trenton, NJ: Africa World Press, 2007.

Nwakanma, Obi. *Christopher Okigbo, 1930–67: Thirsting for Sunlight*. London: James Currey, 2010.

Nwankwo, Chimalum. *Feet of the Limping Dancers*. Enugu: ABIC Publishers, 1987.

Nwapa, Flora. *Never Again*. Trenton, NJ: Africa World Press, 1992.

Nwosu, Maik. *Markets of Memories: Between the Postcolonial and the Transnational*. Trenton, NJ: Africa World Press, 2011.

Nwosu, Maik. *Invisible Chapters*. revised edition. Lagos: Beacon Books, 2015.

Nwosu, Maik. *A Gecko's Farewell*. Lagos: Parrésia Books, 2016.

Obasanjo, Olusegun. *My Command: An Account of the Nigerian Civil War 1967–70*. London: Heinemann, 1981.

Obasanjo, Olusegun. *My Watch*. Vol. 1. Lagos: Prestige, 2014.

Obiechina, Emmanuel. "Poetry as Therapy: Reflections on Achebe's 'Christmas in Biafra' and Other Poems." *Callaloo*, Vol. 25, No. 2 (Spring, 2002): 527–558.

Odumegwu-Ojukwu, Emeka. *Because I Am Involved*. Ibadan: Spectrum Books, 1989.

Ofeimun, Odia. *The Poet Lied*. Lagos: Update Communications, 1989.

Ogazimorah, Igbonekwu. *New Roads to Biafra: The Igbo Man's Burden*. Enugu: Centre for Public Affairs Research and Development, 1997.

Ohaeto, Ezenwa. *Chinua Achebe: A Biography*. London: James Currey, 1997.

Ojukwu, Emeka. "The Ahiara Declaration (the Principles of the Biafran Revolution)." www.biafraland. com/Ahiara_declaration_1969.htm Accessed 10 September 2019.

Ojukwu, Emeka. "Why We Lost." Interviewed by Comfort Obi and Maik Nwosu. *The Source* (June 2, 1997): 6–14.

Okara, Gabriel. *The Fisherman's Invocation*. Benin City: Ethiope Publishing, 1979.

Okigbo, Christopher. *Labyrinths*. London: Heinemann, 1977.

Okocha, Emma. *Blood on the Niger: An Untold Story of the Nigerian Civil War*. Washington, DC: USA Africa in association with Gom Slam, 1994.

Okpewho, Isidore. *The Last Duty*. Essex, England: Longman, 1988.

Omotoso, Kole. *Just before Dawn*. Ibadan: Spectrum Books, 1988.

Reader, John. *Africa: A Biography of the Continent*. New York: Vintage Books – Random House, 1999.

Remarque, Erich Maria. *All Quiet on the Western Front*. New York: The Heritage Press, 1969.

Saro-Wiwa, Ken. *Sozaboy: A Novel in Rotten English*. Port Harcourt: Saros International Publishers, 1985.

Saro-Wiwa, Ken. *On a Darkling Plain: An Account of the Nigerian Civil War*. Port Harcourt: Saros International Publishers, 1989.

Soyinka, Wole. *Madmen and Specialists*. London: Methuen, 1971.

Soyinka, Wole. *The Man Died: Prison Notes*. London: Rex Collings, 1972.

St. Jorre, John de. *The Brothers' War: Biafra and Nigeria*. Boston: Houghton Mifflin, 1972.

Uwechue, Ralph. *Reflections on the Nigerian Civil War: Facing the Future*. New York: Africana Publishing Corporation, 1971.

PART VI

Literature and disability

21

CHILDREN WITH DISABILITIES AS NEGOTIATORS OF SOCIAL RESPONSIBILITY

A critical study of 'redemption' in Meshack Asare's *Sosu's Call*

Dike Okoro

Introduction

Ato Quayson argues elegantly that "[o]ne of the most abiding interests of African literary criticism has been to demonstrate the continuity that African literature written in European languages has with indigenous sources" (1). His statement is valid and supports the narrative framework deployed in Meshack Asare's *Sosu's Call*, which is written in English. First published in 2002, *Sosu's Call* is a very popular African children's story book that shares a trajectory of lived experiences when placed in context of Asare's childhood experiences. Asare himself knew people who lived with disability and empathized with their condition as a minority within the world where class and stereotypes make others normal. This logic brings to the forefront the idea of disability stories as a form of minority literature. Are the disabled a minority? The idea that disabled people are given a place in literature unlike that reserved for people that are not disabled makes them not to belong to the mainstream. They are the other in a way. They are almost like a class of themselves. Is a literature about them what people look forward to reading? The African society has no ADA (Americans with Disabilities Act). The disabled are erased. In fact, it is only an act of heroism that earns them recognition. This is what we notice in Asare's book, where Sosu, the protagonist, is rewarded with a wheelchair only after he saves the village from being swept away by waters rising. His singular act of crawling to the drum shed from where he beats out a rhythm to alert the men in the fields to return home from their work to assist in saving the old and the young who stayed home represents a timely decision taken to avert an impending disaster. Telling the disabled's story is part of telling them they are part of humankind. Their acts of heroism make them liked by others. This fact is further proof of Asare's book being an example of minority literature, given that it echoes the ideas in the definition of minor literature, that it is "literature that produces an active solidarity in spite of skepticism . . . The literary machine thus becomes the relay for a revolutionary machine-to-come, not at all for ideological reasons but because the literary machine alone is determined to fill the conditions of a collective enunciation that is lacking elsewhere in this milieu" (Delueze et al. 18). It is evident from Asare's plot that the theme of 'redemption' is a central message in his book and functions with the hopes and struggles of his protagonist, Sosu, who views the world from the hindsight of a child dealing with the challenges of disability in an African society.

Influences

Retroactively, Asare, over the years, has credited his early influences for his writings to his family, fated meetings with strangers, and his willingness to leave a legacy worth remembering for Africa's children. Involved in his analysis of the relationship between the writer's lived experiences and the creative imagination is a space occupied by the notion of the literary influence. This is particularly evident in the chronological order of events that direct his children's book stories. Asare's influences emerge from an oral source that gave him a grounding as a storyteller. In his essay, "Culture to Free Our Children: Looking Back at My Work over Five Decades," published in *World Literature Today*, Asare notes:

> As a child, I enjoyed our folktales, which I often heard firsthand from my parents and grandparents – it was possible at that time. Unfortunately, by the time I had my own children, this privilege that I enjoyed had changed considerably, owing mainly to urbanization and the consequent disintegration of traditionally family systems. Nowadays, many children in Ghana only know some folktales from textbooks and TV programs.

As Asare's statement genuinely implies, the possibilities of his emergence as a writer have roots that extend to his childhood. His indebtedness to the oral tradition in Africa is particularly influential in his development as a children's literature author. He learned early to recognize the advantages at his disposal as a child and diverted his interest in those opportunities that were bound to favor him later in life. This is what he hints at, stating:

> unlike most other children in the small town in Ghana where I grew up, I had a father who loved to read, so there were many books and magazines at home. Unfortunately, there were no "children's books" beside school textbooks, and even those, too, were scarce . . . My goal then was to create books in which local children engaged in their usual activities and real-life experiences in environments and conditions that were familiar to them.
>
> *("Culture to Free Our Children")*

Indeed, the very act of children engaging in their usual activities and real-life experiences permeated the circumstances that many of Asare's readers encounter in *Sosu's Call*. Perhaps the argument could also be made that if history has taught the African any lesson through literature, it is that there is redemption after deprivation. This fact finds a classic case in the character Sosu. Asare does not only postulate, he gouges his own past to authenticate the messages in his story book.

Another source of influence on Asare's storytelling technique in his children's books is talent as an artist. In his essay "Culture to Free Our Children," which appears in *World Literature Today*, Asare reflects on how his beliefs and training as an artist influenced his writing:

> My training in art taught me to observe the world around me with keen interest. And possibly, one of the most powerful spells of influence I came under as a child was

a man that I had met at my grandfather's house. He claimed to know the language of everything and often told us what he claimed to be conversations between dogs, cats, trees, fowl, pots and pans, etc., that he had overheard. I thought he must be an extremely clever man and would have liked to be a little bit like him. That was a while before I turned five. I was told years later by my mother that the man was in fact a patient at the local psychiatric hospital, but it still did not bother me. It gave me a fairly multiple and composite perspective on knowledge and tolerance, essentially "multi-literacy."

Studying carefully the many lessons from Asare's early experiences in life that later act as catalysts for his children's story books, one can find in the phenomena of his success overlapping parallels that characterize the work of a gifted mind. *Sosu's Call* is not only a success for children but serves as a lesson for adults on understanding disability.

Ann Katz, in an essay published in a scholarly book titled *Lessons in Disability: Essays on Teaching with Young Adult Literature*, observes:

> I read Meshack Asare's *Sosu's Call* (2002) to a small group. This book is about Sosu, a young African boy who is unable to walk. He joins his dog Fusa in helping to save their village when a great storm threatens the community. For many years, Sosu saw the world from behind the family's fence. Many villagers thought he was not capable of achieving very much and that he should remain in the house. However, when the storm approaches Sosu retrieves a drum so that he can alert his villagers in enough time to save his community members. Sosu becomes a hero, and now he can go to school and be "just one of the boys in the small village, somewhere between the sea and the Lagoon." After the reading of the book, students engaged in a discussion regarding how Sosu was represented initially in the book, and how he was represented as the book evolved.
>
> *(22–23)*

The lesson in Katz's intimation can be found in the heartfelt appreciation admitted for *Sosu's Call* as a book that engages children in a narrative with meaning and lessons for all, regardless of age. Her decision to share the story with children in her classroom is marked with both sincerity and inspiration. In the boy Sosu and his dog Fusa, the children see a child and his trusted friend. Nevertheless, the plot of the story seems to offer the reader a chronological order of events that reveal its central character's instinctive gift for surviving challenging moments and circumstances.

Next, the storyline of *Sosu's Call* has a familiar trail of events that Africans living in the urban city can identify with, despite their upbringing that seems a distant world from what generally occurs in the village. Deanne Paiva, a teacher who adopted *Sosu's Call* for her third grade students, notes this influential aspect of the book after observing two of her students who are originally from Ghana:

> Two students were cousins from Ghana and so I was thrilled when I found an international book from Ghana, *Sosu's Call* (Asare 2002). Sosu is physically handicapped and not accepted by his rural village because he is not able to walk. Sosu helps save his village from a devastating flood by dragging himself to the village drums and calling out to the adults working the land. The two students native to Ghana shared that they did not live like Sosu in the country, but they lived much like we do in Dallas with houses

and apartments and their parents went to jobs in the city and did not farm. However, Crystal did enjoy telling us that her cousin Wadie did "run around with no shoes in Ghana like Sosu." I liked how their information helped broaden students' views of Ghana so the students would not assume everyone lives like Sosu.

(30)

Paiva's intimation presents one way that students, irrespective of culture or place of domicile, can view children's literature from Africa and appreciate the lessons absorbed through the characters and their actions for personal value. More importantly, too, it shows how teachers in the West can also use insider knowledge, given that the two students referenced are from Ghana and were candid in their views of the book. Both students specified the sociocultural and class differences in Ghana, as well as the difference between those living in the city and those living in the village, to enable the teacher to also gain some level of knowledge for the book. Perhaps this exposure to the knowledge shared by students from Ghana, concerning the characterization and setting of Asare's *Sosu's Call*, resulted in an American student admitting, "I think that Sosu's life is going to be good because he is a hero and now everybody likes him. Now since he saved a village, they might donate money so people can build a hospital there because some people may be sick and they don't have medicine so they will die" (Paiva 30).

Sosu's Call

The book itself depends on a child's ability to adapt to the peculiar circumstance in which he finds himself as a disabled person in a village that offers no support for people with disabilities, much less children. Hence, Sosu, a resident of a Ghanaian village on the shores of the lagoon, with his family and his dog, Fusa, improvises a strategy to get by:

> The dog always returned, panting, his eyes shining with the satisfaction of having been outside. It was this, more than anything else, which made Sosu envious. "What use is a boy without a pair of good, strong legs?" he thought.
>
> *(p. 7)*

As Asare makes clear to his reader through finely crafted paintings, Sosu stays home while his siblings attend school. His fisherman father represents a positive force in Sosu's life, for he takes him on fishing trips. However, this thoughtful decision that makes the boy revel in the bonding he develops with his father soon comes to an end when other fishermen object. This act of depriving a child of spending quality time with his father during fishing outings demonstrates the attempt by the other fishermen to be both critical of Sosu's disability and pander to age-long notions of seeing disability as both a form of weakness and bad omen. Many critics of African literature have written about this aspect of the literature, zeroing in on the very fact that it is a space that allows African writers to share real-life experiences that are embodied through the published text. Barbara H. Solomon and W. Reginald Rampone Jr, in their introduction to the book of African short stories, *An African Quilt*, averred, "In some interactions, characters try to exploit or take advantage of another whom they perceive as weaker or lacking in power or status" (xviii). The logic in their assertion becomes true when applied to the situation Sosu's father faces when his fellow fishermen discourage him from taking his son along with him to fish. Perhaps the idea of 'exploiting' or 'taking advantage of another,' as Asare's storyline demonstrates, works in revealing the complexity of the claim made by Solomon and Rampone Jr. As a result, his father stops taking him with him. Asare, even at this point of the story, tweaks his plotline in a way that does not make the boy an object of pity while he stays at home. Besides reveling in the company of Fusa, Sosu develops an affinity for life, waiting at home to make lunch for his siblings who return from school. They, in return, teach him what they learn in school. Soon the boy takes to learning and understanding how to read and write, a sort of escape from the boredom that is expected for someone of his age who feels as though life is useless since people with good legs do everything, while those living with his kind of disability feel as though they are useless to their family and community.

The awareness Sosu gains from learning new things his age mates who are privileged to go to school learn whenever his siblings return home gives him a sort of redemption. As the story pushes on, he learns to appreciate the importance of family as they show him care that shapes his life. It is arguable that this experience transforms Sosu and helps him to develop the sense of social responsibility he displays in admirable actions and decisions toward the end of the book. 'Social responsibility,' by definition, presupposes that "an organization or individual has an obligation to act to benefit society at large" (Bartleby). As an extension of human behavior, possessing a sense of 'social responsibility' is also akin to being morally conscious in the way one acts. Hence Sosu's reaction in a time of grave danger for others, even though he has his limitations as a disabled person who crawls, demonstrates his natural instinct to be a helper of others in time of trouble. This is what we learn from *Sosu's Call* when Asare states:

> He could think only of the many people and animals that were in serious danger. The look in Fusa's eyes told Sosu, "Don't be afraid. We will be all right!"
>
> With Fusa leading the way, Sosu crawled out of the yard and into the storm. The water reached up to the dog's heels. The screaming wind blew and tore at everything in its way.
>
> *(22)*

The boy shows empathy and consideration for others and follows the lead of his friend, the dog Fusa. His physical challenges do not derail his intent or discourage him from carrying out his intended goal. Instead he sets out with his dog, ignoring completely the danger of drowning as "the water reached up the dog's heels". Another reason for Sosu's instinctive and timely reaction could be Asare's deployment of a narrative scheme that is associated with African storytelling technique. Solomon and Rampone Jr, for good reasons, share the following:

> Several seemingly disparate stories are embedded in detailed descriptions of the characters' daily lives. While the crisis depicted in each is very different – sometimes a trivial event and sometimes a horrifying threat – in each case the problem is dramatized against a vivid pattern of days with characters who know very well (or soon learn) what to expect when they set out from home.
>
> (An African Quilt *xv*)

There is hardly any doubt as to the veracity of the statement by both critics. The individual, as Sosu's character is represented, is caught not in a state of panic or fear but in a moment of decision. He must act in relation to his others and his environment. He observes his dog's reaction and notes the natural changes taking place as a result of the water rising. The fact that Asare points to the bravery the boy sees in a dog's eyes as he imagines hearing, 'don't be afraid,' is a mark of the writer commemorating the value in relationships humans share with pets, in this case a dog. This value, given this instance, is redemptive, for it leads to an outcome that benefits not just one but an entire community.

Furthermore, Asare depicts in his book a boy who chooses 'the right moment' in the narrative to show his responsibility to the plight of those facing danger. To add vitality to his protagonist's character, Sosu is presented as one who possesses courage and the will to survive. We note this aspect of his personality when he approaches the sea:

> Somehow, he managed to drag himself along, against the howling wind and the churning water. To this day, Sosu does not know where the strength came from to move his frail limbs, or the courage that drove him on
>
> *(22)*

In assessing Sosu's reaction previously, we are compelled to consider what makes a boy of his age and with his physical condition to display the kind of courage that drove him on. Asare is giving us every bit of information to make us believe that the boy is first responsible and, second is aware of the benefit of 'good' judgment. He had no adult to supervise him, in which case he might have been told to stay indoors because of his disabled condition. Also, Asare operates with a notion of the disability as a heritage of change. This notion of heritage of change informs his description of Sosu that takes on a psychological representation, given that every thought that races through the boy's mind energizes him and "to this day [he] doesn't know where his strength came from." Nevertheless, he assumes the role of the helper and therefore fits the mold of the kind of person with the moral responsibility that Tamara Ayrapetova describes when she argues,

> When any of us is judging any kind of action we usually tend to give this action a value of "good" or "bad" and assign a responsibility for this action to someone who was involved. Responsibility comes from moral obligations and certain commitments and obligations we have to each other.
>
> *(Ayrapetova 34)*

Sosu's actions during the impending flood help us appreciate the strength of his character. Anna Chitando reminds us that "Children's literature represents an important resource for understanding the needs, wishes and aspirations of young people" ("Imagining"). Without idealizing children's views, it can be discerned from Sosu's actions that he places the safety of others in his community in high regard and thus sees his participation in the protection of others, regardless of his physical limitations, as a responsibility and moral obligation to which he is indebted.

As indicated previously, inspiration is one virtue that pushes Sosu to take on the initiative to go in search of the drum to alert the village community of danger. Asare probably paints this picture to give his protagonist a redeeming quality. There is no time to waste when one is faced with danger, more so when the danger puts family members and people that are known, especially villagers, in a place of uncertainty. Therefore Asare's narrative is both inspiring and teaching. As a story about redemption, it also rekindles in us the value in acknowledging redemption in life. Much as we learn about Sosu's drive to extend a helping hand to others, we are also made aware of his unflinching urge to act as a hero for his community, even when it involves following the lead of his dog Fusa:

> They reached the drum shed dripping wet, but safe. The shed was dry inside, and Fusa looked very pleased. As the dog stood, wagging its tail, Sosu was faced with another problem. He had never played a real drum before and did not know how to make it

talk. But Fusa, as if to say, "There is no time," stood on his hind legs and began to scratch at a medium-size drum with his paws.

(24)

The boy's imitation of the dog as he reaches for the drum is symbolic of unity in mission. Both Sosu and his dog share the goal of rescuing the villagers. We note this in the following scene:

He played slowly at first, but the storm, the pounding waves, the young children, the sick, the old, the animals, the crashing fences and the snapping trees, all came rushing towards him like moving pictures! He struck the drum harder and faster until he could hear it above the shrieks and howls of the wind.

(27)

Besides the act of striking the drums to alert others of danger, Sosu's act helps him to fulfill an instinctive commitment to the preservation of human lives. Even with his disabled condition, and considering how judgmental others are of him, he bears no grudge. In addition to his innocence as a child, Asare situates him as a thinker and problem solver. Sosu's rescue act was probably imagined by Asare as a timely deployment that will give a positive image to his book's protagonist. On top of that, Sosu's actions to help also justify Asare's good judgment in telling a story that changes lives and the way people see things, thus validating Chinua Achebe's claim that "Creative writers have long been associated with vision and the quest for social transformation" (1988). Social transformation in this case means acting to benefit others.

Perhaps in *Sosu's Call* Asare opted to create a world where the person least expected to help or be a hero turns out to be a hero. That the eventual hero turns out to be a person who had been written off, especially because of his disability status, makes the story all the more remarkable. Nobody in Sosu's village expects him to be a leader until they all experience his act of kindness. Sosu's act mobilizes villagers in the end to accept people with disabilities. These same villagers have shown intolerance towards him in the past. For example, we note their intolerance in the following quote:

But one day while fishing with Da, two stern-looking men drew up alongside Da's canoe. One of them said harshly, "We don't think it is wise to bring that boy of yours out here. It is bad luck to have the likes of him in our village. We doubt if the Lagoon Spirit is pleased to have him sitting here as well! You must keep him in your house."

(9)

It is also quite troubling to accept that adults in Asare's world of fictional characters in children's books do not always make the right decision. In the previous quote, both men are critical of Sosu and have displayed a neglect for his kind. The idea here is troubling and shows Asare's authorial deftness at exposing an African problem. The victim of the harsh statement made by both men is a child. Yet, as African history has taught us, especially in light examples, human beings will always display their vileness. Historically, African writers have been scrupulous in their attempts to capture these forms of vileness, which they also perceive as institutional. They are always there and never seem to go away. Barbara H. Solomon and W. Reginald Rampone Jr revisit this aspect of the literary. In their introduction to *An African Quilt*, they state thus: "A considerable number of African stories and novels depict the historical and contemporary oppression and institutional brutality of much of the continent" (xxi). Yet one good thing about Asare's book is that even at the very moment when a disturbing turn of events seems to be dominant, a redemptive thing occurs. This is what one senses when the likes of the same men who spoke harshly about Sosu join in singing praise in the end when they discover he is their savior:

> The drum was heard by those at the farthest end of the lagoon, working in the fields. They said, "The drumming is coming from our village. There must be trouble there. Let's go!" The neighboring village also heard the drum. They too said, "The drumming is from the village on the sandbar. They must be in trouble. Let's go!" Through the rain and the wind, they all came rushing to Sosu's village.
>
> *(29)*

The previous scene describes the impact of the drum that Sosu beats and the villagers' reaction to the echoes that catch their attention. Asare has utilized the effectiveness of an African music instrument, an ancient one at that, to draw attention to Sosu who, though disabled, thought it wise to reach out to people after realizing his voice was ineffective in the midst of a storm, as he tried to shout. What follows is a display of appreciation from the villagers upon returning to their respective homes:

> And what a shock awaited them! Waves as high as roofs were pounding the village! Some houses were so flooded that it took a number of strong men to reach them. They worked hard, moving from house to house, searching for those who might be trapped. "We were just in time, thanks to drummer," they said. "But who was the drummer?" somebody asked.
>
> *(31)*

In the end, one can easily discern the merits of Asare's story. The same people that condemned Sosu because of his disability status offer profuse thanks to him. Also, change has come to the village community by way of the rejected child's act of courage. This aspect of the story lends profoundness to Asare's vision. In fact, it evokes the kind of ideology Shehu Musa Yar'Adua intended to pass on in his foreword to *Black & African Writing: The Festac Anthology*, where he posits:

> Unlike the historian, the literator uses not only actual happenings as motif but also creates situations and influences by his works the course of events. In the process, he is sometimes prophetic. Therefore, unlike history, literature is also an instrument of *protest* and a catalyst in the processes of change.
>
> *(xvii)*

The idea here is that Asare makes this story both one that teaches life lessons and serves as an example of redemption. Sosu's story is an example of minority discourse; his actions have endeared him to his detractors and earned him respect and admiration. Even Asare admits that he writes children's stories to make a point. To him, writing stories for Africa's children is relevant because it is both empowering and beneficial to his people. He thus uses examples from real-life experiences in Africa to make his art powerful. In addition to using real-life experiences in his writing, Asare has also emphasized the importance of culture as a catalyst for informing and educating others. This is what he hints in the essay "Culture to Free Our Children":

> I have come to believe seriously that culture is, actually, essential knowledge which gives us freedom to live and act and behave and express ourselves in ways that are

recognized and accepted by society. Primarily, it frees us, especially children and young people, from ignorance. This is very much so in Ghana and Africa, and for that reason, culture is a theme that cuts right through and across the entire landscape of my work.

As Asare himself would attest, his fondness for writing stories that empower and inspire children did not occur at midlife or without a point of reference. Like many African writers, he seems to view his passion for writing for children as a way of filling a gap that existed when he was yet a child.

Conclusion

Sosu's Call places Meshack Asare in the category of African writers who use art not for art's sake but as a recourse to promote social change and attitudes. As a form of minority discourse, the book achieves its aims because it advocates for social change and attitudes, especially against people who ridicule children with disabilities. Furthermore, the storyline is essential because it crosses cultural boundaries and has a universal appeal. Asare's book is written for children but also targets adults since they are expected to act as either parents or guardians to children and therefore stand the chance of learning life-changing lessons from Asare's protagonist Sosu and the other characters in the book, who change after seeing the wise actions of a disabled child whom they have ridiculed. Through this book, Ghanaian and African literature are empowered. The story is liberating and identifies common social problems and attitudes that are traceable to modern African society.

Asare's images in the book also work well and display his artistic gift. He colors the characters and landscape in a way that imitates real life and evokes the African setting which he writes about. When he says, "My training in art taught me to observe the world around me with keen interest," he is saying the obvious among writers who see art as a commitment. In this case, his commitment is to an African destiny (Asare "Culture"). He is telling the world outside of Africa that numerous stories abound in Africa that have their root in the idea of the child learning from the elders. This resembles his assertion that "As a child, I enjoyed our folktales, which I often heard firsthand from my parents and grandparents . . . Unfortunately, by the time I had my own children, this privilege . . . had changed considerably, owing mainly to urbanization and the consequent disintegration of traditional family systems" (Asare "Culture to Free Our Children"). Asare is in fact candid with this remark. To him, the African writer has an obligation not only to his African audience and society but also to the destiny of the continent. His work reflects his conscious decision to change attitudes about certain issues and to inspire children to read stories from which they can learn useful things about life. And in presenting Sosu, a disabled boy whose heroic action rescues a village facing impending danger, Asare is able to use a narrative influenced by oral African storytelling technique and impressionistic paintings to display resolve in a postcolonial African world that is constantly changing. Sosu represents every child's hope, regardless of culture. His ability to sense danger and act on initiatives that end up saving lives, both human and animals, suggests his character assuredly symbolizes that aspect of social responsibility that every human society needs to appreciate the values of living in harmony.

Thus, when Vivian Yenika-Agbaw declares that "Asare succeeds in drawing attention to Ghanaians' attitude toward people with disabilities" and "captures the mood of the story and does succeed in representing a certain aspect of Ghanaian culture realistically" (106–107), she is taking a necessary stand. First, she is acknowledging Asare for assuming the responsibility of informing society of the wrong that occurs when children with disabilities are treated harshly; second, she is probing Ghanaian/African society through the lens of literature. Furthermore,

Yenika-Agbaw's statement about Asare confirms Tanure Ojaide's contention that "[l]iterature in Africa has traditionally played a transformative role" (7). Her conclusion helps us to begin to see why African children's story books, as presented in *Sosu' s Call*, portray Africans as multidimensional characters and realistic. In the story, Asare finds the need to present Sosu's siblings as supportive, because they teach him what they have learned in school each day they return home. However, in the fishermen who meet Sosu and his father when they go fishing, Asare shows the negative side of the society he writes about, given that both men view Sosu as bad luck (Asare, *Sosu' s Call* 9). From a critical perspective, Asare's intentions as a writer are alluded to by Yenka-Agbaw, because his decision to write about Ghanaians while focusing on real-life experiences that inspire humans, irrespective of culture, goes to show his ingenuity in using examples from a culture he knows so well to tell Africa's story. This aspect of his writing reinforces Chinua Achebe's argument that "the story we [Africans] had to tell would not be told for us by anyone else, no matter how gifted or well-intentioned" (*Morning Yet on Creation Day* 123).

Asare arguably ranks among Africa's celebrated authors. His numerous awards include the internationally recognized NSK Neustadt Prize for Children's Literature (2015), for which he is noted as the first African to win the award, and the 1999 UNESCO Prize for Children's and Young People's Literature in the Service of Tolerance for his book *Sosu's Call*. He has received numerous local and global awards for his children's books, and there is much to be said about the multiplicity of critical responses and awards that *Sosu's Call* has received. The themes associated with the book include redemption, courage, social responsibility, and bravery. The book has earned Asare praises for his mastery of the craft of storytelling and other forms of critical discourse relating to the ideological framework of his stories. *Sosu's Call* is not only regarded highly in Africa but elsewhere. In his article "Weaving Gold," published in *World Literature Today*, Asare maintains that *Sosu's Call* was listed at the top of the list, alongside Chinua Achebe's *Things Fall Apart*, as "one of the 100 most influential books written by Africans and published around the world"; the book's global appeal as a children's story with multicultural accessibility greatly enhances Asare's reputation as a writer with a profound influence. Put simply, *Sosu's Call* is a children's story with a strong social message and lesson for every child and adult who reads it and finds in its messages human values that are made relevant through the literary text.

Works cited and references

Achebe, Chinua. *Hopes and Impediments: Selected Essays: 1955–1987*. London: Heinemann, 1988.

"Africa's 100 Best Books of the 20th Century." *African Studies Center Leiden*. <https://www.ascleiden.nl/content/webdossiers/africas-100-best-books-20th-century≥

Asare, Meshack. *Sosu's Call*. Accra: Sub-Saharan Publishers, 1997.

Asare, Meshack. "Culture to Free Our Children: Looking Back at My Work over Five Decades." *World Literature Today*. Jan 2016. Web.

Asare, Meshack. "Weaving Gold." *World Literature Today*. Jan 2016. Web.

Ayrapetova, Tamara. "Does Individual Responsibility Lead to Collective Moral Responsibility for Organizations?" *CRIS-Bulletin for the Center for Research and Interdisciplinary Studies*. Feb 2012. <www.degruyter.com/downloadpdf/j/cris.2012.2012.issue-2/v10284-012-0002-2/v10284-012-0002-2.pdf>

Bartleby Writing. "What Is Social Responsibility?" 29 Jan 2018. <www.bartleby.com/essay/What-is-Social-Responsibility-F33CF44CDMRA>

Chitando, Anna. "Imagining A Peaceful Society: A Vision of Children's Literature in a Post-Conflict Zimbabwe." Uppsala: *Nordiska Afrika Institute*, 2008.

Deleuze, Gilles and Felix Guattari. *Kafka: Toward a Minor Literature (Theory and History of Article V. Literature)* Minneapolis: University of Minnesota Press, 1986. Print.

Katz, Anne. "Disability, Young Adult Literature and Pedagogical Strategies." *Lessons in Disability: Essays on Teaching with Young Adult Literature*. Jacob Stratman, Editor. Jefferson: McFarland & Co Publishers, 2016.

The Neustadt Prizes. "Meshack Asare Announced as the 2015 Winner of the Prestigious NSK Neustadt Prize for Children's Literature." <https://www.worldliteraturetoday.org/blog/news-and-events/meshack-asare-announced-2015-winner-prestigious-nsk-neustadt-prize-childrens>.

Ojaide, Tanure. "Examining Canonization in Modern African Literature." *Contemporary African Literature: New Approaches.* Durham: Carolina Academic Press, 2012.

Paiva, Deanne L. "Students' Views of the Values of Characters in International Children's Literature." *WOW Stories: Connections from the Classroom.* Vol. 3. Issue 2. July 2011. <https://wowlit.org/wp-content/media/WOW-Stories-3.2-FINAL-ilovepdf-compressed-1.pdf>

Quayson, Ato. "Introduction: African Literature and the Question of Orality." *Strategic Transformation in Nigerian Writing.* Oxford: James Currey, 1997.

Solomon, Barbara H. and W. Reginald Rampone Jr. (Eds). "Introduction." *An African Quilt.* London: Penguin Books, 2012.

Yar'Adua, Shehu Musa. "Foreword." *Black & African Writing: A Festac Anthology.* Ed. Theo Vincent. Lagos: Lagos: The Centre for Black and African Arts and Civilization National Theatre, 1981.

Yenika-Agbaw, Vivian. *Representing Africa in Children's Literature: Old and New Ways of Seeing.* New York: Routledge, 2008.

22

BEYOND 'HARMLESS LUNACY'
African women writers (w)riting madness

Pamela J. Olubunmi Smith

What do they know about madness? What if mad people weren't mad? What if certain types of behaviour which simple, ordinary people call madness, were just wisdom, a reflection of the clearsighted hypersensitivity of a pure, upright soul plunged into a real or imaginary affective void?

(Warner-Vieyra, *Juletane*, 2)

Madness need not be all breakdown. It may also be breakthrough. It is potential liberation and renewal as well as enslavement and existential death.

(R. D. Laing *The Politics of Experience*, Ch. 16)

As Sandra Gilbert and Susan Gubar observed in the preface to *The Madwoman in the Attic*, their extensive study of Victorian women writers, the topic of "madness" was considered a female malady in nineteenth- and twentieth-century British and American literatures. Thus, it has generally been viewed as a thing of female concern and preoccupation, written on by mainly women writers about privileged female characters. Thus, writers and critics have not only engaged and bequeathed to the literary world the Brontean tradition and theme of the "madwoman in the attic," but, comparatively speaking, have also more recently opened up the study of the subject of "madness" beyond its medical scope to encompass its psycho-sociological dimensions. Comparatively speaking, although there is a dearth of literature providing us with an all-but-accurate view of the psychology and mental health of the black woman whose experiences have been circumscribed simultaneously by colonization, racism, and sexism, Gilbert and Gubar's discovery early in their work is illuminating (but not surprising). Despite huge time spans and clime and spatial differences, they record their early discovery thus:

We were surprised by the coherence of theme and imagery that we encountered in the works of writers who were often geographically, historically, and psychologically distant from each other. Indeed, even when we studied women's achievements in radically different genres, we found what began to seem a distinctly female literary tradition, a tradition that had been approached and appreciated by many women readers and writers but which no one had yet defined in its entirety. *Images of enclosure and escape, fantasies in which maddened doubles functioned as asocial surrogates for docile selves,*

> *metaphors of physical discomfort manifested in frozen landscapes and fiery interiors – such patterns recurred throughout this tradition, along with obsessive depictions of diseases like anorexia, agoraphobia, and claustrophobia.*
>
> (ix, my emphasis)

Simply, this observation speaks universally to the 'woman question' in all its historic, geographic, cultural, and yes, hegemonic, feminist formulations.

The resurgence of the (re)new(ed) voices of African and diaspora black women's writings of the 1970s and 1980s whose "inside view" of the female experiences of "normality" and "abnormality" now provide us with a revisionist, other-than-Euro-American paradigm for understanding the relationship between the condition of black women in patriarchal societies and what we impute as "madness."

Reading the works of African women writers, the issue of "madness" is not as central a theme in their works as it was in eighteenth- and nineteenth-century British literature or late twentieth-century African American literature by women. This is not to infer that African women writers have been less concerned about what for many centuries was designated "the female malady." Perhaps it would be safe to say that, unlike the British women writers' preoccupation with the "mad woman in the attic" theme, twentieth-century African women writers have dealt with the issue of women and madness and of 'madness as illness' in less clinical, less analytical ways than did such British and American writers as Virginia Woolf, Susan Sontag, Katherine Ann Porter, and Sylvia Plath. This, in part, may be the case because the issue of patriarchy and the woman question has become a delicate one among African women writers and Western feminist scholars, which partly explains the absence, for instance, of schizophrenic protagonists in African women's writings of the seventies and eighties, except Bessie Head's protagonist, Elizabeth, in *The Question of Power*.

Unlike African American literature by women in which psychic suffering is engendered by racism and sexism, African literature by women deals with introspective, interior suffering and anguish engendered by social constraints and traditions of patriarchy, which, as late Senegalese writer Mariama Ba argues, "religions or unjust legislations have sealed" (88). While African American women writers have for the past three decades shown how the mainstream American ideals of true womanhood have fractured the lives of black women who are often excluded from the ideal of blond beauty, African women writers have shown the debilitating effects of "abandonment"[1] as it dislocates modern African women characters from their spaces of reality into spaces of unreality, which often leads to conditions of "disequilibrium" and "madness." While race, sex, and class account for much of the situations of illness and suffering of African American women characters,[2] it is especially the role of sex and gender in patriarchy that is at the heart of illness and psychic suffering of African women characters. Not only do the compulsions imposed by tradition and religious precepts compound African women's suffering, as Ba argues, but isolation and loneliness, a mental and/or physical exile, also push women to the edge of darkness, to the realm of dislocation that can be construed as "madness."

What is the nature of this madness in African literature by African women writers? The concern in this chapter is not with the clinical aspect of insanity as much as it is about the conditions, the causes of the anguish, the disequilibrium that leads to behavior commonly attributed to madness. Therefore, I find useful here Flora Veit-Wild's caveat in her monumental work, *Writing Madness: Borderlines of the Body in African Literature* (2006), "Unless 'madness' is carefully limited to the discussing of the structural narrative features of a text, or radically redefined to signify anything but insanity, a study of madness in African literature risks sliding into an affirmation of old, yet persistent, colonial stereotypes of African irrationality" (Newell 483). Thus, I make the distinction here between physical illness symptomatic of disease in the clinical/psychosis sense and physical suffering, which is that pervasive fragmentation of the psyche caused by societal, existential conditions. In other words, it is important to stress the distinction between mental "disease" in the traditional medical sense of the term and *dis-ease* as a condition of disequilibrium outside the normative. This distinction is intended to establish a clear difference between psycho-neurosis caused by mental imbalance and a sociopsychologically induced mental imbalance which leads to disintegration and what we describe as mental breakdown, as in the case of the "harmless lunatic" whose behavior violates societal codes of behavior in response to patriarchal and social pressures. This latter condition, in many cases, is or can be temporary once the cause of the suffering, usually identifiable, is stemmed and other alternatives, sometimes including medical ones, are sought and pursued.

Five representative works by four African women writers – anglophone and francophone – are examined here: Buchi Emecheta's *The Joys of Motherhood* (1979); Mariama Ba's two novels, *So Long a Letter* (1981) and *Scarlet Song* (1986); Yvonne Warner-Vieyra's *Julatane* (1987); and Tsitsi Dangarembga's *Nervous Conditions* (1988). While in the later four novels, the authors were more nuanced in their presentation of the conditions that drive women to "madness," Emecheta plunges directly into the more obvious – something akin to what is often referred to as the cause effect of "post-partum blues" in Western parlance. In *The Joys of Motherhood*, the result of what could very well be likened to "post-partum" disintegration (though not proven or thus named) begins early, indeed in the very first sentence of the shortest chapter (three pages) of the book. In fact, it is these pages that frame the disintegration the narrative will unfold in the book's remaining 17 chapters.

The story is about the complex life of Nnu Ego, a simple, seemingly docile daughter of a strong, free-minded mother, Ona, and a powerful village chief, Agbadi. But there is nothing simple about the cosmic web of relationships that circumscribe Nnu Ego's life. Right from childhood, she is marked by a retributive curse placed on her father's household by a servant-girl whom he ordered buried alive in accordance with his senior wife's traditional burial rites. As the slave girl dies, she defiantly promises to return and does so as an embodiment of Nnu Ego, becoming her "chi" in fulfillment of that promise. The "curse" begins to manifest early, first in Nnu Ego's early loss of her mother and then as a married woman with an infertile womb. To right these early existential manifestations, Agbadi steps in to "rescue" Nnu Ego from the wicked "chi" who was responsible for her "childless" and unhappy first marriage. A remarriage is quickly arranged with Nnaife, a podgy washer man in Lagos whom she abhors but grudgingly accepts if he can make her "a woman/mother." After the heartbreaking loss of her first-born child, a boy, her "chi" unleashes a bevy of "babies," and she gives birth to eight children, including two sets of twins, in rapid succession. Trials and tribulations abound throughout the rest of her life, and "the mother of so many sons" dies alone – a childless mother – at a crossroads, poor and unloved.

Disheveled, physically and emotionally distraught, disoriented at the beginning of the novel, she remains the same at the end, but this time older. In this existential wilderness of home and community, Emecheta lays bare unceremoniously Nnu Ego's condition of *dis-ease*, preparing the reader for her protagonist's unequivocal intent on ending the emotional pain of an unrelenting kaleidoscopic life journey of disasters. The cause of her self-imposed suicide judgment is failure to immortalize her husband. At the beginning, "Nnu Ego backed out of the room, her eyes unfocused and glazed, looking into vacancy. Her feet were light and she walked as if in a daze, not conscious of using those feet. She collided with the door, moved away from it and across the veranda, on the grass that formed part of the servants' quarters" (7). But like the slave-girl "chi," she was not planning on going down quietly – not without a confrontation with her unrelenting chi, "the unforgiving princess," whose own cruel fate at the hands of tradition had, in turn, circumscribed Nnu Ego's life from birth.

What else but destiny/fate could ensure a life of such tragic proportions with a hint at perhaps some genetic flaw? Otherwise, how does one explain the fact that the liaison between Ona, an impetuous, stubbornly arrogant "male-daughter" mother and Agbadi, an imperious, domineering father, can produce no more than an affable but painfully passive offspring? Fate dealt a cruel but philosophical hand in ensuring that the sins of the father (the father's household) shall be visited on the daughter. Indeed, there is a flaw in Nnu Ego's character, not necessarily genetic but fate generated by a ritual curse. Nnu Ego's life shall be a sacrifice, an atonement for the atrocious murder of the slave girl who becomes her "chi." The (birthmark) lump on her forehead at birth, a living symbol of the atrocities of her father's household, brands Nnu Ego for life. The equation is set: A strangely contentious "love child" birth; a gentle, easy-going personality conditioned by traditional custom to be submissive/passive under the strictures of patriarchy; an unnatural, motherless childhood, overshadowed by an ultraconservative upbringing; a male-dominated adolescence and adulthood, pervaded by a prenatal curse – hardly an ominous damnation list, which begs the question: Is this the stuff madness is made of?

Young, firm, able-bodied, virtuous, desirable, yet Nnu Ego is infertile. Paradoxically infertile, yet the potential for "birthing" is simulated in the ability of an anxiety-wracked body to *lactate* without the actual experience of birthing. Nnu Ego's mental/emotional and physical health is diminished by this experience of paradoxical infertility, which "had become her problem and hers alone." With much communal and familial nurturing, and a father's elaborate ritual atonement for his sins, her emotional health responds as her physical health is restored. The much-needed, life-bearing "juices" return to replace the dryness, lack-lusterness, and ill-humouredness stamped by the constraints of traditional values. Even the doting patriarchal father, Agbadi, recognizes that emotional love, patience, and understanding, "the art of love," of a mature man, could gradually coax out the (unnatural, unacceptable) imperfection in his daughter and effectively bring her "restless ripeness" to fruition. However, Nnaife, unfortunately, is the ill-chosen choice to fulfill this all-important role as Nnu Ego embarks on her quest for (m)otherhood, a quest she seeks with a singleness of purpose characteristic of her personality.

The ironies and cruelties of Nnu Ego's life begin to unfold, first with the premature joy of motherhood and the resulting suicide attempt and the mixed blessings of a paradoxical fruitfulness which brings her children in rapid succession but with the nagging reality of her unrewarding years of sacrificing everything for and "giving all" to her children. The anguish of Nnu Ego's creative impulse is subtly fulfilled by having children. The frequent pregnancies; Nnaife's emasculation; his long absences; his inability to provide financially for the family; his multiple marriages in the face of difficult subsistence living under the chi's unrelenting, looming presence conspire to complicate Nnu Ego's simple acceptance of, search for, and fulfillment of *Motherhood*, that formulaic patriarchal definition of female fulfillment. Did not the tradition promise fulfillment and many rewards in the honorific status of motherhood, particularly motherhood that has been graced with not one but three sons? Literally banking on her natural, creative accomplishment after the birth of her first son, Oshia, "she was now sure, as she bathed her baby son and cooked for her husband, that her old age would be happy; that when she died there would be somebody left behind to refer to her as 'mother'" (54). Nnu Ego's naive belief in the promise of yields on her investment is buoyed by her blind adherence to tradition, a tradition that conveniently bends its own rules without warning. All too soon, Nnu Ego begins to wrestle with reality, the ironic reality that indeed "a woman with many children could [still] face a lonely old age and maybe a miserable death all alone, just like a barren woman" (224). Contradictions abound in defining the self in motherhood and losing the self in motherhood.

The economic, sociopolitical, and cultural imperatives of tradition have shifted, and the motherhood investment no longer provides a security or even the sense of it. In fact, at every turn, particularly with the last two of nine births, the shortcomings of the tradition-bound system become disappointingly glaring. Nnu Ego slowly begins to see and acknowledge the reality of the tradition she blindly adheres to:

> Men – all they were interested in were male babies to keep their names going. But did not a woman have to bear the woman-child who would later bear the sons? "God, when will you create a woman who will be fulfilled in herself, a full human being, not somebody's appendage?" . . .
>
> After all, I was born alone, and I shall die alone. What have I gained from all this? Yes, I have many children, but what do I have to feed them on? On my life. I have to work myself to the bone to look after them. I have to give them my all. And if I am lucky enough to die in peace, I even have to give them my soul. They will worship my dead spirit to provide for them: it will be hailed as a good spirit so long as there are plenty of yams and children in the family, but if anything should go wrong, if a young wife does not conceive or there is famine, my spirit will be blamed. When will I be free? . . .
>
> But even in her confusion, she knew the answer: "Never, not even in death."
>
> *(186–187)*

Cri de coeur monologues such as this begin to emerge and give voice to the foreboding essence of her lament during her temporary nervous breakdown preceding her suicidal attempt, as she laments the loss of the societally imposed legitimizing badge of her personhood, indeed her humanity, at the beginning of the novel: "But I am not a woman anymore! I am not a mother anymore. The child is there, dead on the mat. My chi has taken him away from me. I only want to go in there and meet her" (62). The anguish inherent in her lament as a first-time mother (though short-lived) is foreshadowed and forebodingly re-echoed in the novel's paradox of all paradoxes: that it is motherhood (and wifehood) that strip(s) her of a confident center of being.

Metamorphosized by her association with Adaku, her co-wife, she begins to give voice to the ironies and cruelties of her life, recognizing that it is both an unrelenting chi and the imperious hand of patriarchy that have combined to deviously manipulate the prescription to a happy, abundant life in old age:

> I am a prisoner of my own flesh and blood. Is it such an enviable position? The men make it look as if we must aspire for children or die. *That's why when I lost my first son I wanted to die, because I failed to live up to the standard expected of me by the males in my life, my father and my husband – and now I have to include my sons. But who made the law that we should not hope in our daughters? We women subscribe to that law more than anyone. Until we change all this, it is still a man's world, which women will always help to build.*
>
> *(my emphasis, 187)*

"With the first flush of youthful energy gone," she realized the folly of having sacrificed friends to the exclusive building-up of her "joys" as a mother. Little did she realize that the all-consuming nature of motherhood necessarily precludes what would seem to be a natural integration of motherhood and otherhood, hence (m)otherhood. Total and exclusive investment in unreciprocating sons and a complete denial of life's comforts in the name of 'motherhood' ensures not the guaranteed self-fulfilled and a happy old age which social conventions promise but a shrine and the posthumous joy of having given all to (your) children. If only she had the presence of mind to set aside her jealousy of her rival, Adaku, who understands and articulates in no uncertain terms to her senior co-wife the stuff of which madness is made as she resolves to nip the potential blossom of madness in the bud by leaving Nnaife. Primal survival instinct overrules the filial duty to family and community of this mother of two-daughters-but-no-sons as she exclaims:

> My chi be damned . . . I don't care for the life he or she gave me . . . I am not prepared to stay here and be turned into a mad woman just because I have no sons . . . the more I think about it the more I realize that we woman set impossible standards for ourselves. That we make life intolerable for one another. I cannot live up to your standards, senior wife. So, I have set my own.
>
> *(168–169)*

Dogged by a motherless "unconventional" childhood, buffeted in the hands of patriarchy – from father to husbands to sons – and shrouded by a 'chi' determined to legitimize herself through revenge, staunch traditionalist Nnu Ego walks the fine line between sanity in a confusing world and madness, the status of her physical and emotional health never really certain. Ostracized by the Owulum family, penniless, alone (though three children still remain), clutching onto vague memories of two successful sons instead of her children's or grandchildren's hands: "She became vague, and people pointed out that she had never been strong emotionally" (224). Physically and emotionally exhausted, lonely, displaced in the familiar Ibuza surroundings, her childhood home, meaninglessly engaged in wandering around, telling people about her two prized sons abroad, and finally disoriented,

> She died quietly . . ., with no child to hold her hand, no friend to talk to her. She had never really made many friends, so busy had she been building up her joys as a mother . . . And her reward? Did she not have the greatest funeral Ibuza had ever seen? It took Oshia three years to pay off the money he had borrowed to show the world what a good son he was. That was why people failed to understand why she did not answer their prayers, for what else could a woman want but to have sons who would give her a decent burial?
>
> *(224)*

Broken-spirited and confused, Nnu Ego dies alone with the title that legitimizes her but does not give her life, having perceived her children as her life, but not as part of her life. The specter of the childless, bereft young woman at the beginning of the novel looms grievously in the pitiable tragedy of the "childless mother" at the end of the novel.

Although we do not get an intense introspection of Nnu Ego's subconscious, we glimpse through rare, but sufficient, insightful monologues her *dis-ease* with contradictory patriarchal imperatives as she probes the nature of her tragic dilemma. Her recognition of her enslavement to patriarchal tradition of complete filial obedience to the men in her life – father Agbadi, husbands Amatokwu and Nnaife, and (now) sons Oshia and Adim – the role women play in their own fragmentation, and the rampant inequities inherent in male-female relationships, metamorphosized her. Unfortunately, this metamorphosis materialized far too late to track her in the road to the self-fulfillment and 'otherhood' she assumes are inherent in the honorific status of 'mother.' The totality of loneliness, mental and territorial exile, frustrated love, abandonment, an acquiescence to the reality of her pre-suicide lament as well as a haunted, personal natal history and a lack of knowledge of some personal strengths and maternal attributes which she could have gained from her mother, Ona, but did not, culminated to plunge her into an abysmal pre-death and post-death silence. And the calamitous result is that even though "Nnu Ego had it all, yet still did not answer prayers for children" (224). Strangely and grievously, in her silence, the many "why?" and "why not?" stories are encapsulated in madness.

Silence and madness, madness and silence? "What if her silence," as Warner-Vieyra marvels in *Juletane*, "were a reflection of the clear-sighted hypersensitivity of a pure, upright soul plunged into a real or imaginary affective void?" (2). In some respects, Emecheta, Warner-Vieyra, Ba, and Dangarembga echo the same concerns about the causes of women's *dis-ease*, naming as major culprit the combination of patriarchal institution of marriage, family, and colonial exploitation. Unlike Emecheta's extended narrative form, Warner's and Ba's terse, epistolary form in *Juletane* and *So Long a Letter*, respectively, offers the immediacy of the protagonists' introspective voices.

Juletane is the personal account of Juletane, a young West Indian woman exile who meets and marries Mamadou Moustapha, a Senegalese student in Paris. Aware of his Islamic background but kept in the dark about his marital status until she finds out by happenstance just a few days before she is to return with Mamadou to live in Africa, Julatane finds herself trapped and "struggling in the depths of an abyss, alone, defenseless" (38). The diary she keeps is the account of her physical and psychological breakdown and subsequent madness caused by the anguish, dislocation, and abandonment of Mamadou's straight-faced betrayal. In the study of the causes of madness, individual and collective histories play a significant role. Like Nnu Ego, Juletane chronicles burdensome circumstantial individual and collective histories. Juletane, like Nnu Ego, is dogged by a peculiar nascent circumstance, being ominously conceived on a Lenten day, after which she is soon orphaned a few years later. Confused and sheltered, her growing-up years are shrouded in geographic and mental dislocation and disillusionment. "An only child, an orphan," with no friends, no natal family (after her godmother's sudden death), she engages full force her childhood longing for connectedness, filial affection, centeredness, and self-fulfillment. However, she begins this earnest journey bearing the burdens of personal ambiguity, shrouded in a shameful and embarrassing race history, on an "outsider/intruder" status. Here is how she circumscribes herself: "I have no children. I have neither parents nor friends. And not even a name" (13).

The backdrop to Juletane's search for self is a telling framework to the cause and nature of her eventual self-described madness. Her conception on a Lenten day is ominous, accounting, she believes, for the "abnormality" of her puberty and adolescence at the hands of her godmother and the weighty imperious anguish of orphanhood and dislocation.

Overwhelmed by this notion of a destiny which has been decided at her birth and circumscribed by history, Juletane ascribes herself the role of victim of a hostile, unnurturing environment – "a victim of the elements." She becomes extremely vulnerable. In her relationship with Mamadou, she is affectionate, trusting, and open. Holding back nothing, she transfers all filial affection to Mamadou as husband, father, friend, entrusting to him her very soul. Until the fateful revelation of Mamadou's deplorable deception, at sea, on the second day of their journey home to Senegal, Juletane's previously ambiguous, dislocated world is temporarily contained in the affectionate, protective, pre-Senegal world of Mamadou. Until she discovers the reality of Mamadou's cowardly and inhumane act of luring her into his snare with professed love, Juletane has almost convinced herself of the manageability of the pre-Mamadou world that nurtures her insecurity and sense of rootlessness. With spontaneous naïveté, she believes that Mamadou and, finally, the return to Mother Africa, "land of [my] forefathers," will provide that confident center of being which her fragmented natal history and geographic dislocation have displaced. But in Senegal, the social realities of traditional Muslim life of husband-sharing and burdensome, incessant family demands reawaken the old insecurities and anguish of orphanhood. Her miscarriage and knowledge of her irreversible barrenness are the final death knell which drives Juletane into unendurable extremes of loneliness, complete alienation, and subsequent madness, at least as her co-wife, Ndeye, sees it.

In *Juletane*, madness is writ large. Madness is the dis-ease of being a foreigner, an outsider who has nothing to do but turn over memories of days on end; Juletane, the stranger who has only one voice – her own – to listen to until it becomes an obsession (78). Madness is the dis-ease caused by failure, the death of love, a physical and mental fragmentation, rootlessness, a double physical and mental exile, shrouded by a pervasive, strange natal history. Madness is the dis-ease of abandonment which causes a debilitating physical and psychological breakdown. Madness is the dis-ease of compulsions imposed on women by tradition and women themselves who wear the oppressive mantle as 'keepers of tradition.' Madness is suffering compounded by the sense of isolation and loneliness from family, the community, and society in general. Madness is being stripped of name, of essence, by and in a household in which the pervasive presence and patronage of the male dominates, decentering everything that does not conform to the imperatives of patriarchy. Madness is schizophrenia, inaccurately diagnosed neurosis, manic depressions, asylums. Madness is being drugged with injections, medications, and artificial rest. Madness is written up diagnoses that circumvent the real issues of "(her)stories – the loneliness, the hurt, the pain." Juletane's "madness" is faulty diagnosis invoked and ascribed by others and circumstances.

Overwhelmed by circumstances and unable to forge any alliances with other women, Juletane passively accepts her victimization, ironically holding her co-wives, Awa and Ndeye, and not Mamadou, responsible for her anguish. Ironically, rather than a common-goal "subversive sisterhood" response to this ill-placed 'victims blaming fellow victims' while the victimizer looks on bemused and unscathed, the co-wife victims squander their ace venom in the service of upholding the very patriarchal system that oppresses them. However, unlike the co-wives she blames for her condition, Juletane finds, in her seclusion, the creative impulse – other natural impulses such as sexual, maternal, and romantic having been unnaturally silenced in her. By the stroke of crayon and a snitched exercise book, Juletane begins to journal her anguish in a monologue to Mamadou who, unfortunately, does not live long to read it. Nonetheless, the very exercise of writing, Juletane rationalizes, "will shorten my long hours of discouragement, will be something for me to cling to and will give me a friend, a confidante" (5). In the private sphere of her madness, Julatane remains supreme, inadvertently charting, shaping, directing, and understanding her journey through the past to the present. Through the diary, Juletane can chronicle the past, reorder her reality and (w)rite herself back from the precipice, the deep dark hole, the valley of dark despair. Providentially, through writing, she gives "birth," though not naturally, but symbolically, to a hidden self. Through her diary, Juletane can tear off the artificial labeling and naming which her victimizers throw at her and at once retrieve her own true name. Patriarchal institutions of marriage, family, and motherhood ascribe madness, which is a convenient, categorical description for behavior that deviates from the norm. Owning that historical displacement and geographic dislocation and a haunted childhood history as potentially significant influences on one's personality is one thing, but wearing the cloak of someone else's ascription is another. Even in ascribed insanity as Juletane ponders the fatalistic acceptance of mysterious, premature death in Muslim belief, she assesses her ascribed condition, her assigned madness, and lays its origin and cause squarely not at Allah's feet but on Mamadou's household:

> This fatalism has always amazed me. I know that in this particular case, Allah is not the only one involved . . . And what about my madness, whose will was that? That is if I could be considered mad. For the moment I am neither the mad woman of the village

313

nor the neighbourhood. *My madness is the private property of Mamadou Moustapha's house and in particular of Ndeye, his favourite and third wife.* This beloved Ndeye loses nothing by waiting.

(62, my emphasis)

Institutionalized polygyny, its process, its effects, and its inherently inequitable nature are problematic and cause pain for the modernized woman even when some co-wives show good-will. In instances where the modern woman is non-Moslem, non-African, and outside the ethnic group, honesty in explaining expectations *prior to* a marriage commitment, respect for the foundation of mutual trust on which the relationship is based, and a sensitivity to the potential pain of cultural differences are simple, sensible courtesies, if not imperatives. Blatant betrayal of trust, deceptive and surreptitious communication about status, and indifference: these are the volatile elements which easily rattle and derail an already fragile, not-so-confident personality. Juletane, a new, enthusiastic, foreign bride, not only finds out surreptitiously her husband, Mamadou's marital status a few weeks *into* the marriage, but she does so after they were already on a boat at sea, en route to their new home in Senegal. What effect should Mamadou assume such emotional trauma, this betrayal of trust, this violation of mutual respect will have on Juletane's psyche, especially since he explains it with the simple lie that he intends to dissolve his child-marriage to Awa? Naturally, pangs of jealousy would and do give rise to fits of delirium and suicidal contemplation.

Finally, it is through writing that Juletane recognizes that "if there is a slightest glimmer of hope buried in the depths of your being, you can overcome the greatest difficulties" (68). Juletane (w)rites herself, as it were, out of the destructive actions, decisions, and self-destructiveness into which anguish had plunged her. In writing, Juletane speaks her silence and (w)rites/rights her silenced repression. However, she is only partially empowered since the very nature of the diary form as a confession bereaves her of the full power of her self-actualization. She defers to Mamadou, the authority, addressing her desire to be understood – she promised him undeserved salvation, perhaps as she resigns herself to the belief in the possibility of the triumph of love.

Fully aware of her faculties, and finally reaching out to fellow inmates dumped by relatives at the asylum (where many of them do not belong in the first instance), Juletane listens to and encourages a community of women – Oumy, Naboou, and others like herself, "all victims of a selfish world which crushes them carelessly" (75) – to "take stock of oneself," to tell/write their stories of exile, alienation, loneliness, and madness. Unfortunately, the very human beings like Mamadou and all upholders of oppressive patriarchal institutions and practices to whom these *cri de coeur* stories of alienation, loneliness, and madness are addressed never get to read/hear these stories. Mamadou will not live to read the diary; he mysteriously dies from a car accident late at night after dropping off Juletane at the hospital/sanatorium. Sadly, Juletane dies only four months later, her body found lifeless by a nurse. Her exhausted heart has simply stopped (79).

What is madness after all? Since the major cause of what is often described as female insane behavior results directly from women's response/reaction to one patriarchal imperative or another, does the assessment of female insanity not suggest a corollary re-examination of "patriarchal sanity?" Juletane laments her inability to adjust to the condition of forced polygyny to which Mamadou has deceptively subjected her:

I had put on mourning and cut off my hair the day I stopped living with Mamadou. For me, the world had ended on that day. Here I am today, after four years reprieve, finally, really, all alone in the world, my heart bereft of hope. Had my life been worth living? What had I contributed, what had I given? Oh, how I long to fall asleep too, to have a long, restful night! To wake up in another world where mad people are not mad, but wise and just.

(78)

Alas, the destructiveness of abandonment – that art of betrayal of promise.

It is perhaps Senegalese writer Mariama Ba who best develops this issue of polygyny as a significant root of physical and psychological fragmentation in African women's lives. In *So Long a Letter* and *Scarlet Song*, two short but significant texts about Senegalese society, Ba lays bare at once the root cause of and solution to the malady that afflicts African women, traditional and modern, in marriage. While she does not name polygyny as a major cause of women's madness as such in *So Long a Letter*, she points squarely to *abandonment*, a hallmark of the common practice of *polygyny*, as a major *dis-ease* which undermines the physical and mental welfare of African women in modern Africa in her second novel, *Scarlet Song* (published posthumously).

Although Ramatoulaye, the protagonist of *So Long a Letter*, does not go mad in or as a result of her polygamous marriage as did Nnu Ego in *The Joys of Motherhood* and Juletane in *Juletane*, the potential for a breakdown belies the anguish echoed throughout the formal "long letter" she writes to Aissatou, her "sister soulmate" who, like her, has suffered a similar fate of abandonment by her husband, Mawdo. Ba's choice of the epistolary as agent to convey the depth of her heroine's suffering is purposeful. The epistle begins on the fortieth and final day of remembrance for the dead, according to "the precepts of Islam."

The story of a 30-year marriage (25 of it seemingly normal and blissful, producing 12 children, and the last 5 years characterized by abandonment) is reduced to an 89-page letter of anguish addressed to a divorcee best friend, Aissatou, on the official day that the mourning spouses of the dead man shed their garments, their yoke of mourning. In this Senegalese culture, the institution of marriage, with its stultifying inhibitions and restrictions, remains the sole definer of woman's destiny. In it, despite preparation by and adherence to the 'precepts of Islam,' marriage, husband, and children remain woman's only means of self-actualization, making "wifehood," that subversive agent of her objectification, in a patriarchal institution she inadvertently serves as an accomplice.

Thus, on this final day of her emancipation, Ramatoulaye breaks her silence when she finally breaks from the solitary confinement of widowhood, mourning vestment and all, giving voice to her long-held pain and suffering from physical and psychological abandonment by her dead husband, Modou. Her unburdening is not unlike the universal "cry everywhere, everywhere in the world" which Ba recognizes as the unmistakable anguish not only "from the heart of the Senegalese women . . . But . . . also a cry which can symbolize the cry of women everywhere."[3] Consequently, Ba harps relentlessly on what she identifies as the root cause of this malady in Senegal society in both her novels. *So Long a Letter* and *Scarlet Song* both constitute her glaring critique of 'Islamic polygyny,' particularly the insidious practice of 'abandonment,' which is at its core.

In his study, Mbaye Cham observed that 'abandonment,' in both novels, is "an issue in the sociocultural settings," noting that:

> [It] is not the result of a single act even though it may be a unilateral act, nor is it to be confused with divorce or repudiation even though it may share with the latter certain causal factors. *Abandonment is a social disease.* It is the cumulative result of a process

that could be referred to as the gradual opening and enlargement of the emotional/ sexual circle that originally binds two partners (a husband and a wife) to introduce and accommodate a third partner (a second wife) *in a manner so devious and deceptive that a new process is set in motion.* This new process itself culminates in a state of mind and body that forces the first female partner to reevaluate the whole relationship by either reluctantly accepting or categorically rejecting the enlarged circle.

(92, my emphasis)

This, unfortunately, aptly describes the primary reality of most of Ba's (married) women characters. Both novels are rife with the evil machinations of: conniving in-laws, engaged in cruel social and economic power plays; conniving young ladies in search of "sugar daddies" to liberate them from financial ghettos; greedy mothers eager to sacrifice and use their daughters as bait for big-catch cash-cows to lift them out of poverty; unscrupulous, spineless married men unable to resist the lure of young girls to rejuvenate themselves; mean-hearted, jealous mothers-in-law who undermine their daughters-in-law; and so on. The antagonistic role of all these players, themselves victims of male lust and vanity and female greed and jealousies, is the root cause of abandonment, a social ill which breeds child exploitation, encourages child marriage, and engenders the abuse and problems of polygyny.

The theme-script is all too familiar; the characters run the entire social class gamut. The higher the social class, the more scandalous the effect. The power play is constant: older, established males (victims of lust and vanity), ditching long-established marriages to lure and marry innocent girl-children seeking socioeconomic transformation. Thus, in *So Long a Letter*, the protagonist Ramatoulaye is abandoned by Modou, her husband of 25 years, for a younger woman, Binetou, their oldest daughter's classmate and best friend. Put up to it by her greedy mother, Dame Belle-Mere, Binetou turns out to be the sacrificial lamb, offered to ensure her mother's accession from poverty to elite class status. Like Ramatoulaye, Aissatou, her sister/best friend, was abandoned by Mawdo, her physician husband, for a young, hand-picked cousin by Tante Nabou, under the pretext that Aissatou's vulgar background as a mere blacksmith's daughter unacceptably taints Mawdo's noble origin. However, Aissatou calls her bluff, rejecting her pitiful, spineless husband who cannot stand up to and reject his mother's meddling in their marriage, and walks away from the marriage, clothed in her dignity. While Aissatou walks away from her marriage and thrives with her four sons, her sister-friend Ramatoulaye chooses to stay notwithstanding the act of disavowal in the loathsome way Modou's marriage to Binetou is announced to her – its betrayal looming large amid the insult of being asked to be an ally to his "polygamic instinct." She is like one of the many women, "despised, relegated or exchanged, . . . abandoned like a worn-out or outdated boubou" (41), despite the fact that, as is the case, Ramatoulaye has lived her life strictly according to the precepts of Islam concerning polygamic life and has prepared herself for equal sharing (46). Notwithstanding all entreaty, Modou not only abandons his family, he cuts off all maintenance funds, cleaning out the joint bank account to purchase and furnish a new flat for his new wife and mother-in-law. Neither Ramatoulaye nor any of the twelve children see nor hear from him for five years until he dies of a heart attack. Ramatoulaye's abandonment is unusual and complete, like "a fluttering leaf that no hand dares to pick up" (52).

Here, then, is the complete act of betrayal and downright violation of Koranic Law, which requires equal sharing in all things uxorial and domestic. Divorce would have been a better 'opium' than the pain and disgrace of abandonment. Yet, as Ramatoulaye rationalizes it, as "one of those who can realize themselves fully and bloom only when they form part of a couple" (55), she "accepted" and waits, and cries a lot through sleepless nights, waiting, wondering, hoping; she remains faithful to the love of her youth, longing to be a part of 'something.' Unlike some of the abandoned, her luck holds steady, helping her skate by without any major calamity. A busy household of raising twelve children keeps her from insanity.

Unfortunately, unlike Ramatoulaye, the beautiful and lovestruck but headstrong Madame Jacqueline Diack is not as lucky. Nowhere are the double effects of the pain of abandonment by spouse and ostracism from in-laws more focused than in Ba's story of Jacqueline, the Ivorian married to Samba Diack, a Senegalese doctor. Ironically, Ba's broken-hearted protagonist is the lucky, clear-eyed one in the end who knows one has to "[b]race oneself to check despair and get it into proportion!" (41). She has observed other casualties of abandonment to know that:

> A nervous breakdown waits around the corner for anyone who lets himself wallow in bitterness. Little by little, it takes over your whole being."
>
> Oh, nervous breakdown! Doctors speak of it in a detached, ironical way, emphasizing that the vital organs are in no way disturbed. You are lucky if they don't tell you that you are wasting your time with the ever-growing list of your illnesses – your head, throat, chest, heart, liver – that no X-ray can confirm. And yet, what atrocious suffering is caused by nervous breakdowns!
>
> *(41)*

Having heard of too many misfortunes not to understand her own, Ramatoulaye recalls the sad story of Jacqueline Diack and the ironic weight of cultural myopia, among many nuptial constraints, which sends her to the psychiatric wing of a hospital. How ironic that Jacqueline, "a black African [who] should have been able to fit without difficulty into a black African society" becomes the unfortunate patient with undiagnosable cultural infirmity:

> Jacqueline truly wanted to become Senegalese, but the mockery checked all desire in her to cooperate . . . *Her husband, making up for lost time, spent his time chasing slender Senegalese women, as he would say with appreciation, and did not bother to hide his adventures, respecting neither his wife nor children* . . . Jacqueline cried; Samba Diack 'lived it up'. Jacqueline lost weight; Samba Diack was still living fast. Jacqueline complained of a disturbing lump in her chest, under her left breast . . . she fretted . . . eagerly Jacqueline took tablets, tortured by the insidious pain. The bottle empty, she noticed that the lump remained in the same place . . . to feel the pain just as acutely as ever.
>
> *(42, my emphasis)*

Alas the dangers of psychosomatic illnesses and their endless "guesswork" diagnoses. Alarmingly, the ironies mount, turning the story of the once-lively Madame Diack, wife of Samba Diack, medical doctor, into little more than the cautionary tale of the hell-hole that is indeed the Samba Diack household. What commonsense diagnosis other than "stress" could not have eventually "guessed" at the obvious ailment that takes its toll so thoroughly, robbing a woman in a troubled marriage of her (well)beingness? More specifically, what difficult-to-diagnose ailment could so doggedly fly undetected under sophisticated medical diagnostic radar other than the all-too-obvious 'wifehood/motherhood blues' derived from the "anxiety-laden" household of Samba Diack? Rather than automatically assume any and all forms of woman's manifested anxieties as categorically diagnosable, Ramatoulaye (Ba) offers the medical profession insightfully, experientially, not guesswork but common sense, with the humanitarian caveat:

> Strange and varied manifestations of neuro-vegetative dystonia. Doctors, beware, especially if you are neurologists or psychiatrists. Often, the pains you are told of have their

root in moral torment. Vexations suffered and constant frustrations: these are what accumulate somewhere in the body and choke it.

(44)

Ironically, it would take a mature, more experienced physician, the head of the Neurology Department, to buck the Senegalese patriarchal system and finally name the root cause of Jacqueline's ailment and unchoke "the source of the distress disrupting her organism" (45). The "heart of her illness," he assured her, was a casualty of Diack-induced anxiety, the result of "mental alienation" (45). Simply, gently, reassuringly giving hope, he explains:

> Madame Diack, I assure you that there is nothing at all wrong with your head. The X-rays have shown nothing, and neither have the blood tests. *The problem is that you are depressed, that is . . . not happy.* You wish the conditions of life were different from what they are in reality, and this is what is torturing you. *Moreover, you had your babies too soon after each other; the body loses its vital juices, which haven't had the time to be replaced.* In short, there is nothing endangering your life.
>
> *(45, my emphasis)*

First, the simple diagnosis, then the equally uncomplicated cure: 'You must react, go out, give yourself a reason for living. Take courage. Slowly, you will overcome. We will give you a series of shock treatments with curare to relax you. You can leave afterwards' (45).

The simple but sage-like words of assurance, uttered in a matter of minutes (not months), hit at the core of the problem, providing the healing balm the myriad previous diagnoses failed woefully to produce (in months). The older doctor's simple diagnosis hits on the truth of Jacqueline's and (by extension) Senegalese women's lives: attendant marital and domestic problems, exacerbated by Islamic polygamic practices and abandonment processes. The inevitable conclusion: they do take a heavy physical and psychological toll on Senegalese women's psyche and bodies. Thus, first-hand knowledge of the very loneliness that was viewed as the byproduct of Jacqueline's (near) insanity is the very tool Ramatoulaye deftly uses to "manage" her own choice of aloneness.

Ba lays bare the choices, offering one more example of how yet another woman character handles her own experience of abandonment. As was the case in *So Long a Letter*, Ba again takes up the issue of the debilitating process and its conflation with insanity in *Scarlet Song*, probing further, with damning precision, the duplicitous role women play, especially mothers-in-law, in the demise of other women. While Senegalese society is patriarchal, it needs its womenfolk, acting variously as 'handmaids' and 'sugar-babies,' to provide the sturdy legs on and with which patriarchy stands and thrives.

Scarlet Song is the love story of Ousmane, a Senegalese man, and Mireille, a French woman who moves from France to live in Dakar after their marriage. The union of the Black Senegalese man to the White, affluent French woman, it appears, is doomed from the start. If it had any prospects of surviving at all, it could only do so at the whim and caprice of one individual: Yaye Khady, Ousmane's mother, who meddles with impunity in the couple's marriage. Sworn to wrest her son from the clutches of the white woman she views as "a cultural outcast," "a usurper," "intruder," Yaye Khady leaves no proverbial stone unturned in her dogged efforts to misuse the privileges of tradition and the institution of the mother-in-law to supplant Mireille by any means necessary. Absolutely no effort at Mireille integrating into Senegalese society is good enough to stave off Yaye Khady's unmasked dislike for Mireille, not only as a white daughter-in-law but also for what she views as the foreigner's role in denying her the long-calculated and expected cultural privileges and material pay-offs due her as a mother-in-law in traditional

Senegalese society. Consequently, she engineers a plan, fully sanctioning a polygynous marriage between Ousmane and Ouleymatou that is designed to drive Mireille insane.

In an unstable environment where displacement and alienation are the only options to one who, unfortunately, has foolishly burned the bridges of family and her French culture, Mireille finds herself at the crossroads of sanity and madness, facing the apprenticeships of "married life and . . . being a black man's wife in Africa" (99). Unfortunately, an anonymous letter and a year-long tracking of the Ousmane-Ouleymatou marriage liaison and its new domestic arrangements soon confirms Ousmane's betrayal to a lonely, demoralized Mireille, sending the hysterical prodigal off the edge into a rage in which she first poisons her son, Gorgui, before ambushing and viciously stabbing her husband. Turned into a fury at such a heinous crime of deception, Mireille's madness strikes at the heart of Ba's issue with the role women play in deliberately sabotaging other women's happiness in patriarchal societies, "killing another woman's daughter" (152) for their own self-interest, as Soukeyna, Yaye Khade's first daughter and Ousmane's sister, bold-facedly reminds her own family.

Although lamentations on the ills of patriarchy in the narratives of African women's subjugation are an all-too-common theme in African women writers' novels, the contextual details of these lamentations differ only in the historical and sociopolitical and religious tenets that inform and frame them. While patterns of women's responses to their conditions of subjugation may be similar in accordance with Ba's described "cry of women everywhere," patriarchal machinery wears different cloaks according to the traditions and whims from which it is impended. In other words, although patriarchy formed the basis of most African traditional cultures prior to their collision with the different colonial powers, what emerged thereafter are institutions sanctioned by gerontocratic systems of coercion planted in religion and tradition. We see Islamic polygyny in Ba's and Warner-Vieyra's francophone Senegal and, likewise, a self-centered and authoritative patriarchal social order in Emecheta's anglophone Nigeria.

The shifts from Emecheta's rural, traditional Ibuza, to Warner-Vieyra and Ba's Dakar, to Tsitsi Dangarembga's 'Homestead' and 'The Mission' in *Nervous Conditions* present a different set of dynamics. Comparatively a late-comer to the literary scene than her senior sister-compatriots – their late 1970s and 1980s decades versus her 1988 debut – Dangarembga grabbed the literary limelight in the forefront of post-war Zimbabwe with her brazen, head-on exposure of patriarchy and colonialism's self-centered and authoritative infiltration of colonial ideals. Right from its debut, her work has gained a reputation as the most daring, unapologetic, and vociferous centerpiece indictment of the insidious nature of colonization and its devastating double-yoke effects on Zimbabwean women. It is also in this novel that women openly name, expose, and lay siege ti the source-cause of their 'hysteria.' By design, this was Dangarembga's primary agenda in *Nervous Conditions*: to expose the mechanism of male domination in Zimbabwean society.

Intent on putting colonialism and patriarchy, its attendant partner-in-crime, on notice, the novel's grievance-filled opening statement explodes unabashedly with an affront: "I was not sorry when my brother died" (1), followed declaratively a few lines later with the purpose of the narrative outlined:

> For though the event of my brother's passing and the events of my story cannot be separated, *my story is not after all about death, but about my escape and Lucia's; about my mother's and Maiguru's entrapment; and about Nyasa's rebellion – Nyasa, far-minded and isolated, my uncle's daughter, whose rebellion may not in the end have been successful.*
>
> *(1, my italics)*

Historically, in the transition period during and between colonial Rhodesia to independent Zimbabwe, neither colonized native male nor female was spared the psychological whipping rod of colonialism, its impact putting their condition in a constant state of "nervousness," especially that of the female, who endured the double jeopardy of colonial and patriarchal oppression. Therefore, the story is not about one male's death but about the welfare of the remaining five casualties, the trapped females, "whose needs and sensibilities . . . were not considered a priority, or even legitimate" (12) and who continue to suffer from "the poverty of blackness on the one side and the weight of womanhood on the other" (16) as well as from a list of other "conditions" developed from a collusion of Shona patriarchal social structure and colonial oppression. Some of these oppressive conditions produce serious anxieties with life-threatening, foreign symptoms, as in the case of Nyasha. For example, Mainini, Tambudzai's mother, develops deep-seated anxieties from fear of the English culture that not only kills her son, Nhamo, but poses imminent danger to her four remaining children; Nyasha ends up with a cultural-alienation ailment resulting in *anorexia nervosa*, a Western disease common in Europe and America but rarely known in Africa; Maiguru, Babamukuru's British-educated wife, struggles under the weight of Shona patriarchy that demands traditional Shona uxorial loyalty and adherence to Shona culture; Lucia, Mainini's sister, faces and struggles against restricting gender structures; and Tambudzai, under deep cultural pressure, claws her way through the entanglement of subjugation and degradation as well as gender and economic inequality at the hands of her uncle, Babamukuru, the "hallowed headmaster and revered patriarch" (197). All these entrapped women suffer from/react to various kinds of psychosomatic symptoms.

The conditions of nervousness in which Zimbabwean women find themselves are not only social and gendered but are also economic ones which are exacerbated by what Mainini describes as "the poverty of Blackness." This is the manifestation of the colonial economic exploitation from which "[a]ll the characters suffer, in a variety of ways and to certain degree levels of entrapment that the narrator identifies as the entrapment of poverty, the weight of womanhood, and 'the Englishness' that Tambu's mother cautions against" (Uwakweh 79).

Astonishingly, it is Mainini, the uneducated, lowest-on-the-totem-pole of the Siguake women who, eventually, shows an insightful albeit intuitive understanding and articulation of the nature of "Englishness," her pseudonym for colonialism, a.k.a. Western education. While others – Nhamo, Nyasha, Maiguru, Tambudzai, and even Babamukuru – are either blind or simply acquiesce to its brutal nature and hypocrisy, Mainini experientially looks on quietly – through her son, Nhamo's, transformation – and sees its precision, its means and moments of coercion. Her analysis and verdict immediately upon hearing Babamukuru announce Nhamo's death – her worst fears eventually come to pass: "First you took his tongue so that he could not speak to me . . . you bewitched him and now he is dead . . . *You and your education have killed my son*" (54) my emphasis.

Education is the killer; specifically, Western education which, at its social level, steals the natives' language, hence his voice, and, at its economic level, slices through the native's being. Nhamo, then, is the clear case-study of English education's fatalistic result which ends in the subject falling victim to cultural alienation. Simply stated, cultural alienation is the real killer hidden behind Nhamo's embrace of the bread-and-butter filler diet of the Mission in rejection of the homestead's culturally rich and nourishing sadza diet and all it represents spiritually. Mainini got it right all along after all. The two-part travesty of "Englishness" is its virulence, which methodically first ensures the loss of language that will in turn result in the inevitable loss of the self.

Of the five texts examined in this essay, it is *Nervous Conditions* that provides more than a glimpse of patriarchy and its workings. Whereas Emecheta, Ba, and Warner-Vieyra show the effects of patriarchal oppression and how women respond to these conditions, thus giving us but a glimpse of its "what" and "how," Dangarembga gives a sustained portrait of patriarchy-at-work in Shona/Zimbabwean culture through the characterization and navigation of Babamukuru's use and abuse of patriarchal power. Babamukuru is at the center of Shona traditional culture, what remnants of it that he has not denied or willed away after its brutal battering by colonialism. As the eldest son of the Sigauke family, he is its patriarch in every sense of the word – its benefactor, final arbiter, its god, "as nearly divine as any human could ever hope to be" (164). In his position as principal of the Mission School, he is the embodiment of colonial power on the one hand and, on the other, the symbol of absolute patriarchal power over his homestead's extended family, especially the womenfolk. Tambudzai captures this crucial point earlier in the story when she describes him simply as "God" (70), whose "identity was elusive" (102). He has "Plenty of Power. Plenty of money. A lot of education. Plenty of everything" (50). Despite his benevolence, born more out of obligation to the extended family than from heartfelt charity, Tambudzai recalls the chilly, mirthless home life: "We hardly ever laughed when Babamukuru was within earshot, because, Maiguru said, his nerves were bad. His nerves were bad because he was so busy. For the same reason we did not talk much when he was around either" (102). These are the same "bad nerves" which quench his daughter Nyasha's exuberant nature, turning her into a rebellious, self-destructive child who suffers a nervous breakdown at the end of the novel.

As traditional head of the Homestead, Babamukuru presides over every single aspect of the lives and affairs of his relations, male and female. In this role "[h]e was a rigid, imposing perfectionist, steely enough in character to function in the puritanical way that he expected, or rather insisted, that the rest of the world should function" (87). His very presence as the living symbol of masculinity emasculates all the other male members of his extended family, notably his shiftless younger brother Jeremiah and Takesure, his nephew, whose laughable claim to manhood is in their feeble joint effort trying to find "a good strategy to outsmart that woman [Lucia]" (145). And the women? All entrapped! Except for Nyasha's full-throated verbal and physical affront to Babamukuru's authority, Mainini, Tambudzai, Lucia, Maiguru, Nyasha (the five-named entrapped women), and all the other females of the homestead tow the line despite one or two squeaky attempts at revolt. Although it is evident that the women are keenly aware of their double colonization and exploitation, it is also clear that their sometimes intense women palavers, their lack of complete female solidarity, and their fear of patriarchy (Maiguru's nervousness and morbid fear of Babamukuru, for example) not only expose the wiles of patriarchy but ironically also feed it in the process of this exposure.

Of all Babamukuru's heavy-handed acts of hearing and settling disputes, presiding authoritatively over family meetings, or parceling out assignments, the most cruel and egregious is the calculated and brutal act of humiliating Jeremiah, his feckless brother, and Mainini, his wife of nineteen years and mother of their five children. If the authorities think Babamukuru was a "good African", it is because his almost complete adoption of the English way of life – language, culture, and religion – to the disapproval and rejection of his Shona culture "strengthens the belief of the colonial system in its own superiority because his behavior supports the very message of the inferior African (Shona) culture the colonizers had tried to implant in the minds of the colonized" (Berndt 102). Taken in by the white colonizers, the holy "wizards"/missionaries whose farms he works by day in return for education in their "wizardry" by night, Babamukuru has imbibed Christianity since age nine, and has proved himself "good" and capable of "yield(ing) harvests that sustain the cultivator" (19). In response to his mother's pleadings, "the holy wizards had prepared him for life in their world" all right. Unfortunately, "good and capable" are not good enough passports to citizenry claims to English culture. His efforts, including, unfortunately, an exorcising of what remained of traditional Shona culture after its colonial bastardization, do not mitigate his desire to be *of* the culture rather than merely being *in* the culture, domestically as well as professionally.

Apparently, in all his hypocritical Christian piety, he sees nothing brutal in constantly attacking his own daughter Nyasha's womanhood and damning her to whoredom for standing up to authority – his authority. Little wonder, then, that Babamukuru, in a typical take-full-charge moment, finds the right, punitive solution in the tenets of "English" culture to his junior brother Jeremiah's irresponsible behavior. Conveniently invoking the ghost of their mother's long-ago wish that "Jeremiah must have a church wedding," Babamukuru damns Jeremiah and Mainini to a "white wedding" (with all its trappings) after nineteen years of traditional Shona sanctioned marriage because Jeremiah has been and is still living in sin all these years and has "not been married in Church before God" (147). In effect, Jeremiah's and all such Shona traditional marriages must be adjudged illegitimate and the offspring from those marriages damned to 'bastard' status. The damning order, then, intended to shame and put Jeremiah (and his Shona ilk/generation) on the straight and narrow path delegitimizes Shona traditional marriage rites and practices. In a matter of minutes, Babamukuru has gone from Shona patriarch excoriating a father-of-five sinner/brother-child to a pious Christian church preacher, offering absolution for sins past while winning souls for and advancing the evangelizing-acculturation cause of "the holy wizards."

Ironically, with her parents, home, and person so thoroughly demoralized by this decreed sham church wedding foisted on her parents by their tyrant/patriarch/benefactor, Tambudzai finally finds in this unforgiving display of insensitivity and disrespect the possibility of cracks to an otherwise solid, almost impenetrable wall of gratitude to Babamukuru's benevolence despite the heavy-handedness and arbitrariness of his patriarchal abuses. This is evidence of yet another female's resolve to thwart the unjust act of patriarchy at the corporal cost of fifteen lashes and two weeks of maid-takeover chores.

In the end, in their own individual ways, each of the "entrapped" women of the beginning chapter of *Nervous Conditions* finds her strategy for combating the threatening ills in patriarchy that disrupt women's organism and cause "madness" in them.

Conclusion

If the women characters in African literature of the fifties and early sixties (mainly by male writers) were portrayed in one-dimensional stereotypic roles – usually as prostitutes, concubines, priestesses, barren women, or as mothers, and so on – their transformation in the hands of African women writers in the subsequent five decades has been phenomenal. Along with the emergence of these women writers in the mid/late 1960s came the deconstruction of stereotypes and the reconstruction of dynamic heroine character portrayals. While fifties and early sixties literature depicted women struggling within traditional African societies, literatures by women writers of the eighties and nineties depicted self-conscious African women at the crossroads of tradition and modernity, "those on the verge of social change (whose) problems range from the choice of a husband, to infertility, desertion and the paradox of being economically successful at the expense of marital joy" (Kolawole 84). Because the African woman is as much on the verge of change as her society, the "song" African women writers sing about the lives of their women characters as well as their own in their respective cultures must keep time with the tune of change.

Unfortunately, that has not been the case, as African women writers have had to hoe a hard row with fellow male writers and publishers alike, not only in getting their voices heard and their "songs" legitimized but also in fending off testy, unwarranted, even ill-placed criticism of masculine stereotypes, the likes of which Femi Ojo-Ade levied personally against Ba's Ramatoulaye in *Une si Longue Lettre*.[4] However, what is clear is that these women writers have blazed trails finally. They have finally channeled their "women songs" convincingly enough such that one cannot but wonder if some of their male counterparts have not taken guidance from them in their own portrayal of African women characters. It is difficult to ignore the crucial agency role women writers have played as *de facto* guardians of culture. As storytellers, they are perforce change makers. If they are to be the keepers of culture as expected by virtue of their gendered division of labor, they must and do approach their tasks with diligence. Therefore, in their guardianship role and as change agents, they are tasked to sing songs of joy when there is joy and songs of sorrow when no other words fully begin to describe the condition of the state.

Four major African female writers were selected for this chapter, not because they are the only ones or the best known. Indeed, there were many pioneers before them in the early sixties. They were selected for the multi-dimensional richness of their vision. From Emecheta to Warner-Vieyra to Ba to Dangarembga – anglophone Nigeria, francophone Caribbean/Senegal, anglophone/Shona-Zimbabwe – different milieux, different nomenclatures but together similarly demonstrating the power/heavy-handed effects of patriarchy/patriarchal institutions on women's lives.

It is critical to note that in the face of social problems made more complex by the dogged digging in of patriarchy in the name of tradition, this quartet of arbiters of societal ills offered transformative and reformist, less complex solutions, upbraiding with equal condemnation and criticism both male and female "misuse and distortion of power and privilege in a socio-cultural milieu" (Cham 90). For instance, Ba "remain[ed] persuaded of the inevitable and necessary complementarity of man and woman" (88). Emecheta made Ona ask that her child, Nnu Ego (and by extension women) be allowed "a life of her own, a husband if she wants one . . . and be 'allowed to be a woman'" (28). Even less subtly, through her mouthpiece character, Adaku, Emecheta resolutely supports alternatives for a woman to leave a bad marriage if the alternative to staying in it is 'madness'. Suggested solutions to the issues of polygyny are more complex, especially made so in the context of Islamic religion and old patriarchal traditions. And to stem the interference of mothers-in-law and female relatives, those notorious abettors of polygynous marriages, freedom to 'choose' rather than be forced into a polygynic relationship is an important caveat. To this end, all four writers echo the resounding expression of "genie-out-of-the-bottle" liberation shouts in the war against "the power of patriarchal socialization to render a woman powerless" (Stratton 166).

The nature of women's dis-ease, their disequilibrium, has been known but has remained unacknowledged for so long. Almost seventy years of ample narrative "data" speak to the reality of women's claims of abuse and repression under the patriarchal state. Presently, the past claims of women's "voicelessness" are no longer tenable. Patriarchy, the source of women's dis-ease, has been named for *what* it is and *why* it is. The power and effects of its disequilibrium have been exposed, disrobed. It remains to see *how* the present crop of African women writers chronicle the cure for the disquieting "vexations . . . and frustrations" of patriarchal practices which accumulate somewhere in and "choke" women's bodies, driving them to madness.

Notes

1 Used in the African cultural, Moslem religion context to denote a breach of socioreligious precept and uxorious duty by the male in a polygynous arrangement.

2 See, for example, Gayle Jones. *Eva's Man*. Boston: Beacon Press, 1976.

3 During her acceptance speech in Paris on winning the Noma Prize Award for her first book, *Une si Longue Lettre*. In essay "Feminize Your Canon: Mariama Ba." *The Paris Review*. May 13, 2019.

4 In his blistering discussion of *So Long a Letter* in which he conflates author (Ba) with character/mouth piece (Ramatoulaye), Ojo-Ade took issue with Ramatoulaye's accusatory statement "Man, the unfaithful husband; Man, the womanizer; Man, the victimizer" as overboard, stereotypic condemnation (73).

Works cited

Arndt, Susan. "It Is Immoral for a Woman to Submerge Herself: Being a Woman as Seen in Buchi Emecheta's *The Joys of Motherhood.*" *The Dynamics of African Feminism: Defining and Classifying African Feminist Literatures.* Trans. Isabel Cole. Trenton: Africa World Press, Inc., 2002, pp. 125–136. Print.

Arndt, Susan. "Women Who Undermine Women's Happiness in Mariama Ba's *Une Si Longue Lettre.*" *The Dynamics of African Feminism: Defining and Classifying African Feminist Literatures.* Trans. Isabel Cole. Trenton: Africa World Press, Inc., 2002, pp. 116–124. Print.

Azodo, Ada Uzoamaka, ed. *Emerging Perspectives on Mariama Ba: Postcolonialism, Feminism, and Postmodernism.* Trenton: Africa World Press, 2003.

Ba, Mariama. *So Long a Letter.* Trans. Modupe Bode-Thomas. London: Heinemann, 1981. Print.

Ba, Mariama. *Scarlet Song.* Trans. Dorothy S. Blair. London: Longman, 1986. Print.

Berndt, Katrin. "The Bildungsroman: Nervous Conditions." *Female Identity in Contemporary Zimbabwean Fiction.* Bayreuth: University of Bayreuth African Series, 2005, pp. 80–117. Print.

Cham, Mbye. "Contemporary Society and the Female Imagination: A Study of the Novels of Mariama Ba." *Women in African Literature Today* 15 (1987): 89–101. Print.

Chukwuma, Helen. "Positivism and the Female Crisis: The Novels of Buchi Emecheta." *Nigerian Female Writers: A Critical Perspective.* Otokunefor, Henrietta & Obiagele Nwodo. Lagos, Nigeria: Malthouse Press Ltd., 1989, pp. 2–18. Print.

Dangarembga, Tsitsi. *Nervous Conditions.* Seattle: The Seal Press, 1988. Print.

Emecheta, Buchi. *The Slave Girl.* Glasgow: Fontana/Collins, 1977. Print.

Emecheta, Buchi. *The Joys of Motherhood.* London: Heinemann, 1979. Print.

Frank, Kathrine. "The Death of the Slave Girl: African Womanhood in the Novels of Buchi Emecheta." *World Literature Written in English* 21.3 (1982): 476–497. Print.

Frank, Kathrine. "Women without Men: The Feminist Novel in Africa." (Omolara Ogundipe-Leslie, special guest editor), *Women in African Literature Today* 15 (1987): 14–34. Print.

Garman, Emma. "Feminize Your Canon: Mariama Ba." *The Paris Review.* May 13, 2019. Print.

Gilbert, Sandra, and Susan Gubar. *The Madwoman in the Attic: The Woman Writer and the Nineteenth-Century Literary Imagination.* New Haven: Yale University Press, 1979. Print.

Mugambi, Helen Nabasuta. "Reading Masculinities in a Feminist Text: Tsitsi Dangarembga's Nervous Conditions." Chikwenye Okonjo Ogunyemi and Tuzyline Jita Allan, eds. *Twelve Critical Readings by African Women.* Athens: Ohio University Press, 2009, pp. 199–218.

Ogundipe-Leslie, Omolara. "The Female Writer and Her Commitment." (Eldred Durosimi Jones, Eustace Palmer & Marjorie Jones, editors) *Women in African Literature Today* 15 (1987): 5–13. Print.

Ogunyemi, Chikwenye Okonjo, and Tuzyline Jita Allan, eds. *Twelve Critical Readings by African Women.* Athens: Ohio University Press, 2009.

Ojo-Ade, Femi. "Still a Victim? Mariama Ba's *Une si Longue Lettre.*" *African Literature Today: New Writing, New Approaches* 12 (1982): 71–87. Print.

Ojo-Ade, Femi. "Madness in the African Novel: Awoonor's This Earth, My Brother . . ." *African Literature Today: Retrospect & Prospect* 10 (1979): 134–152. Print.

Olaogun, Modupe. "Aesthetics, Ethics, Desire, and Necessity in Mariama Ba's So Long a Letter." Chikwenye Okonjo Ogunyemi and Tuzyline Jita Allan, eds. *Twelve Critical Readings by African Women.* Athens: Ohio University Press, 2009, pp. 177–198.

Opara, Chioma. "The Emergence of the Self: The Liberating Pen in Mariama Ba's *Une Si Longue Lettre* and Sembene Ousmane's *Lettre de France.*" Aduke Adebayo, ed. *Feminism & Black Women's Creative Writing: Theory, Practice, Criticism.* Ibadan: Graduke Publishers, 2015, pp. 153–167. Print.

Oriaku, Remy. "Buchi Emecheta: If Not a Feminist, Then What?" Aduke Adebayo, ed. *Feminism & Black Women's Creative Writing: Theory, Practice, Criticism.* Ibadan: Graduke Publishers, 2015, pp. 72–90. Print.

Proulx, Patrice. "Alienation, Madness and Rebirth in Warner-Vieyra's *Juletane.*" Unpublished paper, presented on panel, "Exile and Madness: A Third World Womanist Epistemology" at the Third World Studies Annual Conference, University of Nebraska at Omaha, 1993. Print.

Stratton, Florence. "The Shallow Grave: Archetypes of Female Experience in African Fiction." *Review of African Literature* 19.2 (1988): 143–169. Print.

Uwakweh, Pauline Ada. "Debunking Patriarchy: The Liberational Quality of Voicing in Tsitsi Dangarembga's *Nervous Conditions.*" *Research in African Literatures* 26.1 (New Voices in African Literatures (Spring 1995): 75–84.

Veit-Wild, Flora. *Writing Madness: Borderlines of the Body in African Literature.* Oxford: James Currey, 2006 (Stephanie Newell, reviewer).

Warner-Vieyra, Myriam. *Juletane.* Trans. Betty Wilson. London: Heinemann Caribbean, 1987. Print.

23

MENTAL HEALTH, MINORITY DISCOURSE AND TANURE OJAIDE'S SHORT STORIES

Stephen Ese Kekeghe

Introduction

Mental health narratives, no doubt, occupy a marginal position in Nigerian literary scholarship. This limitation may have been engendered by the general poor attitudes to mental patients in Nigeria. Until recently, there were series of unhealthy management and demonization of the mentally impaired globally. Ingram compiled autobiographical accounts, from the 15th to 18th centuries, "representing mental illnesses as demon possession" (2). Narratives like Margery Kempe's *The Book of Margery Kempe* (1436) and Hannah Allen's *A Narrative of God's Creation Dealing with That Choice Christian* (1683) are notable religious accounts that present the mad as people possessed by demonic spirits. Kekeghe reveals that "narratives of madness shifted from the obviously religious to a quasi-secular and apparently secularization of mental condition" (35). From the autobiographical to the fictionalized accounts of madness, one comes across a repulsive portraiture of characters with mental disabilities. While countries in Europe and North America may have developed some humanizing skills in handling mentally challenged people, Nigeria has not really improved on the treatments of psychiatric patients. The theme of mental illness, in Nigerian literature, considering its rarity, can be discussed within the context of minority discourse.

Contemporary African literary and cultural studies have shown impressive interests in minority discourse. Minority narratives, the world over, have helped to unfold regional oppression and resentments as well as cultural peculiarities. Oyeniyi Okunoye observes that minority discourse, as a concept, "consolidates the expressions of marginality in the cultural artefacts of district minorities living in different parts of the world" (413). Postcolonial realities, such as socioeconomic, historical and cultural experiences, are believed to have thrown the so-called minority people to the margin. The voices of the minorities, in literary expression, reveal the artistic distinctiveness and social experiences of people in a plural world of manifold sensibilities.

The response to the sociocultural surroundings is a major obligation of the writer, especially, in the African context, where social consciousness and commitments are the drivers of literary productions. On this note, Edward Said illustrates that "no production of knowledge in human societies can ever ignore or disclaim its author's involvement as a human subject in his own circumstances" (11). This is why Okunoye emphasizes that "the literary practices of African countries with considerable cultural and social diversity engage more issues and problems that reflect their own challenges" (414). In the process of narrating one's experiences against a particular cultural background, different topicalities, which may have universal significance, are conveyed. It is, therefore, not surprising that Tanure Ojaide of the Niger Delta, a minority region of Nigeria, uses his short stories to express mental health situations and challenges, a relevant area of human endeavor not commonly explored by Nigerian writers.

Narratological strategies have been effectively deployed in conveying mental illnesses through literature. There are many pathographies by mental patients, who narrate their plunging into madness as well as their sordid experiences in asylum. In the process of recounting their gradual descent into psychosis, such writers connect to reality by reclaiming their dissolving egos. It has also been recognized that the narrative tools adopted by the novelist are similar to the diagnostic strategies utilized by the psychiatrist in the process of analyzing the mental states of his/her patients. This point is aptly made by Allan Beveridge when he avers that "the techniques involved in understanding and analyzing a novel can be applied to the understanding of patient discourse" (5). Beveridge adds that by recreating mental illnesses through fictional narratives, "one can become more sensitive to the nuances and subtexts of a patient's communication" (5). Both the autobiographical and fictionalized accounts of madness are aimed at encouraging mental wellbeing in the society.

Literature has, over the years, maintained a good status as a potent instrument in medical education, a point that has been made by scholars like Faith McLellan, Anne H. Jones, Paul O'Malley, William Carlos Williams, Femi Oyebode, Martyn Evans and Louis A. Sass. This is given the fact that literature humanizes through empathizing and felicitous language. According to Femi Oyebode, through the literary representation of mental illnesses, "psychiatrists can deepen [their] own understanding of the nature of these conditions and acquire a more felicitous language both to engage our patients with or to assimilate the subjective reality of their conditions" (viii). Oyebode's assertion attests to the healthy collaboration which literature and psychiatry share in the 21st century in Europe and North America.

The depiction of mental diseases in literary texts is within the ambit of literature and psychiatry, which is a subspecialty of literature and medicine. As a domain of medicine, psychiatry focuses on the diagnosis, analysis and cure of psychological diseases, like affective, behavioral, cognitive and perceptual conditions. This is a common definition found in the works of notable psychiatrists like Sass, Oyebode, Olatawura, O'Malley and Mbanefo. Since every field of human endeavor has a history of existence, the emergence of literature and psychiatry as a discipline has also been traced to the pioneering narratives of Heraclitus, Plato and Aristotle, who examine the interplay of the unconscious and human's manifestations. The philosophical narratives of these great philosophers, laced with literary texture, help to establish the close interaction between the human's mind and physical disposition.

There are pockets of works by pioneering African novelists that explore the manifestations of mental challenges through characters' utterances and conducts. For instance, Achebe's "The Madman," Armah's *Fragments*, Head's *A Question of Power* and Sadawi's *A Woman at Point Zero* explore different mental symptoms which are elicited by socioeconomic pressures. Studies by Jacqueline McDaniel, Flora Veit-Wild and Ayobami Kehinde, on some of the social triggers of psychoneuroses in African literature, are worthy of note. Soyinka's play, *Madmen and Specialist*, is, obviously, the most studied Nigerian text on the theme of madness. In other words, the pioneering writers, whose works may have birthed myriads of themes in African literary scholarship unrelated to madness, also foreground features of mental degeneration. On this note, Kekeghe submits that "since human existence raises the constant question of mental and physical wellbeing, the writers' social obligation cannot discard human health situations" (1).

Though an unpopular subject, the representation of mad characters permeates a good number of African literary texts. Writers' effort to narrate the inward quality of characters, in relation to socioeconomic experiences, is psychologically realistic – an individual's inner life manifests in his/ her conduct and social motivations. This chapter examines mental episodes in five short stories by Tanure Ojaide, which are: "I Used to Drive a Mercedes," "Nobody Loves Me," "Sharing Love," "Blacked Out Nights of Love" and "Married at Last." The symptoms of mental dissolution represented in the examined stories are induced by marital pressures, dissatisfactions and anguish.

Literary diagnoses of mental illnesses in the selected short stories

Perhaps, due to the characteristic brevity of the short story subgenre, it is the most suitable for the analysis of characters' mental states. After all, psychiatric pathographies, which are regarded as the first layer of literature and psychiatry, are usually terse narratives. It is therefore interesting that Ojaide consciously or unconsciously depicts characters' psychological conditions in his short stories by highlighting external factors that are capable of eliciting neuroses and psychoses. The five short stories examined in this essay are critically analyzed, bringing to the fore indices of mental abnormalities such as depressive and schizophrenic symptoms. Ojaide also narrates the various socioeconomic and cultural experiences that give rise to different levels of mood disorders manifested by the characters. The narration of mental conditions within the conjugal domain shows Ojaide's artistic commitments to humanize marital experiences in Africa.

Born in 1948 in Okpara, Delta State, Nigeria, Tanure Ojaide is an outstanding poet usually classified within the second generation of African writers. A former fellow in writing at the University of Iowa, Tanure Ojaide was educated at the University of Ibadan, where he earned a bachelor's degree in English and later an MA in creative writing and a PhD in English at Syracuse University. He has won numerous national and international awards. He has over eighteen volumes of poetry collections to his credit. He has also written prose fiction (short stories and novels). Ojaide taught for many years at the University of Maiduguri (Nigeria), and he is currently the Frank Porter Graham Professor of Africana Studies at the University of North Carolina at Charlotte, where he teaches African/pan African literature and art. Ojaide believes that one way in which the writer manifests his social obligation is by writing about mental health situations and challenges. He once avowed in an interview with this researcher:

> I will say that the short story or fiction is a viable medium of conveying psychosocial problems. It narrates and describes the behavior and actions of characters. After all, it is from one's behavior or action that madness can be conveyed. Even though I have quoted in my poetry a Warri madman who says "This sun go make man crazy" as preface to "Of humidity and hydration" in *Songs of Myself*, it is the fictional mode that affords me the opportunity to talk about madness. Fiction deals with the individual and society and it is the society that defines madness and ironically can also induce psychiatric problems. Social pressures on an individual can lead to psychiatric problems as in "I Used to Drive a Mercedes." At the same time, one's own low self-esteem and lack of awareness of self can lead to schizophrenic episodes as in "Nobody Loves Me" in *The Old Man in a State House*. So basically, social, economic, and emotional pressures could drive people to break down and become crazy.
>
> *(Kekeghe, 190)*

Ojaide's "I Used to Drive a Mercedes" narrates the pathetic experiences of Major Alfred Tobrise, a military man, who experiences mental breakdown following what he regards as his wife's betrayal of his unfettered love. In the light of Tobrise's unrestricted love for Sarah, he accepts her request to further her education to the university level, with the understanding that it is necessary to complement Sarah's beauty with a university degree. Having been spoilt with so much money by Major Tobrise, Sarah, on getting to the University, adopts an ostentatious lifestyle. She meets glamorous campus girls who introduce her to the most recent fashion styles and trends and she hides her wedding ring so as to live like a single girl. Thereafter, she weaves up flimsy excuses on why she no longer has time for Major Tobrise. In her trip to London on a summer vacation, she meets one Alhaji Mohammed, who impresses her with his seemingly inexhaustible wealth, and on getting to Nigeria, she finds faults in all that Major Tobrise does. Following her demands for the continuation of her gaudy lifestyle and her subsequent demand for a Mercedes Benz, Major Tobrise sells his blossoming poultry farm cheaply just to make his wife happy. Sadly and unfortunately, after selling the farm, he is involved in a conflict with campus students who beat him up and set his car containing the money ablaze. Major Tobrise, from this moment, unhappy that he will not be able to fulfil his promise to Sarah, experiences a mental breakdown.

In this story, Ojaide foregrounds mental conditions that can be generated by betrayal of love. Tobrise, in this story, is experiencing schizophrenia, which escalates from anxiety and depressive neuroses. This implies that there is a gradualism in the way madness manifests in people. The degree of love which Major Tobrise has for his wife is so intense that he cannot comport himself. From the beginning of the story, the reader is amazed by the low mental capacity displayed by Major Alfred Tobrise, who timidly accepts the flimsy demands of Sarah – he is so enthralled by Sarah's beauty that he is ready to do anything that will make her happy, even at the expense of his own happiness. Believing that "one has to work on beauty to sustain it" (52), Major Tobrise gives Sarah money with which she "bought cosmetic and fashionable dresses and looked great in them" (52). Tobrise loses the wit and wisdom to question and moderate his wife's excesses. He displays signs of nervousness and stupidity, even when the wife scolds him unnecessarily and unjustifiably. Major Tobrise's irrational behaviour in his relationship with his wife nauseates his relations:

> As Major Tobrise's relations saw it, their son was in his wife's pocket and they predicted that a marriage in which a man worshipped his wife would end up hurting the man irreparably. They believed in their hearts and said it openly that Sarah had prepared some charms to make their son senseless.
>
> *(52)*

It is Tobrise's love for Sarah that makes him to approve her proposal to further her education at the university and, sadly, it is in the university that Sarah begins to express physical and emotional distance from the Major. She once exclaims: "I'm glad my eyes are now open" (54). Sarah's association with unmarried ladies increases "her growing appetites for trendy wear" and other trivialities (54). Having met and seen sophisticated women who wear expensive dresses and perfumes in the university, Sarah affirms that "the Army Barracks fashion was no fashion at all" (54). This unsavoury incident of emotional betrayal, manifested by Sarah, tears Major Tobrise's mind apart:

> Major Tobrise remained in shock for months and did not accept that Sarah had left him for good. Alone at home, he called her name as if that would make her come back. He had heard of Bini and Urhobo medicine-men who made charms to or cast spells

to bring men back to women, and such medicine-men could bring women to their men, he believed.

(58)

Major Tobrise's eventual sale of his poultry farm to buy a Mercedes Benz for Sarah, which he regards as "the charm that would reverse his failed marriage into fresh love" (58), is informed by his unrestrained emotional attachment to Sarah. This is why he becomes extremely depressed over Sarah's deliberate emotional and physical separation from him. Tobrise's display of disinhibition and aggression at the university female hostel, where he goes to pick Okon Ekaite, a girl he met a few days before, attests to his dysophoric mood. His arrogance, engendered by his own depression, makes him shout at the president of the Students' Union Government, Paul Ighodaro, who has come to make peace between Major Tobrise and the porters. Showing anger, Major Tobrise exclaims: "shut your mouth there. I attended U.I., the premier university, not this high school slum of a university" (61). It is this spiteful statement that triggers the rage of the students, who swarm on Major Tobrise and give him a severe beating, after which they set his car ablaze together with the five hundred and fifty thousand naira which he had hoped to use to buy a Mercedes Benz for Sarah.

After this unpalatable experience, Major Tobrise loses his mind completely. The narrator reveals that Tobrise was "revived from a seeming death, but (was) never a sane man again" (59). From this moment, Major Tobrise begins to show symptoms of schizophrenia such as disorders of thoughts, gait, utterances and motor skills. The narrator unfolds:

> He marched, almost in military precision to an imaginary martial band. However, his legs moved a little too swiftly for a ceremonial occasion. He wore no uniform, but had on partly torn clothes. He would pass for a roadside motor mechanic if he did not appear too excited and uncontrollable.
>
> "I used to drive a Mercedes. Give way and let me pass", he bellowed hoarsely.

(50)

The previous excerpt shows the extent of damage done to his psyche. The narrator reveals that "Alfred would use his right hand to foot an imaginary horn and shout, pio-pio-pioooo!" (50). It is evident from this excerpt that the Major's ego has dissolved, and he is manifesting schizophrenic episodes, which shows that he has completely drifted from reality. This is given credence subsequently:

> This time his madness appeared permanent. Neither the Army he had served for twelve years nor his family paid attention to his plight anymore. He disappeared at night and reappeared in the morning. During the day, he drove his imaginary Mercedes through Ring Road, turned to mission Road, and back.

(5)

The author uses this part of the story to talk about the negative attitude of Nigerians towards any form of mental health depreciation. Besides the demonization of madness which is a common feature in Nigeria, there is little or no attention to the mentally sick in Nigeria. As a result, the mad are left to wander along the Nigerian streets, constituting an eyesore. No wonder, in Major Tobrise's case, concerned people would ask emotively: "why can't they take him to Uselu? Are they waiting for him to tear off his clothes and be naked before they do something for him?" (50). Uselu is an area in Benin-City where a mental asylum is located. It is evident from Ojaide's short story "I Used to Drive a Mercedes" that emotional betrayal and loss of fortune can engender mental disturbances.

In the second story, "Nobody Loves Me," Ojaide narrates anxiety and depressive neuroses manifested by Ngozi, an educated spinster, who restlessly craves a romantic life but is disappointed by the fact that no suitor comes her way. Harboring a feeling of reproach, Ngozi seeks the service of a native doctor through the advice of her friend, to make her attractive to men, a move that irrevocably worsens her problem – men continue to keep away from her. Ngozi's display of anxiety neurosis escalates to melancholia and severe depression, which eventually results in suicide. The inscription, "Nobody loves me," which she writes before committing suicide, attests to her mood disorder, otherwise known as dysphoria.

When Ngozi's subjection to despondency persists, she begins to experience mental ruminations which eventually trigger reactive depression. She recalls the confession of her aunt, who said she had cursed all the daughters of her mother. Given the fact that her forty-five-year-old elder sister, who lives in Aba, is not yet married, Ngozi's mind is burdened by what she regards as the real manifestations of the spell on her mother's daughters. Thus, her mind floats, gradually losing touch with peace and leading to brokenness:

> She remembered that her elder sister was still a spinster at forty-five in Aba. Is it true that the female children of her mother were jinxed not to have men? Did anybody place any evil charm on her to be loathed by men? An old aunt had died after confessing that nothing could be done to remove the curse she had placed on her mother's female children.
>
> (107)

Ngozi's persistent mental probing leads to self-talks and thought-broadcasts, which attest to her gradual mental crumbling. Her intense pondering on the narrative surrounding the aunt's curse prepares a room for mental disorientation, which eventually culminates in a hazy mood. By implication, the persistent prodding of Ngozi of her condition engenders her psychic numbness and depression. The feeling of worthlessness she exhibits is a result of her psychological and emotional commitment to her unrealized libidinal drives and wishes. The narrator captures the gradual psychological breakdown of Ngozi:

> She started to lose interest in everything. She did not like the food she prepared. She did not buy food outside either. She picked any dress from her wardrobe and sometimes went out with awful combinations of dress, shoes and handbags.
>
> After the heavy traffic of the Friday, Saturday and Sunday nights did not change her plight, despite parading like a real prostitute outside the compound gate, Ngozi decided to stay indoors. She knew that her mind was being destroyed by unfulfilled desires. She was not a lady, it appeared. She became weak and could not carry herself to work on Monday.
>
> (108)

Her remaining indoors and display of introverted features of a schizoid are potent evidence of her mental disorientation. Unlike her fellow tenants, who constantly receive male visitors, no man comes Ngozi's way, much less strikes up a conversation with her. It is evident that Ngozi's depressive state and her obvious show of mood and thought disorder are elicited by her inability to attain her restless desires for emotional and sexual contact. The narrative reveals that:

She needed the warmth of another body. She wanted her body to be admired, wanted her expensive bras to be complimented by a man when she undressed for him. She wanted to be embraced, she wanted to be kissed, and, above all, she wanted somebody to share her life with.

(107)

The mental dislocation of Ngozi, as foregrounded in the narrative, is triggered by her restless cravings for libidinal fulfillment – it is her constant hankering for sexual contact and emotional satisfaction, and the failure to realize her longing, that elicit her depression. Ngozi's anxiety to satisfy her rising libido makes her chase after men, some of whom are her co-tenants' suitors. The dialogue subsequently conveys this:

"Na my man you wan take? You no fit get man for yourself?" Vicky asked Ngozi, who felt ashamed of herself.
  "Sorry, I was trying to ask him whom he was looking for," she lied to Vicky.
  "Just be careful with other people's men," Vicky admonished her.

(106)

Ngozi might have lost control of herself to engage in the shameful act of chasing after the suitors of her neighbours. This is because she constantly harbours a feeling of hollowness, since, unlike her, "every other woman she knew in the compound had a boyfriend, man friend, or suitor" (106). The more she ponders on the inability to meet her emotional desires, the more psychologically numb she becomes. Her emphasis on details, in her reflection to ascertain the cause of her worthlessness, gives rise to her own depression and melancholia. The excerpt subsequently greatly attests to this:

Ngozi searched for a reason why she did not appeal to any man with so many men there seeking women. She knew that men drove around Effurun and stopped to pick girls on the street. She had walked, two weeks earlier in the evening, instead of taking a bus, but no man in a car stopped for her. She started to feel that she was not a complete woman or fate was unfair to her.

(106)

Because of Ngozi's drive to satisfy her libido, she always engages in masturbation. We are made to understand that "she was tired of fondling her own body and however long and hard she did it, it never gave her the pleasure that she expected from a man" (107). An intense obsession to gratify libidinal drives can activate severe depression like in the case of Ngozi, who commits suicide due to her inability to meet her sexual and emotional desires. Suicide is a common symptom of depression (Olatawura, 160). Ngozi's mental condition is triggered by lack of sexual satisfaction.

In the "Blacked out Nights of Love," Ojaide explores traumatic memories that are generated by unhappy marriages and death of spouses. The story revolves around the awful and despairing marital experiences which Mukoro Nomaso and Ufuoma Metitiri had in their past separate relationships. Mukoro has a terrible wife, whose aggressive conducts and disrespect towards him lead to his despondency. It is Mukoro's manifestation of disinhibition, as a result of depression, that leads to his killing of his wife. Rather than mourning the wife's demise, Mukoro privileges her death as his freedom from marital agony. Like Mukoro, Ufuoma has shocking episodes in her former marriage. In her case, her lovely husband dies of a heart attack on their first night as a married couple. Besides the anguish of losing her husband, society constructs her as a witch or some evil woman who sucks men's blood. This demonization adds to her pain, making her exhibit a form of aloneness or introvertedness that characterizes a schizoid condition. Ufuoma, therefore, harbors a feeling of worthlessness and delusion. Worthlessness is a symptom of depression, and it is elicited by traumatic memories. In this story, Ojaide x-rays the tragedy which the lack of marital peace and death of loved ones engender.

A major mental condition foregrounded in the story "Blacked out Nights of Love" is depression, which is exhibited by both characters. In this story, Ojaide is exposed to us as a writer who is conscious of the psychosocial significance of family happiness. Hence, he uses the short story as a convenient medium of conveying mental burdens that are elicited by lack of harmony and satisfaction in the marital domain. The narrative transmits the hellish and traumatic nature of Mukoro's former marriage, which leads to his own display of depressive symptoms:

> Before he moved from Warri to Okpara, Mukoro had gone through many terrible experiences until things became unbearable. He had expected marriage to bring stability and happiness to his life. Rather, it brought him misery.
>
> *(69)*

Ojaide's characterization of Mukoro's former wife reveals the dangerous scars which verbal insults could leave on an individual's mind. The persistent attacks on Mukoro's economic status by his nagging wife leave him feeling reproached, making him emotionally numb. The following excerpt, where she manifests her usual badgering, highlights the ruinous nature of her vocal slights on Mukoro's psyche:

> "You think I would have married you if I knew what I now know about you," she would tell him. The man did not know what to say in response to his wife's disappointment at his life. "I didn't know I was coming to suffer by marrying you. You don't even look at your mates to see what they do for their wives", she would tell him, in a deliberate strategy to humiliate him.
>
> *(70)*

Mukoro's wife constantly fumes because her cravings for an extravagant lifestyle cannot be met by her husband's moderate financial state. In order to show her anger, she insults and deprives him of sexual contact – they sleep in separate rooms. The persistent affronts which she frequently unleashes on Mukoro trigger in him anger and depressive episodes. When Mukoro kills his wife in one of their usual quarrels, he is under the influence of anger which manifests in the form of aggression and disinhibition. Constructing the wife's death as his freedom from a hellish marriage shows that Mukoro is experiencing depersonalization – a display of lack of feelings, caused by the wife's constant attacks of his ego. This idea is captured in the excerpt subsequently:

> They were having one of their usual late evening quarrels . . . In his account of what had happened, he did not mention the quarrel or the pushing which he had done. Outsiders were told she went to take a bath before they went to bed and slipped. From Mukoro's mourning of her, those who knew him thought he deeply felt the loss of his wife rather than the relief it was to him, there was no child in the marriage.
>
> *(71)*

Here, Ojaide exposes the mental burden which unhappy marriage generates. However, in Ufuoma's case, the death of her husband on the very night of her marriage leaves a terrible shock on her mindscape. She finds it difficult to overcome the anguish of a honeymoon turned funeral. The narrator's voice, laced with the tenor of despair, reveals how Ufuoma's husband, Otebele, died in Yola, leading to her relocation to Delta State:

> As a twenty-five-year-old bride, her thirty-three-year husband had a heart-attack on their first night as a married couple; only several hours after the reception party. Some strange illness that she still could not fathom struck the vivacious man dead even before he could penetrate her. It was supposed to be a honey moon for them but turned into sudden grief that paralyzed her emotionally for so many years.
>
> *(75)*

While Mukoro is depressed by an unhappy marriage caused by a nagging wife, Ufuoma's distress is engendered by the death of her lovely husband during romantic moments on a honeymoon. In both cases, Ojaide uses the short story "Blacked out Nights of Love" to express mental disturbances that can be caused by unhappy marriages and the death of loved ones. It has been acknowledged that the death of loved ones and other social pressures can trigger post-traumatic stress disorder (PTSD). This is the condition of Ufuoma in the story. A significant dimension to the story is the mental therapy generated by Ufuoma's meeting with Mukoro, which lights up the foggy moods of both characters – to the widower and widow, they have seen a real love that will correct the grief of the past through the sharing of positive and refreshing affection. Ojaide's bringing together of Mukoro and Ufuoma as lovers shows the resuscitation of their wounded minds. In this short story, Ojaide discloses both the ruinous and invigorating nature of love to the human mind.

"Sharing Love" exposes us to the anxiety and obsessional neuroses that are elicited by intense desire for romantic and sexual contact. The story centers on Kena, a lady possessed by a spiritual husband, who often torments her at night. This makes it difficult for her to marry her earthly love, despite the degree of love they share. Even their elopement to the United States cannot secure their relationship – Kena's spirit husband has accompanied her abroad and torments her with a severe headache which affects Kena's limbs. The sickness defies bioscientific knowledge – tests for migraine, arthritis and different forms of pain therapy show negative results on her condition. This indicates that Kena's condition is spiritual. As soon as Kena is sent back to Nigeria, she regains her health and falls into the arms of the jealous spirit-husband.

In this short story, Ojaide captures the anxiety neurosis that is elicited by love and the passionate longing for romance and sexual engagement. One in love, as Ojaide reveals in this story, manifests mental conditions like anxiety, obsession and hallucination. These psychological traits are exhibited by the earthly lover of Kena in the story, who is the narrator. He reveals:

> We had both waited anxiously for the moment that would swathe us at night in one bed . . .
>
> I then would imagine the cherry fruit falling for me when it was ripe. The cherry fruit only fell when it was ripe and only for its favorite to pick.
>
> *(53)*

The narrator likens his anxiety for Kena to his childhood yearning for cherry fruit, "whose flesh and juice had such a wonderful and hallucinating taste" (53). The cherry fruit and the childhood restlessness to "arrive at the lone tree's shaded ground to pick fruits that had fallen overnight" (53) allegorically foregrounds the private anxiety and the hallucinatory episodes manifested by the narrator, which are engendered by the intense fever of sensual and sexual desires. Here, Ojaide reveals that mental rumination is a characteristic of the workings of the human mind in relation to episodes of love and lust. The id, the unconscious compartment of the narrator's mind, does all the psychological musings. The apprehension displayed by the narrator conveys the mental commitment that is required in the longing for sexual gratification. Again, he says:

> Knowing that she was madly in love with me too, as I was with her, I expected she would not delay for too long to get intimate with me. The cherry fruit, I knew, would not wait for too long before showering ripe fruits on its favorite some early morning.
>
> *(54)*

Anxiety is a major mental symptom displayed by the narrator as a result of his intense desire for sexual and romantic contact with Kena. The narrator confirms his mental cogitation when he says: "I had Kena on my mind when she was not with me and was dazed by her beauty while she was around" (56). For instance, when Kena narrates how she was wooed by a Shell staff member, the narrator feels insecure and tries to manage his nervousness by assuming a positive thought that Kena is his:

> We both knew the time was approaching for us to spend more time together, for her to pass the night at mine. I would relish telling and sharing stories with her, as I would like to share hers too. "Don't be in a hurry", she told me again.
> "When you are ready, I will be ready", I said.
> I knew that she would soon be ready for me. I imagined the cherry tree would not hold back for too long again before showering its ripe fruits on its favorite.
>
> *(58)*

Through the deployment of suspense, we are exposed to the apprehension of the narrator, as he craves a sexual relationship with Kena. Sadly, the long-awaited night takes a negative twist – Kena is omotedjo, the daughter of Mami Wata, already married to a spirit husband who haunts her every night. When Kena eventually visits, she gives an excuse that she will relax in bed a little before the narrator should join her, a pretext meant to create some time with the spirit husband, who makes love with her every night. In order to nurse his libido and nervousness, the narrator consumes some amount of alcohol:

> I thought there was some trepidation in her mind about sleeping with me for the first time. I also had my anxiety but was ready to go through the suspense of seeing her naked, as she would also see my naked body.
>
> *(58)*

> After she left, I went to the refrigerator for a bottle of Gordon's Spark, my favorite drink . . . the drink surely calmed me considerably and made me ready to go to bed.
>
> *(59)*

Alcohol, like other hallucinogens, triggers psychosis as it drifts the mind away from reality, leading to a gradual dissolving of the ego and super-ego. It is under the influence of alcohol that the narrator summons courage and fondles Kena's breast. At this point, it dawns on him that Kena has a spirit husband who has possessed her, and her lifeless body does not respond to his romantic escapades. The narrator, therefore, nurses psychological and emotional dissatisfaction:

> Her possession by the spirit was complete because she could not respond to me beside her. I was jealous of an invisible man, or whoever that person was, who was getting the better side of the woman I called my girlfriend and I wanted to marry.
>
> *(60)*

The spirit husband possesses Kena both emotionally and spiritually. From this moment, the narrator's restlessness heightens. He engages in self-talk or thought-broadcast, which is a symptom of schizophrenic psychosis: "I did not have the ability to keep off my rival, an invisible gentleman I could not reach to tell to leave my love to me alone" (62). The narrator's fears and anxiety are aggravated when Kena's parents confirm to him that Kena is already married to a spirit being. As an artist, Kena is possessed by the spirit husband to draw her portrait. In a dialogue with the narrator, Kena reveals: "I don't even know the man I am drawing, but it possesses my pencil and yet will not lead me to have a full profile of him" (55). Here, Ojaide explores the interface of mental rumination and spirituality on the business of creative upsurge.

In order to avert any sharing of his love with a spiritual husband, the narrator perfects plans to elope with Kena to the United States. The narrator believes that the influence of Kena's spiritual husband will not transcend the domain of Africa, where it is believed to operate. He is thus disappointed that "a severe headache that paralyzed Kena emotionally took over within a few days of [their] arrival abroad" (64). Different medical diagnoses are carried out to spot the condition, but nothing is detected – Kena's illness defies all modern medical interpretations:

> She was referred to different doctors, who were said to be specialists in pain therapy, but the hammering of the skull at night intensified . . . She suffered from neither arthritis nor migraine. All tests for known painful diseases proved negative.
>
> *(64)*

Due to the inability to detect Kena's health condition, Mary-Jane, a pain therapist, says the illness "must be in [Kena's] mind" (65). Here, Ojaide foregrounds the mental health situations that follow the diagnostic criteria of migraine, a severe headache, which is a symptom of depression. The conflicting but fluid relationship between the medical and the superstitious, modern and indigenous, are brought to the fore in Ojaide's exploration of how geographical boundaries could determine human existence and experiences differently.

The appropriation of medical parlance, of the psychopathological domain, which constitutes the texture of the narrative, shows Ojaide's quest to create mental health awareness, especially within the marital sphere. For instance, given the challenges faced by Kena and the lover-narrator, they manifest episodes of depression such as insomnia (intense sleeplessness) and dysphoria. The narrator reveals that, like Kena, he, too, is exposed to sleeplessness as a result of reactive depression:

> Soon Kena was suffering from chronic insomnia. The pain had murdered her sleep. The night became a hell to her and we were scared when night was approaching like one dreading the appearance of the plague.
>
> *(65)*

I suffered the pain and the insomnia too but surely not at the level as she did. I could never grasp the vehemence with which the hammer blows knocked her skull, much as I felt her pain.

(66)

Severe headache and insomnia have been diagnosed as symptoms of depression (Olatawura, 162). While Kena's sleeplessness may have been provoked by the excruciating ache in her head, the narrator's case is caused by his constant thought of Kena's condition and the quests to offer a lasting solution to it so as to secure his love. Ojaide's blend of the supernatural and scientific in his portrayal of Kena's health condition underscores his manifestation of dual consciousness which is the result of postcolonial experiences in Africa.

Furthermore, in "Married at Last," the last story examined in this chapters, we are exposed to the mental burden suffered by Ese, a forty-two-year-old virgin, who gets married to an impotent man called Victor. Ese, a highly religious and chaste lady, has sworn that she will keep her virginity for her husband. When she eventually gets married at forty-two, she is extremely happy, hoping that her husband will satisfy all the cravings for sexual contact she has been suppressing over the years. Sadly, Mr. Victor is impotent – he cannot make love with her. The moment Ese discovers this, she becomes emotionally numb and resigns to fate. This is because her religion does not give room for divorce.

In this story, Ojaide conveys libidinal drives and anxiety which individuals manifest while longing for sexual gratification. The narrator coveys Ese's anxiety for a sexual and emotional relationship in the night after her wedding:

> She walked out gracefully from the wardrobe, a sensuous woman bristling with smiles. She was already warm and melting inside of her. She felt it would not take long for the man to make her come.
> She entered the bed and drew Victor to herself.
> "I told you I am tired," Victor told her.
> He got out of the bed like a deflated tire of a car in motion. Her warm body suddenly turned cold.
>
> *(124)*

Victor's cold response to Ese's hunger for sex devastates her mind – she expected a prolonged moment of sexual ecstasy that would take care of all the years she had deprived herself of sex. She thought that her husband would make her reach many orgasms. Since her religion will not allow her to divorce Victor, she will be subjected to a life without sexual pleasure. Thus, Ese becomes melancholic as she reflects on the sad reality that confronts her marital life. As a result of her despondency, she engages in self-talk, revealing her disappointment. The subsequent excerpt underscores her foggy mood:

> She had hoped for a sex feast after holding back for so long, but she soon discovered that she would not taste that luscious dish at all. She was already married to Victor and could not leave him, according to her religion. "That's life", she muttered to herself, accepting her condition but not happy about it.
>
> *(125)*

Here, again, Ojaide reveals that libidinal drive is a significant constituent of the human's psychosocial domain. The satisfaction of one's cravings for sexual contact, as foregrounded in the story, is important in maintaining the state of one's mental health. Ese, no doubt, is experiencing depression, which is generated by her inability to realize sexual gratification.

Conclusion

Tanure Ojaide's narration of mental health experiences, a marginal or minority discourse, in Nigerian literature, is a rewarding effort. As learned from the short stories examined in this chapter, spousal betrayal, love lost and the death of loved one in the marital domain are capable of eliciting traumatic memories, which may escalate to a severe mental breakdown like depression and schizophrenia. The anxiety and melancholia elicited by sexual libido are conveyed in stories like "Sharing Love," "Married at Last," and "Nobody Loves Me." Also, lover's betrayal, lack of marital peace and the death of a spouse can activate post-traumatic stress disorder, as found in stories like "I Used to Drive a Mercedes" and "Blacked out Nights of Love." Ojaide, in the selected stories, pays close attention to characters' portraiture and events – from the sociological, rhetorical and psychological dimensions of reality, the stories express convincing human conditions. The conduct and utterances of the characters, which are brought to the fore through realistic dialogue and narrative pulse, reveal the socioeconomic and religious factors that engender the mental disintegration of the characters that people the stories.

A suitable conclusion to be drawn from this discussion is that Ojaide is conscious of psychological and emotional dissatisfactions in matrimonial relationships in the 21st century and deploys the short story subgenre as a convenient medium of creating mental health awareness in the marital sphere.

Works cited

Allen, Hannah. *A Narrative of God's Creation Dealing with That Choice Christian* London: John Wallis, 1683.

Beveridge, Allan. "The Benefits of Reading Literature". In *Mindreadings: Literature and Psychiatry*. Ed. Oyebode, F. London: RC Psych Publications, 2009. 1–14.

Evans, Martyn. "Roles of Literature in Medical Education". In *Mindreadings: Literature and Psychiatry*. Ed. Oyebode, F. London: RC Psych Publications, 2009. 15–24.

Freud, Sigmund. *Studies on Hysteria (1895)*. London: Hogarth Press, 1955.

Jones, Hudson Anne. "Literature and Medicine: Narrative of Mental Illness". *Lancet* 350, 1997, 359–361.

Kehinde, Ayobami. "Patriarchal Suppression and Neurosis: African Women Plight in J. M. Coetzee's *In the Heart of the Country*". *African Study Monograph* 27(4), 2006, 169–185.

Kekeghe, Stephen Ese. "Psychiatric Conditions in Selected Nigerian Literary Texts". *Ph.D Thesis*. Department of English, Ibadan: University of Ibadan, 2018.

Mbanefo, Ejiofo S. *Psychiatry in General Medical Practice in Nigeria*. Ibadan: University Press, 1991.

McDaniel, Jacqueline. "'Madness' in Exile Literature: Insanity as a Byproduct of Subjugation and Manipulation in Bessie Head's *A Question of Power*". In *Seton Hall University Dissertation and Theses (ETDS) Paper 10*, 2011.

McLellan, Faith M. "Literature and Medicine: Physician-Writers". *Lancet* 349, 1997, 564–567.

Ojaide, Tanure. "Blacked Out Nights of Love". In *The Old Man in State House*. Lagos: African Heritage Press, 2012.

Ojaide, Tanure. "I Used to Drive a Mercedes". In *God's Medicine-Men & Other Stories*. Lagos: Malthouse, 2003.

Ojaide, Tanure. "Married at Last". In *The Old Man in State House*. Lagos: African Heritage Press, 2012.

Ojaide, Tanure. "Nobody Loves Me". In *The Oldman in the State House*. Lagos: African Heritage Press, 2012.

Ojaide, Tanure. "Sharing Love". In *The Old Man in State House*. Lagos: African Heritage Press, 2012.

Okunoye, Oyeniyi. "Alterity, Marginality and the National Question in the Poetry of the Niger Delta". *Cahiers d'Etudes Africaines* 191, 2008, 413–436.

Olatawura, Michael. O. *Psychology and Psychiatry*. Ibadan: Spectrum Books Limited, 2008.

O'Malley, Paul. "Literature and Psychiatry". *Med Hum Review* 9(1), 2000, 9.

Omobowale, Emmanuel Babatunde. Literature and Medicine: A Study of Selected Creative Works of Nigerian Physicians. Thesis. Ibadan: University of Ibadan, 2001.

Oyebode, Femi. "Autobiographical Narrative and Psychiatry". In *Mindreadings: Literature and Psychiatry*. Ed. Oyebode, F. London: RCPsych Publications, 2009. 25–41.

Oyebode, Femi. *Madness at the Theatre*. London: RCPsych Publications, 2012.

Said, Edward W. *Orientalism*. New York: Pantheon Books, 1978.

Sass, Louis A. *Madness and Modernism: Insanity in the Light of Modern Art, Literature and Thought*. New York: Basic Books, 1992.

Veit-Wild, Flora. *Writing Madness: Borderline of the Body and in African Literature*. Oxford: James Currey, 2006.

PART VII

Recent trends of marginalities

Timely and timeless

24

NOT YET SEASON OF BLOSSOM

Writing Northern Nigeria into the global space

Sule Emmanuel Egya

Introduction

The first part of my title deliberately echoes Abubakar Adam Ibrahim's *Season of Crimson Blossoms*, a novel that emerged from northern Nigeria in 2015 to great acclaim, winning the much coveted NLNG Prize for Nigerian Literature in 2016, enjoying rave reviews and rapidly penetrating global literary consciousness.[1] This success story reminds us of Zaynab Alkali's *The Stillborn*, published in 1984, whose immediate reception at home and abroad was also resounding. The celebration of Alkali as a writer was unprecedented, mainly because she was from northern Nigeria, a region that had not produced any 'significant' (female) writer writing in English before her. Beyond the reception similarity, there is the more crucial similarity (which, one might conjecture, accounts for the reception): both novels are about a woman attempting to break out of a patriarchal and religious convention. Li in *The Stillborn* and Hajiya Binta in *Season of Crimson Blossoms* are northern Nigerian women caught in the dilemma of either accepting the status their society has confined them to or resisting it and negotiating their own emancipatory status. How are these novels important to my discussion of Anglophone northern Nigerian literature as minority writing? The two novels, in the context of this chapter, are symbolic points at which northern Nigerian literature in English (Anglophone literature about northern Nigeria, written by people from northern Nigeria) enjoyed worldwide recognition.[2] In spite of that, this literature faces institutional domination in Nigeria and on the global stage. The struggles of the protagonists of these novels to emancipate themselves from conventional structures that limit their lives and aspirations, it seems to me, are figurative of the struggle of northern Nigerian literature to liberate itself from the cultural powers – from within and outside northern Nigeria – that limit its growth. Using *Season of Crimson Blossoms* as a point of literary reference, therefore, I would like to examine the minority status of northern Nigerian literature in the context of Anglophone Nigerian literature: the factors responsible for this status, institutional efforts made so far to deal with its domination and the possibilities of gaining more recognition and visibility. The prognosis from this historical-critical analysis is that, drawing from the figurative force of Ibrahim's novel, northern Nigerian literature in English is blossoming and has the potential to confront and transcend home- and self-imposed restrictions in the north and the institutional denigration from southern Nigeria, "on whose pivotal work the canon of modern Nigerian literature was based" (Abubakar 7).

It is, however, imperative to, from the outset, clear up some conceptual issues concerning the notion of minority about northern Nigerian literature. Northern Nigeria, in this work, is conceived as the broad geographical space comprising the conveniently and politically zoned north-central, north-east and north-west. Conversely, southern Nigeria is the geographical space that includes south-east, south-south and south-west.[3] The problematic this immediately poses is that within the northern region, the literature is heterogeneous, with the attendant problem of domination within. But this does not undermine (it rather accentuates) the invisibility that this literature, as a collective of heterogeneous voices, suffers. And with our focus on literature from northern Nigeria written in English, not in indigenous languages, another problem arises. To privilege Anglophone literature is to occlude those in indigenous languages, especially literature in Hausa, which has enjoyed some growth and visibility. With the awareness that the notion of minority is shifting depending on where one stands, I would like to map out the terrain of this discussion as having to involve the colonial and postcolonial forces that influence the production of Anglophone northern Nigerian literature and its relatively slow development in the context of Nigeria as arguably the literary capital of Africa. Also, it is noteworthy that the concept of minority literature here should be qualified with region and ethnicity. In other words, it is minority literature because it is regional – and this is to distinguish this shade of minority from the one dealing with a particular language or writer. Gilles Deleuze and Felix Guattari are often credited as the first to talk about "minority literature", but they obviously use the shade that deals with a marginalised writer since their study is on Franz Kafka, considered a minority within the geographical and sociopolitical space he operated (see *Kafka: Toward a Minor Literature*). Literature of African-America, from a racial perspective, has also been viewed as a minority literature (JanMohamed 102–123). However, our understanding of minority here is marked by regionality; northern Nigeria is taken as a region of different ethnic groups, collectivised by a literary experience that renders them minor on the Nigerian literary scene.

Northern Nigerian literature as minority

Anglophone northern Nigerian literature, like all Anglophone literatures in postcolonial societies, is a product of colonial contact. That is to say, the literature began in the wake of the British colonial government's incursion into northern Nigeria in the late eighteenth century. But there had been Arab contact in northern Nigeria centuries before, which had enabled an Arab literary tradition in the region. Ousseina Alidou writes,

> The introduction of Islam in Hausa populated areas of West Africa around the early twelfth or thirteenth century in particular led to the adoption of the Arabic language in local compositions. Though originally a product of religious discourse, writing in Arabic later became an established literary tradition, especially in poetry, that continues to this day.
>
> *(140)*

The tradition, over the years and through different sociopolitical eras, has flourished, giving northern Nigeria a non-Anglophone literature that dates back to the sixteenth century (Abubakar 1–15; Tsiga 13–51). Writing was mostly done in Arabic but also in *Ajami* – "an adaptation of the Arabic script for writing in indigenous languages" (Alidou 138). To cite just one example, Nana Asma'u (1793–1865), daughter of the founder of the Sokoto Caliphate Usmanu dan Fodio, had produced "about ninety . . . published works . . . in Arabic, Fulfulde, Hausa and Tomashek, the languages spoken by prominent scholars within her locality in her time" (Tsiga 22).

Most of these works have appeared in Jean Boyd and Beverly Mack's *The Collected Works of Nana Asma'u*. Asma'u's feat as a literary figure (Tsiga [13–15] classifies her writing as mainly belonging to the genre of literary life-writing) is indicative of the robust literary tradition in northern Nigeria before British colonialism.

The fact of an established education and writing tradition in Arabic, Fulfulde and Hausa – a product of Islamic conquest – would influence the reception of Western education and literary tradition in northern Nigeria.[4] The northern elite and scholars viewed Western education as synonymous with Christianity and were thus reluctant to accept it in order not to jeopardise Islam. To confront this Islam-Arabic establishment, among others, the British colonial government resorted to the Indirect Rule strategy, a form of concession that recognised the established mode of education and literary expression.[5] Rather than send their children to schools established by the British colonial institution, people in the north, mostly succumbed to Usman dan Fodio's jihad, continued to patronise Islamic education and civilisation. This rejection by the elite and institutions in the north would be the beginning of the minoritisation of Anglophone northern Nigerian literature, which is a corollary of the denigration Western education and civilisation suffered in the north. With a strong literary tradition premised on what Ousseina Alidou calls "quadruplet, rather than dual, arena of literary articulation" (138), namely (1) indigenous oralities, (2) Arabic script, (3) *Ajami* script and (4) Western-Roman script, literature from northern Nigeria ought to have been more developed than literature from southern Nigeria since it would have been built on an already existing intellectual structure. But this is not the case because of the conflict arising from the clash between the Arabic civilisation and the Western civilisation.

With the amalgamation of the southern and northern protectorates by the colonial government in 1914, leading to the creation of Nigeria, the north became a regional part of Nigeria, thereby causing the decline of Islam's educational and political forces. To operate within this entity called Nigeria, constituted as a secular state, northerners needed Western education. This was, one might guess, a sudden realisation, given their widespread opposition to this form of education. By the time they started taking Western education seriously in order to function nationally, the southerners had long begun to operate in it, already benefitting from the privileges it offered. It was not only that the first Western schools and colleges were built in southern Nigeria but also the first publishers and reading publics. In this regard, south-west Nigeria was privileged as the colonial government established Yaba Higher College, Lagos, in 1932 and University College, Ibadan, in 1948. It was arguably at Ibadan that the first literary minds that would constitute the canon of modern Nigerian literature germinated. Ibadan as a pioneer institution also attracted Western publishing outfits such as Heinemann, Longman, Spectrum and University Press that would nurture Nigerian literature in English. This development further deepened the disadvantage of the north so that when Anglophone Nigerian literature emerged in the 1940s or thereabouts, there was hardly any voice from the north in spite of its established literary tradition. This was worsened by the colonial project of erasing (at best, excluding) what had existed before colonialism which resulted in shutting off the oral literary traditions vibrant in southern Nigeria before the emergence of the Anglophone literary tradition.

The canon of Nigerian literature in English, one might contend, took its life in the 1960s, not only with poetic works by Gabriel Okara and Christopher Okigbo, dramatic works by J. P. Clark and Wole Soyinka and fictional works by Chinua Achebe and Cyprian Ekwensi, among others, but also with the inception of a critical tradition constituted by the works of pioneer critic-scholars such as Bernth Lindfors, Taiwo Oladele, Robert M. Wren, Dan Izevbaye, Abiola Irele and Charles Nnolim, among others. As it turned out, the making of the canon at this pioneering stage has no participants from northern Nigeria, as all the major names both in literary writing and critical discourse are from southern Nigeria and abroad. The silence from northern Nigeria was disturbing in critical works such as Oladele Taiwo's *An Introduction to West African Literature* published in 1967 and *Culture and the Nigerian Novel* published in 1976. This can be explained by the fact that at the time these pioneer writers, usually regarded as the first generation of modern Nigerian writers, were producing their early works, the colonial government in northern Nigeria was only able to persuade the literati to accept the Roman script in which English was written. One of the strategies adopted by the colonial institution was to encourage the reproduction of works in Hausa literature (written in Arabic or *Ajami*), using the Roman script. Alidou reports that:

> Between 1911 and 1913, for example, Frank Edgar, then a British colonial administrative officer in Sokoto, published three impressive volumes, *Litafin Tatsuniyoyi na Hausa* [Book of Hausa tales and traditions], composed of transliterations of oral folktales from Sokoto collected and transcribed in *Ajami* by the *malammai*, the teachers trained within *Ajami* tradition.
>
> *(143)*

This was to enable the Hausa literati to get used to the Roman script but also to produce school instructional materials in the script. This move would gain a major boost with the establishment in 1930 of the Translation Bureau in Zaria by the northern Nigerian education department. The Bureau was headed by Rupert M. East, a teacher in northern Nigeria. In 1933, the Bureau organised a literary competition aimed at getting the Hausa literati to take an interest in the Roman script as well as in the Western form of storytelling, which was not acceptable to the northern elite. Manuscripts selected from this competition would result in, among others, Abubakar Tafawa Balewa's *Shaihu Umar*, Bello Kagara's *Gandoki*, Muhammadu Gwarzo's *Idon Matambayi* and Abubakar Imam's *Ruwan Bagaja*. Of these writers, Abubakar Imam would become quite famous among northern Nigerian readers of the Roman script. Even with the competition, and subsequent efforts, the Romanisation of the Hausa script, itself a step towards instituting the English literary tradition in the literary consciousness of northern Nigeria, was a very slow process. As Alidou points out, "all laureates of the 1933–1934 competitions were graduates of Katsina Teachers Training College where Rupert [East] himself taught" (143), which indicates its limited reception in spite of the Bureau's efforts. This phase of the Romanisation of Hausa script, resulting in the transformation of Hausa literature in the Hausa language, not yet in the English language, coincided with the formation of the pioneering phase of Anglophone Nigerian literature in southern Nigeria, another way of saying that northern Nigeria is conspicuously absent in this phase.

In the aftermath of the Nigerian civil war (1967–1970), Nigeria would witness a boom in literary production, triggered by the war experience (Amuta 85–92). Perhaps to capture the magnitude of Anglophone literature inspired by the war, Olu Obafemi concludes that "[t]he Nigerian civil war has given birth to what could be called a national literature in Nigeria" (3). The conceptual fault of this conclusion is glaring if one takes into consideration the regional origin of the authors who have concentrated on the war. Nearly all the post-war literary works on the war experience are from the south, among which are *Girls at War and Other Stories* by Chinua Achebe, *Casualties* by J. P. Clark, *The Last Duty* by Isidore Okpewho, *Heroes* by Festus Iyayi and *The Poet Lied* by Odia Ofeimun. Although many northern Nigerians (as soldiers, as businessmen and contractors, as watchers) participated in the war, literary response to the war from the north remains to today poor. In fact, there are just a couple of literary works fully dealing with the condition of the war, such as Dul Johnson's *Shadow and Ashes*, published in 1998. Nevertheless, the post-war phase in Nigerian literature could be regarded as the one in which Anglophone literature from northern Nigeria emerged. Notable pioneers here would be Mohammed Sule, whose *The Undesirable Elements* appeared in 1977, followed by *The Infamous Act* in 1982, and Tukur Muhammad Garba, whose *The Black Temple* appeared in 1981, followed by *Stop the Press* and *Forgive Me Maryam* in 1983 and 1986, respectively. These novels appeared in the Pacesetter series run by Macmillan Publishers, aimed at producing a popular literary culture, mainly targeted at the youth. This posed a canonical problem since institutional critics and scholars of the period ignored the Pacesetter series and favoured the African Writers Series run by Heinemann Publishers. Edited by the renowned novelist Chinua Achebe, the African Writers Series, whether or not by design, had no presence from northern Nigeria in its heyday. (Heinemann's Frontline Series has Atabo Oko's *The Secret of the Sheikh* published in 1988, perhaps the only one from the north.) It is understandable that the series was focused on 'literary' stories, targeted at the emerging African elite, thereby midwifing serious African fiction in the spirit of high modernism. But two novels, which would be regarded as 'literary' stories, appeared in 1984, namely Zaynab Alkali's *The Stillborn* and Ibrahim Tahir's *The Last Imam*, published by Longman and Kegan Paul International, respectively. That these novels did not appear in the African Writers Series, at the time most of such novels appeared in the series, is symptomatic of the politics of canon-making that literature from northern Nigeria had faced.

At this juncture, it is important to stress the role the critical establishment in Nigeria played in othering literature from the north. The flowering of literary writings from northern Nigeria from the 1980s has not been met with sufficient critical attention. Two possible explanations can be adduced here. The first is that departments of literary studies in higher institutions in northern Nigeria in the 1970s and the 1980s, up to the 1990s, were mainly manned by scholars from southern Nigeria, a region that has produced established literary scholars such as Dan Izevbaye, Charles Nnolim, Abiola Irele and Kolawole Ogungbesan, among others, who would be regarded as the first generation of indigenous scholars of Nigerian literature. These scholars would claim (and perhaps correctly) that there was no tangible literary production from the north deserving of scholarly attention. But they were known as scholars less concerned about non-Anglophone literary traditions, not willing to pay attention to Nigeria's rich oralities (this will change with the coming of Isidore Okpewho); they were rather fascinated by and promoted the tradition of Anglo-American formalism within which they studied (see Jeyifo, Ezenwa-Ohaeto, Egya). The second explanation is tied to the first, namely the colonial shaping of curriculum for literary studies as a scaffolding for the 'civilising mission' that must be undertaken in Nigeria. The regular diet consisted of mainly Anglo-British and Greco-Roman classics. When attention eventually shifted to Nigerian literature, it was easier to focus on writers from the south who had made their marks such as Okigbo, Achebe, Soyinka, Clark and Okara. In the post-war era, a fresh set of literary voices compellingly drew the attention of critics and scholars. These voices would come to be represented by the powerful voices of, among others, Odia Ofeimun, Tanure Ojaide, Niyi Osundare, Femi Osofisan and Festus Iyayi. A critical trend framed by the Marxist theoretical persuasions, on one hand, and by Feminist theoretical persuasions, on the other, characterised the critical tradition of Nigerian literature in the 1980s and the 1990s. Within this tradition, Zaynab Alkali is immediately noticed, her feminist aesthetics valorised as a welcome instance of womanism (see Adebayo 37–56), but especially as a feminist voice from the late-comer region on account of which she received "sympathetic" reviews (Ojinmah and Egya). Although in the 1980s literary scholars, such as David Ker, Olu Obafemi and Yakubu Nasidi, had emerged in northern Nigeria, they paid little or no attention to emerging voices from northern Nigeria. In addition to Alkali, there had been Abubakar Gimba, whose first novel *Golden Apple* (later published as *Sacred Apple*) was published by Vintage Press, New York, in 1997.

It is fair to say that literary production in the north – that is, the output of Anglophone literary works – is not a match for that of the south, and this may be the case even in the present time, especially if we consider the ethnic origins of works published in the decades between the 1980s and the 2000s, a period that witnessed a great output in Anglophone Nigerian literature. Yet one can argue that the critical establishment is rather blind to the increasingly blossoming Anglophone literature coming out of the north. The notion that the north in Nigeria is less developed intellectually, less receptive of Western ideas and ideals (which is a historical fact) is often used as a rationalisation for excluding literary voices from the north by way of preconceived dismissal. This discourse of underdevelopment, Abdul R. JanMohamed and David Lloyd (1–16) point out, is one of the means through which a literature can be inferioritised. Being blind to the textual manifestations of a literature, or symbolically erasing them from existence, is also a strategy of the critical establishment to diminish the status of northern Nigerian literature. The guest-edited volume of the South African journal *English in Africa* (volume 32, number one), captioned "Nigeria's Third Generation Writing: Historiography and Preliminary Theoretical Considerations" is significant for projecting the robust literary imaginations (especially in the poetry genre) shaped by the despondency that marked the decades of military oppression in Nigeria. The journal presents younger Nigerian writers, mostly born during the oil booms of 1970s, who had had to face the oil doom and military despotism of the 1990s, and then transformed their suffering and precarity into an efflorescence of literary works. Crucial as it is in defining what the editors call the "third generation" of Nigerian writers, the volume is blind to writings and literary trends from northern Nigeria. Pius Adesanmi and Chris Dunton, the guest editors, claim that:

> The decade that saw the emergence and the domestic consideration of the generation, 1985–1995, was almost exclusively dominated by poets who emerged in parallel formations in the two cities that have acquired a reputation in Nigeria's literary history for being sites of generational beginnings: Ibadan and Nsukka.
>
> *(8)*

The claim is supported in the journal by two seemingly commissioned essays on the creative ferments and literary exuberance that shaped this "generation". The first is "Ibadan and the Memory of a Generation: From the Poetry Club to the Premier Circle", written by Remi Raji. The second is "Children of the Anthill: Nsukka and the Shaping of Nigeria's 1960s Literary Generation", written by Maik Nwosu. Other essays in the journal focus on the individual works of poets and novelists, who are all from southern Nigeria. There is no essay in the journal about similar literary ferments, or any writer, in the north, giving the impression that the region is barren at the time. On the contrary, University of Maiduguri, Maiduguri, where Tanure Ojaide, already a well-known poet of international repute, and Zaynab Alkali mentored writers, such as Idris Okpanachi, Abubakar Othman, Razinat Mohammed and Idris Amali, among others, could have been mentioned as a site of beginning for the third generation. Okpanachi, Othman, Mohammed and Idris have been active in the thematic and stylistic landscape of the third generation and any historical mapping that does not mention them could be regarded as faulty. Besides them, there have been other contemporaneous northern writers such as Maria Ajima, Audee T. Giwa, Joseph Mangut, Ismail Bala, B. M. Dzukogi and Denja Abdullahi, who would have featured among the voices considered the third generation of Nigerian writing. In the same vein, the 2008 summer issue of *Research in African Literatures* (volume 39, number 2), specially themed "Nigeria's Third-Generation Novel: Preliminary Theoretical Engagements", occludes northern Nigerian writers. The concession here is the inclusion of Unoma Azuah, understandably because her mother hails from Delta state, south-south Nigeria, where she grew up and later moved to University of Nigeria, Nsukka, for her degree studies. Whether or not by design, the symbolic erasure of literary voices from northern Nigeria, as demonstrated in the those two journals, is a function of systematic othering by the critical establishment, mostly through the discourse of the "backward" or "undeveloped" or "uncivilised" north. And yet it ironically indicates the parochialism characterising the views of those who deploy such discourse. As JanMohamed and Lloyd point out, "[t]he 'inadequacy' or 'underdevelopment' ascribed to minority texts and authors by a dominant humanism in the end only reveals the limiting (and limited) ideological horizons of that dominant, ethnocentric perspective" (6).

Breaking out of the minority status

Writers and literary scholars in northern Nigeria are not insensitive to the disadvantaged condition of their literature, to the canon-making machineries that systematically exclude them. Efforts have been made at individual and systematic levels to confront the situation. With the liberalisation of higher education in Nigeria thereby opening up the space for state and private universities, most, if not all, states in northern Nigeria have established universities, nearly all of them running a degree in English studies. The indigenisation policy that structures such state-run universities empowers them to train indigenous faculty members. Such trainings have been yielding results, and the significance of this to literary development in northern Nigeria is that literary studies departments have been fortified with scholars that pay special attention to northern Nigerian literature. At the individual level, the scholars put literary texts by northern authors on their reading lists, develop curriculums on northern Nigerian literature and, in most cases, take as subjects of their higher degree theses the works of writers from northern Nigeria.[6] Students are also encouraged to write their undergraduate long essays and higher degree theses on northern Nigerian literature. The poet and scholar Ismail Bala has been consistently collecting books for a bibliography of writings from northern Nigeria. In his "A Bibliographic Listing of Northern Nigerian Novel and Short Story in English 1967–2016", there are about two hundred and fourteen titles (228–241).

Two organisational efforts to support the development of literature in northern Nigeria are worth mentioning here. The first is the annual Conference on Literature in Northern Nigeria, whose twelfth edition was held in 2018. The formation of this conference at Bayero University, Kano, was made possible by the efforts of these prominent northern Nigerian scholars: Prof. Shuaib Oba AbdulRaheem, Prof. Ismaila Tsiga and Prof. Abubakar Rasheed, among others. The conference is today co-funded by Bayero University, Kano; Kwara State University, Malette and Kaduna State University, Kaduna. Papers from the conference over the years have been collected in proceedings that offer a great resource to students of northern Nigerian literature. Some of the titles are *Literature, History and Identity in Northern Nigerian Literature*, edited by Ismaila A. Tsiga and M. O. Bhadmus; *Literature, Integration and Harmony in Northern Nigeria*, edited by Hamzat I. AbdulRaheem, Saeedat B. Aliyu and Reuben A. Akano and *Writing, Performance and Literature in Northern Nigeria* edited by Sa'idu B. Ahmad and Muhammad O. Bhadmus. By focusing on the contents and forms, the historical realities, the critical trends and the diverse indigenous arts that shape northern Nigerian literature, the conference offers northern Nigerian scholars, scholars from southern Nigeria and indeed the entire world an avenue to follow the development of writing in the north. Far more crucial, perhaps, is the critical tradition it initiates and sustains, providing a discourse platform for the theorising and readings of contemporary

Anglophone northern Nigerian literature. This achievement is complemented by the establishment of the Northern Nigerian Writers Summit, the second organisational effort, in 2008. It is also an annual summit. The poet B. M. Dzukogi and members of the Association of Nigerian Authors, Niger State chapter, are credited for taking this significant step. The Summit's attention is more focused on creative writers (with much emphasis on the young, budding ones), on how to realise the potentials of creative writing in the north and on engaging with the northern publics in the development of arts. In its third edition, held in Borno State in 2018, the scholar Tanimu Abubakar in his keynote address draws a connection between the Conference on Northern Nigerian Literature and the Northern Nigerian Writers Summit:

> The bigger underlying motive [for the Summit] is the creation of enabling reading and writing formations that support the "growth" of Literature in Northern Nigeria. This is a strategically significant endeavour which should dovetail into the efforts to evaluate, discuss and propagate Literature in English and indigenous Languages through the regular Conferences on Literature in Northern Nigeria organised by Bayero University, Kano, and Kwara State University, Malette, and Kaduna State University, Kaduna.
>
> *(2)*

The contributions of the Conference and the Summit have resulted in greater visibility for northern Nigerian literature, in both the English language and indigenous languages. Indeed, their impact is being strongly felt among the literati, in higher institutions of learning and in literary circles across northern Nigeria and beyond.

A roadmap for greater visibility

In the same keynote address quoted previously, Tanimu Abubakar suggests a roadmap to the Summit's participants on how northern Nigerian literature can further inscribe itself in global literary consciousness. In his words,

> The Roadmap should be instrumental in propelling the authors and the texts of Northern Nigeria onto the world literary scene and to the attention of leading academic and scholarly reading publics. This entails developing strategies for building viable reading formations as well as boosting their capacity to blend the best of inherited English Tradition with the disquisitions and poetics of Postcolonial Literature in order to attain the highest possible level of literary merit.
>
> *(6–7)*

Of significance is the instrumentation of authors and texts in any design to enhance the visibility of northern Nigerian literature. Beyond the communal spirits and aspirations collectivised in a regional manifesto aimed to politically, socially and economically support northern Nigerian literature, the basis on which northern Nigerian literature can be reckoned with is the quality of its textual manifestations. That is to say, the quality and ideological force of literary works from northern Nigeria should remain the most vital factor for its recognition.

In dwelling on the literary-ideological strengths of writings from northern Nigeria, I return to Ibrahim's *Season of Crimson Blossoms*, a text I consider metaphorical in interrogating the self-imposed, constructed religious and cultural narratives that have, besides institutional neglect, inhibited the development of northern Nigerian literature from within. The novel traces the life of Hajiya Binta, a middle-aged widow, her husband having died in the recurrent religious crises in Jos. The first sentence of the novel is a revelation: "Hajiya Binta Zubairu was finally born at fifty-five when a dark-lipped rogue with short, spiky hair, like a field of miniscule anthills, scaled her fence and landed, boots and all, in the puddle that was her heart" (3). This highly metaphorical expression is a revelation, not to the reader, but to Hajiya Binta herself – a kind of self-discovery that opens up a new world of liberation: a liberation from her religion-backed self-imposed prison of ethical rules, but also from the ruthlessly puritanical society. At the heart of the drama of this liberation is sexuality, her individual choice to bind or unbind her sexual desire. But it is not much of a choice, as she lives in northern Nigeria where individual choices do not matter, where individuals are forcefully rendered subjects of religion. The "dark-lipped rogue" who breaks into Hajiya Binta's heart, who penetrates her prison of ethical rules, is a burglar; he jumps the fence to burgle her house, finds her inside the house and from their initial body contacts a mutual sexual desire is born. A dutiful Muslim, a dedicated student of the adult Islamic school, Hajiya Binta is not expected to commit fornication, and yet she finds herself succumbing to her desire to have sex not even with a responsible person but a street rogue. In the end, a troubled love affair will define her life, but the novel is keen in showing how having sex with a rogue (to the point of watching pornography together) is a form of releasing her body from the prison of ethical rules, "of moistening her long-abandoned womanhood" (26). There is no doubt that she invites Hassan, the rogue, to help release her from that prison:

"Would you like to . . . have some water or something. I mean, I'm all alone, here . . . for now." She was looking down at the damp bed of petunias Hadiza [her daughter] had so lovingly planted to add colour to the yard that hosted little birds at sunrise. That was the precise moment, Binta would reflect later, that the petals of her life, like a bud that had endured half a century of nights, began to unfurl.

(47)

Although Hajiya Binta, as a result of her choice of breaking out of the prison, faces disgrace, what is of utmost importance to her is that she can now enjoy sex, having been brought up with the belief that a woman is not supposed to enjoy it. Through the flashback device, the novel sharply contrasts her newfound freedom with her imprisonment. She never enjoys any closeness to her mother because she is the firstborn, and her culture does not allow a woman to openly show love to her first child. Despite her love for education and her dream of becoming a teacher, she is, at the age of sixteen, sent off to her husband Zubairu in Jos, a man she hardly knows. Before travelling to meet her husband, the following sexual rules are spelt out to her: "Don't look your husband in the eyes . . ., especially when you are doing it [having sex]. Don't look at him down there. And don't let him look at you there, either, if you don't want to have impious offspring" (51–52). Life with Zubairu thrusts her deeper into the prison of religious and cultural rules, sex with him is dryly functional: "Zubairu was a practical man and fancied their intimacy as an exercise in conjugal frugality. It was something to be dispensed with promptly, without silly ceremonies" (54). Her experience with Hassan the rogue is different, as she is allowed to explore her body's desires; attaining sexual orgasm for her signifies her liberation from the prison. *Season of Crimson Blossoms* is a rude affront on the northern Nigerian Islamic and cultural establishment, its constructed narratives of morality and its iron grip on the region's social psyche. It explores subjects that would be considered taboo in northern Nigeria.

The point I attempt to make with this brief reading of Ibrahim's novel is that unless northern Nigerian writers, males and females, begin to deconstruct anti-human religious and cultural conventions, especially in the radical manner Ibrahim has done with this novel, northern

Nigerian literature will continue to suffer self-limitation. This self-limitation is often deployed by reading publics in southern Nigeria to denigrate writings from the north. If literature, with its unlimited potentials for the formation of alterity, for harnessing transgressive forces, is used, as it appears to be the case in northern Nigeria, to endorse constructed religious and cultural narratives that constrict human freedom, it may be difficult for it to attract national and international reading publics. One would therefore find disturbing Abdul-Rasheed Na'Allah's contention that:

> In particular, Hausa rhetorical and literary corpuses involve a process of cultural arrangement that makes every composer conscious of two important requirements: an affirmation of societal truth, even when vigorously re-examining it, and an avowal of the consequence of deviance from it. Although the poetics is a community-wide cultural perspective, every composer, critic and the consumer often consciously engage these binary yardsticks to ensure that the society continues to project acceptable ethics, truth and other forms of community morality.
>
> *(5)*

What Na'Allah seems to be implying here is that northern Nigerian writers, following the received literary didacticism of pre-Western, Islam-based literature, should endorse and promote "acceptable ethics, truth and other forms of community morality." Rather than "ensure that the society continues to project" such 'ethics' and 'truths', northern Nigerian writers, in my view, should shift the paradigm from continuing the "acceptable ethics" to challenging them, the way Ibrahim's novel, I believe, has done.

Conclusion

New voices are emerging on the northern Nigerian literary scene, and this should be seen as an affirmation of the rich literary tradition of the region, dating back to the precolonial period. As I researched for this paper at the turn of 2019, two poetry collections, among others, hit the shelves: Richard Ali's *The Anguish and Vigilance of Things* and Umar Abubakar Sidi's *The Poet of Dust*. Yet literature from northern Nigeria has continued to suffer neglect from the critical establishment in Nigeria. This neglect may be as a result of the late entry of the region's literature into the national literary consciousness. But it is also the result of critical blindness or symbolic erasure. Northern Nigerian writers and scholars have therefore been making efforts to increase the visibility of this literature not only at the national level but also at the international level. Using Ibrahim's *Season of Crimson Blossoms* as an example, I have suggested that the most crucial means by which northern Nigerian literature can transcend self-limiting forces and institutional denigration that undermine its exuberance and richness is to demystify religious and cultural structures that stand in the way of human freedom in northern Nigeria. If literature, of whatever region, whatever society, has any use for humanity at all, it is to subvert institutional powers, in any disguise, that circumscribe subjectivity and agency.

Notes

1 NLNG stands for Nigeria Liquefied Natural Gas; its literature prize, established in 2004, comes with the value of USD100,000, making it the richest and most sought-after prize in Nigeria.
2 This remark is not to discount the fact that other northern Nigerian writers/works have also enjoyed global attention. We know, for instance, that the works of Helon Habila, Unoma Azuah, E. E. Sule and Elnathan John, among others, have also received world recognition.

3 The demarcation of Nigeria into six zones (north-central, north-east, north-west, south-east, south-south and south-west) in the 1990s was done for political reasons, to enable the rotation of power; hence they are referred to as "geo-political zones".

4 Usmanu dan Fodio's jihad (ca. 1804–1808) represents the Islamic conquest, as it is responsible for the spread of Islam in northern Nigeria.

5 For more on Indirect Rule and generally on the challenges of British rule in northern Nigeria, see Robert Heussler's *The British in Northern Nigeria*.

6 I wrote my masters dissertation on the work of Zaynab Alkali at Benue State University, Makurdi. I am aware that Dr. Audee T. Giwa wrote his PhD thesis on the work of Zaynab Alkali at Ahmedu Bello University, Zaria, and Prof. A. K. Babajo wrote his PhD thesis on the work of Abubakar Gimba. These are just a couple of examples.

Works cited

Abubakar, Tanimu N. "Postcolonial Literary Tradition and Its Expanding Space in Northern Nigeria." 3rd Summit of Northern Nigerian Literature: Developing a Blueprint for the Growth of Literature in Northern Nigeria: A Roadmap to Book Development and Distribution in the Region, 19–22 July 2018, Borno, Command Guest House.

Adebayo, Aduke. "Tearing the Veil of Invisibility: The Roles of West African Female Writers." Ed. Aduke Adebayo. *Feminism and Black Women's Creative Writing*. Ibadan: AMD Publishers, 1996. 37–56.

Alidou, Ousseina. "Gender, Narrative Space, and Modern Hausa Literature." *Research in African Literatures*. 33.2 (2002): 137–153.

Alkali, Zaynab. *The Stillborn*. London: Longman, 1984.

Amuta, Chidi. "Literature of the Nigerian Civil War." Ed. Yemi Ogunbiyi. *Perspectives on Nigerian Literature: 1700 to the Present*. Vol. 1. Lagos: Guardian Books, 1988. 85–92.

Bala, Ismail. "A Bibliographic Listing of Northern Nigerian Novel and Short Story in English 1967–2016." *Lapai Research in Humanities*. 5.1 (2018): 228–241.

Boyd, Jean and Beverly Mack. *The Collected Works of Nana Asma'u, Daughter of Usman dan Fodio (1793–1864)*. Ibadan: Sam Bookman, 1999.

Deleuze, Gilles and Felix Guattari. *Kafka: Toward a Minor Literature*. Trans. Dana Polan. Minneapolis: University of Minnesota Press, 1986.

Egya, Sule E. *Niyi Osundare: A Literary Biography*. Makurdi: Sevhage Publishers, 2017.

Ezenwa-Ohaeto. *Winging Words: Interview with Nigerian Writers and Critics*. Ibadan: Kraft Books, 2003.

Heussler, Robert. *The British in Northern Nigeria*. Oxford: Oxford University Press, 1968.

Ibrahim, Abubakar Adam. *Season of Crimson Blossoms*. Lagos: Parresia Books, 2015.

JanMohamed, Abdul R. "Negating the Negation as a Form of Affirmation in Minority Discourse: The Construction of Richard Wright as Subject." Eds. Abdul R. JanMohamed and David Lloyd. *The Nature and Context of Minority Discourse*. Oxford: Oxford University Press, 1990. 102–123.

JanMohamed, Abdul R. and David Lloyd. "Introduction: Towards a Theory of Minority Discourse: What Is to Be Done?" Eds. Abdul R. JanMohamed and David Lloyd. *The Nature and Context of Minority Discourse*. Oxford: Oxford University Press, 1990. 1–16.

Jeyifo, Biodun. *Wole Soyinka: Politics, Poetics and Postcolonialism*. Cambridge: Cambridge University Press, 2004.

Na'Allah, Abdul-Rasheed. "Literature, History and Identity: Theories, Contents and Perspectives". Eds. Ismaila A. Tsiga and M. O. Bhadmus. *Literature, History and Identity in Northern Nigeria*. Ibadan: Safari Books, 2014. 1–11.

Obafemi, Olu. *Nigerian Writers on the Nigerian Civil War*. Ilorin: J. Olu Olatiregun Company, 1992.

Ojinmah, Umelo and Sule E. Egya. *The Writings of Zaynab Alkali*. Abuja: RON Publishers, 2005.

Taiwo, Oladele. *An Introduction to West African Literature*. London: Nelson, 1967.

Taiwo, Oladele. *Culture and the Nigerian Novel*. London: Macmillan, 1976.

25

AFROPOLITAN LITERATURE AS A MINORITY DISCOURSE IN CONTEMPORARY AFRICAN LITERATURE

Razinat Talatu Mohammed

Introduction

Since the turn of the new millennium, African diasporic literature has drastically been on the increase and, with it, the new conflated concept of Afropolitanism. The term Afropolitan, unlike its older brother, Pan Africanism, came forth as a relatively new terminology used to refer to a class of African elites who are either born or brought up in the diaspora or those who have adopted citizenship of countries other than their original African homelands. Taiye Selasi's short but relevant seminal essay (2005), "Bye-Bye Babar (Or What is Afropolitan?)", puts forward the meaning of the term "Afropolitan" in an emotional exposition that brings forth the complexities in the lives of these "children of the world." These are children like her, who were born abroad and have lived all their lives in countries which are theirs only because they were born and raised there. They are transnational and transcultural and are constantly struggling for the right identity for themselves because the multiplicity of their nationalities makes them citizens of more than one country while living in many other countries. These new waves of young Africans have jettisoned their geographical and racial inhibitions and are taking the world in a sweep because they think as universal entities rather than as black or white.

Afropolitanism is the child of the New World Order. Nuttall and Gevisser view the term "Afropolitan" to mean "a place or city with a pluralism of African cultures in one geographical space" (qtd. in Sarah Balakrishnan, 2017). Achille Mbembe (2007) gives the term an elaboration that refers to the existence of "the elsewhere in the here," that is, the interconnectivity of different cultures in a single given space. However, Selasi's notable contribution of formulating a vivid definition of the term has come to represent the origin of the coinage "Afropolitan" for many literary enthusiasts and critics. For her,

> They (Read: we) are Afropolitans – the newest generation of African emigrants, coming soon or collected already at a law firm/chem lab/jazz lounge near you. You'll know us by our funny blend of London fashion, New York jargon, African ethics and academic successes. Some of us are ethnic mixes, e.g. Ghanaian and Canadian, Nigerian and Swiss; others merely cultural mutts: American accent, European affect,

African ethos . . . we understand some indigenous tongue and speak a few urban vernaculars. There is at least one place on the African continent to which we tie our sense of self: Be it a nation-State (Ethiopia), A city (Ibadan) . . . We are Afropolitans: not citizens, but Africans of the world.

(2005)

To a large extent, this definition emphasizes the notion of a socially reconstructed identity for the African in the New World Order. Africans have become fluid in their abilities to migrate and claim other nationalities while yet holding tight to cultural values from their original home fronts. The dynamism displayed by Afropolitans has created a divide in the discourse relating to it. In this regard, the term has not been received wholeheartedly by critics like Binyavanga Wainaina and a number of other African elites. According to Alpha Abebe (2015), Wainaina has expressed concerns with Afropolitan discourses on the basis that it "reflects an elitist representation of African Diasporas, which depoliticizes social relations and commodifies African cultures" (2). Minna Salami (qtd. in Mark Tutton, CNN feature, 2012) states that "Afropolitans are a group of people who are of African origin or influenced by African culture, who are emerging internationally using African cultures in creative ways to change the perceptions about Africa." For some critics, Salami's view refers to Africa's consumerism or unrefined cultural commoditization, whereby creative minds have found a platform for a variety of preoccupations like the Afropolitan Magazine and Afropolitan shop (which Salami founded) that feature typically African products seen from a commercialized world view. For Wainaina, this stance is contrary to the ideals of Pan Africanism, which is essentially to promote everything that can change the reality of the black race and benefit Africans and people of African descent, not for the benefit of the West.

Dabiri (2016, 106) insists that the image that Afropolitans project of Africa appears like "an Instagram-friendly Africa," meaning that they are out to window-dress Africa in most unrealistic ways, while Grace Musila (2016, 112) agreeing with this view, likens it to Coke Lite: "Afropolitanism seems to promise Africa lite," that is, without the "unhealthy" or "intoxicating" elements that define the continent. These fears are, perhaps, founded on the belief that the last three or four decades have marked the beginning of the end of the Pan African movement, and scholars are wondering if, indeed, it will not pay off to re-energize the Pan African movement rather than coining a counter-movement to compete with it. However, the discourse around Afropolitanism is centered within the larger discourse on Cosmopolitanism or the New World Order with its multiplicity of nationalities and cultures which require definite classifications in order to explain the obvious formation of identities along different dimensions of race, nationality, and culture which Selasi proposes. Africans, like other peoples of the world, are migratory in nature, and reasons for such migrations are many. Richard K. Prieb (2005) describes Africans as "the most transcultural and transnational group of individuals anywhere in the world" (57). And Ojaide (2012, 31) sees African writers as becoming "part of the worldwide phenomena of migration and globalization with the attendant physical, socio-cultural, psychic and other forms of dislocation, which permeate their individual writings." When seen as a part of a constantly mobile world, Afropolitanism becomes relevant (even as a minority view) because it shares in its African minority form the context and identities found in a cosmopolitan setting anywhere in the world. However, caution should be exercised in giving the term an extended definition which the Zimbabwean editor of Afropolitan Magazine, Brendah Nyakudya, attempts to do when she states that the term Afropolitan refers to "someone who has roots in Africa, raised by the world, but still has interest in the continent and is making an impact, is feeding back into the continent and trying to better it." But she continues that the term can apply to non-Africans: "We like to think that it doesn't matter where you were born, if you find yourself on the continent and you love the continent, that makes you an Afropolitan." (Tutton 2012). Nyakudya's expansion of the term to include everyday Africans is important to this study; however, to include non-Africans who love the continent is nothing but an attempt to neutralize the Afropolitan ideology. These new citizens of the world are like the free radicals, unweighted by any single nationality, culture, or language. They are emboldened characters who do not linger for long on incidences that see them as victims because they have moved past such fixations. By and large, these are the kinds of characters that we encounter in the works of some African diaspora writings. Afropolitanism, although a minority discourse, is a vibrant and new concept in African literature that is poised to celebrate African identities and values in the face of challenging globalized values.

This study will examine *Americanah* (2013) by Nigerian Chimamanda Ngozi Adichie, *Ghana Must Go* (2013) by Nigerian/Ghanaian Taiye Selasi, and *We Need New Names* (2014) by the Zimbabwean writer NoViolet Bulawayo. The choice of these novels is primarily determined by the fact that they are all written by Anglophone African diaspora writers and for the fact that they were published after the turn of the millennium because Afropolitanism, a conflated concept, also came into being during the same period.

Chimamanda Ngozi Adichie's *Americanah* (2013) was selected by the *New York Times* as one of the Ten Best Books of 2013 and won the National Book Critics Circle Fiction Award. *Americanah* is about a love affair that starts between two adolescent Nigerian students, Ifemelu and Obinze, in the city of Lagos. Soon after secondary school, Ifemelu migrates to the United States of America to attend university, while Obinze remains behind with the hope of joining her when his visa application is approved. Ifemelu's stay in America brings her face to face with racism, as she is refused employment because of her race. She struggles at this point to make ends meet and falls victim to sexual abuse at the hands of a white employer. Afterwards, filled with shame and self hate, she is not able to talk to Obinze, and that causes a break in their relationship. Not long after this, she gets a babysitting job and soon begins to date a handsome white American, Curt. In his company, she enjoys luxury and exposure, but soon, driven by her impulse and suspicion of infidelity, she betrays him and soon ends the comfortable relationship. She becomes a blogger on racial issues in America, during which time she meets Blaine, an African American professor. On impulse, after some years, Ifemelu closes her very successful blog and returns to Lagos, where she successfully breaks Obinze's marriage to reunite with him.

Americanah has a powerful ability to change one's views on not only interracial love but also intraracial relationships. Elizabeth Day (2013), in the Guardian review, says the book has the power to combine both telling a "great story as well as make you change the way you look at the world." Also, David Fish, in his 2017 review of the book, agrees that it has the power "to change your perspective, but only if you allow it to do so." Caroline Lyle (2018, 1) sees Selasi's concept of Afropolitanism in *Americanah* as open to expansion to include female Afropolitans with a "racialized sexual identity." For Shoba Jini. V (2018, 1), *Americanah* depicts the fact that despite the hybridity of nationality, race, and culture that defines Afropolitans, the Africans in the diaspora still "have strong bonding for their roots." Other reviewers have noted the problem of race taking on a serious dimension in the novel because the America that was the dream country for Ifemelu and her schoolmates back in Lagos turns out not to be true after all.

Afropolitanism and the loss of African identity and values in Chimamanda Ngozi Adichie's *Americanah*

African migrants living in cosmopolitan cities of the world have had liaisons that promoted a fusion with other people of different ethnicities or races either through marriage or simply a connection through a shared history or experience. Over a period of time, the younger generations of African descent have become hybridized, thus giving rise to the Afropolitans. This curious tribe has evolved from shared experiences, and they are not anxious to put claims to one location because they are very mobile entities who do not "belong to a single geography, but feel at home in many" (Selasi 2005, 1).

However, Chimamanda Ngozi Adichie has refused to be identified as an Afropolitan for reasons that seem logical to her. She questions the singling out of Africa from the rest of "humanity that they must be designated by a particular word when they travel or are found in the capitals of the world" (Santana 2016, 122). In spite of her minority position, her novel *Americanah* expounds the ideals of the theory of Afropolitanism. The novel highlights Ifemelu's inner struggles as an African immigrant in a racially conscious place like America. Some of her experiences are painfully derogatory and others condescending, and yet she forges ahead in pursuit of her American dreams. During her courtship with Curt, she is exposed to luxury and world travel, and all of these portrayals make *Americanah* come clean as an Afropolitan text. This view is also shared by Caroline Lyle (2018, 2), who considers the novel "a text that perfectly lends itself to the expansion of Selasi's theory of Afropolitan identity and formation." This analysis will, therefore, examine the select African diaspora texts for those ideals which Selasi puts forward rather than for having been written by African diaspora writers.

At the Trenton platform, amid an array of people of different ages and sizes, the reader is immediately conscious that the novel will invariably be based on a set of multicultural characters. A Caribbean driver; an African American fat woman; and, in the braiding room, the melting pot of West African diaspora are all working to make ends meet, and, according to Nyakudya's definition that an Afropolitan is "someone who . . . is feeding back into the continent and trying to better it" (qtd in Tutton, 2012). Going by this definition, Afropolitanism is not always about elitism. Everyday Africans who are in the diaspora and continue to struggle against obvious odds like cultural adulteration and overcoming racial discrimination while at the same time continuing to foster links with their countries of origin and send back monies to better it are also Afropolitans. It is important also to state that spatial mobility, which is often enhanced by the financial statuses of the immigrants, is only possible, as Chielozona Eze (2015) asserts, because there exists an underlying "symptomatic interior mobility" (116). In other words, spatial mobility is predetermined by interior or internal mobility. The mobility and other changes that Afropolitans spot are driven by some inner forces which may not really be class related. In this regard, these West African women who live and make their living in America are multilingual; Mariama speaks French, the local Wollof and Americanized English; Aisha, a Senegalese, is taken to Ifemelu because her boyfriend is Igbo and she desperately wants to get married to him – they are living in the diaspora and making impacts in their own ways. They visit their countries or send monetary assistance to their families back home while they remain in the diaspora and form a new identity which is seen in their struggle with poor living conditions and the debilitating heat on the one hand and their incoherent and hybridized Americanized English on the other (8–9). After many years of living in these cosmopolitan cities, the African diaspora evolves into hybridized entities that are often neither purely African nor truly American. These traits of hybridization are often reflected in the literature of migration.

Ifemelu and other diaspora characters, like Aunty Uju, struggle through self-debasing circumstances, all in the bid to survive in America. They change their African accent to a strange Americanized one just so that they can be understood. Aunty Uju pronounces her own name as "you-joo instead of oo-joo" (104). And at the grocery store, she changes her accent, "*Pooh-reet-back*" whenever she is in the presence of white Americans. And Ifemelu observes that with "the hybridized accent emerged a new persona, apologetic and abasing" (108).

The issue of identity formation in the diaspora is seen in the changes that obvious challenges impose on migrants. When Ifemelu is faced by challenges later in Philadelphia, her struggles leave long-lasting effects on her life. At the first registration point in school, the desk officer, Cristina Tomas, to Ifemelu by condescendingly overenunciating emphasizing every syllable which intimidates her and pushes her to start learning the American accent (135).

Ifemelu's struggle with finances caused by her joblessness is heightened each time the phone rings and she receives yet another rejection while faced by unpaid rents and depleted groceries. These pressures push her to accept an offer from her tennis coach, which, sadly, turns out to be the turning point in her life. It is true that pressure from all fronts pushes her into his arms, but she goes to his house prepared for whatever the tennis coach wants because she takes time to "shave her underarms, dug out the lipstick she had not worn since the day she left Lagos, . . . what would happen with the tennis coach? He had said 'massage', but his manner, his tone, had dripped suggestion" (153). In her drive for identity formation as a member of the African diaspora, she believes that only through finding an immediate solution to her financial problems could she survive, and when she picks up the phone to call the tennis coach, she knows she is submitting herself to his "abuse," if it can be said to be an abuse because although, "she did not want to be here, did not want his active finger between her legs, did not want his sigh-moans in her ears, and yet she felt her body rousing to a sickening wetness. Afterwards, she lay still" (154). It is only after the act that she realizes how low she has sunk. She feels no longer worthy of Obinze's love and decidedly ends their childhood relationship in a moment of impulsive decision.

Also, her relationship with the ebullient Curt, the rich white American, affords Ifemelu a view of the new person she has evolved into, "She became, in her mind, a woman free of knots and cares, a woman running in the rain with the taste of sun-warmed strawberries in her mouth." She lives in luxury, enjoying her identity as an Afropolitan, traveling around Europe without inhibitions.

Afropolitans often adopt identities to achieve life purposes. Ruth advises Ifemelu to straighten her hair to get a job in Baltimore, and Ifemelu remembers that "Aunty Uju had said something similar in the past, and she had laughed then" (202–203). After her saloon experience, the hairdresser's comment completes Ifemelu's identity formation: "But look how pretty it is. Wow, girl, you've got the white-girl swing!" (203). As for Curt, after realizing that she has burned her scalp, he is horrified: "It is so fucking wrong that you have to do this." But for her, that identity of having her hair "straight and sleek, parted at the side and curving to a slight bob at her chin" serves the purpose, for when, after the interview, "the woman shook her hand and said she would be a 'wonderful fit' in the company, Ifemelu wondered if the woman would have felt the same way had she walked into the office wearing her thick, kinky, God-given halo of hair, the Afro" (203–204). Ifemelu is living a hybridist lifestyle which defines the Afropolitan's life. She has changed her personality several times in the course of a very short period. It is not surprising, therefore, when her Ethiopian taxi driver thinks that she needed to be careful or "America will corrupt you" because he is unable to tell from her looks where she is from; he says: "I can't place your accent. Where are you from?" When her reply comes and she claims Nigeria, he quickly opines, "You don't look African at all . . . because your blouse is too tight" (206). From this point on, Ifemelu has lost her identity and arrived at the full definition of an Afropolitan; "We are Afropolitans: not citizens, but Africans of the world" (Selasi, 1). She no longer is recognizable as belonging to any particular part of the world.

Also, Kimberly's sister, Laura, taunts Ifemelu about Nigeria's 419 stories and how America's money is wired to Nigeria. Ifemelu knows that Laura's interest about Nigeria "was an aggressive, unaffectionate interest," (163) but she handles Laura's taunting with the Afropolitan attitude of not playing the victim to her racist comments but to face the situation bravely. Ifemelu tells the story of a corrupt driving instructor she met in Brooklyn. She concludes by observing: "It was a strange moment for me, because until then I thought nobody in America cheated" (164). Her response is meant only to goad Laura.

While in London, Obinze also struggles for diaspora identity. Working under a borrowed identity, his experiences are very bitter because in spite of his privileged upbringing, he ends up cleaning toilets in London while Emenike, his old friend, would rather show off his achievements as an Afropolitan (marriage to an Englishwoman and postgraduate degree) than help him sincerely (246–247). Like many in the novel, Emenike is living a conflicted identity and not ready to identify with his past.

When Ifemelu and Obinze reunite in Lagos and rekindle their suspended relationship, she is invited to a gathering of returnees from Europe and America who call their union the Niger-politan Club, a local flavor of Afropolitan consisting of a group of diaspora Nigerians who have formed other identities abroad while living in transnational and transcultural cities. Their accents remain foreign, real or fake, and some of their laments tend toward the ludicrous; for example, one of them decries the lack of vegetarian restaurant in Lagos. Although these returnees are physically living in Nigeria and both or one of their parents may be Nigerian, they choose to maintain other identities that perhaps, have defined them, thus keying into Selasi's definition of Afropolitans, "others'cultural mutts" (1). Indeed, these are examples of culturally altered Africans.

As an Afropolitan, the link that Ifemelu maintains with Nigeria pulls her to self-fulfillment in the end. Ifemelu makes recourse to her roots, which, again, defines the fluidity of the Afropolitans because "ultimately, the Afropolitan must form an identity along at least three dimensions: national, racial, cultural" (Selasi 2005, 2).

In this regard, Ifemelu, the young African diaspora member who struggles with racism, unrequited love, and other forms of deprivation in America is compelled to return to her country, where there is between her and Obinze, "a weightless, seamless desire. . . . There was an awakening even in her nails, in those parts of her body that had always been numb" (447). Realizing these inadequacies in her dream country, America, she settles back in Lagos.

Afropolitanism and the loss of African identity in Taiye Selasi's *Ghana Must Go*

Taiye Selasi came into the limelight with the publication of her seminal essay "Bye-Bye Babar." *Ghana Must Go* is her debut novel, and it tells the story of a brilliant Ghanaian surgeon, Kweku Sai, and his family and how the loss of his job through unfair racial considerations in Boston causes him to betray his family. His departure, without confronting his wife with the true reasons why he is leaving America, plunges the family of six into a long, conflicted relationship that traverses continents. The novel actually begins with the death of Kweku Sai and the return of his four children from the United States for his funeral in Ghana.

The children's return to Africa reopens existing conflicts between them and their mother. Olu, the eldest of the four children, is living with the fear of turning out like his father, although he takes after him professionally. Taiwo and Kehinde are twins, brilliant and beautiful. They are broken from their incestuous experiences in Lagos while staying with their maternal uncle, Femi. Sadie, the youngest of them, is struggling to fit into the records of her siblings just as the rest of them consistently seek to define one another. The severance of their roots at some point becomes worrisome for Sadie, who laments her lack of roots. In the end, a decision is made by Fola, their mother, to keep the family together by her symbolic submerging of Kweku's urn in the ocean rather than scattering the ashes in the wind.

Taiye Selasi's novel is expectedly Afropolitan in conception. It is a careful construct intended to explain the Afropolitan concept, which she coined in 2005. Elizabeth Busby (2013) refers to it as an arresting first novel that "comes garlanded with mighty expectations" (1). The book has received praise from high quarters. She was the literary protégé of Toni Morrison, who believes that Selasi has taken an uninhibited risk "with language and allusions which sets it [*her work*, my emphasis] apart." Furthermore, she states that Selasi's seminal essay on "Afropolitan" is "inspirational . . . to cover those – like herself – whose geographical and cultural hybridity allows them to shape-shift fearlessly, carrying with it the need for constant self definition" (2). Diana Evans (2013) states that *Ghana Must Go* "is one of the most hyped debuts of recent times." She goes on to say that Selasi draws on the consciousness of the novel by bringing to the fore the "rootlessness passed down through generations of immigrants and interpreted in myriad subjectivities" (3). For Zainab Quadri (2015), *Ghana Must Go* brings to the fore "the importance of fathers in our societies." If Kweku Sai had not left his wife and children, Quadri believes that "Taiye [sic] and Kehinde would never have lost their innocence, they would never have witnessed so much sadness and bitterness in their lives" (1).

The term "Afropolitan," for Selasi, must refer to that young generation of Africans living in cosmopolitan cities in the West, interacting with people from multiple other countries with transcultural influences: this young and vibrant generation is multilingual, has the capacity to traverse the world, and is able to engage in the politics of the world around them and media, music, and arts rather than the safe and traditional professions of their parents, which were medicine, law, accountancy, and so on. The construction of this novel takes into cognizance the definition and ideals of the term "Afropolitanism" because it is, after all, her first novel.

First, *Ghana Must Go* depicts an elitist family of six. The father, Kweku, and elder son, Olu, are both talented surgeons; the mother, Fola, a law school graduate turned florist; the twins, Kehinde and Taiwo, a successful painter and one of the best law students at Oxford University and writer, respectively; and the youngest of the Sais, Sadie, is conscious of the family's academic achievements and fears failing them. Kweku and Fola are the older generation, who are safe in the traditional professions of medicine and law, while the younger generation, like Kehinde and Taiwo, are "not shy about expressing our African influences (such as they are) in our work" (Selasi 2).

Like all other members of the African diaspora, migrants suffer levels of racism and condescending comments about their persons or where they come from. In *Ghana Must Go*, the characters equally suffer from such condescending comments: "You live your whole life in this world, and you know what they think of you" (305). But rather than play the victim and pretend they are not aware that they are looked at as inferior or being taunted, they stand their ground because they have formed their identities around these new worlds; they see themselves as belonging with them.

Also, cosmopolitanism is a major consideration for Afropolitan ideals. The six major characters in the novel are cosmopolitan in conception. The parents, Kweku and Fola, were already fully integrated into the American culture before the arrivals of their children. The children, having been born in cosmopolitan America, are by right American citizens who naturally internalize the American nuance. When the twins Kehinde and Taiwo arrive in Lagos, they see a "urban grey, the sky smoggy and muted and clogged with tall buildings" (167).

Multilingualism is a trait which stems from interracial and tribal marriages or other forms of interactions that form important identity traits for the Afropolitans. The Sais are African descendants, who, in addition to English, speak some other tongues, like Twi (Ghana), Yoruba (Nigeria), and Mandarin (Chinese). To be multilingual necessarily means that one is also culturally integrated into more than one culture. Fola represents the melting pot of biracialism and multiculturalism in the novel because she is the granddaughter of an Igbo man, John Nwaneri, from the Eastern part of Nigeria who married a Scottish woman, and her own father, Kayo Savage, married her mother, Somayina, the biracial daughter of this Igbo/Scot marriage, and the union between Kayo Savage and Somayina brought forth Folashade, who in turn marries a Ghanaian. Additionally, her son Olu, who has the blood of his mother's lineage running through his veins, decides to marry a Chinese American. This is a perfect picture of an Afropolitan hybridized genealogy which Selasi traces in her seminal essay. This hybridization is also seen in the characters' behaviors and world views. Fola and Taiwo wear Western attire and combine it with African accessories. A typically hybridized outfit is seen in Taiwo's appearance when she goes to interview Dean Rudd for the magazine the *Law Review*; she comes out in the cultures that have defined her existence, Western and African. Like Selasi's Afropolitans, the "cultural hybrid: kente cloth worn over low-waisted jeans," (1) Taiwo is "in blue velvet blazer, dress cum dashiki . . . quarter Yoruba priestess, quarter prim British school girl" (130). Fola, like Taiwo, clearly identifies with her Africanness, and in spite of other condescending diasporian challenges, they keep strong because they are proud to live both identities.

The fluidity of Afropolitans advances the notion of the absence of geographical or national fixations. Afropolitans are rootless. For instance, Fola and her children are affected by what Selasi herself calls "weightless, without gravity, completely unbound." Fola is orphaned early in life, blamed by her grandparents for presumably causing her mother's death; the raging civil war that takes her father away plunges her into a life of mobility both internal and spatial. Her arrival in the United States is with the hope of excelling academically and settling down and starting a family. At first, she creates her identity around the family that she and Kweku started. Kweku, too, a migrant from Ghana, is detached from his homeland identity. In America, Kweku imbues himself with hope; he dares to become someone, an "excellent surgeon," but when he suffers injustice at his workplace and he becomes disillusioned, he decides to remove himself, the head of the family, from that shared identity. They have only one dream because Kweku himself makes clear that Fola does not need a dream other than his: "One dream's enough for the both of us" (73). But Kweku punctures that dream and with it the ego of the family that he has built, thus sending everyone into an abysmal character formation, which Emylia Hall (2013) refers to as a fractured family constantly seeking "to define and redefine one another and themselves throughout the novel, handing out roles and assuming them, shackling and being shackled" (1). After Kweku's departure, Fola is not able to handle the pressure of life alone, and she sends her twins, Kehinde and Taiwo, to her brother, Femi, in Lagos, Nigeria, thereby exercising one very important Afropolitan ideal, spatial mobility. Unknown to her, however, Femi is a perverted man because the twins are subjected to some heinous experiences at his insistence. Also, although Kehinde and Taiwo connect with Femi, like their mother, they would never think of Nigeria as a place to link their identities to. This is a pointer to the Afropolitan belief that a migrant's identity cannot always be traced back to his/her origin but should be determined by where one chooses as home or that place where one's identity formation can be traced to, that is, the cosmopolitan cities of the world. In this regard, Selasi's characters, although belonging to one family, are each at liberty to choose where to append his/her identity.

For Kweku and Fola, they are the old generation, whose main achievement is in the fact that they raised their four Afropolitan children in the light of Selasi's conception: "Kweku looked like a man on his own . . . a surgeon, a Ghanaian, . . . just a man in a cord with an odd sort of bearing; a stranger in Accra as in Boston. Alone" (248). Perhaps in his dying moments, his hopes lie with his children, for whom he has suffered hard work and devotion in America. In other word, the sacrifices of the parents (Kweku and Fola) will be harnessed by his Afropolitan children.

There is obvious and deliberate mobility in the novel, especially when the news of Kweku's death is made known to Fola, who had also moved to Ghana. She calls her older son, Olu, in Boston; he calls his sister Taiwo in New York; she goes to pick up her sister, Sadie, in New Haven; and together they meet Kehinde in Brooklyn, from where they all fly to Ghana for their father's funeral. The struggles and challenges of the African diaspora that are commonly seen in their existential crises are seen within the Sai family in *Ghana Must Go*.

There is tension and a huge sense of lack in the Sai children. The youngest child, Sadie, struggles to meet the uphill standard set by her siblings, and always the overbearing knowledge that they are a family that has no history, no traceable lineage or tree of descent, continues to haunt her. In a sense, this is the very concept/circumstance that makes them Afropolitans. However, when Sadie's sense of inadequacy is critically examined, it may seem that she envies her best friend Pilae. The tone of Selasi's seminal essay is that of acceptance on the part of the Afropolitans: they are who they are, free and hybridized world citizens who are able to take up any challenge and claim any form of identity because they are not always obliged to belong to their parents' origins. The Sai family has no "roots spreading out underneath them, with no living grandparent, no history, a horizontal – they've floated, have scattered, drifting outward, or inward, barely noticing when someone has slipped off the grid" (146–147). Here, Selasi makes the Sai children bemoan their lack of traceable history in spite of the fact that they are accomplished Afropolitans scattered all over the civilized West. Sadie faults her own family in comparison to her friend's, for she claims that "Philae's family is heavy, a solid thing, weighted," while her own family represents the opposite of that, it is "weightless . . . a family without gravity, completely unbound" (146). Taiwo remains by the window staring at people's windows, where she imagines "successful families" (124) are living, totally bonded, a kind of family that she does not have. In like manner, Olu spends much time staring at his friends' family pictures each time he visits, and "He'd tour their homes aching with longing, for *lineage*, for a sense of having descended from faces in frames" (251). This longing for a solid family is not shared by Kehinde, however, because, for him, his family represents a typical New World Order, and he is not bothered by any definitive lineage; in other words, a true Afropolitan. However, the last part of the novel sees this weightless family coming together and reconciling their differences. Even the youngest child, Sadie, discovers family talents and resemblances. But the final decision by Fola to commit Kweku's urn to the ocean rather than scattering the ashes may be suggesting that the family has finally come together through the death of its head; therefore, scattering the ashes will send the family on their different ways again because: "The idea of him scattered seems wrong in some way. *We've been scattered enough*" (314).

However, in the end, it is in Ghana that the Sai five begin to find answers to their alienated identities. Sadie discovers that she is a good dancer and has a lot in common with her Ghanaian aunt and also reconciles with her mother; Taiwo and Kehinde reconcile; and Olu decides to finally start his own family. It does seem like Selasi's Afropolitanism has been domesticated to wear a Ghanaian identity at this point, bringing her assertion of the "willingness to complicate Africa" to mind.

Afropolitanism in NoViolet Bulawayo's *We Need New Names*

NoViolet Bulawayo is a Zimbabwean novelist who came into the limelight in 2011 after winning the Caine Prize for African Writing. *We Need New Names*, published in 2013, is her first novel. The novel is in two parts. The first part is about the exploits of six children all under the age of fourteen. These children all live in Zimbabwe's shantytown (ironically called Paradise), where poverty, diseases, and promiscuity reign. The children have no schools to attend because the paramilitary policemen have destroyed their schools, and Darling, through whose point of view the narration runs, remembers that once her family lived in a normal home. Since the children are left with nothing developmental to engage in, they roam the entire province of Budapest, an area reserved for the whites and rich blacks, stealing guavas from their gardens. The second part of the novel tells the story of Darling's escape to America through the assistance of her maternal aunt, Fostalina, who lives in America. In America, Darling sees so much food luxury and remembers her family and friends back in Africa living in dire need. Her stay in America also exposes the inherent racism and the diaspora fever of getting ones *papers* right, whatever one has to do.

Since its publication in 2013, *We Need New Names* has received critical reviews. Helon Habila (2013) wonders if the novel does not actually overstate the sufferings of the African continent. He agrees that, like other parts of the world, Africa has its dark and ugly parts, "but we don't turn to literature to confirm that" (3). For Nereah Obimbo (2018), the novel represents the escape of an African girl to America, the land of plenty and, paradoxically, this "America's abundance is hard to reach" (2). Leyla Sanai (2013) sees the novel as a relevant place to view the lives of immigrants who are engaged in doing "the menial jobs," with "the obligation to send money home . . . their westernized children, who grow up to be distant and dump their parents in nursing homes" (2).

Afropolitanism and the loss of African identity and values in *We Need New Names*

We Need New Names is another African migration novel. In the second part, Bulawayo states thus: "Look at them leaving in droves, the children of the land . . . When things fall apart, . . . They flee their own wretched land so their hunger may be pacified in foreign lands" (147–148).

> She expresses with clarity the many issues in migrating to other people's lands. She says: "They will never be the same again because you just cannot be the same once you leave behind who and what you are."
>
> *(148)*

This poignant statement is relevant because, consciously or unconsciously, migrants form new identities and can never be the same again. In this regard, this novel reveals the transcultural identity of the migrant protagonist, Darling, who, over the period of her stay in America, constantly reverts to her memories of back home in the evaluation of her new environment. The novel presents two types of Afropolitans: the born and raised in the West type and the migrated to the West type. The migrated to the West type are those who come with their minds formed on experiences from their places of origin, determined to achieve their dreams of living better lives in their chosen abodes in Europe and America.

From her exploits with the gang, back in Paradise in Zimbabwe, Darling's new life in America is hybridized and her memories fluid; for example, when she is confused about Aunt Fostalina's obsession with looking like the skinny American women, she wonders why her Aunt should keep walking in one spot like MaDube the mentally ill woman back in Paradise (150). For Uncle Kojo, Aunt Fostalina's obsession with counting calories is not African. "I actually don't understand why you are doing all this. . . . Kick.

And punch. And punch. Look at you, bones. . . . All bones" (153). For Aunt Fostalina, identifying culturally with her environment and looking skinny and having a live-in partner in Uncle Kojo are some of the Afropolitan choices that she makes.

Cultural condescension of African immigrants in the West is another aspect that Afropolitans constantly have to deal with. When Darling sets foot in Washington, kids her age make her life difficult because they "teased me about my name, my accent, my hair, the way I talked or said things" (167). This taunting continues until the young Darling adopts the western culture of dressing like American children of her age and speaking with the American accent: "the TV has taught me just how to do it" (196). At this point, Darling can be said to have developed a new racialized identity in her young mind. She is made aware of her inadequacies from the majority white children. This challenge represents as, Lyle (2018) says, "Afropolitans' inner struggle between their Africanness and the challenges which life in Western cultures bring about" (2). Also, Chielozona Eze (2015) asserts that "spatial mobility is only symptomatic of our interior mobility" (116). In America, Darling discovers that study is easy because "I've been getting all As in everything, even maths and science, . . . because school is so easy in America even a donkey would pass". (169) Darling's success is a proof of the Afropolitan concept of "You'll know us by our funny blend of London fashion . . . academic successes" (1).

Furthermore, Dumi, the handsome Zimbabwean, agrees to marry a grotesquely obese white lady, not for love, obviously, but to enable him get his papers. These behaviors again, point potentially to Selasi's statement that the modern "African is tasked to forge a sense of self from wildly disparate sources" (2).

For Bulawayo, children like Darling or those born in the West do not truly represent the African migrants because "they grow and we squint to see ourselves in them . . . They did not want to hear the stories our grandmothers had told to us around village fires" (250–251). They have become what Selasi refers to as "Africans of the world," true Afropolitans who are "lost in translation" (1–2).

In the same vein, Darling's mother accuses her of forgetting them in the squalor of Paradise under the excuse of being busy. This excuse does not go down well with the mother, as she sarcastically tells her daughter, "Yes, you've been busy because I hear now you have a job. . . . And I see that America has taught you to speak English to your mother, and with that accent. He-he-he, so you are trying to sound white now!" (208). At this point, Darling's assimilation is clear. Her stay and interactions in the new world have caused her affected accent, which the mother notices immediately. Whether this identity formation is reached consciously or unconsciously, Selasi's claim that Afropolitans choose, "which bits of a national identity (from passport to pronunciation) we internalize as central to our personalities" (2). Hence, Darling's alienation from her old life is complete and proves the affectation of her new world. This new sense of the "self" creeps in when her friends call from back home. Darling becomes irritable and hates the questions that she is asked: "I just don't know how to deal with all these crazy questions" (210). And when the doorbell rings while she is still talking to Stina, she asks him to hold on, "knowing I will not be picking up the phone. It's hard to explain, this feeling; it's like there's two of me. One part is yearning for my friends; the other doesn't know how to connect with them anymore, as if they are people I've never met. I feel a little guilty but I brush the feeling away" (212). This conflicted feeling is caused by the interjection of the new and the old cultures. Therefore, Darling has consciously formed her identity along at least two national and cultural dimensions, all of which represent her Afropolitan status.

In conclusion, these three diaspora novels have been examined for their tilt in the direction of the discourse on Afropolitanism and its minority status in African literature. Often, the challenges that African migrants face in the West have help in the formation of individual and sometimes collective identities of characters as depicted and often highlighting the Afropolitans' refusal to accept playing the victim and languishing in self pity. This is a strong and positive point because rather than allowing heart-wrecking experiences ruin their self worth, they struggle through and fight back to accomplish their dreams. Ifemelu's encounter with the tennis coach is a good example of this high point. The fact that the African diaspora has to relate to more than one identity can be tasking both in the physical form as well as in the psyche, which is the reason for the identity crisis that most characters in these novels suffer. They are daily struggling to understand their positions in the world of multiculturalism, a kind of definition for their existence in a transnational space. They have the desire to feel accepted or simply proclaim that they belong to the societies in which they live because they are hybridized citizens of not just one space but of multiple spaces. In all of these, Selasi's "willingness to complicate Africa" can then mean that, as much as the Afropolitans want to be "Africans of the world," they are still rooted to their African identities: "The acceptance of complexity common to most African cultures is not lost on her prodigals. Without that intrinsically multi-dimensional thinking, we could not make sense of ourselves" (Selasi 2005, 3). No wonder Ifemelu does not find fulfillment in her sojourn in America (in spite of her later accomplishments and associations) but must return to her roots and change jobs and lovers, thus representing the mobility of the Afropolitans in both spatial and internal terms. Darling makes a detour to Paradise in her Zimbabwean homeland at the end of the novel and, of course, the Sai family convenes in Ghana to reinvent another identity for themselves. Is Selasi then suggesting that the Afropolitans can deconstruct socially formulated stereotypes that are related to identities of the African diaspora and then make a detour to celebrate their roots?

Works cited

Abebe, Alpha. (2007). "Afropolitanism", in Njami Simon and Lucy Duran (Eds.), *Africa Remix: Contemporary Art of a Continent*. Johannesburg: Johannesburg Art Gallery: 26–30.

Abebe, Alpha. (2015). "Afropolitan: Global Citizenship with African Routes." http://blog.politics.ox.ac.uk/afropolitanism-global-citizenship-african-routes/. (Retrieved: 28/07/2019).

Adichie, Chimamanda N. (2013). *Americanah*. Lagos: Kachifo Limited.

AF Spagnuolo. www.surrey.ac.uk. (Retrieved 8/6/2019).

Annand, David. (2013). "Americanah by Chimamanda Ngozi Adichie: Review." www.telegraph.co.uk/culture/books/fictionreviews/9986831/Americanah-by-Chimamanda-Ngozi-Adichie-review.html.

ASSUMPTA. (2017). "TBBNQ Reads: *Ghana Must Go* by Taiye Selasi." www.thebookbanque.com/literary/review/ghanamustgo-selasi. (Retrieved: 15/8/2019).

Balakrishnan, Sarah. (2017). "The Afropolitan Idea: New Perspectives on Cosmopolitanism in African," *History Compass*. https://scholar.harvard.edu/files. (Retrieved: 23/07/2019).

Boelhover, Q. William. (1981). "The Immigrant Novel as Genre," *Melus*, 8(1), 3–13.

Bulawayo, NoViolet. (2014). *We Need New Names*. New York: Back Bay Books.

Busby, Elizabeth. (2013). "*Ghana Must Go* by Taiye Selasi." www.independent.co.uk/arts-entertainment/books/reviews/ghana-must-go-by-taiye-selasi-8553725.html. (Retrieved: 15/8/2019).

Dabiri, Emma. (2016). "Why I Am (Still) Not an Afropolitan," *Journal of African Cultural Studies*, 28(1), 104–108.

Day, Elizabeth. (2013). "*Americanah* by Chimamanda Ngozi Adichie-Review." www.theguardian.com. (Retrieved: 30/07/2019).

Emecheta, Buchi. (1974). *Second Class Citizen*. Oxford: Heinemann.

Evans, Diana. (2013). "*Ghana Must Go* by Taiye Selasi." www.theguadian.com/books/2013/apr/03/ghana-must-go-selasi-review. (Retrieved: 15/8/2019).

Eze, Chielozona. (2015). "We, Afropolitans," *Journal of African Cultural Studies*, 28(1), 115–119. Taylor & Francis. doi:1080/13696815.1100065.

Falola, Toyin. (2014). *African Diaspora: Slavery, Modernity and Globalization*. Rochester, NY: University of Rochester Press.

Fish, David. (2017). "Book Review: *Americanah* by Chimamanda Ngozi Adichie." https://medium.com/"dsfish/book-review-americanah-by-chimamanda-ngozi-adichie-a84ddb3d2250. (Retrieved: 30/07/2019). (12/06/2019).

Habila, Helon. (2013). "*We Need New Names* by NoViolet Bulawayo – Review." www.theguardian.com/books/2013/jun/20/need-new-names-bulawayo-review. (Retrieved: 10/8/2019).

Hall, Emylia. (2013). "*Ghana Must Go* by Taiye Selasi." https://africainwords.com/2013/6/27/ghana-must-go-bytaiya-selasi-review/. (Retrieved: 15/8/2019).

Jini, V. Shoba. (2018). "Afropolitanism in Chimamanda Ngozi Adichie's *Americanah*." www.johnfoundation.com/journals/sparkling/article/SIJMRS VIII 04.php. (Retrieved: 3/8/2019).

Killingray, David. (2011). "Origins of Pan Africanism: Henry Sylvester Williams, Africa, and the African Diaspora." www.tandfonline.com. (Retrieved: 18/8/2019).

Knudsen, Eva Rask, and Ulla Rahbek. (2016). *In Search of the Afropolitan: Encounters, Conversation and Contemporary Diasporic African Literature*. Lanham: Rowman & Littlefield International.

Lyle, Caroline. (2018). "Afropolitanism for Black Women: Sexual Identity and Coming to Voice in Chimamanda Ngozi Adichie's *Americanah*." www.aspeers.com/2018/lyle. (Retrieved: 4/08/2019).

Mbembe, Achilles. (2007). "Afropolitanism", in Simon Njami and Lucy Duran (Eds.), *Africa Remix: Contemporary Art of a Continent*. Johannesburg: Jacana Media: 26–31.

Musila, Grace. A. (2016). "Part-Time Africans, Europolitans and 'Africa Lit'", *Journal of African Cultural Studies*, 28(1), 109–1313.

Obimbo, Nereah. (2018). "Book Review: *We Need New Names* by NoViolet Bulawayo." www.potentash.com/2018/10/02/we-need-new-names-noviolet-bulawayo/. (Retrieved: 10/8/2019).

Ojaide, Tanure. (2012). "Migration, Globalization and Recent African Literature," in *Contemporary African Literature: New Approaches*. Durham: Carolina Academic Press, 2012.

Omotayo, Joseph. (2013). "*Americanah*." http://criticalliteraturereview.blogspot.com/2013/07/americanah-by-chimamanda-ngozi-adichie.html. (Retrieved: 22/7/2019).

Phiri, Linda. (2016). "Reviving Afropolitanism: The Negotiation of African Global Identity: What Is Lost in Translation?" www.semanticscholar.org. (Retrieved: 26/07/2019).

Prieb, K. Richard. (2005). "Literature, Community and Violence: Reading African Literature in the West, Post-9/11," *Research in African Literature RAL*, 36(2), 46–58.

Quadri, Zainab. (2015). "*Ghana Must Go* by Taiye Selasi." www.pulse.ng/book-review-ghana-must-go-by-taiye-selasi/j06fyvw. (Retrieved: 15/8/2019).

Salami, Minna. (2013). "Can Africans Have Multiple Subcultures? A Response to 'Exorcising Afropolitanism'." www.msafropolitan.com/2013/04/canafricans-hve-multiple-subcultures-a-response-to-exorcising-afropilitanism.html. (Retrieved: 27/06/2019).

Salami, Minna. (2014). "Why Afropolitanism?; Afropolitanism 101", *Open Space*, 1(1), 8–10.

Sanai, Layla. (2013). "Review: We Need New Names, by NoViolet Bulawayo: Humour in a Shanty Town? Godknows." www.independent.co.uk/arts/entertainment/books/reviews/we-need-new-names-by-noviolet-bulawayo-8772475.html. (Retrieved: 10/8/2019).

Santana, B. Stephanie. (2013). "Exorcizing Afropolitanism: Binyavanga Wainaina Explains Why 'I Am a Pan-Africanist, Not an Afropolitan' at ASAUK 2012." (Retrieved: 27/6/2019).

Santana, B. Stephanie. (2016). "Exorcising the Future: Afropolitanism's Spectral Origins," *Journal of African Cultural Studies*, 28(1), 120–126. Also on http://africanwords.com. (Retrieved: 23/07/2019).

Selasi, Taiye. (2005). "Bye-Bye Babar," *The Lip Magazine*. thelip.robertsharp.co.uk. (Retrieved: 30/07/2019).

Selasi, Taiye. (2013). *Ghana Must Go*. London: Penguin Books.

Soyinka, Wole. https://quotes.yourdictionary.com. (Retrieved: 1/09/2019).

Tutton, Mark. (2012). "Young, Urban and Savvy, Meet the Afropolitans – CNN.Com", *CNN*. www.cnn.com/2012/17/world/Africa/who-areafropolitans/index.html. (Retrieved: 30/07/19).

Wikipedia. "Afropolitan." www.google.com. (Retrieved: 27/07/2019).

26

TANELLA BONI'S *MATINS DE COUVRE-FEU*

Environmentalism and ecocriticism in African literature

Honoré Missihoun

Introduction

Consonant with ecocriticism as an interdisciplinary study of literature and the environment, Tanella Boni's *Matins de couvre-feu* presents the complex intersections existing between environment and culture. The examination of human experience and the world of an imaginary African country called Zamba reveals the existence of issues that are natural and fabricated. A central impetus in Boni's writings is the resistant reading of power – in its complex colonial, neocolonial, patriarchal, discursive, and material manifestations – in order to unsettle its epistemology, its claims to truth, and its strategies of representation. In this regard, Boni is part of a community of writers who use minority discourse platform and subaltern communication perspectives of mediation that examine the means by which marginalized people have a voice in society by re-focalizing and subverting hegemonic discourse through narrations that unambiguously articulate their identities, interests, anxieties, and dedications. In alignment with these perspectives, in her minority literary discursive aesthetics, Boni explores diverse thematic concerns, particularly the environment, Mother Nature, and patriarchy, and contributes in diverse ways to literature, culture, society, and politics.

Drawing on critical perspectives informed by postcolonial ecocriticism, ecofeminism, and minority discourse theories, this chapter focuses on cultural attitudes towards nature and women. It examines, among others, how the role that nature plays in Tanella Boni's *Matins de couvre-feu* (*Mornings under Curfew*) reflects environmental concerns the author expresses in other works. The chapter will tap Boni's thoughts from her work "The Polluting of the World and the Silence of African Writers", a text which might be well interpreted as an environmentalist manifesto for African writers and which encapsulates Boni's environmental consciousness.

Highlighting the writer's ecological consciousness and her approach to ecological issues in *Matins de couvre-feu*, my analytical strategy will use a socioliterary methodology: the analysis will allow more elbow room for recourse to out-of-text elements, particularly history, sociodiscursive borrowings, and eco-sociology. The analysis, in its broad shaping of thinking, will comprise three major parts: theorizing to integrate *Matins de couvre-feu* in the broad interdisciplinary field of criticism of discourse known in environmental literary studies as postcolonial ecocriticism and ecofeminism to which, for this analytical circumstance, I incorporate "subaltern communication". After summarizing the novel and highlighting its discursive typology, the analysis will concentrate on deciphering Tanella Boni's environmental consciousness.

Postcolonial ecocriticism and ecofeminism: *Matins de couvre-feu* as a minority discourse

Ecocriticism as environmentalist cultural criticism moves beyond science, geography, and social science into the humanities. As subaltern communication in minority discourse in postcolonial literary production, environmental disputes raise the questions of neo-colonialism, the political power of multinational corporations, and the industrialization of developing countries. Boni's environmentalism is subaltern communication in minority discourses in African literature, as "The Polluting of the World and the Silence of African Writers" (*Eco-Imagination*, 27–39), a story exposing a scandal of Western deliberate pollution in the Third World became part of her memory. In 2006, a multinational company, Trafigura, was involved in a deadly polluting scandal in Abidjan, the capital city of Côte d'Ivoire. Trafigura dumped toxic wastes in the city, in neighboring districts, and around the edge of the lagoon. Hundreds perished, and thousands suffered contamination and long-term damages. This example shows the extent to which Africa has become a dustbin for the West to dump its toxic wastes. These postcolonial realities of the new devastating trends of global capitalism in the South find their way into the literary representation of minority discourses. This analysis will expand its environmentalist, ecocritical, and ecofeminist literary project by delving deeply into Boni's *Matins de couvre feu*.

Richard Kerridge's view on literature in *Writing the Environment* is interesting when he states that most of the concerns raised in the environmental disputes do not belong readily to the conventional domain of 'literature', so much as to 'science' or 'politics', indeed, relegating environmental sensibilities to the category of subaltern communication. He goes on to mention that literature, like the other arts, has been positioned in British education as one of the 'humanities', a humanizing sphere, a refuge from the harsher, depersonalized cultures of technology and business. He is of the view that sometimes this can be too neat a separation, consigning literature to a part of life called 'leisure', from which it has little influence on 'real life'. There are similarities between this treatment of literature and the construction of 'nature', in pastoral, as a separate space, a place of refuge from the urban and the modern.

In theorizing literature as representation, Kerridge and Mitchell share the view that even purely "aesthetic" representation of fictional persons and events can never be completely divorced from political and ideological questions; one might argue, in fact, that representation is precisely the point where these questions are most likely to enter the literary work. Mitchell summarizes his argument as "If literature is a 'representation of life,' then representation is exactly the place where 'life,' in all its social and subjective complexity, gets into the literary work" (15). This argument enhances the postcolonial perspective of subaltern communication, and Boni is eloquent in her agreement with Kerridge and Mitchell in her work "Polluting of the World" when she writes "Literature as any other form of expression of thought and sensibility cannot exist outside its time. Like other subjects, literature . . . has to borrow from the trends of its era, the worries, happy moments and aspirations of the moment" (*Ecoimagination*, 35).

Expanding on literature as art in *The Literary Artist as Social Critic*, Thomas Kakonis and Barbara Desmarais quote the poet-philosopher Friedrich Nietzsche's "no artist tolerates reality" and Albert Camus, the existentialist writer who agreed to this, but added that "no artist can get along without reality" (1). Indeed, reality provides the basis for even the most abstract and imaginative of the artist's conceptions, and the shared experience of reality permits him to communicate with other men. However, the artist does not only stop at reproducing reality. Kakonis and Desmarais make the point that "with the tool of his medium, the artist goes on not only to represent but to shape reality, for in essence the function of the artist is not reproductive but creative: he arranges, he orders, he selects. In short, he imposes form." To impose form is to alter reality, and to the extent that he does so, every artist, particularly the literary artist, becomes a critic of the world he observes around him. Boni is that literary artist and social critic who represents minority sensibilities through subaltern communication in her environmentalism.

Furthermore, accounting for literature as representation, art, and tool of his medium, Kerridge brings the literary artist to task by stating: "So the challenge environmentalism poses to literature is this: show how it feels, here and now. Dramatize the occurrence of large events in individual lives. Make contact between the public and the personal, in accordance with the Green maxim: 'Think globally, act locally'" (6). Boni's concept of "habitability of the world" aligns well with the Green maxim.

This slogan espouses well the concept of subaltern communication and echoes the feminist principle that "the personal is political". Each challenges a dominant ideology that draws boundaries and declares things separate. However, environmentalism has a political weakness in comparison with feminism. In this regard, Kerridge wrote in *Writing the Environment*:

> Green politics cannot easily be, like feminism, a politics of personal liberation and empowerment . . . Nevertheless, there is an important body of thought in feminism, which argues that the beliefs and institutions that oppress women are largely those that cause environmental damage, and that feminism and ecology can make common cause under the heading 'ecofeminism'.
>
> *(5)*

In the production of postcolonial literary representation of Mother Nature through ecocriticism and ecofeminism, feminist ecologists have looked at the male tradition of identifying women with nature. While some feminists have rejected the pairing of women with nature, demanding access to the traditionally male domains of scientific rationality, ecofeminists and environmentalists have explored its history and the advantages that lie in retaining it, turning a negative to a positive. Environmentalism, through ecocriticism and ecofeminism, brings rationalist science and technological capitalism under intense scrutiny, questioning through literary representations and demands a revaluation of qualities traditionally associated with both nature and women.

Just as Kerridge brings the literary artist to task in his view on literature, Boni interrogates the role of the writer and literature. On the heels of Trafigura large polluting scandal, releasing a skeptical sigh in the face of the environmental disaster, Boni stated: "What can writers and their words say in favor of the protection and preservation of the environment in Africa? Even if they make their voices heard, would they be listened to? And who will?" (35).

Tanella Boni and environmental consciousness

The literary critic and poet Tanure Ojaide says: "literature is a cultural production" (3). Considering Ojaide's thought, Boni expresses her frustration as today's African literature is barely fulfilling its role as cultural production, and contemporary writers are showing paucity in aesthetic sensibilities as culture producers and social critics. Literature is produced and received in agreement or disagreement with the dominant ideas and the media, as well as all means of production and broadcasting used at a given period of society's evolution. Paradoxically, as important meetings on the environment and global warming are held in rapid succession internationally, African literature is shy in ecological engagement which will narrate the concerns of scholars and decision-makers. Boni expresses her worries on the paucity of young African writers' thoughts on the environment in the following words: "Although, social and political difficulties can be omnipresent, the 'habitability of the world' will continue to be in question and pollution in Africa is to me a crucial topic which must be foregrounded" (36).

Indeed, a glance at Boni's fiction or her integrating environmentalism to literary text shows strong concerns for the environment, what Raymond Hounfodji calls "conscience écologique" [ecological consciousness]. According to Hounfodji, "ecological consciousness" is the interest and attention for the thematic trilogy: nature, environment, and ecological problems. Therefore, writers demonstrate ecological consciousness when their works display ecoimagination, when their imaginary and literary creation overarches that trilogy. Developing ecoimagination in the work purports embracing nature and the environment; it is an engagement with environmental preoccupations and, at times, with problem-solving commitment. It is important to draw once again attention to Boni's consciousness by repeating, "Each Human Being is the Source of Time", where she reminded the young person she creates of the changing climatic conditions from one century to the other and the unavoidable reality floods and droughts have become.

The environmentalist concern of Boni is not only local. It is also global. Her environmentalism is a consistent focus in 1999 UNESCO publication project whose book's title was *Letters to Future Generations*. The challenge was to project oneself into the future, as the question raised was "What message would you have for people who would live in 2050?" For the book, scholars, philosophers, and writers proposed texts in which the concept of responsibility appeared clearly. In fact, twentieth-century thinkers from the five continents acknowledged that they were leaving behind, among others, a world threatened by all sorts of dangers, particularly the degradation of the environment.

On a par with other environmentalists worldwide, Boni remains a fervent advocate for issues akin to the environment. A career philosopher, she is also one of the most prolific writers of sub-Saharan Africa. Her multi-generic work covers essays, poetry, and fiction. Her ecocritical sensibility shows a high environmental consciousness. Indeed, her profound environmental sensibility reflects Julia Tosic's definition of ecocriticism, which emphasizes the relationships humans maintain with nature in which they live. We capture Boni's environmental sensibility through the titles of some of her works: *Les baigneurs du lac rose* (1995), *La fugue d'Ozone* (1992), *Gorée île baobab* (2004), *Grain de sable* (1993), *Labyrinthe* (1984). The composition and combination of the terms of these titles refer one way or the other to the lexical and semantic field of nature and environment. Pondering these para-textual elements along with the contents of the texts highlights the writer's sharp interest in environmental health and preoccupation with ecology.

My work, in its broad shaping, will comprise two major parts: after summarizing the novel and highlighting its discursive typology, the analysis will concentrate on deciphering Tanella Boni's environmentalism as subaltern communication in minority discourses.

Matins de couvre-feu and discursive typology

In "Exploring the Gendered Nature of National Violence: The Intersection of Patriarchy and Civil Conflict in Tanella Boni's *Matins de Couvre-feu* (Morning under Curfew)" (Wagadu 125–147), Janice Spleth wrote a synoptic account on the novel. Spleth's textual summary inspires the first part of this analysis, and the focus is only on Boni's environmentalism as subaltern communication in minority discourse.

Various types of discourses form the enunciative plot of the novel and articulation of its many stories. In his reflection in "Conscience écologique dans *Matins de couvre-feu*", Hounfodji has recourse to *L'Archéologie du savoir* by Michel Foucault. He elaborates on the Foucauldian literary theory, which advances and theorizes the notion of "discursive formations" defined as "a kind of unifying network of social discourses" (108). We should understand the expression "social discourse" within the context literary theorist, Marc Angenot, uses it, that is, the conglomerate of everything that society says and writes. It is then faithful to his notion of discursive formations that Foucault claims in *L'Ordre du discours* that "One and same literary work may contain, simultaneously, very distinct types of discourses" (26). This postulate underscores that the literary discourse in general and the novelistic in particular is a constellation, a conglomerate of diverse discourses that thrive by fertilizing one another. *Matins de couvre-feu* is not an exception to the rule; it presents itself, above all, as a discursive and narrative complex of subaltern communication of minority discourse, including environmentalism.

Matins de couvre-feu, indeed, is a narrative complex in the sense that it is made up of various stories woven the one into the other to form the four major parts of the story or stories of the novel that opens up on admonition and closes on epilogue. The novel shares the characteristics of a polyphonic and polysemous narrative complex, as there are many narrative voices who tell many stories that gravitate around the one narrated by the protagonist-narrator. The logical results of this narrative complexity are that the novel accumulates many types of discourses. However, to remain in the main of this analysis, focus will be on the discourse relating to the triptych "nature-environment-ecological problems".

Matins de couvre-feu: deciphering Tanella Boni's environmental consciousness

As a discourse on the environment, the novel operates and systematizes the ecological consciousness of Tanella Boni. Owing to politics, ecoimagination does not have the lion's share of the novel. However, through the pages, though martyred by the troubling political situation of her country fallen prey to the devils of division and war, the protagonist-narrator of the novel does not hesitate to bring, as much as possible, environmental concerns to the forefront. Just by coincidence, one of the narrator's brothers she has never met before is an expert in ecology, whereas she herself has a passion for nature and the environment. Attentive reading reveals that the environmental discourse in the novel is organized into two key movements of ideas. The narrator, in fact, portrays nature and the environment as sources of well-being for all living entities, and urbanization, an environmental tsunami, destroying everything in its path.

To illustrate the nature/urbanization dualism in the novel, I will have recourse to Guy Midiohouan, who identifies three eras in the evolution and treatment of African literary discourse: the period of stability, the period of rupture, and the period of the search of the lost paradise. Two important observations appear clear from Midiohouan's view. Although the institutionalization of African literature dates back to just a few decades, African writers, right from the inception, tackled the environmental challenge confronting them and their countries. How they represent those problems varies from one period to the other and reflects above all the sociological climate and geopolitical debates that inspire them. The second observation is that there is a perfect synchronism between the third point of the conclusion and the ecological discourse in *Matins de couvre-feu*.

This leads back to the first movement of ideas relating to Boni's environmental consciousness in the novel. She professes her generous exaltation for the environment and her intimate proximity with nature. To bolster my reflection on Boni's work, similar to Hounfodji, I will expand my view on nature and the environment in literature by referring to J.-J. Rousseau. Like Rousseau and many other writers of their different eras, Boni considers nature, her "intimate environment", an abode of peace and harmony where she takes refuge from the stifling surrounding world. The following metaphoric lines from her text "Le secret du papayer" in her *De l'autre côté du soleil* are quite eloquent to that end: "The sun is at its height. A young boy plays in the green grass. He seems to be having a refreshing bath in a water stream, or in a river, or in the sea; he feels very happy. Now and then, he stretches himself, walks slowly, scratches his head" (5).

We apprehend the intentions of the writer in these lines as an apologetic speech for the environment. She underscores the harmonious connection of peace and refreshment that the "young boy" entertains with that abode, the "intimate environment". The boy makes out of "the green grass" a protective shield from the harmful heat of the sunrays and the stifling surroundings. We then understand lauding the benefits of the natural environment constitutes a recurrent paradigmatic thematic in Boni's fiction. It is recurrent in *Matins de couvre-feu*.

In fact, reading into her childhood life, the protagonist-narrator recalls her obsession with nature as follows: "This is how since my tender childhood, I have learnt to explore my intimate environment. I met the animals; I spoke with them; I also followed the fowls and turkeys with their extraordinary parading that captured my attention hours on end" (164). This reminding of the narrator's past life and her love for the company of animals is quite emblematic of her adult life. In the chain of the living entities on earth, the fauna represent the species closest to humans. Nevertheless, as the years of modernity unfold, the cousinship links dwindle and weaken more and more. From natural companions, most of the animals have become play objects for men. When we have not confined them to zoological parks for visitors' voyeuristic pleasure, we then park them in poaching reservations. This allusion of the narrator to her childhood and her close connection to animals takes the form of a love cry to reconnect the broken secular links between human and animals. For instance, she considers her dog Jupiter a faithful guardian, "fidèle gardien" (76). There is woven between them an ontological link of mutual dependence and confidence.

We understand the childhood life conditions of the protagonist-narrator; as a country girl, she cultivated a profound relationship with her natural environment. She might inherit her strong passion for nature from her mother who, despite all the constraints of traditions, comforts herself that "Nature is radiant with joy" (136). This explains the narrator's disorientation and lack of comfort in the urban milieu where artificial commodities have, largely, replaced the true nature. Moved by that new reality and undergirded by a nostalgic and gregarious spirit, she decided to remedy the lack of nature in her urban life setting. Having "green fingers", she recreates a corner for nature in her house and even goes as far as offering herself a well, even though there are running water taps installed everywhere in the house. Because she loves all that pertains to nature, she prefers the water from the well.

Nevertheless, in an attempt to cast more light on the environmental consciousness of Tanella Boni, I will return later to the water plastic bags, the "artificial commodity" part of the water-selling strategy she deploys to survive house arrest confinement. At this juncture, my analysis will be focused on how Boni represents the trees of her garden, an integral part of the nostalgic, gregarious ecosystem of the childhood rural environment she is trying to transplant to her urban setting. She presents her garden:

> Every morning, I go and see, with by my side, Jupiter, my faithful guardian, if my fruit trees are faring well. The lemons start ripening. I am not sure whether to utilize them for fresh juices in the restaurant or, as I think of it, leave my door open for possible home clients. Nobody forbids this, anyway. The passion fruit are still green. There are

yet those mango trees in flowers, that coconut tree, and that frangipani tree which, in the dry season, fills the front of the house with its scent.

(76)

The protagonist-narrator presents here panoplies of advantages nature offers, particularly trees.

For her, nature is not only a source of wellbeing and protection; it is also a source of good health and nourishing food. Furthermore, it is a source of income. Drawing from natural pharmacopeia, the narrator variously boasts the virtues of lemon. Her emphasis on the therapeutic qualities of lemon throughout the novel borders on mnemonics. She seems to inculcate in the readers that the lemon source of C vitamin is natural, within the reach of everyone, and practically free of charge.

As this first movement of ideas reveals in the novel, Boni's environmental consciousness narrows down to the passion, the attachment of the protagonist-narrator to the environment and all she finds positive in nature. She affirms this eloquently in "Nothing is worth the proximity of the mountain or of the sea so far away, inaccessible to the eyes, so close to the heart, so beneficial to the skin" (30). It is out of her deep passion for the environment that she is a dedicated advocate for nature. For according to the narrator, the world is an ecosystem where everything has its place, its role and importance. The elements of that infinite ensemble are, up to some extent, correlated, and when disrupted, the chain ceases functioning naturally. We understand the narrator has a good apprehension of the environmental ecosystem. This is why she proceeds to the creation of a corner for nature in her house to benefit from its effects. Throughout the novel, she explains the important place her orchard has in her personal life during her nine-month house arrest. She takes refuge there not only to shield from the stifling political atmosphere of Zamba but more to remedy somewhat the annoyances caused by urbanization. In the cycle of nine months, she gives birth to new nourishing ideas on the living environment and nature.

Tanella Boni: environmental consciousness and the phenomenon of urbanization

Referring to Midiohouan's *Mots Pluriels*, the preceding considerations on Boni's environmental consciousness logically lead to the second movement of ideas in the writer's ecological consciousness in *Matins de couvre-feu*. Here, her environmental consciousness emanates from a scathing criticism of the phenomenon of urbanization and its very damaging implications for nature and living beings. Recurrently, the protagonist-narrator's speech is an indictment of the encroaching urbanization of her country and its effects on ecology. Taking the narrator at her words, big cities kill the environment and traditions:

In Zambaville, the daily life of the people has changed at a break-neck speed. Everyone feels like living in the city while memories continue to cling to old stories which no longer have any connection with the habits of the megalopolis, Zambaville, where there is no sacred forest, where community life, in the open air, has become so difficult; where the extended brotherhood cannot be what it once was. Animals have gone extinct and ancestral worship rituals going downhill.

(24–25)

This passage substantially condenses all the environmental discourses of the novel. It is a concentrated epitome of criticism and exposure of the ecological issues Boni is eager to use to sensitize the reading audience and, more probably, the policy decision-makers. The characterization of urbanization in Zamba, and likely in most African nations, is a tsunami. It destroys everything in its path with unspeakable consequences. It is the cause of the overpopulation of cities fueled by the youth drift to town, deserting rural communities. Everybody goes to the city in quest of a better life, of an illusory prosperity, of a deceitful happiness. It is a pure mirage that barely considers social realities.

If we still consider the critical extent of the passage, urban centers, the new Eldorado, in the eyes of immigrants, create more problems than they resolve. They offer a completely different climate of life where traditions encounter contradictions, which literally lead to extinction. They present new existential social settings where community life and effective goodwill lose their traditional meanings and quintessence and give way to the selfish logic, gangrene of modern societies.

Furthermore, in order to answer certain needs, such as the construction of road and estate infrastructure, nature bears the toll. Nature suffers lethal blows because the flora is subject to highway construction erosion; it is driven into a corner or, in the worst-case scenario, entirely wiped out. The loss of trees and forests implies a paucity of the fauna. However, the violence done to nature by man through city construction is not recent. It dates back to colonial times when the new colonists started building broader ways to replace the snaking rural paths in the woods and savannahs. Speaking of the different environmental changes that occurred while her mother awaited the uncertain return of her father from the war he volunteered to fight in Europe, the protagonist-narrator says ten years growing, she witnessed the disappearance of the forest, in the literal as well as the metaphoric sense, tall trees fell one after the other, except the kapok trees of which everybody is scared, even the Whites; there were roads and tracks everywhere. (133)

An attentive reading of the narrator's message, however, reveals that she is not criticizing urbanization just for the sake of doing so. In fact, as a social critic, she centers her scathing remark above all on urbanization without conscience and unplanned development. A nation may develop well by harmoniously integrating traditions and modernity; in a nutshell, by preserving nature and the environment, albeit building modern infrastructures.

Boni's environmental consciousness as subaltern communication in a minority discourse of postcolonial ecocriticism and ecofeminism reflects environmental concerns of some new sociocritical African environmentalists. Questions raised by critic Obari Gomba's "Niger Delta Dystopia" (*Eco-Critical Literature*, 239–271) support Boni's nation-building plea for the harmonious integration of traditions and modernity. In his analysis of "The Goat Song" in Ojaide's *The Tale of the Harmattan*, Gomba draws attention to the issues of the environment and industrialization with rhetorical questions: "Is it possible for industry and modernity to treat the environment with care? Could there be a better way to extract oil . . .? Are there examples to prove that development can be sensitive to nature?" The poem "Transplants" shows that the persona finds development does not necessarily have to be destructive. "I see transplants of my youth's landscape," says the poem, "first at Hawthorden and now at Steepletop: the pristine streams, the multi-ethnic population of plants, costumed birds, and graceful game."

Hawthorden and Steepletop prove that development is not a negation of environmental protection. Boni and Gomba, in the community of postcolonial ecocritical and ecofeminist writers of subaltern communication in minority discourses, agree that enterprise must understand the need for "all members of the natural world – humans, animals, plants, rocks, oceans, winds – to live healthier and happier lives in a vigorously healthy earth" (McDowell 26).

Tanella Boni: environmental consciousness and politics

After the broad criticism built against urbanization and its implications for the natural environment, the protagonist-narrator also takes the political leaders of her country to task and exposes their nonchalance in tackling ecological urgencies. Lacking in adequate environmental and political planning, government seems to close its eyes on ecological problems and gives the impression of not caring about them. In an effort to denounce governmental inertia to ecological urgency, the narrator repeatedly evokes those issues through strident descriptions and allusions in *Matins de couvre-feu*. It is in this thread of ideas that she depicts at length her visit to the slummiest areas of Zambaville. This is her account of the social realities she encounters:

> I saw Zambaville as I had never seen before, a squalid city swarming with maggot-like crowds on heaps of refuse. I needed to witness this to measure the gap between the fantastic speeches of the redeeming Angels of Zamba sent to rid the people off all the misfortunes of the world and the maggot lives adjacent to polluted waters, dustbins of all the miseries of Zamba piled up in the Bas-fonds, a name well found for a neighborhood just above or almost under water. Yet, it is where I found women standing tall, aware of their fates and interests, not of the maggots or animals.
>
> *(185–186)*

Passages of the kind are legion, and their recurrence sounds alarms and highlights the environmental consciousness of the writer. As an attentive observer, through this depiction of the city and its seediest areas, the narrator brings to light the ecological unconsciousness, the environmental illiteracy of the political elite. They seem to have resigned their leadership responsibility in the face of the environmental challenge confronting their city. Indeed, the description of the Bas-fonds that the narrator characterizes in other terms as a "squalid corner" or "very little comforting, unhealthy environment" shows that this neighborhood and its dwellers are squarely abandoned to their fate. The image of fetidity that presents the hyperbolic comparison expressed in the second sentence of the passage paints the true feelings of the narrator. The Bas-fonds vegetates in a state of total rottenness, and its dwellers live and work in inhuman, totally unacceptable conditions. In this environment of garbage and miseries, sanitary risks are incalculable: "And malaria found there, all year round, a favorable environment for its fast expansion" (187). In short, for the narrator, social realities contradict the political discourses of the leaders. If the latter are not showing bad faith, they then seem to not truly apprehend the value of nature, the imminent conditions of the environmental dangers, and the looming ecological disaster.

The examples and passages that I have so far presented in this reflection show without a shred of ambiguity that *Matins de couvre-feu* is an environmentalist discourse, which supports the ecological consciousness of Boni. She is undoubtedly environmentalist. However, it is fair to draw a critical attention to her environmentalism, which presents some boundaries we do not see in feminism and ecofeminism. In support of my criticism, I will once again quote Kerridge from *Writing the Environment*: "Green politics cannot easily be, like feminism, a politics of personal liberation and empowerment. Often it seems to be the reverse: a politics insisting on restraint and self-denial, the curbing of consumption and pleasure" (5). In fact, *Matins de couvre-feu*, while striving to be sociorealist and subaltern communication in minority discourse in the representation of the environment and social life of the dregs of society in the Bas-fonds of Zambaville, raises important theoretical and conceptual questions, which coincide with the third point of Midiohouan's conclusion on African literature and the environmental discourse of *Matins de couvre-feu*.

Boni's ecological consciousness: environmentalism and ecofeminism border-crossing

The genuine engagement of *Matins de couvre-feu* in the salvation of nature, indeed, presents an ironically sour note that flies in the face of Boni's environmentalism. We understand that the protagonist-narrator of the novel nourishes a fervent passion for the environment while exhibiting profound disarray for the aftermaths of improvised and ill-conceived urbanization. She also blames the nonchalant and ecologically unconscious political leadership of the country. Nonetheless, she is not totally guilt free with regard to the problems that confront the environment. Consciously or unconsciously, she contributes to the pollution she is denouncing; she is a polluting agent who is not aware. The following passage vindicates this assertion:

> I sold also clean water that, as it were, tasted like mineral water. My water was of an exceptional quality compared with all the other polluted waters selling in the city, coming out of rusty pipes or smelling chlorine. I put it in bottle or, for the poorest who could not give but coins, I filled with water plastic bags of all sizes and there were for every purse.
>
> *(163)*

Through this passage, the narrator explains why she sells drinking water: she exposes government inability to provide the same quality of water to the people. She puts the blame on the governing authorities because not only are they not capable of providing the people with clean water, moreover, they cannot even maintain in good hygienic conditions the hydraulic installations that need renewing. The narrator is of the good faith she has found a simple solution for a problem government deems not urgent to resolve.

However, even if she is able to do what the municipal authorities are incapable of performing, that is, providing her neighbors or the people of her neighborhood with clean water from her well, "the plastic bags of all sizes" she uses are serious polluting problems in Africa. In a brief antithetic approach to the protagonist-narrator's environmental consciousness, to illustrate the imminence of the hazards posed by the plastic bags in *Matins de couvre-feu*, Hounfodji's analysis refers to a series of articles published on the Internet site on *UN Volontaires*. For instance, considering the case of Burkina Faso, "7000 Hours in the Service of Volunteering for the Environment" exposes in detail the ecological dangers posed by the excessive usage of plastic bags. The analysis clearly expresses that the uncontrolled usage of plastic bags constitutes an issue of collective consciousness. The following observations bring more to light the collateral dangers of the modern commodity plastic bags have become:

> Plastic bags are a plague in most of sub-Saharan Africa. In Burkina Faso, quasi every public space is a true heap of rubbish where plastic bags abound and create serious environmental hazards. Data show that 30% of cattle mortality is due to ingestion of plastic . . . Plastic bags are incinerated in rustic depots, releasing polluting toxic gas into the atmosphere. Furthermore, spread all over the ground, plastic bags hamper water infiltration. This may undermine the development of agriculture.

Usage of plastic bags has reached endemic proportions across the globe. Thanks to their handy convenience, plastic bags lure many environmentalists such as the protagonist-narrator into using them unaware. In fact, it is clear that the ecological dangers that plastic bags represent for her so-cherished "intimate environment" escapes the narrator. At this juncture, I will bring into focus the ambivalent anthropocentric development the narrator presents in her thought, which straddles Grey Williams's patriarchal Green Philosophy and Val Plumwood's critical challenge to that cosmic anthropocentrism.

In fact, bringing the "polluting water bags" into focus is a wedge in Boni's environmental consciousness to show that even though the novel sometimes leans towards objective realism and subaltern communication, such as its graphic depiction of the social realities of the Bas-fonds, it remains an imaginary world where creativity allows vision and intentionality. Thanks to its literary and creative breadth, and sociocritical multi-facetedness, *Matins de couvre-feu*, indeed, presents an anthropocentric facet, which deserves critical attention.

Theorist Val Plumwood maintains that feminist and ecofeminist exposure of masculinism in environmental thinking is sometimes portrayed as carping (327). This portrait overlooks the positive theoretical improvements feminist theory brings to environmental thought as it applies feminist models and understandings to the concepts of environmental philosophy. Theorizing anthropocentrism in *Matins de couvre-feu*, I will have recourse to William Grey (1993), the latest of those who declare the search for a non-anthropocentric ethic "a hopeless quest." The protagonist-narrator in *Matins de couvre-feu* does not declare the hopelessness of the non-anthropocentrism of Green philosophy. However, her ecological unawareness of the imminent hazards "water bags" represent for the natural environment illustrates anthropocentrism at the individual and microcosmic level. Expanding my criticism, it is easy to assert how global capitalism, through consumerism, expansion of lucrative ventures of mineral, forest felling and crude oil extraction, and over-predation of marine life, has become a threat to the global ecosystem. In this regard, Boni is cognizant of the ecological tragedy in Nigeria's Niger Delta. She also stridently denounces Trafigura's toxic wastes dumping in Abidjan early this century. (*Ecoimagination*, 27–39)

Plumwood's criticism of Grey's anthropocentrism is that Grey's eco-philosophy reminisces about 17th-century scientific revolution logic, which laid out the premises for industrial revolution and western imperialism and predation on the colonized world. Though Grey's reflection on anthropocentrism may somewhat be vindicated by *Matins de couvre-feu* protagonist's money-making venture to survive house arrest, Plumwood's argument is strong enough to challenge Grey's capitalistic implication for nature across the globe. Also, Boni's own "The Polluting of the World and the Silence of African Writers" (*Ecoimagination*) is an eloquent challenge to cosmic anthropocentrism.

Plumwood is of the view that ethical consideration, to the extent that it involves treating others with sensitivity and consideration for their welfare, often seems to require some version of putting ourselves in the other's place, seeing the world from the perspective of a creature with its own needs and experiences rather than our own. Here, Plumwood echoes Boni's environmentalism. This may involve some form of transcendence of our own location, but it does not require us to eliminate our own location, rooting out any trace of our own experience and concern for our own needs. Indeed, it will be fair enough to envision the protagonist-narrator's "water bags" episode in this context of "location". If we assumed moral consideration to require eliminating our own location, the argument would seem to lead towards ethical solipsism or egoism in the human case just as much as in nonhuman. Critical thinking illuminates. Plumwood's argument challenging Grey's Green philosophy mitigates the protagonist-narrator's necessity to maintain, somewhat, "a location" where survival under house arrest requires her to venture into bagged water selling.

Boni's environmentalism and the limitations of ecocriticism and ecofeminism

The intersection of patriarchy and environmental consciousness in Boni's *Matins de couvre-feu* shares the view that certain attributes are intrinsically feminine within the gendered universe of the text. Despite the changing roles of women, Boni's narrator shares at least one important characteristic with her mother, that of nurturer, a concept dear to the environmentalism of subaltern communication and minority discourse, which is at the core of environmentalism in African literature and culture. She is, after all, the proprietress of a restaurant. During the period of her isolation when she can no longer depend on the restaurant for income, she has to find some way of supporting herself. Again, we come to the water well in her home, a dynamic semantic. Not written in stone, the well expands the protagonist-narrator's social role to the traditional function of woman in society. It allows selling drinking water to her neighbors and also making and selling juices from her own fruit trees. This is not only a means of assuaging their thirst but also a way of raising their spirits. She said "The poor folk know that it is necessary to care for the heart and the liver in order to stand up to the chaos caused by the lengthy curfew" (2005). She also distributes water and juices to children who come to play in her house. She has become a good woman in her turn without really having the temperament. By becoming the guardian of the land producing the water and the fruit juices that serve as source of sustenance and refreshment for her neighbors, she is a representation of Gaia, an African deity of the environment and place. As such, she refuses reductionism to the "other" as would theorize western ecofeminism, and she epitomizes the social agent of subaltern communication Boni represents in her environmentalism of minority discourse.

The idea that woman protects nature is a fundamental principle of ecocriticism and ecofeminism. The concept of ecofeminism is relevant in *Matins de couvre-feu*. It supports my analysis not only because many of its branches, including cultural ecofeminism, that view women as having an inherently protective role with respect to nature but also because ecofeminism responds to the hierarchical dominance of patriarchy and represents both woman and nature as victims of masculinity. In this vein, M. Mies and V. Shiva (1993) wrote, "We see the devastation of the earth . . . by the corporate warriors as feminist concerns. It is the manifestation of the same masculinist mentality, which would deny our right to our own bodies and sexuality, and which depends on multiple systems of dominance and state power to have its way" (14).

Some forms of ecocriticism and ecofeminism draw a parallel between man's tendency to construct nature as irrational, chaotic, and needing to be controlled and the propensity to impute similar characteristics to women. My analysis of *Matins de couvre-feu* is a way to take western ecocriticism and ecofeminism to task by showing their intellectual limitations as literary and critical theories in the humanities. Tanella Boni's environmentalism reflects the subaltern communication so prevalent in minority discourses, particularly in African literary tradition, an important segment of which is environmentalism. Boni's environmentalism challenges the strict female/male dualism through *Matins de couvre-feu* as minority discourse. The novel is subaltern communication, a perspective of mediation that examines the means by which marginalized entities have a voice in their existing setting by re-focalizing and subverting hegemonic discourse through narrations that authentically articulate their identities, interests, anxieties, and dedications. Within this framework of subaltern communication and minority discourse, women, men, and the natural environment perceive one another as rational, ordered, and capable of providing control and direction for one another.

Conclusion

In "Pollution as a Threat on Every Type of Life" (*Ecoimagination*, 28–31), Tanella Boni presents environmental pollution not as just affecting one individual but thousands of people. It can be considered a phenomenon whose causes and consequences can be determined, responsibility established, and solutions offered so it does not reoccur. There are international rules, declarations, and agreements to this effect. However, to avoid polluting our environment, action depends on local political decisions. Boni refers pragmatically to the type of pollution that is not only imaginary or mythic but also one that can be thought about rationally as a dateable and historical fact that has quantifiable and disastrous consequences which may be unquantifiable in the long run.

From a philosophical standpoint, one may think about environmental pollution phenomena as consequences of modern life apprehended in the epistemological context of "taking control and possession" of nature, an idea expressed by Descartes in the 17th century. A new concept of work and production came to light, and man manufactured and consumed on scales never known before. Thus, pollution is, to a large extent, linked to the ecological marks man has left on nature that he no longer worships nor respects. However, it is well known that some regions in the world resisted for a long time the idea of letting technology rule nature. Africa was one of such places where human beings still tried to live in harmony with nature. Yet, today, the breakdown seems to be total, with colonization, independence, development, and all kinds of misunderstood or ill-applied ideologies in the continent. Africa is now part of a fast-changing world which cannot escape the pollution of the planet Earth regardless of its causes.

Reading critic Hounfodji, I found Catherine Ndiaye's *Gens de sable* interesting. In the post face of the novel, she declared: "I am not a victim of the myth of purity; I admire A. Malraux for being political without this obliterating his style. But it appears that, in the Third World, politics always ends up devouring everything" (158–159). This presumption gets on the wrong side of *Matins de couvre-feu*. A synoptic view of the typology of the novel discourses in this work reveals that the era of purely political novels is long gone. While tackling serious political problems affecting her country and Africa, Boni's sociocritical attention is also on other issues, such as those concerning women and the environment. The ecological discourse running through *Matins de couvre-feu* translates the environmental consciousness of the writer. Nature, for her, is a very precious entity that must be preserved at all costs for all the benefits it yields.

Matins de couvre-feu, as subaltern communication, eloquently informs Val Plumwood's ecocritical and ecofeminist theory on Green philosophy by taking ecofeminism to task, challenging androcentrism and anthropocentrism, and expressing the devastating effects global capitalism has on the natural environment. Boni makes the point stridently in the novel that we rely on nature to provide us a place to live, food to eat, and water to drink. Without it, we would not survive.

Works like *Matins de couvre-feu* help us to further our understandings of how we write and think about the environment. Boni points out how the natural environment shapes gender identities and the ways in which environmental literature represents the experiences of women and nature in capitalist and patriarchal cultures. Ecocritical analysis of *Matins de couvre-feu* helps us to understand the conceptual framework for the study of the relationships between literature and the physical environment. Works such as Tanella Boni's ecological fiction, particularly *Matins de couvre-feu*, encourage us to reflect on the environment and our relationships with it.

Works cited

"7000 heures au service du volontariat pour l'environnement". 15 Déc. 2009. Web. 27 Sept. 2012. www.unv.org/fr/activites/pays/burkina-faso/doc/7-000-heures-au.html.

Boni, Tanella. *Matins de couvre-feu: Roman*. Paris: Serpent à plumes, 2005. Print.

Boni, Tanella. *Labyrinthe*. Lomé: Editions Akpagnon, 1984.

Boni, Tanella. *La fugue d'Ozone*, Paris: NEA-EDICEF, 1992. Print.

Boni, Tanella. *Grains de sable* (poems). Limoges: Le bruit des autres, 1993.

Boni, Tanella. *Les baigneurs du Lac rose* (novel). Abidjan: Nouvelles Editions Ivoiriennes, 1995. Paris: Editions du Serpent à Plumes, 2002.

Boni, Tanella. *Gorée île baobab* (poems), Trois-Rivières, Québec: Limoges & Ecrits des forges, 2004.

Boni, Tanella. "Ecrire dans l'urgence ou le partage inégal du sensible." *Museum International*, 61 (5), 2009, 44–53.

Boni, Tanella. *Que vivent Les Femmes d'Afrique?* Paris: Panama, 2008. Print.

Boni, Tanella. "The Polluting of the World and the Silence of African Writers." In *Ecoimagination: African and Diasporan Literatures and Sustainability*. Eds. Assiba d'Almeida, T. Pinto, & L. Viakinnou-Brinson. Trenton: Africa World Press, 2013, pp. 13–25.

Foucault, Michel. *L'archéologie du savoir*. Paris: Gallimard, 1969. Print.

Foucault, Michel. *L'ordre du discours*. Paris: Gallimard, 2003. Print.

Gomba, Obari. "Niger Delta Dystopia and Environmental Despoliation in Tanure Ojaide Poetry." In *Eco-Critical Literature: Regreening African Landscapes*. Ed. Ogaga Okuyade. London: African Heritage Press, 2013, pp. 252–253. Print.

Grey, William, "Anthropocentrism and Deep Ecology" *Australasian Journal of Philosophy* 71 (4), 1993, 463–475.

Hounfodji, E. Raymond. "Conscience écologique dans *Matins de couvre-feu*, Roman de Tanella Boni." In *Ecoimagination: African and Diasporan Literatures and Sustainability*. Eds. Assiba d'Almeida, T. Pinto, & L. Viakinnou-Brinson. Trenton: Africa World Press, 2013, pp. 105–122. Print.

Kakonis, Thomas E., & Barbara G.T. Desmarais. "Introduction." In *The Literary Artist as Social Critic*. Beverly Hills: Glencoe Press, 1969. Print.

Kerridge, Richard, & Neil Sammells. Eds. *Writing the Environment: Ecocriticism and Literature*. New York: Zed Books Ltd, 1998. Print.

McDowell, Michael. "Talking about Trees in Stumpton: Pedagogical Problems in Teaching Ecocamp." In *Reading the Earth: New Directions in Study of Literature and Environment*. Eds. Michael P. Branch, Rochelle Johnson, Daniel Patterson, & Scott Slovic. Idaho: University of Idaho Press, 1998, pp. 19–28. Print.

Midiohouan, Guy Ossito. "Le créateur négro-africain et l'environne ment: de la contemplation à l'engagement." *Mots Pluriels*. 11 Sept. 1999. Web. 27 Sept. 2012. http://motspluriels.arts.uwa.edu.au/MP1199gom.html.

Mies, Maria & Vandana Shiva. *Ecofeminism*. Halifax: Frenwood Publications, 1993. Print.

N'Diaye, Catherine. *Gens de sable*. Paris: P.O.L., 1984. Print.

Ojaide, Tanure. *The Tale of the Harmattan*. Cape Town: Kwela Books, 2007. Print.

Ojaide, Tanure. *Contemporary African Literature: New Approaches*. Durham, NC: Carolina Academic Press, 2012.

Plumwood, Val. "Androcentrism and Anthropocentrism: Parallels and Politics." In *Ecofeminism: Women, Culture, Nature*. Ed. Karen J. Warren. Bloomington: Indiana University Press, 1997, pp. 327–351. Print.

Spleth, Janice. "Exploring the Gendered Nature of National Violence: The Intersection of Patriarchy and Civil Conflicts in Tanella Boni's *Matins de couvre-feu* [*Mornings under Curfew*]." *Wagadu: Journal of Transnational Women's and Gender Studies*, 18, Winter, 2017, 125–147.

27

FUTURISTIC THEMES AND SCIENCE FICTION IN MODERN AFRICAN LITERATURE

Dike Okoro

Introduction

According to John Mbiti, Africa's religious worldview is anchored on the existence of spirit beings, spirits and the living-dead or spirits of ancestors (Mbiti 75). This claim is evident in the narratives by many African fiction writers whose stories incorporate characters and traits found in science fiction or fantasy fiction, two genres often mistaken as one and obviously similar in the ways they explore the supernatural, myths, magic and mystery. Over the years, works of fiction by distinguished authors born in Africa and those with parental links to Africa have embodied features that resonate with SF and fantasy fiction. For example, Ben Okri admits: "*The Famished Road* is . . . a perpetual story into which flowed the great seas of African dreams, myths and fables of the world, known and unknown" (*Guardian*). In a recent article published in *The New York Times*, Alexandra Alter describes the novels of Nnedi Okorafor and concludes that they are "Magic, ritual and secrecy are threads that run through . . . a head-spinning menagerie of otherworldly spirits and deities drawn from Nigerian myths and legends." All of these bring back the idea of current trends in modern African fiction and the now widely discussed area of Afrofuturism. The statements by Okri and Alter are apt and help to situate the Afrofuturism in their works and postulate the existence of Afrofuturist modern Africa fiction. I argue in this chapter that much as Afrofuturism in fiction exists in America, based on its definition by Mark Dery, it is essentially associated with black speculative fiction written by African American SF writers. A number of reasons have prompted this argument. First, Dery's definition locates Afrofuturism within the confines of the black experience in the Americas. He states thus: "Speculative fiction that treats African-American themes and addresses African-American concerns in the context of 20th century technoculture.". His definition primarily centers on the existence of black lives in America and has no space allocated to the postcolonial experience in Africa or the myths that exist in indigenous African narratives. I am aware that an argument can be made along the line that the black experience in the Caribbean is similar in myths and spirituality to the black experience in Africa. However, the focus in this chapter hinges on the definition by Dery that isolates the African aspect of Afrofuturism. Therefore, I propose the existence of "Africanfuturism" in modern African fiction, based on examples from specific novels and stories by African writers that are arguably examples of science fiction or fantasy, to argue that "Africanfuturism" does exist and is identifiable in works of fiction by first-generation African fiction writers and the succeeding generations that follow their trail.

African science fiction/fantasy and the question of origin

Prior to the publication and general acceptance of Dery's definition of Afrofuturism, there had been instances of the existence of Afrofuturism in works by black authors. In fact, a lot has been written lately about "Afrofuturism" as both an artistic and cultural movement. From its growing followership in the United States among science fiction writers to its widespread influence in the works of black artists recognized for their Afrocentric and space-related paintings as well as comic strips, the movement seems to have gained ground in the present decade as a result of attempts by culture-conscious blacks in America who see in its rise a valid attempt at the resurgence of the black arts in America and across the globe. The question of what qualifies as African science fiction can be contested, but the argument made by Mark Bould as he traces examples of African authors and books that typify this genre cannot be overlooked. Here is what he wrote: "Depending on your definitions, African science fiction includes some of the most highly regarded of the continent's authors" (Bould). He goes on to name "Algerian Mohammed Dib's *Who Remembers the Sea* (1962), South African J.M. Coetzee's *Waiting for the Barbarians* (1980), Congolese Sony Labou Tansi's *Life and A Half* (1977), Kenyan Ngũgĩ wa Thiong'o's *Wizard of the Crow* (2006), and South African Nadine Gordimer's *July's People* (1981)," among others, as books with elements of fantasy and "imagines an alternate world in which African nations colonised Europe." As an additional background to his argument, Bould also cites "D.O. Fagunwa's *Forest of a Thousand Daemons* (1939) and Amos Tutuola's *The Palm-Wine Drinkard* (1952) to Ben Okri's *The Famished Road* (1991)," as works that frequently verge on the science-fictional. His claims settle any doubt as to the veracity of science in African literature. Much as the term "science fiction" does not occupy a historical platform in the African canon, African writers have produced works that are saturated with features and characters that are synonymous with science fiction or the fantasy genre.

While these developments have in one way or another helped to stir interest in the movement beyond cultural boundaries, there remains to be seen how the movement will take shape in an exclusively African context. Several factors prompt this thought, chief among which is the definition of Afrofuturism. Mark Dery, a white American, is credited with coining the word "Afrofuturism," "but the ideas go much further (indeed, a century-old WEB Dubois science fiction story was discovered just this week" (Thrasher). Thrasher's claim is valid because African science fiction is not a new development in African literature. It has always been there but never recognized. Mark Bould attempts to justify the presence of science fiction in African narratives to support this assertion as he states thus:

> And so it is really no surprise that now, when African science fiction suddenly seems to be everywhere, the media, as prone to amnesia as they are averse to research, presume it did not exist before they condescended to notice it and blithely label it "afrofuturism". But African science fiction can be traced back more than a century, at least as far as Egyptian Muhammad al-Muwaylihi's timeslip satire, *A Period of Time*, which began newspaper serialisation in 1898, and South African Joseph J. Doke's 1913 lost race novel, ‹*The Secret City: A Romance of the Karroo*›.
>
> *(Bould)*

Bould's remark is fascinating and reminds us of how wide a space serious scholarship can be, especially as it positions its implicit argument within the many possibilities that exist in African literature.

Crosscontinental influences and the reclaiming of tradition

Some of the African science fiction writers known today have tapped into orature and the African writers of the past to add vigor and structural relevance to their stories. Nnedi Okorafor's young adult novels are a good example that achieves this blending of traditions so well. In her works that are set in African landscapes, one can find tropes that link her ideas to both an Ibo destiny/Nigerian experience and African writers such as Amos Tutuola. Whether this trend is a deliberate attempt to maintain a relationship with the Nigerian roots in her writing and vision remains open to examination. Perhaps these aspects of her science fiction have been pointed out by Mark Bould, who states thus: "Okorafor's *Zahrah the Windseeker* (2005) is set in the Ooni kingdom, where technology is based on plant-life and some of the plants are intelligent." He goes on to name two other young adult novels by Okorafor and concludes:

> Each of these young adult novels involves a quest and a coming-of-age in a world in which revenant colonial power relations are imbricated into West African postcolonies, into worlds – like those of Tutuola – in which the mythical and supernatural is part of every reality. *Who Fears Death*, which explicitly references *The Palm-Wine Drinkard*, is set in a post-apocalyptic Sudan. The story follows Onyesonwu, a child of wartime interethnic rape shunned by her mother's people and subjected to female genital mutilation, as she develops the magical powers with which to defeat her evil sorcerer father.

The forebears and African futurism

Before I will go on to expound my argument, it is pertinent that I reference the writers whose works represent the founding link connecting those writing science fiction and fantasy in Africa today and their forebears. And, it is understandable to look to past publications in African literature as a source of influence and nurturing role for those writing today. As such, landmark works of such imposing literary forebears such as Daniel O. Fagunwa and Amos Tutuola, both of whom are renowned for their seminal publications, *Forest of A Thousand Daemons* and *The Palm-Wine Drinkard*, respectively; too, the works of Elechi Amadi (*The Concubine*) and Cyprian Ekwensi (*An African Night's Entertainment*) are examples of narratives that possess African futurism. These engaging books deftly utilize characterization, setting, and myths to engage readers with plausible representations of myths and supernatural forces that reflect African reality and society.

Much as African society and reality are linked to an African futuristic ideal, they serve as sources of inspiration for those African writers whose fiction deploy features of magic, myth, superstition, and other identifiable features of Afrofuturism. Not to be excluded from these features are fables addressing African conditions such as military dictatorships, tyranny, corruption in government offices, and others. This bring us to the question of definition. What is African futurism in fiction? Recently, many scholars and writers have made attempts at coming up with a definition, but it is Pamela Satsimo Sunstrum's attempt to situate a definition in her essay "Afro-mythology and African Futurism: The Politics of Imagining and Methodologies for Contemporary Creative Research Practices" that set me thinking when she states that she is "interested in locating an African sensibility with regards to futurism" (114) and goes on to add, "In African futurism, major concerns include postcolonialism, neocolonialisms, transglobal identities, transcultural identities and, . . . [the] transcendence of these historical, geographical, national, political, cultural, economic, and temporal specifiers" (114). I agree with Sunstrum's assessment that African futurism deals with each of the subcategories that she points out. More importantly, I am drawn to the reference to postcolonialism, an area that many African states are still facing.

Another aspect of African futurism that has been explored widely is the age-old experiences of war. The wars that have been witnessed by the continent have been covered in both science fiction and fables. Ngugi wa Thiong'o does a thorough job in *Wizard of Crow* and, according to Mark Bould, "Ugandan filmmaker Dilman [Dila's] *A Killing in the Sun* is arguably the first single-author collection of African science fiction short stories, concerned with the complex identities produced in the postcolony . . . Characters are often adrift in the confusions of war." Nigeria experienced a bloody war in the sixties that obviously appeared uneven, given the swift run to victory claimed by the Federal troops over the Biafran army.

Festus Iyayi's *Heroes* stands on the side of postcolonialism and serves as both a political, historical, and cultural specifier. The protagonist Osime displays a vision that takes neither the Biafran nor Nigerian side but rather accepts that being humanity overrides any other quality in a time of war. He states thus:

> I was on the side of neither the Biafrans nor the Federal troops. I was made neutral by my hatred for both, that is, after the Federal troops took my pass at the stadium and kicked me in my testicles, after they murdered Ndudi's father in cold blood as he ran for the river, after I saw the headless bodies of men, women and children, butchered by the Biafrans. I saw these things and I was neutralized by my hatred for the soldiers and told myself that the Nigerian had an innate natural tendency to inflict pain.
>
> *(142)*

The concerns shared by Iyayi's lead character impose on the reader the need to beware of the consequences of war, in this case, the wars that take place in a postcolonial African reality. Nigeria's case is unique for so many reasons. However, within the concerns raised here, we sense a sort of anxiety for the future seems marred by ethnic conflict and hatred that seemed tied to geographical and cultural lines. The predominantly Ibo east wanted a cession and tried earnestly to achieve that goal but failed. Almost sixty years later, the story of the war is still being told in Nigeria, and the issue of a possible Biafran state has surfaced with the recent agitation for secession. These politicized struggles have a futuristic tie and have been visited for debate since the end of the Nigerian civil war. But at the bottom of this very issue also lies corruption in the corridors of government, a postcolonial dilemma that is linked to Africa futurism. The entire continent struggles with it, and Nigeria's struggles have been well documented in the fiction produced by many of her finest writers. Iyayi points to it when Osime laments:

> Corruption always begins from the top. Before the war, corruption was in the very breath of the ministers and presidents and businessmen and politicians and traditional rulers and church leaders and army generals and police commissioners. It was there and we all reeled in it. It is still there now and we are still reeling in it . . . Let the war end and the corruption will resurface.
>
> *(142)*

As if speaking prophetically, Iyayi's last comments define the present-day political and economic reality of Nigeria, as corruption has been the main focus of the ruling government. Iyayi's character Osime was hinting at an issue that would persist five decades later and is being touted as a problem with the leadership in the country and elsewhere on the continent. These are instances of African futurism and have constantly been part of conversations across continents by citizens of the country who straddle two continents while embracing "transglobal identities" like Sundstrum had mentioned.

Current events in African futurism and traits

In 2017, the Nigerian-American writer, Deji Bryce Olukotun admitted that "There can be entertainment value in creating a pan-African vision of the continent, like the kingdom of Wakanda in Marvel's Black Panther series . . . The Black Panther is a thoughtful celebration of African achievement." In the same provocative article published online, he added: "My first novel *Nigerians in Space* drew upon noir traditions, combined with some fantastical folklore, to depict South Africa and Nigeria as I saw it. But noir didn't work for me in depicting Nigeria today. The extreme contrasts in the country – of inequality, of the adaptation of technology – were too epic in scope to reduce to a hardboiled plot." His proclamation is a sincere assessment of futuristic themes in sf (science fiction) in African literature and invites a candid assessment of the genre which has recently seen a catapulting in publications by authors such as Kojo Laing, Deji Bryce Olukotun, Lauren Beukes, and Nnedi Okorafor, among others.

Strikingly, the works of the aforementioned authors will lack a defined tradition without an examination of the link that connects African science fiction to speculative narratives from Africa that enriched their conflicts and characters' actions with myths, fables, magic, magical realism, and fantasy. Authors whose works demonstrate this tradition include Elechi Amadi, Kojo Laing, Ngugi wa Thiong'o, Zakes Mda, Ben Okri, and Benjamin Kwakye, among others. These authors in one way or another situate their works around the narratives that address Africa's sociopolitical and postcolonial conditions.

Africans writing SF and fantasy fiction are writing imaginative material influenced by the belief systems of the culture they were either born into or that already exist in the culture they were born into. Put simply, they are incorporating aspects of the reality of their culture into the creative works they are producing. Furthermore, these authors recreate an African world where social, political, and economic situations share symbiotic ties to the beliefs or mythical realities presented through narrative techniques such as magical realism or fantasy tales. Hence, magical realism is used by these authors as an aesthetic of necessity to situate postcolonial realities and imagined worlds that satirize or illustrate social realism and other forms of postcolonial African crisis. Their concerns are not distant from the concerns of their counterparts in the West but remains unique in terms of ideas.

A common thread that runs in the work of the current generation of African science fiction and fantasy writers is the need to utilize "specificity" in their plot and setting. Deji Bryce Olukotun attempts to explain this pivotal aspect of African science fiction and fantasy writers when he admits, "Nigeria's size and history beckons specificity. In that specificity, there are compelling stories and there is beauty. So I set my novel in Houston, Texas and in Kano, a city in the north of the country." This narrative technique has been deployed by many other African sf and fantasy writers effectively. Perhaps the very idea of "specificity" opens doors to a wide range of possibilities in present-day Africa. Two factors that dominate its emergence are the digital age and technology in an African society threatened by waves of violence. Nnedi Okorafor's new creation, *Blessing in Disguise*, a book published by Marvel, features a superheroine named Ngozi. Set in Lagos, Nigeria, the story is inspired by the adoption of the Chibok girls in 2014. The selection of Lagos, again, brings forward the role of "specificity" in the futuristic narrative genre. This trend is very similar to that employed by other authors from Africa resident in the West. Benjamin Kwakye's novel *Clothes of Nakedness* features a mysterious character by the name of Mystique Mysterious, whose atrocities in a postcolonial Ghanaian society in Accra include "introducing free narcotics to drug-free clubs and extorting money from men after finding them employment" (*Publishers Weekly*). Like Kwakye, Nigerian-American author Dike Okoro weaves the kind of pan-Africanist ideology hinted by Deji Bryce Olutokun in his book *Letter to Aisha*, where two women who grew up in Port Harcourt, Nigeria, find themselves exchanging letters as adults, reflecting on their husbands cheating and marital pitfalls, with the narrator ending up empathizing with Moji, her childhood friend, declaring,

> I know these days you are probably still wishing you could get over it all. The hang-overs from being the diplomat's wife. Take heart. Life never settles for a fair score with anyone. I remember even you told me that. Many, many years ago. So, today as you face the mirror and search for a spot to place a finger, I ask that you take solace in the joy of the moment. Your husband is a good man. He chose a profession that gives him joy. And I know he loves you much. His absence at home for almost six months out of a year is excusable. After all, we used to pledge to ourselves in primary school how we looked forward to marriages that afforded us the freedom to travel the world and know places we only visited in books and news stories. The tall tales enriching the wives' tale. Well, you have no excuse now. As far as I know, you live the dreams of many like me. The friends you grew up with and with whom you tasted the often bitter waters of being a young woman.
>
> (9)

The imagining of a hopeful future resonates in the previous lines quoted from Okoro's book to highlight the futuristic element of his narrative. The story is set in Port Harcourt but shifts to Chicago to fulfill Okoro's attempt at situating his story within the kind of speculative fiction that demonstrates the role of futuristic writing in Africa today.

Historically, the relationship of African fiction writers and the science fiction/fantasy tradition probably spans five decades or more. Post-independence works and recent works by African novelists and short story writers posit the ways the neocolonial experience influences novelists and short story writers whose stories embody features that today are defined as traits of speculative fiction and represent what might be categorized by critics as "African futurism." From oral stories harping on the interplay between humans and spirits to speculative prose that mirrors the reality of a society in transition, African fiction writers have strived to engage society and the world beyond their[1] boundaries with narratives detailing disparate lives in conflict-laden imagined places linked both to the real and the supernatural. In their engaging narratives, which are often fables or fantasy, they have passionately illuminated memorable characters, timeless places, and intriguing conflicts that uplift the human spirit in the face of harsh human conditions. These are interlaced with themes such as gender, poverty, magic, patriarchy, war, tyranny, varying forms of human and environmental exploitation, and many more that have saturated the vision of authors from the continent.

African writers belonging to post-independence generation such as Elechi Amadi, Ngugi wa Thiong'o, Ben Okri, Kodjo Laing, Zakes Mda, Syl-Cheney Coker, and Benjamin Kwakye deploy narrative styles that mix fables and magical realism to expose postcolonial conditions in their countries or imagined settings. The novels and stories by these authors showcase characters with supernatural abilities and transformative roles, and quite often the enemies these characters confront appear in either human or nonhuman/spirit forms. The conflicts these characters face carry on until they have found peace and solution to their disparate circumstances. The historical reach of their narratives stretches from slavery through colonialism to the post-independence period. In particular, the geographical location is Africa and other imaginary worlds, but the authors also deploy characters whose struggles in the real world clash with the magical. There is also the representation of the living and the dead coexisting in imagined spaces that present oppression, manmade conflicts with ties to the spirit world, and varying forms of the human quest for freedom. Some of the books that imbue neocolonial experiences with speculative narratives and tropes enriched with magic are Ben Okri's *The Famished Road*, Kojo Laing's *The Woman of the Aeroplane*, Zakes Mda's *Ways of Dying*, Syl-Cheny Coker's *The Last Harmattan of Alusine Dubar*, and Buchi Emechetta's *The Rape of Shavi*. Ngugi's *Wizard of the Crow* and Coker's *The Last Harmattan of Alusine Dunbar* are fabled tales about the plundering of their homelands. Like both authors, South Africa's Zakes Mda's *Ways of Dying* addresses a present predicament by focusing deeply on his country's post-apartheid world and the living conditions of South Africans.

Possible futures, myths, and alternate realities

Within this context, one might find validation in Anderson's definition and Eshun's theoretical statement by looking no further than the novel *Legacy of Phantoms* by Accra-born US-based author Benjamin Kwakye, whose novel is described by Sola Adeyemi as follows:

> 'Legacy of Phantoms' has a lot to offer in fashioning a new direction for African literature. The style is engaging and the use of idioms and metaphor rich. Perhaps the greatest contribution this novel will make to the corpus of African literature is its psychoanalytical appraisal of the past through the smoky lens of the present, with the future in sight.
>
> *(Sola Adeyemi blurb in* Legacy of Phantoms*)*

I agree with Adeyemi's statement and yet see the need to scout certain territories in African literature that have already been explored by Kwakye's progenitors. One author who readily comes to mind here is the Nigerian novelist Elechi Amadi. In the essay book *Bloom's Modern Critical Views: Alice Walker*, American Alice Hall Petry credits Amadi for having influenced Walker's *In Love & Trouble* and *You Can't Keep A Good Woman Down*, two of Walker's notable publications that also included references to Ahurole, a character in Amadi's *The Concubine*. In the essay, Petry states:

> The first epigraph, a page-long extract from *The Concubine* by Elechi Amadi, depicts a girl, Ahurole, who is prone to fits of sobbing and "alarmingly irrational fits of arguments": "From all this her parents easily guessed that she was being unduly influenced by agwu, her personal spirit." It is not until the end of the extract that Amadi mentions casually that "Ahurole was engaged to Ekwueme when she was eight days old."
>
> *(34)*

In taking a similar stand on Amadi's work, African American novelist and poet Alice Walker, in her book *The Cushion in the Road: Meditation and Wandering as the Whole World Awakens to Being in Harm's Way*, speaks admirably of Amadi: "I remember reading *The Concubine* by Elechi Amadi . . . and just being stunned" (226). Walker's view of Amadi's work is very admirable, given that Amadi belongs to the first generation of African authors, a point expanded upon by Somak Ghoshal, who, writing for *The Telegraph*, a Calcutta, India, newspaper, links Chimamanda Ngozie Adichie's emergence to the footprints left by Amadi's generation in an article titled "The African Writer and the Burden of History," stating, "Adichie comes out of the tradition of modernist African literature initiated by Chinua Achebe and enriched by Buchi Emecheta, Elechi Amadi, Chukwuemeka Ike and others" (Ghoshal).

Amadi's novels are populated with memorable characters whose daily struggles have links to worlds outside of their immediate reality. In his stories, myths and superstitions dictate his characters' conflicts. For example, in *The Concubine*, Madume's actions are dictated by external forces. After he fights with Emenike, the husband to Ihuoma, the beauty who is also Amadi's female protagonist, he learns an unforgettable lesson when he visits Emenike's compound, just days after the latter's death, to court his widow. Thus, a severe injury to his toe when he visits the dead Emenike's compound teaches him a lesson. Several critics of Amadi's work have attempted to unravel the mystery of Madume's injury and the role traditional belief systems play in the outcome of events that shape human conditions. Emmanuel Obiechina, in his book *Culture, Tradition and Society in the West African Novel*, reiterates:

> Idyllic pictures are attractive because they offer a dream escape from the realities of the World one knows and lives in. But if Amadi has overplayed the stability and decorum, he has handled the intervention of the supernatural in traditional life most convincingly. It is not simply that gods and spirits mingle freely with the people, shaping their destinies for good or ill; Amadi's tale conveys this effect with ease and conviction, as in the scene in which Madume consults Anyika the dibia after cutting his toe in Emenike's compound. Emenike had died after a fight with him, so the event is more than a coincidence.
>
> *(Obiechina 146)*

Obiechina's suggestion supports why Amadi finds relevance in deploying traditional life and belief systems in his works to give importance to African reality. People consult *dibia*, another name for the medicine man, to uncover secrets to happenings that are beyond human understanding. Perhaps Amadi, even as the writer of this story, reminds us in a speech he delivered titled "Literary Criticism and Culture" that "every novel is a recounting of human situations. Every human situation teaches us a lesson or two" (36). Furthermore, Madume's consultation of Anyika for possible purification reaffirms Amadi's own belief in African tradition, an issue he visits in his essay, "Background of Nigerian Literature," stating, "An Ikwerre proverb says: to set up a shrine the dibia must have a piece of earth. This means that he must have a strong and stable link with his community in order to practice his art of spiritual and physical healing" (2).

The Concubine possesses every charm one might find in a narrative that could easily pass as science fiction and fantasy fiction projecting the features of African futurism. It centers on the beauty of a woman that seems to be downfall of every man who marries her. Ihuoma, the lead character, is a beauty admired by all. Yet it is the same beauty of hers that is directly linked to the deaths of her husbands and suitors, with Amadi providing a trope that gives his reader the indication that Ihuoma, after all, might be married to the sea god. As mystical and unbelievable as this aspect of the plot seems, there are reasonable twists within the narrative itself that justify the possibility of this suspicion. In fact, many critics and reviewers have stressed this aspect of Amadi's novel, heaping praise on his artistic vision. Alistair Niven claims that:

> Amadi first gained serious attention as a writer with the publication of *The Concubine*, an early contribution (number 25) to the great Heinemann African Writers Series . . .

Amadi's novel explored the boundary between myth and reality, its protagonist Ihuoma being revealed as the wife of the Sea King and hence only a concubine to her male partner.

(Niven)

The boundary between myth and reality is also explored in Benjamin Kwakye's novel *The Clothes of Nakedness*, which *Publishers Weekly* describes this way:

Evil lurks in the streets of Accra, Ghana, and it goes by the name of Mystique Mysterious. He can turn the sober to drink, persuade the faithful to cheat and rally the masses to hysteria . . . this allegory introduces its abstractly villainous Mephistopheles to an Accra suburb, where he proceeds to destroy the lives of as many townspeople as possible by introducing free narcotics to drug-free clubs and extorting money from men after finding them employment.

Interplay of the realistic and fantastic

Narration, in particular from an African context, not only approximates conflicts enunciating the birth or emergence of protagonists and antagonists but involves a sequence of conflicts that build from very believable sources, even triggered by acts readers might find puzzling. These narrative features are thrust in the tales of enviable merit that occupy the desks of many teachers of literature in the schools across the African continent today. These signature aspects of the widely promoted fiction genre illustrates the thematic trends, conflicts, and characterization situated within the discourse of authors such as Ben Okri, Elechi Amadi, Nnedi Okorafor, and Benjamin Kwakye.

One writer whose novels and short stories continue to provide an aesthetic appeal that elicits ideals suitable to African futurism is Ben Okri. In his Booker Prize-winning novel *The Famished Road*, we notice the impressionable narrator Azaro, who at 7 years old takes on bringing incidents in the narrative within the framework of arbitrary shifts. Okri's greatest achievement with this book is his ability to impose on his craft the deftness of indigenous beliefs. Azaro from the onset announces himself as no ordinary child. His diction and vision merit that of children the Yoruba tradition would describe as abiku, which literally translates as spirit children who retain contact between the real world and the spiritual one or, as Ato Quayson puts it, "a child in an unending cycle of births, deaths and rebirths" (122). In the Igbo mythology system, such a child is branded as ogbanje, which, according to Chidi Maduka, "denotes a person who acts in a weird, capricious, callous and even sadistic way" (qtd in Quayson 1997).

Blending past, present, and future

Many of the narrative ideas espoused in the previous exchange elicit a multiplicity of experiences that are increasingly seen in African literary works addressing an openness to a wider dialogue on gender issues. The attainment of independence by many African nations coincided with a universally accepted criteria to reconsider the role and place of women in African society. By and large, this decision has been relayed in individual works with ranging takes on the relationships between wives and husbands and the effective modes of the female voice actively studying domestic issues and the many parts of marital conflicts. How this is idealized in the Afrofuturistic narrative can be best understood through the various ways the African region is represented on the world stage. Ben Okri says in an interview titled "Talking with Ben Okri,"

> I was told stories, we were all told stories as kids in Nigeria. We had to tell stories that would keep one another interested, and you weren't allowed to tell stories that everybody else knew. You had to dream up new ones.
>
> And it never occurred to us that those stories actually contained a unique worldview. It's very much like the river that runs through your backyard. It's always there. It never occurs to you to take a photograph or to seek its mythology. It's just there; it runs in your veins, it runs in your spirit.
>
> *(Emeagwali)*

Conclusion

Africanfuturism in fiction is real and exists in the novels written by renowned African fiction writers as well as those written by current authors specializing in the science fiction genre. What makes each of these authors relevant is not their works but their insistence on tapping into the rich oral resources of the continent to infuse myths, the supernatural, and other forms of spirituality referenced by Mbiti to make their stories uniquely African. In an age of globalization and technology, these practices might seem normal, and indeed it is, for Africa has always played catch-up to the west in terms of maintaining a status quo for recognition. Ben Okri, Nnedi Okorafor, Ngugi wa Thiong'o, Elechi Amadi, and many others explore postcolonial Africa in ways that lend importance to their stories as not just familiar narratives but narratives reinforcing the importance of using fables or sf to articulate memorable tales. This, among other aspects of their stories, has made indigenous beliefs and myths and the supernatural central to the African experience in fiction. The level of conflicts they traverse within the framework of the narratives from which they symbolically replicate patterns of common events and the realities of African societies illustrate the deftness and clarity of vision by the aforementioned authors to dissect eroding morals, push forward indigenous beliefs, and embellish their narrative structure with ideological musings amplified by ironic twists, tragedy, and narrators whose ambitions are guided by their consciousness.

In the end, science fiction and fantasy in African literature, especially in the novel and short story genre, have not flourished as one would expect. Nevertheless, the argument can be made that authors born to African-born parents in the West, in particular Tom Adeyemi and many others, and those writing in the continent such as Efe Okogu, Tendai Hushu, and others, address futurist themes in different ways that explore African myth, society, and culture. Also, conflicts and events that the authors whose works illustrate the deployment of characters and plotline that easily pass for SF and fantasy fiction have earned praises because the conflicts they recreate engage readers with the realities of the societies they depict. After all, one does not have to believe in the supernatural to believe it is often, if not occasionally, cited in the flurry of stories that float in the newspapers and daily gossip in the African continent. Perhaps it is safe to say that even those who do not believe in these realities have a sense of the way they are anchored in the myths that are in circulation in the various cultures of Africa.

Note

1 Nnedi Okorafor, born in the United States to Nigerian immigrants, both bridges this breach and fills it. She appears on lists of black sci-fi on either side of the Atlantic. And while she says that she has "issues with [the label] Afrofuturism," she is one of the most prolific black writers of speculative fiction out there and has set several of her fantasy and science fiction novels on the continent. Okorafor, in other words,

is Afropolitan *and* African American: she insists that her "flavor of sci-fi is evenly Naijamerican (note: 'Naija' is slang for Nigeria or Nigerian)." Yet in an essay on the Science Fiction and Fantasy Writers of America website, Okorafor herself bemoans the scant canon:

> Here's my list of "African SF." It's really short . . . How do I define African SF? I don't. I know it when I see it . . . The main fact is that this list DOES exist. Africans ARE writing their own science fiction, contrary to what some may think. But the fact is that Africans need to also write more of it. (Okorafor, *Science Fiction and Fantasy Writers of America*) and (Okorafor, *Native*).

NATIVE: How would you define your identity as an African Nigerian with a wide range of inspirations?

NNEDI: I would define it as just me . . . I do 'AfricanFuturism', not Afrofuturism, Africanfuturism (one word). That falls under science fiction. I've written what I call Juju fantasy (laughs). I think it's a little different because a lot of the things considered fantasy aren't fantasy. There are things people believe in that would be in there with the stuff I have made up

Okorafor, Nnedi.

"The native exclusive: Nnedi okorafor on Africanfuturism and the challenges of pioneering." Interview by Edwin Okolo, Toye Sokunbi and Tomiwa Isiaka. *Native*, 5 Nov. 2018.

https://thenativemag.com/interview/native-exclusive-nnedi-okorafor-africanfuturism-challenges-pioneering. Accessed 2 October, 2019

Okorafor, Nnedi.

"Can you define African Science Fiction?" Science Fiction and Fantasy Writers of America. 10 March, 2010.

https://www.sfwa.org/2010/03/16/can-you-define-african-science-fiction. Accessed 2 October, 2019

Works cited and references

Adeyemi, Sola. "Blurb." In *Legacy of Phantoms*. Trenton: Africa World Press, 2011.

Alter, Alexandra. "Nnedi Okorafor and the Fantasy Genre She Is Helping Redefine." *The New York Times.* 6 Oct. 2017. Web.

Amadi, Elechi. *The Concubine*. Oxford: Heinemann, 1966.

Amadi, Elechi. *Speaking and Singing*. Port Harcourt: University of Port Harcourt Press, 2003.

Amadi, Elechi. *Elechi Amadi: Collected Plays*. Port Harcourt: Pearl Publishers, 2004.

Bloom, Harold. "Alice Walker: The Achievement of the Short Fiction." In *Bloom's Modern Critical View: Alice Walker*. New York: Chelsea House, 2007: 33–34.

Bould, Mark. "From Afrofuturism to AfroSF." 01 Feb. 2016. Accessed 5 Oct. 2017. www.fabrikzeitung. ch/from-afrofuturism-to-afrosf/#/.

Ekwensi, Cyprian. *An African Night's Entertainment*. London: John Murray Publishing, 1996.

Emeagwali, Philip. "Talking with Ben Okri." 19 July 1992. Accessed 5 Oct. 2017. Web.

Eshun, Kodwo. "Further Considerations on Afrofuturism." *CR: The New Centennial Review*, 3:2, 2003, 287–302.

Fagunwa, Daniel O. *Forest of a Thousand Daemons: A Hunters Saga*. Translated by Wole Soyinka. San Francisco, CA: City Lights Books, 2013: 140.

Gayland, Gerald. *After Colonialism: African Postmodernism and Magical Realism*. Johannesburg: Wits UP, 2005.

Goshal, Somak. "The African Writer and the Burden of History." *The Telegraph*. 10 Aug. 2007. Accessed 11 Mar. 2017. Web.

Kalisa, Marie-Chantal. Review of Calyxthe Beyala's *The Sun Hath Looked upon Me*. Oxford: Heinemann, 1996. H-AfrLitCine, July, 1997.

Kalisa, Marie-Chantal. Review of Calyxthe Beyala's *Your Name Shall Be Tonga*. Portsmouth, NH: Heinemann, 1988. H-AfrLitCine, July, 1997.

Kirkus Reviews. "Woman of the Aeroplanes." 23 May 1990. www.kirkusreviews.com/book-reviews/kojo-laing/woman-of-the-aeroplanes/.

Kwakye, Benjamin. *Legacy of Phantoms*. Trenton: Africa World Press, 2011.

Kwakye, Benjamin. *The Clothes of Nakedness*. Trenton: Africa World Press, 1998.

Laing, Kojo. *Woman of the Aeroplanes*. New York: William Morrow & Co, 1990.

Namwali, Serpell. "Africa Has Always Been Sci-Fi." *Lithub.com*. 01 Apr. 2016. https://lithub.com/africa-has-always-been-sci-fi/.

Niven, Alastair. "Elechi Amadi Obituary." *The Guardian*. 22 Aug. 2016 Accessed 7 Oct. 2017. Web.

Nyawalo, Mich. "Afro-Futurism and the Aesthetics of Hope in Bekolo's Les Saignantes and Kahiu's Pumzi." *Journal of the African Literature Association*, 10:2, 209–221. DOI: 10.1080/21674736.2016.1257499. http://dx.doi.org/10.1080/21674736.2016.1257499.

Obiechina, Emmanuel. *Culture, Tradition and Society in the West African Novel*. London: Cambridge University Press, 1975.

Okoro, Dike. *Letters to Aisha and Other Stories*. Milwaukee: Cissus World Press, 2015.

Okri, Ben. *The Famished Road*. New York: Anchor Books, 1991.

Okri, Ben. *Stars of the New Curfew*. New York: Vintage Books, 2010.

Petry, Alice Hall. "Alice Walker: The Achievement of Short Fiction." In *Bloom's Modern Critical Views*. Edited and with an Introduction by Harold Bloom. New York: Chelsea House, 2007: 34.

Publishers Weekly. "A Review of *Stars of the New Curfew*." Reed Business Information, 1989. Web.

Quayson, Ato. *Strategic Transformations in Nigerian Writing*. Oxford: James Currey/IUP, 1997: 122, 123, 125.

Sunstrum, Pamela Phatsimo. "Afro-Mythology and African Futurism: The Politics of Imagining and Methodologies for Contemporary Creative Research Practices." *Paradoxa Journal*, 'Africa SF', ed. Michael Bould, 25, 2013, 199–136.

Thrasher, Steven W. "Afrofuturism: Reimagining Science and the Future from a Black Perspective." *The Guardian*. 7 Dec. 2017. Accessed 7 Oct. 2017. Web.

Walker, Alice. *The Cushion in the Road: Meditation and Wandering as the Whole World Awakens to Being in Harm's Way*. New York: The New Press, 2013: 226.

28

WRITING THE SELF

Indian women writers from South Africa

Rajendra Chetty

Introduction

South African Indian women's writings form an integral component of the African literary historiography and bring to light the role of women activists in the struggle for liberation and commitment to social justice and equality. Key women writers within this subgenre include Kesaveloo Goonam (*Coolie Doctor*), Fatima Meer (*Prison Diary: One Hundred and Thirteen Days, 1976*), Pregs Govender (*Love and Courage: A Story of Insubordination*) and Phyllis Naidoo (*Footprints beyond Grey Street*). These writers, marginalised twofold by the regime as black persons and as women, root themselves in a South African identity concomitant with a shift from the individual to an ethnocommunal consciousness that implies a widening in the perspectives under which a new kind of deterritorialised African identity should be evaluated. A major feature of the Indian women's writing is the concern with place, displacement, myths of identity and authenticity, and the engagement with these themes has added radical new dimensions to African resistance writings.

The exclusionary practices in South African literary history have failed to accommodate the writings of black writers (African, coloured and Indian), as well as women writers. A re-thinking and re-positioning of writings within the new democratic South Africa, after an era of repression, is not possible without profound understanding of the narratives that need to be revived, recreated and excavated. Post-1994 writers were able to engage with history and the 'writing of the self' in a more candid manner and to reflect on the apartheid era without fear of being harassed by the regime. The black women writers' perceptions and experiences restore memory and foster a new humanity, and perhaps it is justice in its deepest sense. The subaltern speak for themselves in these stories; there is a 'talking back', a reclaiming of memory, bringing to light the blanked-out areas of their identity and, in the case of prisoners (Fatima Meer) and exiles (Phyllis Naidoo), of their lives. They stress their essential humanness in their self-narratives; there is a recovering of a consciousness and a reflection of their role as interventionist historian.

The colonial history of South Africa and its legacy of cultural and linguistic domination have resulted in a situation where the literatures of blacks (African, Coloured/mixed race and Indian) were relegated to the margins of institutional, social and cultural life (Chetty 2002:9). Exclusion of writings of the 'other' was the principal mode by which power was exercised within the white-dominated academe and apartheid society. It is within this context of the marginalised black writers that this chapter engages with the writings of South African Indian women in an attempt to shift a component of the excluded other to the centre. I regret perpetuating the old apartheid categories in this chapter, but the different life experiences created for the various ethnic groups in the pre-1994 racist society are likely to have resulted in different forms of writings and literature. In discussing South Africa, one is also unfortunately obliged to use its system of racial categorisation, without affirming any of its implications. Indian people were classified earlier as Coolies, later as Asians, politically as non-white or black people and more recently as simply South African.

It is not appropriate to homogenise South African Indian women's writings or to make sweeping generalisations on this subgenre of writing. A second source of the danger of homogenising any group of writers is the tendency to find just what we set out looking for. I find broad similarities among a wide range of works by South African Indian women writers, especially the dominant trope of resistance to the racist regime, but I hope that the similarities are illuminating ones, not based on ignorance or difference. Gayatrie Spivak, like Michel Foucault (1972), cautions against unifying differences and striving towards a unity of discourse and contends that commonness can only be built on and out of difference – the place where, indeed, all human beings are similar is seen to be lodged in their being different (Spivak 228).

Part one

Sister outsiders

It is imperative to place South African Indian women's writings in their historical and cultural contexts since there is an essential relationship between literary forms and their historical context. The majority of South African Indians are the descendants of indentured workers brought to Natal between 1860 and 1911 to work in the sugar belt. The indigenous Zulu people, relatively secure in their tribal economy, refused to market their labour. It was also the time in Natal when the Zulu warriors would victoriously wash their spears in the blood of over 1500 British soldiers at Isandhlawana. A new form of slavery of Indian subjects was thus sanctioned by the British. As indentured labourers, most Indian people started life in South Africa as slaves of their white masters. They were (like the African people) deprived of citizenship rights and subjected to gross exploitation by the British colonial authority and later by the apartheid government until the advent of democracy in 1994.

The publishing houses were all owned by whites, and, coupled with apartheid conditioning, they saw books by the 'other' of little use and feared that they would not sell. Publishing houses like the Lovedale Press restricted publication to works with a Christian message, and this further excluded the Indian community, which was overwhelmingly Hindu and Moslem. It was the literary magazine *Staffrider* that served as an effective avenue for alternate black writings in view of the limited publishing capacity for excluded writers. The first South African Indian women writer who was encouraged in *Staffrider* and went on to publish individual volumes was Jayapraga Reddy.

The autobiographical impulse of the nation is evident in the large number of life narratives by South African Indian women that have emerged post-1994 in an attempt to recover the past. They include works by Zarina Maharaj, Zuleikha Mayat, Neela Govender, Farida Karodia, Agnes Sam, Muthal Naidoo, Sumayya Lee, Raazamah Pillay, Prabha Moodley, Mariam Akabor, Kogi Singh, Devi Rajab and Sherin Ahmed. Farida Karodia foregrounds strong women in an interview on the launch of *Other Secrets*:

Women always had the power to change and create. They are the most important elements in my stories. I come from a family with very strong women. That was the influence on me. It was a natural progression to write about strong women.

(Chetty 2003)

The engagement with writings of liberation activists like Meer, Goonam, Naidoo and Govender encourages a re-thinking of conventions and roles of women and their courage, power and resilience to challenge repressive structures and patriarchal norms of colonialism and apartheid.

Write about South Africa and you write about politics; it is less a choice than a dilemma. Literature serves as a valuable source of information about the experiences, struggles, feelings and thoughts of a society. It gives access to the area in which historical process is registered as the subjective experience of individuals in society: fiction gives us 'history from the inside' (Clingman 1). Most South African black writers had a morbid fascination with politics, and opposition to apartheid motivated their writings. South African writings clearly demonstrate the fact that political impetus of the postcolonial begins well before the moment of independence (Ashcroft, Griffiths & Tiffin 83). Most South African Indian women's writings gave attention to documenting the atrocities perpetrated by the apartheid government, for example, the dispossession and relocation of Indian communities is central to their writings, together with the detention and struggle of political prisoners. Political activists like Fatima Meer and Phyllis Naidoo wrote of their incarceration, frequently accompanying torture and unwarranted death of comrades. Peck (9) notes that the invasion of the private realm by politics meant that even writers who might usually have ignored politics were forced to deal with it. The personal relationships that might otherwise have been their focus were moved into the political realm, as was the case with Meer.

It was the theatre and playwriting that was the initial form of artistic expression and writings in English among the South African Indian women, and this first took root in the 1960s. The diaspora's fascination with the works of India's literature laureate Rabindranath Tagore led to the production of *Sacrifice*, *Muktha Dhara* and Kalidasa's *Shakuntala* with Ansuyah Singh and Devi Bughwan. These productions had a great influence on the actors, and they were the catalyst for the first published play by a South African Indian woman, Ansuyah Singh's *Cobwebs in the Garden*. The Durban Academy of Theatre Arts was formed in 1962, and the company included three Indian women who carved out illustrious careers as academics and writers in South Africa; Muthal Naidoo, Fatima Meer and Devi Bughwan. Muthal Naidoo, in her 'search for a cultural identity', records the theatre history succinctly in her *Indic Theatre Monograph* (1993). Naidoo's interrogation of the concept 'Indian' is illuminating:

> Though origins have influenced the perception of 'Indians', I believe material conditions in South Africa have been the major factor in influencing cultural patterns. What 'Indians' have in common with all other groups is the culture of apartheid. Being black people, we have been subjected to a dominant culture, and had to adopt customs and behaviours of the dominant culture and developed an ambivalence towards our origins.
>
> What we have gained from the apartheid culture is a sense of inferiority, disempowerment and a concern for self preservation at the expense of human rights. Those who repudiate the role of victim have developed a fighting spirit which takes them outside the community and into alliances across ethnic barriers.
>
> *(2)*

Shobna Poona breaks the silence of the Indian woman poets in her collections *Words on a Blank Page* and *In Search of Rainbows*. Poona provides a feminist perspective to the experiences of women in the patriarchal and sexist South African society. Poetry was the genre favoured by black writers during the Black Consciousness period of the 1970s. Another preferred genre was the autobiography, and it served as a vehicle for South African Indian history. Zuleikha Mayet's *A Treasure Trove of Memories* provides poignant reflections on growing up in an Indian ghetto while the grand dame of resistance politics, Kesaveloo Goonam, charts the trajectory of Indian resistance in *Coolie Doctor* (1971). Fatima Meer's biography of Nelson Mandela, *Higher than Hope*, remains an extraordinary account of Mandela and his time and covers the most significant period of the African National Congress (1940–1960). Kogi Singh's *A Labour of Love: The Biography of Shishupal Rambharos* is an example of a biography of a prominent activist in fields other than politics. More recent autobiographical writings that chronicle resistance are Fatima Meer's *Prison Diary*, which is chosen for intensive discussion in Part 2 of this chapter, and Phyllis Naidoo's *Footprints beyond Grey Street*. Neela Govender's childhood reminiscences are portrayed in *Acacia Thorn in my Heart*, which was published in France and provides a glimpse of rural itinerant farming life in Pietermaritzburg.

Farida Karodia, who spent three decades in Canada, has produced three novels – *Daughters of the Twilight*, which deals with the deleterious effects of apartheid; *A Shattering of Silence*, which examines the effects of the war in the neighbouring country of Mozambique and *Other Secrets*, which explores the mother-daughter relationship in the post-1994 South Africa. The theme of the tensions of race and class is further portrayed in Karodia's short story collection *Coming Home*. Jayapraga Reddy introduces the everyday life of South African Indian society in her collection *On the Fringe of Dreamtime*. Writers like Fatima Meer and Kesaveloo Goonum relocate the South African Indian woman as an integral part of the country's landscape. In demonstrating the unique position of the South African Indian as part of the oppressed and committed to the liberation of the country, these writers help to restore to Indians a credibility lost during their extradition from central and north African countries as well as the shameful collaboration with the regime by unscrupulous politicians.

Agnes Sam's collection, *Jesus Is Indian and Other Short Stories*, reflects the interrelationship between characters of different racial groups and their attempt to come to terms with the effects of apartheid. The tension in her stories is between the political and the aesthetic function of literature. The story 'High Heels' deals with the struggle of Indians to maintain their religious and cultural practices within the context of colonisation. The role of the church in separating Hindu converts from their traditional and cultural practices is interrogated by Sam. The story 'And They Christened It Indenture' is not only a mocking attack on Christian-practice among Hindus but also a critical reflection on the abhorrent history of indenture. Many of Sam's stories also provide an autobiographical account of her exile and an examination of gender issues. Sam's discovery that her marginalised status as a black person is replicated in England is a turning point in her life. Both Sam and Karodia displace vociferously the perception of women as subordinate and dependent. The contribution of Indian women in the struggle for liberation and their role in the democratic government and society are indeed a corrective to patriarchy.

Exile, race, identity and gender are central to Karodia's writings. Much of the writings of the exiles were banned in South Africa during apartheid. It is therefore understandable why 'return' was a recurrent theme that dominated the national agenda since 1994: the return of detainees from prison, the most famous being Mandela, the return of the bantustans through incorporation into the new democracy, the return of land and homes of those forcibly removed by the regime (albeit to a limited extent) and the return home of the exiled artists and freedom fighters like Zarina Maharaj and Phyllis Naidoo.

Part 2

Fatima Meer: apartheid activist

At just seventeen, Fatima Meer threw herself into resisting racism, the first public act of defiance in a long and pioneering political life. She played a significant part in the history of political thought and action in South Africa. Speaking out against injustice was a political act with dire consequences for her and led to her imprisonment, house arrest and ostracism by the apartheid regime. Her writings span a wide diversity of interests and concerns which include sociological, political and historical aspects of Indian life in South Africa; resistance against apartheid and experiences of working-class women. Fatima Meer was profoundly concerned with exposing and opposing the illegitimacy of South Africa's legal system, which was deeply flawed in its treatment of blacks. Meer's landmark publication as a sociologist was her book entitled *The Mis/Trial of Andrew Zondo*. In her plea for extenuating circumstances at the trial of Zondo, who planted a bomb in the Amanzimtoti (a town on the south coast of the Kwazulu Natal province) shopping centre on 23 December 1985, Meer defends Zondo on the grounds that the court that charged him with terrorism had not taken into account the sociological circumstances and political injustices which prompted Zondo to plant the device. Lalu and Harris note that:

> Meer's book seems to have been an intervention in, and a challenge to, the procedures of legal institutions in South Africa, especially their positivist metalanguage, and the workings of the 'repressive and ideological state apparatus'. Meer claims that the trial omitted an understanding of the context, which prompted Zondo's act.
>
> *(26)*

Meer's understanding of the significance of the sociological context of a legal ruling was ground-breaking in many ways: it shattered the myth of law as a realm unto itself and broke the male authority of white racist laws. Terrorism is not necessarily terrorism if the perpetrator can demonstrate the predicament of living in a social cage of illegality. The same legality of context may well apply to Lydia, the so-called murderess, who befriended Meer in prison (*Prison Diary*) and who had her own personal, historical and political reasons for killing the male-constructed patriarchal legal apparatus of their day. In a connotative understanding and contextual estimation of their work, Meer, like the Egyptian writer Nawal El Saadawi, may be charged with homicide: of challenging and annihilating male hegemony.

A curious coincidence in the history of the incarceration of female political activists in twentieth-century Africa is that Fatima Meer in South Africa at the southern end of the continent and Nawal El Saadawi in Egypt at the northern edge, were both imprisoned for their liberal political views and both befriended women in prison who had killed men. Meer came to know Lydia, who had killed her husband with a spade, while El Saadawi's fellow inmate Fathiyya killed her husband with a hoe. Both political prisoners, Meer and El Saadawi, were detained unlawfully under structures of male hegemonic domination. Both so-called 'murderesses', Lydia and Fathiyya, were held as criminal prisoners: their actions against male abuse were far more brutal yet may, in important ways, be classified within the same reactive bounds as the standpoints of the two political prisoners.

Badassy points out in her study of crimes of passion between master/mistress and servant relations, between whites and Indians in Natal's British colonial occupation that relations were often so brutalised and poisoned between worker and employer that occurrence of murder or physical

injury was inevitable rather than shocking. Badassy employs the same logic of contextual instiga-
tion that Meer relied upon in defending and explaining the act of Andrew Zondo. Criminal acts
and causes for such action cannot be removed from the political, social, economic and emotional
housing in which they exist. Badassy describes the nature and attitude of white male racist settlers:

> Peter Spiller has shown, in his study on the District and Supreme Courts of the colony
> of Natal, juries were extremely racially biased and were most often uninterested in
> cases where the accused were Indian or Black and, most importantly, they resented the
> fact that their time was taken up by sitting in on these cases, especially since verdicts
> were predetermined by the powerful influence of settler racism.
>
> *(176)*

In the pre-1994 South African racist legal system, black subalterns who were exploited within
that structure were seldom granted fair legal rights, and similarly, within a male hegemonic system, females are disadvantaged. Prosecution of blacks and females in the South African apartheid
legal system was unjust. In the case of political detainees such as Meer and her fellow prisoners
like Winnie Madikizela Mandela and Phyllis Naidoo (all three women were incarcerated in the
Johannesburg jail in 1976), male hegemony is impugned and its legal purchase negated.

Meer's criticism of the political and social systems of the day in South Africa caused grave
discontent and retribution from the patriarchy that controlled the country. She was imprisoned
for her political activism. Meer's incarceration was the enactment of her liberal resistance. Her
behaviour while in prison was determined by her ethical and egalitarian codes. Her belief in a
common humanity and the rights of all human beings was transferred into action when she was
humiliated, insulted and isolated in jail. The acuity of her critique of government and the precision of her observations guaranteed her enmity from patriarchy.

At every turn, Meer resisted the minute instruction of white male hegemonic rule. Although
she was determined not to be the victim, the psychological attrition of being in a cell away from
her family did affect her:

> Vesta complains that I am sulking and not talking to the others. I am depressed. I don't
> want to talk to anyone. I have curled up on my mattress, my eyes are sore, but my
> problem is my mood. It has taken hold of me and I can't shake it off . . . Vesta wants to
> know if I am cross with them. Why will I not talk to them? I have no answer for her;
> I am sunk in my depression.
>
> *(94)*

In order to break the chains of apartheid, one of the most complete systems of white male
hierarchical control, Meer determines to assert her agency as a non-male, a non-Christian and
non-white: she has to convince herself that she can psychically resist the urge to capitulate, sink
into misery and self-pity:

> Today, for the hell of it, for the fun of it, just to prove to them and to myself that I
> could, if I wished to, violate the prison rules, I violated one. The gate to our yard was
> open; I walked out of it and out of our yard.
>
> *(94)*

Meer returns to her own yard: her gallantry has broken the dark spell of a regime which sentences her to being, acting and thinking as an *untermensch*. Her small act of defiance, a single

degree of disobedience 'for the hell of it, for the fun of it', has assured her inwardly of the justice and righteousness of her cause: both for women and for blacks in South Africa. The war of the will takes a crucial step in Meer's sudden refusal to sink into the despondency that her tormentors wish to impose: 'My dark mood is broken. I have entered the world of my fellow detainees again' (94). Meer's ability to evade the trap of self-pity, her sheer exercise of the will, intimates a far larger existential war for female agency: entering the world of her fellow inmates tells of the vital solace of women's community and arguably the peculiarly female wisdom of recognising the value of such sisterhood. Her escape from depression is a rite of passage, and her re-entry into the company of survivors is a personal badge of honour. Vesta, her fellow prisoner's, concern for her is part of a life-saving membrane of care woven between the prisoners. On her first night in prison, Meer sinks into despondency but is awoken by the caring knock of Sibongile Kubeka in the next door cell:

> My headache has returned. I lie cold, sick and miserable in my improvised bed. I turn my face to the wall. I hear a muffled knock. All my senses are on alert . . . I return the knock. "How are you?" the voice comes in a loud whisper.
>
> *(35)*

This concern and bonding are significant of much greater issues: an egalitarian social linking that breaches barriers of class, race, profession and stigma of criminality among women. Vesta and Sibongile provide evidence of a uniquely female instinct to care, communicate and support. They both know instinctively when and how to contact a sister (Fatima) in pain and danger. Meer repays these moments of care by reaching out to help other women in moments of crisis: she pleads for the teenage girls who are imprisoned on little proof of wrongdoing. Meer is distraught at the sobbing of one of the teenagers and records the confusion, anxiety and desperation she hears:

> I do not know when I fell asleep, but towards morning I woke up to the terrible sobbing of little Baleka locked up by herself. She was calling for her mother and for her home. From across the yard and from across the other cells, Jane Pakathi called to the child in consolation and then called on us to console her.
>
> *(101)*

This statement points to formation of bonds of support in an organic and spontaneous way which demonstrates the emergence of a new kind of society and a novel way of recording that emergence. Meer is quick to observe that the thirteen-year-old Baleka is braver and more effective in her sobbing than older inmates: Baleka disturbs the peace, challenges the continuity of male domination and refuses to 'be a good girl'. Meer remarks astutely:

> A child is teaching us to protest and has jerked us out of the way we accommodated our imprisonment. It is no place for her. It is no place for us. Baleka must go on crying, for crying is terrible to hear; it tears the silence and wrings the conscience. "I'm dying, let me out!" Baleka pleads in Sotho through her tears, "Mother! Oh mother! I'm dying!"
>
> *(101)*

Meer senses that Baleka's protest is braver than her own meek 'accommodation' of prison life: she is ashamed that she did not, like the young detainee, howl in grief and anger against her incarceration. The child has 'jerked us out of the way' of mild acceptance. Meer realises that her protest, the ethical reasons for her being imprisoned are undercut by her slippage into a patriarchal and patronising system which wishes to dull prisoners' senses, anaesthetise women's minds and, mainly, silence them. Baleka's call to her mother awakens responses in the prison and alerts Meer not to relapse into the minutest degree of co-operation with the hierarchy of white men. Meer's resistance is re-ignited by Baleka's plangent call at night: it is a call to arms. The young teenager's cry represents a general call between women: against barbarity, lack of feeling and chauvinism. The nature of Meer's response cuts across boundaries of class, education, religion and age. All women are drawn together by her fight for freedom. Meer was elected the leader of the Black Women's Federation in December 1975 in Durban and spearheaded its attack on white male privilege. Meer lived in a long tradition of Indian South African women freedom fighters that includes feisty women like the sixteen-year-old Valiamma Moodliar, who was killed in prison while participating in a protest march under the leadership of Gandhi. Incidentally, the Andrew Zondo case resurfaces in 1991 at the University of Natal where Meer was an academic. The university was the first to confer on the newly released Nelson Mandela a honorary doctorate, but Meer convinced Mandela not to accept the degree from the university's chancellor, Ramon Leon, whom Meer labelled a 'child killer' as he served as the judge during the Zondo trail and sentenced him to death. Mandela heeded Meer's call and did not attend the university graduation.

Meer accesses different cultures, classes and languages during her imprisonment and writes a cross-cultural discourse in her prison diary. Jacobs cites Wolfgang Iser in defining the emergence of a new form of intercultural expression at a time of acute political crisis:

> Operating at the interface between different cultures as well as between a culture's past and its present, such a discourse "establishes a network of interpenetrating relationships" which both allows for "mutual impacting of cultures upon one another " and functions as "a clearing station in which cultural differences are juxtaposed and sorted out" rather than smoothed over.
>
> *(179)*

It could well be claimed that the writings of Meer written at such a nexus point in her country's history (during the children's revolt in Soweto 1976) does create a network of interpenetrating relationships which allow for mutual impacting of cultures, race, age and gender. Meer and El Saadawi's inclusion of fellow women in their prison memoirs, specifically women that killed men, rebukes and re-writes a history of exclusion. Their writings create an egalitarian blueprint for a more just society: the centrality of their work makes its critical neglect more inexplicable.

Meer's close friendship with Nana Weinberg speaks of Meer's alliances across all boundaries. Weinberg was a rich Jewish woman from the plush northern suburbs of Johannesburg, and her affiliation with the Black Consciousness Movement grew from her own parents' fight against Nazism in Europe. Such paradoxical alignments across racial boundaries were facilitated by women's bonding. Weinberg was a source of hope and sustenance for Meer in her grim prison days. She arranged for food to be sent to Meer. From the very start of Meer's incarceration, she saw to tiny details that gave some comfort to Meer:

> She came my way at Wits when I first started university in 1949. She came like a ray of light today, when I was feeling desolate. I was moved to tears when a packet came, marked Meer, and in it was my nightie, left so many months ago at her house. It was left providentially for this day. My dearest friend Nana will never forsake me. I am

almost certain she battled to get it through to me. There is no message; nothing to say from whom it came – the nightie is the message.

(41)

The title of Maimela's central work, 'Black Consciousness and White Liberals in South Africa: Paradoxical Anti-Apartheid Politics', points to the many unexpected associations that formed during the turmoil of the anti-apartheid struggle in South Africa. Meer lived out the catholic and egalitarian manifesto which she proclaimed publically; she proved her own individual probity. Her ability to forge friendships across all barriers in prison was her own enactment of her private charter of human rights.

Whether in prison, in the community of letters or societies throughout Africa, women support each other in an often unspoken understanding of the need to oppose a common enemy. In their introduction to *African Women Writing Resistance*, De Hernandez et al. review commonalities between African women who are alert to their own rights, liberty and autonomy:

> For women across the African continent, resistance frequently takes more subtle forms, "To me, resistance means challenging beliefs, traditions, and values that place women below men in terms of being heard, making decisions and choices," says Zambian contributor Ellen Banda-Aaku. Kenyan Ann Kithaka agrees, saying that "resistance means saying 'no' to the patriarchal system and values that continue to disempower, subjugate, and undermine my personal dignity. In all stages of my life, my thoughts and actions have been subject to societal dictates, where 'society' denotes the male figure – my father, my husband, my boss, my brothers, my pastor." Marame Gueye of Senegal defines resistance simply as "the political, moral, intellectual, and spiritual refusal to succumb to any form of violence or oppression."

> *(6)*

The desire to kill male dominance amounts to homicide, which women commit in intention, writing and intellectual impulse. Possibly the most agonising and coherent articulation of female homicide is El Saadawi's novel *Woman at Point Zero*, in which she interviews Firdaus, a female prisoner in Cairo, who murdered a man claiming to have been her pimp. Arguing along the lines of Meer's plea as expert witness in the case of Zondo, that social inequalities may not be ignored but must be assessed as mitigating causation, these women warriors aim to rectify the imbalances of a legal system founded on male advantage.

Female community may be employed as a legal term which binds the rights of women, exposes the historically biased legislation and chauvinistic social mindsets which caused and continue to cause so many women to reach point zero in their lives. Female community may signify an inherited consciousness of women warriors who preceded Fatima Meer and handed her a mantle of duty: the courageous women who had marched with Gandhi in the passive resistance protest against the Jan Smuts government. Sixteen-year-old Veliamma Moodliar died in detention during this protest. Female community speaks as well of the literary awareness of women who are able to communicate their predicaments through writing and share solutions to male injustice, implementing and living out an ordered homicide in their conscious and sustained resistance. Female community indicates the mutual support and instinctive, often unspoken, apprehension of fellow women's crises. Such material female community is evidenced in El Saadawi's planting of food crops in her small prison vegetable garden, aided by the convicted 'murderess' Fathiyya and using a hoe, this time an instrument of bucolic purpose rather than one of blood-stained retribution against men. Meer gives her prison rations to women prisoners convicted of criminal rather than political crimes, although such actions are forbidden (95). But possibly the single incident that most clearly encapsulates the indomitable and uniquely female quality of women's particular type of community and resistance is best left in Meer's own words as she describes the celebration of fellow inmate Jeanie's birthday:

> Our cell doors are opened and we pour out in our night clothes and sing and dance, "IjaalileImothando Section Ten – "There is love in the jail in Section Ten". We give Jeanie her skirt and cards. The dancing continues. I arrange the flowers. The dancers dance to the backyard to alert the detainees in Winnie's yard. I leave my flower arranging to join them but stop when Winnie and company, still in their night gowns, come dancing through the gate into our yard. We are wild with joy, waving our hands, singing and dancing towards us, and then we join together, forming one long chain.
>
> *(145)*

This particular type of resistance, joyful celebration of female comradeship, is as effective as invective, armed struggle or exile. To raise this energy of happiness in one of the grimmest penitentiaries, Johannesburg gaol, during a time of one of the most systemic and brutal regimes of white male suppression, is a potent testimony to the nature of female resistance. 'One long chain', a concatenation of unbreakable strength between like-minded women intent upon homicide in every sense.

Conclusion

The exclusive nature of minority studies and the focus in this chapter on South African Indian women's writing may be critiqued as 'coolie ghettoizing' given the need to reconcile the ravages of apartheid on the literary landscape with its unfortunate racial enclaves of white writings and black writings. The critique is valid, as projects like this may reinforce the exclusivity of contemporary South African literary history based on race. However, I maintain that there is great value in challenging the dominant ideas of literature and culture and addressing matters of race, gender, identity, place and ethnicity in minority writings within the new nation-state. The categories of diaspora versus domicile, global versus local, colonisation and indigenous cultures and neo-colonialism and new cultural formations are all relevant, especially in postcolonial developing contexts. The shift of South African Indian women's writings to the centre, an objective of this chapter, is a strategy to strengthen and enrich the country's literary historiography and is necessary for the creation of a culturally rich and just society.

The writings of South African Indian women like Fatima Meer provide a re-thinking of conventions and roles, enabling women to challenge the power structures and patriarchal norms of a racist society. The dialectic of place and displacement is a defining feature of their stories. Indian women's writings form an integral component of the African literary historiography and bring to light the role of women activists in the struggle for liberation and commitment to social justice and equality. The focus on this minority community revealed how they voiced their efforts of becoming fully human in an exclusionary society and highlighted the resistance and resilience of marginalised women within an oppressive space. They were marginalised twofold by the apartheid regime as black persons and as women. However, they embedded themselves in an African identity together with a shift from the individual to an ethnocommunal consciousness that implies a widening in the perspectives under which a new kind of deterritorialised African identity should emerge in the new nation-state. The engagement with the themes of protest and struggle added radical new dimensions to African resistance writings.

References

Ashcroft, B., Griffiths, G. & Tiffin, H. *The Empire Writes Back: Theory and Practice in Post-Colonial Literatures*. London: Routledge. 1989.

Badassy, P. And My Blood Became Hot! Crimes of Passion, Crimes of Reason: An Analysis of the Crimes against Masters and Mistresses by Their Indian Domestic Servants in Natal 1880–1920. Unpublished doctoral thesis. University of Kwazulu Natal. 2005.

Chetty, R. *South African Indian Writings in English*. Durban: Madiba Publishers. 2002.

Chetty, R. Farida Karodia's Other Secrets. In M.K. Ray (Ed.) *Studies in Commonwealth Literature*. New Delhi: Atlantic Press. 2003, 19–27.

Clingman, S. *The Novels of Nadine Gordimer*. London: Allen & Unwin. 1986.

De Hernandez, J.D. et al. (Eds.). *African Women Writing Resistance Contemporary Voices*. Wisconsin: Wisconsin University Press. 2010.

El Saadawi, N. *Woman at Point Zero*. London: Zed Books. 2007.

Foucault, M. *The Archaeology of Knowledge and the Discourse of Language*. New York: Pantheon Books. 1972.

Goonam, Kesaveloo. *Coolie Doctor: An Autobiography*. Durban: Madiba Publishers. 1971.

Govender, N. *Acacia Thorn in My Heart*. Paris: Gaspard Nocturne. 2000.

Govender, P. *Love and Courage: A Story of Insubordination*. Johannesburg: Jacana. 2007.

Lalu, Premesh. & Harris, Brent. Journeys from the Horizons of History: Text, Trial and Tales in the Construction of Narratives of Pain. *Current Writing*, 8(2): 24–38. 1996.

Maimela, M. Black Consciousness and White Liberals in South Africa: Paradoxical Anti-Apartheid Politics. Unpublished PhD thesis. University of South Africa. 1999.

Meer, Fatima. *The Trial of Andrew Zondo*. Johannesburg: Skotaville. 1987.

Meer, Fatima. *Prison Diary: One Hundred and Thirteen Days 1976*. Cape Town: Kwela. 2001.

Naidoo, Muthal *Indic Theatre Monograph Series 1*. Durban: Asoka Theatre Publications. 1993.

Naidoo, Phyllis. *Footprints beyond Grey Street*. Durban: The Brewery. 2007.

Peck, Richard. *A Morbid Fascination: White Prose and Politics in Apartheid South Africa*. London: Greenwood Press. 1997.

Reddy, Jayapraga. *On the Fringe of Dreamtime and Other Stories*. Johannesburg: Skotaville. 1987.

Sam, Agnes. *Jesus Is Indian and Other South African Stories*. London: The Women's Press. 1989.

Singh, Ansuyah. *Cobwebs in the Garden and a Tomb for Thy Kingdom*. Durban: Purfleet Publications. 1966.

Singh, Kogi. *A Labour of Love: The Biography of Dr Shisupal Rambharos*. Durban: Atlas Printers. 2000.

Spivak, Gayatri C. Remembering the Limits: Difference, Identity and Practice. In P. Osborne (Ed.) *Socialism and the Limits of Liberalism*. London: Verso. 1991.

POSTSCRIPT

Tanure Ojaide

After reading through the many chapters in which literary scholars discussed different forms of minority discourses, also called "minor literatures" and "studies" in African literature, the book needs to end with remarks that are themselves not a form of conclusion but reflections on the state and future of African literature and this type of study. Each of the chapters of this book opens new vistas that could lead to further explorations. The Introduction has defined "minority discourse," which is the focus of every chapter. That definition cannot be exhaustive enough to cover the more flexible meanings given to it in this book. One can always continue to expand this definition beyond what scholars like Gilles Deleuze and Felix Guattari have done in their *Kafka: Toward a Minor Literature* and Abdul R. JanMohamed and David Lloyd in their edited *The Nature and Context of Minority Discourse*. Theories are sociocultural productions and may not have the same results when applied to literary works produced outside cultures that inform them. If, for instance, Michel Foucault researched 19th-century Europeans on conformity and resistance or sexuality and Karl Jung on Swiss patients in a psychiatric clinic to form their respective theories, such findings might not have the same validity outside those sociocultural areas. So, one might understand why this Handbook has expanded the meaning of "minority" as different from those in the two texts quoted previously. However, while such studies are based on societies, they are also on human beings, whose humanity is also validated. This only means that any study of African literature should not forget this.

By Deleuze and Guattari's definition, all modern African literature is a "minor literature," since it is written in colonial foreign languages of English, French, and Portuguese. Fortunately, no scholar claims every literature in the English language to be English or British literature. One can understand the frustration of a writer like Salman Rushdie, who says that there is no Commonwealth literature of which English/British literature and American literature are not part. English literature has its own tradition to which other literatures written in the English language but from outside Britain do not belong. African literature is one of those literatures "excluded" from the mainstream of English literature. The same holds for the many African literary works in French and Portuguese languages but which are not French or Portuguese literature. Modern African literature displays some of the major features of "a minor literature" in the deterritoriality, politics, and collectivity of expressing the African experience or living reality. What this Handbook shows is that definitions change with time, place, and medium. In the book, any issue that attracts a body of literary responses in the form of works within African literature is a "minority discourse." That is why disability, environmental concerns, gender, sexuality, and regional autonomy, among many others, are treated as separate discourses.

Sub-Saharan Africa can be said to be a non–race conscious society where one does not need to register one's blackness or use it as a form of identity. As stated in the introduction, many Africans did not have to identify themselves as black until they landed in the United States. I was only a human being that did not need any race tag. This is unlike Europe, where treatment of the African as the "other" extended to North America such that in the United States, one has to declare one's whiteness, blackness, or otherwise in official forms. For those who assumed superiority over others for centuries, attempting to have racial representation becomes a way of paying back for centuries of slavery or racial discrimination in the likes of Jim Crow laws. Thus, differences tend to be seen in racial and color terms in the West, unlike in Africa. So, diversity in Africa conjures something different from racial or color representations. Much of the content of *The Nature and Context of Minority Discourse* has that racial background in mind with the hope that multiculturalism will remedy a racial society into a diverse one.

The West is creating differences in African literature by its notions of what Africa is to them and not what Africans are to themselves. That notion of Africa as "the other" which inspired Joseph Conrad's *Heart of Darkness* and Joyce Cary's *Mister Johnson* persists to this twenty-first century. It is mostly in the publishing industry through trade companies headquartered in London and New York in their choices of fictional works that the West is creating the Africa and Africans of its liking, which are very different from African reality. So many decades of African literary productions have attempted to counter or redress that Western, rather negative, image of Africa. This goes back to the publication of Achebe's *Things Fall Apart*. Western publishers determine through their editors what African writers deserve to be published, and that means selecting creative works that create that image of Africa that is much to their liking, however far from the truth and bizarre that might be. As Maximilian Feldner says in his chapter, Western publishers publish, promote, and market what they want of Africa. This is a minor literature they create for their aesthetic interest and is a minority discourse in African literature. It is a literature that is created for European and North American consumption and not for the people whose experiences, environment, sociopolitical background, and other living realities are being interrogated.

The point I am pursuing here has two antecedents that I will discuss. In Africa, there has been the decades-long discussion of "mother tongue" versus "other tongue." Generally, Africans belong to ethnic groups that have their respective languages and cultural practices. However, because the European languages of English, French, and Portuguese are adopted as official by an overwhelming majority of African countries, they became the dominant "other" tongues. This work has attempted to showcase as many literatures in "mother tongues" as possible, but there is a limit to the number of over a thousand ethnic groups whose literary productions one can represent in a book such as *The Routledge Handbook of Minority Discourses in African Literature*. The cases of Swahili, Jola, Amazigh/Berber, Pidgin English, and Afrikaans appear in the Handbook. They reflect the wealth of African languages that are the media of their respective literatures.

Closely related to the "mother tongue" versus the "other tongue" is the place of local/indigenous knowledge versus dominating Western knowledge. Daniela Merolla incorporates this into her discussion of Amazigh/Berber literatures. Frieda Ekotto also suggests this in her call that African scholars should research salvaging African values and practices, the true nature of Africa's pre-colonial experience, that generations of colonial and postcolonial existence of accepting the European and Western ways seem to have occluded. Africans seem to have forgotten how they really lived, and familiarity with the Western lifestyle and decades of denigration of African culture have contorted our own views of the African. This call indirectly asks scholars of modern African literature to also work on their oral literatures and traditions to excavate, to use an archeological term, the so much buried in the past. Issues such as that of women marrying women in traditional Africa could be clarified and not be confused with current Western practices.

Precolonial Africa seems to have placed the collective good ahead of individual profit. Though general, very many folklores and literary works have affirmed this principle. So the concept of power among Africans is different from power among Europeans. Power in traditional Africa is for the general good. It is the power that prompts women to dethrone an unpopular Yoruba oba that men find themselves incapable of doing. It is the power of the community that places no one above the law, as the case of Okonkwo shows in Chinua Achebe's *Things Fall Apart*. This African sense of power is different from European royalties and nobilities, who were placed above the laws of the common people. Thus, in Foucault's *Discipline and Punish*, political power and high social status are above the commoners. It is they who want to keep everybody in line to protect their privileges. It is interesting that the dominant power in traditional Africa is the community's interest. If one violates the rules or regulations, one is compelled to perform a ritual of cleansing or pay a fine to be reinstated into the community. One is not surprised that Okonkwo, for beating his wife, is fined for violating the Week of Peace. And it is noteworthy that Obierika, his best friend, takes part in burning his house after his inadvertent murder as a form of communal cleansing. It can be argued that while it was so in precolonial/early colonial times, the same cannot be honestly said for today, when we have the most corrupt criminals and offenders walking free and even controlling the society or even national government. Salvaging those values of old could help make better contemporary governance in Africa. Some of these details help to ground African literature in the cultural setting of its own and should be approached as such.

This brings to mind the issue of the environment, which also has its body of literature in African literature to form its own discourse. From traditional to contemporary times, the environment has been an important aspect of the African's life. Nature and non-human beings are seen as brothers and sisters to humans. Many features of nature, like rivers, mountains, and trees, are deified and worshiped. In many societies, there are sacred animals or totems whose relationships with society are inscribed into the local folklores. Emmanuel Obiechina, in his scholarly work, *Culture, Tradition, and Society in the West African Novel* (Cambridge: Cambridge University Press, 1975), wrote about the domestication of the European novel in Africa. He paid detailed attention to the culture, tradition, and society which help us understand the African reality. However, recent attention to ecocriticism in the West only started from the late 1980s, despite many Western writers' centuries-long interest in nature. Thus, while there are current terms for studies, one working on African literature should be careful in using the new terms but stick to what gives meaning to the African heritage. Scholars could use ecocriticism, but environmental concerns or appreciation will do well to express the African care for the environment with which there has been a long partnership and a symbiotic relationship.

In "minority discourse," one cannot avoid mentioning the literature of the periphery and that of the metropolitan place. The literature of the periphery is imbued with revolutionary fervor in the diction and idiom, which has a lot of vibrancy. On the other hand, there appears, as a result of the long history, exhaustion in the literature of the metropolis, such as that of Britain, France, and Portugal. These works have been advanced by imperial and colonial promotion to a stature that their current writers have not been able to match. The minor literatures of these European major languages seem not to suffer the same fate of exhaustion as the majority discourses. There is an infusion of new tropes and folklores to insure the linguistic richness of an old language in a foreign setting.

African creative writing continues as the scholarly interrogation of the productions. It is the expectation that a scholarly work such as this has drawn attention to issues that are "minor literatures" that will need further critical investigation. Also expected is that many of the "minorities" in the Handbook will elicit more discourses, counter or not. The fertile imagination of writers should challenge the critical insight of the literary scholar. The sustained intensification of the literature and the scholarship will lead to their growth in a symbiotic relationship.

Finally, there is a need to theorize from the African experience itself rather than swallow hook, line, and sinker the Western epistemologies that the academy promotes. There is room to introduce concepts gained from African thought and knowledge to approach African literature as other humanistic and cultural productions of the continent.

INDEX

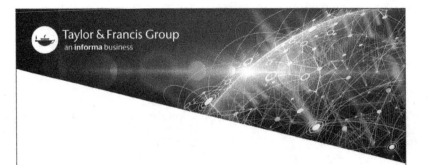